Antique Trader.

AMERICA'S #1 SELLING PRICE GUIDE

Antiques&
Collectibles

2019 PRICE GUIDE 35TH EDITION

Eric Bradley

Published by

Krause Publications, a division of F+W Media, Inc.
5225 Joerns Drive, Suite 2 • Stevens Point, WI 54481
715-445-2214 • 888-457-2873
www.krausebooks.com

**To order books or other products, call toll-free 1-855-864-2579
or visit us online at www.krausebooks.com**

ISSN 1536-2884
ISBN-13: 9781440248764
ISBN-10: 1440248761

Designed by Rebecca Vogel
Edited by Eric Bradley
Printed in the United States of America

10 9 8 7 6 5 4 3 2 1

FRONT COVER:

Grasshopper chair, Eero Saarinen design, 1945, manufactured by Knoll, Model No. 61U, 35-1/2" x 26-1/2" x 33". (Courtesy of Rago Arts and Auction Center, ragoarts.com)

Norman Rockwell (1894-1978), study for *Triple Self Portrait*, 1960. Rockwell's oil study of his self-described "masterpiece" was created for a 1960 cover of the *Saturday Evening Post*, signed and inscribed lower right, oil on photographic paper laid on panel, 11-1/2" x 9-1/4". (Courtesy of Heritage Auctions, ha.com)

Lalique "Bresse" vase, France, des. 1931; cased opalescent aqua glass with white patina; R. LALIQUE FRANCE acid stamp; 4 1/8" x 4". (Courtesy of Rago Arts and Auction Center, ragoarts.com)

BACK COVER:

Star Wars Land Speeder (a.k.a. Landspeeder), #38020, 1978, Kenner, Mint In Sealed Box (characters not included). (Courtesy of Mark Bellomo)

Rare poster of Harry Houdini (1874-1926) depicting him performing his "Chinese Water Torture Cell" trick. Printed in London in 1912, 88" h x 40" w. (Courtesy of Potter & Potter Auctions, potterauctions.com)

CONTENTS

LISTINGS

INTRODUCTION

THE PURSUIT OF fine art, antiques, and collectibles has been called many things by those who have escaped the sticky web of collecting. Despite the number of fleeting television shows about buying and selling grand old things, antiques and collectibles are not a fad. Collecting is an intellectual pursuit (to history's great fortune) and an adventure for the world's curious treasure hunters.

It is through this lens we offer you the market's only, fully-illustrated price and identification guide for thousands of objects (great and small) from the four corners of the world. Every item is photographed to help you compare and contrast it with treasures you can find every day.

With thousands of images across so many categories, the goal of this guide is an ambitious one. It is a practical representation of today's market in terms of its prices, demand, and collecting tastes.

THE HOBBY'S HOTTEST CATEGORIES ARE THOSE ATTRACTING NEW COLLECTORS

First Edition Books — Did you know publishers and collectors have two different definitions of a book's "first edition?" Publishers say the term is the number of copies printed from the same setting of type-pages, while collectors define it as the first commercial publication of a work between its own covers. Either way, the earliest bound copies of famous books by famous authors are reaching record prices. First edition copies of *Harry Potter and the Philosopher's Stone* by J. K. Rowling set three world records at auction in the same year, the latest being an author's presentation copy which sold for more than $140,000.

Contemporary Ceramic Art — Pablo Picasso was a prolific painter, but his 3D designs are leading an important upswing in demand for contemporary ceramic art. Collectors want mid-century studio ceramics, but later pieces are also drawing attention. A ceramic plate painted in 1995 by late Filipino artist Anita Magsaysay-Ho recently sold for $45,000, more than 35 times expectations, and *Menta totem*, an 86-inch tall ceramic sculpture designed by Ettore Sottsass in the late 1960s (but produced in 1985) recently sold for $19,000.

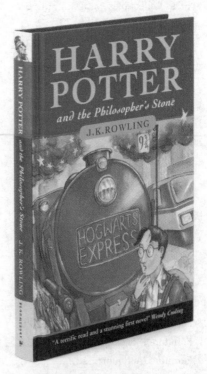

This British first edition of J.K. Rowling's first book in the *Harry Potter* series, *Harry Potter and the Philosopher's Stone*, sold for a record price in 2017...**$142,000**

Courtesy of Bonham's, bonhams.com

Vinyl records, set of eight, 1957-1970, works by Allen Ginsberg, Lawrence Ferlinghetti, Brother Antoninus, W.H. Auden, and a number of others, all read by the authors, from the personal collection of poet Kenneth Rexroth, central figure in the San Francisco Renaissance poetry movement. **$350**

Courtesy of PBA Galleries, pbagalleries.com

Pablo Picasso (1881-1973), Vase deux anses hautes, 1952, partially glazed turned white ceramic vase, painted in black and gray, 15-1/4" h. **$40,000**

Courtesy of Heritage Auctions, ha.com

Vintage Vinyl Records — Last year marks the 12th straight year of record growth in vinyl record sales, topping out at $14 million. Last year's top album to the digital generation was, surprisingly, The Beatles' *Sgt. Pepper's Lonely Hearts Club Band*. Sales figures like this back up what antiques shop owners have been seeing as well: the popularity of vintage vinyl is at an all-time high and shows no signs of slowing. Collectors are seeking top condition to the unconventional — a set of eight LP vinyl albums featuring poets reading their work recently sold at auction for $350.

Asian Fine Art and Antiques — Authentic, period Chinese and Japanese fine art and antiques are once again sparking intense interest. For example, two collectors took notice of a 24-foot-wide Chinese poem scroll that was only expected to sell for $800 in a Rhode Island auction. When the 19th century scroll crossed the block, it sparked a furious bidding war that drove the final price to $72,500. Objects ranging from 15th century Chinese porcelain to 20th century Japanese cloisonné-enameled vases, Asian art regularly fetch six-figure prices.

A bejeweled French doll created in 1868 by Antoine Edmund Rochard set a world record at a 2018 Theriault's auction. **$333,500**

Courtesy Theriault's, theriaults.com

Only expected to sell for $800, this 19th century Chinese archaic poem scroll painting, 24" w x 29" h, brought a much higher price at auction. **$72,500**

Courtesy of Bruneau & Co. Auctioneers, bruneauandco.com

Best of the Best — The best examples in every category continue to rack up world record prices. A $333,500 winning bid set a record for an antique doll sold at auction when collector Carolyn Barry purchased the French rarity for the Barry Art Museum at Old Dominion University in Norfolk, Virginia. The most expensive post-World War II trading card, a mint condition 1952 Mickey Mantle baseball card, sold for a world record $2.8 million, and the current record price for a painting is approximately $450 million paid for Leonardo Da Vinci's *Salvator Mundi* in 2017.

2019 COLLECTING TREND: REDEFINING 'COLLECTORS' ITEMS'

Dealers are Diversifying — Shop keeps who once hung antique chairs from the rafters are increasingly offering fewer items in better condition. Some are positioning creations by living designers and artists next to modernist furniture and post-1960s ceramics, glass, and industrial design. Nearly all antiques dealers have watched prices plummet year after year for "brown furniture," the trade term for most all 19th and early-20th century furniture in mahogany, walnut, or oak.

Shows Are Specialized — Like dealers, even high-end antiques and collectibles shows have opened the floor to contemporary art and design to attract younger buyers and adapt to changing tastes. Gate crowds may be smaller, but dealers are compensating by finding better quality items bursting with eye appeal. Collectors say antiques shows remain a top source of fresh-to-market finds at better prices than if the piece had been offered on an online auction site.

Designers Depend on Vintage — From timeworn kitchen tables to mass-produced wares in plastic, glass, or metal, interior designers always fall back on antiques. Perpetual shoppers of collectibles, designers are expected to blend Flow blue china and Bauhaus lighting

> **...there is one key task to keep in mind before you start buying or selling:**
>
> # Research. Research. Research."

with a Williams-Sonoma sofa all in the same room. This can pose both a challenge and a boon for those with large collections: Selling or buying in a fickle market can bring a loss or a windfall by watching the market.

Prices Prove Collectibles are Finite — There's a limited supply of rare antiques in excellent condition and sophisticated buyers are paying world-record prices for exceptional collectors' items. The tide has irrevocably turned away from quantity in favor of quality. New collectors can jump in more affordably but they approach collecting already knowing a rule it took some of us decades to learn: "Buy the best you can afford because you love it, not because you want to retire on it."

OTHER TRENDS

- Last year's global art economy grew for the first time since 2014 with $63.7 billion in total global sales, a rise of 12% from 2016, according to a report by UBS and Art Basel.
- Post-war and contemporary art make up 46 percent of art auction sales, the largest art sector as it has been every year since 2011.
- A 2017 survey of 2,245 American millionaires and billionaires found that 35 percent of them collected art and antiques, so says research firm Arts Economics.
- The world's first survey on the collectible design market (functional pieces from 1890 to today) shows average sale prices increased 35 percent between 2016 and 2018, according to the DeTnk Collectible Design Report.
- Millennials are embracing the concept that antiques are "green." Decorating with and collecting antiques doesn't leave a carbon footprint like it does when they buy from a big-box retailer.
- For the first time in its 64-year history, New York's prestigious Winter Antiques Show required objects to be noted if they are $10,000 or less, $5,000 or less or $3,000 or less. The change was instituted to help emerging collectors feel less intimidated so they can learn more about antiques.
- Mom and Pop antiques shops are carrying fewer figurines and more pop-culture items as buyers hunt for comic books, toys from the 1950s, and related nostalgia.
- Tastemakers see fast-growing demand for objects with more texture, color, patterns and eclectic style. New collectors are seeing pâte-sur-pâte porcelain with fresh eyes and designers are driving up prices on ornately patterned furniture.

If any of the categories in this book pique your interest, there is one key task to keep in mind before you start buying or selling: Research. Research. Research.

As you'll see, informative features show why some categories are currently irresistible to

Antique Trader.

ABOUT ANTIQUETRADER.COM

We think you'll be impressed with the layout, sections, and information in this year's annual book. Because the antiques world (like everything else) is constantly changing, I invite you to visit AntiqueTrader.com and make it your main portal into the world of antiques.

Like our magazine, AntiqueTrader.com's team of collectors, dealers, and bloggers share information daily on events, auctions, new discoveries, and tips on how to buy more for less. Here's what you'll find at AntiqueTrader.com:

Free eNewsletters: Get a recap of the world of antiques sent to your inbox every week.

Expert Q&A columns: Learn how to value and sell your collections online and for the best prices.

The Internet's largest free antiques library: Dig into thousands of articles on research, prices, show reports, auction results, and more.

Blogs: Get vital how-to information about topics that include selling online, buying more for less, restoring pieces, spotting fakes and reproductions, displaying your collections, and finding hidden gems in your town!

Show guides: Check out the Internet's most visited antiques events calendar for links to more than 1,000 auctions, flea markets, conventions, and antiques shows worldwide.

collectors and the very best items pursued by collectors are identified as Top Lots, marking the ceiling on dozens of categories.

A book of this size and scope is a team project and special thanks are owed to Editorial Director Paul Kennedy; book editor Kris Manty; Antoinette Rahn, content manager and online editor of *Antique Trader* magazine; Karen Knapstein, print editor of *Antique Trader* magazine; designer Rebecca Vogel; and several specialists, dealers, and shops. Ever the professionals, they work year round to make this book a best seller. We also thank the numerous auction houses and their staffs for generously providing images. Their hard work and great ideas are always focused on one goal: selecting the topics, images, and features our readers will find the most fascinating. We hope you enjoy the results.

Eric Bradley is the author of more than a dozen collectibles reference books, including the critically-acclaimed *Mantiques: A Manly Guide to Cool Stuff, Harry Potter - The Unofficial Guide to the Collectibles of Our Favorite Wizard*, and two *Picker's Pocket Guides*: *Signs* and *Toys*. He is a nine-time editor of the annual *Antique Trader Antiques & Collectibles Price Guide*, America's No. 1 selling price guide. A former editor and an award-winning investigative journalist with a degree in economics, he has appeared in *The Wall Street Journal, GQ, PARADE* and *Bottom Line/Personal*, among others. He is the Director of Public Relations at Heritage Auctions, HA.com, the world's largest collectibles auctioneer, and lives near Dallas with his wife and three children.

INTRODUCTION TO

CONSIGNING AT AUCTION

THE AUCTION BUSINESS has changed significantly over the last 30 years due in part to societal changes and to technological advancements. Buying and selling estate goods and collections has never been more accessible. With the advent of the Internet, location is no longer an impediment to selling items that may not be wanted locally, but are in high demand elsewhere. In addition to auction firms' own websites with their online bidding capabilities, LiveAuctioneers, BidSquare, Invaluable, AuctionZip, Proxibid, iGavel, and other online auction platforms are allowing auctioneers to bring buyers and sellers together.

Whether you want to sell a single item or an entire third-generation collection, there are thousands of auction specialists across the country who are dedicated to helping sellers achieve the highest prices possible. During any given week, there are specialists hard at work aiding collectors, heirs and executors in finding new homes for everything from fine art to quirky collections. Without consignments, there would be no auction houses. As Cindy

Stephenson of Stephenson's, in Southampton, Pennsylvania, says, "We are working for the consignor; they're our main customer."

Auction firms are tasked with getting top dollar for the consignors' property. To do that, the auction house invests time in researching, cataloging and advertising before the auction opens. Consignors with quality antiques and collectibles should be drawn to auction houses willing to dedicate those resources to achieve the maximum bid. The percentage the auctioneers charge the consignors (and the premium collected from buyers) is to cover their investment and overhead in selling the consignments. Selling keeps auctioneers in business; a consignment without a sale is wasted effort for everyone.

Stephenson's holds auctions every Friday and has been in business since 1962. The firm, which sells coins, silver and gold, antique and fine decorative arts, and firearms, pulls in consignments from New Jersey, Delaware and Pennsylvania on a regular basis, but have picked up consignments for their specialty auctions from as far away as Florida, Connecticut and California. Cindy Stephenson says her firm only takes items they believe will sell, which is why Stephenson's has a 100 percent sell-through rate. She explains, "If I can't sell it, I'm spinning my wheels and taking up space with that."

LOCATION IS NOT A CONSIGNMENT FACTOR

Many auction houses use online resources not only as bidding platforms, but also to gather information and consignments. In addition to their Signature auctions, Heritage Auctions, based in Dallas, holds weekly online specialty auctions selling books and autographs, comic books, movie posters, sports, luxury accessories, wine, timepieces and jewelry, and various numismatic categories. The firm's online consignment portal puts potential consignors directly in touch with the appropriate category experts.

Becky Dirting, vice president of Collectibles at Heritage Auctions, explains, "In addition to eight offices around the world, Heritage Auctions regularly hosts appraisal events across the United States where collectors can meet with more than a dozen category specialists in one place for free auction evaluations of their treasures. Heritage experts also support various collecting communities around the world with booths and appearances at conventions, trade shows, expos, as well as on radio and television. For large collections and estates, consignment directors are also willing to meet a collector in his or her home or other location for an onsite visit. Our Free Auction Evaluation tool on HA.com makes it easy for clients to request a free estimation of auction value and even allows for the submission of digital photos to aid in the evaluation process."

Deirdre Magarelli, of Pook & Pook Inc., Downingtown, Pennsylvania, points out, "The internet in general has eliminated location as a barrier for both consignors and buyers. Consignors can email digital photographs to us from anywhere in the world."

Representatives from some auction firms periodically attend antiques shows, sports shows and firearms shows across the country where they meet with potential consignors. Dan Morphy Auctions, Denver, Pennsylvania, holds 40 to 50 auctions per year. Dan Morphy reports his firm logs the most miles when it comes to show attendance. "We attend about 150 shows a year. No other auction house comes close to the number of shows we attend each year."

Alex Winter, president of Hake's Americana & Collectibles, says, "We do whatever it takes to get a collection. This includes traveling for it and/or making accommodations to have it delivered."

Jeffrey S. Evans of Jeffrey S. Evans &

Associates explains, "The consignment process doesn't take very long. We ask that potential consignors send photos or a list of the items they are interested in selling." He continues, "The sale date would be determined by the types of materials. We have specialized sales, so we would put the items in the sale deemed most appropriate by our specialists."

COMMUNICATION IS KEY

All the auction houses we spoke with had one belief in common: Clear communication is the key to ensuring that consignors are satisfied with their experience. Before his passing in January 2017, Don Presley, of Don Presley Auctions in Santa Ana, California, said he didn't go anywhere without his iPad so he could educate potential consignors on what items like theirs are fetching at auction. Presley, whose firm deals primarily in antiques, art and higher-end collectibles, told us, "Most consignors are more concerned with how much items will bring." He met with potential consignors and not only educated them by visiting other auctioneers' results on LiveAuctioneers. com, but also showed them how they could research how much money various items are earning at auction.

Cindy Stephenson echoes the belief: "We try to keep them informed from the very beginning. If they have an idea of what the pieces will bring at auction, that's the most important thing. If there's an unrealistic expectation, that's where problems begin."

Greist explains, "We go out of our way to cover all of the details of the process in advance of signing a contract, he said. "In addition, we feel it is very important to be realistic, conservative and absolutely truthful about the estimates that we publish for each item we offer."

Evans says, "We provide a pre-auction estimate in the catalog for every lot, but if a consignor would like an estimate before sending items they would need to ask."

Deirdre Magarelli advises, "Every consignor should have a contract going into any commitment. Read the contract. Make sure you, as the consignor, understand

what the commission rates mean. For example, the commission is taken out of the hammer price, not the realized price. Make sure you understand what these terms mean so you are not surprised when you receive payment."

ESTABLISHING MINIMUM BIDS AND RESERVES

Auction houses research past auction results, not only from their own sales but results from other auction houses as well, to establish realistic presale estimates. Many, including Don Presley Auctions and Jeffrey S. Evans & Associates, set their minimum bids at 25 percent of the low estimate.

When it comes to auction reserves, Evans says, "We only accept reserves on items of significant value; otherwise the minimum bid is started at a quarter of the low estimate." He continues, "Only items with reserves will not sell; if they don't sell there would be a buy-in fee."

Magarelli explains, "If an item does not meet a reserve set by the consignor, the consignor must pay the auction house a fee to cover their expenses (i.e. 5 percent of the reserve amount)."

RECEIVING PAYMENT

Magarelli says, "Make sure you understand when your items are going to be sold and when you will be paid for them. Some auction houses, like ours, pay out within 30 days, but others pay out after several months."

Dirting explains, "At Heritage, 45 days after the auction closes, a settlement check is mailed. Heritage takes great pride in the fact that every consignor has been paid in full and on time since 1976."

Alex Winter says Hake's begins "paying consignors as soon as one week after the close of the auction and typically have all payments issued within 45 days from the close."

Jeffrey Evans explains, "The payout is 30 days after the auction, which allows time for the items to be paid for and any returns to be completed. Dan Morphy also says payment is usually completed within 30 days after close of auction, and that, "From the day someone consigns to the day payment is issued, it's usually a six-month time period."

Don Presley Auctions has an even quicker payout. The firm closes the auction 10 days after the auction is over and issue checks immediately after the consigned item is paid for, usually around two weeks, on average.

IF IT DOESN'T SELL

Items that are put up for auction without reserve will usually sell. If the item is passed, some auction houses will simply return it. Others, like Heritage Auctions and Don Presley Auctions, will list the item as a post-auction buy or will work with the consignor to try to negotiate a private sale or will re-list in a future auction. Deirdre Magarelli explains Pook & Pook's process: "If an item does not sell at auction, the auction house contacts the consignor and gives them two options: The item can be retrieved by the consignor or it can be re-offered in another auction at a lower estimate."

Hake's offers "a post-auction sale of any unsold item. These are posted on our website for as long as the consignor likes, up until the next auction goes live." After all, no sale means no payment for anyone.

EVERYTHING ELSE

Run-of-the-mill household and decorator items are best suited for general estate or merchandise auctions, of which there are hundreds across the United States. Houses such as Don Presley Auctions, Hake's Americana and Jeffrey S. Evans & Associates, are open to consignments with single-item values of a few hundred dollars or even less. Pook & Pook, Don Presley and Hake's even work with other local auction houses in arranging sale of items that are inappropriate for their own firms.

One thing to keep in mind is the lower the item value, the higher the percentage of the auctioneer's fee to cover their costs. For example, Don Presley's commission depends on the value of the item and ranges from 10 to 35 percent, with the average running 25 percent. Presley explained, "I can't sell a $100 or $200 item for 10 percent."

The general estate auction business is booming. When asked how his auction business is doing, one local auctioneer jokes, "People are dying to have auctions with me."

A visit to AuctionZip.com's auctioneer directory (www.auctionzip.com/Auctioneer-Directory/) shows a seemingly endless list, which includes location and contact information. [By registering on the website and logging in, which is free, you can avoid the annoying pop-ups.] South Coast Auctions (www.southcoastauction.net) of Santa Ana, California, reportedly holds the largest weekly merchandise auctions in Southern California, selling everything from bric-a-brac to vehicles and industrial equipment.

Members of younger generations are no longer finding value in estate goods. As a result, demand has waned for many vintage, antique and collectible items. Rather than taking their time to search out a quality-made vintage piece for their new home, a young couple may visit their local Pier 1 Imports, Home Goods or Ikea store and purchase a new item that may or may not survive a relocation in the future.

Decades ago, families were larger and inheritances were a windfall to the heirs, no matter how meager. Surviving family members were often happy to receive items from an estate. A set of special-occasion china inherited from grandparents held both sentimental and practical value; the inheritance meant you had something to remind you of them, and it also meant you didn't have to go out and purchase a "good" set of china yourself. Don Presley said "Limoges dinner sets are now tough to sell for more than a few hundred dollars because they can't go in the dishwasher."

NON-AUCTION OPTIONS

Dirting says, "If Heritage Auctions determines that particular items are not suitable for auction, we try to point collectors to more appropriate resources in their local area and/or online. If a consignor is not convinced the auction method is right for a particular piece or collection, Heritage offers a comprehensive Private Treaty service for those rare and unique objects of value."

Sterling Associates of Closter, New Jersey, also offers estate sale and tag sale services. The firm's Stephen D'Atri explains that the only items they're not interested in selling at their auctions are industrial equipment and non-decorative items. He says although they're not interested in your refrigerator or farm tractor, unlike many other auction houses, they're fine with selling contemporary décor, because "They have to find a home also." D'Atri says they offer local "tag sales and cleanouts as another option for the items that aren't worth transporting if there are enough of those items." Although Sterling Associates won't coordinate donations, they do offer a cleanout service: they organize and empty out the house into a dumpster.

If there is simply no market demand for collectibles, auction consignors may not be happy with the results no matter which auction house they choose. For example, large lots of collector plates and Beanie Babies may bring $1 or $2 apiece. So what should you do if you are told your items are not suitable as auction consignments?

The auctioneers we spoke with had several suggestions, some of which include:

- Try listing on craigslist.org. D'Atri says "It's hard work, but it's a viable option if you want to make a few dollars."
- Outsourcing to a local auction.
- Donating to a thrift store, veterans' group, church or other non-profit

organization. (Speak with your tax adviser or accountant to see how you can maximize the benefit of donating.)
- Selling outright to a dealer.
- Consigning at a local resale store.

Some items are better suited to auction houses that have a successful history selling specialty items, but there is always a place to turn for more information.

When considering selling a specialty item, such as fine art, fine antiques, folk art or any number of other eagerly sought after collectibles, it's in the consignor's best interest to hire an auction house that has the attention of dedicated collectors who actively pursue those items. Consignors need to do their research by contacting consignment specialists themselves so they can make informed decisions.

It's wise to get more than one estimate when considering auction consignment as an option. Weigh the pros and cons when comparing services, rates, references and results.

Communication is key. Before signing a consignment contract, make sure you understand all the details and leave no question unanswered. It's in both the consignor's and auction house's best interest that transactions run as smooth as possible. Content consignors and happy bidders keep auction houses in business and that keeps the collecting market afloat.

— *Karen Knapstein*

ARIZONA

American Auction Company
951 W. Watkins St.
Phoenix, AZ 85007
800-801-8880
Fax: 800-854-1543
www.americanauctionco.com
Established 1995
8:30 a.m.- 5 p.m. PDT
Jacque Weiner
J.Weiner@AmericanAuctionCo.com
800-801-8880
Antiques, fine art, jewelry, estates,
and real estate
Free pre-consignment evaluation
References Upon Request
*Exposure to a local and global buying
audience. You'll reach thousands of qualified
buyers from around the world via our
multinational marketing and web presence.*

EJ's Auction & Consignment
5880 W. Bell Rd.
Glendale, AZ 85308
623-878-2003 Fax: 623-878-2006
www.ejsauction.com
Established 2013
8:30 a.m.- 5 p.m. PDT
Erik Hoyer: info@ejsauction.com
Estate auctions and asset liquidators
Free pre-consignment evaluation
References Upon Request

J. Levine Auction & Appraisal
10345 N. Scottsdale Rd.
Scottsdale, AZ 85253
480-496-2212 Fax: 480-284-4539
www.jlevines.com
Established 2009
9 a.m.-5 p.m.; Sat 10 a.m.-3 p.m. PDT
Josh Levine: reception@jlevines.com
High-end estates and private collections
Free pre-consignment evaluation
References Upon Request

CALIFORNIA

Bonhams
220 San Bruno Ave.
San Francisco, CA 94103
415-861-7500
Fax: 415-861-7500
www.bonhams.com
www.bonhams.com/services/VAC-AUC
Established 1793
9 a.m. - 5 p.m. PDT
Laura King Pfaff
appraisal.us@bonhams.com
415-503-3218
Every major area of art and collectibles

Free pre-consignment evaluation
References Upon Request
Clars Auction Gallery
5644 Telegraph Ave.
Oakland, CA 94609
510-428-0100 Fax: 510-658-9917
www.clars.com
www.clars.com/selling/consignment-
information/
Established 1948
Deric Torres
deric@clars.com
510-428-0100 ext. 122
Fine American and European art, Asian
art, antique, modern, and contemporary
furniture and decorative objects, fine
jewelry, vintage vehicles, rugs, and
collectibles.
Free pre-consignment evaluation
*Clars Auction Gallery is the Western United
States' largest full service auction gallery
offering personalized attention to both
buyers and consignors. Courtesy walk-in
evaluation sessions are offered every
Thursday, from 9 a.m. until noon at the
Oakland gallery.*

Heritage Auctions
9478 West Olympic, First floor
Beverly Hills, CA 90212
800-872-6467 Fax: 310-492-8602
www.ha.com
www.ha.com/consign
9 a.m. - 5 p.m.; Sat By appt. PDT
bid@ha.com
Free pre-consignment evaluation

Heritage Auctions
478 Jackson St.
San Francisco, CA 94111
800-872-6467
www.ha.com
www.ha.com/consign
9 a.m. - 5 p.m.; Sat By appt. PDT
bid@ha.com
Free pre-consignment evaluation

I.M. CHAIT Gallery
9330 Civic Center Drive
Beverly Hills, CA 90201
310-285-0182 Fax: 310-285-9740
www.chait.com
www.chait.com/consign.asp
Established 1969
11 a.m. - 5 p.m. PDT
Jake Chait
chait@chait.com
310-285-0182
Asian art, antiques, fine art, jewelry, and

natural history.
Free pre-consignment evaluation
References Upon Request
*Family run and operated since 1969. Strong
buyer pool of over 50,000, and one of the
first auction houses in America with auctions
exclusively dedicated to Asian art.*

Julien's Auctions
9665 Wilshire Blvd., Suite 150
Beverly Hills, CA 90210
310-836-1818
Fax: 310-742-0155
www.juliensauctions.com
Established 2003
9 a.m. - 5 p.m. PDT
Michael Doyle
info@juliensauctions.com
310-836-1818
Entertainment memorabilia (Hollywood,
sports and rock 'n' roll).
Free pre-consignment evaluation
References Upon Request
*Julien's Auctions is the auction house to the
stars, and we get top prices.*

Los Angeles Modern Auctions (LAMA)
16145 Hart St.
Van Nuys, CA 91406
323-904-1950 Fax: 323-904-1954
www.lamodern.com
Established 1992
9 a.m. - 5 p.m. PDT
Peter Loughrey
peter@lamodern.com
323-904-1950
20th and 21st century modern and
contemporary fine art and design
Free pre-consignment evaluation
*Simply put, we get the best prices for
modern art and design.*

COLORADO

**Artemis Gallery Ancient Art/
Artemis Gallery LIVE**
Online
Boulder County, CO 80027
720-890-7700
www.artemisgallerylive.com
Established 1993
24 Hrs - Online
Teresa Dodge
Teresa@artemisgallery.com
720-890-7700, ext. 1103
Antiquities, ancient and
ethnographic art
Free pre-consignment evaluation
References Upon Request

Leslie Hindman Auctioneers
960 Cherokee St.
Denver, CO 80204
303-825-1855 Fax: 303-825-0450
www.lesliehindman.com
9 a.m. - 5 p.m. MDT
www.lesliehindman.com/about/
appraisals-events
Annie McLagan
anniemclagan@lesliehindman.com
Free pre-consignment evaluation
References Upon Request

CONNECTICUT

Schwenke Auctioneers/
Woodbury Auction
710 Main St. South
Woodbury, CT 06798
203-266-0323 Fax: 203-266-0707
www.woodburyauction.com
Established 2009
9 a.m. - 5 p.m. EDT (Summer hours)
M-Thu 9 a.m. - 1 p.m. EDT
Thomas Schwenke
consign@woodburyauction.com
203-266-0323
American, French, Asian mid-century
modern and contemporary
decorative arts
Free pre-consignment evaluation
References Upon Request
We provide the ultimate in personalized
auction services for both buyers and sellers,
with primary effort given to maximize
property values through careful research,
and aggressive marketing.

FLORIDA

Burchard Galleries
2528 30th Ave. N.
St. Petersburg, FL 33713
727-821-1167
Fax: 727-821-1814
www.burchardgalleries.com
Established 1979
9 a.m. - 5 p.m. CDT
Jeffrey Burchard
mail@burchardgalleries.com
Antiques, fine art, jewelry, and military.
Free pre-consignment evaluation
References Upon Request
Auction firm internationally recognized for
consistently bringing quality estate antiques
and fine art to the marketplace. Thirty
years of personal experience in full-service
estate liquidation, computerized marketing
and online bidding, and extensive pre-sale
evaluation process.

Freedom Auction Company
1601 Desoto Rd.
Sarasota, FL 34234
941-725-2166
www.freedomauctions.com
Established 2008
By appt.
Brian P. Hollifield
brianphollifield@aol.com
Antiques, mid-century, modern, coins,
and jewelry
Free pre-consignment evaluation
References Upon Request
High volume auctions at your place
or ours.

Leslie Hindman Auctioneers
324 Royal Palm Way, Suite 102
Palm Beach, FL 33480
561-833-8053 Fax: 561-833-8052
www.lesliehindman.com
www.lesliehindman.com/about/
appraisals-events
9 a.m. - 5 p.m. EDT
Free pre-consignment evaluation
References Upon Request

Leslie Hindman Auctioneers
850 6th Ave. S.
Naples, FL 34102
239-643-4448 Fax: 239-643-1432
www.lesliehindman.com
www.lesliehindman.com/about/
appraisals-events
9 a.m. - 5 p.m. EDT
Kristin A. Vaughn
kristinvaughn@lesliehindman.com
Free pre-consignment evaluation
References Upon Request

Louis J. Dianni, LLC
11110 W. Oakland Park Blvd., Suite 314
Sunrise. FL 33351
914-595-7013
www.louisjdianni.com
9 a.m. - 5:30 p.m. EDT
Louis J. Dianni
info@louisjdianni.com
Antiques, arms and art
Free pre-consignment evaluation
References Upon Request
Operates out of Florida location from
Oct. 20-April 15.

Palm Beach Modern Auctions
417 Bunker Rd.
West Palm Beach, FL 33405
561-586-5500

Fax: 561-586-5540
www.modernauctions.com
www.modernauctions.com/selling.asp
Established 2011
10 a.m. - 5 p.m. CDT
Rico Baca
info@modernauctions.com
561-586-5500
Mid-century modern art, furniture, luxury
goods, and decorative art
Free pre-consignment evaluation
References Upon Request
We are a full service boutique auction house
specializing in modern, with an established
in-house client base from Palm Beach,
Florida, America's wealthiest zip code.

GEORGIA

Atlanta Auction Company
133 S. Clayton St.
Lawrenceville, GA 30046
www.atlantaauctionco.com
10 a.m. - 4 p.m.; Sat & Sun By appt., CDT
Lori Karlson
lkarlson2@aol.com
404-213-9429
Antiques, art, cars, and business and
estate liquidation
Free pre-consignment evaluation
References Upon Request

ILLINOIS

Leslie Hindman Auctioneers
1338 West Lake Street
Chicago, IL 60607
312-280-1212 Fax: 312-280-1211
www.lesliehindman.com
www.lesliehindman.com/about/
appraisals-events
Established 1982
9 a.m. - 5 p.m. CDT
Mary Kohnke
marykohnke@lesliehindman.com
312-334-4236
Full service
Free pre-consignment evaluation
References Upon Request
Leslie Hindman Auctioneers is one of the
largest full service auction houses in the
nation and an industry leader for more
than 30 years. View a list of experts: Arts
of the American West: Maron Hindman,
maron@lesliehindman.com; Asian Works
of Art: Benjamin Fisher, benjaminfisher@
lesliehindman.com; Fine Art: Zachary
Wirsum, zachary@lesliehindman.com; Fine
Books and Manuscripts: Kathryn Coldiron,
kathryncoldiron@lesliehindman.com; Fine
Furniture and Decorative Arts: Corbin Horn,
corbinhorn@lesliehindman.com; Fine

Jewelry and Timepieces: Alexander Eblen, alexandereblen@lesliehindman.com; Luxury Accessories and Vintage Fashion: Anne Forman, anneforman@lesliehindman.com

Rock Island Auction Company
7819 42nd St. W.
Rock Island, IL 61201
800-238-8022 Fax: 309-797-1655
www.rockislandauction.com
Established 1993
8 a.m. - 5 p.m. CDT
Jessica Tanghe and Kevin Hogan
jtanghe@rockislandauction.com/
khogan@rockislandauction.com
800-238-8022
Firearms, edged weapons and military artifacts
The #1 firearms auction house in the world for 11 consecutive years.

Susanin's Auctioneers & Appraisers
900 South Clinton St., Chicago, IL 60607
312-832-9800 Fax: 312-832-9311
www.susanins.com
Established 1994
info@susanins.com
Free pre-consignment evaluation

IOWA

Jackson's International Auctioneers & Appraisers of Fine Art and Antiques
2229 Lincoln St.
Cedar Falls, IA 50613
800-665-6743 Fax: 319-277-1252
www.jacksonsauction.com
www.jacksonsauction.com/consignments/
Established 1969
8 a.m. - 5 p.m. CDT
Jessica Brogan
consignments@jacksonsauction.com
319-277-2256
All fine art and antiques
Free pre-consignment evaluation
References Upon Request
Jackson's International is one of the country's premiere service providers for the sale and appraisal of fine art and antiques. For over 40 years, Jackson's has assisted clients coast-to-coast successfully appraising and bringing to market hundreds of millions of dollars worth of fine art and antiques.

LOUISIANA

Crescent City Auction Gallery
1330 St. Charles Ave.
New Orleans, LA 70130
504-529-5057 Fax: 504-529-6057
www.crescentcityauctiongallery.com
www.crescentcityauctiongallery.com/

selling.aspx
Established 2008
10 a.m. - 5 p.m. CDT
Adam Lambert
info@crescentcityauctiongallery.com
504-529-5057
Local estates, fine art (particularly Southern or Louisiana interest), bric-a-brac, pottery, silver, jewelry, art glass, American, English and Continental furniture, lighting, and oriental carpets.
Free pre-consignment evaluation
References Upon Request
Crescent City Auction Gallery is a privately owned auction company and one of New Orleans' premier auctioneers of fine art and antiques. CCAG is proud of their participation in the rich history and tradition of the New Orleans auction culture. With the combined experience of 60+ years, CCAG's auctioneers and staff, we pride ourselves in providing the best services to both sellers and buyers.

MAINE

Barridoff Galleries
401 Cumberland Ave.
Portland, ME 04101
207-772-5011 Fax: 207-772-5049
www.barridoff.com
www.barridoff.com/consignments/
form.php
Established 1977
By appt.
Robert Elowitch
fineart@barridoff.com
Fine art of all periods. From Old Master to contemporary, including American, European, Japanese and Chinese works of art.
Free pre-consignment evaluation
References Upon Request
Barridoff Galleries was the first auction house in Maine to specialize in the auction of fine art. It is the only auction house in Maine to offer only works of art at two auctions a year which are held in April and October. The Galleries boasts many world auction records and consistently strong prices in all categories. Barridoff Galleries responds to potential consignors and auction buyers within 24 hours with accurate condition reports.

Thomaston Place Auction Galleries
51 Atlantic Hwy.
Thomaston, ME 04861
207-354-8141 Fax: 207-354-9523
www.thomastonauction.com
Established 1995
8:30 - 5 p.m. EDT

Kaja Veilleux and John D. Bottero
appraisal@kajav.com
207-354-8141
Art, antiques, coins, jewelry, silver, Asian, weapons, vehicles, and real estate
Free pre-consignment evaluation
References Upon Request
Extensive appraisal and auction experience, meticulous research, strategic worldwide marketing, state-of-the-art auction technology, and discreet and caring consignor service.

MARYLAND

Crocker Farm, Inc.
15900 York Rd.
Sparks, MD 21152
410-472-2016 Fax: 877-815-6954
www.crockerfarm.com
www.crockerfarm.com/contact
Established 2004
By appt.
Anthony Zipp
info@crockerfarm.com
410-472-2016
American stoneware and redware pottery
Free pre-consignment evaluation
References Upon Request
The world's leading auction of antique American stoneware and redware.

Mosby & Co. Auctions
5714-A Industry Lane
Frederick, MD 21704
240-629-8139 Fax: 888-815-7740
www.mosbyauctions.com
10 a.m. - 5 p.m. EDT
Keith Spurgeon
keith@mosbyauctions.com
240-629-8139
Toys, advertising, and circus memorabilia.
Free pre-consignment evaluation
References Upon Request

MASSACHUSETTS

Eldred's
1483 Route 6A
East Dennis, MA 02641
508-385-3116 Fax: 508-385-7201
www.eldreds.com
www.eldreds.com/customerservice/
consignment.php
Established 1950
9 a.m. - 4:30 p.m. EDT
Annie Lajoie
annie@eldreds.com

508-385-3116 x114
Americana, paintings, Asian art, Marine, and sporting
Free pre-consignment evaluation
Competitive rates, New England's oldest auction house, prompt payment, and more than 65 years in business.

American Glass Gallery
P.O. Box 227
New Hudson, MI 48165
248-486-0530 Fax: 248-486-0538
www.americanglassgallery.com
Established 2008
John Pastor
jpastor@americanglassgallery.com
248-486-0530
Antiques bottles, flasks, blown glass
Free pre-consignment evaluation
References Upon Request

Leslie Hindman Auctioneers
32 North Brentwood Blvd.
Clayton, MO 63105
314-833-0833 Fax: 314-833-5393
www.lesliehindman.com
www.lesliehindman.com/about/appraisals-events
Bridget Melloy
bridgetmelloy@lesliehindman.com
Free pre-consignment evaluation
References Upon Request

Morphy Auctions, Las Vegas
4520 Arville St., #1
Las Vegas, NV 89103
702-382-2466 Fax: 702-382-6513
www.morphyauctions.com/lasvegas
9 a.m. - 3 p.m. PDT
info@morphyauctions.com
Free pre-consignment evaluation
References Upon Request
More than 40 years experience. Unquestioned integrity and quality of items. Leader in coin-operated devices sold at auction.

21st Century Antiques
210 Ivy Rd.
Beverly, NJ 08010
609-877-6843 Fax: 609-877-6843
www.allthingsold.com
Established 1998
9 a.m. - 5 p.m. EDT. and by appt.

Chris Doerner
dolltoy@hotmail.com
609-877-6843
General antiques collectibles, dolls and toys, and on-site estate auctions
Free pre-consignment evaluation
References Upon Request
We understand that consignor antiques and collectibles are often far more than just "merchandise"; they are fond memories, and deserve to be treated with care and respect, regardless of their value. It is our sensitivity to that and our core value as a support to the customers that make us worth looking into.

Bertoia Auctions
2141 DeMarco Dr.
Vineland, NJ 08360
856-692-1881 Fax: 856-692-TOYS (8697)
www.bertoiaauctions.com
Established 1986
9 a.m. - 5 p.m. EDT
Michael Bertoia
toys@BertoiaAuctions.com
856-692-1881
Antique toys, banks, trains, and dolls
Free pre-consignment evaluation
References Upon Request
Leader worldwide in antique toy auctions for over 30 years.

RSL Auction Company
295 US Highway 22 East, Suite 204 W
Whitehouse Station, NJ 08889
412-343-8733 Fax: 412-344-5273
www.rslauctions.com
Established 2004
M-F 9 a.m. - 5 p.m. EDT
Ray Haradin
raystoys@aol.com
412-343-8733
Antique toys and folk art
Free pre-consignment evaluation
References Upon Request
We are the best at selling early toys and banks.

Sterling Associates Inc.
70 Herbert Ave.
Closter, NJ 07624
201-768-1140 Fax: 201-768-3100
www.antiquenj.com
Established 1987
10 a.m. - 4 p.m. EDT
Stephen D'Atri
sterlingauction@gmail.com
201-768-1140
Estates and antiques

Free pre-consignment evaluation
References Upon Request
Experience, integrity and personalized service.

Cottone Auctions
120 Court St.
Geneseo, NY 14454
585-243-1000 Fax: 585-243-6290
www.cottoneauctions.com
www.cottoneauctions.com/fine-art-and-antique-consignments
Established 1980
9 a.m. - 4 p.m. EDT
Matt Cottone
matt@cottoneauctions.com
585-243-1000
Fine art and antiques.
Free pre-consignment evaluation
References Upon Request
Have a highly successful track record of realizing maximum price results and delivering prompt payments.

Grey Flannel Auctions
13 Buttercup Lane
Westhampton, NY 11977
631-288-7800 Fax: 631-288-7820
www.greyflannelauctions.com
Established 1989
9 a.m. - 5 p.m. EDT
Michael Russek
michael@greyflannelauctions.com
631-288-7800 ext. 230
Premium-quality, game used sports memorabilia
Free pre-consignment evaluation
References Upon Request
We are the world's foremost authenticators and auctioneers of high-profile sports memorabilia, trusted by countless Hall of Famers, sports museums and institutions.

Heritage Auctions
445 Park Ave. Near 57th St.
New York, NY 10022
212-486-3500 Fax: 212-486-3527
www.ha.com
www.ha.com/consign
10 a.m. - 6 p.m. EDT
bid@ha.com
Free pre-consignment evaluation

Louis J Dianni, LLC
982 Main St., Suite 175
Fishkill, NY 12524
914-474-7710 Fax: 888-371-4620
www.louisjdianni.com
Established 1980

Louis J. Dianni
Antiques, arms and art
Free pre-consignment evaluation
References Upon Request
Typical auction has 1,000 to 2,000 lots, 6,000 registered bidders from 70 countries. (In New York from May 1-Oct. 15.)

Swann Auction Galleries
104 East 25th St.
New York, NY 10010
212-254-4710
www.swanngalleries.com
Established 1941
10 a.m. - 6 p.m. EDT
swann@swanngalleries.com
212-254-4710
Fine art, rare and antiquarian books, posters, photography and illustration art. For a complete list of departments, visit our website.
Free pre-consignment evaluation
References Upon Request
Swann has a 75 year legacy as a family-run business. We pride ourselves on our expertise, authenticity and long-standing client relationships.

OHIO

Humler & Nolan
225 East 6th Street
Cincinnati, OH 45202
513-381-2041
www.humlernolan.com
Established 1991
9 a.m. - 4 p.m. EDT
Riley Humler
rhumler@humlernolan.com
American and European art pottery, art glass and paintings. With a special emphasis on Rookwood Pottery.
Free pre-consignment evaluation
References Upon Request
We have been selling Rookwood and other American and European art pottery, art glass and paintings since 1991 and have a stellar reputation for honesty, scholarship and customer service.

Rachel Davis Fine Art
1301 West 79th St.
Cleveland, OH 44102
216-939-1190 Fax: 216-939-1191
www.racheldavisfinearts.com
Established 1987
Tue - Sat 10 a.m. - 5 p.m. EDT
Rachel Davis
rdavis@racheldavisfinearts.com
216-939-1190
Paintings, prints and sculpture

Free pre-consignment evaluation
References Upon Request
Cleveland's oldest auction house specializing in the sale of fine art. We give honest, realistic expectations.

Top Hat Auctions, Appraisals & Sales
3775 Old Columbus Rd. NW,
Suites 103 & 102
Columbus, OH 43213
614-419-9161
Established 2007
Wed - Sun 10 a.m. - 5 p.m. EDT
Michael G. Kraft
tophatsells@yahoo.com
614-419-9161
Pottery, art glass, small antiques and estates
Free pre-consignment evaluation
Top Hat Auctions provides top quality professional auction services.

PENNSYLVANIA

Bullock's Bid 'N Buy
4635 Scrubgrass Road
Grove City, PA 16127
814-786-7129
www.paauctioneerbullock.com
Established 2007
7:30 a.m. - 10 p.m. EDT
Darlene Bullock
dbullock1515@verizon.net
724-372-1066
Antiques and collectibles
Free pre-consignment evaluation
References Upon Request
Because we recognize our number one responsibility is integrity and trust. We are dedicated to accomplishing, educating, and building a rapport with our buyers and sellers, and performing to the highest professional standards.

Cordier Auctions & Appraisals
1500 Paxton St.
Camp Hill, PA 17104
717-731-8662 Fax: 717-731-9830
www.cordierauction.com
Established 1980
9 a.m. - 5 p.m. EDT
info@cordierauction.com
717-731-8662
Antiques, fine art, real estate, firearms, jewelry, coins, sterling, and single consignments and estates.
Free pre-consignment evaluation
References Upon Request
Decades of experience, a full-time professional staff, secure 12,000-square foot auction facility, and many satisfied customers.

Hake's Americana & Collectibles
3679 Concord Rd.
York, PA 17402
866-404-9800 Fax: 717-434-1690
www.hakes.com
Established 1967
9 a.m. - 5:30 p.m. EDT
Kelly McClain
mkelly@hakes.com
866-404-9800 ext. 1636
Pop culture collectibles and Americana
Free pre-consignment evaluation
References Upon Request
Hake's is America's first and most diversified collectibles auction house. Commission rates as low as 10% and no additional fees. We set records in hundreds of collecting categories.

Lark Mountain Auction Co.
369 Johnson St.
Wilkes-Barre Township, PA 18702
570-822-8855
www.auctionzip.com/PA-Auctioneers/339903.html
Established 2013
By appt.
Barbara Conover
bft1317@aol.com
570-301-3107
Antiques and household collectibles
References Upon Request
Ethical, friendly staff, quick payment, and good advertising.

Material Culture
4700 Wissahickon Ave., Suite 101
Philadelphia, PA 19144
215-438-4700 Fax: 215-438-4710
www.materialculture.com
Established 20+ years ago
9 a.m. - 5 p.m. EDT
George Jevremovic
expert@materialculture.com
215-438-4700
Fine carpets and textiles, Asian arts, fine folk and outsider art, ethnographic arts, antiques, modern design, fine books, jewelry and timepieces, and silver and objects de vertu
Free pre-consignment evaluation
References Upon Request
We conduct auctions throughout the year, covering a vast and eclectic array of diverse material, periods, styles and price ranges. Whether you are an individual or a business, seeking to consign a single object, a collection, or an estate; or a museum of university seeking to de-accession items, our specialists and experienced staff will

provide you with individualized attention and service through the entire auction process.

Morphy Auctions
2000 N. Reading Rd.
Denver, PA 17517
877-968-8880 Fax: 717-336-7115
www.morphyauctions.com
Established 1997
M-Sun 9 a.m. - 4 p.m. EDT
Dan Morphy
dan@morphyauctions.com
717-335-4569
Fresh to market collections
Free pre-consignment evaluation
References Upon Request
Record-setting prices realized, strategic marketing campaigns, and unrivaled experts.

Noel Barrett Antiques & Auctions Ltd.
PO Box 300
Carversville, PA 18913
215-297-5109 Fax: 215-297-0457
www.noelbarrett.com
Established 1987
9 a.m. - 5 p.m. EDT
Noel Barrett
toys@noelbarrett.com
Antique toys and advertising
Free pre-consignment evaluation
References Upon Request
Outstanding reputation for honest and fair dealing.

Old Toy Soldier Auctions USA
1039 Lakemont Dr.
Pittsburgh, PA 15243
412-343-8733 Fax: 412-344-5273
www.oldtoysoldierauctions.com
Established 2005
9 a.m. - 5 p.m. EDT
Ray Haradin
raytoys@aol.com
412-343-8733
Toy soldiers
Free pre-consignment evaluation
References Upon Request
We are the only auction house in the world that exclusively specializes in toy soldiers.

Pook & Pook, Inc.
Attn: Consignment Dept.
463 E Lancaster Ave.
Downingtown, PA 19335
610-269-4040 Fax: 610-269-9274
info@pookandpook.com
www.pookandpook.com
Established 1984
Free pre-consignment evaluation

References Upon Request
If you have any questions regarding the consignment process, feel free to call at any time.

Stephenson's Auctioneers & Appraisers
1005 Industrial Blvd.
Southampton, PA 18966
215-322-6182 Fax: 215-364-0883
www.stephensonsauction.com
Established 1962
9 a.m. - 5 p.m.; F 2 p.m. - 9 p.m.;
Sat 9 a.m. - noon EDT
Cindy Stephenson
info@stephensonsauction.com
215-322-6182
Antiques, jewelry, coins, and firearms
Free pre-consignment evaluation
References Upon Request
Full service auction house running weekly auctions year round.

Manifest Auctions
361 Woodruff Rd.
Greenville, SC 29607
864-520-2208 Fax: 864-520-2210
www.manifestauctions.com
www.manifestauctions.com/auction-steps/
Established 2014
9 a.m. - 6 p.m. EST
Manning Garrett
info@manifestauctions.com
864-520-2208
Coins, currency, art glass, pottery, advertising, antiques, and railroadiana
Free pre-consignment evaluation
References Upon Request
Our low rates get consignors more money.

Case Antiques Inc. Auctions & Appraisals
2240 Sutherland Ave., #101
Knoxville, TN 37919
865-558-3033
www.caseantiques.com
Established 2005
By appt.
Sarah Drury
sarah@caseantiques.com
615-812-6096
Fine Art and sculpture, southern regional art and antiques, silver, pottery, and historic documents, maps and weapons.
Free pre-consignment evaluation
References Upon Request

Top-notch customer service, multiple auction records, reasonable commission rates and terms, worldwide marketing, professional photography and cataloging, three accredited appraisers on staff.

Case Antiques Inc. Auctions & Appraisals
116 Wilson Pike Circle, #102
Brentwood, TN 37027
615-812-6096
www.caseantiques.com
By appt.
Sarah Drury
sarah@caseantiques.com
615-812-6096

John W. Coker Ltd.
1511 W. 11-E
New Market, TN 37820
865-475-5163 Fax: 865-475-5055
www.antiquesonline.com
Established 1971
By appt.
John Coker
john@antiquesonline.com
865-475-5163
Pre 1900 antiques and fine art
References Upon Request
More than 40 years experience. Let a knowledgeable dealer deal with it, serving greater Knoxville area.

Heritage Auctions
3500 Maple Avenue
17th Fl.
Dallas, TX 75219
800-872-6467 Fax: 214-409-1425
www.ha.com
www.ha.com/consign
9 a.m. - 5 p.m.; Sat 9 a.m. - 1 p.m. CDT
Holly Culbreath (Inquiries coordinator, Fine & Decorative Arts) 877-437-4824 x1444; Joe Bumpas (Project coordinator, Charity Auctions) 877-437-4824 x1953; David Mayfield (Coins and VP, Heritage Auctions) 800-872-6467 x1277; Dustin Johnston (Director of Currency Auctions) 877-437-4824 x1302; Tom Slater (Director of Americana Auctions) 877-437-4824 x1441; Jill Burgum (Senior Director of Fine Jewelry) 877-437-4824 x1697; Grey Smith (Director of Vintage Movie Poster Auctions) 877-437-4824 x1367; Nate Schar (Director of Luxury Real Estate) 855-261-0573; Chris Ivy (Director of Sports Auctions) 877-437-4824 x1319; Mark Prendergast (Director

of Trusts & Estates) 877-437-4824 x1632; James Gannon (Director of Rare Books) 877-437-4824 x1609; Lon Allen (Managing Director of Comics & Comic Art) 877-437-4824 x1261; Aron Meysteldt (Founder and Director of Intellectual Property) 877-437-4824 x1362; Margaret Barrett (Director of Entertainment & Music Memorabilia) 877-437-4824 x1912; Ed Jaster (Senior VP, Heritage Auctions, Illustration Art & Photography) 877-437-4824 x1288; Barbara Conn (Consignment Director of Luxury Accessories, NY) 877-437-4824 x1336; Craig Kissick (Consignment Director of Fine Minerals) 877-437-4824 x1995; Jim Wolf (Director of Watches & Fine Timepieces) 877-437-4824 x1659; Frank Martell (Director of Fine & Rare Wine) 877-437-4824 x 1753
bid@ha.com

With more than 40 categories, it's easy to secure a free estimation of value from Heritage Auctions Visit Heritage Auctions' easy to use Free Auction Evaluation to select your category, submit a brief description, or even upload snapshots of your rare coins, fine art and collectibles. The most appropriate Heritage specialist will contact you promptly. Learn more at ha.com/consign.
Free pre-consignment evaluation
Founded in 1976, Heritage Auctions is the world's third largest auction house and the world's largest collectibles auctioneer with annual sales of more than $900 million. Heritage clients enjoy unprecedented access to more than 900,000+ online bidder members and unparalleled standards of honesty and transparency as well as the latest advancements in technology via HA.com. Heritage Auctions offers consignors an unmatched depth of expertise with access to 3.4+ million prices realized and a network of 500+ specialist employees around the world. We are always looking to acquire interesting items, whether through consignment or by outright purchase, and we spend or disburse millions of dollars every business day, on average, keeping our clients' demands satisfied.

Kasper Auction Co.
8714B Clearbrook Trail
Austin, TX 78729
512-673-9958
www.kasperauctionco.com
Established 2015
8 a.m. - 8 p.m. CDT
Robin Kasper

robin@kasperauctionco.com
Multifaceted estates and consignments.
Free pre-consignment evaluation
References Upon Request
We are a small auction company and can offer our clients personalized services to meet their needs.

LL Auctions
PO Box 1371
Dickinson, TX 77539
713-248-6186
www.TexasAuctions.biz
Established 2002
8:30 a.m. - 5:30 p.m. CDT
Lisa Gay or John Gay
lisa@texasauctions.biz
713-248-6186
Estates
Free pre-consignment evaluation
References Upon Request
We do online auctions (licensed by the state of Texas) and reach a large group of bidders. We are also a full service company. We can pick up and pack up, offering turn-key service.

Simpson Galleries
6116 Skyline Drive, Suite 1
Houston, TX 77057
713-524-6751 Fax: 713-524-6752
www.simpsongalleries.com
Established 1962
M-Thu 10 a.m. - 4 p.m.; F 10 a.m. - noon CDT
Ray Simpson Jr.
ray@simpsongalleries.com
713-524-6751
Fine art, antiques, and mid-century modern
Free pre-consignment evaluation
References Upon Request
We are a third generation auction house having more than 50 years experience in the marketing and selling of fine art and antiques.

Bremo Auctions
320 Pantops Center
Charlottesville, VA 22911
434-293-1267 Fax: 434-293-0898
www.bremoauctions.com
Established 2013
9 a.m. - 5 p.m. EDT
Cecily Reynolds
info@bremoauctions.com
High-end art, period furniture and accessories
Free pre-consignment evaluation

References Upon Request
Our personalized service is unparalleled and our customer loyalty speaks volumes.

Jeffrey S. Evans & Associates
2177 Green Valley Lane
Mt. Crawford, VA 22841-2430
540-434-3939
www.jeffreysevans.com
info@jeffreysevans.com
Established 2009
9 a.m. - 5 p.m. EDT

Quinn & Farmer Auctions
2109 India Rd.
Charlottesville, VA 22901
434-293-2904 Fax: 888-728-6102
www.quinnfarmer.com
Established 2012
10 a.m. - 4 p.m.; Sat noon - 4 p.m. EDT
Skip Usry
information@quinnfarmer.com
434-293-2904
Fine and decorative art, mid-century modern furniture, coins, and southern material items
Free pre-consignment evaluation
References Upon Request

Quinn's Auction Galleries
360 S. Washington St.
Falls Church, VA 22046
703-532-5632 Fax: 703-552-1996
www.quinnsauction.com
M-Th. 10 a.m. - 4 p.m.; Fri 10 a.m. - 5 p.m.; Sat 10 a.m. - 2 p.m. EDT
David Quinn
info@quinnsauction.com
703-532-5632
Fine and decorative art, mid-century modern furniture, Netsuke, and Asian items
Free pre-consignment evaluation
References Upon Request

Waverly Rare Books at Quinn's Auction Galleries
360 S. Washington St.
Falls Church, VA 22032
703-532-5632 Fax: 703-552-1996
www.quinnsauction.com
Established 1977
Monika Schiavo
monika.schiavo@quinnsauction.com
703-532-5632 x 300
Rare books, maps, autographs, and photos

Free pre-consignment evaluation
References Upon Request

WISCONSIN

Leslie Hindman Auctioneers
525 East Chicago St.
Milwaukee, WI 53202
414-220-9200 Fax: 414-220-9220
www.lesliehindman.com
www.lesliehindman.com/about/
appraisals-events
9 a.m. - 5 p.m. CDT
Sara Mulloy
saramulloy@lesliehindman.com
414-220-9200
Free pre-consignment evaluation
References Upon Request

Paul Auction Co. Inc.
N131 County Rd. S
Kewaskum, WI 53040
262-338-3030 Fax: 262-626-2430
www.paulauction.com
Established 1969
Mike Paul
mike@paulauction.com
262-338-3030
Antiques

Free pre-consignment evaluation
References Upon Request
Sterling reputation for honesty. Broad depth of knowledge in Wisconsin antiques.

CANADA

A.H. Wilkens Auctions & Appraisers
299 Queen St. East
Toronto, ON M5A 1S7 Canada
416-360-7600 Fax: 416-360-8900
www.ahwilkens.com
Established 2009
9 a.m. - 5 p.m. EDT
Asian, silver, decorative arts
Free pre-consignment evaluation
Leading Canadian auction house, with a good online presence

GERMANY

Auction Team Breker
P. O. Box 50 11 19
50971 Koeln, Germany
Otto-Hahn-Str. 10
50997 Koeln (Godorf)/Cologne, Germany
Tel. +49/2236/38 43 40
Fax +49/2236/38 43 430
Tues - Fri 9 a.m.-5 p.m.
www.Breker.com

Auction@Breker.com
U.S. representative: Andrew Truman
207-485-8343
AndrewAuctionTeamBreker@gmail.com
Technical Antiques & Fine Toys

Hermann Historica
Linprunstr 16
D-80335, Munich, Germany
49-89-54726490 Fax: 49-89-547264999
www.hermann-historica.com
Established 1982
10 a.m. - noon/2:30 p.m. - 6 p.m. CEST
Thomas Rief
contact@hermann-historica.com
49-89-54726490
Antique arms and armor, antiquities, orders, militaria, and historical collectibles.
Free pre-consignment evaluation
www.roseberys.co.uk
M-F 9:30 a.m. - 5:30 p.m. BST
Peter Greenway
valuations@roseberys.co.uk
44 (0) 2087612522
Fine art, antiques, and Islamic and Indian arts
Free pre-consignment evaluation

ADVERTISING

TODAY'S MARKET FOR antique advertising items is white hot. Items of a particularly strong interest are porcelain signs, rare tins, advertising trays, pocket mirrors, antique displays, and pinbacks. Strong collecting bases exist for advertising material from the oil and gas, country store, tobacco, and breweriana fields.

Advertising has been called the every man's art, and that art has now rivaled the prices paid for Picasso sketches and Renoir studies.

"It really was the closest people came in those days to real art," said Wayne Yoder, a Wisconsin auctioneer who has watched collector's tastes evolve from glassware to high-end signs. "They were everywhere at the time and they had true art that people still want to own today."

To understand the passion behind collecting advertising, it helps to understand the art and the ad campaigns that created them. Both were not created by chance. These are the end result of market study, product study, consumer sentiment, and return on investment. Advertising items are punchy, beautiful, visually arresting, and designed to capture your attention in a 10th of a second. Even the plainest ad items collected today have some aspect of graphic design that catches a collector's eye, even if the value isn't terribly high.

Advertising items are the wellspring of a consumer-driven economy. The diversity we enjoy today shows just how lucrative that consumer class can be. A robust middle class America was the chief driver of this advertising boom. As such, most ads are for consumer products marketed to this consumption

Buffalo Brewing Co. Bohemian Beer charger, lithographed tin, Victorian woman on a green background, framed by golden lettering, printed by Beach Art Display, 24" dia. **$3,380**

Courtesy of Morphy Auctions, morphyauctions.com

class, such as gasoline, soft drinks, beer, alcohol, food stuffs, and various other consumables. Consumables like these required a steady stream of advertising to maintain sales against competitors. These remain the most popular and most valuable items among collectors.

Objects made to promote goods that are not customarily produced or distributed for sale to consumers are also sought by collectors, but on the whole, they generally do not enjoy the same level of collectability as signs promoting non-consumer goods. For instance, a 27-inch sign for Armour's Animal and Poultry Feeds, which was marketed exclusively to livestock farmers, may currently be found at auction for roughly $800. A 27-inch sign advertising Coca-Cola may be had for roughly $1,900. Both signs may have avid collecting bases but Coke enjoys more household brand awareness than Armour's animal feeds, despite its catchy tagline promising greater profits.

When all of these elements – the talent, the typography, the characters, the slogans, and the calls to action – come together, it's easy to see why advertising items stir such strong passion among collectors.

That passion often translates into big dollars.

▲ Altes Lager Beer advertising painting, original art by Jack Wittrup, 1949, 42" x 23". $1,075

Courtesy of Heritage Auctions, ha.com

Reverse Glass Anheuser Busch Faust light-up sign, scarce early curved glass sign made by The P. Pause & Company, Chicago, 27-1/4" x 15-1/2"..........$12,000

Courtesy of Morphy Auctions, morphyauctions.com

Fan-Taz syrup dispenser, extremely rare, 15-1/2" h. $15,600

Courtesy of Morphy Auctions, morphyauctions.com

Indian Rock Ginger Ale syrup dispenser, 15" h.............$17,220

Courtesy of Morphy Auctions, morphyauctions.com

An Eastman Company porcelain enamel on steel advertising sign for Kodak Camera, circa 1890, 23-3/4" h x 17-3/4" w. $1,625

Courtesy of Heritage Auctions, ha.com

Indian Lake, Ohio, porcelain die-cut sign, extremely rare, 38" x 26-1/2"................$11,400

Courtesy of Morphy Auctions, morphyauctions.com

top lot

Carved Indians were first used in front of tobacco shops in England in the early 1600s. The source of the tobacco supply at that time was from Native Americans and the symbolism easily conveyed the message that the shop sold tobacco. The custom later took root in the United States. Most of the men who carved cigar store Indians came from a shipbuilding background where they specialized in sculpting wooden figureheads for ships. One of these men, considered one of America's finest and most renowned carvers of his time, is Julius Theodore Melchers (1829-1908). Recognized for his attention to detail, the authenticity of Melchers' carved Indian figures is the one feature that excites and inspires collectors. This cigar store Indian that came up for auction recently at Heritage Auctions is one of a few known to be signed by the artist and sold for $81,250. Often damaged because the figures tipped over easily, this example is fully intact and in an excellent state of preservation including most of its original polychrome paint. Also unique are the carver's initials – "J.T.M." – found on the block below the figure's left foot. The figure stands 77 inches tall; the platform is modern, conforming to known period examples. It has been said that Melchers achieved such accuracy with his cigar store Indians by using Native American models, being sure to capture the correct dress and original style.

Melchers immigrated to Detroit from Prussia after studying at Ecole des Beaux Art in Paris. In addition to carving cigar store Indians, Melchers did other types of sculpture. In the late 1860s, Melchers was commissioned to carve the "larger than life" sandstone statues of Detroit's four French pioneers: Antoine Cadillac, Father Jacques Marquette, Robert de LaSalle and Father Gabriel Richard. These were installed at the old Detroit City Hall in 1874 but are now are on view at Wayne State University.

COURTESY OF HERITAGE AUCTIONS, HA.COM

A View to a Kill Michelin Sweepstakes poster, MGM/UA/ Michelin, 1985, James Bond movie featuring Roger Moore, Christopher Walken, Tanya Roberts and Grace Jones, 33" x 49". **$150**

Courtesy of Heritage Auctions, ha.com

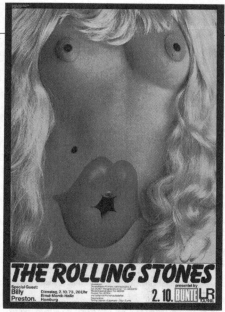

Rolling Stones Frankfurt Concert Poster, 1973, German tour with Billy Preston, design by John Pasche from a photo by David Thorper, 25-1/2" w x 33" h... **$836**

Courtesy of Heritage Auctions, ha.com

Shell Gasoline poster, "Cars Love Shell," 1960, 32" x 40".. **$145**

Courtesy of Heritage Auctions, ha.com

Lucille Ball and Desi Arnaz / Philip Morris advertising standee, 1953, Philip Morris was a sponsor of the *I Love Lucy* TV show from 1951-54; cardboard standee was a store display to promote the Christmas packaging for a carton of Philip Morris King Size cigarettes, 19-1/4" x 26-1/2".. **$478**

Courtesy of Heritage Auctions, ha.com

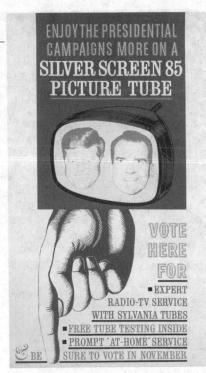

The Empire Strikes Back Coca-Cola poster, 1980. To coincide with the release of *The Empire Strikes Back*, Coca-Cola teamed with 20th Century Fox and commissioned fantasy artist Boris Vallejo to create premium posters that were given to customers who purchased Coca-Cola products. Four works were printed; three offered at fast food chains and one at theaters, including this poster, 27" x 41".. **$717**

Courtesy of Heritage Auctions, ha.com

Sylvania Television Tubes advertising poster promoting John F. Kennedy and Richard Nixon presidential debate, 1960, displayed at television and appliance stores during the campaign, capitalizing on the interest in the televised debates between the two antagonists, 22-1/2" x 39".. **$1,500**

Courtesy of Heritage Auctions, ha.com

Golf pin-up cardboard advertising sign, 1940s, promotes "Braumeister Pilsener," a beverage described as "Milwaukee's Choicest Beer," 17-1/2" w x 22".. **$265**

Courtesy of Heritage Auctions, ha.com

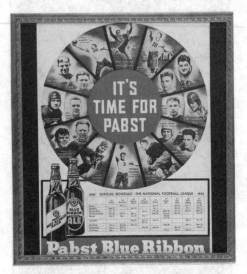

Pabst Blue Ribbon NFL schedule advertising sign, 1935, proof that the marriage of professional football and beer is at least eight decades old, players featured include Hall of Famers Bronko Nagurski and Don Hutson, 22-1/2" x 30". **$1,550**

Courtesy of Heritage Auctions, ha.com

RCA Radio Tubes poster, "RCA Cunningham Radiotron Studio Party," 1933, featuring collage of major radio performers: Burns & Allen, Betty Boop, Bing Crosby, Paul Whiteman, Rudy Vallee, Bert Lahr, Walter Winchell, The Shadow, Al Jolson, Kate Smith, Fanny Brice, Lowell Thomas and Sherlock Holmes, 28" x 43-1/2". **$1,250**

Courtesy of Heritage Auctions, ha.com

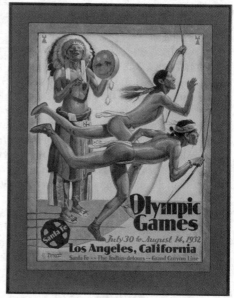

Santa Fe Railroad poster advertising Los Angeles Olympics, 1932, utilizes work of esteemed Santa Fe artist Hernando Villa and encourages travelers to head to the City of Angels for this greatest of international athletic events, classic example of Depression-era advertising, 19-1/2" x 26". **$5,975**

Courtesy of Heritage Auctions, ha.com

Wyandotte Sanitary Clean and Cleanser, tin sign, framed, J.B. Ford Company, 39" h x 28" w. .. **$2,400**

Courtesy of Morphy Auctions, morphyauctions.com

The Ranchmen's Trust Co. reverse glass advertising sign, made by Rawson & Evans Co., Chicago, 41-1/2" x 30". **$9,600**

Courtesy of Morphy Auctions, morphyauctions.com

ASIAN ART AND ARTIFACTS

ASIAN ART (AKA EASTERN ART) is highly prized by collectors. They are attracted by its fine workmanship and exquisite attention to detail, plus the undeniable lure of the exotic.

Often lumped under the generic header "Oriental," Asian art actually embraces a wide variety of cultures. Among the many countries falling under the Asian/Eastern art umbrella: Bali, Bhutan, Cambodia, China, India, Indonesia, Japan, Korea, Laos, Thailand, Tibet, Vietnam, and the Pacific Islands. Also in the mix: art forms indigenous to the native cultures of Australia and New Zealand, and works of art celebrating the traditions of such Eastern-based religions as Buddhism and Hinduism.

A number of auction houses had events in September 2017 to coincide with Asia Week New York, which is a celebration of Asian art.

Christie's New York had a combined total of $43.4 million with seven auctions. According to Christie's, lots of bidding came from Greater China across all categories, in addition to active participation from 33 countries. Among the many highlights were Luohans — a pair of hanging scrolls by Ding Yunpeng and Sheng Maoye — which sold for $1,068,500, more than five times the low estimate; a rare and important Korean gilt-bronze standing figure of Buddha from the United Silla period, which realized $732,500; a seminal painting by Vasudeo S. Gaitonde, which realized $4,092,500 as the second-highest price ever paid for the artist; and a 13th/14th century Nepalese gilt bronze figure of Buddha, which sold for $3.8 million.

Sotheby's Fall 2017 Asia Week featured over 400 lots of collectible and decorative Chinese, Japanese and Korean works of art and paintings including early ceramics, Ming and Qing porcelain, snuff bottles, jade, huanghualiand hardwood furniture, Buddhist sculpture, textiles, paintings and calligraphy. With estimates ranging from $100 to $50,000, there was something for both the novice art enthusiast and the seasoned collector. Highlights include a rare yellow and green-enameled blue and white "Lotus" vase, Qianlong Seal Mark and Period, which sold for $1.1 million; a rare blue and white ewer, Yongzheng Seal Mark and Period, which sold for $936,500; and a rare bronze figure of a Buffalo, Eastern Zhou Dynasty, which sold for $732,500.

Rare yellow and green-enameled blue and white "lotus" vase, Qianlong Seal Mark and Period, pear-shaped body with a slightly compressed belly, waisted neck and flared mouth, painted in deep underglaze-blue tones with a composite lotus and chrysanthemum scroll around the body, framed by a lappet collar below and ruyi-head and C-scrolls borders at the shoulder, neck accentuated with upright lappets below further ruyi and classic scroll borders below the rim, foot encircled by a keyfret band, 8-5/8" h. ..**$1.1 million**

Courtesy of Sotheby's, Sotheby.com

Aggressive bidding among shrewd collectors pushed numerous lots well past their pre-auction estimates in Heritage Auctions' Asian Art Auction in New York, ultimately driving the total realized to nearly $3.3 million.

"We made a big impression during Asia Week New York and these results show it," said Richard Cervantes, director, Asian Art. "Our clients are extremely happy with the scholarship and marketing we put behind their precious objects."

The top lot was a Tibetan thangka depicting two abbots, possibly 13th century, which hammered at $642,500; and a Chinese Tobi Seiji decorated Longquan celadon jar, Yuan Dynasty, 14th century, also eclipsed its pre-auction estimate when it realized $492,500. With a molded three-toe dragon on the lid, the jar includes floral decoration on the rim, continuous scrolling floral and foliage on the body and splashes of iron-brown on the body and lid. A very fine and rare partial set of six Imperial Chinese embroidered silk hundred crane scrolls, Qing Dynasty, 18th century, brought in $212,500.

The top lot at Heritage Auctions' Asia Week auction was this Tibetan thangka depicting two abbots, possibly 13th century, 36" h. **$642,500**

Courtesy of Heritage Auctions, ha.com

The influence of Eastern art on Western art is strong. As Western artisans absorbed the cultural traditions of the East, stylistic similarities crept into their work, whether subconsciously or deliberately. (The soft matte glazes popularized by Van Briggle Pottery, for example, resulted from founder Artus Van Briggle's ongoing quest to replicate the "dead" glazes of the Chinese Ming Dynasty.)

Chinese porcelain was one of the first representations of Asian art to entice buyers in the United States; export of the ware began in the 1780s.

Japanese porcelain, originally billed as "Nippon," began to make its way to U.S. shores near the end of the 19th century. Early Chinese porcelain was often distinguished by a liberal use of blue and white; Japanese porcelain, by a similar reliance on floral and landscape motifs. Consumers found the products of both countries desirable, not only because of their delicacy, but also because pieces of comparable quality were not yet available domestically.

Porcelain was not the only outlet for Eastern creativity. Among the many other materials utilized: ivory, jade, bone, hardstone, marble, bronze, brass, gold, silver, wood, and fabric (primarily silk). Decorative treatments ranged from cloisonné (enamel sections in a pattern of metal strips) to intricate hand carving to the elaborate use of embroidery, gilt, and lacquer.

Asian art in any form offers a unique blend of the decorative and the functional. The richness of the materials and treatments utilized transforms even everyday objects into dazzling works of art. Among myriad items receiving this Cinderella treatment: bowls, vases, planters, chess sets, snuff bottles, rugs, robes, tapestries, tables, trays, jars, screens, incense burners, cabinets, and tea caddies. Even a simple item such as an oil lamp could be reborn through imaginative artistry: A Chinese version from the 1920s, its exterior worked in cloisonné, emerged as a colorful, ferocious dragon.

This multitude of products makes Asian art an ideal cross-collectible. Some may be interested only in the output of a specific country or region. Others may be drawn to a specific type of collectible (kimonos, snuff boxes, depictions of Buddha). There will even be those attracted solely to pieces created from a specific material, such as jade, ivory, or porcelain. Aficionados of any of these categories have a lifetime of collecting pleasure in store.

The timeline of Asian art is a long one, with value often determined by antiquity. Due to age and rarity, minor flaws (jade nicks, porcelain cracks, and chips) are not generally a detriment to purchase. Any restoration should only be done by a professional, and only after careful analysis as to whether or not restoration will affect value.

Asian art continues to be produced and imported today at an overwhelming rate (and often of "souvenir-only" quality). Collectors seeking museum-quality pieces are strongly advised to purchase only from reputable dealers, and to insist on proof of provenance.

Set of two bronze censers, Japan, 19th century, one depicting a standing rooster, the other a hen with two chicks, their pupils depicted in gilt lines, each signed "Miyama," to 13-5/8" h. **$4,305**

Courtesy of Skinner Auctioneers & Appraisers, skinnerinc.com

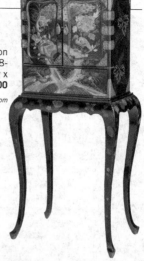

▶ Japanese lacquered chest on stand, Meiji Period, circa 1868-1912, 44-1/2" h x 21-1/2" w x 14" d. **$1,500**

Courtesy of Heritage Auctions, ha.com

Chinese export silvered and cloisonné cricket cage, multi-character marks, 8-3/4" h x 7" w x 3-1/2" d. **$400**

Courtesy of Heritage Auctions, ha.com

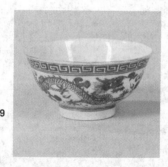

Iron red enameled porcelain "dragon" cup, China, 20th century, two facing dragons below a meander band at rim, gilt and white enameled details, six-character Guangxu mark in overglaze iron red, 1-7/8" h, mouth rim is 3-1/2" dia. **$369**

Courtesy of Skinner Auctioneers & Appraisers, skinnerinc.com

▼ Two large stucco and polychrome Buddhist heads, late Qing Dynasty/20th century, one the head of a guardian with furrowed brow and protruding inlaid eyes, framed by long-lobed ears and hair pulled back in a high topknot, painted in russet, blue and black; the other a head of Buddha, the round face with inlaid black glass eyes and an urna between slender arched brows, framed by long-lobed ears and an ushnisha covered in conical spirals, painted in russet, red, black and white, both mounted on stands, taller one is 24-1/2". **$1,250**

Courtesy of Sotheby's, sothebys.com

◀ Pair of enamel and bronze caparisoned elephants, China, 19th/20th century, elephants with archaic motifs on turquoise ground carrying gu-form vases, wooden stands 12-1/4" h, metal are 11-1/4". **$738**

Courtesy of Skinner Auctioneers & Appraisers, skinnerinc.com

top lot

At Skinner Auctioneers' September 15, 2017 Asian Works of Art auction, more than 500 lots were offered, including Chinese paintings, ceramics and sculpture, an important Nan Edwards collection of cloisonné, an important grouping of jade pieces. Also auctioned was this exceptional Manchu Lady's 19th-century kingfisher headdress, which came with four hatpins, and sold for $110,700 – more than 35 times the low estimate of $3,000 – and was the top lot.

The kingfisher feather headdress, made in China in the 19th century, is semicircular with a flat back and decorated with gilt-brass openwork filigree in the shapes of phoenixes and flowers, and covered with conforming kingfisher feather cutouts, jeweled with precious gemstones, jadeite, tourmaline, and pearly beads, over a wickered frame of satin bands, with five three-string beaded pendants to the back (now all detached); it measures 10-1/4 inches high and 13-1/2 inches wide. The two pairs of brass hairpins each have an openwork phoenix finial and a four-string beaded pendant, (now all detached except one) and are to 9-3/4 inches long.

Kingfishers and phoenixes have special meanings in Chinese art. Centuries ago, kingfisher feather crowns (known as feng guan) decorated with phoenix, dragons and precious stones, were only worn by empresses in China. From the 19th century, however, a headdress such as this one would be worn either by an aristocratic lady on formal occasions, as an indication of her wealth and status, or by a bride on her wedding day.

According to Wikipedia.com, Tian-tsui ("dotting with kingfishers") is a style of Chinese art featuring kingfisher feathers. For 2,000 years, the Chinese have been using the iridescent blue feathers of these birds as an inlay for fine art objects and adornment, from hairpins, headdresses, and fans to panels and screens. Kingfisher feathers are painstakingly cut and glued onto gilt silver, and the effect is like cloisonné, but no enamel was able to rival the electric blue color. Blue is the traditional favorite color in China.

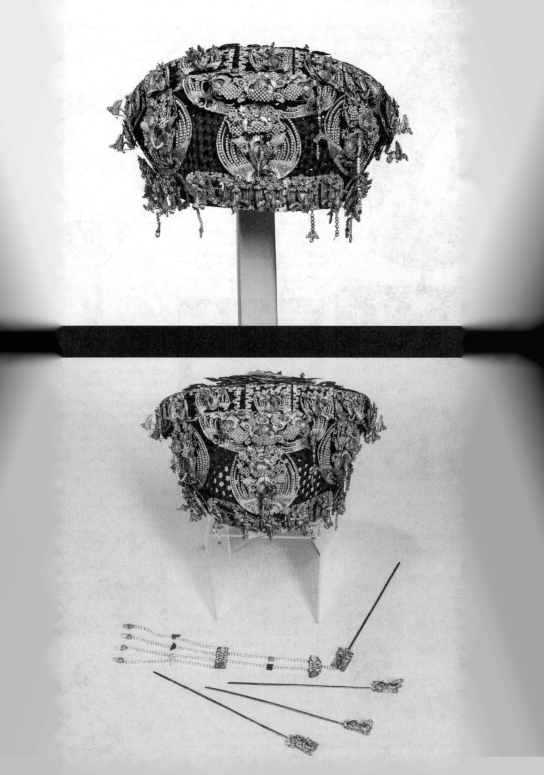

◀ Large Indonesian carved hardwood figure of a fisherman, marks: IWY. MACONG, BR. LANTANGIDUNG, 42" h. **$500**

Courtesy of Heritage Auctions, ha.com

Pair of eggshell porcelain covered jars, China, 20th century, decorated with bird-and-flower designs and calligraphy, the domed cover with an elongated lotus knob, with wood stands, to 4" h.... **$677**

Courtesy of Skinner Auctioneers & Appraisers, skinnerinc.com

A Chinese silver, jade, and agate hand mirror, marks: SILVER, handle with carved and reticulated jade chilong buckle mount, silver frame with bat, carp, lotus, and other motifs in repoussé interspersed with jade and agate cabochons, central carved jade plaque depicting two male elders under tree unraveling scroll, 9-3/4" h x 4-1/2" w. **$2,750**

Courtesy of Heritage Auctions, ha.com

Chinese carved coral female and phoenix group on stand, 96 grams (coral including stand), 5-1/8" h (coral), 6" h (coral including stand). **$2,000**

Courtesy of Heritage Auctions, ha.com

A Japanese Satsuma fishbowl jardinière on Chinese carved hardwood stand, late Meiji-Taisho Period, three-character Shimazu mark, jardinière is 11", 19-1/8" h overall. **$312**

Courtesy of Heritage Auctions, ha.com

▶ Cloisonné snuff bottle, China, 20th century, round jar with two lion head knobs and three ruyi-shape feet, with lotus scroll decorations, gilt details, four-character Qianlong mark on base, 2-1/4" h. **$2,706**

Courtesy of Skinner Auctioneers & Appraisers, skinnerinc.com

▲ Pair of leather and lacquer-decorated drums with stands, China, 20th century, red-lacquered sides decorated with floral meanders, on similarly decorated wooden stands, with two pairs of lacquered drumsticks, drum is 34" h and 42-1/2" with stand, 20" head dia. **$615**

Courtesy of Skinner Auctioneers & Appraisers, skinnerinc.com

Nine-dragon blue-ground robe, China, late 19th/early 20th century, depicting dragons, pearls and clouds above waves, silk metallic threads with a pale blue lining, 56" l..**$2,460**

Courtesy of Skinner Auctioneers & Appraisers, skinnerinc.com

Bronze tripod teapot and openwork wood stand, China, 19th/20th century, turtle shape, with a chilong handle and oval cover with a fish-shaped knob, body decorated with foliate scroll design in relief, 4-1/4" h, 8-1/8" w. ... **$554**

Courtesy of Skinner Auctioneers & Appraisers, skinnerinc.com

Pair of large Japanese Imari porcelain floor vases, 42" h x 14-1/8" dia at mouth.......... **$937**

Courtesy of Heritage Auctions, ha.com

A Chinese ink and watercolor on paper painting, Bird with Berries, 20th century, 12-3/4" x 18".....................**$250**

Courtesy of Heritage Auctions, ha.com

ASIAN ART AND ARTIFACTS

A framed Chinese silk embroidered wall panel, panel is 71-1/2" h x 40-1/2" w, 81" h x 48" w overall, framed. **$6,250**

Courtesy of Heritage Auctions, ha.com

A Chinese lacquered, painted and partial giltwood wall panel, Republic Period, circa 1912-1949, 73" h x 28-1/4" w x 1-1/2" d......................... **$500**

Courtesy of Heritage Auctions, ha.com

Hasui Kawase (Japanese, 1883-1957), Udo Turret, Kumamoto Castle in Rain, 1948, woodblock in colors, 14-3/8" x 9-1/2"........... **$1,750**

Courtesy of Heritage Auctions, ha.com

AUTOGRAPHS

THE MARKET FOR historical and seldom seen autographs remains particularly robust; however, prices are also on the rise for those from celebrities, sports figures, and famous authors. Presidential autographs prior to 1940 remain highly sought after among collectors and institutions alike.

The market for celebrity scientists, modern presidents, and current heads of industry are not commanding high prices in today's market. This makes the opportunity to collect these types of autographs a low-cost hobby before prices increase in the future.

Take, for instance, the autograph of Steve Jobs. In 1992, Jobs signed a rare poster promoting the inaugural Next World Expo in San Francisco. Little did he know his signature would be one of the most coveted among collectors – particularly because Jobs did not sign many documents during his lifetime. The autographed poster sold in 2017 for $16,000.

Like most autographs, the story associated with the signature contributes greatly to the value. In the case of the Jobs poster, Apple purchased NeXT in 1997 for $429 million and $1.5 million shares of Apple stock, with Jobs, as part of the agreement, returning to the company he co-founded in 1976, said Bob Eaton, CEO of RR Auctions, who offered the poster at auction.

For the last few years, autograph collectors have been forced to "branch out" away from traditional clipped signatures so often seen in established collections. Why? Blame the digital age. More digital correspondence means even fewer signatures. Therefore, collectors are pursuing older items such as autographed magazines and period photographs, as well as passports and even driver's licenses. A passport from the private collection of Whitney Houston sold in 2015 for a surprising $15,000.

NEIL A. ARMSTRONG

Neil Armstrong signed photograph, half-length portrait by NASA. On July 21, 1969, Armstrong became the first person to walk on the moon, 8" x 10". **$2,500**

Courtesy Swann Auction Galleries, swanngalleries.com

It may be hard to believe that signatures of Jobs and Houston can command three or four times as much as the signature of Abraham Lincoln or Thomas Jefferson. With autographs, it all comes down to context, clarity, condition, and rarity. Eye appeal helps a great deal, too. A signed cut autograph, so named because the signature is cut from perhaps a check, autograph book, or some other piece of paper, to a signed photo makes a world of difference to collectors.

MOST DANGEROUS AUTOGRAPH TO COLLECT

Not all autographs are safe or easy to get and some are downright dangerous to a collector's checkbook. The Beatles remain at the top of the list of the most often copied and faked historical and entertainment autographs. They are the most heavily forged band in the world. The following list of the most dangerous historical and entertainment autographs to collect is compiled annually by Professional Sports Authenticator, the largest and most trusted third-party grading and authentication company in the world.

1. The Beatles: ($5,000 for a signed cut signature to $15,000 or more for a signed photo.)
2. Elvis Presley: ($1,500 for a signed cut signature to $35,000 or more for a signed contract or letter.)
3. Neil Armstrong: ($1,500 for s singed cut signature to $4,000 or more for a signed photo.)
4. John F. Kennedy: ($1,750 for a signed cut signature to $25,000 or more for a presidential letter/document.)
5. Michael Jackson: ($350 for a signed cut signature to $1,000 or more for a signed photo.)
6. Marilyn Monroe: ($2,500 for a signed cut signature to $15,000 or more for a signed photo.)
7. Led Zeppelin: ($1,200 for a signed cut signature to $4,500 or more for a signed photo.)
8. Jimi Hendrix: ($2,500 for a signed cut signature to $7,500 or more for a signed photo.)
9. The Rolling Stones: ($1,200 and up for a signed photo and $3,500 and up for a signed guitar.)
10. *Star Wars: The Force Awakens* cast ($500 and up for a cast-signed photo and $50 to $250 for individual key cast members.)

Benedict Arnold signed letter, 1772. An early American hero of the Revolutionary War (1775-1783), Arnold later became one of the most infamous traitors in U.S. history after he switched sides and fought for the British. **$5,500**

Courtesy Swann Auction Galleries, swanngalleries.com

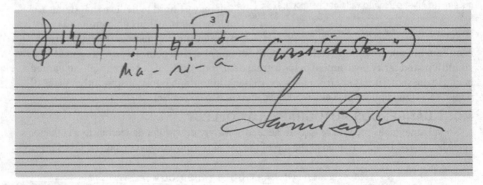

Leonard Bernstein signed musical quotation, two bars from "Maria" in *West Side Story*, 2-1/2" x 6-1/2". **$2,565**

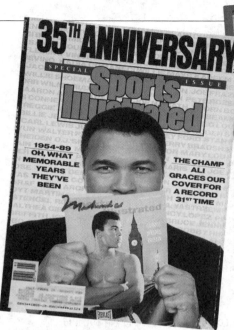

Muhammad Ali signed *Sports Illustrated* magazine, 1989. .... **$264**

Robert James ("Bobby") Fischer signed *Time* magazine cover featuring the 1972 match between world champion Boris Spassky and Fischer. Held in Reykjavik, Iceland, the World Chess Championship was dubbed "The Match of the Century." Fischer won the match, becoming the first American in the United States to win the world title. **$575**

Rudolph Valentino signed photograph postcard, full-length portrait showing him in costume as Vladimir Dubrovsky in the film, *The Eagle* (1925), 5-1/2" x 3-1/2". **$938**

Princess Diana and Prince Charles of Wales signed Christmas card, mounted to page facing inscription is a photograph, showing the two standing on either side of a miniature horse being ridden by their children, Princes William and Harry, 7-1/4" x 5". **$2,000**

AUTOGRAPHS

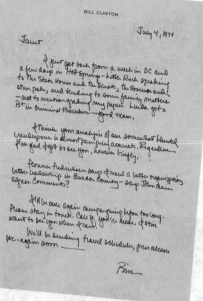

Bob Dylan signed *Nashville Skyline Quadrophonic* album cover (Columbia, 1969). **$1,875**

Courtesy of Heritage Auctions, ha.com

Bill Clinton signed letter, July 4, 1974, to supporter Janet Nelson shortly after graduating from law school. The letter is among an archive of 16 items inscribed and singed by Clinton. William Jefferson Clinton served as the 42nd President of the United States from 1993 to 2001. .... **$8,750**

Courtesy Swann Auction Galleries, swanngalleries.com

Jack Dempsey autographed photograph. Nicknamed "The Manassa Mauler," Dempsey was boxing's heavyweight champ from 1919-1926, 8" x 10". **$113**

Courtesy of Heritage Auctions, ha.com

Thomas Edison signed letter, March 3, 1878, to Western Union President William Orton. In the letter Edison writes "...I did find a 'bug' in my apparatus." Edison is among the first to use the word "bug" to refer to a technical problem...**$12,500**

Courtesy Swann Auction Galleries, swanngalleries.com

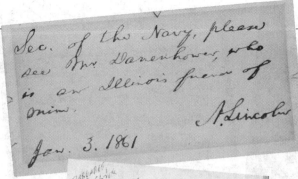

Abraham Lincoln signed note, January 3, 1861, on a small card (2" x 3"). Message reads: "Sec. of the Navy, please see Mr. Danehower, who is an Illinois friend of mine." **$5,670**

Courtesy Swann Auction Galleries, swanngalleries.com

Bruce Springsteen signed Freehold Regional High School (Freehold, New Jersey) annual yearbook, 1967. Springsteen signed by his senior class picture: "Margaret, Best of Luck, Stay Cool – Bruce." **$1,900**

Courtesy of Heritage Auctions, ha.com

Amelia Earhart signed and inscribed *The Fun of It*, "To Admiral Susan in appreciation of a week end," 1932 .... **$1,375**

Courtesy Swann Auction Galleries, swanngalleries.com

Helen Keller signed photograph, January 25, 1947. Photo shows Keller seated beside her assistant Polly Thomson and a dog at her feet. . **$530**

Courtesy Swann Auction Galleries, swanngalleries.com

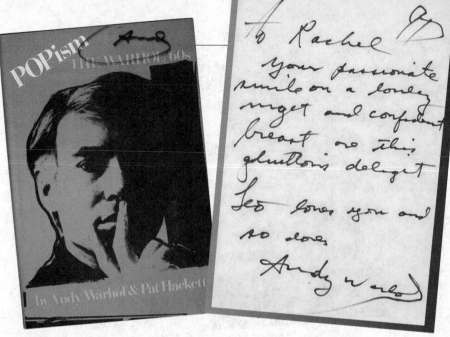

Andy Warhol signed and inscribed *Popism*, first edition, first printing, 1980... **$2,295**

Courtesy Swann Auction Galleries, swanngalleries.com

George Gershwin signed and inscribed copy of *Tin Pan Alley* by Isaac Goldberg; also signed by conductor Charles Previn and tenor James Melton, both in pencil. Also included is a program celebrating the 10th anniversary of "Rhapsody in Blue" February 5, 1934, featuring Gershwin on piano, Melton and Previn conducting the Leo Reisman Symphonic Orchestra..................... **$2,125**

Courtesy Swann Auction Galleries, swanngalleries.com

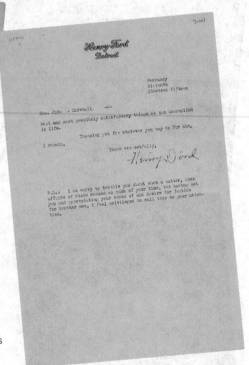

Henry Ford signed letter asking the Vice President to intervene on behalf of a parole who worked for Ford, Feb. 11, 1915................................... **$1,625**

Courtesy Swann Auction Galleries, swanngalleries.com

BANKS

MOST COLLECTIBLE BANKS were designed for one purpose: to encourage children to save money. How well the bank accomplished this task makes all the difference in making it collectible by later generations.

Manufactured from the late 1800s to the mid-1900s, mechanical, still, and register banks (which indicate the value of the coins deposited) are marvels of ingenuity made of tin, lead, or cast iron. Although banks come in all makes and functions, the most desirable banks employ a novelty or mechanical action when a coin is placed inside. Banks are sought after because they so efficiently represent the popular culture at the time they were made. This is evident in the wartime register banks sporting tin lithographic decorations of superheroes or animation characters or the cast iron figures that propagated racial stereotypes common from 1880 to 1930. Many early cast iron bank models have been reproduced during the years, especially in the 1950s and 1960s. A key indicator of a reproduction is fresh, glossy paint or dull details in the casting.

I always tell new collectors that they should buy what they like. Even if you pay a little more than you should for a bank, the value in the enjoyment of owning it will more than offset the high price one may pay." – Dan Morphy

According to 10 years of sales data on LiveAuctioneers.com, most mechanical banks sell at auction for between $500 and $1,000. Morphy Auctions is the world leader in selling mechanical banks.

"There are a dozen or so collections that I know of that would bring over $1 million," said Dan Morphy, owner and founder of Morphy Auctions. "There are dozens of other bank collections that would fall in the six-figure ranges."

Morphy says condition – like all other categories of collecting – is king. "Banks in top condition seem to be the trend these days," he said.

On the basis of affordability, now is the time to start a collection.

Germania Exchange mechanical bank, J. & E. Stevens Co., c 1880s, made of cast iron with a painted lead goat on top, by placing a coin on the goat's tail and turning the faucet, this allows figure to deposit coin and seemingly present the depositor with a stein of beer, very attractive in scarcer paint scheme colors..............................**$42,500**

Courtesy of Bertoia Auctions, bertoiaauctions.com

A top on Morphy's list to offer at auction is a Darkey & the Watermelon mechanical bank. Otherwise known as the Football Bank, it was designed and patented by Charles A. Bailey on June 26, 1888. Known as the leader in mechanical bank design, Bailey's Darkey & the Watermelon bank incorporated all of his imagination and design talents: When the right leg of a figure is pulled back into position, a coin is then placed in a small football; a lever in the figure's coattails is pressed and the football with coin is kicked over into a large watermelon. Only four of these banks are known to exist.

"That would be my dream bank," Morphy said, "in that I would also want to buy it!"

Like their predecessors crafted nearly 150 years ago, contemporary banks blur the line between tool and toy. Some modern banks that may make interesting collectibles in the future include digital register banks that tabulate coin and paper money deposits or those licensed by famous designers. But beware – antique banks are still being reproduced and can be found cheaply at lesser-quality flea markets or sold online.

For more information on banks, see *The Official Price Guide to Mechanical Banks* by Dan Morphy (morphyauction.com).

Dark Town Battery cast iron mechanical bank, 1888, the most popular of all baseball-related mechanical banks, features a pitcher, catcher and batter in a design that speaks to the pervasive racism of 19th century America, all three characters move when the mechanism is pressed: The pitcher sends the coin flying out of his underhanded pitch to the catcher, who moves his head and hand and opens up a hole to accept the coin; the batter moves his head and raises his bat into the air. All parts work properly and bank is in excellent condition, 10" x 7-1/2" x 2-1/2"............... **$2,580**

Courtesy of Heritage Auctions, ha.com

Lot of two banks: Cabin, made by J. & E. Stevens Company, shows an African American figure in the doorway, when a coin is placed at his feet and the lever is released, he does a flip and the coin goes into the slot on the roof, in working condition; and a mule and barn, coin is placed between the mule's legs and when the lever is pressed, a dog come out frightens the mule and he kicks the coin into the barn, mule's tail is missing but the bank is still in working condition. **$625**

Courtesy of Heritage Auctions, ha.com

Teddy and the Bear cast iron mechanical bank, original paint, wear, missing trap, 7-1/2" h, 10" l **$550**

Courtesy of Cottone Auctions, cottoneauctions.com

Cast iron figural George Washington bank, unpainted, approx. 6-1/2" h **$25**

Courtesy of Auction Gallery of Boca Raton, LLC, liveauctioneers.com

Milking/kicking cow cast iron mechanical bank, J. & E. Steven, in good overall condition and working, 5-1/4" h x 9-1/2" w x 3-1/2" d. **$850**

Courtesy of Fontaine's Auction Gallery, fontainesauction.com

Mechanical bank, cast iron lion and monkeys, manufactured by Keyser & Rex, coin is placed on the larger monkey's hand, when the lever is pulled, the smaller monkey jumps up and the hand goes forward allowing the coin to slide down the lion's mouth, working condition. **$625**

Courtesy of Heritage Auctions, ha.com

Vintage Marx metal budget bank, 5-3/4" x 2-1/2" x 3-1/2". **$14**

Courtesy of Pioneer Auction Gallery, liveauctioneers.com

J & E Stevens cast iron mechanical bull dog bank, 1880s, with inlaid glass eyes, original trap, approx. 7-1/2" h...**$200**

Auction Gallery of Boca Raton, LLC, liveauctioneers.com

Cast iron house bank, approx. 4-1/2" x 5-1/2" x 6" h. **$23**

Courtesy of M.J. Stasak Jr. Auction and Appraisal Service, stasakauctions.com

A cast iron "Doughboy" or Boy Scout still bank, circa 1920, original enamel paint, no maker's marks, very good condition, 7" x 2-1/2". **$50**

Courtesy of Soulis Auctions, dirksoulisauctions.com

Vintage Bank of Republic cast iron piggy bank, 7" h. **$45**

Courtesy of Ole Hound Auction House, liveauctioneers.com

Cast iron Mr. Peanut bank, 5-1/2" x 11".........................**$90**

Courtesy of Echoes Antiques & Auction Gallery, Inc., echoesauctions.com

THE BEATLES

THE FIRST WAVE OF BEATLEMANIA broke over the U.S. in 1964 when The Beatles appeared on The Ed Sullivan Show. More than 50 years after that historic evening, that storm has swelled into a tsunami as a new era of Beatlemania has hit the collecting world hard.

"The Beatles rule the world of music and entertainment memorabilia like few others," says Noah Fleisher, author of *The Beatles: Fab Finds of the Fab Four*. "I might even venture to say, having watched the market for the best Beatles material explode in the last five years, that they may well be the only sure-fire bet in music memorabilia that a collector could have right now."

Recent auction results support Fleisher's contention. At auction, John Lennon's lost Gibson J-160E guitar sold for $2.4 million; the drum head on Ringo Starr's drum kit from the *Ed Sullivan Show* sold for more than $2 million; and a Beatles-signed *Sgt. Pepper's Lonely Hearts Club Band* album gatefold sold for nearly $300,000.

Everything from autographs to photos, albums, clothing, licensed plastic Beatles guitars and especially the real things are hotly pursued.

"The music was the doorway and the merchandising was the fix," Fleisher says. "We're all so fascinated by how they did what they did that we got personally involved with their stories and their images. How do you feel close to your idols? To people that you love with all your heart and soul but to whom you have almost no chance of ever meeting? You buy the stuff."

When it comes to selling Beatles memorabilia there are few, if any, who can match Darren Julien, the CEO and president of Julien's Auctions in Los Angeles.

"The Beatles are so popular because their music is still relevant and their fan base is not only global but it transcends all age groups," Julien says. "Their fan base only continues to increase and, for many, buying an item from their life or career is like buying a memory from their past.

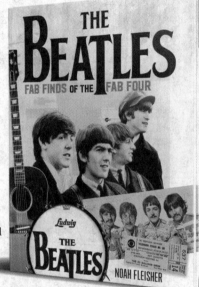

More than 50 years after exploding onto the American music scene, The Beatles remain one of the hottest tickets in entertainment collectibles. See *The Beatles: Fab Finds of the Fab Four* for more information.

"Beatles memorabilia is the blue chip of the collectibles market. Items from their career tend to go up gradually and consistently, unlike some celebrities who spike high and sometimes end low."

As a matter of debate, there may be no better investment in the memorabilia market today than a Beatles item.

"The items that bring the most and are the most sought-after are items that were used/worn on stage," Julien says. "The market for these items has dramatically increased. For instance, guitars that Christie's sold for around $100,000 in recent years, we now sell for more than $500,000. Beatles garments have also dramatically increased in recent years as museums and investors now look for iconic items that can be on display or that will increase in value."

"The Beatles are not going anywhere. I think their legendary status and collectability will only continue to increase. Items that we see selling for $500,000 now, I believe, will someday soon be worth $2 million to $3 million."

The value of the memorabilia mirrors the band's career to a tee, Fleisher says.

"The early part of their fame can be documented by massive amounts of material that was released with their names and images on it, much of which they didn't control," Fleisher notes. "The middle period, when they stopped touring, and the end, saw a good bit less of the trinket-type pop-culture material. Their image was more mature and the market in memorabilia matured the same way, focusing on autographs, records and more personal material. The end of the band saw very little material, and you can see in the book it's much more scarce from the final period of the band's time together and more valuable for that scarcity."

Items closely tied to The Beatles demand top dollar. Band-used gear — guitars, drums, even cases that carried equipment – is the ultimate prize for the biggest players in the Beatles memorabilia field.

"With this band, it all comes back to the music," Fleisher says. "They are working now on their fifth successive generation and the music sounds as fresh, innovative and inspiring as it ever has. As long as the tunes these men wrote and recorded together continue to sound so damn good, I cannot imagine that the attendant memorabilia won't continue to bring a premium. The $2.4 million paid for John's Gibson J-160E is going to look like a bargain in 20 years."

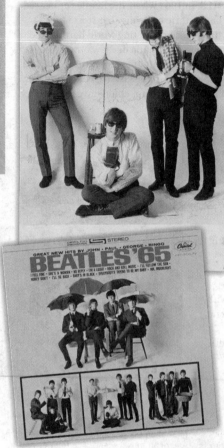

Black-and-white autographed photograph from the Beatles '65 album cover shoot, circa 1964, from original negative, shot taken by photographer Robert Whitaker during the sessions for the album's cover at London's Farringdon Studio, 12" x 15". **$16,250**

Courtesy of Heritage Auctions, ha.com

Beatles "Official Beatles Fan" pinback button, Green Duck/NEMS, 1964, featuring photo images of Paul McCartney, Ringo "Rings" Starr, George Harrison, and John Lennon, 4". **$55**

Courtesy of Heritage Auctions, ha.com

The Beatles 1963 EMI *Parlophone Records* promo poster (UK, 1963), pristine condition, 15" x 12".
.... **$525**

Courtesy of Heritage Auctions, ha.com

Movie poster, *A Hard Day's Night* (United Artists, 1964), one sheet, 27" x 41"...................... **$1,195**

Courtesy of Heritage Auctions, ha.com

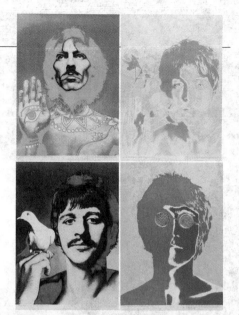

Full set of Richard Avedon psychedelic posters of The Beatles, 1968. In 1967, The Beatles commissioned famed fashion photographer Richard Avedon to do a set of portraits distributed through three publications: *LOOK* magazine in the US, the *Daily Express* newspaper in the UK, and *Stern* magazine in Germany. This set is from *Stern*, with text in German along the bottom borders. The psychedelic posters measure 18-3/4" x 27"... **$3,750**

Courtesy of Heritage Auctions, ha.com

Sgt. Pepper's Lonely Hearts Club Band Gold Record from the Record Industry Association of America, commemorating more than $1 million worth of sales for The Beatles' 1967 release, *Sgt. Pepper's Lonely Hearts Club Band*, an album that spent 175 weeks on the American charts...... **$8,125**

Courtesy of Julien's Auctions, juliensauctions.com

Abbey Road Gold Record from the Record Industry Association of America, commemorating more than $1 million worth of sales for The Beatles' 1969 release, *Abbey Road*, an album that spent 129 weeks on the American charts............... **$5,937**

Courtesy of Julien's Auctions, juliensauctions.com

top lot

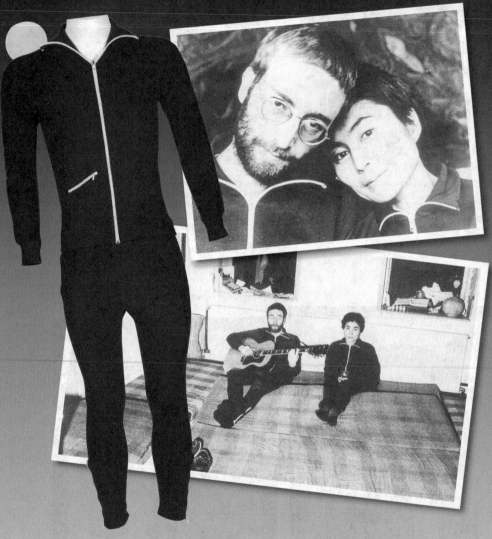

In 1970, John Lennon and Yoko Ono spent most of January in Denmark to be with Yoko's daughter, Kyoko. The couple stayed with film producer Tony Cox, Yoko's second husband, and his new wife, Melinde. It was a time of personal renewal for both John and Yoko. While staying in Denmark, Lennon decided to have his hair cropped shorter than at any time in his adult life. Yoko followed suit. The day was January 20, 1970. The precise reason for the haircuts is unclear, but both were in the midst of a lengthy peace campaign and were keen to remain in the public eye. During their stay in Denmark, John and Yoko wore Danish running suits almost all the time: hers red and his blue. John's blue running suit sold at Heritage Auctions for $37,500.

Courtesy of Heritage Auctions, ha.com

Beatles signed group photo taken in Bahamas during the filming of *Help!*, circa February-March 1965, glossy black-and-white image, 8" x 10".
.... **$9,375**

Courtesy of Heritage Auctions, ha.com

The Beatles Flip Your Wig Game, 1964, Milton Bradley, includes game board, cardboard cutouts for each member of The Beatles, numbered die and two decks of cards................................... **$140**

Courtesy of Heritage Auctions, ha.com

Beatles unused ticket to their last performance on *The Ed Sullivan Show*, August 14, 1965, with original folder, transmittal letter and envelope. This performance was taped on September 12, 1965. Other than later promotional clips supplied to Sullivan, it was the Beatles' fourth and last "live" appearance on the show and they performed six songs. The first set: "I Feel Fine," "I'm Down," and "Act Naturally." They closed the show with: "Ticket to Ride," "Yesterday" (Paul, introduced by George, performing solo on guitar with string accompaniment), and "Help." **$9,375**

Courtesy of Heritage Auctions, ha.com

Beatles publicity photograph, 1962, by Peter Kaye, Liverpool. The leather jackets are gone, replaced by the suits that would come to define their early rise to fame...**$2,240**

Courtesy of Julien's Auctions, juliensauctions.com

Beatles wrist watch, Bradley Time, 1964, dial bears the group's individual portraits placed at the 12:00, 3:00, 6:00, and 9:00 positions with the text: "The Beatles," "Shockproof" and "Made in Gt Britain." **$656**

Courtesy of Heritage Auctions, ha.com

Beatles Bobb'n Head figures, Car Mascots, Inc., 1964, with original box and cardboard insert that keeps the heads from "bobb'n." **$1,075**

Courtesy of Heritage Auctions, ha.com

Beatles Record Player, NEMS, 1964, four-speed portable record player with carrying case. With only about 5,000 produced, the record player is considered by most collectors to be one of the ultimate pieces to own of all commercial Beatles memorabilia. **$2,750**

Courtesy of Heritage Auctions, ha.com

"With the Beatles" Perfume, UK, circa 1963, manufactured by Olive Adair Ltd., Liverpool, rare, elusive collectible from the earl days of Beatlemania, 2-1/4" x 3-1/4". **$3,750**

Courtesy of Heritage Auctions, ha.com

Beatles blue lunchbox with original matching Thermos, Aladdin, 1965, first Aladdin lunchbox dedicated to a rock group. **$750**

Courtesy of Heritage Auctions, ha.com

Beatles School Bag, Burnel Ltd. of Canada, 1964, gusseted tan vinyl school bag with handle and shoulder strap with Beatles images in brown below the flap and on either side of the latch with facsimile signatures between the images, 12" x 9". **$1,750**

Courtesy of Heritage Auctions, ha.com

Beatles sealed coloring set, UK, 1964, manufactured by Kitfix Hobbys Ltd. According to the box — which features detailed color portraits of the visage of each Beatle — the set includes "5 Numbered Ready to Colour Portraits of John, Paul, George, Ringo, and the Group" with "6 Brilliant Coloured Pencils." Box measures approximately 13-3/4" x 9". **$2,375**

Courtesy of Heritage Auctions, ha.com

BOOKS

WITH AN EXCESS of 100 million books in existence, there are plenty of opportunities and avenues for bibliophiles to feed their enthusiasm and build a satisfying collection of noteworthy tomes without taking out a second mortgage or sacrificing their children's college funds. With so many to choose from, the true challenge is limiting a collection to a manageable size and scale, adding only volumes that meet the requirements of bringing the collector pleasure and holding their values.

What collectors are really searching for when they refer to "first editions" are the first printings of first editions. Every book has a first edition, each of which is special in its own right. As Matthew Budman points out in *Collecting Books* (House of Collectibles, 2004), "A first represents the launching of a work into the world, with or without fanfare, to have a great impact, or no impact, immediately or decades later ... Holding a first edition puts you directly in contact with that moment of impact."

Devon Gray, director of Fine Books and Manuscripts at Skinner, Inc., skinnerinc.com, explains the fascination with collectible books: "Collectors are always interested in landmarks of human thought and culture, and important moments in the history of printing."

What makes a first edition special enough to be considered collectible is rarity and demand; the number of people who want a book has to be greater than the number of books available. So, even if there are relatively few in existence, there has to be a demand for any particular first edition to be monetarily valuable.

As is the case with so many collectibles, condition is paramount. If a book was published with a dust jacket, it must be present and in great condition to attain the maximum value.

"A book with a very large value basically has further to fall before it loses it all," Gray says. "A great example is the first edition of the printed account of the Lewis and Clarke expedition. In bad condition, its value is in the four-figure range; in better condition, it gets up to five figures; and in excellent condition, six figures."

Ken Kesey, *One Flew Over the Cuckoo's Nest.* New York: The Viking Press, 1962, first edition, first printing, inscribed by Kesey: "For / Darrel / Kesey / 1993," 311 pages. **$8,365**

Courtesy of Heritage Auctions, ha.com

A signature enhances a book's value because it often places the book in the author's hands. Cut signatures add slightly to a book's value because the author didn't actually sign the book – he or she may have never even held the book with the added cut signature. When the book itself is signed, even if with a brief inscription, it holds a slightly higher value. If the author is known for making regular appearances and accommodating all signature requests, the signature adds little to the value of the book because the supply for signed examples is plentiful.

"Real value potential comes into play with association material," Gray explains. "For example, a famous novelist's Nobel-winning story is based on a tumultuous affair he had with a famous starlet under his heiress-wife's nose, and you have the copy he presented to his wife, with her 'notes.'"

Even a title that has been labeled as "great," "important," or "essential" doesn't mean a particular edition – even a first edition – is collectible or monetarily valuable. After all, if a much-anticipated book is released with an initial print run of 350,000, chances are there will be hundreds of thousands of "firsts" to choose from – even decades after publication. Supply far outweighs demand, diminishing value.

The overly abundant supply of book club editions (which can be reprinted indefinitely) is just one of the reasons they're not valued by collectors. Some vintage book club editions were also made from inferior materials, such as high-acid paper using lower quality manufacturing processes.

Determining if a book is a book club edition is easier than determining if it is a first edition. Some of the giveaways that Matthew Budman lists in *Collecting Books* include:

- No price on dust jacket
- Blind stamp on back cover (small impression on the back board under the dust jacket); can be as small as a pinprick hole
- "Book Club Edition" (or similar notation) on dust jacket
- Books published by the Literary Guild after World War II are smaller format, thinner and printed on cheap paper.

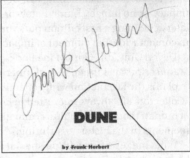

Frank Herbert, *Dune*. Philadelphia and New York: Chilton Books, [1965]. First edition, signed by the author on the title page, first novel in the *Dune* series, winner of the 1965 Nebula and 1966 Hugo awards for best novel. **$15,000**

Courtesy of Heritage Auctions, ha.com

TIPS FOR IDENTIFYING FIRST EDITIONS

Learning how to recognize first editions is a key to protecting yourself as a collector; you can't take it for granted that the person you are buying from (especially if he or she is not a professional bookseller) has identified the book properly. Entire volumes have been written on identifying first editions; different publishing houses use different means of identification, many utilizing differing methods and codes. However, Richard Russell, who has been collecting and selling books since 1973, offers these clues in his book, *Antique Trader Book Collector's Price Guide*:

- The date on the title page matches the copyright date with no other printings listed on the copyright page (verso).

- "First Edition," "First Printing," "First Issue," or something similar is listed on the copyright page.

- A publisher's seal or logo (colophon) is printed on the title page, copyright page, or at the end of the text block.

- The printer's code on the copyright page shows a "1" or an "A" at one end or the other (example: "9 8 7 6 5 4 3 2 1" indicates first edition; "9 8 7 6 5 4 3 2" indicates second edition).

Fledgling book collectors should also be aware of companies that built a burgeoning business of publishing a copious number of "classic" and best-seller reprints; just a few on the long list are Grosset & Dunlap, Reader's Digest, Modern Library, A.L. Burt, Collier, Tower and Triangle. Many of these companies' editions are valued only as reading copies, not as collectibles worthy of investment.

Proper care should be implemented early when building a collection to assure the books retain their condition and value. Books should be stored upright on shelves in a climate-controlled environment out of direct (or even bright indirect) sunlight. Too much humidity will warp covers; high temperatures will break down glues. Arrange them so similar-sized books are side-by-side for maximum support, and use bookends so the books don't lean, which will eventually cause the spines to shift and cause permanent damage.

A bookplate usually will reduce a book's value, so keep that in mind when you're thinking of adding a book with a bookplate to your collection, and avoid adding bookplates to your own volumes. Also, don't pack your volumes with high-acid paper such as newspaper clippings, and always be careful when placing or removing them from the shelf so you don't tear the spine.

Building a book collection – or any collection, for that matter – on a budget involves knowing more about the subject than the seller. Learning everything possible about proper identification of coveted books and significant authors involves diligence and dedication, but the reward is maximum enjoyment of collecting at any level.

– Karen Knapstein

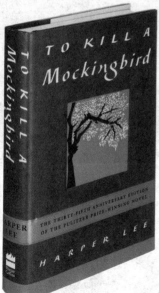

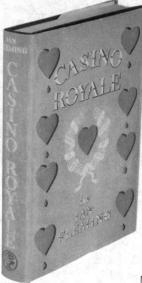

Harper Lee, *To Kill a Mockingbird*. New York: Harper Collins, 1995. Thirty-fifth anniversary edition, later printing, signed by the author. **$300**

Courtesy of Heritage Auctions, ha.com

Ian Fleming, *Casino Royale*. London: Jonathan Cape, [1953]. First edition. Publisher's black cloth, spine lettered in orangish-red, central heart-shaped device stamped in orangish-red on front board, first James Bond novel, from the Collection of Daniel J. King. **$23,750**

Courtesy of Heritage Auctions, ha.com

Margaret Mitchell, *Gone with the Wind*. New York: The Macmillan Company, 1936, first edition, signed by the author on the front free endpaper, best-selling novel and winner of the Pulitzer Prize for Fiction in 1937, and the basis of one of the most successful Hollywood films ever made. From the James C. Seacrest Collection. **$21,250**

Courtesy of Heritage Auctions, ha.com

top lot

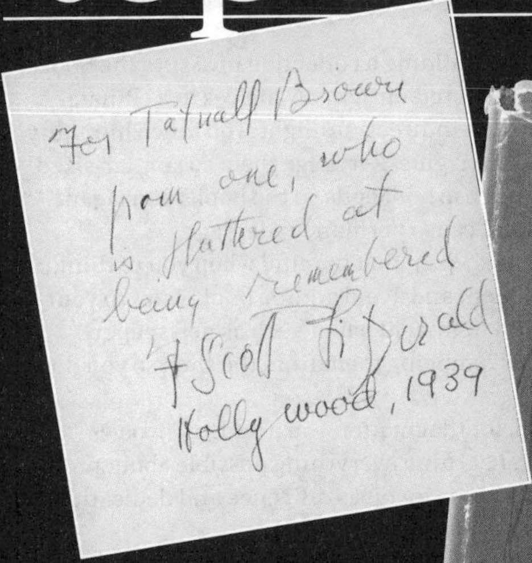

> For Tatnall Brown
> from one, who
> is flattered at
> being remembered
> F Scott Fitzgerald
> Hollywood, 1939

F. Scott Fitzgerald (1896-1940) is considered one of America's greatest writers. His classic novel, *The Great Gatsby* (Charles Scribner's Sons, 1925), has sold millions of copies and is required reading in high schools and colleges. A first edition, first printing of the book is a great find among collectors. And this one from the James C. Seacrest Collection is no exception. Making this copy of *The Great Gatsby* even more desirable is the front endpaper inscription by Fitzgerald, who writes: "For Tatnall Brown / from one, who / is flattered at / being remembered / F Scott Fitzgerald / Hollywood, 1939."

The timing of the signature is significant. Fitzgerald moved to Los Angeles to write for the movie industry, but it did not go well. After a few years struggling in Hollywood to see his projects realized, Metro-Goldwyn-Mayer terminated Fitzgerald's contract in 1939 after a single screenwriting credit. Inscribed at his professional nadir, no longer with MGM and his books out of print and languishing in warehouses, Fitzgerald clearly summarized his feelings about his state for Tatnall Brown, a banker and former Harvard College dean, in this copy of his most popular book. Fitzgerald died the next year at 44. This cherished book sold at auction for a remarkable $162,500.

COURTESY OF HERITAGE AUCTIONS, HA.COM

10 Things You Didn't Know About **Margaret Brundage**

1 Margaret Brundage was the primary designer of covers for the pulp fiction magazine *Weird Tales* throughout much of the 1930s and into the 1940s. She was a pioneer of the pulp era, becoming its first female cover artist. Her covers drew attention and sparked controversy. They often depicted scantily clad female characters — many times in treacherous situations — associated with one of the magazine's 'tales.'

2 Sizeable original cover art by Brundage illustrating the story, "The Carnal God," for the June 1937 issue of *Weird Tales* sold for $47,150 (including buyer's premium) at auction on March 17, 2016. The pastel artwork appeared on illustration board, was framed, and measured 26-1/8" x 30-1/8", before selling during the auction presented by Hake's Americana & Collectibles.

3 Her various informal monikers, which include "The First Lady of Pulp Pinup Art" and "The Queen of the Pulps," speak to her claim to fame. However, her post-secondary education and early work was in fashion design and illustration.

4 *Weird Tales* continues to appeal to fans of pulp fiction, as well as collectors. Among the *Tales* receiving considerable interest are those featuring stories of Conan, written by Robert E. Howard. From 1932-1936, 17 stories featuring Conan appeared in *Weird Tales*, with nine of those appearing on the cover. Brundage, who signed most of her work M. Brundage, drew all nine Conan covers. This was well before Frank Frazetta began drawing covers of Conan for paperbacks.

5 During a 2012 auction by Heritage Auctions, original pastel on board cover art for "Abd Dhulma, Lord of Fire," which appeared on the cover of *Weird Tales* in December 1933, commanded $32,500.

6 In an interesting twist, Brundage crossed paths with Walt Disney while the two were in high school and students at the Academy of Fine Art in Chicago, according to an article on fastcocreat. com, referencing the book, *The Alluring Art of Margaret Brundage: Queen of Pulp Pin-Up Art*, by J. David Spurlock and Stephen D. Korshak (bit.ly/AT_TenThings021517).

Original cover art of *Weird Tales'* "The Six Sleepers." **$19,375**

Courtesy of Heritage Auctions, ha.com

7 Although she was frequently criticized for her depiction of women as helpless damsels in her cover art, she was well known for her innovative actions as a member of various progressive organizations including the College of the Complexes and the Dil Pickle Club in Chicago during the 1950s and '60s. Her then husband, Myron "Slim" Brundage, founded the College of Complexes. It's reported she participated in antiwar protests, the woman's suffrage and civil rights movements, crusaded for free speech and sought to help people living in lower income communities to utilize their artistic talents.

Original cover art for "The Carnal God." **$47,150**

Courtesy of Hake's Americana & Collectibles, hakes.com

Original pastel cover art for "Abd Dhulma, Lord of Fire." **$32,500**

Courtesy of Heritage Auctions, ha.com

8 Brundage created her art using pastels on illustration board, a departure from the way many of her peers approached creating cover art.

9 The original cover art of *Weird Tales*' "The Six Sleepers," from October 1935, a pastel on paper by Brundage, sold for $19,375 during a 2013 auction by Heritage Auctions.

10 Between 1933 and 1945, Margaret Brundage sold 66 original pulp cover illustrations to *Weird Tales*.

– Compiled by Antoinette Rahn

Sources: quod.lib.umich.edu/s/sclead/umich-scl-hobohemia?view=text; anageundreamedof.com/2012/12/collecting-robert-e-howard-part-3.html; ha.com; fastcocreat.com;anageundreamedof.com; chicagology.com

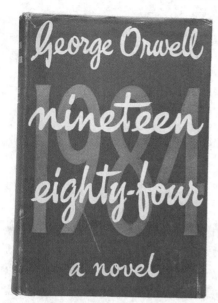

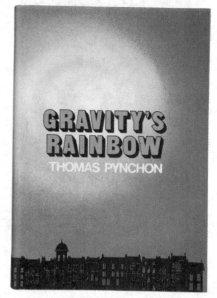

George Orwell, *Nineteen Eighty-Four* [1984].
London: Secker & Warburg, 1949, first edition,
"First Published 1949" stated on copyright page,
312 pages. **$4,480**

Courtesy of Heritage Auctions, ha.com

Thomas Pynchon, *Gravity's Rainbow*. New York:
Viking, 1973, first edition, first printing, inscribed
and signed by Pynchon on half-title page, "10/86
/ To Michael Urban, / Best Wishes, / Thomas
Pynchon," 760 pages. **$16,250**

Courtesy of Heritage Auctions, ha.com

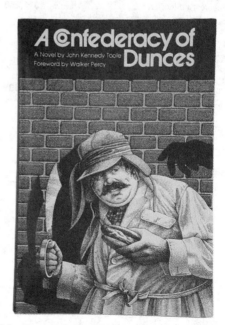

H. A. Rey, *Curious George*. Boston: Houghton
Mifflin, 1941, first edition, quarto, unpaginated,
illustrations by author, publisher's brick red cloth
with Curious George vignette in black on front
board and lettering in black on spine, illustrated
endpapers, original dust jacket with $1.75 price.
....**$26,290**

Courtesy of Heritage Auctions, ha.com

John Kennedy Toole, *A Confederacy of Dunces*.
Baton Rouge: Louisiana State University Press,
1980. Foreword by Walker Percy, first edition
signed by Walker Percy, 338 pages............... **$4,482**

Courtesy of Heritage Auctions, ha.com

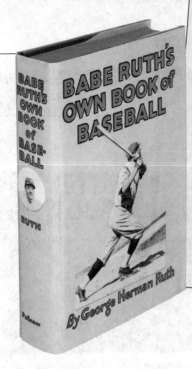

George Herman "Babe" Ruth, *Babe Ruth's Own Book of Baseball*. New York: G. P. Putnam's Sons, 1928. First edition, limited to 1,000 copies, of which this is number 384, and signed by the author, and seemingly less common than a 1,000-copy limitation would suggest. From the James C. Seacrest Collection. **$11,250**

Courtesy of Heritage Auctions, ha.com

▼ Eric Hodgins, *Mr. Blandings Builds His Dream House*. New York: Simon and Schuster, 1946, first edition, signed and inscribed by author on front endpaper. **$538**

Courtesy of Heritage Auctions, ha.com

▲ J. D. Salinger, *The Catcher in the Rye*. Boston: Little, Brown and Company, 1951. First edition, tenth printing, presentation copy, inscribed by the author on the front free endpaper: "Dec. 24, 1951 / To Susan Bishop- / with best wishes, / J. D. Salinger." From the James C. Seacrest Collection. **$27,500**

Courtesy of Heritage Auctions, ha.com

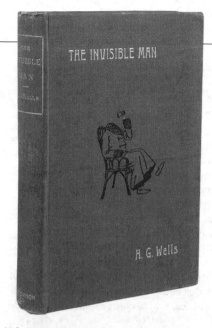

H.G. Wells, *The Invisible Man*. A Grotesque
Romance. London: C. Arthur Pearson Limited,
1897, first edition, 245 pages plus two pages
of advertisements. **$538**

Courtesy of Heritage Auctions, ha.com

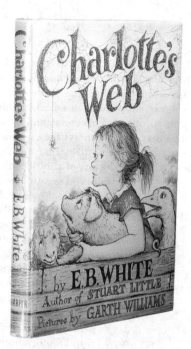

E.B. White, *Charlotte's Web*. New York: Harper
and Brothers, 1952, first edition, pictures by
Garth Williams, 1953 Newberry Award
winning book.. **$1,554**

Courtesy of Heritage Auctions, ha.com

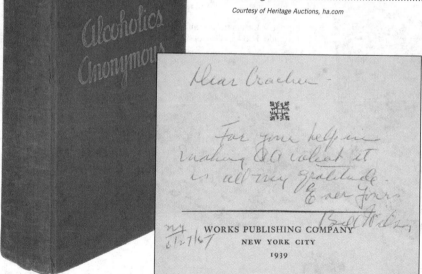

[Bill Wilson]. *Alcoholics Anonymous*. New York City: Works Publishing Company, 1939. First
edition of the famous Big Red Book, presentation copy, inscribed by Bill Wilson on the title-page:
"Dear Cracker- / For your help in / making AA what it / is, all my gratitude. / Ever Yours / Bill Wilson /
NY / 6/27/67." **$30,000**

Courtesy of Heritage Auctions, ha.com

BOTTLES

INTEREST IN BOTTLE COLLECTING continues to grow, and more collectors are spending their free time digging through old dumps and foraging through ghost towns, digging out old outhouses, exploring abandoned mine shafts, and searching for their favorite bottles at antiques shows, swap meets, flea markets, and garage sales. In addition, the Internet has greatly expanded, offering collectors numerous opportunities and resources to buy and sell bottles with many new auction websites, without even leaving the house.

Most collectors, however, still look beyond the type and value of a bottle to its origin and history. Researching the history of a bottle is almost as interesting as finding the bottle itself. In addition to numerous bottle auctions, along with 15 to 20 antique bottle shows held each month by bottle clubs across the United States, England, Australia, and Europe, there have been major archeological finds, shipwreck discoveries in the Gulf of Mexico and the Baltic Sea, bottles found in attics, and of course many great bottle digs across the country.

All of this good news demonstrates that the hobby is not only strong, but continues to gain popularity while bringing an overall greater awareness to a wider spectrum of antiques collectors.

For more information on bottles, see *Antique Trader Bottles Identification & Price Guide*, 8th edition, and *Picker's Pocket Guide: Bottles*, both by Michael Polak.

Litthauer bitters bottle, milk glass, "Litthauer Stomach Bitters / Invented 1864 by / Joseph Loewenthal, Berlin," 9-1/2". **$138**
Courtesy of Holabird Americana, holabirdamericana.com

Amber pistol bottle, "C.C.P. Co. / PAT-D APP FOR," original screw cap, c. 1890-1900, 5" x 8". **$81**
Courtesy of Holabird Americana, holabirdamericana.com

VISIT WWW.ANTIQUETRADER.COM

WWW.FACEBOOK.COM/ANTIQUETRADER

Figural beer bottle, clear,
Italian, marked "Made in Italy"
on bottom, 11-1/2" h............**$25**

Courtesy of Holabird Americana,
holabirdamericana.com

Ink bottle, First Higgins, aqua,
"Chas. M. Higgins & Co., New
York," "16oz" with original
paper label in recessed band
in the center, founded 1880,
thought to be the first (or one
of the first) Higgins ink bottles,
c. 1885, 3" dia., 7-1/2" h. . . **$138**

Courtesy of Holabird Americana,
holabirdamericana.com

Indian bitters bottle,
medium amber, "BROWN'S
/ CELEBRATED / INDIAN
BITTERS // PATENTED / FEB.
11 / 1868," small bruise
potstone on back, 12-1/4". . **$469**

Courtesy of Holabird Americana,
holabirdamericana.com

Six-log amber Plantation
Bitters, 9-3/4" h.................**$115**

Courtesy of Holabird Americana,
holabirdamericana.com

Medicine bottle, clear, "J. A.
MULLER /DRUGGIST / OPP.
POST OFFICE, CARSON CITY,
NEV.," seldom seen, 6" h. ..**$186**

Courtesy of Holabird Americana,
holabirdamericana.com

BOTTLES

▶ Highrock Congress Springs mineral water, amber, "HIGHROCK CONGRESS SPRING/ 1767(small numbers)/ C & W/ SARATOGA N. Y.," 1/4"chip on rear. **$310**

Courtesy of Holabird Americana, holabirdamericana.com

Lynch & Clarke mineral water, "LYNCH & CLARKE/ NEW YORK," unknown variety, possible pontil scar. **$279**

Courtesy of Holabird Americana, holabirdamericana.com

Pearson Bros. soda bottle, aqua, "PEARSON BROS / BODIE" [Calif.]," with original glass stopper, c. 1880. .... **$2,108**

Courtesy of Holabird Americana, holabirdamericana.com

Pint, Pitkin Swirl, dip mold, open pontil, curved crosshatch design, yellow-green, 6-1/2" x 5". **$563**

Courtesy of Holabird Americana, holabirdamericana.com

Italian soda bottle, pint, cobalt, "ITALIAN / SODA WATER / MANUFACTORY / SAN FRANCISCO." **$1,054**

Courtesy of Holabird Americana, holabirdamericana.com

Highrock Congress Springs mineral water, pint, amber, "HIGHROCK CONGRESS SPRING CO/ 1767(large number)/ C & W/ SARATOGA NY.," molding issue on the lip similar to a smooth chip. **$248**

Courtesy of Holabird Americana, holabirdamericana.com

Hutch soda bottle, cobalt blue, E. Ottenville, tooled top, Nashville, Tennessee. **$200**

Courtesy of Holabird Americana, holabirdamericana.com

Hutch soda bottle, Stockder & Co., aqua, Canon City, Colorado. **$94**

Courtesy of Holabird Americana, holabirdamericana.com

California Gold Rush soda, medium cobalt blue, pontiled, "M. R. / Sacramento // (Misspelled "Sacrimento")" 1851-1863, rare. **$1,313**

Courtesy of Holabird Americana, holabirdamericana.com

Scarce Coca Cola Bottling Works, Phoenix, Ariz. crown top, aqua green, 1914-1915. **$37**

Courtesy of Holabird Americana, holabirdamericana.com

▲ Royal Velvet back bar bottle, raised white enamel Royal Velvet. Prior to 1895, this distillery operated under the name Mayflower Distillery Co. In 1892, it was purchased by Dick Meschendorf, who changed the name to Old Kentucky Distillery and produced different brands of whiskey including "Royal Velvet" and many others. The Old Kentucky Distillery operated from circa 1880 until it was shut down due to Prohibition in 1919. .... **$94**

Early 1900s Coca-Cola soda bottle, rare light aqua, "Coca Cola Bottling Works, Phoenix, Ariz.," 1908-09. .... **$24**

Courtesy of Holabird Americana, holabirdamericana.com

Courtesy of Holabird Americana, holabirdamericana.com

BRASS COLLECTIBLES

BRASS IS A yellow alloy mainly of copper and zinc but it can include other metals. Generally used for decorative articles, brass' durability makes it ideal for inlays, wall insets and tools. The inexpensive, yet strong metal makes it ubiquitous across many cultures and objects for thousands of years. In modern times, brass was particularly favored during the Art Deco Movement of the 1930s and the modernist movement of the 1960s and '70s, the complete opposite of the darkly patinated copper and bronze used during the Arts and Crafts and Art Nouveau movements. It was also a favored metal to use for accenting firearms and swords. The metal's ability to withstand strong pressure and heat made it ideal for lanterns and locomotive pressure gauges.

Among the most heavily collected items today include chandeliers, figurines, and statues, nautical items, clocks, and pocket watches, and even microscopes. All of these items can be readily found at your local thrift store and flea markets. In fact, there are sellers on Etsy.com who specialize in bringing unique brass items to market.

The market for brass has been remarkably steady, but is showing signs of an upswing. Younger buyers who are attracted to simple forms and uses, particularly bookends, affordable jewelry, designer candlesticks and even furniture, favor the color. Generally, vintage examples of mass-produced bookends can be found between $5 and $50, depending on the venue. Brass figurines make attractive décor items and many brass items were produced with a practical use in mind, so many of the antiques can still be used for their intended purpose.

Solid examples of bookends are commanding higher prices these days, particularly figural examples of animals and people. High-quality castings are back in style. Low-quality castings are also holding their values (even if those values are not particularly high to begin with).

With brass, the older the object, the more value it offers to the decorator or collector. Home items from the late 1700s and early 1800s are collected based on their use. Several artists who worked in brass continue to see their values climb. Artists such as Franz and Karl Hagenauer, Josef Hoffman, Wiener Werkstatte, Peter Muller-Munk and Harry Bertoia all used brass as a medium due to its versatility. Most all of Bertoia's musical sculptures employ brass.

Unlike other decorative mediums such as silver, gold or bronze, brass can tarnish and pit heavily if left in salt water or when exposed to some household cleaning solutions such as ammonia. Interestingly, many people are introducing artificial patinas to common, low-value brass objects for decorative effects. This can be achieved by applying vinegar, salt, some window cleaners and even hardboiled eggs. The brass object is placed into an airtight container for several hours to acquire the desired coloration, such as a ruddy, rust or green or even bronze look. Collectors should be aware of these artificial patinas if they are on the lookout for authentic pieces.

Since it is easy to make a new piece look old, it's not surprising to learn Chinese and Japanese brass objects are being heavily reproduced. Both cultures were adept at using the metal in objects and tools, but many items were made for religious ceremonies. Again, the learned collector should study commonly used designs and castings before investing a lot of resources here. Sloppy or blurry castings are a sure sign the piece is new and is only worth décor value. The market for Indian brass has plummeted due to the mass amounts of imports flooding into the country. Brass from India should only be purchased from a reputable dealer or auction house.

The key to collecting quality brass items is based on careful observation. First, a quality brass item should not have any machining or mold marks or any other evidence that modern machinery was used in the making of the piece. Second, try to find out as much as possible about the time period in which a piece was made. This will help you understand the composition of the item and where is likely came from. The best quality brass items often have maker's marks, which gives collectors much interesting stories and a source where the item was made. Unlike silver, these makers' marks are most often found on the bottom of the piece or even hidden behind felt padding on the bottom.

Pair of table mirrors, in easel form, cherubic decorations flank the sides, 18" h x 14"w. **$130**

Courtesy of Susanin's Auctions, susanins.com

Three-arm hanging chandelier, Rochester Brass, patent Sept. 14, 1886, lacking chain, multiple flea bites to shades, 36-1/2" h x 8-1/2" w. **$625**

Courtesy of Gray's Auctioneers, graysauctioneers.com

Welded sculpture with leaves and enamel butterflies, by Brutalist artist Curtis Jere, signed "C. Jere," one leaf appears to be missing, 55" h x 30" w. **$227**

Courtesy of Susanin's Auctions, susanins.com

Two antique hot water urns, lever on the taller of the two urns is broken, tallest 17"h. **$260**

Courtesy of Susanin's Auctions, susanins.com

Sectioned footed censer, elephant figural feet and peacock statuettes on lids, five separate sections each with a lid, 4" h x 5" w x 5" l................... **$127**

Courtesy of The Benefit Shop Foundation, Inc., thebenefitshop.org

National Cash Register Model No. 50, circa 1906, finish C, top plate features a dolphin pattern ornamentation on sides and impressed "Amount Purchased," three glass panes for money figures viewing over a plate with impressed patent information including the serial number of "542949" over "50," hinged lift-up cover with a key and glass windows displaying "Dollars/Cents," "Customer Counter," and "No Sale," fifteen push-down keys with various figures, marble table, wooden drawer with brass plate, underside of drawer bears original manufacturer's paper label marked with matching serial number and built for "Atlanta Soda Co., Atlanta, GA," very good condition, one push-down key with a detached plate, one side with a spot of oxidation, 21-1/4" h x 10-1/4" x 16"... **$685**

Courtesy of Jeffrey S. Evans & Associates, jeffreysevans.com

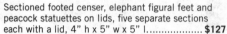

◄ Russian gilt can antique samovar by the Brothers Varonsovy, featuring a foliate spout handle, wood-enhanced ring handles, and stamped in several places with images of the medals it won, with a later Soviet drip bowl and under tray, can has a few shallow dents and the interior bears marks of minor water encrustation, 23-1/2" h x 12-1/2" w over handles................ **$600**

Courtesy of Auctions At Showplace, nyshowplace.com

Reticulated footed fire fender, used to protect the space in front of the fireplace free from ash, debris and a stray log from the fire, and to help keep children and pets away from the fire, 47" l. **$150**

Courtesy of Langston Auction Gallery, langstonantiques.com

Vintage Imhof mantel or boudoir clock, with a brass body and a hand-painted face featuring a medieval scene in enamel, mid-20th century, minor age-appropriate wear, 7-1/4" h. **$1,000**

Courtesy of Auctions At Showplace, nyshowplace.com

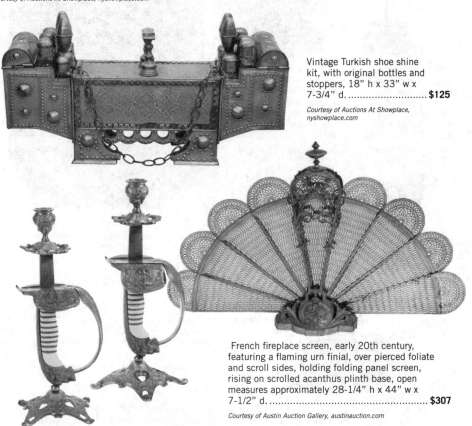

Vintage Turkish shoe shine kit, with original bottles and stoppers, 18" h x 33" w x 7-3/4" d. **$125**

Courtesy of Auctions At Showplace, nyshowplace.com

French fireplace screen, early 20th century, featuring a flaming urn finial, over pierced foliate and scroll sides, holding folding panel screen, rising on scrolled acanthus plinth base, open measures approximately 28-1/4" h x 44" w x 7-1/2" d. **$307**

Courtesy of Austin Auction Gallery, austinauction.com

Imperial German Navy sword hilt pair of candlesticks, each featuring a lion's head with red eyes and original wire-wrapped grip, anchor on the hinged guard, mounted on a brass base and candle socket; thought to be assembled from unissued leftover swords and sold as souvenirs after World War I, circa 1925, undamaged condition, 11" h. **$187**

Courtesy of Jeffrey S. Evans & Associates, jeffreysevans.com

Ink stand with lizard figure nestled among the foliage, features double crystal inkwells, removable, 3-1/2" x 10". **$156**

Courtesy of Hudson Valley Auctions, hudsonvalleyauctions.com

Vintage bush sculpture, attributed to Harry Bertoia, made of heavy brass rods, mid-century modern design, 81" h x 31" d....................**$12,600**

Courtesy of Joshua Kodner, joshuakodner.com

Gilt brass fox head doorstop with swirling rope handle ending in a devil tail, sitting atop a black-painted metal base, 18" h.......... **$250**

Courtesy of Auctions At Showplace, nyshowplace.com

Gilt wall mirror, circa 1940s, features an octagonal hammered frame, with scroll and acanthus accents to corners, holding beveled mirror, weighs 15-1/4 pounds, 27-1/4" h x 20-1/4" w x 1" d. **$400**

Courtesy of Austin Auction Gallery, austinauction.com

◀ German Baroque Altar Navicula (Christian censer) on integral stand, in repoussed brass, showing signs of generations of use, with several old riveted repairs to hinge and lid, wonderful patina of veneration, roughly 7" x 7" x 3-1/2". **$84**

Courtesy of Thomaston Place Auction Galleries, thomastonplace.com

Sand cast polished brass and wrought iron fire poker with turquoise inlaid, for Pepe Mendoza, Mexico City, circa 1965, Surrealist design in Aztec-style female figure with an upraised hand, a roosting chicken atop her right hand, with wings on her hips, standing atop a turquoise inlaid circular band with a pair of wings at each side and an Aztec style astrological dial, over a pair of scroll brackets, joining tapering stacked discs, 39-3/4" h x 5-1/4" w x 2" d..................**$872**

Courtesy of Simpson Galleries, LLC, simpsongalleries.com

CERAMICS

belleek

THE NAME BELLEEK refers to an industrious village in County Fermanagh, Northern Ireland, on the banks of the River Erne, and to the lustrous porcelain wares produced there.

In 1849, John Caldwell Bloomfield inherited a large estate near Belleek. Interested in ceramics and having discovered rich deposits of feldspar and kaolin (china clay) on his lands, he soon envisioned a pottery that would make use of these materials, local craftspeople, and waterpower of the River Erne. He was also anxious to enhance Ireland's prestige with superior porcelain products.

Bloomfield had a chance meeting with Robert Williams Armstrong, who had established a substantial architectural business building potteries. Keenly interested in the manufacturing process, he agreed to design, build and manage the new factory for Bloomfield. The factory was to be located on Rose Isle on a bend in the River Erne.

Bloomfield and Armstrong then approached David McBirney, a highly successful merchant and director of railway companies, and enticed him to provide financing. Impressed by the plans, he agreed to raise funds for the enterprise. As agreed, the factory was named McBirney and Armstrong, then later D. McBirney and Co.

Although 1857 is given as the founding date of the pottery, it is recorded that the pottery's foundation stone was laid by Mrs. J. C. Bloomfield on Nov. 18, 1858. Although not completed until 1860, the pottery was producing earthenware from its inception.

With the arrival of ceramic experts from the (William Henry) Goss Pottery in England, principally William Bromley, Sr. and William Wood Gallimore, Parian ware was perfected and, by 1863, the wares we associate with Belleek today were in production.

With Belleek Pottery workers and others emigrating to the United States in the late 1800s and early 1900s, Belleek-style china manufacture, known as American Belleek, commenced at several American firms, including Ceramic Art Co., Colombian Art Pottery, Lenox, Inc., Ott & Brewer, and Willets Manufacturing Co.

Throughout its Parian production, Belleek Pottery marked its items with an Irish harp and wolfhound and the Devenish Tower. Its second period began with the advent of the McKinley Tariff Act of 1891 and the (revised) British Merchandise Act as Belleek added the ribbon "Co. FERMANAGH IRELAND" beneath its mark in 1891. Both the first and second period marks were black, although they occasionally appeared in burnt orange, green, blue, or brown, especially on earthenware items. Its third period begin in 1926, when it added a Celtic emblem under the second period mark as well as the government

Shell-form round compote sits atop a spiral stem and a six-lobe base including three shell bowls separated by horses emerging from the base, all with green decoration throughout, bears first Belleek mark (1863-1891), along with retailer's stamp for John Mortlock, 204 Oxford Street, London, and the outside rim of the base also showcases the impress of "BELLEEK/CO FERMANAGH," bowl is 9-3/4" d, 9-3/4" h. **$1,722**

Courtesy of William Bunch Auctions & Appraisals, bunchauctions.com

CERAMICS

trademark "Reg No 0857," which was granted in 1884. The Celtic emblem was registered by the Irish Industrial Development Association in 1906 and reads "Deanta in Eirinn," and means "Made in Ireland." The pottery is now utilizing its 13th mark, following a succession of three black marks, three green marks, one gold mark, two blue marks, and three green marks. The final green mark was used only a single year, in 2007, to commemorate its 150th anniversary. In 2008, Belleek changed its mark to brown. Early earthenware was often marked in the same color as the majority of its surface decoration. Early basketware has Parian strips applied to its base with the impressed verbiage "BELLEEK" and later on, additionally "Co FERMANAGH" with or without "IRELAND." Current basketware carries the same mark as its Parian counterpart.

Woven strand round bowl with applied flowers on top rim, looped handles, marked Belleek / R / CO FERMANAGH on two pad, 11" d.................... **$148**

Courtesy of William Bunch Auctions & Appraisals, bunchauctions.com

Pink lace charger platter with gold accents, first makers' mark black (1863-1890), 14-1/2" d.**$1,200**

Courtesy of Turkey Creek Auctions, antiqueauctionsfl.com

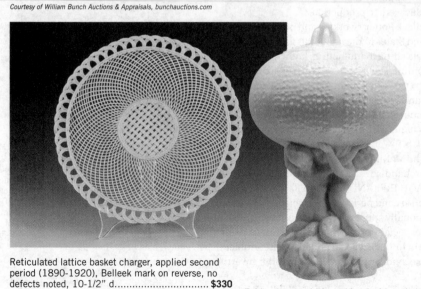

Reticulated lattice basket charger, applied second period (1890-1920), Belleek mark on reverse, no defects noted, 10-1/2" d.............................. **$330**

Courtesy of Cordier Auctions & Appraisals, cordierauction.com

Echinus mermaid footed bowl with a sixth period makers mark, in green, excellent shape, approx. 8" w... **$132**

Courtesy of Turkey Creek Auctions, antiqueauctionsfl.com

Grass ware teapot, first period Belleek makers' mark, bird head spout, no damage noted, 4-1/4" h. **$400**

Courtesy of William Bunch Auctions & Appraisals, bunchauctions.com

Lobster and shell bowl, pink interior, 1st black makers' mark, some damage to one small shell at base, minor glaze roughness at a small area on top rim, 4-1/2" w x 3-1/2" h. **$738**

Courtesy of William Bunch Auctions & Appraisals, bunchauctions.com

Bulbous-body ewer with an angled spout and gilded thorn leaf handle in cream tones featuring gold enamel floral and leaf designs, 8" h x 7" w.
.... **$240**

Courtesy of Woody Auction, woodyauction.com

Honey pot with lid, twig handle, three-leg tree trunk base, worn mark appears to be second makers' mark black, very good condition, 5-3/4" h x 4-3/4" sq. **$338**

Courtesy of William Bunch Auctions & Appraisals, bunchauctions.com

First Period Irish Belleek vases each with two fish wrapped around base with applied butterflies, on layered slab bases with shell decoration, one butterfly wing detached but present, first black mark, 12" h. **$984**

Courtesy of William Bunch Auctions & Appraisals, bunchauctions.com

CERAMICS

Premiere vase featuring ornate hand-made roses and foliage appearing on the front and back of the vase, sits atop a pedestal base, bears green makers mark (1946-1980), 13" h x 7" w x 5" d................... **$160**

Courtesy of J. Garrett Auctioneers, jgarrettauctioneers.com

Center vase with applied porcelain flowers, sixth green makers' mark (1965-1980), clover, pearl and polychrome glaze, signed under the base, 11" h.......................... **$354**

Courtesy of Dirk Soulis Auctions, dirksoulis.com

▲ Twin-handled vase with crenulated lip above a baluster body, decorated with shell motifs and flanked by classic dolphin figures, 6" h. **$49**

Courtesy of Aalders Auctions, aaldersauctions.com

Figure of Venus, 1863-1891, depicted in kneeling form on a partially glazed rockery plinth and seated on a clam shell with gilt arm bands, first black makers' mark back stamp, 18-1/4" h... **$3,120**

Courtesy of Jackson's Auction, jacksonsauction.com

CERAMICS

buffalo

INCORPORATED IN 1901 as a wholly owned subsidiary of the Larkin Soap Co., founded by John D. Larkin of Buffalo, New York, in 1875, Buffalo Pottery was a manufactory built to produce premium wares to be included with purchases of Larkin's chief product: soap.

In October 1903, the first kiln was fired and Buffalo Pottery became the only pottery in the world run entirely by electricity. In 1904, Larkin offered its first premium produced by the pottery. This concept of using premiums caused sales to skyrocket and, in 1905, the first Blue Willow pattern pottery made in the United States was introduced as a premium.

The Buffalo Pottery administrative building, built in 1904 to house 1,800 clerical workers, was the creation of a 32-year-old architect named Frank Lloyd Wright. The building was demolished in 1953.

By 1910, annual soap production peaked and the number of premiums offered in the catalogs exceeded 600. By 1915, this number had grown to 1,500. The first catalog of premiums was issued in 1893 and continued to appear through the late 1930s.

John D. Larkin died in 1926, and during the Great Depression, the firm suffered severe losses, going into bankruptcy in 1940. After World War II, the pottery resumed production under new management, but its vitreous wares were generally limited to mass-produced china for the institutional market.

Among the pottery lines produced during Buffalo's heyday were Blue Willow (1905-1916), Gaudy Willow (1905-1916), Deldare Ware (1908-1909, 1923-1925), Abino Ware (1911-1913), historical and commemorative plates, and unique hand-painted jugs and pitchers. In the 1920s and 1930s, the firm concentrated on personalized wares for commercial clients including hotels, clubs, railroads, and restaurants.

For more information on Buffalo Pottery, see *Antique Trader Pottery & Porcelain Ceramics Price Guide*, 7th edition.

Buffalo Pottery Deldare Ware candle holders, lot of three, comprising one candlestick and two low candle holders with loop handles, all having polychrome designs of "Ye Olden Times," candlestick artist-signed by "K. Caird," black printed mark on bases with Buffalo over sign reading "MADE AT / ye / BUFFALO / POTTERY / DELDARE WARE / UNDERGLAZE," dates include 1909 and 1925, early 20th century, candlestick is 9" h. **$200**

Courtesy of Jeffrey S. Evans & Associates, jeffreysevans.com

CERAMICS

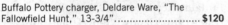

Buffalo Pottery charger, Deldare Ware, "The Fallowfield Hunt," 13-3/4"............................ **$120**

Courtesy of Strawser Auction Group, strawserauctions.com

Buffalo Pottery Albino Ware mug, hand-painted with sailboats and schooners at sea, signed C. Harris, 4-1/4" h.. **$75**

Courtesy of John McInnis Auctioneers, mcinnisauctions.com

Buffalo Pottery Deldare Ware "Ye Lion Inn" humidor, artist-signed M. Gryhardt, dated 1909, Very Good condition, 7"h................................ **$400**

Courtesy of Conestoga Auction Company Division of Hess Auction Group, hessauctiongroup.com

Buffalo Pottery Deldare Ware pitcher, stamped "Made at Buffalo Pottery," Excellent condition, 12" h. **$175**

Courtesy of Dan Morphy Auctions, morphyauctions.com

Buffalo Pottery Deldare Ware emerald plaque, elaborate peacock in the center and "emerald" design on edge, printed mark on base "1911 / BUFFALO / POTTERY / DELDARE / WARE / UNDERGLAZE," early 20th century, 12" d........**$350**

Courtesy of Jeffrey S. Evans & Associates, jeffreysevans.com

Buffalo Pottery Deldare Ware tankards, lot of four, including two miniature tankards, designs include "The Fallowfield Hunt" and "At the Three Pigeons," black printed mark on bases with Buffalo over sign reading "MADE AT / ye / BUFFALO / POTTERY / DELDARE WARE / UNDERGLAZE," dates include 1908 and 1909, early 20th century, 2-3/8" and 4-1/4" h. $300

Courtesy of Jeffrey S. Evans & Associates, jeffreysevans.com

◄ A rare and hard to find Brown Transferware "Marine" jug by Buffalo Pottery, c. 1907, marked on bottom with Buffalo Hallmark including date, cream background with sailors, ships and lighthouse transfer, 9-1/4" h............................ **$170**

Courtesy of Charleston Estate Auctions, charlestonestateauctions.com

▲ Buffalo Pottery Marine jug with blue decoration of sailors, lighthouse, ships, etc.. Good condition, 9" h... **$275**

Courtesy of Americana Auctions, americanaauctions.com

Buffalo Pottery brown and white Transferware jug, marked 1907 Buffalo Pottery, underglaze, trademarked, "The Whaling City Souvenier of New Bedford Mass," words on inside of spout, images of whales, sea themes, tall sail ships, marked 1329, maritime and nautical themes, rope design on handle, 6-1/4" h, 6" w. **$150**

Courtesy of The Benefit Shop Foundation, Inc., thebenefitshop.org

Buffalo Pottery porcelain spittoon, green floral, marked on bottom "Semi-Vitreous," 8-1/4" x 7". **$175**

Courtesy of Showtime Auction Services, showtimeauctions.com

CERAMICS

capodimonte

KING CHARLES OF BOURBON waxed passionate about porcelain upon wedding Maria Amalia, whose family was associated with the first hard paste porcelain factory in Europe: Meissen. The Meissen formula, which rivaled expensive, highly desirable Chinese porcelain, remained a closely guarded secret. Yet in 1743, after successfully creating pieces of equal quality, Charles founded a factory of his own, the Royal Capodimonte ("Top of the Mountain") Porcelain Factory in Naples, Italy.

According to Louise Phelps, associate director of the European Ceramics and Glass Department at Christie's auction house, "Though Capodimonte designs were inspired by Meissen production, their shapes tend to be slightly more flamboyant, and the porcelain, which is soft paste, is creamier and not as white as Meissen hard paste pieces.

"The most sought-after Capodimontes from this period were traditionally figures and groups modeled by Giuseppe Gricci, Antonio Flacone and others," Phelps said. "Italian comedy figures are especially attractive to collectors, as are figures of fishermen, spaghetti-eaters, and groups [that] show 'local' life." Many of these figurines feature characteristically small heads in proportion to their bodies.

While some Capodimonte figurines can be found for under $10,000 each, exceptional ones in prime condition command far more. Non-figural pieces of this era, like enamel and gilt dresser boxes, wall plaques, covered jars, trinket boxes, and decorative vases, many of which feature brightly colored, high relief classic images or military scenes, are collectible as well. While some are unmarked, others bear painted or impressed fleurs-de-lis in blue or gold.

During this period, Capodimonte, like other companies across Europe, also produced wildly popular, lifelike, handmade, applied porcelain flowers arranged in porcelain vases. Indeed, King Charles' Porcelain Room reputedly bloomed with bouquets of exquisite, hand-wrought, delicately tinted blossoms. Due to their extreme age and fragility, however, few of

Collectors who are charmed by authentic Capodimonte creations, but can't afford their high price tags, may consider collecting modern pieces, such as this one. Capodimonte, 20th century, "Smoke Time," modeled as three boys sharing a smoke by a tree, mark: under-glaze N with a crown, porcelain, made in Italy, circa 1980, 12-1/2" w. **$150**

Courtesy of AB Levy's Palm Beach, ablevys.com

these earliest non-figural Capodimontes have survived. In light of their rarity — and because this porcelain is considered the finest in Italy — they consistently command premium prices at auction.

From 1759 on, when Charles left Naples to become the king of Spain, the Royal Capodimonte factory continued production under direction of his son, Ferdinand. Though Ferdinand's porcelains followed earlier shapes and styles, he favored classic, mythological, and significant historical decorative themes. During this era, his figurines, which often depicted royalty or the emerging middle class, became more lifelike. The Capodimonte blue crown over Neapolitan "N" trademark also came into use. With Napoleon's occupation of Naples in the early 1880s, however, the Golden Age of Capodimonte drew to a close.

According to Stuart Slavid, senior vice president and director of European Furniture & Decorative Arts, Ceramics, and Fine Silver at Skinner, Inc., "Rarely, if ever, do Ferdinand-period Capodimonte porcelains reach the market." The majority, along with earlier ones that have survived, reside in museums and private collections.

As the fame of this unique porcelain spread during the 19th and 20th century, ceramic manufacturers across Italy began producing similar wares. Those labeled "in the Capodimonte style," however, vary greatly in technique, craftsmanship and value.

Moreover, since the original Capodimonte trademark was not fully protected, many bear misleading marks. Some may not even be porcelain. In recent years, for example, low-quality knock-offs from the Far East have reached the market. So prior to purchase, collectors are advised to consult with qualified experts regarding a Capodimonte's material, age and origin.

People who are charmed by authentic Capodimontes — but not by their high cost — may consider collecting modern ones.

— Melody Amsel-Arieli

CELEBRITIES COLLECT CAPODIMONTE, TOO

This Capodimonte piece owned by famed English pop singer Engelbert Humperdinck was sold at auction in November 2017 at Julien's Auctions. The porcelain figural, depicting The Last Supper, is set with a pierced giltwood and on a plinth base. It is signed "Cortese," and measures 13" x 33" x 15". **$2,000**

Courtesy of Julien's Auctions, juliensauctions.com

Capodimonte porcelain hinged box, late 19th or early 20th century, of oval form, the lid depicting a high relief scene of four classical female nudes alongside putti on a terrace, framed in a gilded shell motif border, above the bronze central latch and lined rims, opening to a fitted compartment, the base depicting two different scenes of putti in bucolic settings, the whole terminating to a conforming band of gilded shells, marked underneath, 6"h x 13-1/2" w x 10" d. **$1,800**

Courtesy of Great Gatsby's Auction Gallery, Inc., greatgatsbys.com

Capodimonte porcelain hinged box, late 19th or early 20th century, of undulating rectangular form, depicting a high relief bacchanalian scene on the lid bordered in a polychrome foliate motif, above the central bronze latch and lined rims, opening to a fitted velvet lined compartment, the base depicting male masks interspaced by goats and scrolling florals, marked underneath, 3" h x 12-1/2" w x 9" d. **$1,300**

Courtesy of Great Gatsby's Auction Gallery, Inc., greatgatsbys.com

A large capodimonte charger featuring four battle scenes, maintains original hand-painted embellishments, 23" h, 23" w, 4" d. **$500**

Courtesy of Kamelot Auctions, kamelotauctions.com

► Capodimonte porcelain eagle in flight with outstretched wings, affixed to a wooden stand, made in Italy, circa 1980, 12" h. **$100**

Courtesy of AB Levy's Palm Beach, ablevys.com

Capodimonte figural grouping, c. 1860-1875, faint crown mark on underside, depicts man and woman serenading each other as dog and lamb look on, 9" x 10" x 5-1/2". **$125**

Courtesy of A-1 Auction, a-1auction.net

A large Capodimonte porcelain plaque depicting a battle scene from the Italian Wars, 19th century, plaque is 21" dia, framed measurements are 27" h x 26" w... **$400**

Courtesy of Heritage Auctions, ha.com

◀ A mid-20th century Capodimonte porcelain Passover plate decorated with gildings, a Star of David in the center surrounded by fruit, gold Hebrew inscriptions on the rim of the Passover foods and hand-colored reliefs of biblical scenes, marked, 38" dia. **$300**

Courtesy of Ishtar Antiques LTD, ishtararts.com

▼ A set of eight Capodimonte armorial plates, circa 1900, each with a Baccanalian scene molded in relief on rim and with a different hand-painted coat-of-arms on cavelto, blue underglaze crown N marks, 10-3/4" dia.. **$500**

Courtesy of Jackson's Auction, jacksons-auction.com

81

CERAMICS

◀ Capodimonte covered tankard, with a figural
female handle, the lid with a draped female
surmount, the relief sides depicting Bacchanalia
revelry, 11-1/4" h, 8" w, 4-1/4" d................. **$150**

Courtesy of Crescent City Auction Gallery, crescentcityauctiongallery.com

▲ Pair of French Capodimonte porcelain covered
urns, colorfully hand-painted with festive scenes
of male and female figures with putti on the front
and back and ram's head handles on the sides,
lids have large figural finials with two children
embracing, signed on the bottom with a 5 point
crown over "N" and marked "France," 31-1/4
pounds, 24" h x 14" w x 11" dia................. **$1,750**

Courtesy of Fontaine's Auction Gallery, fontainesauction.com

Antique Capodimonte vase once in a
collection owned by Egypt's King Farouk,
accompanied by a 1988 auction catalog
from which the piece was obtained, 9-1/2" h,
10-1/2" w...................................... **$350**

Courtesy of Blackwell Auctions, blackwellauctions.com

Pair of Ginori quality Capodimonte vases, land
and seascape scenes with putti, seahorses, trees,
beautiful feathered bottom third, blue crown and
"N" mark, 9"................................... **$125**

Courtesy of A-1 Auction, a-1auction.net

CERAMICS

CERAMICS

chinese export

LARGE QUANTITIES OF porcelain have been made in China for export to America from the 1780s, much of it shipped from the ports of Canton and Nanking. A major source of this porcelain was Ching-te-Chen in Kiangsi province, but wares were also made elsewhere. The largest quantities were blue and white. Prices fluctuate considerably, depending on age, condition, decoration and other variables.

Rare circular dish from the Lee of Coton Hall service, circa 1735, famille rose and grisaille porcelain, considered the finest armorial service ever ordered by an English family. The border showing early scenes of London viewed from the south bank of the Thames with London Bridge at the right and the dome of St. Paul's visible on the left, alternating with panels of Canton seen from the Pearl River with the city walls to one side and the Dutch folly fort to the other, both in soft grisaille, arms are those of Lee quartering Astley, circa 1735, and an example is illustrated in Howard/Ayers Masterpieces of Chinese Export Porcelain and represented in the collections of the State Department, Victoria & Albert, The Metropolitan Museum, Winterthur and The Reeves Collection at Washington and Lee University. The motto, "Virtus vera est nobilitas" translates to: "Virtue is the true nobility." A dish from this service is also illustrated on the cover of Oriental Export Market Porcelain by Geoffrey A. Goddon, 1-3/8" h, 9-7/8" dia. **$14,000**

Courtesy of Schwenke Auctioneers, liveauctioneers.com

Qing Dynasty famille rose bowl with hunting scene design details, 18th century, 8-1/2" d. **$1,000**

Courtesy of Pennington Antiques & Consignment, LLC, liveauctioneers.com

Silver card case, 19th century, "C" mark, indicative of the late China Trade Period, 1840-1885 A.D., 4.03 oz, 4" h x 2-1/2" w............... **$950**

Courtesy of Bruce Kodner Galleries, brucekodner.com

Armorial plate, circa 1740, painted with the arms of Van Herzeele, the rim decorated in grisaille and gilding, 9" dia... **$2,125**

Courtesy of Heritage Auctions, ha.com

Candle lanterns, circa 1790, with reticulated sides with polychrome painted floral and European Crest with motto reading, "Fortie In Bello," with gilt trim and ring handles, 5-1/2" dia x 10" h. . **$160**

Courtesy of Forsythes' Auctions, LLC, forsythesauctions.com

Chinese export blue & white porcelain jar, 9" h x 8" l. **$4,500**

Courtesy of WR Auction Gallery, Inc., liveauctioneers.com

Pair of famille rose porcelain phoenix birds, Qing Dynasty (1644-1911), modeled standing on rockwork molded with peonies, bases filled, 12-1/4" h, overall height with stands 13-1/4".. **$700**

Courtesy of Neal Auction Company, nealauction.com

Punch bowl, famille rose, circa 1820, with figural scene panel in center, with alternating figural scene and bird and floral scene on inside and outside of bowl, resting on carved wood stand, 7-1/2" h, 15-1/2" w. **$400**

Courtesy of Twine Services LLC. Twineservices.com

Canton lacquer sewing box, second half 19th century, of eight-sided form, decorated to the exterior with panels containing figural scenes, with scrolling floral designs in the surround, the hinged cover opening to reveal a compartmentalized interior, over a single drawer, the whole raised on four claw feet. ... **$425**

Courtesy of New Orleans Auction Gallery, neworleansauction.com

► Pair of 19th c stands with marble tops and mother-of-pearl inlay, 25" h. **$275**
Courtesy of Kaminski Auctions, kaminskiauctions.com

◄ Large porcelain water jug and cover, circa 1850, of pear shape with loop handle, painted with Chinese figures in landscape, reserved on a gilt vine ground, the cover decorated with two similarly reserved cartouches with flowers, the knop molded as a blossom, 15-1/2" h.............................**$875**
Courtesy of Sotheby's, sothebys.com

▲ Three large "Imari" tankards, circa 1725, each of slightly tapered form with a splayed base, decorated in an Imari palette with peonies and chrysanthemums beneath a trellis border, the handle painted with a flower spray in underglaze blue and iron-red, 6-1/4" h. **$2,375**

Courtesy of Sotheby's, sothebys.com

Famille Juane porcelain umbrella stand, 19th-20th century, decorated with a scrolling scene of birds and flowers, 24" h x 8-1/2" dia. **$550**

Courtesy of Bruneau & Co. Auctioneers, bruneauandco.com

Pair of porcelain vases, Qing dynasty, famille rose, painted with blue and white, and gold decorated desk objects, and multicolor birds, flowers, and fruits, all on a light celadon crackle ground, 13" h. **$1,200**

Courtesy of WR Auction Gallery, Inc., liveauctioneers.com

CERAMICS

coalport porcelain

COALPORT PORCELAIN WORKS (John Rose & Co.) operated at Coalport, Shropshire, England, from about 1795 to 1926. In 1926, production was moved to Staffordshire. Since 1951 the firm has operated as Coalport China, Ltd., producing bone china.

English Coalport serving bowl, 19th c., the baluster sides with entwined handles, with hand painted floral cartouches and gilt and green enamel decoration, 4-3/4" h, 12" w, 10-1/8" d. **$175**

Courtesy of Crescent City Auction Gallery, crescentcityauctiongallery.com

Coalport Imari master sugar bowl, sugar with lid and under plate, ca. 1780................................ **$30**

Courtesy of Premier Auction Galleries, premierauctiongalleries.com

Lot of six Coalport Chinese Willow chargers, 11" w. **$225**

Courtesy of Lewis & Maese Antiques, lmauctionco.com

Set of eight Coalport of England dessert plates in the "Hong Kong" pattern, all marked with the Coalport stamp to the back, each approximately 9" dia.. **$170**

Courtesy of Bremo Auctions, bremoauctions.com

Twelve Coalport china teacups and saucers in the purple "Oak Leaf" pattern, gilt accents, saucers are 4-1/2" dia... **$125**

Courtesy of Alex Cooper, alexcooper.com

Coalport china dinner service in Ming Rose pattern, approx. 61 pieces including 10 dinner plates (10-3/4" dia), nine salad plates (8"), four luncheon plates (7-1/4"), seven bread plates (6-1/4"), nine soup bowls, nine flat cups and nine saucers, oval platter 11" x 14", flower frog, two posie pots. **$400**

Courtesy of Burchard Galleries, Inc., burchardgalleries.com

Coalport perfume bottle, hand decorated with avian motif and gilt accents, c. 1814, 5-1/2" h x 4" w x 2-3/4" d. $40

Courtesy of Alderfer Auction, alderferauction.com

Pair of English Coalport porcelain urns, vases are cobalt covered with a beautiful dark cobalt blue glaze and white panels decorated with roses and other flowers, urns are trimmed in gold gilt flowers, lattice work, etc., handles are attached to urns with lion mask, unsigned, 9-1/2" h x 7-1/4" dia.. $275

Courtesy of Kennedys Auction Service, kennedysauction.com

Coalport lidded porcelain vase with a portrait of John Paul the II on the front and Saint Peters Basilica on the reverse, limited edition of 10 of 100, hand-painted by Malcolm Harnett, 20th century mark, England, 9-1/2" h. $125

Courtesy of Whitleys Auctioneers, whitleyauction.com

Pair of jeweled Coalport porcelain vases and covers, England, late 19th century, acanthus scroll handles to an ivory ground with turquoise enamel jeweling to gold panels, a polychrome enameled landscape cartouche to each, artist signed "E.O. Ball," printed factory marks, 7" h...$1,000

Courtesy of Louvre Antique Auction, liveauctioneers.com

CERAMICS

contemporary

Jean Cocteau charger, limited edition, red, blue, yellow, black and white enameled designs depicting a bull with wide eyes, flaring nostrils and horns all against a gray pottery background, signed on the front "Jean Cocteau 1957" and "Villefranche," marked on the underside "Edition Originale de Jean Cocteau Atelier Madeline-Jolly 3/25," accompanied by Certificate of Authenticity, VG to Ex condition, 12-5/8" dia. **$3,630**

Courtesy of James D. Julia Auctioneers, jamesdjulia.com

Wayne Higby (b. 1943) Landscape series bowl, Alfred, N.Y., late 20th c, Raku-fired earthenware, chop mark, excellent condition, 7" x 12-1/4" **$2,250**

Courtesy of Rago Arts and Auction Center, ragoarts.com

THE PROLIFIC TREND of contemporary ceramics appearing in museum exhibits, auctions, and at shows the last few years has not gone unnoticed. In many cases, American ceramic art is gaining respect and preference as the medium of choice of many of today's most popular artists. The versatile and inexpensive material is easy to manipulate. The artist may express fine details of figurative sculptures or ugly mugs, such as popular face jugs, which were first made as early as the 14th century.

"We are just now adopting the perception of ceramics as fine art," said Katie Nartonis, director of 20th & 21st Century Art at Heritage Auctions in Dallas. "California gave rise to an active American ceramic art scene since the 1950s, and studio ceramics are getting a second glance from collectors as well."

It is always easy to find modern ceramics at garage sales and thrift stores, but it's not always easy to recognize the artist or an object's potential value upon first inspection. That fact almost cost the Caddo Indian Nation a rare piece of pottery that turned up in a Goodwill thrift store donation box. Goodwill placed the pear-form, 7-1/2-inch piece of pottery, decorated with two rows of symmetrical raised spikes, up for bids on shopgoodwill. com, the charity's online auction website. A few astute historians alerted Goodwill of its potential historical value and sure enough, tucked deep inside was a note that stated the item was "found in a burial mound near Spiro, Oklahoma, in 1970."

Historians think the simple ceramic pot originated from Oklahoma's Spiro Mounds archaeological site and could be thousands of years old. Goodwill returned the piece to the tribe.

Several 20th century modern and contemporary artists known more for their watercolors or oils expanded into ceramics. Collectors avidly pursue Wassily Kandinsky's glazed porcelain cups and saucers, which he produced in 1923. A pair recently sold for $1,250, an affordable sum compared to the artist's famed geometric and abstract paintings, which have sold for $1.6 million.

Warren MacKenzie (American, b. 1924), lidded jar, stoneware, artist's stamp on base, 450 inscribed on underside, 10-1/4" h. **$840**

Courtesy of Cowan's Auctions, cowans.com

Cliff Lee (b. 1951) fine vase with lotus flowers and dragonflies, celadon glaze, Stevens, Pa., 2007, carved and glazed porcelain, signed and dated, excellent condition, 5-1/2" x 6-1/4". **$2,500**

Courtesy of Rago Arts and Auction Center, ragoarts.com

Jean Cocteau charger, oval, limited edition, stylized figure of a man with oval face, black enameled hair, eyebrows and eyes and red enameled mouth and nostrils against a matte background with blue pastel shadowing and an orange glazed border around the rim. Signed on the front "Jean Cocteau," marked on the underside "Edition Originale de Jean Cocteau Atelier Madeline-Jolly 9/35," accompanied by Certificate of Authenticity, VG to Ex condition, 10-1/2" x 15".
.... **$3,328**

Courtesy of James D. Julia Auctioneers, jamesdjulia.com

Tom McCanna stoneware figural of large golden elephant leaping over a large pierced blue, white and yellow teapot, seemingly held together with McCanna's signature steel wire wrappings. Made in 1994, marked with applied "Thoym, Rebusi Studio" lozenge on the side of the teapot, excellent condition, 15 lbs, 14-1/2" x 15" l. **$1,200**

Courtesy of Mark Mussio, Humler & Nolan, humlernolan.com

Jack Earl (b. 1934), "HAND MADE TeaPot" on stand, Ohio, 1993, glazed hand-decorated earthenware, signed, dated, and titled, one short glazed-over firing line to rim of teapot (in making), 12" x 12" x 5".
.... **$1,500**

Courtesy of Rago Arts and Auction Center, ragoarts.com

Tim Eberhardt vase, green grass and blue flowers against a cloud-filled sky, 2001, sold at Pottery Lovers in Zanesville, Ohio, marked on bottom "Tim Eberhardt St. Louis 5-9-'01, #508" in blue, personal message to the purchasers in black, fine overall crazing, 7" h. **$225**

Courtesy of Mark Mussio, Humler & Nolan, humlernolan.com

CERAMICS

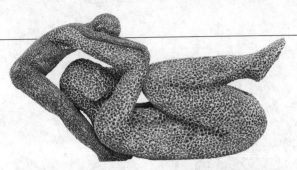

Adrian Arleo (b. 1960), Mother and Child teapot, Montana, 1994, glazed earthenware, signed and dated, excellent condition, 9-3/4" x 18" x 6"..**$4,375**

Courtesy of Rago Arts and Auction Center, ragoarts.com

Cindy Kolodziejski (b. 1962), "Artificial Lure" teapot, Venice, Calif., 1993, glazed hand-decorated earthenware, signed, dated, and titled, excellent condition, 9-1/2" x 6" x 4". **$1,250**

Courtesy of Rago Arts and Auction Center, ragoarts.com

▶ Three common ground pottery vases by Eric Olson, clockwise from top: green leaves, 7-3/4" h; white flowers, 2004, 11-3/8" h; butterflies, 2002, 9-1/2" h. All in excellent condition, all incised with the artist's signature and date. **$450**

Courtesy of Mark Mussio, Humler & Nolan, humlernolan.com

◀ Warren McKenzie large stoneware bottle vase, beige and rust glazes, imprints of the artist's hand and fingerprints on either side, impressed with the artist's M monogram along the base rim, purchased directly from McKenzie, 11-3/8" h x 5" dia. **$200**

Courtesy of Mark Mussio, Humler & Nolan, humlernolan.com

▶ Paul Katrich vase, luster glaze, with patches of heavy volcanic glazes, marked with raised Grecian Sphinx trademark and sticker noting this vase as #1606, excellent condition, 7" h. **$450**

Courtesy of Mark Mussio, Humler & Nolan, humlernolan.com

Stephanie Young three-handled vase, carved, painted and incised with Jellyfish decoration, 2013, divided into six panels with jellyfish whose tentacles interlock and intertwine, signed in black slip on the bottom, "Large Jellyfish vase with handles 2013 Boston Fired" along with the SY logo of the artist, excellent condition, 16-1/4" h. **$700**

Courtesy of Mark Mussio, Humler & Nolan, humlernolan.com

Tim Eberhardt vase with snow falling on flowers décor, marked in blue slip "Tim Eberhardt St. Louis 4-1-02 #596, Made for 'Pottery Lovers '02' Inspired by Matsui's woodblock prints!" Excellent condition, 6-7/8" h. **$200**

Courtesy of Mark Mussio, Humler & Nolan, humlernolan.com

Don Reitz (American, 1929-2014), blue-skirted vessel, salt-glazed stoneware, signed at base under skirt, 27" h. ... **$2,160**

Courtesy of Cowan's Auctions, cowans.com

Lidya Buzio (Uruguayan-American, 1948-2014), Cityscape Vessel, ceramic, signed, dated 1985, numbered XV 85 and inscribed NYC on underside, 14-1/4" h. **$4,200**

Courtesy of Cowan's Auctions, cowans.com

Pablo Picasso (Spanish, 1881-1973), "Sujet Colombe, Mat," unglazed ceramic, inscribed and stamped Edition Picasso, stamped Madoura Plein Feu, and numbered 82/100 on underside, 6-3/4" h x 10-3/4" l. **$9,000**

Courtesy of Cowan's Auctions, cowans.com

Harding Black Yellow Sunburst and Flame Red glazed terracotta vase and bowl, San Antonio, Texas, 1972, marks: Harding Black, 1972, both good condition, 6-1/4" h. **$625**

Courtesy of Heritage Auctions, ha.com

CERAMICS

cowan

R. GUY COWAN opened his first pottery studio in 1912 in Lakewood, Ohio. The pottery operated almost continuously, with the exception of a break during World War I, at various locations in the Cleveland area until it was forced to close in 1931 due to financial difficulties. Many of the 20th century's finest artists began with Cowan and its associate, the Cleveland School of Art. This fine art pottery, particularly the designer pieces, is highly sought after by collectors.

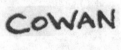

Many people are unaware that it was due to R. Guy Cowan's perseverance and tireless work that art pottery is today considered an art form and found in many art museums.

For more information on Cowan pottery, see *Antique Trader Pottery & Porcelain Ceramics Price Guide*, 7th edition.

Early Cowan Pottery vase, hand-painted, monogrammed RGC, numbered 553 on bottom, sage and opalescent yellow flambé glaze, 7-1/4" h. **$160**

Courtesy of Rachel Davis Fine Arts, racheldavisfinearts.com

Cowan Pottery swan form flower frog, designed by Waylande Gregory, special ivory glaze, marked on bottom with Cowan logo as well as "Cowan" impressed in block letters and the shape number F-7 in pencil, very fine overall crazing, 11-3/4" h. **$170**

Courtesy of Rachel Davis Fine Arts, racheldavisfinearts.com

Drexler Jacobson Cowan Pottery sculpture, "Giulia," c. 1928, mat glaze, impressed Cowan logo verso, 10" h. **$550**

Courtesy of Rachel Davis Fine Arts, racheldavisfinearts.com

Cowan Pottery vase, 1922, Mahogany-Marigold flambé glaze, early Cowan stamp, 7-1/4". **$110**

Courtesy of Rachel Davis Fine Arts, racheldavisfinearts.com

Cowan Pottery candlestick, 1925, made for the Rowfant Club of Cleveland, Ohio, depicting a groundhog holding a branch in one arm and an open book in the other, designed by Frank M. Wilcox (American, 1887-1964), marked "Rowfant Club / 1925 / #14 of 156 copies / R.C. Cowan" on underside, light wear, 9" h x 5" dia. **$984**

Courtesy of Cowan's Auctions, cowans.com

Cowan Pottery hand-decorated vase, no. 932, plum and green gloss glaze, impressed mark on bottom, 8" h. **$250**

Courtesy of Rachel Davis Fine Arts, racheldavisfinearts.com

Cowan Pottery tobacco jar, designed by Thelma Frazior Winter, 1929-30, ribbed sides, melon green glaze, 5-1/2"... **$110**

Courtesy of Rachel Davis Fine Arts, racheldavisfinearts.com

Unusual Cowan vase with volcanic-like glaze, Black over April Green Flambé, marked with Cowan die impressed logo, excellent condition, 7" x 11".
.... **$100**

Courtesy of Mark Mussio, Humler & Nolan, humlernolan.com

Cowan Pottery candy dish, carved floral design, attributed to Raoul Joseph and Jose Martin, melon green glaze, die impressed mark, 6-1/4" w x 4" h.
.... **$100**

Courtesy of Rachel Davis Fine Arts, racheldavisfinearts.com

Cowan pottery bowl with ornate brass frame drape, excellent condition. **$160**

Courtesy of Milestone Auctions, milestoneauctions.hibid.com

CERAMICS

10 Things You Didn't Know
About Viktor Schreckengost

1 Viktor Schreckengost was born in Sebring, Ohio, in 1906. He learned clay sculpting from his father, a commercial potter. Schreckengost died in Florida in 2008 at the age of 101. In 2005, Crain's Cleveland Business reported the designer's impact on the United States economy at more than $200 billion.

2 In 1933, Viktor Schreckengost, known as "The American DaVinci," established the first modern industrial design department in the United States at the Cleveland Institute of Art, where he taught for 70 years. As a teacher, he led his students "through the process of self-discovery."

3 Schreckengost was the first artist from Cleveland to show his work at the Metropolitan Museum of Art. Schreckengost said his goal was always "to make products that are both beautiful and affordable, and to make an emotional connection with the customer."

4 Viktor Schreckengost was prolific in his design and influence. Former students credit Schreckengost with elevating ceramics to a fine art form and elevating the sense of quality in your life through design, making everyday objects more pleasurable to use. Many of his students went on to illustrious careers of their own — some in the automobile industry. For example, Joseph Oros, who graduated from the Cleveland Institute of Art in 1939, led the team that created the 1965 Ford Mustang.

5 Early in the 1930s, on behalf of a "special customer," the Brownell-Lambertson Gallery in New York City placed an order with Cowan Pottery for a punchbowl with a "New Yorkish" style. According to an article on cleveland.com, "Schreckengost pulled the order out of a job jar at Cowan, and went to work on what the dealer had said was a special punch bowl ordered by a New York housewife." Schreckengost's design was inspired by the energy of New Year's Eve in New York's Times Square. He was able to capture the feel of the neon lights, the fun and excitement at the dance halls, and glasses of contraband champagne, among other details. The "special" customer turned out to be Eleanor Roosevelt, and she adored her punchbowl with black and vibrant blue design — so much that she ordered two more. Later, the Jazz bowl went into limited production. Selling for $50 apiece during the Great Depression, fewer than 50 bowls were made. One of these production bowls sold for more than $250,000 at Sotheby's in 2004.

6 Questions foremost in Schreckengost's mind when planning a design were: "Who will use it?" and "How will it be used?" For example, before Schreckengost's innovations in pedal vehicle design, most people couldn't afford the ride-in toys. However, in the early 1940s, Schreckengost made pedal cars much less expensive to by designing the car body, made from sheet metal, to act as its own frame, rather than attaching parts to a frame as regular automobiles — making them affordable for the middle class. Also, he designed his pedal airplane to fit through a standard door frame so children could ride inside as well as outside.

7 At age 37, Viktor Schreckengost enlisted in the U.S. Navy during World War II to help the Allies. He was awarded the Secretary of Navy's commendation for developing a system for detecting radar. After the war, he helped develop prosthetic limbs. After the war, he joined the Naval Reserves, and when he retired, he held the rank of captain.

8 After graduating from the Cleveland Institute of Art in 1929, Schreckengost was awarded a partial scholarship to study ceramics in Vienna, Austria. To supplement his scholarship, Schreckengost played saxophone with several jazz groups and became fairly well known.

9 By the end of the 1930s, Schreckengost was the lead designer for the Murray Ohio Company, a name well known in bicycle circles. His first bicycle, the "Mercury,"

Aspire Auctions sold this authorized, signed replica of a Pursuit pedal plane for $748 in May 2014. Designed by Viktor Schreckengost for the Murray Company, the pedal plane was originally issued in 1941 and is 26" x 33" x 40".

Courtesy of Aspire Auctions, aspireauctions.com

was displayed at the 1939 World's Fair in New York. In the 1960s, Schreckengost invented the "banana" seat and added the "sissy bar" to bicycles to keep kids from falling off — especially when learning stunts.

10 A sit for a drink: According to John Spirk, an industrial designer who is one of Schreckengost's former students at the Cleveland Institute of Art, as quoted in an article in *Cleveland* magazine, when developing the "Beverly Hills" lawn chair at the Murray-Ohio Company, Schreckengost molded a prototype of a chair out of clay covered in plastic (plastocene) and asked each employee to sit on it. "It was a chair designed for bottoms, by bottoms," the article says. "A day's worth of body warmth Spirk estimates hundreds of people sat there — softened the clay into a seat custom-designed for comfort." (Each employee who sat in the chair received a token for a free drink from the Murray Company's commissary.)

Bonus Trivia: Schreckengost, loosely translated, means "rightening guest" in German ("erschreckender Gast").

– Compiled by Antoinette Rahn

Viktor Schreckengost red Astro Flight bicycle, 1965, Murray Ohio Manufacturing Company, enameled steel, rubber, lot includes original box from Murray, appears to have never been used, slight lifting of the Murray label, 43" x 68-1/2". **$3,750**

Courtesy of Heritage Auctions, ha.com

▲ Viktor Schreckengost Cowan "Jazz" bowl, Ohio, ca. 1931, glazed earthenware, artist signature to body, base stamped "COWAN," 8-1/4" x 13-3/4". **$15,000**

Courtesy of Rago Arts and Auction Center, ragoarts.com

Sources: *Success By Design: The Schreckengost Legacy*; cmgww.com; nytimes.com; cleveland.com ("Cowan Pottery's legacy as a Cleveland institution and an art form"); clevelandhistorical.org; *Cowan Pottery and the Cleveland School* by Mark Bassett and Victoria Naumann (Schiffer Publishing, 1997).

CERAMICS

CERAMICS

dedham

DEDHAM POTTERY was originally organized in 1866 by Alexander W. Robertson in Chelsea, Massachusetts, and became A.W. & H. Roberson in 1868. In 1872, the name was changed to Chelsea Keramic Art Works and in 1891 to Chelsea Pottery, U.S.A. About 1895, the pottery was moved to Dedham, Massachusetts, and was renamed Dedham Pottery. Production ceased in 1943. High-fired colored wares and crackleware were specialties. The rabbit is said to have been the most popular decoration in blue on crackleware.

Dedham Pottery plate, Dedham, Mass., c. 1896-1928, Asian-influenced with cranes in flight over breaking waves, white with dark blue lines, ink-stamped Dedham Pottery label, 8-1/2" dia.... **$2,214**

Courtesy of Skinner, Inc., skinnerinc.com

Dedham Pottery duck plate, Dedham, Mass., c. 1898-1928, border of ducks in blue and white on crackle ground, Dedham mark and one foreshortened rabbit, 8-3/8" dia...................... **$123**

Courtesy of Skinner, Inc., skinnerinc.com

Two Dedham Pottery plates, two-eared rabbits, approx. 8-1/2" dia., approx. 6" dia. **$75**

Courtesy of Keystone Auction LLC, auctionsbykeystone.com

VISIT WWW.ANTIQUETRADER.COM

WWW.FACEBOOK.COM/ANTIQUETRADER

Dedham Pottery elephant ashtray, light wear, excellent condition, 4" dia. **$120**

Courtesy of Milestone Auctions, milestoneauctions.com

Dedham Pottery rabbit bowl, signed, mint condition, 2-1/4" h x 5-1/2" dia. **$100**

Courtesy of California Historical Design, acstickley.com

Arts & Crafts horse chestnut plate, Dedham stamp on back, relief border, signature fine overall crazing, approx. 8-1/2" dia. **$75**

Courtesy of Keystone Auction LLC, auctionsbykeystone.com

Four Dedham Pottery plates, 1896-1929, Grape pattern, all with blue rabbit stamp, one also with marked R on base, three with 9" dia., fourth 8-1/2" dia. **$584**

Courtesy of Cowan's Auctions, cowans.com

Hugh Robertson Dedham Pottery vase, signed, 6" h. **$650**

Courtesy of California Historical Design, acstickley.com

Six Dedham pottery plates including turtles, lobster, and crab, 7-3/4" to 8-1/2" dia. **$1,200**

Courtesy of Nadeau's Auction Gallery, nadeausauction.com

Six Dedham Pottery items: All white crackle ground pieces encircled by a blue border of rabbits, comprising a pitcher, a creamer, a sugar, a tray, a bowl, an egg cup, tallest 5-1/4" h; creamer 3-1/2" h; open sugar 3-1/2"; tray 10" l x 6-1/2" w; bowl 2-1/2" h; egg cup 2-3/8" h. **$200**

Courtesy of Michaan's Auctions, michaans.com

▶ Three Dedham Pottery items: "Morning/Night" creamer, crowing rooster, owl with prey, dated 1931, 4-3/4" h; plates 8-1/2" dia and 8-3/8" dia. **$325**

Courtesy of Milestone Auctions, milestoneauctions.com

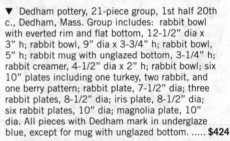

Eight Dedham Pottery items: Four rabbit plates, two rabbit cups, two rabbit saucers, each with white crackle ground with blue rabbit border, large plates 12" dia; small plates 6" dia; cup 2" h x 3-7/8" dia, saucer 6" dia; cup 2-7/8" h x 3-1/2" dia; saucer 6-1/4" dia....................................**$200**

Courtesy of Michaan's Auctions, michaans.com

▼ Dedham pottery, 21-piece group, 1st half 20th c., Dedham, Mass. Group includes: rabbit bowl with everted rim and flat bottom, 12-1/2" dia x 3" h; rabbit bowl, 9" dia x 3-3/4" h; rabbit bowl, 5" h; rabbit mug with unglazed bottom, 3-1/4" h; rabbit creamer, 4-1/2" dia x 2" h; rabbit bowl; six 10" plates including one turkey, two rabbit, and one berry pattern; rabbit plate, 7-1/2" dia; three rabbit plates, 8-1/2" dia; iris plate, 8-1/2" dia; six rabbit plates, 10" dia; magnolia plate, 10" dia. All pieces with Dedham mark in underglaze blue, except for mug with unglazed bottom. **$424**

Courtesy of James D. Julia Auctioneers, jamesdjulia.com

CERAMICS

delft

IN THE EARLY 17TH CENTURY, Italian potters settled in Holland and began producing tin-glazed earthenwares, often decorated with pseudo-Oriental designs based on Chinese porcelain wares. The city of Delft became the center of this pottery production, and several firms produced the wares throughout the 17th and early 18th century. A majority of the pieces featured blue-on-white designs, but polychrome wares were also made. The Dutch Delftwares were also shipped to England, where eventually the English copied them at potteries in such cities as Bristol, Lambeth, and Liverpool. Although still produced today, Delft peaked in popularity by the mid-18th century.

For more information on Delft pottery, see *Antique Trader Porcelain & Pottery Ceramics Price Guide, 7th edition.*

Framed Delft blue and white tiles, each decorated with wine harvesters carrying grapes, consisting of one with six framed tiles, another with two, together with two single tiles depicting lush characters, one gambling, the other seated on a wine barrel, largest 12" h x 17" w. $175

Courtesy of Clars Auction Gallery, clars.com

Joost Thooft & Labouchere Delft portrait charger after Rembrandt van Rijn, scalloped foliate rim, 16" dia.. **$175**

Courtesy of Clars Auction Gallery, clars.com

Delft blue and white porcelain charger, Dutch scene with windmills and a canal, signed C. Summerville, Delft mark on underside, 15" dia. . **$70**

Courtesy of DuMouchelles, dumouchelle.com

Delft blue and white pottery charger, 17th/18th c., Dutch, decorated to imitate Chinese porcelain, old paper inventory label to underside, 15" dia. **$2,250**

Courtesy of Millea Bros., milleabros.com

Unusual Delft (de Porceleyne Fles) attempt at Oxblood glaze having an amazing range of colors interspersed with the copper red, marked with the de Porceleyne Fles ink stamp logo and the name Delft both in black, 3-7/8" h. **$250**

Courtesy of Mark Mussio, Humler & Nolan, humlernolan.com

Delft blue and white porcelain chargers, 11-1/4" dia and 13-3/4" dia, pair. **$150**

Courtesy of DuMouchelles, dumouchelle.com

Pair of Delftware jars mounted as lamps, each ovoid form decorated on one side with floral decor, the reverse depicting a woman, the other a man, fitted with shades, 18" h x 8" w x 5" d. **$2,250**

Courtesy of Michaan's Auctions, michaans.com

Delft blue and white porcelain urn, parrot on lid, hallmarked (1764-1771), Made in Weesp, 22-1/2" x 9" x 8".............. **$150**

Courtesy of Don Presley Auctions, donpresley.com

Dutch delft polychrome charger, c. 1800, together with a stein with a pewter lid, charger is 14-1/4" dia, stein is 10" h. **$183**

Courtesy of Pook & Pook, Inc., pookandpook.com

CERAMICS

doulton & royal doulton

DOULTON & COMPANY, LTD., was founded in Lambeth, London, around 1858. It operated there until 1956 and often incorporated the words "Doulton" and "Lambeth" in its marks. Pinder, Bourne & Co. Burslem was purchased by the Doultons in 1878 and in 1882 became Doulton & Co., Ltd. It added porcelain to its earthenware production in 1884. The "Royal Doulton" mark has been used since 1902 by this factory, which is still in operation.

John Doulton, the founder, was born in 1793. He became an apprentice at the age of 12 to a potter in south London. Five years later he was employed in another small pottery near Lambeth. His two sons, John and Henry, subsequently joined their father in 1830 in a partnership he had formed with the name of Doulton & Watts. Watts retired in 1864 and the partnership was dissolved. Henry formed a new company that traded as Doulton and Co.

In the early 1870s the proprietor of the Pinder Bourne Co., located in Burslem, Staffordshire, offered Henry a partnership. The Pinder Bourne Co. was purchased by Henry in 1878 and became part of Doulton & Co. in 1882.

With the passage of time, the demand for the Lambeth industrial and decorative stoneware declined whereas demand for the Burslem manufactured and decorated bone china wares increased.

Doulton & Co. was incorporated as a limited liability company in 1899. In 1901, the company was allowed to use the word "Royal" on its trademarks by Royal Charter. The well-known "lion on crown" logo came into use in 1902. In 2000, the logo was changed on the company's advertising literature to one showing a more stylized lion's head in profile.

Today Royal Doulton is one of the world's leading manufacturers and distributors of premium grade ceramic tabletop wares and collectibles. The Doulton Group comprises Minton, Royal Albert, Caithness Glass, Holland Studio Craft, and Royal Doulton. Royal Crown Derby was part of the group from 1971 until 2000, when it became an independent company. These companies market collectibles using their own brand names.

Royal Doulton bronze mounted table lamp, Wisteria pattern, England, early 20th century, vase is mounted so that the light from the bulbs highlights the hand-painted wisteria flower decorations, vase is approx. 10", 23" overall..........................**$550**

Courtesy of Bruneau & Co. Auctioneers, bruneauandco.com

VISIT WWW.ANTIQUETRADER.COM

WWW.FACEBOOK.COM/ANTIQUETRADER

Royal Doulton "Promenade" figurine, HN2076, approx. 8" h.. **$375**

Courtesy of Premier Auction Galleries, premiereauctiongalleries.com

Royal Doulton "Fortune Teller" figurine, 7" h x 5" w. **$110**

Courtesy of Martin Auction Co., martinauctionco.com

Royal Doulton Lambeth jardinière with basket weave pattern and floral border, artist signed FJ, #4885, 9" x 7-5/8".. **$225**

Courtesy of Echoes Antiques & Auction Gallery, Inc., echoesauctions.net

Doulton Lambeth blue stoneware Aesthetic jardinière, England, circa 1883, decorated with a raised flower pattern between aestheticized banded patterns in relief, underside bears an impressed Doulton Lambeth mark, 1883 date stamp, and Barlow family signature, 7-1/4" h, 7-1/4" dia at opening. **$100**

Courtesy of Bruneau & Co. Auctioneers, bruneauandco.com

A Royal Doulton Flambé figure of an elephant, depicted in stride with trunk raised, decorated in red and black with white tusks, stamped manufacturer's mark in black underneath, with "OCK" and impressed illegible number at one foot, 11" h, 18" l. **$650**

Courtesy of Schmidt's Antiques Inc., schmidtsantiques.com

CERAMICS

Royal Doulton Bayeux pitcher, "Battle of Hastings" pattern, 7-1/2" h, 5-3/4" w. **$90**

Courtesy of Schwenke Auctioneers, woodburyauction.com

Doulton polychrome Faience "Indian" octagonal pedestal, late 19th c., removable top and side panels in an exotic relief, 26-1/2" h, 13" dia. . **$800**

Courtesy of Neal Auction Co., nealauction.com

▼ Royal Doulton Burslem tea service with tray, 16 pieces, circa 1891-1901, hand-painted floral motifs, includes teapot (4-3/4" h x 8-1/2"), open creamer, covered sugar, 6 teacups and saucers, tray with scalloped edge (19-1/2" x 14-3/4"). .. **$450**

Courtesy of Burchard Galleries, Inc., burchardgalleries.com

Doulton Burslem pitcher and basin, English, 19th century, 9" h x 13" dia. **$150**

Courtesy of Nye & Company, nyeandcompany.com

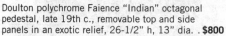

Large Doulton Burslem umbrella stand with raised relief dragon, 11-1/2" x 25".**$350**

Courtesy of Echoes Antiques & Auction Gallery, Inc., echoesauctions.net

Doulton & Co. polychrome faience "Indian" urn, late 19th c., marked "Doulton Lambeth," modeled in Hispano-Moresque style with panels of flowers and foliage interspaced with elephant masks, 17-1/2" h, 20-1/2" w, 20-1/2" d..**$1,900**

Courtesy of Neal Auction Co., nealauction.com

Doulton Lambeth blue and gilt stoneware vase decorated by Marion Holbrook, England, circa 1895, decorated with an incised gilt floral and foliate pattern with blue and white accented leaves throughout, neck and rim are finished in a faux tortoise shell glaze, underside bears an impressed Doulton Lambeth mark, numerals "9987," Doulton & Slaters patent mark, and Marion Holbrook's incised signature, 17-1/2" h. **$150**

Courtesy of Bruneau & Co. Auctioneers, bruneauandco.com

Doulton Lambeth stoneware bottle vase, 1881, impressed mark, monogram "WP" for William Parker (act. 1879-1892), incised brown, blue, green and yellow foliage, 8-3/4" h, 5-1/2" dia. **$100**

Courtesy of Neal Auction Co., nealauction.com

Large square Royal Doulton "Sung" flambé fish vase, fish are highlighted in gold, as are many of the plants on each side, Royal Doulton back stamp, early 20th century, England, 10-1/2" h x 5" d.**$2,750**

Courtesy of Whitleys Auctioneers, whitleyauction.com

107

CERAMICS
===

fiesta

THE HOMER LAUGHLIN China Co. originated with a two-kiln pottery on the banks of the Ohio River in East Liverpool, Ohio. Built in 1873-'74 by Homer Laughlin and his brother, Shakespeare, the firm was first known as the Ohio Valley Pottery, and later Laughlin Bros. Pottery. It was one of the first white-ware plants in the country.

After a tentative beginning, the company was awarded a prize for having the best white-ware at the 1876 Centennial Exposition in Philadelphia. Three years later, Shakespeare sold his interest in the business to Homer, who continued on until 1897. At that time, Homer sold his interest in the newly incorporated firm to a group of investors, including Charles, Louis, and Marcus Aaron and the company bookkeeper, William E. Wells.

Under new ownership in 1907, the headquarters and a new 30-kiln plant were built across the Ohio River in Newell, West Virginia, the present manufacturing and headquarters location.

In the 1920s, two additions to the Homer Laughlin staff set the stage for the company's greatest success: the Fiesta line. Dr. Albert V. Bleininger was hired in 1920. A scientist, author, and educator, he oversaw the conversion from bottle kilns to the more efficient tunnel kilns.

In 1927, the company hired designer Frederick Hurten Rhead, a member of a distinguished family of English ceramists. Having previously worked at Weller and Roseville potteries, Rhead began to develop the artistic quality of the company's wares, and to experiment with shapes and glazes. In 1935, this work culminated in his designs for the Fiesta line.

Fiesta was produced until 1973, when waning popularity and declining sales forced the company to discontinue the

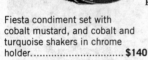

Fiesta condiment set with cobalt mustard, and cobalt and turquoise shakers in chrome holder.............................. **$140**

Courtesy of Strawser Auction Group, strawserauctions.com

FIESTA COLORS AND YEARS OF PRODUCTION TO 1972

Antique Gold.................................... 1969-1972	Mango Red (same as original red)............1970-1972
Chartreuse 1951-1959	Medium Green................................ 1959-1969
Cobalt Blue..................................... 1936-1951	Red... 1936-1944
Forest Green 1951-1959	& 1959-1972
Gray 1951-1959	Rose... 1951-1959
Green (often called light green when comparing it to other green glazes; also called "original" green) 1936-1951	Turf Green....................................... 1969-1972
	Turquoise.. 1937-1969
Ivory.. 1936-1951	Yellow.. 1936-1969

line. But renewed appreciation of Art Deco design, coupled with collectors scrambling to buy the discontinued Fiesta on the secondary market, prompted the company to reintroduce the line on Fiesta's 50th anniversary in 1986, spawning a whole new generation of collectors.

For more information on Fiesta, see *Warman's Fiesta Identification and Price Guide* by Glen Victorey.

FIESTA COLORS

From 1936 to 1972, Fiesta was produced in 14 colors (other than special promotions). These colors are usually divided into the "original colors" of cobalt blue, light green, ivory, red, turquoise, and yellow; the "1950s colors" of chartreuse, forest green, gray, and rose (introduced in 1951); medium green (introduced in 1959); plus the later additions of Casuals, Amberstone, Fiesta Ironstone, and Casualstone ("Coventry") in antique gold, mango red, and turf green; and the striped, decal, and Lustre pieces. The colors that make up the "original" and "1950s" groups are sometimes referred to as "the standard 11." In many pieces, medium green is the hardest to find and the most expensive Fiesta color.

Assorted yellow items marked Fiesta: mixing bowl, 5-1/2" x 8-1/2"; mixing bowl, 3-1/2" x 9-1/2"; divided plate, 10-1/4". **$80**

Courtesy of Woody Auction LLC, woodyauction.com

Fiesta sweets compote, turquoise, signed HLC.... **$45**

Courtesy of Strawser Auction Group, strawserauctions.com

Fiesta complete mixing bowl set, #1 to #7, all red, excellent condition, #6 with minor rim nick. **$950**

Courtesy of Strawser Auction Group, strawserauctions.com

Fiesta two-pint jug, rare gray with floral and gold décor. **$250**

Courtesy of Strawser Auction Group, strawserauctions.com

Five Fiesta HLC cups and saucers, set of 5, 6" dia. **$25**

Courtesy of Auctions By B. Langston, LLC, liveauctioneers.com

Fiesta sauce boat, green, circa 1937-1969,
4-1/4" h. **$30**

Courtesy of Auctions By B. Langston, LLC, liveauctioneers.com

Fiesta marmalade, turquoise. **$75**

Courtesy of Strawser Auction Group, strawserauctions.com

Marked Fiesta yellow milk pitcher, 5-3/4" h. **$20**

Courtesy of Woody Auction LLC, woodyauction.com

Red-orange Fiesta
carafe pitcher,
10" h. **$70**

*Courtesy of Auctions
By B. Langston, LLC,
liveauctioneers.com*

Fiesta water carafe, with unusual green mottled
glaze, no stopper, chips to base under glaze.
.... **$325**

Courtesy of Strawser Auction Group, strawserauctions.com

Fiesta 12" compartment plate, rare ivory with red
stripe... **$2,200**

Courtesy of Strawser Auction Group, strawserauctions.com

Rare green shell-shape plate, listed in Fiesta
pattern book as shape No. 1203, 9-1/2". **$130**

Courtesy of Strawser Auction Group, strawserauctions.com

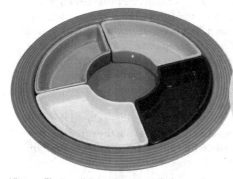

Vintage Fiesta relish tray, orange, missing center,
11" dia... **$150**

Courtesy of Auctions By B. Langston, LLC, liveauctioneers.com

Fiesta relish tray, ivory tray with only known
maroon inserts, extremely rare, minor rim nick to
tray... **$3,500**

Courtesy of Strawser Auction Group, strawserauctions.com

CERAMICS

CERAMICS

frankoma

JOHN FRANK STARTED his pottery company in 1933 in Norman, Oklahoma, but when he moved the business to Sapulpa, Oklahoma, in 1938, he felt he was home. Still, he could not know the horrendous storms and trials that would follow him. Just after his move, on Nov. 11, 1938, a fire destroyed the entire operation, which included the pot and leopard mark he had created in 1935. Then in 1942, the war effort needed men and materials, so Frankoma could not survive. In 1943, John and Grace Lee Frank bought the plant as junk salvage and began again.

The time in Norman had produced some of the finest art ware that John would ever create and most of the items were marked either "Frank Potteries," "Frank Pottery," or to a lesser degree, the "pot and leopard" mark. Today these marks are avidly and enthusiastically sought by collectors. Another elusive mark wanted by collectors shows "Firsts Kiln Sapulpa 6-7-38." The mark was used for one day only and denotes the first firing in Sapulpa. It has been estimated that perhaps 50 to 75 pieces were fired on that day.

The clay Frankoma used is helpful to collectors in determining when an item was made. Creamy beige clay known as "Ada" clay was in use until 1953. Then a red brick shale was found in Sapulpa and used until about 1985 when, with the addition of an additive, the clay became a reddish pink.

Rutile glazes were used early in Frankoma's history. Glazes with rutile have caused more confusion among collectors than any other glazes. For example, a Prairie Green piece shows a lot of green but it also has some brown. The same is true for the Desert Gold glaze; the piece shows a sandy-beige glaze with some brown. Generally speaking, Prairie Green, Desert Gold, White Sand, and Woodland Moss are the most puzzling to collectors.

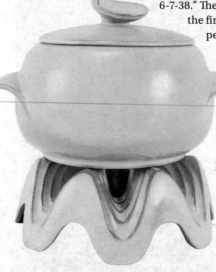

Chaffing dish and stand, dish and base separate, some crazing, 11" h x 10-1/2" d. **$13**

Courtesy of Westport Auction, westportauction.com

In 1970, the government closed the rutile mines in America, and Frankoma had to buy it from Australia. It was not the same, so the results were different. Values are higher for the glazes with rutile. Also, the pre-Australian

Woodland Moss glaze is more desirable than that created after 1970.

After John Frank died in 1973, his daughter Joniece Frank, a ceramic designer at the pottery, became president of the company. In 1983, another fire destroyed everything Frankoma had worked so hard to create. They rebuilt, but in 1990, after the IRS shut the doors for nonpayment, Joniece, true to the Frank legacy, filed for Chapter 11 (instead of bankruptcy) so she could reopen and continue the work she loved.

In 1991, Richard Bernstein purchased the pottery, and the name was changed to Frankoma Industries. The company was sold again in 2005 to Det and Crystal Merryman. Yet another owner, Joe Ragosta, purchased the pottery in 2008.

Frankoma Pottery was closed for good in 2010 with a factory closeout auction in Oklahoma in 2011.

Vase, Prairie Green color, 12" h. $87
Courtesy of Thomas Cornell Galleries, LTD, thoscornellauctions.com

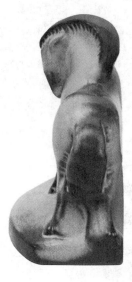

Ceramic "Lazy Susan," mid-20th century, matte gray-green glaze with brown highlights throughout, features a central well surrounded by four lobed wells, sits atop a composite turning mechanism, marked on base "Frankoma" and "No 818," 3" h x 12-1/2" w. $30
Courtesy of Farmer Auctions, farmer-auctions.com

Pair of vintage pottery charger horse bookends with tan and brown glaze, features dark red unglazed clay for the base, unmarked, excellent condition with no cracks, chips, or crazing, 6" x 3-1/2" x 6-1/2". $74
Courtesy of MG Neely Auction, neelyauction.com

CERAMICS

Seldom-seen unglazed puma figures set, 7-1/4" h. $30

Courtesy of Summit Auction Gallery, facebook.com/summitauctiongalleries

Lot of three pottery pieces including a dealer sign boasting a frothy rich brown glaze, and a creamer and open sugar, both impressed "Frankoma" and 7A and 7B respectively, excellent condition, sign 2-3/4" h x 8" w, creamer and sugar 3-7/8" h. ...$101

Courtesy of Humler & Nolan, humlernolan.com

Pair of ceramic objects including a bowl and a flower frog, both covered in an ivory mat glaze; the bowl bears impression FRANKOMA in the style dating to the early 1930s, and there is a tiny nick at the foot ring, while the flower frog piece is in excellent condition, bowl 3-1/8" h x 11" l, frog 1-1/2" h x 5" l..............$101

Courtesy of Humler & Nolan, humlernolan.com

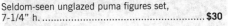

Group of Frankoma including four trivets bearing indications of "Cattle brands," "Sequoyah," "Good Luck," and one depicting a rooster marked "94TR"; beehive honey jar with green glaze and wooden dipper; two wagon wheel pitchers; matte green rectangular planter; cream glazed planter marked on bottom "B3"; all signed; measure 3/4" to 4" h...$85

Courtesy of Wickliff Auctioneers, wickliffauctioneers.com

CERAMICS

fulper

FROM THE "GERM-PROOF Filter" to enduring Arts & Crafts acclaim — that's the unlikely journey of Fulper Pottery, maker of the early 20th century uniquely glazed artware that's become a favorite with today's collectors.

Fulper began life in 1814 as the Samuel Hill Pottery, named after its founder, a New Jersey potter. In its early years, the pottery specialized in useful items such as storage crocks and drainpipes fashioned from the area's red clay. Abraham Fulper, a worker at the pottery, eventually became Hill's partner, purchasing the company in 1860. Renamed after its new owner, Fulper Pottery continued to produce a variety of utilitarian tile and crockery. By the turn of the 20th century, the firm, now led by Abraham's sons, introduced a line of fire-proof cookware and the hugely successful "Germ-Proof Filter." An ancestor of today's water cooler, the filter provided sanitary drinking water in less-than-sanitary public places, such as offices and railway stations.

In the early 1900s, Fulper's master potter, John Kunsman, began creating various solid-glaze vessels, such as jugs and vases, which were offered for sale outside the pottery. When Chinese art pottery started attracting national attention, Fulper saw an opening to produce similarly styled modern ware. Dr. Cullen Parmelee, who headed the ceramics department at Rutgers, was recruited to create a contemporary series of glazes patterned after those of ancient China. The Fulper Vasekraft line of art pottery incorporating these glazes made its debut in 1909. Unfortunately, Parmelee's glazes did not lend themselves well to mass production because they did not result in reliable coloration and in 1910, most of these glazes disappeared from the line, and a new ceramic engineer, Martin Stangl, was given the assignment of revitalizing Vasekraft. His most notable innovation: steering designs and glazes away from reinterpretations of ornate Chinese classics and toward the simplicity of the burgeoning Arts & Crafts movement. Among his many Vasekraft successes: candleholders, bookends, perfume lamps, desk accessories, tobacco jars, and even Vasekraft lamps. Here, both the lamp base and shade were of pottery; stained glass inserts in the shades allowed light to shine through.

Always attuned to the mood of the times, William Fulper realized that by World War I,

Rare Vasekraft vessel, fine Mission Matte glaze, Flemington, NJ, 1910s, rectangular ink stamp, 12-1/4" x 5". **$5,000**

Courtesy of Rago Arts and Auction Center, ragoarts.com

the heavy Vasekraft stylings were fading in popularity. A new and lighter line of Fulper Pottery Artware, featuring Spanish Revival and English themes, was introduced. Among the most admired Fulper releases following the war were Fulper Porcelaines: dresser boxes, powder jars, ashtrays, lamps, and other accessories designed to complement the fashionable boudoir.

Fayence, a popular line of solid-color, open-stock dinnerware eventually known as Stangl Pottery, was introduced in the 1920s. In 1928, following William Fulper's death, Martin Stangl was named company president. The artware that continued into the 1930s embraced Art Deco as well as Classical and Primitive stylistic themes. From 1935 onward, Stangl Pottery became the sole Fulper output. In 1978, the Stangl assets came under the ownership of Pfaltzgraff.

Unlike wheel-thrown pottery, Fulper was made in molds; the true artistry came in the use of exceptionally rich, color-blended glazes. Each Fulper piece is one-of-a-kind. Because of glaze divergence, two Fulper objects from the same mold can show a great variance. While once a drawback for retailers seeking consistency, that uniqueness is now a boon to collectors: Each Fulper piece possesses its own singular visual appeal.

Fulper art pottery Ibis bowl, circa 1909-16, blue-green glazed bowl supported by three Ibis supports, stamp mark, 5" h, 9-1/2" dia. **$450**

Courtesy of Alex Cooper, alexcooper.com

Fulper early Arts & Crafts style hooded candle shield covered in a deep blue crystalline glaze and having all three of the original glass inserts including two triangular white and one rectangular blue, marked on the bottom with the die-stamped "incised" mark and having a small remnant of an original paper label, this shape is seldom seen and typically will be missing one or more of the glass inserts, 10-5/8" h. **$1,000**

Courtesy of Humler & Nolan, humlernolan.com

Pair of Fulper Sleepy Reader Bookends, American, early 20th century, mottled green glaze, each with a male figure with spectacles on head, sleeping in a seated position with open book in lap, signed "Fulper" on base, 6 x 5-1/2 x 6 in. **$400**

Courtesy of Brunk Auctions, brunkauctions.com

A scarce Fulper parrot perfume lamp, circa 1930, two-piece porcelain, lighted base, rim of the foot signed Fulper, 9" x 6-1/2" x 9-1/4".. **$700**

Courtesy of Soulis Auctions, dirksoulisauctions.com

Fulper Art Deco vase, circa 1920s, matte blue glaze, marked Fulper 851, very good condition, 9-1/2" h............. **$200**

Courtesy of Treasureseeker Auctions LLC, treasureseekerauction.com

A rare Fulper glazed earthenware and leaded glass Vasekraft table lamp, Flemington, New Jersey, circa 1911-1918, the mushroom-form lamp with Chinese blue flambé glaze, leaded glass inserts in blue and yellow to the shade, marks: FULPER, 18-1/2" h x 14-1/4" dia..**$5,500**

Courtesy of Heritage Auctions, ha.com

Fulper Arts & Crafts floor vase, mottled green matte glaze, vertical signature, 7" dia x 17" h. **$350**

Courtesy of Forsythes' Auctions, LLC, forsythesauctions.com

Unsigned Fulper stoneware pitcher with cobalt blue bird decoration, scarce form, no lid, 5" h......... **$350**

Courtesy of Conestoga Auction Company, Division of Hess Auction Group, hessauctiongroup.com

Nice early Fulper pottery gloss finish blue and brown glaze handled vase, rectangular ink stamp mark, 8" h x 7" w... **$175**

Courtesy of Kraft Auction Service, kraftauctions.com

Fulper pottery avocado-shaped vase with a purplish-blue glaze over matte pink, signed, mint condition, 3-3/4" h x 3" d.............................. **$100**

Courtesy of California Historical Design, acstickley.com

A Fulper Arts & Crafts turquoise ceramic two-handled vase, Flemington, New Jersey, early 20th century, marks: FULPER, 6" h......................... **$100**

Courtesy of Heritage Auctions, ha.com

CERAMICS

grueby

FINE ART POTTERY was produced by the Grueby Faience and Tile Co. established in Boston in 1891. Choice pieces were created with molded designs on a semi-porcelain body. The ware is marked and often bears the initials of the decorators. The pottery closed in 1907.

Grueby three-tile tableau with well-detailed galleon in the center in two shades of green, yellow, brown and black; matching tiles on either side with seagulls and waves, marked on the back with typical initials in green including EA, MMC and MD, typical crazing with very minor roughness to high points, each tile 8" x 8" **$3,000**

Courtesy of Mark Mussio, Humler & Nolan, humlernolan.com

Grueby scarab paperweight, medium green matte glaze, impressed circular Grueby logo, small open glaze bubble on side, 1-1/8" h x 2-1/8" w x 3-1/8" l. **$450**

Courtesy of Mark Mussio, Humler & Nolan, humlernolan.com

Grueby tile decorated in cuerda seca with ship (framed), Boston, Mass., 1910s, excellent condition, tile only: 6" sq. **$2,750**

Courtesy of Rago Arts and Auctions Center, ragoarts.com

CERAMICS

Grueby tile decorated in cuerda seca with penguins, Boston, Mass., 1910s, signed PS to back, excellent condition, 4" sq. **$3,000**

Courtesy of Rago Arts and Auctions Center, ragoarts.com

C. Pardee Works tile, a view of the sea beyond a house surrounded by trees, using a format originally done by Grueby, impressed "The C. Pardee Tile Works" on the back and painted in heavy slip, "XMM," three minor edge-corner glaze nicks. Pardee took over the failing Grueby Pottery in 1919, continuing with Grueby designs and Grueby's rich colors. This tile is most likely an early transition piece given the marks on the back, 4-1/4" x 4-1/4" square. **$425**

Courtesy of Mark Mussio, Humler & Nolan, humlernolan.com

Grueby tulip tile, deep yellow and green mounted in Tiffany bronze frame, only marks are the number 21737 on the underside of the bronze mount, excellent condition, 6" h x 6" w. **$4,100**

Courtesy of Mark Mussio, Humler & Nolan, humlernolan.com

Grueby tile decorated in cuerda seca with oak tree (framed), Boston, Mass., 1900s, unmarked, some large chips to back of tile, tile only: 6-1/8" x 6-3/4" x 1". **$2,625**

Courtesy of Rago Arts and Auctions Center, ragoarts.com

Marie Seaman, Grueby short vase with leaves, Boston, Mass., c. 1905, circular Pottery stamp, incised MS, excellent condition, 4-1/2" x 5-1/2" **$875**

Courtesy of Rago Arts and Auctions Center, ragoarts.com

Grueby squat vase, curdled green matte glaze, impressed on bottom with circular Grueby logo, minor stilt pull not visible from the side, 3" h x 6-1/4" dia.. **$350**

Courtesy of Mark Mussio, Humler & Nolan, humlernolan.com

Grueby miniature gourd vase, rich organic green leathery glaze inside and out, impressed with Grueby Pottery, Boston and tulip logo, excellent condition, 3" h.. **$350**

Courtesy of Mark Mussio, Humler & Nolan, humlernolan.com

Monumental Grueby vase, an Auguste Delahersche derivation of tri-petal flowers rising above overlapping leaves covered by a rich, gloopy organic matte green glaze, impressed Grueby Faience Co., Boston, USA with tulip circular logo, excellent condition, 13-3/8" x 9-1/2".......... **$4,100**

Courtesy of Mark Mussio, Humler & Nolan, humlernolan.com

Grueby side ribbed vase, rich organic matte green leather glaze, impressed with circular logo and incised ERG designer monogram, 9-1/2" h.... **$2,000**

Courtesy of Mark Mussio, Humler & Nolan, humlernolan.com

◀ Grueby vase with leaves, Boston, Mass., c. 1905, circular pottery stamp, incised FR, tight, short hairline from rim, darkened firing line to interior of neck (in making), some flecks to high points on leaves, 8" x 7"............................. **$3,750**

Courtesy of Rago Arts and Auctions Center, ragoarts.com

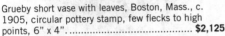

Grueby short vase with leaves, Boston, Mass., c. 1905, circular pottery stamp, few flecks to high points, 6" x 4". **$2,125**

Courtesy of Rago Arts and Auctions Center, ragoarts.com

Grueby early tall vase with yellow buds, Boston, Mass., c. 1900, circular faience stamp/23, 11-1/2" x 5-1/4". **$4,375**

Courtesy of Rago Arts and Auctions Center, ragoarts.com

Wilhelmina Post, Grueby five-handled vase with leaves, Boston, Mass., c. 1905, circular pottery stamp, incised WP [Wilhelmina Post], post-manufacture drill-hole to base, fine leathery glaze, crisp edges, 1/4" chip to rim, some minor flecks/small chips to high points and one handle, a large and rare version, 11" x 6-1/2". **$5,625**

Courtesy of Rago Arts and Auctions Center, ragoarts.com

Grueby vase with blossoms, Boston, Mass., c. 1905, circular Pottery stamp, incised GBS, excellent condition, 8" x 4-1/4". **$938**

Courtesy of Rago Arts and Auctions Center, ragoarts.com

▶ George P. Kendrick, Grueby gourd-shaped vase with modeled leaves, Boston, Mass., c. 1905, circular Pottery stamp/34, invisible touch-ups to a few minor chips on top row of leaves, 12" x 8-1/4". **$33,750**

Courtesy of Rago Arts and Auctions Center, ragoarts.com

▲ Grueby early lobed vase with buds, Boston, Mass., c. 1902, circular faience stamp, couple of flecks to high points, 8-1/4" x 5-1/2" x 4-1/4". **$938**

Courtesy of Rago Arts and Auctions Center, ragoarts.com

CERAMICS

hampshire

HAMPSHIRE POTTERY was made in Keene, New Hampshire, where several potteries operated as far back as the late 18th century. The pottery now known as Hampshire Pottery was established by J. S. Taft shortly after 1870. Various types of wares, including art pottery, were produced through the years. Taft's

brother-in-law, Cadmon Robertson, joined the firm in 1904 and was responsible for developing more than 900 glaze formulas while in charge of all manufacturing. His death in 1914 created problems for the firm, and Taft sold out to George Morton in 1916. Closed during part of World War I, the pottery was later reopened by Morton for a short time and manufactured white hotel china. From 1919 to 1921, mosaic floor tiles became the main production. All production ceased in 1923.

Hampshire Pottery Arts & Crafts two-color bowl, unusual colors with a leaf and bud design, marked "Hampshire Pottery 57 M," 3" x 10". **$175**

Courtesy of Dan Morphy Auctions, morphyauctions.com

Green Arts & Crafts oil lamp with a green Handel #2325 ice shade, base is 11" w x 7-1/2" h, shade is 12" dia, overall 20" h. **$600**

Courtesy of Tremont Auctions, tremontauctions.com

Hampshire Pottery, vase, #35, Keene, NH, matte glazed ceramic, impressed mark, 8" w x 5-1/2" d x 5-1/2" h...$75

Courtesy of Treadway Gallery, treadwaygallery.com

Hampshire Pottery curdled matte yellow vase, mint condition, 6-3/4" h x 4" d. $350

Courtesy of California Historical Design, acstickley.com

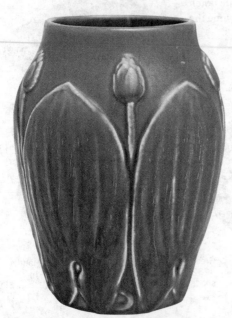

Hampshire Art Pottery vase, stylized leaves in matte green, with maker's mark on underside, 7-1/4" h. $250

Courtesy of Auctions at Showplace, nyshowplace.com

Hampshire Arts & Crafts vase, green matte glaze with stylized leaves and flowers, stamped "Hampshire/Pottery/33," with M inside a circle, 6-3/4" h. $150

Courtesy of Forsythes' Auctions LLC, forsythesauctions.com

Hampshire Pottery matte green vase with an incredible slightly curdled matte green glaze, signed, perfect condition, 5-3/4" h x 6-3/8" d. **$425**

Courtesy of California Historical Design, acstickley.com

Hampshire Pottery matte blue vase, signed, stabilized tight hairline, otherwise perfect condition, 8-1/2" h x 6-1/2" d **$300**

Courtesy of California Historical Design, acstickley.com

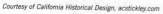

Hampshire Pottery matte green vessel, having stylized leaf form decoration, marked, 9-1/2" x 7-1/2" **$650**

Courtesy of Ashcroft and Moore, ashcroftandmoore.com

Hampshire Pottery matte green vase, signed, a couple of small glaze bubbles at base, otherwise perfect condition, 4-1/4" h x 3-1/4" d **$175**

Courtesy of California Historical Design, acstickley.com

CERAMICS

kpm

KPM PLAQUES ARE highly glazed, enamel paintings on porcelain bases that were produced by Konigliche Porzellan Manufaktur (KPM), the King's Porcelain Factory, Berlin, Germany, between 1880 and 1901.

Their secret, according to Afshine Emrani, dealer and appraiser at www.facebook.com/wwwsome-of-my-favorite-thingscom-156030115618/, is KPM's highly superior, smooth, hard paste porcelain, which could be fired at high temperatures.

"The magic of a KPM plaque is that it will look as crisp and beautiful 100 years from now as it does today," he said. Even when they were introduced, these plaques proved highly collectible, with art lovers, collectors, tourists, and the wealthy acquiring them for extravagant sums.

KPM rarely marketed painted porcelain plaques itself, however. Instead, it usually supplied white, undecorated ones to independent artists who specialized in this genre. Not all artists signed their KPM paintings, however.

While most KPM plaques were copies of famous paintings, some, commissioned by wealthy Americans and Europeans in the 1920s, bear images of actual people in contemporary clothing. These least collectible of KPM plaques command between $500 and $1,500 each, depending on the attractiveness of their subjects.

KPM pate-sur-pate charger, central reserve decorated with a satyr assisting two maidens raise a pillar on green ground, surrounded by an enameled foliate border, Germany, late 19th c, signed "HM" and marked, 13-3/4" dia. **$13,750**

Courtesy of Rago Arts and Auction Center, ragoarts.com

Gilded, hand-painted plaques featuring Middle Eastern or female Gypsy subjects and bearing round red "Made in Germany" stamps were produced just before and after World War I for export. They command between $500 and $2,000 each. Plaques portraying religious subjects, such as the Virgin Mary or the Flight into Egypt, command higher prices but are less popular.

Popular scenes of hunters, merrymakers, musicians, etc., generally fetch less than $10,000 apiece because they have been reproduced time and again. Rarer, more elaborate scenes, however, like "The Dance Lesson" and "Turkish Card Players" may be worth many times more.

Highly stylized portraits copied from famous paintings – especially those of attractive children or décolleté women – allowed art lovers to own their own "masterpieces." These are currently worth between $2,000 and $20,000 each. Romanticized portrayals of cupids and women in the nude, the most desirable KPMs subjects of all, currently sell for up to $40,000 each. Portraits of men, it must be noted, are not only less popular, but also less expensive.

Size also matters. A 4- by 6-inch plaque whose subject has been repeatedly reproduced may sell for a few thousand dollars. Larger ones that portray the same subject will fetch proportionately more. A "Sistine Madonna" plaque, fashioned after the original work by Rafael and measuring 10" x 7-1/2", might cost $4,200. One featuring the identical subject but measuring 15" x 11" might cost $7,800. A larger plaque, measuring 22" x 16", might command twice that price.

The largest KPM plaques, measuring 22" x 26", for example, often burst during production. Although no formula exists for determining prices of those that have survived, Emrani said that each may sell for as much as $250,000. Rare plaques like these are often found in museums.

The condition of a KPM plaque also affects its price. Most, since they were highly glazed and customarily hung instead of handled, have survived in perfect condition. Thus, those that have sustained even minor damage, like scratches, cracks, or chips, fetch considerably lower prices. Those suffering major damage are worthless.

KPM painted plaques arouse so much interest and command such high prices that, over the last couple of years, unscrupulous dealers have entered the market. According to dealer Balazs Benedek, KPM plaques are "the mother of all fakes. About 90 percent of KPM plaques are mid-to-late-20th century reproductions. And about 70 percent are not hand painted."

Collectors should be aware that genuine KPM paintings always boast rich, shiny, glazes that preserve their colors, and though subject matter may vary, they typically feature nude scenes, indoor portraits of women, or group gatherings in lush settings. Anything wildly different should raise suspicion.

Genuine KPMs, on their backs or edges, feature small icons of scepters deeply set in the porcelain, over the letters KPM. These marks are sometimes accompanied by an

KPM porcelain inkwell in the form of an armadillo with removable shell, Germany, late 19th c, marked on shell and base, overall good condition, 4-1/4" x 7-1/2" x 3". **$1,500**

Courtesy of Rago Arts and Auction Center, ragoarts.com

KPM porcelain jardinière, hand-painted, two-handled, colorful fruit decor on white, marked "KPM." Model #3686, good condition, 6-3/4" x 7". **$175**

Courtesy of Woody Auction, woodyauction.com

"H" or some other letter, which may indicate their production date or size. Some are imprinted with the size of the plaque as well, which facilitated sorting or shipping. Shallow or crooked imprints may reveal a fake.

— *Melody Amsel-Arieli*

KPM porcelain plaque, "Hagar & Ishmael in the Wilderness," Germany, c. 1900, signed "A. Knys" and marked, plaque: 12-1/2" x 16-1/2". **$2,000**

Courtesy of Rago Arts and Auction Center, ragoarts.com

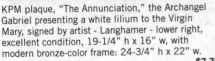

KPM plaque, "The Annunciation," the Archangel Gabriel presenting a white lilium to the Virgin Mary, signed by artist - Langhamer - lower right, excellent condition, 19-1/4" h x 16" w, with modern bronze-color frame: 24-3/4" h x 22" w. **$7,700**

Courtesy of Mark Mussio, Humler & Nolan, humlernolan.com

KPM porcelain plaque, "Dolce Foir Niente," portrait of young woman in long pink robe, signed "Ullmann," set in ornate 14" x 12" gilt wooden frame, good condition, plaque 9-1/2" x 7-1/2". **$800**

Courtesy of Woody Auction, woodyauction.com

KPM porcelain plaque, seven naked children lugging a heavy garland of fruit through a landscape, signed lower right "A.J.," in a painted gold carved wood frame, the back having impressed scepter mark "KPM," VG condition, plaque: 10" x 12-1/2"; overall: 13-1/2" x 16". **$8,470**

Courtesy of James D. Julia Auctioneers, jamesdjulia.com

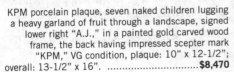

KPM porcelain plaque, young woman with blond hair and blouse draping off her shoulder with a blue throw wrapped around her, oval plaque housed in gilt frame with scroll design on the rim and beaded trim around the oval opening, plaque is signed on the backside with impressed scepter mark "K.P.M.," plaque retains an original handwritten paper label, plaque is VG to Ex condition, frame has some missing beaded trim and has cracks in corners; plaque: 7-1/2" w x 5-3/4" h; overall: 12-1/4" w x 14" h. **$726**

Courtesy of James D. Julia Auctioneers, jamesdjulia.com

KPM porcelain plaque, classical scene of two figures at doorway, one decorating a large urn, the other looking on, signed "Wagner" lower left, impressed scepter mark "KPM" on verso, in gold painted gesso decorated frame with velvet liner, scrapes to surface and consolidation in upper left, plaque: 7" x 5"; overall 14" x 11-1/2". **$1,271**

Courtesy of James D. Julia Auctioneers, jamesdjulia.com

KPM porcelain plaque, "Erbluht" (Coming into Blossom), portrait of young nude, dark green background, no signature visible, set in original 17" x 12-1/2" gilt wooden frame, frame has slight edge damage, plaque good condition and 8-3/4" oval. **$2,500**

Courtesy of Woody Auction, woodyauction.com

CERAMICS

CERAMICS

limoges

"LIMOGES" HAS BECOME the generic identifier for porcelain produced in Limoges, France, and the surrounding vicinity. More than 40 manufacturers in the area have, at some point, used the term to describe their work, and there are at least 400 different Limoges identification marks. The common denominator is the product itself: fine hard-paste porcelain created from the necessary components found in abundance in the Limoges region: kaolin and feldspar.

Until the 1700s, porcelain was exclusively a product of China, introduced to the Western world by Marco Polo and imported at great expense. In 1765, the discovery of kaolin in St. Yrieixin, a small town near Limoges, made French production of porcelain possible. (The chemist's wife credited with the kaolin discovery thought at first that it would prove useful in making soap.)

Limoges entrepreneurs quickly capitalized on the find. Adding to the area's allure: expansive forests, providing fuel for wood-burning kilns; the nearby Vienne River, with water for working clay; and a workforce eager to trade farming for a (hopefully) more lucrative pursuit. Additionally, as the companies would be operating outside metropolitan Paris, labor and production costs would be significantly less.

By the early 1770s, numerous porcelain manufacturers were at work in Limoges and its environs. Demand for the porcelain was high because it was both useful and decorative. To meet that demand, firms employed trained as well as untrained artisans for the detailed hand painting required. (Although nearly every type of Limoges has its fans, the most sought-after — and valuable — are those pieces decorated by a company's professional artists.) At its industrial peak in 1900, Limoges factories employed over 8,000 workers in some aspect of porcelain production. The heyday of quality French Limoges lasted roughly into the 1930s. Production continues today, but after WWII, designs and painting techniques became much more standardized.

Limoges cake set, seven pieces: 12" round tray with six matching 8-1/2" plates, green tones with large pink poppy and gold highlights, artist signed "Roby," good condition. ...**$250**

Courtesy of Woody Auction, woodyauction.com

Vintage Limoges is highly sought-after by today's collectors. They're drawn to the delicacy of the porcelain as well as the colors and skill of decoration; viewing a well-conceived Limoges piece is like seeing a painting in a new form. Valuation is based on age, decorative execution and, as with any collectible, individual visual appeal.

For more information on Limoges, see *Antique Trader Pottery and Porcelain Ceramics Price Guide*, 7th edition.

Large punch bowl and stand, Tressemann & Vogt, late 19th century, marks: T&V, LIMOGES, FRANCE, DEPOSE; LIMOGES, 1764, Sabots de Venus, some rubbing, feet slightly uneven, 9" h x 14-1/8" dia. **$188**

Courtesy of Heritage Auctions, ha.com

Limoges charger, scene of young woman at lake side playing mandolin, heavy gold highlights, artist signed "N. Gilbert," good condition, 12-3/4" dia.. **$150**

Courtesy of Woody Auction, woodyauction.com

Limoges plaque, hand-painted portrait of "Chief Shooting Hawk," artist signed, good condition, 12-1/2"... **$450**

Courtesy of Woody Auction, woodyauction.com

Limoges scenic porcelain plaque, scene of man and woman seated on bench, marked "LRL" Limoges, artist signed, good condition, 12-1/2". **$80**

Courtesy of Woody Auction, woodyauction.com

CERAMICS

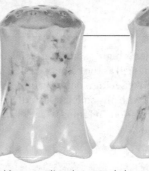

Limoges salt and pepper shakers, unmarked, yellow tone with pink floral decor, good condition, 2-3/4" h. $5

Courtesy of Woody Auction, woodyauction.com

Limoges painted and gilt charger, porcelain, by M. Redon, hand-painted scene of women and putti in center and gilt borders, marked MR / France on underside, with attached hanging wire, wear consistent with use, 12-1/4" x 12" x 1-1/2". $31

Courtesy of Cowan's Auctions, cowans.com

▶ Two Limoges game plates, one marked Coronet Limoges, artist signed "Fredo," other marked "Limoges L.R.I," artist signed "Valentine," good condition, 10-1/4" dia. .... $90 pair

Courtesy of Woody Auction, woodyauction.com

▼ J.P. Limoges vase, French, 20th century, hand-painted irises, 14" h x 8-1/2" w x 7-1/2" d. $123

Courtesy of Cowan's Auctions, cowans.com

Limoges vase depicting a man reading under a tree, France, late 19th c, stamped "HAVILAND & CO. Limoges 52/4," touched-up chips around base, firing lines on short sides corresponding to mold lines, a few chips to high points, 10-1/2" x 7" x 3"... $2,250

Courtesy of Rago Arts, ragoarts.com

Limoges porcelain dresser set, 20th century, six-piece set with floral decor, each marked, largest 7-1/2" h. $92

Courtesy of Cowan's Auctions, cowans.com

Limoges porcelain cache pot and lidded jars, all decorated with floral designs, each signed by three different artists, including Eleanor Gordon Weston, Riley, and B. Arigel, each marked on the underside, the largest marked Limoges, tallest 8-3/4" h x 9-1/4" dia.............$123

Courtesy of Cowan's Auctions, cowans.com

CERAMICS

majolica

IN 1851, ENGLISH POTTER HERBERT MINTON had high hopes that his new interpretation of a centuries-old style of ceramics would be well received at the "Great Exhibition of the Industries of All Nations" set to open May 1 in London's Hyde Park.

His father, Thomas Minton, had founded a pottery works in the mid-1790s in Stoke-on-Trent, Staffordshire, and Herbert had designed a "new" line of pottery, while his chemist, Leon Arnoux, had developed a process that resulted in vibrant, colorful glazes that came to be called "majolica."

Trained as an engineer, Arnoux also studied the making of encaustic tiles, and had been appointed art director at Minton's works in 1848 and his job was to introduce and promote new products. Victorian fascination with the natural world prompted Arnoux to reintroduce the work of Bernard Palissy, whose naturalistic, bright-colored "maiolica" wares had been created in the 16th century. But Arnoux used a thicker body to make pieces sturdier and gave it a coating of opaque white glaze, which provided a surface for decoration.

Pieces were modeled in high relief, featuring butterflies and other insects, flowers and leaves, fruit, shells, animals, and fish. Queen Victoria's endorsement of the new pottery prompted its acceptance by the general public.

When Minton introduced his wares at Philadelphia's 1876 Centennial Exhibition, American potters also began to produce majolica.

For more information on majolica, see *Warman's Majolica Identification and Price Guide* by Mark F. Moran.

Minton majolica compote/centerpiece, lobed dish supported by two cherubs/putti with swags of laurel and two doves between them, exterior of base impressed "MINTON" with additional numerals and letters on base, third quarter 19th c, areas of professional restoration, small manufacturing flaw on outside of footrim, 6-5/8" h. **$322**

Courtesy of Jeffrey S. Evans & Associates, jeffreysevans.com

Large George Jones giraffe and stag centerpiece, c. 1875, giraffe and stag standing beneath turquoise bowl decorated with branches and leaves, tree trunk pedestal, rare, 14" h x 14" w. **$29,000**

Courtesy of Strawser Auction Group, strawserauctions.com

Minton majolica cheese dish and cover, c. 1870, cover modeled as a yellow straw beehive with trailing blackberries, branch forming handle, 13-1/2" h x 10" w. **$19,000**

Courtesy of Strawser Auction Group, strawserauctions.com

▼ Majolica George Jones ceramic dish, c. 1870, England, heart shape with scalloped edge, leaf and floral design on interior with bird perched on edge of dish, impressed with registration mark on base, George Jones & Sons, Stoke-on-Trent, Staffordshire, England, areas of professional restoration, 10-1/2" x 9-1/4" x 5-1/4"............. **$556**

Courtesy of Jeffrey S. Evans & Associates, jeffreysevans.com

Wedgwood majolica ceramic game dish/casserole, England, molded rabbit finial with birds on cover, garlands of grapes and vines on sides with game birds, c. 1880, impressed "WEDGWOOD" on base with additional letters, one minute flake on interior flange, some crazing, 6-1/4" h............. **$322**

Courtesy of Jeffrey S. Evans & Associates, jeffreysevans.com

Monumental Hugo Lonitz majolica model of a hawk, c. 1875, glass eyes, perched on rocky ground with ferns and branches on entwined branch base, rare, 24" h. **$30,000**

Courtesy of Strawser Auction Group, strawserauctions.com

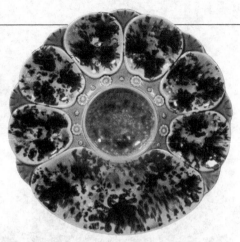

Minton majolica ceramic oyster plate, England, central well surrounded by embossed flowers and small lobed wells for oysters, mottled glaze and green surround, impressed "MINTON" on base with additional symbols and numerals including one pretzel-like stamp, third quarter 19th c, 9" dia. **$761**

Courtesy of Jeffrey S. Evans & Associates, jeffreysevans.com

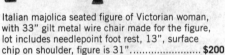

Italian majolica seated figure of Victorian woman, with 33" gilt metal wire chair made for the figure, lot includes needlepoint foot rest, 13", surface chip on shoulder, figure is 31".......................... **$200**

Courtesy of Woody Auction, woodyauction.com

Majolica Brownfield "Isle of Man" figural ceramic teapot, England, three-legged man in blue coat with black top metal hat perched on a tree with one of his legs as the spout, c. 1880, unmarked, 9-5/8" h. **$199**

Courtesy of Jeffrey S. Evans & Associates, jeffreysevans.com

Majolica jardinière and pedestal, Albert Radford, pedestal with three long strap handles along with three-dimensional birds and flowers, jardinière has the same bird motif along with flowers and ruffles, both pieces signed A. Radford on the side, glazed-over chip on the foot of the pedestal along with a bruise on the edge of its platform, both pieces with fine overall crazing, 41-1/2" h. **$425**

Courtesy of Mark Mussio, Humler & Nolan, humlernolan.com

Majolica Thomas Sargent ceramic vase, c. 1880, France, large bird with spread wings opening its beak toward a black and yellow snake wrapped around an open tree stump, impressed "TS" on base, several small scattered flakes and chips on sharp edges, 10-3/8" h. **$211**

Courtesy of Jeffrey S. Evans & Associates, jeffreysevans.com

Wedgwood majolica pottery fan-shaped umbrella rack, Burslem (Stoke-on-Trent), Staffordshire, England, circa 1900, marks: WEDGWOOD, (registry mark), scattered hairlines, overglaze application near hairlines now yellowed, 24-3/8" h x 19" w x 11-1/2" d. **$625**

Courtesy of Heritage Auctions, ha.com

Continental majolica figural camel ceramic vase, camel with two urns on the sides of its back, mounted on a raised based, impressed "EE" above a garland with additional impressed numerals on base, second half 19th century, areas of professional restoration, minute flake on one ear, 7" h, base 5-1/2" x 4". **$187**

Courtesy of Jeffrey S. Evans & Associates, jeffreysevans.com

Pair of Fives Lille majolica convolvulus wall pockets, c. 1880, each modeled as a large purple convolvulus flower with applied butterfly, against a back plate of green leaves, 14" h. **$4,000**

Courtesy of Strawser Auction Group, strawserauctions.com

CERAMICS

PALISSY WARE ON THE RISE

When is a plate laden with snakes, frogs and lizards an object of admiration, not revulsion? How could a charger filled with snails, bugs and seaweed be an example of opulence? When it's a piece of finely executed Palissy ware.

As a potter, 16th century Renaissance man Bernard Palissy (France, 1510-1590) developed a distinctive style of earthenware, creating naturalistic scenes of plants and animals and finishing them off with polychrome glazes inspired by nature. He called his three-dimensional creations of lifelike flora and fauna "Art of the Earth" and "rustique," and they came to be known as "rustique figulines." Recognizing his talent, the queen of France, Catherine de Medici, brought Palissy to Paris and bestowed upon him the title "The King's Inventor of Rustic Figurines."

Since their incarnation, Palissy-style wares have been creating an air of extravagance, and they are realistic enough that they seem ready to hop, slither, or crawl from whatever platform on which they lay. The observer can see each scale on a snake, each rib in a fish's fin, each vein running through a leaf because the figures are often cast from master molds created from creatures themselves. The wares often exhibit extraordinary detail and complexity. Although we may see closely matched pairs of urns, vases, or platters, subtle differences in glazing, placements and textures assure each piece is unique.

The use of many individual molds for components means creating Palissy-style wares is far more complicated than many other ceramics. Geoffrey Luff has been creating Palissy-style ceramics in the heart of the Loire Valley in France since 1993. He says each piece takes 10 to 15 days over a period of two to three months to complete because of drying time. Individual molds are used to create each element, which then becomes part of the composition. He says he has made more than 500 molds for creating individual elements. "My first mold was of a frog and that mold is still producing frogs today; it must have made over one thousand five hundred frogs."

Luff continues: "As you can imagine, getting hold of a frog in France is relatively easy, but some of the other creatures were a bit more difficult. I have to thank the cat for catching the lizard but in doing so the lizard ejected its tail so now on many of my pieces you will see a little leaf covering the joint. In fact putting little bits of leaf over lizards' tails is quite a common feature on both 16th and 19th century Palissy ware."

He says the hardest creature to get was the viper. "Not that they are particularly rare but their habitat makes them hard to see and they can be dangerous – not to mention protected." Whereas Luff relies on road kills for the majority of his creatures, he theorizes, "Palissy must have gone out to capture his creatures himself or had people who collected them for him. Interestingly enough, you can still see to this day on plates that are over 400 years old that mark on the snake made by the stick used to dispatch it," which is a statement that gives new meaning to the phrase "impressions of the past."

On the secondary market, Luff's 20th and 21st century pieces are within reach of many collectors. One doesn't have to search long to find them, either. In October 2015, one of Luff's Palissy ware centerpieces (with minor damage), measuring approximately 14 by 18 by 18 inches, sold through Heritage Auctions in Dallas for $1,563 including the buyer's premium. No two views are the same for the centerpiece, which is in the form of a modeled and textured oak stump, rock, and fern, with applied snakes, frogs, salamanders, butterflies and lizards.

Geoffrey Luff (English, 20th Century), Palissy ware centerpiece, the modeled and textured oak stump, rock, and fern centerpiece with applied snakes, frogs, salamanders, butterflies, and lizards throughout, signed to base: GL, IV, 14" x 18" x 18".. **$1,563**

Courtesy of Heritage Auctions, ha.com

Charles Jean Avisseau Palissy grotto, c. 1856, polychrome, modeled as a naturalistic forest floor scene, depicting a snake, lizard and frog climbing on rocks around a watery hole with lilies, ferns and grasses, a gnarled branch and oak leaves to the rear, a tablet to the front inscribed "Avisseau a tours 1856," 6-1/2" h x 10" w. Avisseau is recognized for rediscovering Bernard Palissy's lost secrets 250 years after Palissy's death. Together with his brother-in-law, Joseph Landais, he was the pioneer of the 19th century Palissy Revival. .**$14,000**

Courtesy of Strawser Auction Group, strawserauctions.com

Although Bernard Palissy died in the dungeons of the Bastille more than four centuries ago, the style of naturalistic pottery he first created continues to be appreciated, emulated, and eagerly sought by collectors. His contemporaries became so adept at recreating his style that it's difficult to identify which 16th-century works in the rustique manner are from Palissy's workshop, and which are imitators.

Majolica aficionado Nicolaus Boston has been buying, selling and studying majolica and Palissy ware for 34 years, and for the last three, he has been partnering with Michael Strawser of Strawser Auctions to hold an annual majolica auction. Combined, the partners have ceramics experience of nearly 70 years and have a worldwide reputation as the top experts in their field.

Boston explains there are many different manufacturers in the world of Palissy, with most being in France or Portugal; however, some are more pursued than others. "The most important 19th century Palissy revivalist and commands the highest prices, would be Jean-Charles Avisseau from Tours in France, who is recognized as being the potter to rediscover the lost secrets of Bernard Palissy, who took them to his grave two hundred years earlier. Palissy himself referred to his work as creating 'Art of the Earth' and it was Avisseau whose creations were true Palissy 'Art of the Earth,'" Boston said.

He said other noteworthy French potters are Joseph Landais (Avisseau's cousin), a golden name for Palissy collectors, having produced high quality, highly glazed basins of fish, snakes, and crustacea, and Alfred Renoleau, another Palissy master, who created huge oval dishes and plaques covered in huge lobsters, crabs and fish, all extremely life like.

In Strawser Auctions' October 2016 majolica auction, a lot of two large Victor Barbizet Palissy planters, circa 1875, sold for $6,765, including buyer's premium. Each rectangular planter, measuring 16-1/2 inches wide by 10 inches high, was profusely decorated with leaves, fauna, shells, mushrooms, frogs, nests of birds eggs and snakes, all creating a sumptuous Art of the Earth scene. In April 2016, a Jean-Charles Avisseau Palissy ware platter with central decorations of crossed fish and eel, with a crayfish to the border, sold through Skinner, Inc., for $2,460 including buyer's premium. The large, 20-1/2-inch-long platter was inscribed "Avisseau Tours 1862," and exhibited scattered minor restorations and firing lines. A recent Heritage Auctions sale saw a 19th century French Palissy-style glazed earthenware platter, 14 inches high by 17-1/4 inches wide, sell for $1,125 including buyer's premium. The oval platter in organic color scheme featured applied frogs, vines, flowers, lizards, mushrooms, and foliage to the rim, with a winding snake applied to the center.

Palissy wares from Portuguese ceramists also rate highly with collectors. Mainly produced in Caldas Da Rainha, Boston says Portuguese Palissy can often be distinguished from its French counterparts by the ground; Portuguese examples are often covered in a green "grass," created "by forcing clay through a mincing machine rather like producing spaghetti."

"The two most famous and collected Portuguese Palissy companies were Manuel Mafra and José Cuhna. Their work is very similar, generally circular plates covered in green grass which are decorated with snakes, lizards, shells, moths, worms, frogs," Boston said.

When considering the Palissy wares market overall, Boston is optimistic. He said that the economic crisis of seven or eight years ago had a severe effect on majolica and Palissy, which are significant sections of the decorative arts market. He said prices "remained poor for five or six years." However, sales results are again on the upswing.

— Karen Knapstein

CERAMICS

CERAMICS

marblehead

MARBLEHEAD POTTERY WAS organized in 1904 by Dr. Herbert J. Hall as a therapeutic aid to patients in a sanitarium he ran in Marblehead, Massachusetts. It was later separated from the sanitarium and directed by Arthur E. Baggs, a fine artist and designer, who bought out the factory in 1916 and operated it until its closing in 1936. Most wares were hand-thrown and decorated and carry the company mark of a stylized sailing vessel flanked by the letters "M" and "P."

Marblehead fine and rare scenic tile by Arthur Baggs (1886-1947), Marblehead, MA, ca. 1908, stamped ship mark MP, original paper label, 1" x 6" sq.
.........................**$10,000**

Courtesy of Rago Arts and Auction Center, ragoarts.com

Marblehead low bowl with berries, Marblehead, MA, 1910s-20s, stamped ship mark/MP, 2" x 7-1/2". **$900**

Courtesy of Rago Arts and Auction Center, ragoarts.com

◀ Marblehead Pottery matte blue bookends with sailing ship motifs, signed with paper labels, mint condition, each is 5-1/2" h x 5-1/2" w x 2-1/2" d. **$325**

Courtesy of California Historical Design acstickley.com

Marblehead rare vase with circles by Arthur Baggs (1886-1947) and Sarah Tutt (1859-1947), Marblehead, MA, 1920s, stamped ship mark MP, incised AB/T, 4" x 4 1/2". **$1,600**

Courtesy of Rago Arts and Auction Center, ragoarts.com

Marblehead Pottery, landscape tile with original frame, Marblehead, MA, glazed ceramic, with original sticker, 4-1/4" w x 4-1/2" h; framed: 6" sq...**$1,400**

Courtesy of Treadway Gallery, treadwaygallery.com

Marblehead vase by Arthur Hennessey and Sarah Tutt (1859-1947), with stylized trees, Marblehead, MA, 1910s, impressed ship mark MP, signed HT, 6-3/4" x 4". **$4,000**

Courtesy of Rago Arts and Auction Center, ragoarts.com

Large Marblehead matte blue cylinder vase, signed, mint condition, 9-1/2" h x 5-1/4" d. **$475**

Courtesy of California Historical Design, acstickley.com

CERAMICS

Four pieces in various glazes, Marblehead, MA, early 20th c., all with ship mark, one with remnants of original paper label, vase is 3-1/4" x 8-1/8" dia. **$400**

Courtesy of Rago Arts and Auction Center, ragoarts.com

Tapering vase incised with stylized flowers, Marblehead, MA, 1910s, stamped ship mark MP, 3-3/4" x 4-1/4" dia. **$900**

Courtesy of Rago Arts and Auction Center, ragoarts.com

Marblehead matte blue three-handle candlestick, signed, mint condition, 5-1/2"h x 5"d. **$225**

Courtesy of California Historical Design, acstickley.com

CERAMICS

martin brothers

MARTINWARE POTTERY DATES from 1873 and is the product of the Martin brothers — Robert, Wallace, Edwin, Walter, and Charles — and is often considered the first British studio pottery. From first to final stages, the hand-thrown pottery was completely the work of the team. The early wares may be simple and conventional, but the Martin brothers built their reputation by producing ornately engraved, incised, or carved designs as well as rather bizarre figural wares. The amusing face jugs are considered some of their finest work. After 1910, the work of the pottery declined and can be considered finished by 1915, though some attempts were made to fire pottery as late as the 1920s.

Martin Brothers glazed stoneware double-sided face mug, c. 1900, engraved "R. W. Martin + Bros., London + Southall," light yellowing of glaze at base, 4-5/8" h. **$1,375**

Courtesy of Heritage Auctions, ha.com

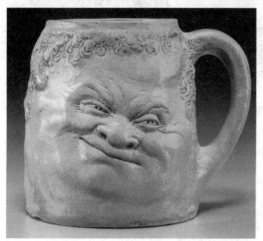

CERAMICS

◀ Martin Brothers vase with fish, crab, and seahorses, England, 1904, glazed stoneware, incised "9-1904 Martin Bros. London + Southall," excellent condition, 10-1/4" x 4"................... **$1,875**

Courtesy of Rago Arts and Auction Center, ragoarts.com

▼ Robert W. Martin (1843-1923), two-handled vase with cat heads, England, 1883, glazed stoneware, incised "RW Martin & Bros London + Southall 4-1883," excellent condition, 9" x 6"............ **$2,750**

Courtesy of Rago Arts and Auction Center, ragoarts.com

▲ Martin Brothers glazed stoneware baby bird vase, c. 1880, etched "MARTIN, London + SOUTHALL," excellent condition, 9-3/4" h. **$15,000**

Courtesy of Heritage Auctions, ha.com

Martin Brothers pitcher with leaves, England, 1883, glazed stoneware, incised "Martin Bros. London + Southall 3-83," excellent condition, 8" x 5-1/4". **$600**

Courtesy of Rago Arts and Auction Center, ragoarts.com

CERAMICS

mccoy

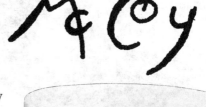

THE FIRST MCCOY with clay under his fingernails was W. Nelson McCoy. With his uncle, W. F. McCoy, he founded a pottery works in Putnam, Ohio, in 1848, making stoneware crocks and jugs.

That same year, W. Nelson's son, James W., was born in Zanesville, Ohio. James established the J. W. McCoy Pottery Co. in Roseville, Ohio, in the fall of 1899. The J. W. McCoy plant was destroyed by fire in 1903 and was rebuilt two years later.

It was at this time that the first examples of Loy-Nel-Art wares were produced. The line's distinctive title came from the names of James McCoy's three sons, Lloyd, Nelson, and Arthur. Like other "standard" glazed pieces produced at this time by several Ohio potteries, Loy-Nel-Art has a glossy finish on a dark brown-black body, but Loy-Nel-Art featured a splash of green color on the front and a burnt-orange splash on the back.

George Brush became general manager of J. W. McCoy Pottery Co. in 1909. The company became Brush-McCoy Pottery Co. in 1911, and in 1925 the name was shortened to Brush Pottery Co. This firm remained in business until 1982.

Separately, in 1910, Nelson McCoy, Sr. founded the Nelson McCoy Sanitary and Stoneware Co., also in Roseville. By the early 1930s, production had shifted from utilitarian wares to art pottery, and the company name was changed to Nelson McCoy Pottery.

Vintage bowl with Pinecone pattern, marked "McCoy" on bottom, 6-1/2" x 7".............**$30**

Courtesy of Desert West Auction, desertwestauction.com

Designer Sydney Cope was hired in 1934, and was joined by his son, Leslie, in 1936. The Copes' influence on McCoy wares continued until Sydney's death in 1966. That same year, Leslie opened a gallery devoted to his family's design heritage and featuring his own original art.

Nelson McCoy, Sr. died in 1945, and was succeeded as company president by his nephew, Nelson McCoy Melick.

A fire destroyed the plant in 1950, but company officials — including Nelson McCoy, Jr., then 29 — decided to rebuild, and the new Nelson McCoy Pottery Co. was up and running in just six months.

Nelson Melick died in 1954. Nelson, Jr. became company president and oversaw the company's continued growth. In 1967, the operation was sold to entrepreneur David Chase. At this time, the words "Mt. Clemens Pottery" were added to the company marks. In 1974, Chase sold the company to Lancaster Colony Corp., and the company marks included a stylized "LCC" logo. Nelson, Jr. and his wife, Billie, who had served as a products supervisor, left the company in 1981.

CERAMICS

In 1985, the company was sold again, this time to Designer Accents. The McCoy pottery factory closed in 1990.

For more information on McCoy pottery, see *Warman's McCoy Pottery*, 2nd edition, by Mark F. Moran.

Baskets, lot of three, all with various molded designs on sides including oak leaf and acorn, and embossed "McCoy / USA" on base, circa 1945, 5-3/8" to 9-1/2" h.................**$20**

Courtesy of Jeffrey S. Evans, jeffreysevans.com

Planters, lot of four, including one rectangular planter with five Scottie dogs molded across the front, and one dog "stretch animal," two unmarked, one with "NM / USA" and one with embossed "McCoy," circa 1940, 3-7/8" to 5-3/4" h...**$40**

Courtesy of Jeffrey S. Evans, jeffreysevans.com

Yellowware pitchers, lot of two, comprising a Hall Boy jug pitcher, and a Fancy pitcher, each with Nurock mottled glaze, Brush-McCoy Pottery, Roseville, Ohio, first quarter 20th century, 7" and 7-1/4"...........................**$40**

Courtesy of Jeffrey S. Evans, jeffreysevans.com

146

McCoy porcelain tea set, four pieces including teapot, sugar pot, and creamer pitchers, teapot is 5-3/4" h x 9-3/4" l..**$20**

Courtesy of Robert Slawinski Auctioneers, Inc., slawinski.com

Large Brush-McCoy turtle, 16". **$250**

Courtesy of Strawser Auction Group, strawserauctions.com

Calla Lily vase, depicting three calla lilies on rectangular base, circa 1940-1960, bearing McCoy maker's mark on underside, 7" h x 3" w x 6-1/2" l. **$50**

Courtesy of Auctions at Showplace, nyshowplace.com

CERAMICS

CERAMICS

CERAMICS

meissen

KNOWN FOR ITS finely detailed figurines and exceptional tableware, Meissen is recognized as the first European maker of fine porcelain.

The company owes its beginning to Johann Friedrich Bottger's 1708 discovery of the process necessary for the manufacture of porcelain. "Rediscovery" might be a better term, since the secret of producing hard paste porcelain had been known to the Chinese for centuries. However, Bottger, a goldsmith and alchemist, was the first to successfully replicate the formula in Europe. Soon after, The Royal Saxon Porcelain Works set up shop in Dresden. Because Bottger's formula was highly sought after by would-be competitors, in 1710 the firm moved its base of operations to Albrechtburg Castle in Meissen, Saxony, in fortress-like surroundings. Because of that move, the company name eventually became one with its locale: Meissen.

The earliest Meissen pieces were red stoneware, reminiscent of Chinese work, and incised with Chinese characters. Porcelain became the focus in 1713; early releases included figurines and tea sets, the decorations reminiscent of baroque metal. In 1719, after Bottger's death, artist J. J. Horoldt took over the firm's direction. His Chinese-influenced designs, which employed a lavish use of color and decoration, are categorized as chinoiserie.

By the 1730s, Meissen employed nearly 100 workers, among them renowned modelers J. G. Kirchner and J. J. Kandler. The firm became known for its porcelain sculptures; subjects included birds, animals, and familiar figures from commedia dell'arte. Meissen dinnerware also won acclaim; in earlier attempts, the company's white porcelain had only managed to achieve off-white. Now, at last, there were dazzling white porcelain surfaces that proved ideal for the exquisite, richly colored decoration that became a Meissen trademark.

Meissen porcelain figure of frolicking children on teeter-totter, repair to back of neck of white bust and pedestal, 10-1/2".............................. **$500**

Courtesy of Strawser Auction Group, strawserauctions.com

Following Horoldt's retirement in the mid-1700s, Victor Acier became Meissen's master modeler. Under Acier, the design focus relied heavily on mythological themes. By the early 1800s, however, Meissen's popularity began to wane. Changes were instituted, especially technical improvements in production that allowed Meissen to operate more efficiently and profitably, and Meissen designs, which had remained relatively stagnant for nearly a century, were refurbished. The goal: to connect with current popular culture. Meissen's artists (and its porcelain) proved perfectly capable of adapting to the prevailing tastes of the times. The range was wide: the ornate fussiness of the Rococo period; the more subdued Neoclassicism of the late 1700s; the nature-tinged voluptuousness of early 20th century Art Nouveau; and today's Meissen, which reinterprets, and builds on, all of these design eras.

VISIT WWW.ANTIQUETRADER.COM

WWW.FACEBOOK.COM/ANTIQUETRADER

Despite diligent efforts, Meissen eventually found its work widely copied. A crossed-swords trademark, applied to Meissen pieces from 1731 onward, is a good indicator of authenticity. However, even the markings had their imitators. Because Meissen originals, particularly those from the 18th and 19th centuries, are both rare and costly, the most reliable guarantee that a piece is authentic is to purchase from a reputable source.

Meissen figural candelabra, German, late 19th century, man and woman holding baskets of flowers, each with floral decorations and gilding, each marked on underside, man missing pointer finger on raised hand, small chips to flower petals and loss to gilding on each, 13" h x 9" w x 4-1/2" d. **$185**

Courtesy of Cowan's Auctions, cowans.com

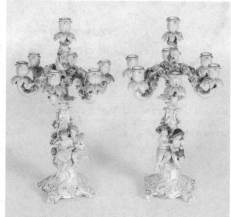

Meissen candelabra, 19th century, pair of seven-light Meissen candelabra with floral decoration and figures seated on base, mark to underside of each base, multiple, significant repairs to each arm, each 20" h. **$1,107**

Courtesy of Cowan's Auctions, cowans.com

Meissen Blue Onion compote, 9-1/2". **$100**

Courtesy of Strawser Auction Group, strawserauctions.com

Meissen Blue Onion compote, 8-1/2". **$150**

Courtesy of Strawser Auction Group, strawserauctions.com

Meissen figures, pair, Germany, late 19th/early 20th c., man and woman seated beside large open pitchers with lid, bright painted polychrome floral designs and raised modeled flowers, marked with blue underglaze crossed swords, additional incised, impressed, and painted numerals, 7-1/4" h, 7-1/2" h.. **$819**

Courtesy of Jeffrey S. Evans & Associates, jeffreysevans.com

Meissen luncheon set, white with cobalt blue trim, colorful floral border, three pieces, blue crossed swords mark. **$125**

Courtesy of Woody Auction, woodyauction.com

Meissen Blue Onion platter, 20" x 15". **$75**

Courtesy of Strawser Auction Group, strawserauctions.com

Meissen Blue Onion platter, with ribbon and bow, 12-1/2" x 11"... **$75**

Courtesy of Strawser Auction Group, strawserauctions.com

Meissen Blue Onion server, shell form, three wells with finger-loop handle, 13". **$70**

Courtesy of Strawser Auction Group, strawserauctions.com

Meissen large oval tray, floral center, embossed border, minor rim nicks, 16-1/4"..................... **$650**

Courtesy of Strawser Auction Group, strawserauctions.com

Meissen Blue Onion tureen, 20-1/2" w x 9-1/2" h. **$200**

Courtesy of Strawser Auction Group, strawserauctions.com

CERAMICS

mettlach

CERAMICS WITH THE name Mettlach were produced by Villeroy & Boch and other potteries in the Mettlach area of Germany. Villery & Boch's finest years of production are thought to be from about 1890-1910.

Mettlach #2739 etched and glazed plaque, Munich Child shield in center with Munich buildings around plaque, mint, 19"...**$2,200**

Courtesy of Fox Auctions, foxauctioncompany.com

Mettlach #2141 etched 1/2
liter stein, Tubingen city scene,
inlay lid, mint...................... **$800**

Courtesy of Fox Auctions, foxauctioncompany.com

Mettlach #2134 etched 1/2
liter stein of dwarf in the nest,
Schlitt, inlay lid, mint. **$900**

*Courtesy of Fox Auctions,
foxauctioncompany.com*

Mettlach #2634 cameo 3 liter
Rodenstein, knights drinking,
conical inlay lid, mint. **$800**

Courtesy of Fox Auctions, foxauctioncompany.com

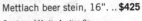

Mettlach beer stein, 16". .. **$425**

*Courtesy of Martin Auction Co.,
martinauctionco.com*

Mettlach #2001-F 1/2 liter
stein with books design.
.... **$100**

*Courtesy of Fox Auctions,
foxauctioncompany.com*

Mettlach #514 relief beaker, floral, 4"............. **$160**

Courtesy of Fox Auctions, foxauctioncompany.com

Pair of Mettlach #3338 etched candlesticks, strong Art Deco design, 5-1/4"........................ **$270**

Courtesy of Fox Auctions, foxauctioncompany.com

Rococo design pitcher with hand-painted gnomes drinking in forest scenes, ca. 1896, 8" x 17".........**$225**

Courtesy of Echoes Antiques & Auction Gallery, Inc., echoesauctions.net

Mettlach #7044 cameo framed plaque of a man and maiden, mint, 8" x 15-1/2". **$700**

Courtesy of Fox Auctions, foxauctioncompany.com

Mettlach punch bowl, 1895, figural drinking scene, medallions and serpent handles, scene initialed "M.SCH & H.S.," 18" x 12"...**$225**

Courtesy of Echoes Antiques & Auction Gallery, Inc., echoesauctions.net

CERAMICS

mochaware

MOCHA DECORATION IS found on basically utilitarian creamware or yellowware articles and is achieved by a simple chemical reaction. A color pigment of brown, blue, green, or black is given an acid nature by infusion of tobacco or hops. When this acid nature colorant is applied in blobs to an alkaline ground color, it reacts by spreading in feathery seaweed designs. This type of decoration is usually accompanied by horizontal bands of light color slip.

Produced in many Staffordshire potteries from the late 18th until the late 19th centuries, its name is derived from the similar markings found on mocha quartz. In addition to the seaweed decoration, mocha wares are also seen with earthworm and cat's-eye patterns or a marbleized effect.

English decorated piggy bank, early 19th century, in tones of brown and teal swirl glaze over a cream body, craquelure and minor losses to glaze, otherwise good overall condition, 4" l x 2-1/4"h. **$31**

Courtesy of Bruneau & Co. Auctioneers, bruneauandco.com

Unusual-form beaker, late 19th century, covered in fine crazing, 2-7/8" h x 2-3/4" w..................**$71**

Courtesy of Jasper52, jasper52.com

Bowl by famed historian and ceramist Don Carpentier, impressed signature with date 1993, 3-1/2" h x 6-1/2" d. **$254**

Courtesy of Material Culture, materialculture.com

Scarce mixing bowl featuring seaweed décor, 19th century, extra large in size, excellent condition with tight spider, 14-1/2" w...........................**$254**

Courtesy of Terri Peters & Associates Auction and Estate Marketing Co., terripetersandassociates.com

Bowl, black seaweed slip over tobacco-colored band on soft paste porcelain pearlware, 19th century, has a crack and two checks, 3-1/2" h x 7-1/4" w.. **$180**

Courtesy of Duane Merrill & Company, merrillsauction.com

Waste bowl, 19th century, 3-1/4" line on side and 1/4" line on base-ring, 3" h x 5-1/2" w............ **$100**

Courtesy of Jasper52, jasper52.com

Earthroom slip decorated bowl, good condition overall, 7-1/2" d x 3-3/4" h............................... **$221**

Courtesy of Hartzell's Auction Gallery, Inc., hartzellsauction.com

Jug and underplate, 19th century, very good condition, jug 6-3/4" h, underplate 8-1/4" d.... **$168**

Courtesy of Ancient Objects, ancientobjects.com

Pearlware pepper pot, late 19th century, 4" h x 1-5/8" d.
.... **$396**

Courtesy of Jasper52, jasper52.com

▲ Pitcher with brown and white cable or slip decoration over bands of blue and gray pearlware soft paste porcelain, minor nick on base, 5-3/4" h x 6" w.................................. **$840**

Courtesy of Duane Merril & Company, merrillsauction.com

▶ Mustard pot with lid, black dendrite decoration on an olive green slip band, with sky blue lines for highlight, foliated handles and pearlware glaze, lid sits a little high in the well of the pot, but decoration and colors are identical, mid-19th century, condition is good to very good, base of pot has no cracks, lines or repairs, some edge rubbing, two chips on edge, 3" h x 2-7/8" d....................... **$187**

Courtesy of Jasper52, jasper52.com

CERAMICS

moorcroft

WILLIAM MOORCROFT WAS first employed as a potter by James Macintyre & Co., Ltd. of Burslem, Staffordshire, England, in 1897. He established the Moorcroft pottery in 1913. Walter Moorcroft, William's son, continued the business upon his father's death and made wares in the same style. The majority of the art pottery wares were hand thrown, resulting in a great variation among similarly styled pieces. Colors and marks are keys to determining age. The company initially used an impressed mark, "Moorcroft, Burslem"; a signature mark, "W. Moorcroft," followed. Modern pieces are marked simply "Moorcroft," with export pieces also marked "Made in England."

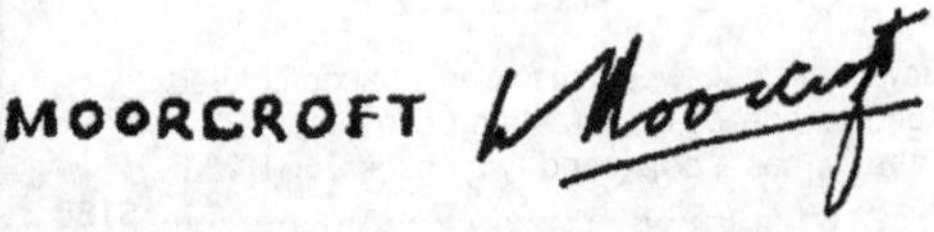

MOORCROFT

Moorcroft cream and sugar with floral designs, approx. 2-1/2" and 2-3/4" $75

Courtesy of Turkey Creek Auctions, antiqueauctionsfl.com

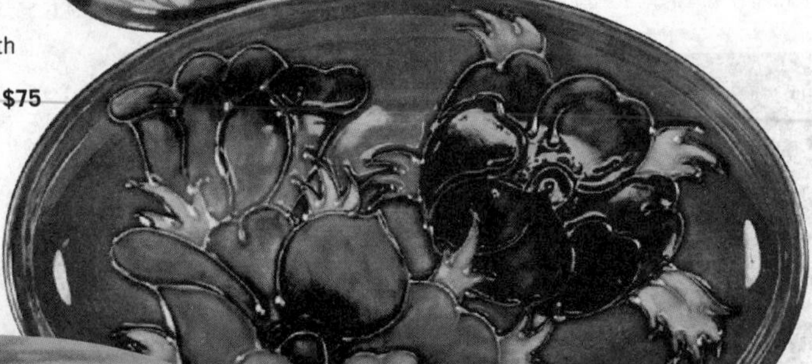

▲ Moorcroft floral-decorated dish, England, good condition, approx. 9" w. $45

Courtesy of Premier Auction Galleries, premierauctiongalleries.com

◄ Moorcroft covered dish with blue base color and floral decoration, approx. 7" w.......................$75

Courtesy of Premier Auction Galleries, premierauctiongalleries.com

VISIT WWW.ANTIQUETRADER.COM

WWW.FACEBOOK.COM/ANTIQUETRADER

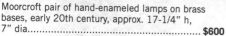

Moorcroft pair of hand-enameled lamps on brass bases, early 20th century, approx. 17-1/4" h, 7" dia.. **$600**

Courtesy of Ahlers & Ogletree Auction Gallery, aandoauctions.com

Moorcroft vase, with original paper label, approx. 4-1/2" h. **$120**

Courtesy of Premier Auction Galleries, premierauctiongalleries.com

Moorcroft vase, circa 1920, painted with red poppies and pendant fruit on a blue ground, undersides marked, 10" h and 8-1/4" h. **$325**

Courtesy of AGOPB, agopb.com

Moorcroft art pottery moonlit blue vase, circa 1924, impressed on the underside "Moorcroft, Made in England," good condition, 4" h x 2" w.**$850**

Courtesy of Myers Fine Art, myersfineart.com

CERAMICS

Moorcroft vase, squat shape, green and blue toned anemone, impressed "Burslem" mark and signature, 6-1/4" h x 5"................................. **$300**

Courtesy of Burchard Galleries Inc., burchardgalleries.com

W. Moorcroft for Liberty cylindrical pomegranate vase, mottled green ground pomegranate and grapes motif, cylindrical shape with flared rim and base over foot, painted "W. Moorcroft," stamped "Made for Liberty & Co.," impressed 153, 9-1/2" h x 3-1/2".. **$1,800**

Courtesy of Burchard Galleries Inc., burchardgalleries.com

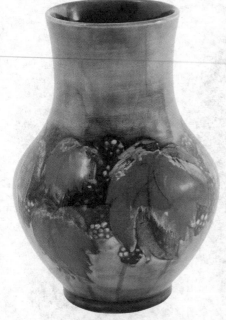

Moorcroft vase, mottled green ground with polychrome grapes and grape vine motif, impressed and signature mark, 8-3/4" h x 6-1/2".
.... **$450**

Courtesy of Burchard Galleries Inc., burchardgalleries.com

Moorcroft double-handled vase, mottled red to green ground, polychrome freesia or lilies, impressed, signature marks, 10" h x 7" dia. **$800**

Courtesy of Burchard Galleries Inc., burchardgalleries.com

CERAMICS

newcomb college

THIS POTTERY WAS established in the art department of Newcomb College in New Orleans in 1897. Each piece was hand-thrown and bore the potter's mark and decorator's monogram on the base. It was always a studio business and never operated as a factory. Newcomb College pieces are scarce, with the early wares eagerly sought. The pottery closed in 1940.

Newcomb College bowl, Corinne Marie Chalaron, 1924, marks: Newcomb logo, date code (OG 73), initials of Joseph Meyer and shape 67, Chalaron's incised CMC, 3-7/8" h x 6" w. **$650**

Courtesy of Mark Mussio, Humler & Nolan, humlernolan.com

Rare Newcomb College lidded teapot, scenic version by Anna Frances Simpson, 1930, deeply carved with cascading Spanish moss, with matching lid, impressed marks: Newcomb College logo, shape number 191, the monogram of potter Jonathan Hunt, date code for 1930, SG 44, also marked with the incised monogram of the artist, excellent condition, 5-1/4" h. **$5,000**

Courtesy of Mark Mussio, Humler & Nolan, humlernolan.com

Newcomb College carved matte glaze bowl with apple blossoms, 1926, Sadie Irvine, marks: Newcomb logo, date code for 1926 (PK 50), shape 70, initials of Joseph Meyer and the artist, couple of unobtrusive grinding nicks off the base, 2-5/8" h x 4-3/4" w. **$425**

Courtesy of Mark Mussio, Humler & Nolan, humlernolan.com

Newcomb College pitcher, Sadie Irvine, 1931, impressed Newcomb logo, date code (TD 81), shape number 224, initials of Jonathan Hunt and artist's monogram, tight line at rim near spout, handle repaired, 2-5/8" h. **$325**

Courtesy of Mark Mussio, Humler & Nolan, humlernolan.com

CERAMICS

Newcomb College Arts & Crafts oil lamp, olive green over golden brown glaze, impressed with company logo, an M for potter Joseph Meyer, stilt pull below base, accompanied by an electric converted oil canister insert with cord, Newcomb-style 16" copper shade, hand constructed with five sides having roses in relief against a stippled backdrop and hammered closed-in top, hand-thrown body 7-1/2" h x 11 1/2" dia, 16" h overall. **$900**

Courtesy of Mark Mussio, Humler & Nolan, humlernolan.com

Newcomb College round vase revealing trio of mature foliaged trees dripping with Spanish moss, by Anna Frances Simpson, incised with Simpson monogram, date code FQ 8 and company logo, stamp mark for potter Joseph Meyer, lower body L-shape crack, total length approximately 6" plus a few shorter body cracks, 6-3/8" x 9" dia. **$900**

Courtesy of Mark Mussio, Humler & Nolan, humlernolan.com

▶ Newcomb College deeply carved and painted mat finish vase with Spanish moss and a moon visible through the trees, Sadie Irvine, 1928, impressed marks include the Newcomb Pottery logo, the date code for 1928 (RE 85) the initials of potter Jonathan Hunt and shape number 319, Irvine has incised her monogram along with the impressed marks, 7-7/8" h. **$1,900**

Courtesy of Mark Mussio, Humler & Nolan, humlernolan.com

Newcomb College candlestick, Sadie Irvine, 1919, carved cherry blossom décor, bands of blossoms encircle the piece, mauve-tinted matte glaze, marks: Newcomb logo, date code (KA80), shape 232 and artist's monogram, excellent condition, 7-3/8" h. **$90**

Courtesy of Mark Mussio, Humler & Nolan, humlernolan.com

◀ Unusual Luster glaze Newcomb College vase and separate stand, Sadie Irvine, 1931, drip glaze with lustrous qualities has shades of rose, peach, green and tan throughout, marks include the Newcomb College logo, the date code (SY) for 1931, the initials of potter Jonathan Hunt and the incised monogram of the artist. The matching base has only an incised monogram (probably that of the artist), there is light, faint crazing, 8-1/8" h overall... **$1,500**

Courtesy of Mark Mussio, Humler & Nolan, humlernolan.com

Newcomb College vase, Henrietta Bailey, 1918, carved and painted green leaves and pink flowers on a blue ground with a mauve tint, marks: Newcomb logo, date code for 1918 (JS 26), shape 236 and initials of Joseph Meyer, Bailey's monogram incised, uncrazed, 4-1/8" h. **$1,000**

Courtesy of Mark Mussio, Humler & Nolan, humlernolan.com

Newcomb College matte glaze vase with morning glory decoration, Anna Frances Simpson, 1922, impressed Newcomb logo, date code (MN26), shape 73, JM for potter Joseph Meyer and Simpson's incised monogram, 6-1/8" h. **$1,000**

Courtesy of Mark Mussio, Humler & Nolan, humlernolan.com

Newcomb College vase with wild roses at the shoulder against a rich blue ground, Sadie Irvine, 1927, impressed with the Newcomb logo, shape 102, date code PZ17, potter Joseph Meyer's initials and incised with Irvine's monogram, 5-3/8" h.**$1,500**

Courtesy of Mark Mussio, Humler & Nolan, humlernolan.com

Newcomb College carved vase with floral designs, 1922, likely by Sadie Irvine, marks: Newcomb logo, date code MQ, obscured potter's mark, shape 29 and what appears to be Irvine's incised monogram, faint crazing, 4-7/8" h. **$750**

Newcomb College small two-handled vase with stylized blossoms, New Orleans, La., 1924, NC/OC79/254/JM/illegible artist cipher, excellent condition, 4" x 5". **$1,125**

◀ Newcomb College matte glaze vase, 1918, carved and painted by Anna Frances Simpson, decoration of overlapping pink irises and green stems on a medium blue ground, marks: Newcomb logo, date code (JU 46), shape 233, initials of Joseph Meyer and the artist, 8-3/4" h. **$2,100**

Courtesy of Mark Mussio, Humler & Nolan, humlernolan.com

▼ Newcomb College buttressed vase with jonquil decoration, 1917, Anna Frances Simpson, impressed Newcomb logo, date code (IQ 58), shape 272 and initials of Joseph Meyer and the artist, excellent condition, 5-1/8" h. **$1,500**

Courtesy of Mark Mussio, Humler & Nolan, humlernolan.com

Newcomb College vase, Sadie Irvine, 1911, carved and painted with pale blue irises, semi-matte finish, impressed company logo, monogram for Joseph Meyer, incised monogram for Sadie Irvine, hand painted EW-47 date code and B for buff clay, flat 3/4-inch chip on foot ring, faint crazing, 12" h. **$1,800**

Courtesy of Mark Mussio, Humler & Nolan, humlernolan.com

◀ Double-signed Newcomb high glaze vase, carved with eight stems of budding white roses arranged about the shoulder and set against a bluish green backdrop with cobalt highlighting the recesses, combined effort of Anna Francis Simpson and Maude Robinson, 1910, impressed marks: Newcomb College logo, monogram of potter Joseph Meyer and the letter K for a clay body used with glossy Newcomb, date code for 1910 [DT-56] written in cobalt slip, as are decorators' marks that include the monogram for Anna Francis Simpson and the signature for Maude Robinson, unobtrusive stilt marks visible on underside of foot ring, rare, 6" x 5" across the shoulder. **$11,000**

Courtesy of Mark Mussio, Humler & Nolan, humlernolan.com

CERAMICS

nippon

THE JAPANESE NAME for Japan is Nippon and Nihon, but only one has become known as the collectible porcelain produced in a variety of styles. From teapots to humidors, Nippon porcelain was made in Japan from 1891 to 1921. This 30-year span is often called the Nippon Era. It saw countless porcelain makers and decorators produce items for the export market. The category is currently seeing soft sales as tastes change, but this represents an ideal time for collectors to jump in and begin accumulating wonderfully decorated articles for a fresh collection.

Nippon is actually a general term that was used following the 1891 McKinley Tariff Act, which required that all wares exported to the United States carry a mark indicating their country of origin. The Japanese decided to use the word Nippon. By 1921, import laws changed and the words "Made in" were required for all markings. The law also required the country to replace the word Nippon with the English name "Japan" on all wares sent to U.S. markets.

WORLD WAR I

The boon in Nippon porcelain can be credited to World War I. With European imports at a standstill Japan became the supplier to fill the void in the marketplace. The affordable china appealed to mid-market households seeking pretty objects for the home. Nippon should not be confused with higher-end Japanese porcelain such as Imari, which appealed to a more affluent collecting base, which were also produced during the Nippon era.

Many Japanese factories produced Nippon porcelain, much of it hand-painted or transfer ware floral decorations. Heavy gold or gilded accents were used, as was applied slip-glaze beading (used most notably for moriage Nippon porcelain). As a result, most collectors of Nippon specialize in European-styled porcelains.

Nippon porcelain rose cracker jar, raised on three feet, two vignettes of hand-painted polychrome "Palette Roses" design and gilding over a green ground, blue maple leaf and "Hand / Painted" mark on base, late 19th/early 20th c, wear to gilding, 7-1/2" h. **$410**

Courtesy of Jeffrey S. Evans & Associates, jeffreysevans.com

Like today, Nippon porcelain was produced almost exclusively to satisfy American tastes. At the time it was much less expensive than its European counterparts, which led to a boon in production and consumption overseas. This explains why today's thrift stores

CERAMICS

Nippon porcelain moriage owl humidor, overall tapestry surface with polychrome landscape, moriage owl on branch in foreground on sides, blue maple leaf and "Hand / Painted" mark on base. Late 19th/early 20th century, several small areas of loss to moriage design on outer rim of cover, 6" h. **$1,053**

Courtesy of Jeffrey S. Evans & Associates, jeffreysevans.com

and antiques shops are awash in Nippon porcelain still at highly competitive prices. Knowledgeable collectors familiar with the various marks are able to discern the exact date period within the Nippon era, as some markings were used in the early years where as others were used in later years.

Although much of Nippon's decoration focused on standard florals, there were three distinct lines that appealed to those seeking exotic art from the East.

MORIAGE

Moriage is a special type of raised decoration used on some Japanese pottery, practically dripping with pastel ceramic accents. Sometimes pieces of clay were shaped by hand and applied to the item; sometimes the clay was squeezed from a tube in the way we apply cake frosting. The result is a beautiful mix of raised relief against a sold colored ground. The effect is quite beautiful and prices remain strong for elaborate examples. A 12-inch vase covered in pink and magenta roses and entwined with heavily ornate moriage detail is valued at $500 to $600 if it retains 95 percent of the original applied and slip-glaze decoration.

DRAGONWARE

Decorated in dark grays and blues, Nippon-era Dragonware was marketed as an exotic, mid-market decorative item from the Orient. Dragons were applied in the moriage fashion and accented with slip-glazed decoration.

The style was used primarily on tea and coffee service sets, which are now available affordably. Prices of Dragonware rise for unusual forms, rather than decoration. A bulging, covered container can bring more than $500. Light-colored variations of the Dragonware line from early in the period can bring $300 or more at a well-attended auction.

NORITAKE

Noritake wares produced during the Nippon era have been highly collectible for many decades. The Noritake Company was first registered in 1904. Until 1917 the word Nippon appeared on the back-stamp (this differs from Nippon as used in denoting the country of origin). From 1918, "Noritake" appeared on the back stamp. Highly collectible items were produced between 1921 and 1940, prior to the United States' involvement in World War II.

Unlike Dragonware, the chief value factor of Noritake is the extent the artist produced floral patterns on the pieces of porcelain. With Noritake, design is king. A stunning Nippon/old Noritake Coralene vase can sell for more than $2,000 in today's market.

TODAY'S PRICING

Nippon porcelain is far from its peak in the early 1980s; changing tastes have affected this market in a deep and substantial way. Only extraordinary and finely painted examples of exotic locations or subjects are commanding top dollar in today's market. Items that once sold for $175 to $225 can now be had for less than $50. In today's market, prices are based on the size of the piece, rather than the art painted on its surface. Objects smaller than 10 inches may be purchased for as little as $20, whereas prices for large vases larger than 12 inches can exceed $100.

New collectors are advised to be aware that a number of Nippon markings are being reproduced on new porcelain wares.

Nippon porcelain moriage thistle humidor, hand-painted purple thistles over dark ground behind raised white moriage thistle and butterfly designs on sides and cover, blue maple leaf and "Hand / Painted" mark on base, late 19th/early 20th c, 5-5/8" h. **$351**

Courtesy of Jeffrey S. Evans & Associates, jeffreysevans.com

Nippon porcelain moriage wisteria pitcher, straight-sided with flared foot, hand-painted polychrome and moriage paste wisteria floral design on sides, blue maple leaf and "Hand / Painted" mark on base, late 19th/early 20th c, several small areas of loss to the moriage design, 10-1/4" h. **$410**

Courtesy of Jeffrey S. Evans & Associates, jeffreysevans.com

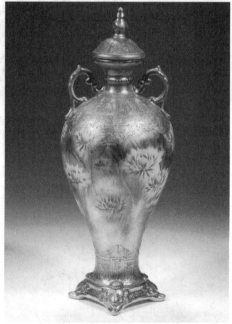

Nippon porcelain cobalt bolted urn, intricate beaded and gilt decoration over cobalt ground, hand-painted landscape on two sides, blue maple leaf and "Hand / Painted" mark on base, late 19th/early 20th century, wear to gilding, 20" h.
.... **$1,638**

Courtesy of Jeffrey S. Evans & Associates, jeffreysevans.com

Nippon porcelain covered urn, baluster form with squared flared foot, ornate handles and small cover with molded finial, white aster floral design over green ground with gilding, unmarked, first quarter 20th c, some wear to finial and handles, 12-1/2" h. **$439**

Courtesy of Jeffrey S. Evans & Associates, jeffreysevans.com

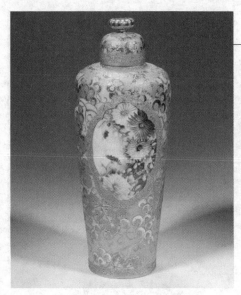

Nippon porcelain gilt-covered urn, tapered form, intricate and elaborate raised gilt design over yellow ground on sides and cover, a small vignette of hand-painted polychrome flowers on one side, blue maple leaf and "Hand / Painted" mark on base, late 19th/early 20th c, light wear to gilding on finial, 12-1/2" h. **$702**

Courtesy of Jeffrey S. Evans & Associates, jeffreysevans.com

Nippon porcelain large bolted urn/floor vase, late 19th/early 20th c, high-shouldered ovoid form with elaborately molded bolted base and handles, hand-painted polychrome vignettes of two women in a garden on one side and flowers on the opposite with gilding over green, off-white, and red grounds, wear to tops of handles, bolt slightly loose, unmarked, 26" h............................... **$1,053**

Courtesy of Jeffrey S. Evans & Associates, jeffreysevans.com

Nippon porcelain seascape vase, ovoid form with flared foot and flared rim, ornate molded gilt handles, hand-painted polychrome vignette of a fisherman and his family at a wharf on one side, alternating panels of lustre gingko leaves over a white ground and polychrome and gilt decorations, green "M" within a wreath for Morimura Brothers, 1911-1921, wear to gilding, 12-3/4" h. **$351**

Nippon porcelain moriage veiled portrait vases, lot of two, both with baluster form with mottled blue around base, hand-painted polychrome floral and portraits on shoulders over with gilding and raised white moriage design and "veil" over portraits, marks: largest with blue maple leaf and "Hand / Painted" first quarter 20th century, wear to gilding on handles, smaller with break and repair to one handle, 4-1/8", 9-7/8" h. **$1,170**

Courtesy of Jeffrey S. Evans & Associates, jeffreysevans.com

Courtesy of Jeffrey S. Evans & Associates, jeffreysevans.com

Nippon porcelain black vase, lower half with black glaze, a central band of swagged gilding and blue beading with flower basket and shield designs, upper half with hand-painted polychrome landscape and flared rim, green "M" within a wreath for Morimura Brothers, 1911-1921, wear to gilding on rim, 12-1/2" h. **$140**

Courtesy of Jeffrey S. Evans & Associates, jeffreysevans.com

Nippon porcelain wisteria vase, paneled sides, high squared handles, flared foot, with hand-painted polychrome wisteria floral design on sides, alternating blue and brown rectangles with gilt overlay designs on shoulder and at base, green "M" within a wreath for Morimura Brothers, 1911-1921, little wear to gilding, 14-3/8" h. .. **$410**

Courtesy of Jeffrey S. Evans & Associates, jeffreysevans.com

Nippon porcelain swan four-handled vase, squared neck, ovoid form, flared molded foot with polychrome hand-painted landscape and swans on one side, green "M" within a wreath for Morimura Brothers mark on base, 1911-1921, scattered small losses to moriage design, 8" h. **$263**

Courtesy of Jeffrey S. Evans & Associates, jeffreysevans.com

Nippon porcelain vase, low, wide base with molded, flared foot, "pretzel" loop handles, flared ruffled rim, white aster floral design over green ground with gilding, green maple leaf and "Hand / Painted" mark on base, late 19th/early 20th c, some wear to gilding, 9-1/2" h........................ **$322**

Courtesy of Jeffrey S. Evans & Associates, jeffreysevans.com

CERAMICS

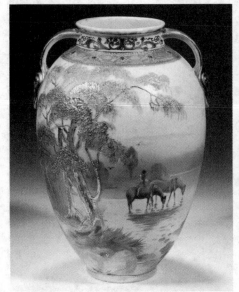

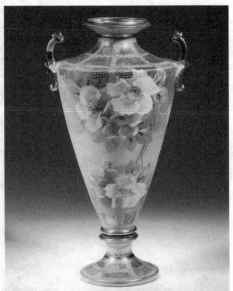

Nippon porcelain horses vase, ovoid form, two handles with molded design at base, hand-painted polychrome image of a man on a horse in water with landscape, intricate gilt design on shoulder with polychrome beading, green "M" within a wreath for Morimura Brothers, 1911-1921, wear to gilding on handles and rim, minute manufacturing flaw on exterior of foot mostly covered with gilding, 10" h. **$410**

Courtesy of Jeffrey S. Evans & Associates, jeffreysevans.com

Nippon porcelain floral bolted vase, wide shoulder, tapered base, flared foot with high molded handles, pastel hand-painted polychrome floral design on sides and gilding on neck, handles, and base with some gilt pinecone designs, blue maple leaf and "Hand / Painted" mark on base, late 19th/early 20th c, very little wear to gilding, 14-5/8" h. **$410**

Courtesy of Jeffrey S. Evans & Associates, jeffreysevans.com

Nippon porcelain Texas Rose vases, pair, high shoulders, wide base, hand-painted polychrome "Texas Rose" design on sides, green and blue maple leaf and "Hand / Painted" marks on bases, late 19th/early 20th c, wear to gilding, 12-1/4" h. **$585**

Courtesy of Jeffrey S. Evans & Associates, jeffreysevans.com

Nippon porcelain moriage vases, pair, both with bulbous form with wide flared foot and two arching handles opposite one another, polychrome hand-painted pansy design with green and gilt ground, raised white and green moriage designs, unmarked except for artist signature on base of both, late 19th/early 20th c, small areas of loss to moriage decoration, some wear to gilding, 8-3/4" h. **$468**

Courtesy of Jeffrey S. Evans & Associates, jeffreysevans.com

CERAMICS

george ohr

GEORGE OHR, THE eccentric potter of Biloxi, Mississippi, worked from about 1883 to 1906. Some think him to be one of the most expert throwers the craft

GEO. E. OHR
BILOXI, MISS.

will ever see. The majority of his works were hand-thrown, exceedingly thin-walled items, some of which have a crushed or folded appearance. He considered himself the foremost potter in the world and declined to sell much of his production, instead accumulating a great horde to leave as a legacy to his children. In 1972, this collection was purchased for resale by an antiques dealer.

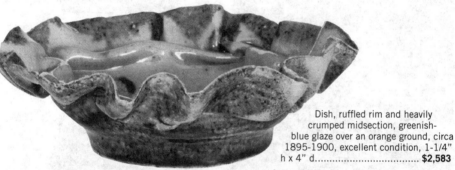

Dish, ruffled rim and heavily crumped midsection, greenish-blue glaze over an orange ground, circa 1895-1900, excellent condition, 1-1/4" h x 4" d...................................**$2,583**

Courtesy of Crocker Farm, crockerfarm.com

Extremely uncommon maritime plaque, inscribed "OHR," Biloxi, Mississippi origin, circa 1895-1905, slab constructed depicting a view of the Mississippi Sound, featuring a hand-sculpted relief scene of a man in a sailboat with hoisted American flag, above an underwater scene depicting swimming fish, seashells, and a blue crab, with brown pelican flies to the right of the boat, two sailboats and a steamship visible in the distance, surface glazed in various shades of blue, green, black, brown, and white, incised "OHR" on a raised area of ocean floor at base, in-the-firing loss to corner – partially glazed, some small additional chips to edge, 10-1/2" l x 10" w..**$3,998**

Courtesy of Crocker Farm, crockerfarm.com

CERAMICS

Bisque vase, squat bulbous form with in-body twist, base hand-signed "(illegible) from/ N.O. Street/ G E Ohr/ 1905," 2-1/2" h x 4" d......... **$704**

Courtesy of Neal Auction Company, nealauction.com

Large vase, green and gunmetal blister glaze, stamped G.E. OHR, Biloxi, Miss., 1897-1900, few scratches and one kiln kiss to shoulder, 6" h x 5-1/2" w.. **$3,125**

Courtesy of Rago Arts and Auction Center, ragoarts.com

Vase, straight neck over large bulbous body, green, ochre and raspberry speckled glaze, base impressed, "G.E. OHR/BILOXI, MISS," 4-3/4" h x 5-1/2" d. **$1,920**

Courtesy of Neal Auction Company, nealauction.com

Small glazed vessel, stamped verso "G.E. Ohr Biloxi, Miss., some crazing in the glaze especially on the inside of the vessel and other minor areas throughout, there are small chips to the underside as if the piece was on a stand at some point, all the points at the top are in tact with no visible chips or cracks to the ceramic, 3-1/2" h x 3-1/4" d. **$444**

Courtesy Michaan Auctions, michaans.com

Vessel with folded-in rim, green, ochre, gunmetal, and raspberry sponged-on glaze, stamped G.E. OHR, Biloxi, Miss., 1897-1900, 3" h x 4-1/2" w. **$4,375**

Courtesy of Rago Arts and Auction Center, ragoarts.com

Mississippi clay-handled jug, late 19th-early 20th century, apparently unsigned, flake to lip with associated hairline, crazing, other small flake to lip, some firing flaws, with wear commensurate with age and use, 4-3/4" h. **$812**

Courtesy of Heritage Auctions, ha.com

Mug incised with a wave pattern and covered in shiny dark brown and ochre metallic glazes, impressed Geo. E. Ohr, Biloxi, Miss. beneath, tiny glaze to neck at base of rim, 3-3/8" h.............. **$819**

Courtesy of Humler & Nolan, humlernolan.com

Pottery puzzle mug, glazed stoneware with a deep brown tone, script incised signature to the bottom, Biloxi, MS, circa 1898-1910, 3-5/8" h x 5-3/8" l x 4" w. **$4,000**

Courtesy of Elite Auctioneers LLC, eliteauction.com

Mug, high glaze waisted form, 1896, script signature "G E Ohr" and "3-18-96" on bottom, and inscribed presentation for Joseph Jefferson "Heres your Good and your Family's and May They All Live Long and Prosper, J. Jefferson." Jefferson was a famous actor and resident of New Iberia, Louisiana, and a visitor to Ohr's studio, 6-1/4" h x 5-3/4" w x 4-1/2"....................................... **$3,125**

Courtesy of Crescent Auction Gallery, crescentauction.com

Jug with small baluster body with applied ribbon handle, rough bisque glaze, base impressed "G.E.O. E. OHR/BILOXI," 4-1/2" h............... **$1,088**

Courtesy of Neal Auction Company, nealauction.com

CERAMICS

overbeck

THE OVERBECK STUDIO POTTERY was founded by four sisters, Hannah, Mary Francis, Elizabeth and Harriet, in the Overbeck family home in Cambridge City, Indiana, in 1911. A fifth sister, Margaret, who worked as a decorator at Zanesville Art Pottery in 1910, was the catalyst for establishing the pottery, but died the same year.

Launching at the tail end of the Arts & Crafts movement and believing "borrowed art is bad art," the sister potters dedicated themselves to producing unique quality pieces with original design elements, which often were inspired by the natural world. Pieces can also be found in the Art Nouveau and Art Deco styles, as well as unique figurines and grotesques. The studio used several marks through the years, including an incised O and incised OBK, often accompanied by the artist's initials. The pottery ceased production in 1955.

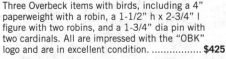

Three Overbeck items with birds, including a 4" paperweight with a robin, a 1-1/2" h x 2-3/4" l figure with two robins, and a 1-3/4" dia pin with two cardinals. All are impressed with the "OBK" logo and are in excellent condition. **$425**

Courtesy of Humler & Nolan, humlernolan.com

Pair of candlesticks with berries, Cambridge City, IN, 1920s, glazed earthenware, both incised "OBK," one incised "E," 2-1/2" x 3-1/4". **$600**

Courtesy of Rago Arts and Auction Center, ragoarts.com

VISIT WWW.ANTIQUETRADER.COM

WWW.FACEBOOK.COM/ANTIQUETRADER

Cockatoo figure, marked on base with the
"OBK" logo, excellent condition, 4-1/2" h. **$275**

Courtesy of Humler & Nolan, humlernolan.com

Lot of four figurines: three gentlemen and a
flamingo, Cambridge City, IN, hand-built glazed
earthenware, all incised "OBK," tallest is
4-1/4" h. **$550**

Courtesy of Rago Arts and Auction Center, ragoarts.com

Granny with Basket of Apples figure, marked
on the bottom with the Overbeck "OBK" logo,
excellent condition, 4-1/8" h. **$250**

Courtesy of Humler & Nolan, humlernolan.com

Colonial figures seated in chairs, both impressed
with the Overbeck "OBK" mark, excellent
condition, man is 3-7/8" and the woman 3-3/8".
.... **$600**

Courtesy of Humler & Nolan, humlernolan.com

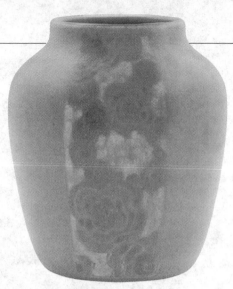

Floral vase, Cambridge City, IN, incised and painted matte glazed ceramic, impressed mark, artist signed "EH," 3-1/2" dia x 4" h. **$1,700**

Courtesy of Treadway Gallery, treadwaygallery.com

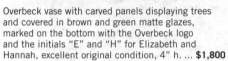

Overbeck vase with carved panels displaying trees and covered in brown and green matte glazes, marked on the bottom with the Overbeck logo and the initials "E" and "H" for Elizabeth and Hannah, excellent original condition, 4" h. ... **$1,800**

Courtesy of Humler & Nolan, humlernolan.com

Squatty shouldered form vase in a mottled blue turquoise and brown glaze, marked "BK," good condition, 6" h..**$250**

Courtesy of Jaremos, jaremos.com

Vase with birds, Cambridge City, IN, incised "OBK/E/H," 5-3/4" x 5-3/4".......................... **$3,250**

Courtesy of Rago Arts and Auction Center, ragoarts.com

CERAMICS

paul revere pottery

PAUL REVERE POTTERY may appear sporadically in today's auction market, but there is no mistaking it once you get a glimpse.

The playful designs — sometimes with wisdom-infused illustrations, depictions of nature, and daily life of the early 20th century — and practical quality construction seem to be what defines this form of pottery, but there is much more to it.

Paul Revere Pottery is, in fact, a glorious extension of a greater educational effort that began with three women in late 19th century Boston. In the midst of tremendous social and cultural change and economic disparity among people, Edith Brown (1872-1932), Edith Guerrier (1870-1958), and Helen Storrow (1864-1944) came together to provide young immigrant women in the North End neighborhood of Boston with opportunities to experience various facets of life, and in turn gain new skills.

The Saturday Evening Girls (SEG) Club grew out of the Saturday Evening Girls Story Hour, which was established by Guerrier in 1899 as part of the North Bennet Street Industrial School (NBSIS). The school was established for the purpose of training newly arrived immigrants in the North End neighborhood (largely Italian and Jewish families) in skilled trades. Not only was the Boston Public Library branch of the NBSIS the place where the Saturday Evening Girls Club took shape, it was the first trade school in America, according to the book, *Saturday Evening Girls*, by Meg Chalmers and Judy Young (Schiffer Publications).

Guerrier (a librarian and writer) and Brown (an artist) met while attending the Museum School of Boston's Museum of Fine Arts. In the early 20th century, the two women, who were living together by this time, met Helen Osborne Storrow, a longtime philanthropist in Boston. With a shared focus of social and political reform, empowerment of women, and the importance of honing various skills and creative endeavors, the three formed a bond that would change the lives of many and eventually bring Paul Revere Pottery into existence.

In the early years, the club incorporated lessons in practical business and trade skills, with

Three Saturday Evening Girls pottery bowls: One larger bowl with stylized decorative band around the interior against a light blue glaze, signed "P.R.P. 1026" [Paul Revere Pottery] with a cross within a circle, 7-1/2" dia; and two smaller bowls with cream-colored acorn-type band surrounding the interior edge of the bowl, against a darker blue background, signed on the underside "SEG" and numbered, 4-7/8" dia...**$1,210**

Courtesy of James D. Julia Auctioneers, jamesdjulia.com

CERAMICS

Saturday Evening Girls covered bowl, circular landscape design, signed and dated "10-21" for October 1921, includes rare ceramic strainer, 8-1/4" dia x 4-1/4" h..................................... **$475**

Courtesy of California Historical Design, acstickley.com

Saturday Evening Girls swan bowl decorated by Sara Galner, dated 2-14 for February 1914, crisp decoration, tight hairline, 10-3/4" dia x 4-1/4" h. **$950**

Courtesy of California Historical Design, acstickley.com

Saturday Evening Girls bowl, circular duck design, signed and dated 2-20 for February 1920, 6-1/2" dia x 2-3/4" h. **$225**

Courtesy of California Historical Design, acstickley.com

creative programs such as storytelling and dance. Following a trip to Europe in 1906, Guerrier and Brown began researching the possibility of incorporating pottery-making classes into their club curriculum. Upon seeing some of the early pieces the group created, Storrow purchased a home in the

North End of Boston. This provided space to designate individual rooms for the pottery-making process, an area to sell the pottery, and rooms for club meetings. On the upper floor were apartments, including one where Guerrier and Brown lived.

Given that this new "headquarters" was located near the Old North Church, the same place Paul Revere had instructed his fellow Sons of Liberty to hang lanterns to signal movement of British troops ahead of the American Revolution, the brand would become Paul Revere Pottery.

By 1915, Paul Revere Pottery by Saturday Evening Girls was attracting widespread interest, and expansion of the program and its operation was necessary. With the incorporation of the Paul Revere Pottery Co. in 1916, it became a full-time business and remained as such until operations ceased in 1942.

Interest in Paul Revere Pottery, as limited as its exposure may be, is represented in prices paid at auction. Having brought many examples to auction — including a record-setting glazed ceramic fireplace depicting a wooded landscape by Saturday Evening Girls artists Fannie Levine, Albina Mangini, and Brown that sold for $219,750 (with buyer's premium) in 2013 — David Rago, principal of Rago Arts and Auctions Center, explained some of what sets this style of pottery apart.

"Little material better describes the Arts & Crafts [movement] in America," Rago said. "Conceived by women, decorated by women, focusing on kitchen ware, centered on designs that are both sophisticated and simple, the intent of SEG was to better the lives of women who needed a boost by involving them in the arts."

In February 2015, during a sale by Rago, an SEG wall pocket with a poppies design measuring 6 inches x 4 inches sold for $2,750. In Chalmers & Young's book, samples of 1921 Paul Revere Pottery catalog pages show that a wall pocket of this size sold for between $2.50 and $4, depending on the design.

"The appeal of Saturday Evening Girls Paul Revere Pottery is tied in with the general interest in Arts & Crafts pottery because it is handmade, often hand-thrown and decorated by a known person," said Riley Humler, principal of Humler & Nolan. "The main appeal still has to do with the quality of the art and often, although simple in design, the better pieces are stunning in execution and composition, and most often done in soft, matte glazes."

Today the market for Paul Revere Pottery is thin, as pieces are scarce, according to Rago and Humler. As the market for early 20th century decorative art has narrowed, it has pushed the cream to the top, which is true of most of the pottery from the Arts & Crafts period, Rago said.

"That prices for the best, rarest work have risen so dramatically hasn't necessarily translated to more pieces coming to market," Rago said. "The people who own it, love it because it is truly fine and lovable ware, spiritually wrought and well designed, and they remain loathe to sell it."

The seldom-seen scenic pieces with no lettering are most sought-after or garner the most interest at auctions, Humler said.

"Lots of pieces were made for children's breakfast sets with bowl, pitcher, mug or plate, and often these have dates and children's names included with the design," he said. "The best pieces will be scenic or floral pieces that do not reference anyone. And as in most art pottery, if an item is of great quality, big is better than small."

One aspect of Paul Revere Pottery that lends itself to identification, and, in turn, avoiding reproductions is the signature and markings on each piece.

"Because the work is almost always signed, artist signed, and dated, this makes determining (the period of a) piece a fairly easy matter," Rago said.

Becoming as familiar as possible with the subject of Paul Revere Pottery, or any work for that matter, is a primary step before buying anything, advised Humler and Rago. In addition to being well-versed in the various types of signatures, gaining knowledge about the materials used in the development of the pottery and attributes of the different periods, along with seeking out reputable people to buy from, go a very long way to ensuring the opportunities one has to acquire historic SEG works are positive.

"I cannot emphasize enough the importance of scholarship when being a collector," Humler said. "Know your area better than the people from whom you buy, and you should be way ahead of the game."

— Antoinette Rahn

Saturday Evening Girls cup and saucer, lotus decoration, 1917, cup marked "S.E.G.," "E.G." and "11-1-17" in black slip, saucer marked in black slip: "S.E.G., 2-17" and "K," saucer 5-3/4" dia, cup 2-1/8" h. **$300**

Courtesy of Mark Mussio, Humler & Nolan, humlernolan.com

Saturday Evening Girls Art Deco covered inkwell, green glaze, hand-signed "SEG" with the monogram "TK" below the base, crazing, corner shoulder chip, 2-1/2" x 4" x 3". **$130**

Courtesy of Mark Mussio, Humler & Nolan, humlernolan.com

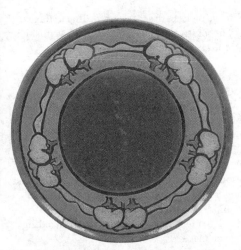

Saturday Evening Girls trivet tile, incised
landscape design, dated 6-17 for June 1917,
invisible professional repair to small edge chip,
6-1/2" dia.. **$400**

Courtesy of California Historical Design, acstickley.com

Saturday Evening Girls vase, speckled green glaze
with a frothy blue glaze dripped from the rim,
marked on bottom in black slip "S.E.G., 10-22"
and initials that appear to be "L E," 5-1/4" h... **$300**

Courtesy of Mark Mussio, Humler & Nolan, humlernolan.com

Saturday Evening Girls Pottery blue pitcher
decorated with carved white swans encircling rim,
signed, 4-1/4" h x 4-1/4" w............................ **$375**

Courtesy of California Historical Design, acstickley.com

Saturday Evening Girls tall vase, Boston, Mass.,
1930, Paul Revere stamp "DECEMBER 1930
SR," marked "BSE," 13-1/2" x 8-1/4". **$17,500**

Courtesy of Rago Arts and Auction Center, ragoarts.com

CERAMICS

red wing pottery

VARIOUS POTTERIES OPERATED in Red Wing, Minnesota, starting in 1868, the most successful being the Red Wing Stoneware Co., organized in 1877. Merged with other local potteries through the years, it became known as Red Wing Union Stoneware Co. in 1906 and was one of the largest producers of utilitarian stoneware items in the United States.

After a decline in the popularity of stoneware products, an art pottery line was introduced to compensate for the loss. This was reflected in a new name for the company, Red Wing Potteries, Inc., in 1936. Stoneware production ceased entirely in 1947, but vases, planters, cookie jars, and dinnerware of art pottery quality continued in production until 1967, when the pottery ceased operation altogether.

For more information on Red Wing pottery, see *Warman's Red Wing Pottery Identification and Price Guide* by Mark F. Moran.

Red paneled sponge bowl, rare, smallest size made, strong red/blue sponge color added in the 1930s, excellent condition, very scarce size, 5" dia. **$250**

Courtesy of Rich Penn Auctions, richpennauctions.com

Red Wing bulldog, chestnut brown glaze, c. 1895, excellent condition, 6-1/2" h x 8-3/4" l **$450**

Courtesy of Rich Penn Auctions, richpennauctions.com

VISIT WWW.ANTIQUETRADER.COM

WWW.FACEBOOK.COM/ANTIQUETRADER

Red Wing advertising water cooler from Minnesota, 5 gal, salt-glazed finish with the original spout and bale handles, front is marked "5 Water Cooler / St. Paul Book & Stationery Co. St. Paul, Minn," lid missing, good condition, 13" dia, 14-1/4" h. **$130**

Courtesy of North American Auction Company, northamericanauctioncompany.com

Red Wing bank, Hamm's Beer bear, excellent condition, 12" h. **$450**

Courtesy of Rich Penn Auctions, richpennauctions.com

Cobalt-decorated crock, 5 gal, attributed to early Red Wing, with flared script "f" and Red Wing-like cobalt flower decoration.......................... **$250**

Courtesy of Stony Ridge Auction, stonyridgeauction.com

Red Wing butter churn, 4 gal, salt-glaze leaf, with lid and dasher, faint hairline on back, chip on base, VG+ overall condition, 16-1/2" h. **$150**

Courtesy of Rich Penn Auctions, richpennauctions.com

Red Wing Overland Rye whiskey crock jug from the Montana Liquor Company in Butte, Montana, 2 gal, two-tone salt-glazed finish with original label that reads "Overland Rye / Montana Liquor Co. / Butte," bottom marked "Red Wing Stoneware," good overall condition, 8" dia, 9-1/4" h.. **$175**

Courtesy of North American Auction Company, northamericanauctioncompany.com

Red Wing crock, 12 gal, dated 1905, with metal and wood handles, good condition, 17" h, 17" dia............................. **$100**

Courtesy of Jay Anderson Auction, jayandersonauction.com

Set of Red Wing dishes
including a coffee pot, mugs
and coffee cups,
good condition.
........................$10

*Courtesy of Donley Auctions,
donleyauctions.com*

Red Wing green planter with
pink flowers and tree bark,
7-1/2" d x 6" h. $35

*Courtesy of Long Auction Company, LLC,
longauction.com*

Planter with oak leaf and acorn
design, 4-5/8" d, 8" w, 5" dia.
....$45

*Courtesy of Long Auction Company, LLC,
longauction.com*

Red Wing Sam's Saloon jug,
"From Sam's Saloon-Tripoli,
IA," few Red Wing jugs are
found promoting a saloon and
the small quart size make it
desirable, flawless condition,
7-1/2" h. $1,500

*Courtesy of Rich Penn Auctions,
richpennauctions.com*

Red Wing pottery vase, marked
"1107," 7-1/4" h, 4-1/4" dia.$35

*Courtesy of Auctions By B. Langston, LLC,
liveauctioneers.com*

Early Red Wing crackle-glaze
vase with two female nudes for
handles, marks include raised
shape number "249" and "Red
Wing Art Pottery" circular ink
stamp logo in blue, 11-3/8" h.
....$300

Courtesy of Humler & Nolan, humlernolan.com

Rare Red Wing large art pottery
vase, features an organic
modernist form in a lime green
glaze with pleasing circular
crazing patterns, slightly
tapered square base, marked
"Red Wing USA," pattern
number is marked on the base
and looks to read "1366,"
but first two digits are weakly
impressed, 18" h................$125

*Courtesy of Hill Auction Gallery,
hillauctiongallery.com*

CERAMICS

CERAMICS

redware

RED EARTHENWARE POTTERY was made in the American colonies from the late 1600s. Bowls, crocks, and all types of utilitarian wares were turned out in great abundance to supplement pewter and hand-made treenware. The ready availability of the clay, the same used in making bricks and roof tiles, accounted for the vast production. The lead-glazed redware retained its reddish color, although a variety of colors could be obtained by adding various metals to the glaze. Interesting effects occurred accidentally through unsuspected impurities in the clay or uneven temperatures in the firing kiln, which sometimes resulted in streaks or mottled splotches. Redware pottery was seldom marked by the maker.

Redware charger decorated with a yellow slip ABC in the center, early 19th century, surface chips to slip, otherwise good condition, 13-1/4" d. **$250**

Courtesy of Hyde Park Country Auctions, hpcountryauctions.com

Slip-decorated and glazed redware bowl, 19th century, cream and green decoration, deaccessioned from New England museum, 11" w x 2-1/2" h.. **$275**

Courtesy of Stony Ridge Auction, stonyridgeauction.com

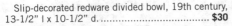

Slip-decorated redware divided bowl, 19th century, 13-1/2" l x 10-1/2" d. **$30**

Courtesy of Stony Ridge Auction, stonyridgeauction.com

VISIT WWW.ANTIQUETRADER.COM

WWW.FACEBOOK.COM/ANTIQUETRADER

Redware glazed flower pot, 19th century, attached saucer base, ruffled rim, tapered body with incised lines and ruffled saucer base, 4-7/8" h x 5-5/8" dia.. **$275**

Courtesy of Conestoga Auction Company Division of Hess Auction Group, hessauctiongroup.com

▲ I.S. Stahl green-glazed redware jar, incise tulip decoration, dated 1948, 7" h. **$500**

Courtesy of Conestoga Auction Company Division of Hess Auction Group, hessauctiongroup.com

◄ Redware loaf dish, early to mid-19th c., drape-molded construction, with plain rim, line and dot yellow slip design, glaze pop to front, approx. 1-3/4" h, 11-1/2" w, 9" d. **$3,250**

Courtesy of Austin Auction Gallery, austinauction.com

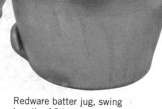

Glazed redware quart-size jug, New England, 19th century, 7-1/4" h. **$225**

Courtesy of Conestoga Auction Company Division of Hess Auction Group, hessauctiongroup.com

Glazed redware manganese decorated stoneware jug, circa 1860, attributed to Porter Pottery, Wiscasset, Maine, footed base, incised double ring at neck, applied hand to neck, 9" h. **$175**

Courtesy of Stony Ridge Auction, stonyridgeauction.com

Redware batter jug, swing handle, 19th century, 9-1/4" h. **$90**

Courtesy of Stony Ridge Auction, stonyridgeauction.com

Redware cream pitcher, 19th century, mottle glazed, bulbous body with raised band, pinched spout, applied loop ribbed handle and molded base rim, mottled manganese glaze on reddish orange glazed ground, 5-1/8" h...................... **$225**

Courtesy of Conestoga Auction Company Division of Hess Auction Group, hessauctiongroup.com

Two-tone glazed redware cream pitcher, Pennsylvania, 19th century, bulbous form with pinched spout and applied loop handle, inscribed on base "Manufactured while in procession Feb. 22, 1832 Centennial Anniversary of the Birth of Washington," Lester Breininger Estate, 5" h. **$1,600**

Courtesy of Conestoga Auction Company Division of Hess Auction Group, hessauctiongroup.com

Manganese redware sander, 19th century, 3-1/2" dia. **$170**

Courtesy of Conestoga Auction Company Division of Hess Auction Group, hessauctiongroup.com

Mottle-glazed redware tub, 19th century, unsigned but possibly Bell pottery, straight sided with flared rim and open rope twist handles, 6" h x 9" dia. **$350**

Courtesy of Conestoga Auction Company Division of Hess Auction Group, hessauctiongroup.com

American Studio Pottery modern lamp base vase, redware pottery with opaque white glaze, modern incised graphic design, not marked, 11-1/4" h, 10" w, 10" d. **$225**

Courtesy of Uniques & Antiques, Inc., uniquesandantiques.com

Lot of two American redware plates, 19th c., one with coggled edge and yellow-slip trailed design, chips and losses, approx. 1-1/4" h, 8-1/4" dia; the other with lightly coggled edge and yellow-slip trailed foliate design, chips at rim, approx. 1-1/2" h, 9-1/4" dia. **$300**

Courtesy of Austin Auction Gallery, austinauction.com

Three yellow slip-decorated redware plates, Pennsylvania, 19th century, two have Sotheby's Park Bernet labels, largest measures 10-1/4" dia. **$450**

Courtesy of Conestoga Auction Company Division of Hess Auction Group, hessauctiongroup.com

CERAMICS

rockingham

THE MARQUIS OF ROCKINGHAM first established an earthenware pottery in the Yorkshire district of England around 1745, and it was occupied afterwards by various potters. The well-known mottled brown Rockingham glaze was introduced about 1788 by the Brameld Brothers and became immediately popular. It was during the 1820s that the production of true porcelain began at the factory, and it continued to be made until the firm closed in 1842.

Since that time the so-called Rockingham glaze has been used by various potters in England and the United States, including some famous wares produced in Bennington, Vermont (see Bennington Pottery). Similar glazes were also used by potteries in other areas of the United States including Ohio and Indiana, but only wares specifically attributed to Bennington should use that name. The following listings include mainly wares featuring the dark brown mottled glaze produced at various sites here and abroad.

Glazed yellowware book-form flask, impressed with "Departed Spirits" on spine, very good condition, 6" h. **$307**

Courtesy of Conestoga Auction Company, a Division of the Hess Auction Group, hessauctiongroup.com

Jasperware pitcher with a snake figure as the handle and the spout, circa 1815, impressed "15" on the base, a couple scuffs and firing cracks to lower side, 7-1/2" h x 10-1/4" w. **$317**

Courtesy of Schwenke Auctioneers, woodburyauction.com

Molded figure of a lion attributed to Haig Pottery, circa 1871-1881, reclining on oblong base with surface decorated with streaked reddish-brown glaze over a light clay ground, hand-incised details throughout, raised letter "H" on the base for Haig, 9-1/8" l..**$338**

Courtesy of Crocker Farm, crockerfarm.com

top lot!

A scarce Rockingham-glazed piece took the top lot at a March 2018 Crocker Farm auction. The very rare Anna Pottery pig bottle with incised railroad map, Wallace and Cornwall Kirkpatrick, Anna, Illinois, circa 1880, sold for $2,706. The 7-1/4-inch long bottle is molded in the form of a reclining pig with snout and hooves, and on one side is inscribed advertising "from/Sanford Wells & Co. / N 214 N. Main St. / St. Louis Mo" along with the slogan, "with a little Fine old Bourton in a." The remainder of the pig is incised with a railroad map of the Midwestern U.S., with landmarks including "Anna Pottery" and "Chicago the corn crib." The surface is covered in a visually-appealing streaked reddish-brown glaze over a yellowish clay body. There is some loss to the back edge of one rear leg, a chip to the bottom of edge of opposite rear leg, losses to ears, chipping to base of tail.

COURTESY OF CROCKER FARM, CROCKERFARM.COM

▲ Three glazed yellowware covered butter tubs, good condition with minor wear.......$124

Courtesy of Conestoga Auction Company, a division of Hess Auction Group, hessauctiongroup.com

◀ A 19th century glazed Staffordshire recumbent lion pen holder, with manufactured holes in top of the heads, crazing, scattered chips, 6-1/2" x 8-1/4" x 4"; and a pair of smaller recumbent lion pen holders, 3-1/2" x 5" x 3"............... $576

Courtesy of Brunk Auctions, brunkauctions.com

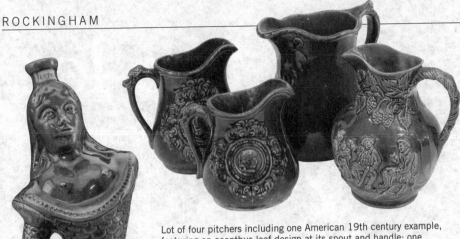

Lot of four pitchers including one American 19th century example, featuring an acanthus leaf design at its spout and handle; one vintage Arthur Wood pitcher, 20th century with a hop motif around the spout and handle, depicting men drinking over the phrase "Willie brewed a peck o'malt"; two 19th century American pitchers, with a 19th century medallion with cameo-style profile of a lady; measuring 9-3/4" h, 9-1/4" h, and 8-1/4" h, respectively. **$86**

Courtesy of Austin Auction Company, austinauction.com

Glazed stoneware mermaid flask, 19th century, glaze flake to tip of nose, old labels to spout and reverse, with wear commensurate with age and use, 7-1/2" h x 4" w. **$125**

Courtesy of Heritage Auctions, ha.com

Pitcher with beavers and maple leaf images on the body and lid, 19th century Canadian, tight fitting lid, glaze crazing on inside, around and on base, very minor roughness to spout edge and a few lid edge flakes, many filled with dirt over time, very good condition, 7" h. **$271**

Courtesy of Miller & Miller Auctions, millerandmillerauctions.com

Bennington signed flint enamel pottery pitcher and basin, both feature paneled sides, Rockingham-style glaze with splashes of green and blue enamels, impressed on base "Fenton's/ENAMEL/PATENTED/1849/BENNINGTON, VT," circa 1850, restoration to two hairlines in basin, and several lower ribs and small area of rim of pitcher, 12-1/2" h. **$403**

Courtesy of Jeffrey S. Evans & Associates, jeffreysevans.com

CERAMICS

rookwood

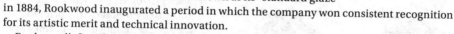

MARIA LONGWORTH NICHOLS founded Rookwood Pottery in 1880. The name, she later reported, paid homage to the many crows (rooks) on her father's estate and was also designed to remind customers of Wedgwood. Production began on Thanksgiving Day 1880 when the first kiln was drawn.

Rookwood's earliest productions demonstrated a continued reliance on European precedents and the Japanese aesthetic. Although the firm offered a variety of wares (Dull Glaze, Cameo, and Limoges for example), it lacked a clearly defined artistic identity. With the introduction of what became known as its "standard glaze" in 1884, Rookwood inaugurated a period in which the company won consistent recognition for its artistic merit and technical innovation.

Rookwood's first decade ended on a high note when the company was awarded two gold medals: one at the Exhibition of American Art Industry in Philadelphia and another later in the year at the Exposition Universelle in Paris. Significant, too, was Maria Longworth Nichols' decision to transfer her interest in the company to William W. Taylor, who had been the firm's manager since 1883. In May 1890, the board of a newly reorganized Rookwood Pottery Co. purchased "the real estate, personal property, goodwill, patents, trade-marks ... now the sole property of William W. Taylor" for $40,000.

Under Taylor's leadership, Rookwood was transformed from a fledgling startup to successful business that expanded throughout the following decades to meet rising demand.

Throughout the 1890s, Rookwood continued to attract critical notice as it kept the tradition of innovation alive. Taylor rolled out three new glaze lines — Iris, Sea Green, and Aerial Blue — from late 1894 into early 1895.

At the Paris Exposition in 1900, Rookwood cemented its reputation by winning the Grand Prix, a feat largely due to the favorable reception of the new Iris glaze and its variants.

Over the next several years, Rookwood's record of achievement at domestic and international exhibitions remained unmatched.

Throughout the 1910s, Rookwood continued in a similar vein and began to more thoroughly embrace the simplified aesthetic promoted by many Arts & Crafts figures. Production of the Iris line, which had been instrumental in the firm's success at the Paris Exposition in 1900, ceased around 1912. Not only did the company abandon its older, fussier underglaze wares, but the newer lines the pottery introduced also trended toward simplicity.

Unfortunately, the collapse of the stock market in October 1929 and ensuing economic depression dealt Rookwood a blow from which it did not recover. The Great Depression took a toll on the company and eventually led to bankruptcy in April 1941.

Rookwood's history might have ended there were it not for the purchase of the firm by a group of investors led by automobile dealer Walter E. Schott and his wife, Margaret. Production started once again. In the years that followed, Rookwood changed hands a number of times before being moved to Starkville, Mississippi, in 1960. It finally closed its doors there in 1967.

CERAMICS

Rookwood console bowl, ivory mat glaze, with an Art Deco-style female at either end, a Louise Abel design, cast in 1929, marks: Rookwood logo, date, shape 2923 and Abel's mold monogram, some minor penciling, 6-7/8" h x 12-1/2" l. **$160**

Courtesy of Mark Mussio, Humler & Nolan, humlernolan.com

Pair of small rook bookends, deep blue mat glaze, a William McDonald design, cast in 1919, marks: Rookwood logo, date and shape 2275, excellent condition, 5" h. **$160**

Courtesy of Mark Mussio, Humler & Nolan, humlernolan.com

Pair of donkey bookends, white mat glaze, William McDonald design, done in 1936, marks: Rookwood logo, date, shape number 6216 and cast in monogram of designer, William McDonald, uncrazed with minor pepper spot or two on each, 6-1/8" h. **$550**

Courtesy of Mark Mussio, Humler & Nolan, humlernolan.com

ROOKWOOD MARKS

Rookwood employed a number of marks on the bottom of its vessels that denoted everything from the shape to the size, date, and color of the body, to the type of glaze to be used.

COMPANY MARKS

1880-1882

In this early period, a number of marks were used to identify the wares.

1. "ROOKWOOD" followed by the initials of the decorator, painted in gold. This is likely the earliest mark, and though the wares are not dated, it seems to have been discontinued by 1881-1882.
2. "ROOKWOOD / POTTERY. / [DATE] CIN. O." In Marks of American Potters (1904), Edwin AtLee Barber states, "The most common marks prior to 1882 were the name of the pottery and the date of manufacture, which were painted or incised on the base of each piece by the decorator."
3. "R. P. C. O. M. L. N." These initials stand for "Rookwood Pottery, Cincinnati, Ohio, Maria Longworth Nichols" and were either painted or incised on the base.
4. Kiln and crows stamp. Barber notes that in 1881 and 1882, the trademark designed by the artist Henry Farny was printed beneath the glaze.
5. Anchor stamp: Barber notes that this mark is "one of the rarest."
6. Oval stamp.
7. Ribbon or banner stamp: According to Barber, "In 1882 a special mark was used on a trade piece ... the letters were impressed in a raised ribbon.
8. Ribbon or banner stamp II: A simpler variation of the above stamp, recorded by Herbert Peck.

1883-1886

1. Stamped name and date.
2. Impressed kiln: Appears only in 1883.

1886-1960

Virtually all of the pieces feature the conjoined RP monogram. Pieces fired in the anniversary kilns carry a special kiln-shaped mark with the number of the anniversary inside of it.

1955

A diamond-shaped mark that reads: "ROOKWOOD / 75th / ANNIVERSARY / POTTERY" was printed on wares.

1960-1967

Occasionally pieces are marked "ROOKWOOD POTTERY / STARKVILLE MISS"; from 1962 to 1967 a small "*" occasionally follows the monogram.

DATE MARKS

Unlike many of their contemporaries, Rookwood seems early on to have adopted a method of marking its pottery that was accurate and easy to understand.

From 1882-1885, the company impressed the date, often with the company name, in block letters (see 1883-86, No. 1).

Although the date traditionally given for the conjoined RP mark is June 23, 1886, this marks the official introduction of the monogram rather than the first use.

Stanley Burt, in his record of Rookwood at the Cincinnati Museum, noted two pieces from 1883 (Nos. 2 and 3) that used the monogram. The monogram was likely designed by Alfred Brennan, since it first appears on his work.

From 1886 on, the date of the object was coded in the conjoined "RP" monogram.

1886: conjoined "RP" no additional flame marks.

1887-1900: conjoined "RP" with a flame added for each subsequent year. Thus, a monogram with seven flames would represent 1893.

1900-1967: conjoined "RP" with 14 flames and a Roman numeral below the mark to indicate the year after 1900. Thus, a monogram with 14 flames and the letters "XXXVI" below it signifies 1936.

CLAY-TYPE MARKS

From 1880 until around 1895, Rookwood used a number of different colored bodies for production and marked each color with a letter code. These letters were impressed and usually found grouped together with the

Rookwood Standard glaze humidor, Lenore Asbury, 1897, decorated with a pair of turtles, marks: Rookwood logo (indicating the date), shape 812, a triangle-shaped esoteric mark and Asbury's incised initials, fine overall crazing, missing lid, 3-7/8" h x 6-1/4" dia.. **$300**

Courtesy of Mark Mussio, Humler & Nolan, humlernolan.com

Rookwood baby elephant paperweight, Nubian Black glaze, cast in 1951, marks: Rookwood logo, date and shape 6490, tiny nick at the base, 3-7/8" h. **$120**

Courtesy of Mark Mussio, Humler & Nolan, humlernolan.com

Rookwood Limoges-style pitcher, Albert R. Valentien, 1882, decorated with a flock of birds and having lots of fired on gold, marks: Impressed ROOKWOOD, 1882, shape 54, 1, R for Red clay, the anchor mark and Valentien's incised initials, excellent condition, 7-3/8" h. **$750**

Courtesy of Mark Mussio, Humler & Nolan, humlernolan.com

CERAMICS

SOME LINES OF NOTE

- **Aerial Blue:** Commercially, this line was among the least successful. As a result, there are a limited number of pieces, and this scarcity has increased their values relative to other wares.

- **Black Iris:** This line is among the most sought after by collectors, commanding significantly more than examples of similar size and design in virtually any other glaze.
  In fact, the current auction record for Rookwood — over $350,000 — was set in 2004 for a Black Iris vase decorated by Kitaro Shirayamadani in 1900.

- **Iris:** Uncrazed examples are exceptionally rare, with large pieces featuring conventional designs commanding the highest prices. Smaller, naturalistically painted examples, though still desirable, are gradually becoming more affordable for the less advanced collector.

- **Production Ware:** This commercial and mass-produced artware is significantly less expensive than pieces in most other lines.

- **Standard Glaze:** These wares peaked in the 1970s-1980s, and the market has remained thin in recent years, but regardless of the state of the market, examples of superlative quality, including those with silver overlay, have found their places in the finest of collections.

- **Wax Mat:** This is among the most affordable of the hand-decorated lines.

shape number, sometimes following it, but more often below it.

The letter "S" is a particularly vexing designation since the same initial was used for two other unrelated designations. As a result, it is particularly important to take into account the relative position of the impressed letter.

R = Red
Y = Yellow
S = Sage
G = Ginger
W = White
O = Olive
P = From 1915 on, Rookwood used an impressed "P" (often found perpendicular to the orientation of the other marks) to denote the soft porcelain body.

SIZE AND SHAPE MARKS

Almost all Rookwood pieces have a shape code consisting of three or four numbers, followed by a size letter. "A" denotes the largest available size, "F" is the smallest. According to Herbert Peck, initial designs were given a "C" or "D" designation so that variations could be made. Not every shape model, however, features a variation in every size.

GLAZE MARKS

In addition to marking the size, shape and year of the piece, Rookwood's decorators also used a number of letters to designate the type of glaze to be used upon a piece. Generally speaking, these marks are either incised or impressed.

"S" = Standard Glaze to be used. (Incised.)

"L" = Decorators would often incise an "L" near their monogram to indicate that the light variation of the Standard Glaze was to be used. (Incised.)

"SG" = Sea Green Glaze to be used.

"Z" = from 1900-1904 designated any piece with a Mat Glaze. (Impressed)

"W" = Iris Glaze to be used.

"V" = Vellum Glaze to be used; variations include "GV" for Green Vellum and "YV" for Yellow Vellum.

Rookwood vase, William Hentschel, 1912, decorated with an incised trio of geese at the shoulder, glazed with green, maroon and brown mat glazes, marks: Rookwood logo, date, shape 131 and Hentschel's incised monogram, also a wheel ground X, faint overall crazing, 5-7/8" h x 9" dia.............**$1,500**

Courtesy of Mark Mussio, Humler & Nolan, humlernolan.com

OTHER MARKS

"S" = If found away from the shape number, this generally indicates a piece that was specially thrown at the pottery in the presence of visitors. (Impressed.)

"S" = If this precedes the shape number than it denotes a piece that was specifically thrown and decorated from a sketch with a corresponding number. Because of the size and quality of pieces this letter has been found on, this probably signifies a piece made specifically for an important exhibition.

"X" = Rookwood used a wheel ground "x" to indicate items that were not of first quality. There has been some suggestion that decorators and salespersons might have conspired to "x" certain pieces that they liked, since this designation would reduce the price. Since there are a number of items that appear to have been marked for no apparent reason, there may be some truth to this idea. Unfortunately, as this idea has gained credence, many pieces with obvious flaws have been listed as "marked x for no apparent reason," and collectors should be cautious.

Generally, the mark reduces the value and appeal of the piece. Peck describes a variation of the "x" that resembles an asterisk as indicating a piece that could be given away to employees.

"T" = An impressed T that precedes a shape number indicates a trial piece.

= These shapes (crescents, diamonds, and triangles) are used to indicate a glaze trial.

"K1" and "K3" = circa 1922, used for matching teacups and saucers.

"SC" = Cream and Sugar sets, circa 1946-1950.

"2800" = Impressed on ship pattern tableware.

Rookwood Vellum vase, Kataro Shirayamadani, 1939, decorated with daffodils against a mottled purple ground, marks: Rookwood logo, date, shape 2746, impressed P and Kataro's Japanese cypher in black slip, excellent condition, 9-1/8" h. **$1,100**

Courtesy of Mark Mussio, Humler & Nolan, humlernolan.com

Rookwood tall Vellum glaze vase, Lenore Asbury, 1918, decorated with tall trees along the banks of a tranquil lake, marks: Rookwood logo, date, shape 917 A, an impressed V for Vellum and Asbury's incised initials, fine overall crazing, 12-1/2" h. **$1,300**

Courtesy of Mark Mussio, Humler & Nolan, humlernolan.com

Rookwood monkey on book paperweight, a Shirayamadani design, cast in 1935, green over light blue mat glazes, marks: Rookwood logo, date and shape 2677, Rookwood showroom label attached, excellent condition, 3-5/8" h. **$325**

Courtesy of Mark Mussio, Humler & Nolan, humlernolan.com

193

Rookwood Design Crystal vase with Picasso-like faces, painted by Jens Jensen, 1948, five faces, all done in Jensen's mature style in which he emulates his favorite artist, Pablo Picasso. Jensen's paintings, done during the next three decades, reflect this style and use the same dark delineating lines and fractured features of his bizarre images. Marks: Rookwood logo and date code, shape number 2720 and Jensen's monogram in brown slip, broad crazing typical of Design Crystal and a tiny glaze nick at the rim, wheel-ground line indicating the piece as a second, rare, 6-1/4" h. **$3,000**

Courtesy of Mark Mussio, Humler & Nolan, humlernolan.com

Rookwood Standard glaze vase, Artus Van Briggle, 1888, daisy decoration, marks: Rookwood logo (indicating the date), shape 464, G for Ginger clay and Van Briggle's incised cypher, fine overall crazing, some areas of dry crazing on the back, a couple of tiny glaze nicks at the rim, 7-7/8" h.... **$250**

Courtesy of Mark Mussio, Humler & Nolan, humlernolan.com

Rookwood Standard glaze handled vase, Daniel Cook, 1895, decorated with a pair of geese, marks: Rookwood logo (indicating the date), shape 459 D, Cook's incised initials, faint crazing, minor stilt pull on the foot ring, 5-1/2" h......... **$400**

Courtesy of Mark Mussio, Humler & Nolan, humlernolan.com

Rookwood porcelain vase, E.T. Hurley, 1926, decorated with exotic birds perched on flowering branches, marks: Rookwood logo, date, shape 2900 and Hurley's monogram in black slip, single craze line, plus a couple of tiny, open glaze bubbles inside the rim, 9-5/8" h. **$1,700**

Courtesy of Mark Mussio, Humler & Nolan, humlernolan.com

◀ Rookwood production vase, William McDonald design, cast 1930, green mat glaze, three levels for flower placement and four classical figures, marks: Rookwood logo, date, shape 6163 and the fan-shaped esoteric mark used during the company's 50th anniversary, excellent condition, 9-1/4" h............ **$160**

Courtesy of Mark Mussio, Humler & Nolan, humlernolan.com

▶ Rookwood Arts & Crafts-style vase, Fred Rothenbusch, 1910, mat glaze, scenic decor in rose and green with trees and vegetation outlined in black, impressed marks: Rookwood logo, the letter V, the date and shape number 950, F. Rothenbusch's monogram in black slip, very faint crazing, 6" h. **$4,800**

Courtesy of Mark Mussio, Humler & Nolan, humlernolan.com

Rookwood Standard glaze vase, Anna Marie Valentien, 1892, ruffled rim and mum decoration, intricate silver overlay by Gorham, marks: Rookwood logo (indicating the date), shape 665, an impressed W for White clay, an incised L for Light Standard glaze and Valentien's incised initials, silver is double stamped Gorham MFG Co with R464, fine overall crazing, 9-3/4" h. **$3,700**

Courtesy of Mark Mussio, Humler & Nolan, humlernolan.com

Rookwood tall Limoges-style vase, Albert R. Valentien, 1883, decorated with a swarm of butterflies, applied golden dolphin handles, gold accented base, marks: Impressed ROOKWOOD, 1883, the kiln mark, G for Ginger clay, incised WA for William Auckland, signed in slip on the side A.R.V., 1883, each of the dolphins appears to have had restoration to the tail, professional repair to the base, several scratches near the restored rim, 24" h. **$3,000**

Courtesy of Mark Mussio, Humler & Nolan, humlernolan.com

Rookwood Black Opal vase, Kataro Shirayamadani, 1929, decorated with pine cones and pine needles, sycamore leaves and seed pods and oak leaves done with incising and slip, a tour-de-force of local trees done in browns, reds, greens and black with the blue hazing associated with Black Opal glaze, marks: Rookwood logo, the date, shape number 614 C, Shirayamadani's cypher in black slip, uncrazed, 12-5/8" h. **$9,750**

Courtesy of Mark Mussio, Humler & Nolan, humlernolan.com

CERAMICS

roseville pottery

ROSEVILLE IS ONE of the most widely recognizable of potteries across the United States. Having been sold in flower shops and drug stores around the country, its art and production wares became a staple in American homes through the time Roseville closed in the 1950s.

The Roseville Pottery Co., located in Roseville, Ohio, was incorporated on Jan. 4, 1892, with George F. Young as general manager. The company had been producing stoneware since 1890, when it purchased the J. B. Owens Pottery, also of Roseville.

The popularity of Roseville Pottery's original lines of stoneware continued to grow. The company acquired new plants in 1892 and 1898, and production started to shift to Zanesville, just a few miles away. By about 1910, all of the work was centered in Zanesville, but the company name was unchanged.

Young hired Ross C. Purdy as artistic designer in 1900, and Purdy created Rozane – a contraction of the words "Roseville" and "Zanesville." The first Roseville artwork pieces were marked either Rozane or RPCO, both impressed or ink-stamped on the bottom.

In 1902, a line was developed called Azurean. Some pieces were marked Azurean, but often RPCO. In 1904 at the St. Louis Exposition, Roseville's Rozane Mongol, a high-gloss oxblood red line, captured first prize, gaining recognition for the firm and its creator, John Herold.

Many Roseville lines were a response to the innovations of Weller Pottery, another Zanesville pottery, and in 1904 Frederick Rhead was hired away from Weller as artistic director. He created the Olympic and Della Robbia lines for Roseville. His brother Harry took over as artistic director in 1908, and in 1915 he introduced the popular Donatello line.

By 1908, all handcrafting ended except for Rozane Royal. Roseville was the first pottery in Ohio to install a tunnel kiln, which increased its production capacity.

Frank Ferrell, who was a top decorator at the Weller Pottery by 1904, was Roseville's artistic director from 1917 until 1954. This Zanesville native created many of the most popular lines, including Pine Cone, which had scores of individual pieces.

Many collectors believe Roseville's circa 1925 glazes were the best of any Zanesville pottery. George Krause, who in 1915 became Roseville's technical supervisor responsible for glaze, remained with Roseville until the 1950s.

Company sales declined after World War II, especially in the early 1950s when cheap Japanese imports began to replace American wares, and a simpler, more modern style made many of Roseville's elaborate floral designs seem old-fashioned.

In the late 1940s, Roseville began to issue lines with glossy glazes. The company also

Roseville Futura Black Flame vase, shape 391-10", unmarked, faint overall crazing and a couple of tiny open bubbles in the glaze, 10" h. **$300**

Courtesy of Mark Mussio, Humler & Nolan, humlernolan.com

VISIT WWW.ANTIQUETRADER.COM

WWW.FACEBOOK.COM/ANTIQUETRADER

tried to offset its flagging artware sales by launching a dinnerware line – Raymor – in 1953. The line was a commercial failure.

Roseville issued its last new designs in 1953. On Nov. 29, 1954, the facilities of Roseville were sold to the Mosaic Tile Co.

For more information on Roseville, see *Warman's Roseville Pottery,* 2nd edition, by Denise Rago.

Roseville Blackberry rectangular bowl, shape number 227-8, unmarked, faint crazing and minor stains inside, 3-3/8" h x 9-3/4" w......... **$150**

Courtesy of Mark Mussio, Humler & Nolan, humlernolan.com

Roseville Baneda jardinière, shape 626-5", green, marked on bottom with Roseville Pottery foil sticker, excellent condition, 5" h.................... **$250**

Courtesy of Mark Mussio, Humler & Nolan, humlernolan.com

Roseville two-sided "Rainbow" dealer's sign, green and tan with black letters, thought to be part of the Futura line, excellent condition, 1-1/2" h x 5-5/8" l. **$1,200**

Courtesy of Mark Mussio, Humler & Nolan, humlernolan.com

Roseville Rozane vase with portrait of a Saint Bernard dog, impressed Rozane, R.P.Co, 812, outside repainted and oversprayed from rim to base, portraiture left untouched, fine overall, 13" h..................... **$325**

Courtesy of Mark Mussio, Humler & Nolan, humlernolan.com

Roseville Majolica-type umbrella stand with molded design of fish and water lilies, unmarked, fine overall crazing, a bruise at the rim and some very minor nicks to the high points of the design, 21" h.. **$475**

Courtesy of Mark Mussio, Humler & Nolan, humlernolan.com

Roseville Pine Cone trial vase, shape 841-7", yellow, marked on bottom Roseville 841-7" having "Trial 18" in black crayon, fine crazing, two chips at rim and a chip at base, largest chip at rim being 1/4"; 7-3/8" h. **$425**

Courtesy of Mark Mussio, Humler & Nolan, humlernolan.com

CERAMICS

BOTTOM MARKS

There is no consistency to Roseville bottom marks. Even within a single popular pattern like Pine Cone, the marks vary.

Several shape-numbering systems were implemented during the company's almost 70-year history, with some denoting a vessel style and some applied to separate lines. Though many pieces are unmarked, from 1900 until the late teens or early 1920s, Roseville used a variety of marks including "RPCo," "Roseville Pottery Company," and the word "Rozane," the last often with a line name, i.e., "Egypto."

The underglaze ink script "Rv" mark was used on lines introduced from the mid-to-late teens through the mid-1920s. Around 1926 or 1927, Roseville began to use a small, triangular black paper label on lines such as Futura and Imperial II. Silver or gold foil labels began to appear around 1930, continuing for several years on lines such as Blackberry and Tourmaline, and on some early Pine Cone.

From 1932 to 1937, an impressed script mark was added to the molds used on new lines, and around 1937 the raised script mark was added to the molds of new lines. The relief mark includes "U.S.A."

All of the following bottom mark images appear courtesy of Adamstown Antique Gallery, Adamstown, Pennsylvania.

Impressed mark on Azurean vase, 8" h.

Raised mark on Bushberry vase.

Ink stamp on Cherry Blossom pink vase, 10" h.

Wafer mark on Della Robbia vase, 10-1/2" h.

Gold foil label and grease pencil marks on Imperial II vase, 10" h.

Impressed mark on Iris vase.

Ink stamps on Wisteria bowl, 5" h.

Impressed marks on Rozane portrait vase, 13" h.

Massive Roseville Topeo vase, shape 666-15", blue, marked on bottom with the shape number in orange crayon and having a Roseville Pottery foil sticker, faint overall crazing, 15-1/8" h. **$600**

Courtesy of Mark Mussio, Humler & Nolan, humlernolan.com

Roseville Futura Tank vase, shape 412-9", marked with black Roseville Pottery sticker on bottom, two small nicks to the base at the rear, a few tiny glaze pops, rare, 9-5/8" h. **$8,000**

Courtesy of Mark Mussio, Humler & Nolan, humlernolan.com

Roseville Egypto vase embossed with herringbone band low on body and decoration on neck covered with matte green craquelle-like glaze, marked with Rozane Ware Egypto wafer logo, excellent condition, 10" h. **$400**

Courtesy of Mark Mussio, Humler & Nolan, humlernolan.com

Roseville Pauleo vase with marbleized blue and green luster glazes with darker glaze dripped at intervals from the rim, unmarked, excellent condition, 17-5/8" h. **$1,200**

Courtesy of Mark Mussio, Humler & Nolan, humlernolan.com

▲ Roseville Experimental vase with primrose-like flowers having white petals, yellow centers and deeply cut leaves, unmarked, excellent condition, 8-1/8" h. **$2,500**

Courtesy of Mark Mussio, Humler & Nolan, humlernolan.com

▶ Roseville Carnelian II vase, shape 340-18", mottled pink with green dripped from the rim, marked on bottom with shape number in orange crayon, excellent condition, 18" h. **$500**

Courtesy of Mark Mussio, Humler & Nolan, humlernolan.com

Large Roseville Tourist window box showing a woman whose car has a flat tire being attended to by a young man, unmarked, tight lines at two corners, rim and on bottom along with scuffs, scratches and shallow chips to the decal, 8-3/4" h x 11" w x 19-1/4" l. **$1,300**

Courtesy of Mark Mussio, Humler & Nolan, humlernolan.com

CERAMICS

rs prussia

ORNATELY DECORATED CHINA marked "R.S. Prussia" and "R.S. Germany" continues to grow in popularity. According to the Third Series of Mary Frank Gaston's *Encyclopedia of R.S. Prussia* (Collector Books, Paducah, Kentucky), these marks were used by the Reinhold Schlegelmilch porcelain factories located in Suhl in the Germanic regions known as "Prussia" prior to World War I, and in Tillowitz, Silesia, which became part of Poland after World War II. Other marks sought by collectors include "R.S. Suhl," "R.S." steeple or church marks, and "R.S. Poland."

The Suhl factory was founded by Reinhold Schlegelmilch in 1869 and closed in 1917. The Tillowitz factory was established in 1895 by Erhard Schlegelmilch, Reinhold's son. This china customarily bears the phrase "R.S. Germany" and "R.S. Tillowitz." The Tillowitz factory closed in 1945, but it was reopened for a few years under Polish administration.

Prices are high and collectors should beware of the forgeries that sometimes find their way onto the market. Mold names and numbers are taken from Mary Frank Gaston's books on R.S. Prussia.

Center bowl, unmarked, Carnation mold, cobalt blue with gold stencil highlights, good condition, 15" dia. .. **$9,500**

Courtesy of Woody Auction, woodyauction.com

Carnation mold bowl, Winter Season portrait decor, lavender and white, satin finish, good condition, 11" dia. **$1,300**

Courtesy of Woody Auction, woodyauction.com

VISIT WWW.ANTIQUETRADER.COM

WWW.FACEBOOK.COM/ANTIQUETRADER

The "Prussia" and "R.S. Suhl" marks have been reproduced, so buy with care. Later copies of these marks are well done, but the quality of porcelain is inferior to the production in the 1890-1920 era.

Collectors are also interested in the porcelain products made by the Erdmann Schlegelmilch factory, founded by three brothers in Suhl in 1861. They named the factory in honor of their father, Erdmann Schlegelmilch. A variety of marks incorporating the "E.S." initials were used. The factory closed circa 1935. The Erdmann Schlegelmilch factory was an earlier and entirely separate business from the Reinhold Schlegelmilch factory.

Mold #201 bowl, cream center with pink and white rose decor, six portrait medallions including Spring, Summer, Fall and Winter Season portraits, small base ring chip, 11" dia...................... **$3,250**

Courtesy of Woody Auction, woodyauction.com

R.S. Prussia bowl, Floral mold, green and cream center, rose decor, cobalt blue and green border, jeweled highlights, good condition, 11" dia...... **$150**

Courtesy of Woody Auction, woodyauction.com

Bowl, cream and blue tones, flora center portrait, six portrait medallions around edge (Racamier, Potacka, Lebrun I & II), good condition, 10-1/2" dia. **$350**

Courtesy of Woody Auction, woodyauction.com

Creamer and sugar, Ribbon and Jewel mold, Melon Eaters scenic decor, gold ribbons, opal jewels, good condition. **$225**

Courtesy of Woody Auction, woodyauction.com

Creamer, Carnation mold, cobalt blue with gold stencil highlights, unmarked, good condition, 4" **$250**

Courtesy of Woody Auction, woodyauction.com

Creamer, white and green tones with mill scenic decor, gold trim highlights, good condition, 3-3/4" h. **$60**

Courtesy of Woody Auction, woodyauction.com

Cup and saucer, pink and white with pink rose decoration, good condition................................. **$15**

Courtesy of Woody Auction, woodyauction.com

Sugar bowl, two-handled, green and white with castle scenic décor, good condition, 5" h. **$20**

Courtesy of Woody Auction, woodyauction.com

Plate, Mold #343, Spring Season portrait decor, white with red trim highlights, some fading of gold, good condition, 8-3/4" dia. **$225**

Courtesy of Woody Auction, woodyauction.com

Two-handled cake plate, Medallion mold, blue green tones, Old Man in Mountain scenic décor, good condition 11" dia. **$125**

Courtesy of Woody Auction, woodyauction.com

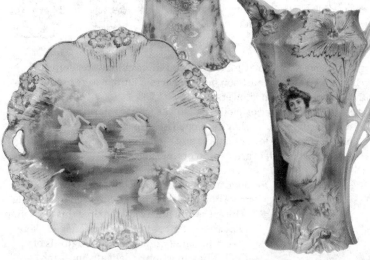

Two-handled vase, Jewel mold, peacock scenic decor, gold trim, opal jewel highlights, good condition, 6" h... **$425**

Courtesy of Woody Auction, woodyauction.com

Two-handled cake plate, Icicle mold, Swan scenic decoration, good condition, 9-3/4" dia............. **$125**

Courtesy of Woody Auction, woodyauction.com

Carnation mold tankard, Summer Season portrait with lavender and pink satin background, good condition, 11" h.. **$2,800**

Courtesy of Woody Auction, woodyauction.com

Celery tray, Medallion mold, cream center with pink and white floral decor, black border with gold tapestry medallions featuring Potacka, Racamier, and Lebrun portraits, good condition, 12-1/4" x 6".. **$650**

Courtesy of Woody Auction, woodyauction.com

Dresser tray, Ribbon and Jewel mold, Dice Throwers scenic décor, some fading on background, good condition, 11-1/2". **$125**

Courtesy of Woody Auction, woodyauction.com

CERAMICS

sèvres

SÈVRES PORCELAIN, THE GRANDEST of ultimate luxury, artistic ceramics, was favored by European royalty, the aristocracy of the 19th century, and 20th century great collectors. Its story begins in 1708, when, following frenzied experimentation, German alchemist Johann Bottger discovered the formula for strong, delicate, translucent hard-paste porcelain. Unlike imported white chinaware, Bottger's porcelain could also be painted and gilded. Soon potteries across Europe were producing decorative items with fashionable gilt and flowers.

French potters lacked an ample source of kaolin, a requisite for hard-paste porcelain, however. So from clay and powdered glass, they developed a soft-paste formula. Soft-paste, though more fragile, could be fired at a lower temperature than hard-paste. This allowed a wider variety of colors and glazes.

The Sèvres porcelain factory was originally founded at Chateau de Vincennes in 1738. Its soft-paste porcelain was prized for its characteristic whiteness and purity. By the time this workshop relocated to Sèvres in 1756, its craftsmen were creating small porcelain birds, figurals of children in white or delicate hues, and innovative pieces with characteristic rosy-hued backgrounds. They also produced detailed allegorical and thematic pieces like "Flute Lesson," "Jealousy," and "Justice and the Republic," which sparkle with transparent, colorless glazes.

The introduction of unglazed, natural-toned "biscuit" porcelain, a favorite of Madame de Pompadour, the mistress of Louis XV, followed. Many of these molded sculptures portray lifelike sentimental or Classical scenes. Biscuit porcelain is extremely fragile.

Madame de Pompadour also adored Sèvres' porcelain flowers, the most delicate item produced during these early years. Legend has it that, to further the company's production, she once presented Louis XV with a profusion of Sèvres vases abloom with colorful porcelain pretties, petal upon tinted

Pair of monumental hand-painted vases, French bronze and porcelain, signed "La Barre," 40" h x 12" w. **$32,00**

Courtesy of Royal Antiques, royalantiques.com

petal atop cunningly wired "stems."

When Louis XV assumed full control of Sèvres porcelain in 1759, he insisted on flawless, extravagant creations, many of which he commissioned for his personal collection. In his travels, he also spread the Sèvres reputation for opulent ornamentation, vivid colors, and fine glazes.

The renowned Sèvres mark, elaborate blue interlaced Ls, was born of his royal patronage and helps determine dates of production. Other marks, either painted or incised, indicate specific Sèvres painters, gilders, sculptors, and potters by name.

Louis XV's successor, Louis XVI, continued to support the royal Sèvres tradition. He not only set prices and arranged exhibitions, but also marketed pieces personally.

Although kaolin deposits were discovered near Limoges in 1768, Sèvres began producing hard-paste porcelain commercially only from 1773. During this period, they continued to produce soft-paste items as well.

After suffering financial ruin during the French Revolution, Sèvres, in addition to creating traditional pieces for the luxury market, began producing simpler, less expensive items. During this period, its craftsmen also abandoned their old-fashioned soft-paste formula for hard-paste porcelain.

Sèvres porcelain regained its former glory under Napoleon Bonaparte, who assumed power in 1804. He promoted elaborately ornamented pieces in the classical style. The Empire's richly decorated, themed dinner sets, for example, were enjoyed by distinguished guests, visiting rulers, and Napoleon himself. These pieces typically feature florals, landscapes, or cameo portraits framed by solid gold edging accented with stylized palm fronds, the ancient Greek symbol of victory.

Along with dinner sets and coffee services, tea services were among Sèvres' most popular creations. During the early 1800s, when passion for that luxury potion peaked, Greek or Etruscan pottery inspired the design of many Sèvres teapots. These were valued not only for their beauty, but also

Bronze-mounted marble top one-door cabinet, caryatid mounted columns and center porcelain vignette of cherubs with basket of flowers, with Marie Antoinette mask and roset-mounted plith, 19th c., 45" h x 32" w x 16-1/2". **$1,200**

Courtesy of Clements, clementsantiques.com

Porcelain demitasse set with silver overlay with tray, rare, tray is 13-1/2" x 9-1/2", pot is 6", creamer 5". **$2,000**

Courtesy of Clarke Auction Gallery, clarkny.com

Pair of jeweled porcelain vases, circa 1850, 11" h. **$2,250**

Courtesy of Louvre Antique Auction, liveauctioneers.com

because, as porcelain, they could withstand the heat.

Many Sèvres shapes, which range from simple cylindrical vases to elaborate perforated potpourri jars, were innovative for their times. Some, like a gondola-shaped vase designed to hold aromatic petals or another with elephant-head handles fitted as candle arms, serve a double purpose. Sèvres also created a wide selection of decorative utilitarian objects, including tobacco jars, lidded ewers and basins, painted plaques, punch bowls, sorbet coolers, and milk jugs.

The range of Sèvres creations is extensive, varying in shape, historical styles, motifs, and ornamentation. Vases typically feature double round, oval, or elliptical finely painted scenes edged in white against pastel backgrounds. One side portrays figures, while the other features flower bouquets. Their lavish gilding, a royal touch reserved especially for Sèvres creations, is often embellished with engraved detail, like flowers or geometric motifs. Many fine pieces like these, if rarely or never used, are still found in pristine condition.

Simple plates and tea wares can be found for a few hundred dollars. Because large numbers were made to accompany dessert services, quite a few Sèvres biscuit porcelains have also survived. These fragile pieces command between $3,000 to as much as $70,000 apiece.

Fakes and pastiches — showy, decorative 'Sèvres-style' imitations — produced during the 19th century in the style of the 18th century are common, so collectors need to be wary and knowledgeable about authentic Sèvres.

— Melody Amsel-Arieli

Hand-painted porcelain column pedestal, with bronze and onyx mounts, large medallion of woman with cherubs, artist signed, surrounded by gold decorations, 11" x 40", column 26" h. **$2,100**

Courtesy of Echoes Antiques & Auction Gallery, Inc., echoesauction.net

Mantel clock with Japy Freres movement and pair of urns, each gilt bronze mounted, jewel-decorated porcelain with central figural reserves and accented with pastoral scenes, France, 19th c.; bronze clock case stamped "Godet," 20" x 12" x 4-3/4". **$3,750**

Courtesy of Rago Arts and Auction Center, ragoarts.com

French cobalt hand-painted bronze and porcelain wall sconces, 19th c., 12-1/2" x 10-1/2" x 5" d... **$1,500**

Courtesy of Royal Antiques, royalantiques.com

◄ ▲ French bronze-mounted and porcelain table, 19th c., 31" x 22" x 32" h. **$8,000**

Courtesy of Royal Antiques, royalantiques.com

◄ Pair of French cobalt porcelain capped urns with gilt bronze mounts, signed center reserves of courting scenes, encompassed with open work "C" scroll raised gold designs, 30" h. **$2,250**

Courtesy of Clements, clementsantiques.com

▲ Cobalt ground and gold gilt highlighted capped palace urn, bronze foliated knop finial on a removable domed porcelain lid resting within a beaded ring having scrolling vine formed ring handles surrounding a central vignette of well-costumed figures, the gent holding a falcon and signed wouvermans, with highly detailed landscape on reverse, resting on a revolving socle with conforming porcelain and bronze stand, 39" h x 18" w. **$9,500**

Courtesy of Clements, clementsantiques.com

CERAMICS

spatterware

SPATTERWARE TAKES ITS NAME from the "spattered" decoration, in various colors, used to trim pieces hand-painted with rustic center designs of flowers, birds, houses, etc. Popular in the early 19th century, most was imported from England.

Related wares, called "stick spatter," had freehand designs applied with pieces of cut sponge attached to sticks, hence the name. Examples date from the 19th and early 20th century and were produced in England, Europe, and America.

Some early spatter-decorated wares were marked by the manufacturers, but not many. Twentieth century reproductions are also sometimes marked, including those produced by Boleslaw Cybis.

Blue spongeware bowl and pitcher, 1840s, mint condition, crazing on both pieces, 4" h x 12-3/4" across, pitcher 9" h. **$165**

Courtesy of William Bunch Auctions & Appraisals, bunchauctions.com

Spatterware purple and black teapot, 19th century, 6"h. **$406**

Courtesy of Wiederseim Associates, Inc., wiederseim.com

English polychrome ceramic teabowl and saucer set, having blue and yellow sponged enamels on exterior of tea bowl and interior of saucer, unmarked, circa 1830, light radial hairline on base of saucer and several small flakes on rim of teabowl, foot rim of saucer with one minor flake, likely from manufacturing, cup 2-1/8" h, saucer 5-7/8" d. **$2,610**

Courtesy of Jeffrey S. Evans & Associates, jeffreysevans.com

Plate with Peafowl design, stamped "Adams," good condition, 8-1/2" dia. **$42**

Courtesy of Thomaston Place Auction Galleries, thomastonauction.com

Five-color rainbow water pitcher with scalloped top, scrolled handle on scalloped bulbous body, flared base, incised "x" on bottom, multiple hairlines to body and base, 9" w x 8" h. **$649**

Courtesy of Cordier Auctions & Appraisals, cordierauction.com

Red spatterware-bordered platter with a green eagle and shield decoration at center, wear includes darkened crazing, two chips to rim, utensil marks, two hairlines to bottom, 17-1/2" x 13-1/2" x 1-5/8"... **$132**

Courtesy of Cordier Auctions & Appraisals, cordierauction.com

Lot of two English peafowl teabowl and saucer sets, red sponged grounds and hand-painted peafowl designs on interior and sides, one saucer impressed "10" on base, otherwise unmarked, circa 1830, both items have minute flakes on the bases of the foot rim, likely occurring during manufacturing, 2-9/16" h. **$342**

Courtesy of Jeffrey S. Evans & Associates, jeffreysevans.com

Transfer-printed ceramic platter, oval shape with red sponged enamel on edge, blue transfer design on interior of a variation on later "Latin Dancers" design made by Clementson Brothers, having a servant with a dog on a leash in the foreground, elaborately-dressed women, and dancers in the background, several impressed numerals, and lightly impressed mark on base with the words "CLEMENTSON" and "HANLEY" visible, circa 1855, excellent undamaged condition with some manufacturing glaze flaws on the front edges, 15-1/2" x 11-3/8." **$124**

Courtesy of Jeffrey S. Evans & Associates, jeffreysevans.com

Two pieces of child's-size Spatterware China, blue, red, and green festoon pattern, blue and red drape pattern, saucer has a tiny pin nip on base, 4" saucer, 2" h x 2-3/4" d. **$738**

Courtesy of Conestoga Auction Company, a division of the Hess Auction Group, hessauctiongroup.com

CERAMICS

spongeware

THE NAME "SPONGEWARE" says it all. A sponge dipped in colored pigment is daubed onto a piece of earthenware pottery of a contrasting color, creating an overall mottled, "sponged" pattern. A clear glaze is applied, and the piece fired. The final product, with its seemingly random, somewhat smudged coloration, conveys an overall impression of handmade folk art.

Most spongeware, however, was factory-made from the mid-1800s well into the 1930s. Any folk art appeal was secondary, the result of design simplicity intended to facilitate maximum production at minimum cost. Although mass-manufacturing produced most spongeware, it did in fact originate in the work of independent potters. Glasgow, Scotland, circa 1835, is recognized as the birthplace of spongeware. The goal: the production of utilitarian everyday pottery with appeal to the budget-conscious. Sponged surface decorations were a means of adding visual interest both easily and inexpensively.

Since early spongeware was quickly made, usually by amateur artisans, the base pottery was often insubstantial and the sponging perfunctory. However, due to its general usefulness, and especially because of its low cost, spongeware quickly found an audience. Production spread across Great Britain and Europe, finally reaching the United States. Eventually, quality improved, as even frugal buyers demanded more for their money.

Spongeware dog figural, elaborate three-color slip decoration, Crooksville, OH origin, late 19th century, molded in the form of a boxer or St. Bernard, depicted with a collar or small liquor barrel around its neck, the surface covered in Bristol slip and decorated with circular blue-green sponging and brushed mustard slip highlights throughout, additional darker cobalt slip highlights to face, tail, feet, and object at dog's neck, excellent condition 6-1/2" h. **$900**

Courtesy of Crocker Farm, crockerfarm.com

The terms "spongeware" and "spatterware" are often used interchangeably. Spatterware took its name from the initial means of application: A pipe was used to blow colored pigment onto a piece of pottery, creating a spattered coloration. Since the process was tedious, sponging soon became the preferred means of color application, although the "spatterware" designation remained in use. Specific patterns were achieved by means of sponge printing (aka "stick spatter"): A small piece of sponge was cut in the pattern shape desired, attached to a stick, then dipped in color. The stick served as a more precise means of application, giving the decorator more control, creating designs with greater border definition. Applied colors varied, with blue (on white) proving most popular. Other colors included red, black, green, pink, yellow, brown, tan, and purple.

Because of the overlap in style, there really is no "right

or wrong" in classifying a particular object as "spongeware" or "spatterware"; often the manufacturer's advertising designation is the one used. Spatterware, however, has become more closely identified with pottery in which the mottled color pattern (whether spattered or sponged) surrounds a central image, either stamped or painted free-hand. Spongeware usually has no central image; the entire visual consists of the applied "splotching." Any break in that pattern comes in the form of contrasting bands, either in a solid color matching the mottling, or in a portion of the base earthenware kept free of applied color. Some spongeware pieces also carry stampings indicating the name of an advertiser, or the use intent of a specific object ("Butter," "Coffee," "1 Qt.").

Spongeware's major appeal is due in large part to the minimalism it represents, which makes it an ideal collectible for those whose taste in 19th century pottery veers away from the overly detailed and ornate.

Large blue spongeware bowl, first half of 20th century, 12" w, 6" h. **$95**

Courtesy of Jasper52, jasper52.com

Blue spongeware ewer, ca 1870, 5-1/2" dia x 7-1/4" h. **$110**

Courtesy of Jasper52, jasper52.com

Blue-banded spongeware chamber pot with lid and handle, 12" h. **$30**

Courtesy of Matthew Bullock Auctioneers, bullockauctioneers.com

Blue spongewear butter crock, 4" x 5-3/4". **$130**

Courtesy of Martin Auction Co., martinauctionco.com

Blue spongeware pitcher, ca 1880, 6-3/4" h x 5-1/4" dia. **$90**

Courtesy of Jasper52, jasper52.com

CERAMICS

CERAMICS

staffordshire

STAFFORDSHIRE FIGURES AND GROUPS made of pottery were produced by the majority of the Staffordshire, England, potters of the 19th century and were used as mantle decorations or "chimney ornaments" as they were sometimes called. Pairs of dogs were favorites and were turned out by the carload, and 19th century pieces are still readily available. Well-painted reproductions also abound, and collectors are urged to exercise caution before purchasing.

The process of transfer-printing designs on earthenware developed in England in the late 18th century, and by the mid-19th century most common ceramic wares were decorated in this manner, most often with romantic European or Asian landscape scenes, animals or flowers. The earliest transferwares were printed in dark blue, but a little later light blue, pink, purple, red, black, green, and brown were used. A majority of these wares were produced at various English potteries right up until the turn of the 20th century, but French and other European firms also made similar pieces and all are quite collectible.

The best reference on this area is Petra Williams' *Staffordshire Romantic Transfer Patterns – Cup Plates and Early Victorian China* (Fountain House East, 1978).

Two Staffordshire covered figural nesting dove boxes with colored highlights, sitting on molded basketweave base, one has small chip on beak, other in good condition, 5-1/2" x 7-1/2" **$90**

Courtesy of Woody Auction, woodyauction.com

Two Staffordshire figural covered boxes, nesting pigeons: one blue and white, one lavender and white (some surface chipping on tail of bird), both fully glazed, each 5-1/2" x 7-1/2".................. **$400**

Courtesy of Woody Auction, woodyauction.com

Staffordshire covered box, pair of full figure doves atop egg-shaped lid, molded basketweave base, colored highlights, good condition, 7" x 7". **$150**

Courtesy of Woody Auction, woodyauction.com

Historical blue Staffordshire Lafayette at Franklin's Tomb coffeepot, flake to spout, shallow 1/2" chip to bottom rim of lid, 12-1/4" h. **$1,159**

Courtesy of Pook & Pook, Inc., pookandpook.com

Staffordshire cow creamer, good condition, 5-1/2" h. **$163**

Courtesy of Pook & Pook, Inc., pookandpook.com

Staffordshire figure of African-American, late 18th century, hand-formed, rare, unmarked; 7" h. **$1,680**

Courtesy of Cowan's Auctions, cowans.com

Staffordshire figure of Dick Turpin, English, 19th century, figure of a man on horseback, labeled Dick Turpin on base, 11-3/4" h. **$92**

Courtesy of Cowan's Auctions, cowans.com

Staffordshire figure of Benjamin Franklin, early 19th century, mislabeled as General Washington, minor paint chips to tie and hat, 15-1/4" h. **$780**

Courtesy of Cowan's Auctions, cowans.com

Two early Staffordshire figural rooster mustard jars, life-like rooster heads with full combs, full figure "chicken foot" spoons, 4-3/4" x 5-1/2". **$800**

Courtesy of Woody Auction, woodyauction.com

Staffordshire blue and white covered tureen, early 19th c., with floral decoration, 13" h, 15-1/4" w. **$519**

Courtesy of Pook & Pook, Inc., pookandpook.com

CERAMICS

Staffordshire historical pottery pitcher, Rowland and Marsellus Co., depicting Declaration of Independence, Liberty Bell, Bunker Hill Monument, 7" h.. **$225**

Courtesy of Woody Auction, woodyauction.com

Staffordshire plate, "Landing of General Lafayette," early 19th century, historical blue Clews plate depicting the Landing of General Lafayette, 10" dia. **$185**

Courtesy of Cowan's Auctions, cowans.com

Blue transfer decorated Canova Staffordshire platter, 19th c., 12-7/8" l, 15-3/8" w.............. **$200**

Courtesy of Pook & Pook, Inc., pookandpook.com

Blue transfer decorated Staffordshire platter, 19th c., with view of a mosque, 12-1/2" l, 15-1/4" w.. **$200**

Courtesy of Pook & Pook, Inc., pookandpook.com

Child's Staffordshire tea service in the Goat pattern, few pieces chipped. **$75**

Courtesy of Pook & Pook, Inc., pookandpook.com

CERAMICS

teco pottery

TECO POTTERY WAS the line of art pottery introduced by the American Terra Cotta and Ceramic Co. of Terra Cotta (Crystal Lake), Illinois, in 1902. Founded by William D. Gates in 1881, American Terra Cotta originally produced only bricks and drain tile.

Because of superior facilities for experimentation, including a chemical laboratory, the company was able to develop an art pottery line, favoring a mat green glaze in the earlier years but eventually achieving a wide range of colors including a metallic luster glaze and a crystalline glaze. Although some hand-thrown pottery was made, Gates favored a molded ware because it was less expensive to produce. By 1923, Teco Pottery was no longer being made, and in 1930 American Terra Cotta and Ceramic Co. was sold.

For more information on Teco Pottery, see *Teco: Art Pottery of the Prairie School* by Sharon S. Darling (Erie Art Museum, 1990).

Teco mug, #298, Chicago, IL, matte green glazed ceramic, two impressed marks, 5" w x 3-1/2" d x 5-3/4" h.
.... **$275**

Courtesy of Treadway Gallery, treadwaygallery.com

A monumental Teco vase by designer W.D. Gates (1852-1935), Chicago, IL, carved, matte glazed ceramic, impressed mark, Fritz Albert (1865-1940) was likely the modeler for this vase, 14-1/2" dia x 26-1/2" h.
....**$25,000**

Courtesy of Treadway Gallery, treadwaygallery.com

Holly and Berry vase by designer Fritz Albert (1865-1940), #136, Chicago, IL, matte green glazed ceramic, impressed mark, 9-1/4" dia x 2-1/4" h. **$150**

Courtesy of Treadway Gallery, treadwaygallery.com

VISIT WWW.ANTIQUETRADER.COM

WWW.FACEBOOK.COM/ANTIQUETRADER

TECO POTTERY

Pair Teco art pottery bookends, Rebecca at the Well design, circa 1920s, modeled as biblical heroine with jar at water pool, cream glaze with green crystalline water pool, impressed mark, 7" h, 5-1/2" w. **$350**

Courtesy of Alex Cooper, alexcooper.com

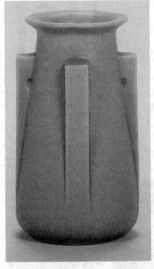

Large Teco matte green vase with four in-body buttress handles, signed, mint condition, 10-1/4" h x 5-1/2" d. **$2,900**

Courtesy of California Historical Design, acstickley.com

Teco floriform vase, rare semi-matte green crystalline glaze, Terra Cotta, IL, ca. 1910, stamped "TECO," 12" x 5". **$2,400**

Courtesy of Rago Arts and Auction Center, ragoarts.com

Teco tall-footed three-lobed vase, Terra Cotta, IL, 1910s, stamped "TECO," 15-1/2" x 7". **$650**

Courtesy of Rago Arts and Auction Center, ragoarts.com

Teco matte green vase with four curved handles at rim, signed, mint condition, 7" h x 4-3/4" d. ... **$950**

Teco oblong wall pocket with violets and leaves in relief, a design by Mrs. F.R. Fuller and covered by a nice charcoal green matte glaze, double-struck Teco on the back, excellent condition, Teco wall pockets not often seen, 7" h x 9-1/2" l **$350**

Courtesy of California Historical Design, acstickley.com   *Courtesy of Humler & Nolan, humlernolan.com*

CERAMICS

teplitz-amphora

ANTIQUE DEALERS AND COLLECTORS
often refer to Art Nouveau-era art pottery produced in the kaolin-rich Turn-Teplitz region of Bohemia (today Teplice region, Czech Republic) collectively as Teplitz. Over the years, however, this area boasted many different potteries. To add to the confusion, they opened, closed, changed owners, merged or shared common designers against a background of changing political borders.

Although all produced pottery, their techniques and products varied. Some ceramicists, like Josef Strnact and Julius Dressler, produced brightly glazed faience and majolica earthenware items. According to Elizabeth Dalton, Furniture and Decorative Arts specialist at Michaan's Auctions, Alameda, California, a strong earthenware body rather than delicate, brittle porcelain allowed more unusual manipulation of the ceramic surface of their vases, flowerpots, and tobacco jars.

Alfred Stellmacher, who founded the Imperial and Royal Porcelain Factory in 1859, produced fanciful, sculptural creations noted for their fine design and quality. Many feature applied natural motifs, Mucha and Klimt-like portraits, or simulated jewels.

"The most collectible Teplitz pieces of all, however, are those manufactured by the Riessner, Stellmacher and Kessel Amphora Porcelain Works (RStK), which was founded in 1892," said Stuart Slavid, vice president and director of European Furniture, Decorative Arts and Fine Ceramics at Skinner Auctions, Boston.

Producing Amphora was time-consuming and prohibitively expensive. Each piece began with an artist's drawing, which would typically include lifelike images of snakes, sea creatures, dragons, maidens, flora, or fauna. Once approved, each drawing was assigned a style number, which would subsequently appear on the bottom of identically shaped pieces, along with the word "Amphora."

Using these drawings as their guides, craftsmen carved and fired clay models from which they created smooth plaster-of-Paris molds. These molds were then lined with thin layers

Amphora figural candlesticks, pair, Art Nouveau maidens with white, flowing gowns rising from a lily pond, each maiden is holding a water lily and a water lily bud, maidens' skin and hair in gold, water lilies in white, blue and green with gilded trim, signed on the underside with impressed mark "Made in Austria," 11" h. **$3,630**

Courtesy of James D. Julia Auctioneers, jamesdjulia.com

of clay. Once the clay dried and the molds removed, the resulting Amphoras were fine-carved, hand-painted, and glazed. Finally they were refired, sometimes as many as 10 times. Since each was decorated in a unique way, no two Amphoras were exactly alike. Since their manufacture was so complex, reproducing one is nearly impossible.

RStK's innovative pieces earned international acclaim almost immediately. After winning prizes at both the Chicago and St. Louis World's Fairs, exclusive establishments, including Tiffany & Co., marketed them in the United States.

In addition to lavish Amphoras, Riessner, Stellmacher and Kessel also produced highly detailed, intricately crafted female busts, both large and small. Virgins, nymphs, and dancers, reflecting fashionable literary, religious, and mythological motifs and themes of the day, were popular choices. Larger busts, because they were so complex

and so rarely made, were expensive from the start. Today these 100-year-old beauties, especially those who escaped the ravages of time, are extremely desirable.

In 1894, leading Viennese porcelain retailer Ernst Wahliss purchased the RStK Amphora. Paul Dachsel, a company designer and Stellmacher's son-in-law, soon left to open his own pottery. Dachsel was known for adorning fairly simple forms with unique, intricate, stylized Art Nouveau embellishments, as well as modern-looking applied handles and rims. These, along with his Secessionist works – those influenced by Austrian exploration of innovative artistic forms outside academic and historical traditions – are highly collectible today.

After Wahliss' death, the Amphora Porcelain Works — now known as the Alexandra Porcelain Works Ernst Wahliss — became known for Serapis-Wahliss, its fine white earthenware line that features intricate, colorful, stylized natural forms.

When Stellmacher established his own company in 1905, the firm continued operating as the Riessner and Kessel Amphora Works. After Kessel left five years later, Amphora Werke Riessner, as it became known, continued to produce Amphora pottery through the 1940s. In 1945, Amphora Werke Riessner was nationalized by the Czechoslovakian government.

Although many Amphoras retail for under $1,000, some are quite costly. Rare, larger pieces, probably commissioned or created expressly for exhibition, were far more prone to breakage in production and display, so they command far more.

Do Teplitz pieces make good investments? According to Stuart Slavid, "Considering their rarity, quality, and decorative appeal, there's still plenty of room for growth, especially at the higher end of the market. I personally think that higher-end Amphoras are exceptional. History says you can't go wrong buying the very best. There will always be collectors at that level."

— *Melody Amsel-Arieli*

Teplitz Dragon jar, late 19th century, lidded jar with dragon handles and owl decoration, marked on underside, minor chips to ears, mouths, and tip of one wing, 8-1/4" h. **$215**

Courtesy of Cowan's Auctions, cowans.com

Ernst Wahliss (Austrian, 1837-1900) porcelain bust, Austria, c. 1900-1915, Art Nouveau, depicting a woman in 18th-century French dress, marked "DEPOSE / EW / Turn Wien / Made in Austria" with crown and impressed "4123 / 7" on underside, 17" h x 12" w x 6-1/2" d. **$185**

Courtesy of Cowan's Auctions, cowans.com

Reissner, Stellmacher and Kessel Amphora vase, pretty young woman standing in a forest with white flowers décor, marked with red R.St.&K. ink stamp logo, impressed 464 and 12, excellent condition, minor wear to gold, 15" h. **$1,200**

Courtesy of Mark Mussio, Humler & Nolan, humlernolan.com

Eduard Stellmacher (1868-1945), Riessner, Stellmacher & Kessel, large Amphora vase with dragon and frog, Turn-Teplitz, Bohemia, c. 1906-07, stamped crown/AMPHORA/ AMPHORA FAIENCE TURN/4536/52, firing lines between wing and vase (in making of), 21-1/4" x 9".. **$8,125**

Courtesy of Rago Arts and Auction Center, ragoarts.com

Ernst Wahliss (1836-1900), large Amphora pitcher with stylized tulips, Turn-Teplitz, Bohemia, 1890s, red "TURN VIENNA EW" stamp, impressed "6384," signed "6384/2444/15," heavy crazing throughout, 12" x 12-1/2" x 10"...... **$1,000-$1,500**

Courtesy of Rago Arts and Auction Center, ragoarts.com

Amphora figural tray, "Leaf Lady" Art Nouveau maiden with long flowing hair and gown with large leaves on each side creating trays, she is wearing a gown in purple at top, shading to white at the bottom while the leaves are shaded in green with gilded veins, base of the figure has another Art Nouveau maiden rising out of the water, signed on the underside with red mark "Turn. Teplitz. Bohemia RSTK Made in Austria"; also marked with impressed "Amphora" within an oval "775 4" and impressed on back of gown near the foot with artist signature, 20" h. **$5,445**

Courtesy of James D. Julia Auctioneers, jamesdjulia.com

Amphora Teplitz figure, woman with assorted acting costume items, 17" h. **$600**

Courtesy of Woody Auction, woodyauction.com

Reissner, Stellmacher & Kessel vase having three-dimensional owl perched on a branch connected to the rim and body, impressed R.St.&K Austria logo on the bottom, faint crazing along with a tight line to a branch under the owl, some restoration to leaves growing out of a branch near the base and a nick to one of the owl's ears, 13-1/8" h. **$750**

Courtesy of Mark Mussio, Humler & Nolan, humlernolan.com

Paul Dachsel, small Amphora vase with dragonflies, Turn-Teplitz, Bohemia, c. 1910, glazed porcelain, raised seal, excellent condition, 6" x 4".............. **$875**

Courtesy of Rago Arts and Auction Center, ragoarts.com

219

CERAMICS

Amphora vase, decorated with a three-dimensional Eastern dragon with body and tail wrapping around the vase and large wings protruding, shaded tan and dark green glaze, signed on the underside with impressed "AMPHORA AUSTRIA" / "TURN," "PARIS 1900" / "4105," artist initials on the side of vase "EST 99" for Eduard Stellmacher 17" h.
.... **$7,260**

Courtesy of James D. Julia Auctioneers, jamesdjulia.com

Eduard Stellmacher (1868-1929), Riessner, Stellmacher & Kessel, large Amphora Grès-Bijou vase with moths and spiderwebs, Turn-Teplitz, Bohemia, c. 1900, red RSTK stamp RSTK DG3789, 17-1/4" x 11"................. **$6,875**

Courtesy of Rago Arts and Auction Center, ragoarts.com

Paul Dachsel; Riessner, Stellmacher & Kessel, large Amphora Confetti vase with trees, Turn-Teplitz, Bohemia, early 20th c., stamped AMPHORA 3729D, 18-1/2" x 10-1/2"......................... **$1,375**

Courtesy of Rago Arts and Auction Center, ragoarts.com

Amphora portrait vase, "Rising Sun," pyramidal form, flared quatrefoil rim decorated with portrait theme of Aurora, Goddess of the Sun, in heavily jeweled headdress facing the rising sun, set against textured green and blue background, all highlighted with gilded accents, signed on underside with red "RStK" logo, impressed Amphora, Crown, and Austria symbols, impressed "3678 60," minor crazing, 6-1/4" h. **$4,235**

Courtesy of James D. Julia Auctioneers, jamesdjulia.com

Amphora figural vase, "Femme Fleur," swirled wave pedestal foot in the form of a reclining maiden holding gilded stems while emerging from green floral buds and salmon colored flower blossoms, all with gilded highlights, signed on underside with red "RStK" logo, "799/56," impressed "737 2 AMPHORA," 11" h. **$1,210**

Courtesy of James D. Julia Auctioneers, jamesdjulia.com

Amphora vase, has applied flowers, stems, and leaves in gold, each flower with applied shaded blue cabochon in the center, all set against mauve iridescent glaze, further decorated with a band around the neck set with dark blue triangular-shaped cabochons framed in gold triangles against a cream colored ground, signed on underside: "BUR Marigold Made in Austria," 11-1/2" h.**$424**

Courtesy of James D. Julia Auctioneers, jamesdjulia.com

CERAMICS

van briggle pottery

THE VAN BRIGGLE POTTERY was established by Artus Van Briggle, who formerly worked for Rookwood Pottery in Colorado Springs, Colorado, at the turn of the 20th century. He died in 1904, but the pottery was carried on by his widow and others. From 1900 until 1920, the pieces were dated. It remains in production today, specializing in art pottery.

Peacock-shaped bookends with a matte turquoise glaze, circa 1922-1926, signed, 1/8" corner chip restoration, 5" h x 6" w x 2" d.......................... **$210**

Courtesy of California Historical Design, acstickley.com

Early matte blue square humidor with stylized tulips, dated 1913, restoration to two or three edge chips, 8-1/2" h x 6-1/4" w x 6-1/4" d. ...**$1,440**

Courtesy of California Historical Design, acstickley.com

Two oval plaques: "Little Star," mauve tones and embossed with Indian maiden image, 5-1/2" d; "Big Buffalo," blue/green tones, no chips, cracks or breaks, 5-1/4".. **$150**

Courtesy of Woody Auction, woodyauction.com

Early vase with poppies, pale blue glaze, 1905, AA VAN BRIGGLE/1905/346/VX, 9-1/4" h x 7" w. **$2,600**

Courtesy of Rago Arts and Auction Center, ragoarts.com

Vase, low wide base with tapered neck, matte green glaze and carved floral designs on side, marked with Van Briggle logo and "Colo Spgs" with additional numerals, circa 1910, 3-3/8" h. **$436**

Courtesy of Jeffrey S. Evans & Associates, jeffreyevans.com

Vase #848 with a rich matte green glaze dated 1914, signed, 7-3/4" h x 5-1/2" d. **$840**

Courtesy California Historical Design, acstickley.com

Anna Van Briggle pottery handled vase or mug, features a modernist or cubist design with a wood-like glazed surface with a frosted rim, mark on base reads Anna Van Briggle Colo. Spgs., good overall condition, 9-1/4" x 5". **$156**

Courtesy Hill Auction Gallery, hillauctiongallery.com

"Despondency" vase early mark and rare glaze, early example, some scuff marks to the glaze, flea bites to the inner rim, 13-1/2" h x 5-1/2" w. **$659**

Courtesy of Appraisal & Estate Sale Specialists, Inc., estatesalemandan.webs.com

Pair of Indian maiden table lamps in Ming Blue glaze, complete with original butterfly shades, circa 1940, brass fittings, laminated composite shades, authentic butterfly wings, both with incised marks, good overall condition, silk-wrapped cords, lower brass ring of one shade is no longer attached, 31-1/2" h x 10" d. **$487**

Courtesy of Rago Arts and Auction Center, ragoarts.com

Early gourd vase, mustard yellow glaze, 1905, marked AA VAN BRIGGLE/VX/1905/319, excellent condition, 5" h x 3-1/2" w. **$715**

Courtesy of Rago Arts and Auction Center, ragoarts.com

Copper-clad vase, 1910, AA Van Briggle, 690, 6-3/4" h x 3 1/2" w. **$1,950**

Courtesy of Rago Arts and Auction Center, ragoarts.com

Lorelei vase, 1905, early AA VAN BRIGGLE 17/1905/L, peppering throughout, some deep crazing lines, one tiny chip to edge of base, 9-3/4" h x 4" w. **$10,400**

Courtesy of Rago Arts and Auction Center, ragoarts.com

Early vase with Virginia creepers, brown and celadon glaze, circa 1904, AA VAN BRIGGLE/1904/V/164, minor scuffs and metal transfer marks to body, 8" h x 6-1/2" w. . **$2,000**

Courtesy of Rago Arts and Auction Center, ragoarts.com

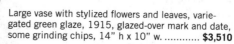

Large vase with stylized flowers and leaves, varie-gated green glaze, 1915, glazed-over mark and date, some grinding chips, 14" h x 10" w. **$3,510**

Courtesy of Rago Arts and Auction Center, ragoarts.com

CERAMICS

wedgwood

WEDGWOOD

IN 1754, JOSIAH WEDGWOOD and Thomas Whieldon of Fenton Vivian, Staffordshire, England, became partners in a pottery enterprise. Their products included marbled, agate, tortoiseshell, green glaze, and Egyptian black wares.

In 1759, Wedgwood opened his own pottery at the Ivy House works, Burslem. In 1764, he moved to the Brick House (Bell Works) at Burslem. The pottery concentrated on utilitarian pieces.

Between 1766 and 1769, Wedgwood built the famous works at Etruria. Among the most-renowned products of this plant were the Empress Catherina of Russia dinner service (1774) and the Portland Vase (1790s). The firm also made caneware, unglazed earthenwares (drabwares), piecrust wares, variegated and marbled wares, black basalt (developed in 1768), Queen's or creamware, and Jasperware (perfected in 1774).

Bone china was produced under the direction of Josiah Wedgwood II between 1812 and 1822, and was revived in 1878. Moonlight Lustre was made from 1805 to 1815. Fairyland Lustre began in 1920. All Lustre production ended in 1932.

A museum was established at the Etruria pottery in 1906. When Wedgwood moved to its modern plant at Barlaston, North Staffordshire, the museum was expanded.

Wedgwood Fairyland Lustre octagonal bowl (pattern 5360), England, 1920s, "WEDGWOOD MADE IN ENGLAND" gilt stamp, signed Z5360i, some wear and losses to gilding, 4" x 8-1/2". **$2,000**

Courtesy of Rago Arts and Auction Center, ragoarts.com

Wedgwood University of California Berkeley dinner service, created for the Diamond Jubilee celebration (49 pieces), comprising 13 dinner plates, 10-1/2" dia; 12 salad plates, 8-1/2" dia; 12 teacups; 12 saucers................................. **$550**

Courtesy of Michaan's Auctions, michaans.com

Wedgwood Fairyland Lustre bowl (pattern Z4968), England, 1920s, "WEDGWOOD MADE IN ENGLAND" gilt stamp, signed Z4968, overall excellent condition, 4" x 9-1/4".......................... **$2,375**

Courtesy of Rago Arts and Auction Center, ragoarts.com

VISIT WWW.ANTIQUETRADER.COM

WWW.FACEBOOK.COM/ANTIQUETRADER

Wedgwood Fairyland Lustre vase, Goblin pattern, brown goblins with blue wings, standing at water's edge, green grass, orange water, underside has Portland vase mark "Wedgwood Made in England," 7" h. **$10,890**

Courtesy of James D. Julia Auctioneers, jamesdjulia.com

Wedgwood banded vase, Keith Murray design, covered in a blue-gray matte glaze, impressed on the bottom, WEDGWOOD, Made in England, D, 1 and Keith Murray WEDGWOOD, Made in England, 11" h. **$375**

Courtesy of Mark Mussio, Humler & Nolan, humlernolan.com

Wedgwood square vase, Butterfly Lustre, 7-3/4" h. **$275**

Courtesy of Strawser Auction Group, strawserauctions.com

Wedgwood Fairyland Lustre covered box, Willow pattern, bronze and coral, with coral fairies flying above an oriental scene of pagodas, junks on the river, and a bridge, signed on the underside with Portland vase mark "Wedgwood Made in England," bronze coloring was skipped on parts of the rim of the lid, one orange enameled bead in the trim on the bottom of the box is missing, scarce, 7" x 4-1/8". **$3,025**

Courtesy of James D. Julia Auctioneers, jamesdjulia.com

Wedgwood Renaissance-style majolica pitcher and underplate, 19th c., marks: WEDGWOOD (various), (artist signature below handle), pitcher with figural bifurcated snake handles, spout with large grotesque mask, body decorated with depiction of the building of Noah's Ark from Raphael's Loggia in the Vatican apartments (c. 1519), underplate with raised center and scrolled decoration throughout, archival numbering to undersides, pitcher 11" h, plate 12-5/8" dia. **$1,875**

Courtesy of Heritage Auctions, ha.com

C

CERAMICS

Wedgwood caneware game pie covered dish, oval shaped with cauliflower finial on lid and continuous grapevine banding on body, early 19th c., with removable baking liner, Wedgwood, Burslem (Stoke-on-Trent), Staffordshire, England, marks: WEDGWOOD, 6-1/4" h x 10-1/2" w x 7-1/4" d. **$500**

Courtesy of Heritage Auctions, ha.com

Wedgwood service plates, suite of 12, claret and raised gilt decorated: each white ground dish form plate with a gilt stenciled spear point reciprocal rim band, enclosed by a rose souffle border with repeating twin raised gilt heraldic griffins with staff, between gilt banding and an inner gilt reciprocal ram's head band enclosing the white ground, stamped on back "Wedgwood Made in England," 10-3/4" dia. **$700**

Courtesy of Michaan's Auctions, michaans.com

Wedgwood Fairyland Lustre plate, Thumbelina pattern, maiden reclining on a large lily pad, a large insect sitting on another lily pad next to her, dragonfly flies above against a flame lustre sky, she appears to have a frog on a leash above her, finished with a Twyford border around the rim, signed on the underside with Portland vase mark "Wedgwood Made in England," scarce, 10-5/8" dia... **$6,050**

Courtesy of James D. Julia Auctioneers, jamesdjulia.com

Wedgwood Fairyland Lustre malfrey pot, Woodland Elves IV, Big Eyes pattern, blue Big Eyes and green fairies all set against a flame orange background, signed on the underside with Portland vase mark "Wedgwood Made in England Z5360," 3-5/8" h x 4-1/2" dia. **$2,118**

Courtesy of James D. Julia Auctioneers, jamesdjulia.com

Wedgwood lavender Jasperware tea set: teapot, creamer, sugar, four cups and four saucers. **$250**

Courtesy of Strawser Auction Group, strawserauctions.com

CERAMICS

weller pottery

WELLER POTTERY WAS made from 1872 to 1945 at a pottery established originally by Samuel A. Weller at Fultonham, Ohio, and moved in 1882 to Zanesville, Ohio.

WELLER Weller Pottery

Weller's famous pottery slugged it out with several other important Zanesville potteries for decades. Cross-town rivals such as Roseville, Owens, La Moro, and McCoy were all serious fish in a fairly small and well-stocked lake. While Weller occasionally landed some solid body punches with many of his better art lines, the prevailing thought was that his later production ware just wasn't up to snuff.

Samuel Weller was a notorious copier and, it is said, a bit of a scallywag. He paid designers such as William Long to bring their famous discoveries to Zanesville. He then attempted to steal their secrets, and, when successful, renamed them and made them his own.

After World War I, when the cost of materials became less expensive than the cost of labor, many companies, including the famous Rookwood Pottery, increased their output of less expensive production ware. Weller Pottery followed along in the trend of production ware by introducing scores of interesting and unique lines, the likes of which have never been created anywhere else, before or since.

In addition to a number of noteworthy production lines, Weller continued in the creation of hand-painted ware long after Roseville abandoned them. Some of the more interesting Hudson pieces, for example, are post-World War I pieces. Even later lines, such as Bonito, were hand painted and often signed by important artists such as Hester Pillsbury. The closer you look at Weller's output after 1920, the more obvious the fact that it was the only Zanesville company still producing both quality art ware and quality production ware.

For more information on Weller pottery, see *Warman's Weller Pottery Identification and Price Guide* by Denise Rago and David Rago.

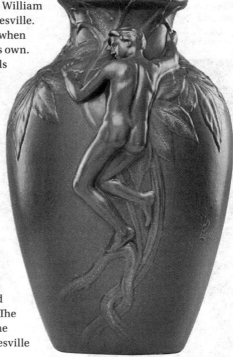

Weller rare and large Fru-Russett vase with nude male and grapevines, Zanesville, OH, ca. 1905, body incised "E .Pickens," based incised "Weller," 18" x 11".......................... **$5,500**

Courtesy of Rago Arts and Auction Center, ragoarts.com

CERAMICS

Weller Roma umbrella stand with dramatic floral design, unsigned, 24" h x 11" w. **$100**

Courtesy of California Historical Design, acstickley.com

Jacques Sicard (1865-1923) for Weller Pottery Company, Sicard vase, Zanesville, OH, metallic glazed ceramic, signed, 5-3/4"dia x 7-1/2" h.**$700**

Courtesy of Treadway Gallery, treadwaygallery.com

Weller "Malverne" wall pocket, circa 1920s, flower and leaf design with multi colors, signed Weller, very good condition, 11" h. **$75**

Courtesy of Treasureseeker Auctions LLC, treasureseekerauction.com

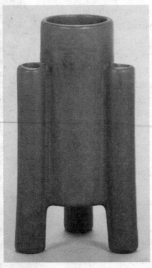

Rare Weller matte green cylinder vase with three cylindrical legs, glazed over signature, mint, 8-1/2" h x 4" d. **$375**

Courtesy of California Historical Design, acstickley.com

Weller Dickensware vase, circa 1905, incised and painted decoration of a lady golfer, a very rare and desirable subject, base marked "Dickensware Weller" and numbered, good condition, 9-1/2" h.............**$425**

Courtesy of Treasureseeker Auctions LLC, treasureseekerauction.com

Weller vase by Hester Pillsbury, Thistle Floral decorated, crazing, signed "H. Pillsbury,"12" h x 7" w. **$425**

Courtesy of Alderfer Auction, alderferauction.com

Weller Coppertone frog center bowl, inkstamp on bottom, 10" x 16". **$325**

Courtesy of Redlands Antique Auction, redlandsantiqueauction.com

Weller jardinière, Woodcraft pattern, adorned with figural woodpecker and squirrel handles, underside is impressed "WELLER," 20th century, 9-1/2" h x 11" dia... **$250**

Courtesy of Bruneau & Co. Auctioneers, bruneauandco.com

Weller matte green two-handle jardinière with cutout finger handles, unsigned, mint condition, 7" h x 10" w... **$1,000**

Courtesy of California Historical Design, acstickley.com

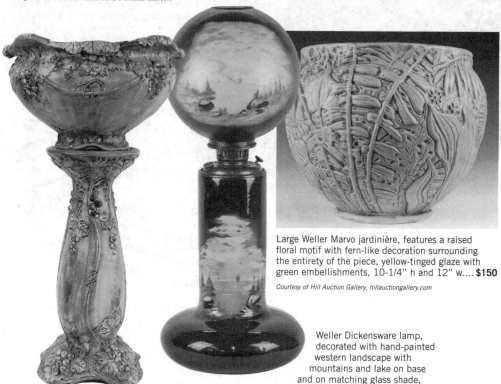

Large Weller Marvo jardinière, features a raised floral motif with fern-like decoration surrounding the entirety of the piece, yellow-tinged glaze with green embellishments, 10-1/4" h and 12" w.... **$150**

Courtesy of Hill Auction Gallery, hillauctiongallery.com

Weller Dickensware lamp, decorated with hand-painted western landscape with mountains and lake on base and on matching glass shade, stamped on base, "Dickensware/ Weller/850," 12-1/2" dia x 32" h.
.... **$275**

Courtesy of Forsythes' Auctions, LLC, forsythesauctions.com

Weller jardinière and pedestal decorated in the Grapevine pattern, with a matte glaze finish, jardinière is 10-1/2" h, 18" dia.; pedestal is 23-1/2" h; approx. 33-3/4" h overall............... **$400**

Courtesy of Auction Gallery of Boca Raton, LLC, liveauctioneers.com

CERAMICS

zsolnay

ZSOLNAY POTTERY WAS made in Pecs, Hungary, in a factory founded in 1862 by Vilmos Zsolnay. Utilitarian earthenware was originally produced with an increase in art pottery production from as early as 1870. The highest level of production employed more than 1,000 workers.

The Art Nouveau era produced the most collectible and valuable pieces in today's marketplace. Examples are displayed in major art museums worldwide. Zsolnay is always well marked and easy to identify. One specialty was the metallic eosin glaze.

With more than 10,000 different forms created over the years, and dozens of glaze variations for each form, there is always something new being discovered in Zsolnay. Today the original factory size has been significantly reduced with pieces being made in a new factory.

Zsolnay bowl with putto and dragonflies, eosin glaze, Pecs, Hungary, ca. 1900, Five churches mark/179, 2" x 7-1/4"............................ **$1,900**

Courtesy of Rago Arts and Auction Center, ragoarts.com

Zsolnay porcelain and orolu cherub sleigh bowl, brass and copper mounts, stamped on the bottom, 6-3/4" h x 4-3/4" w x 14" d.......................... **$400**

Courtesy of Westport Auction, westportauction.com

Zsolnay Porcelánmanufaktúra Zrt, Ophelia charger, 1900, lustre-glazed earthenware, stamped and incised "ZSOLNAY PECS (logotype)/ 470/ 14," 14-1/2: dia................................. **$7,500**

Courtesy of Heritage Auctions, ha.com

Zsolnay-Pecs porcelain jardinière, number 605, mid-19th century, tapered square form having lobed corner design, with polychrome floral motif over a cream ground, has incised Zsolnay mark and blue stamp, made in Hungary circa 1873-1882, approx. 4" h x 6-1/2" l x 4-1/2" w. **$400**

Courtesy of Auction Gallery of Boca Raton, LLC, liveauctioneers.com

Zsolnay glazed and reticulated ceramic centerpiece, Austria-Hungarian, 10" h x 13" l x 7-1/2" w. **$190**

Courtesy of Dargate Auction Galleries, dargate.com

Zsolnay ewer, pink, white and blue tones, reticulated, nice embossed floral design, marked "Fischer J. Budapest," 16-3/4". **$400**

Courtesy of Woody Auction LLC, woodyauction.com

Pair of glazed reticulated ceramic lidded urns, Austria-Hungarian, 10-1/2" h. **$550**

Courtesy of Dargate Auction Galleries, dargate.com

Zsolnay
Porcelánmanufaktúra Zrt,
landscape vase, 1898,
lustre-glazed earthenware,
molded to the underside:
(logotype)/ Zsolnay Pecs,
12-1/8" h. **$7,000**

Courtesy of Heritage Auctions, ha.com

Zsolnay Porcelánmanufaktúra
Zrt, peacock vase, 1906-1908,
lustre-glazed earthenware,
painted to the underside:
(logotype)/ Zsolnay Pecs,
5-1/4" h. **$4,600**

Courtesy of Heritage Auctions, ha.com

Zsolnay large vessel with lizards and cut-out rim,
eosin glaze, Pecs, Hungary, ca. 1900, raised five
churches seal/6436/M, original paper price tag,
7-3/4" x 11-1/2" **$25,000**

Courtesy of Rago Arts and Auction Center. ragoarts.com

Large Zsolnay iridescent red figural
pitcher, impressed "B36, 6986," approx.
16" h. **$1,000**

Courtesy of Time & Again Auction Gallery, timeandagaingalleries.com

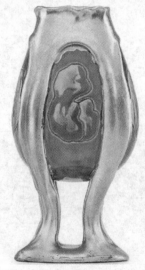

Zsolnay small tulip-shaped vase, eosin glaze,
Pecs, Hungary, ca. 1900, raised five churches
seal, impressed "6174/M," 6-3/4" x 3-1/4".. **$2,300**

Courtesy of Rago Arts and Auction Center. ragoarts.com

Zsolnay fine three-necked vase with daisies,
eosin glaze, Pecs, Hungary, ca. 1900, raised five
churches seal/6172/M/21, 8" x 8" x 6"........ **$4,500**

Courtesy of Rago Arts and Auction Center. ragoarts.com

CHRISTMAS COLLECTIBLES

CHRISTMAS COLLECTIBLES INCLUDE ornaments, kugels, feather trees, candy containers, household décor, art and games, cards and a plethora of ephemera from every corner of the world. The market remains healthy, with demand strong for vintage ornaments and items of yesteryear.

"It's all about supply and demand," said Craig McManus, chairman of The Golden Glow of Christmas Past (goldenglow.org), the main collecting club for fans of vintage holiday collectibles. "Years ago, you couldn't give away a box of Shiny Brites. Things like 1950s plastic Christmas items were usually discarded by collectors as 'junque.' Today, as younger collectors arrive on the scene, those items are now red-hot and collectible."

As newer collectors are exposed to and educated about older collectibles, they eventually trade up to things like figural glass, kugels, and older Christmas items, McManus said. Kugels have set record prices at auction over the last couple years with a few rarer pieces fetching close to $20,000. Dresdens, Nodders, and Belsnickle candy containers have also maintained their values, and are still sought after by longtime collectors.

McManus says people are increasingly collecting things from their childhoods. "Today, we see many newer Glow members interested in buying Shiny Brites (colorful ornaments), '50s plastics, blow molds, and other vintage Christmas lights, ornaments, and decorations from the 1950s and 1960s, even into the 1970s. Seasoned collectors look for older, classic vintage and antique Christmas items like spun-cotton ornaments, figural glass ornaments,

> New collectors to the holiday genre are advised to collect what they like. At Christmas collectible conventions (most often held during the summer) collectors will find almost everything on their shopping list."

Dresdens, kugels, vintage Christmas lighting, holly china, Santas, and ephemera."

"[Collectors should] find those memorable treasures from your childhood and build from there," McManus says. "There are plenty of things for newbies to collect including plastics, and many more common glass ornaments. Even kugel balls from the 1800s in more common colors can be purchased for $40-$50 a piece, or less. Start with more common collectibles, educate yourselves, and build up your collection from there.

Seasoned collectors are zeroing in on top condition.

"The best pieces would be in like-new or very good condition and could include: kugels in rarer colors like amethyst and orange or hard-to-find shapes like ribbed eggs and pears; clockwork nodders (Santa figures and animals like donkeys) that were originally used in store windows in the early 1900s to attract customers," McManus said.

Advanced collectors are paying a premium for 3D Dresden ornaments in uncommon designs; early Christmas figural light bulbs in rare molds and unique Christmas lighting in the original boxes; Belsnickles (originally sold as candy containers) in rare colors like pink, orange, and purple; Christmas pull-toys and windups from the late 1800s or early 1900s, and large, three-dimensional ephemera Nativities.

Nearly 23,000 people now belong to The Golden Glow of Christmas Past's Facebook page. Discussions and photos are shared almost hourly and it is currently the best source to become a stronger Christmas collector.

"Facebook has been a tremendous outreach source for the Glow," McManus said. "While many of the people who like our public Facebook Group are not members, it is a great place for people to learn about the Glow, their Christmas collectibles, and meet other collectors and Glow members. We typically have two or three people joining the Glow as paid members each day, who found us on Facebook."

The group is at facebook.com/TheGoldenGlow.

Board game, c. 1875, lithographed game board with winter and Christmas scenes including Santa Claus, unsigned, 1" d x 19-1/2" w x 10-1/4" l. $675

Courtesy of Soulis Auctions, dirksoulisauctions.com

Figure, Father Christmas, late 19th c., probably German, wool, cloth, composition, from the Leo Lerman and Gray Foy Collection, 25" h. $3,750

Courtesy of Doyle New York, doyle.com

Candy container, late 19th c., Germany, figural "Belsnickle" aka Santa Claus, standing on a snow mound, red robe with gold flecks, blue trim on his hood, feather tree in arm, separates at base for candy retrieval, Tom & Lori Sage Sr. Collection, rare in large size, 18" h. $18,000

Courtesy of Bertoia Auctions, bertoiaauctions.com

Figure, Santa Claus, 1910, cast iron, retaining much of original white and red paint, 4-1/5" h. $375

Courtesy of Teel Auctions, teelauctions.com

Decoration, late 19th c., cardboard, Germany, Dresden, coach with coachman tree decoration, 3-3/4" w. **$1,100**

Courtesy of Ladenburger Spielzeugauktion, spielzeugauktion.de

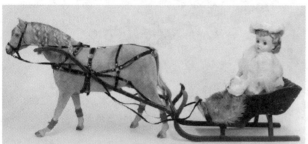

Doll/decoration, circa 1960s ensemble, FAO Schwarz Exclusive, horse-drawn sleigh with circa 1950s Madame Alexander "Elise" doll, sleigh is painted wood in green and red, red velvet lined seat, original faux fur blanket, horse and sleigh, 37" l........ **$900**

Courtesy of Stephenson's Auction, stephensonsauction.com

Decoration, late 19th c., feather tree, blue-green colors, weighted square base with berry-tipped branches, brown paper bark wrapped trunk, base features array of patriotic decorations and ornaments, rare in this coloration, 47" h....... **$1,100**

Courtesy of Bertoia Auctions, bertoiaauctions.com

Ornaments, pre-WWII, Thuringian region of Germany, glass, hand painted, size range from 2-4" l... **$80**

Courtesy of Antico Mondo Auktionen, anticomondo.de

235

Ornament, sterling silver Santa Claus with bag of toys, No. HP-271, 14.7 grams, 20th c., 2-3/4" h x 1-1/4" w. **$165**

Courtesy of IRS Liquidations, treasury.gov/auctions/irs/

Ornament, figural fish ball form, glass, scarce, early 20th c., 2-1/2" l. **$60**

Courtesy of Ladenburger Spielzeugauktion, spielzeugauktion.de

Lamp, opaque white glass fired décor in yellow and brown, head and body of Santa Claus serves as the shade, matching base are the boots, period nickel burner and chimney, rare, made by the Consolidated Lamp & Glass Co., marked "PAT FEB'Y 27.1877," fourth quarter 19th/early 20th c., 9-1/4" h x 4-1/8" h to top of collar, base is 3" dia........ **$6,000**

Courtesy of Jeffrey S. Evans & Associates, jeffreyevans.com

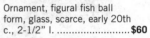

Pinback, depicts Santa Claus accented by holly sprig at left and his toy pack at right, overprinted on his beard is "My Headquarters," early 20th c., no maker name or back paper. **$100**

Courtesy of Hake's Americana & Collectibles, hakes.com

Christmas tree stand, early 20th c., cast iron, North Bros "Yankee," art deco style, gold painted, raised decorations of Christmas trees and geometric designs, eight sockets for light bulbs, signed, 4" h.. **$35**

Courtesy of Leland Little Auctions, lelandlittle.com

Dinner plates, ceramic, made by Sally Merwin, "Days of Christmas" theme, set of 12, 10-1/2" dia.**$12**

Courtesy of Doyle New York, doyle.com

▼ Service plate, "Santa Claws" theme, ceramic, retailed by The Franklin Mint, marked Bill Bell, No. B1390, 8" w.................**$30**

Courtesy of Federal Assets Auctioneers, federalassetsauctioneers.com

Marble, "Sitting Santa" or "Santa on Potty," sulphide, colorless, late 19th/early 20th c., 1-1/2" dia. **$400**

Courtesy of Jeffrey S. Evans & Associates, jeffreysevans.com

◄ Biscuit tin, featuring Santa Claus and holiday scenes and a line from "Twas the Night Before Christmas," marked Tindeco, circa 1920, 2-1/2" d, x 4-3/4" w x 3-1/4" l. **$70**

Courtesy of Soulis Auctions, dirksoulisauctions.com

Movie poster, A Christmas Story (MGM, 1983), one sheet, 27" w x 41" h. **$180**

Courtesy of Heritage Auctions, ha.com

Toy, sheep figure, glass eyes, brass bell, leather ears, wool coat, Santa Claus figure holds feather tree, late 19th c., likely German, 10" h. **$275**

Courtesy of Morphy Auctions, morphyauctions.com

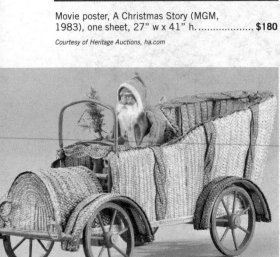

▲ Toy, wicker and wood automobile with seated Santa Claus figure, red robe over composition body, rabbit-fur beard, retaining colors and details, rare, late 19th c., Germany, 28" l. **$2,250**

Courtesy of Bertoia Auctions, bertoiaauctions.com

▶ Advertising poster, grocery store counter display, die-cut, Santa Claus, National Biscuit Co., featuring Santa Claus packing a load of Nabisco-brand cookies, including Barnum's Animals and Sugar Wafers and the since-discontinued Zu Zu Ginger Snaps and Mickey Mouse Cookies, 1937, 17" w x 26" h. **$478**

Courtesy of Heritage Auctions, ha.com

CIRCUS POSTERS

WHILE THE CONCEPT of the circus dates back to Ancient Rome, the circus most of us have come to know featuring clowns, acrobats, and jugglers first appeared in the U.S. in 1793. It wasn't until the late 1880s, however, with the emergence of large circus groups such as Barnum & Bailey and the Ringling Brothers that the circus as entertainment for the masses really blossomed.

Able to move from city to city via railroad and utilizing tents for mobile shows, these large operations captured the imagination of people hungry for spectacle. The introduction of exotic animals such as lions, elephants, and giraffes heightened the appeal.

As a means of advertising shows in advance of their arrival, circus posters played a critical role in the success of shows. Early posters were basic woodblock prints that simply mentioned the circus name, date of show, price of admission and perhaps a few acts. But later, with the advent of lithographic printing processes and more creative design, circus posters featured stupendous acts and promised snarling lions from darkest Africa and elephants from the exotic East. Adding clowns, flamboyant ringmasters, and aerialists performing daring acts — all in vivid color — circus posters took center stage in drawing an audience.

Circus posters are generally divided into two camps: stock or specialty. Stock posters were generic designs that could be used by any circus, and subjects included various clowns, wild animals, circus performers, and just about anything the show might carry.

Ringling Bros. and Barnum & Bailey Combined Circus, featuring Miss Rose Rieffenach, "The Hungarian Queen of Equestrian," circa 1930s, Central Printing and Illinois Litho. Co., Chicago, 27-1/4" x 40".. **$438**

Courtesy of Swann Galleries, swangalleries.com

Specialty posters were designed for specific acts or features and often featured life-like portraits of performers or depictions of specific acts. Specialty posters also include the names of the performers or acts.

Printers offered stock poster designs, allowing the show title and date to be added. Available through catalogs, the stock posters cost much less than specially designed posters. Printers enlisted the services of the finest artists to design posters, although few signed their work. While some artists specialized in particular subjects, most worked in teams to create posters in a more or less assembly line process. Posters became known by the companies that printed them and not by the artists who created them. One of the most prominent printers of circus posters was the Strobridge Lithographing Co., whose roots in Cincinnati, Ohio, stretch back to 1854.

Circus posters featuring exotic acts and famous performers unique to a specific circus are desirable. Reproductions and fakes, however, are common because of the ease and availability of cheap printing. It's always best to do your homework and deal with a reputable source when looking to buy or sell any circus poster of value.

Barnum & Bailey, 1897, 30" x 40"................. **$836**

Courtesy of Heritage Auctions, ha.com

Ringling Bros and Barnum & Bailey Combined Circus, featuring Dorothy Herbert, "World's Most Daring Rider," circa 1935, Erie Litho. and Printing Co., Erie, PA., 40-1/2" x 27-1/4". **$875**

Courtesy of Swann Galleries, swangalleries.com

▼ Ringling Bros and Barnum & Bailey Combined Circus, featuring Dorothy Herbert, circa 1930s, Erie Litho. and Printing Co., Erie, PA., 28" x 40-3/4"... **$500**

Courtesy of Swann Galleries, swangalleries.com

The Great Hagenbeck – Wallace Circus, 1933, Erie Litho. & Printing Co., Erie, PA, 28" x 42-1/4"... **$625**

Courtesy of Swann Galleries, swangalleries.com

◀ Hagenbeck – Wallace Trained Wild Animal Circus, featuring Clyde Beatty, 1934, 27-3/4" x 49-1/2".
.... **$618**

Courtesy of Swann Galleries, swangalleries.com

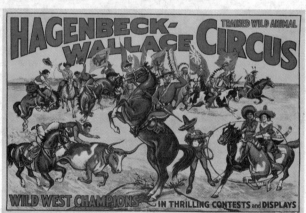

Hagenbeck – Wallace Trained Wild Animal Circus, featuring Wild West Champions, circa 1930s, Erie Litho & Printing Co., Erie, PA, 40-1/4" x 27-1/4"............................. **$325**

Courtesy of Swann Galleries, swangalleries.com

Ringling Bros and Barnum & Bailey Combined Circus poster, featuring Giraffe-Neck Women From Burma, circa 1930s, Central Printing and Illinois Litho. Co., Chicago, 40" x 27-1/4"......................... **$1,250**

Courtesy of Swann Galleries, swangalleries.com

top lot

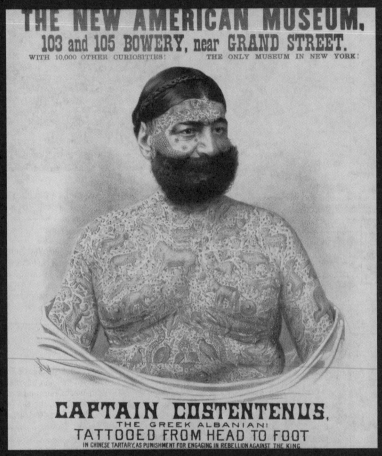

THE NEW AMERICAN MUSEUM,
103 and 105 BOWERY, near GRAND STREET.
WITH 10,000 OTHER CURIOSITIES! THE ONLY MUSEUM IN NEW YORK!

CAPTAIN COSTENTENUS,
THE GREEK ALBANIAN!
TATTOOED FROM HEAD TO FOOT
IN CHINESE TARTARY, AS PUNISHMENT FOR ENGAGING IN REBELLION AGAINST THE KING.

The circus world is known to attract larger-than-life characters with stories to match. Captain Costentenus was just such a character. He claimed to be descended from Greek nobility, dating back to the Ottoman Empire province of Albania. In 1867, he was traveling with an American and a Spaniard in Tartary (central Asia) on a mining expedition. A rebellion arose and the travelers sided with the insurgents. As the story goes, they were taken prisoner and subjected to a three-month-long tattooing session as punishment. After escaping, only Costentenus survived. The tattooing was done with indigo and cinnabar, and covered him from head to foot. The only exceptions were the soles of his feet and parts of his ears. All together he had 387 figures tattooed on his body. Those images ranged from exotic animals and flowers to geometric figures and foreign writing. How much of his story is true is unknown, but it mattered little. The tattoos were real and the man and his story enthralled.

Upon his return to Western Civilization, Costentenus naturally joined the circus. As early as 1874, he was appearing at the Folies Bergère in Paris, and the following year he

ica. After a brief stint at the New American Museum, he began working
ouring with his circus on and off through the end of the decade. It is be
was paid $100 a day to pose for patrons as near naked as legally possi

oster of him on the previous page is likely printed as a blank, as it also
different text on top, promoting his appearance at the Royal Aquarium
e auspices of William Leonard Hunt (the Great Farini), another promine
resario. The poster was printed by H.A. Thomas & Co. Litho, New York,
/2". It sold at a Swann Galleries' auction for $6,750.

fully tattooed Captain seemed to disappear after applying for a passpo
ds after that date reveal nothing of his fate. And yet he has not faded f
Captain Costentenus character, played by Shannon Holtzapffel, is feat
The Greatest Showman, the 2017 film starring Hugh Jackman as P.T. B

Hagenbeck – Wallace and 4 Paw – Sells Bros Combined Circus, featuring Mlle. Rasputin, Daughter of The Mad Monk, circa 1935, Central Printing and Illinois Litho. Co., Chicago, 27-1/2" x 40-1/4". **$1,250**

Courtesy of Swann Galleries, swangalleries.com

Ringling Bros/Barnum and Bailey Circus, featuring "Gargantua, The Great." Ringling featured Gargantua from 1938 to 1949, drawing millions. The gorilla was credited with saving the circus from bankruptcy during the war years. Poster created by The Strobridge Lithographing Co., Cincinnati, OH, 1938, 28" x 42"................. **$1,434**

Courtesy of Heritage Auctions, ha.com

Tom Mix Circus, mid-1930s. Tom Mix appeared in 291 films from 1909-1935, all but nine of them silent movies. He then toured with his own Tom Mix Circus from 1936 to 1938 before dying in a tragic automobile accident on Oct. 12, 1940. Mix is shown on the poster with his horse, Tony, 21" x 28".. **$896**

Courtesy of Heritage Auctions, ha.com

Ringling Bros and Barnum & Bailey Circus, circa 1943, Barbour Street Show Grounds, Hartford, Connecticut, 30-1/4" x 28"............................ **$563**

Courtesy of Skinner Auctioneers and Appraisers, skinnerinc.com

Ringling Bros "World's Greatest Shows" combined with Barnum & Bailey "Greatest Show on Earth," featuring Chas. Patterson, "The Human Airplane," 1916, The Strobridge Lithographing Co., Cincinnati, OH, 38-3/4" x 31-3/4"......................... **$1,750**

Courtesy of Swann Galleries, swangalleries.com

Ringling Bros and Barnum & Bailey Circus, circa 1942, Hartford, CT, with added location banner, 37" x 42". For circus historians, the Hartford location is significant. On July 6, 1944, the Barbour Street Show Grounds was the scene of the worst circus fire in history when a massive, 450-foot-long circus tent caught fire, killing 168 people and injuring another 700....................... **$560**

Courtesy of Skinner Auctioneers and Appraisers, skinnerinc.com

Ringling Bros. and Barnum & Bailey Combined Circus, featuring "The Marvelous Niatto Troupe," circa 1937, with Hartford, Connecticut, attached date banner, 36" x 41".................................. **$178**

Courtesy of Skinner Auctioneers and Appraisers, skinnerinc.com

Ringling Bros/Barnum & Bailey, circa 1940, linen banner, artist Bill Bailey, featuring massive charging rhino, 79" x 117".
....**$3,825**

Courtesy of Heritage Auctions, ha.com

Ringling Brothers and Barnum & Bailey, 1932, linen poster, featuring "5 Big Herds of Performing Elephants," 28-1/4" x 42"............**$2,600**

Courtesy of Heritage Auctions, ha.com

Ringling Bros. and Barnum & Bailey Combined Shows, 1930s, featuring "The Great Arturo." Arthur Trostl traveled with Ringling Brothers and Barnum & Bailey from 1935-1941 thrilling audiences with his many tightrope feats during his solo trapeze act, 41" x 79"
....**$1,015**

Courtesy of Heritage Auctions, ha.com

Cole Bros. Circus, cloth banner, 1930s, Erie Litho. & Printing Co., Erie, PA, unrestored, 78" x 117". **$2,270**

Courtesy of Heritage Auctions, ha.com

CLOCKS

WHEN I SPOTTED the dusty old mantle clock across the store, I wondered what stories it had to tell. Every mechanical mechanism keeps a record of its lifetime. Where was it made? What materials are inside? How was it constructed? Did previous owners care for the inner workings? Can it still be brought back to life?

The clock is one of mankind's oldest inventions. The word "clock" comes from the Latin word "clocca, meaning bell. The first mechanical clocks, driven by weights and gears, were invented by medieval Muslim engineers. The first geared mechanical clock was invented by an 11th century Arab engineer in Islamic Spain. The knowledge of weight-driven clocks was transferred to other parts of the Europe through Latin translations of Arabic and Spanish texts.

In the early 14th century, existing clock mechanisms that used water power were being adapted to take their driving power from falling weights. This movement was controlled by various forms of oscillating mechanisms. This controlled release of power — the escapement — marks the beginning of the true mechanical clock.

The mantle clock I discovered was a standard and common camelback Waterbury mantle clock made in Waterbury, Connecticut. It's neo-classical base and swooping wooden accents at either end of the dial made for an attractive find, despite being gray with years of dust and neglect. I could tell the original shellac finish was under there somewhere and the grime coating the clock's face easily smoothed away with a few rubs of clean thumb.

Brass musical calendar skeleton clock, rare, circa 19th c., France, 5" porcelain dial signed "Chaveau, a Paris," separate brass spring-driven cylinder music box mechanism below the clock, 8 day spring driven skeleton movement, 21" h x 13" w x 8-3/4" d. **$9,000**

Courtesy of Fontaines Auction, FontainesAuction.com

I hoped the inside was clean and the original pendulum was inside. The brass clockwork mechanism was still bright and inside was a lead pendulum still hanging from a suspension spring. For $15, it became my latest mechanical project.

I showed it to my friend, Jim Wolf, the timepiece expert at Heritage Auctions, the world's largest collectibles auctioneer. A familiar smile appeared on his face like he had seen the exact same clock a thousand times before. And in fact, he had. "These are very common at clock shows all over the U.S.," he said. "Years ago you could buy these and almost any other mantle clock you see now in the Sears and Roebuck catalog for a few dollars."

TODAY'S MARKET

Unfortunately, the market for average and common clocks is severely depressed at the moment. Valued at $50 to $200, the standard mantle clock can survive literally a century or more of use. Built to last with basic brass gears and a simple counterweight mechanism, clocks most commonly seen on today's market fall into this value bracket. This includes clocks made as late as 125 years ago. The reason is simple: demand is low and the clocks still

work after years of use. Wear is minimal and although professional clock repair experts are getting harder to find, it doesn't take much time or money to get a vintage mantle clock calibrated to keep accurate time and chime when it's supposed to.

Novelty clocks produced from the 1950s on (think the iconic "Kit-Cat Clock" or the small-dial kitchen clocks of the 1960s) are also not commanding high prices these days. Many vintage styles are being reproduced with new quartz movements rather than the original electric ones. These reproductions have depressed the market for originals to the $20-$50 range for excellent, working examples.

The real value in today's clock market is seen in grandfather clocks made in New England (which are more often purchased as a form of early American woodworking or folk art) as well as high-end brand mantle clocks made by high-end makers or retailers of valuable wristwatches, such as Tiffany, Jager LeCoultre and the like. The movements some clock buyers seek have nothing to do with what's behind the face. Many clocks valued higher are often fashioned in very desirable forms such as Art Deco, Art Nouveau and Mid-Century Modern design movements. Clocks designed as part of these art movements can command prices of $1,000 or more.

The top end of the clock market can reach $1 million. In 2017, an English-made pagoda clock sold for $998,250, just shy of seven figures. That clock, however, was an elaborate automaton in which the clock function was second to the design and craftsman's talent.

My $15 investment clock is worth roughly $50 following a month of fun tinkering and tweaking, staining and resurfacing. Luckily for me, a key was affordable and the "labor of love" keeps decent time, with chimes on the half hour and hour. Nevertheless, our greatest value comes from the strong "tick-tock" heard across our home.

Today's clock market may not be what it was, but there is no mistaking the classic appeal of a bygone day when the family clock had to be wound every seven days.

— *Eric Bradley*

Louis XV-style gilt-metal mounted bracket clock, circa late 19th c., made by Vernis Martin, 17-3/4" h x 10" w, 6-1/4" d. **$625**

Courtesy of Doyle New York, doyle.com

Farmer's time and date shelf clock, circa early 20th c., H.B. Horton patent, mfg. Ithaca Calendar Clock Co., No. 10, mahogany case, two printed dials, 11-1/2" w x 5" d x 21" h. **$275**

Courtesy of Cordier Auctions & Appraisals, cordierauction.com

Wall advertising clock, circa 1885, mfg. by Sidney Clock Co., Owego, NY, model 405, attached tag credits McCray, Kendallville, IND., U.S.A., ad text reads "D.S. Block, A Reliable Jeweler, Opposite Public Square, Cards Change Every 5 Minutes," rare, 28" h x 72" l x 10" d. **$4,500**

Courtesy of Showtime Auction Services, showtimeauctions.com

Shelf clock, late 19th c., interior paper label for Henry Terry, Plymouth Connecticut, eight-day wind, carved mahogany case, paper dial, wooden weight driven time and strike movement, 17-3/4" w x 6" d x 41" h. **$600**

Courtesy of Cordier Auctions & Appraisals, cordierauction.com

▶ Measured time (interval clock case) clock, circa 1932, designed by Isamu Noguchi (American, 1904-1988), mfg. Stevenson Mfg. Co., Bakelite, glass, printed paper, 6-1/8 h x 5-3/8 w x 3" d. **$625**

Courtesy of Heritage Auctions, ha.com

◀ Table clock, early 20th c., Jewish/Judah markings, crown element at top, center are lions, clock face has engraving of Hebrew letters on parchment and a Star of David made of brass, possibly hand assembled from various clock parts, four brass legs, 23" h x 16" w x 13" d. **$350**

Courtesy of Moreshet Auctions, moreshet-auctions.com

▲ Mantle clock, circa 1930s, Gufa, Germany, Westminster chime, art deco design, walnut case, inlaid accents on bun feet, circular metal dial with Arabic numerals, enclosing three key holes, 6 pounds, 8-3/4" h x 10" l x 4-1/5" w. **$90**

Courtesy of Austin Auction Gallery, austinauction.com

▶ Industrial steam engine clock with an automaton, barometer, French, manufactured for the Chinese market, gilt and two-tine patinated bronze, large central cylinder and piston with a vertical connecting rod powers the flywheel with a centrifugal governor assembly, rouge marble base, rare, 40 pounds, 18" h x 14" w x 7" d. **$17,500**

Courtesy of Fontaine's Auction, FontainesAuction.com

▲ Television clock, circa 1950s, figural form of two panthers, with lamp, mfg. Snider Clock Mfg Company, (Toronto, Canada company produced clocks from 1957 to 1976), movement by Sessions Clock Co., 9-1/4" l................**$15**

Courtesy of Specialists of the South, Inc., specialistsofthesouth.com

"Black Forest" clock, 19th c., German, carved walnut, 55" h x 36-1/2" w x 15" d. **$2,750**

Courtesy of Heritage Auctions, ha.com

Biedermeier 30-day Vienna Regulator "Laterndluhr" clock, circa 19th c., Germany, white marble dial, dial signed "Ph. Happacher & Sohn, In Wien," mahogany lantern-style case, 57" h x 14" w x 6-1/2" d.**$13,500**

Courtesy of Fontaines Auction, FontainesAuction.com

Astronomical floor regulator, circa 1875-1877, German, carved walnut floor standing case with ebonized highlights, signed on the rear plate "Gustav Becker, Freiburg i/S" (in Schlesien) with "GB" and crown over anchor mark, front and rear plates are numbered 118702, possibly one-of-a-kind manufactured for display in the 1876 Centennial International Exhibition held in Philadelphia, 109-1/5" h x 34" w x 11" d. **$18,000**

Courtesy of Fontaines Auction, FontainesAuction.com

▲ Carved and adorned clock, mahogany, circa late 19th c., mfg. by Herschede Hall Clock Co., after R.J. Horner, pierce carved arched crest, center cabochon, flanked by angels and flowers, approx. 116" h...............**$20,000**

Courtesy of Great Gatsby's Auction Gallery, GreatGatsbys.com

Regulator wall clock, late 19th c., eight-day movement, original paper label to the back lettered "EIGHT-DAY / SINICO, B.W. / CATHEDRAL GONG. HALF-HOUR STRIKE. TURNBACK / MANUFACTURED BY / WELCH, SPRING & CO., / FORESTVILLE, CONN., U.S.A.," "Cee-Jay's Clocks," Richmond, Va., 45-1/4" l. ... **$400**

Courtesy of Jeffrey S. Evans & Associates, jeffreysevans.com

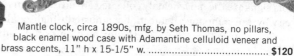

Mantle clock, circa 1890s, mfg. by Seth Thomas, no pillars, black enamel wood case with Adamantine celluloid veneer and brass accents, 11" h x 15-1/5" w. **$120**

Courtesy of Matthew Bullock Auctioneers, bullockauctioneers.com

Mantle clock, circa late 19th to early 20th c., white enamel dial marked "William Wise & Sons, Brooklyn, New York," dome-top, mahogany-veneered marquetry, inlaid blond wood flower and banding, 13-1/4" h x 10-1/4" w x 6" d. **$200**

Courtesy of Auctions at Showplace, nyshowplace.com/live-auctions

Gilt bronze and patinated spelter figural mantle clock, mid-19th c., French, polished steel face, ebonized wood dome base, mfg by Baulier et Fils, Paris, 16" h x 12-1/4" w x 4-5/8" d. **$450**

Courtesy of Crescent City Auction Gallery, crescentcityauctiongallery.com

Figural automaton clock, standing figure of a Chinese man in silk garments, figure moves his arms and eyes with help of a start-stop switch, musical, under a dome, on ebonized base, rare, maker unknown, 25 pounds, 38" h x 17-1/2" w x 12-1/5" d. **$10,000**

Courtesy of Fontaines Auction, FontainesAuction.com

Figural clock, circa late 19th c., carved wood depicting figural "Town Crier," clock mechanism engraved to the interior: PIERRE ROMILLY A GENEVE, 18-1/4" h. **$525**

Courtesy of Heritage Auctions, ha.com

▶ Boomerang-shape wall clock, circa 1960s, mfg. by Empire Art Empire Art Products Co. Inc., #820, 31-1/4" h x 23" w. **$90**

Courtesy of Bremo Auctions, bremoauctions.com

COCA COLA

THE MARKET FOR VINTAGE COCA-COLA items still remains soft, but there appears to be growing interest in original art and exclusive items not available to the public.

Since 1886, Coca-Cola became known for its innovative slogans, designs and tendency to remain on the cutting edge of popular culture – whether 1938 or 2018. Far and away, Coca-Cola signs are the most heavily collected advertising signs in the entire hobby. It's easy to see why: the company's dedication to unusually high-quality images paired with the latest marketing mediums solidified the drink as America's brand and the passion collectors bring to Coke's signs is second to none.

Signs from Coca-Cola's earliest days remain among the most valuable, as seen in recent auction results.

Morphy Auctions of Denver, Pennsylvania, sold off the Robert Newman collection of antique advertising for roughly $1.42 million, mainly on the back of scarce original Coca Cola art. The 1,300-lot sale showed Newman's reverence for Coca-Cola captured the eye of the brand's own archivists when his collection crossed the block in 2016. The collection was the talk of the hobby. Newman did what all successful collectors should do when launching their journey: keep your discipline and focus on the rarest items in the best possible condition.

The top lot of the sale was an amazing original oil painting featuring radio stars Edgar Bergen and Charlie McCarthy peeking inside a cooler full of Coca-Cola. The winning bid of $53,680 (including buyer's premium) was Coca-Cola itself to add the piece to its world-famous archive. The original art from 1949 was acquired by Newman from a gentleman who received it directly from Bergen, and attributed to Haddon Hubbard "Sunny" Sundblom, Coca-Cola's primary artist during the company's 'golden years' of Coca-Cola's signage. Sundblom was also the artist who perfected Coke's depiction of Santa Claus in art spanning the 1930s and 1940s.

Syrup bottle, enamel label,
11" h. **$3,500**

*Courtesy of Duane Merrill & Company,
merrillsauction.com*

Another piece in the auction that far exceeded expectations again stood out for being a one-of-a-kind item that floats at the top of the market: a 1930s sterling silver display bottle on a wood base with master craftsman level detailing sold for $35,380. Touted as "the greatest Coke display bottle made," the display stands 24-1/2 inches high and was crafted and given to a Coca Cola executive that oversaw the building of the ocean-liner inspired Coca Cola bottling plant in downtown Los Angeles.

For more information on Coca-Cola collectibles, see *Petretti's Coca-Cola Collectibles Price Guide, 12th edition,* by Allan Petretti.

Advertisement, c. 1951-1955, set of six die-cut cardboard bottle carrier inserts promoting "The Adventures of Kit Carson," all remain unpunched, scarce Coca-Cola issue, 3-1/2" w x 7-3/4" l............. **$428**

Courtesy of Hakes Americana & Collectibles, hakes.com

Calendar, 1935, Gone Fishing, after Norman Rockwell, lithograph in colors, 17-1/5" h x 11-1/4" w..................................... **$200**

Courtesy of Heritage Auctions, ha.com

Rare 1908 Coca-Cola cardboard calendar, "Good to the last drop," mint condition, framed under glass, 6-7/8" x 14"..................................... **$5,000**

Courtesy of Showtime Auction Services, showtimeauctions.com

Wall clock, 1957, neon, mfg. Cleveland Clock Co., with "Drink - Sign of Good Taste" marquee, Plexiglass front, rare, 31" h x 36" w............. **$2,000**

Courtesy of Weiss Auctions, weissauctions.com

Clock, c. 1950s-1960s, mfg. Cleveland Clock Co., double sided, two different colored neon lighted tubing encircling the face, original hanging mount made of cast iron and formed in a Victorian-style motif, only known example, 51" h x 35" w x 13" d. **$9,500**

Courtesy of Morphy Auctions, morphyauctions.com

Display, 1991, countertop sign, cardboard, 21-1/2" h x 15-1/2" w. **$25**

Courtesy of Morphy Auctions, morphyauctions.com

Mirror, 1906, mfg. Whitehead & Hoag Co., celluloid, scarce, 2-3/4" h.............................. **$382**

Courtesy of Hakes Americana & Collectibles, hakes.com

Sign, c. 1942, "Pause - Go Refreshed," celluloid, button-style, retains original backing and paper maker's mark label, 9" d. **$2,250**

Sign, c. 1938, porcelain, flange-style, double-sided, "Refresh Yourself! Coca-Cola Sold Here Ice Cold," 17" w x 20" h.................................. **$700**

Courtesy of Weiss Auctions, weissauctions.com

Sign, cardboard, original frame, depicts a thirsty cowboy, 20" w x 28" h................................ **$1,900**

Courtesy of Showtime Auction Services, showtimeauctions.com

Publication, March 1946, The Coca-Cola Bottler, "Official Organ of the Coca-Cola Bottlers Association," 60 pages, cover with Bob and Delores Hope, 8-1/2" w x 11" h....................... **$30**

Courtesy of Hakes Americana & Collectibles, hakes.com

Sign, porcelain over metal, 36" h x 12" w........ **$240**

Courtesy of Matthew Bullock Auctioneers, bullockauctioneers.com

▼ Sign, c. early 1940s, cardboard, with embossed cardboard frame and Coca-Cola bottle, lithographed in colors, depicting three members of the U.S. Army's Women's Army Corps., 25" h x 41" w. **$700**

Courtesy of Turkey Creek Auctions, antiqueauctionsfl.com

Advertising display and bottle holder, c. 1960s, wire hanging bottle rack for two Coca Cola bottles, designed to hang on shopping cart, 8" h...............**$60**

Courtesy of Milestone Auctions, milestoneauctions.hibid.com

Hutchinson bottle, c. 1930s, marked "Property of Coca-Cola Bottling Company," 7-1/4" h. **$4,250**

Courtesy of Morphy Auctions, morphyauctions.com

Display, circa 1950s, light up bottle with thermometer, made of wood and composition, script reads "Happy Holidays," 37" h. **$150**

Courtesy of Morphy Auctions, morphyauctions.com

▼ Sign, c. 1960s, aluminum, from distributing plant, 23" h x 62-1/2" w. **$450**

Courtesy of Bright Star Antique Company, brightstarantiques.com

Vending machine, 1956, model H81-B, Serial #61019563, restored with new decals, 59" h x 28" w x 22" d.. **$3,750**

Courtesy of Morphy Auctions, morphyauctions.com

Stand, circa 1950s, with Coca Cola "Place Empties Here" advertising, holds three vintage wood crates, 19" w x 47" h............................ **$190**

Courtesy of Bullock Auctioneers, bullockauctioneers.com

Sign, c. 1960s, made of Vacuform, features "Drink Coca-Cola" button logo held by acrobatic clown, scarce, 12" w x 14-1/4" h. **$118**

Courtesy of Hakes Americana & Collectibles, hakes.com

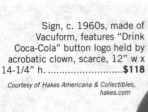

Advertising toy plane, die-cut cardboard, "Spirit of St. Louis," punched, never assembled, rare, 10" l x 8 -1/2" w.**$130**

Courtesy of Oakridge Auction Gallery, oakridgeauctiongallery.com

Toy, c. 1950s, hard plastic free-wheeling Ford delivery truck with six original soda bottle cases, original cardboard logo box, 10-3/4" l. **$359**

Courtesy of Hakes Americana & Collectibles, hakes.com

COIN-OPS

DID YOU KNOW that coin-operated dispensers date back to ancient times when they were used in houses of worship to deliver holy water? You'd be hard-pressed to find one of those offered at auction today, but many other types of coin-operated gadget-like gizmos certainly come up for sale, and there are always eager buyers lining up to add them to collections.

Coin-ops, as they're often referenced by both marketers and aficionados, come in all shapes and sizes and fall into three main categories: gambling, including slot machines and trade stimulators; vending machines with service devices like scales and shoe shiners as a subcategory; and arcade machines. From simple post-World War II gumball and peanut machines that can usually be found for under $100, to rare antique arcade machines that bring to mind the fortune teller amusement working magic in the popular movie *Big* starring Tom Hanks, these are all considered collectible.

Today one of those talking fortune-teller machines can easily bring five figures at auction. Other interesting models without talking features can be purchased more reasonably, in the $1,000-$5,000 range, but none of them come cheap when they're in good working order.

Amusements such as these originated in penny arcades of the late 1800s. There were machines allowing patrons to demonstrate their skill at bowling, shooting or golf, among other pastimes, along with the familiar strength testers that sprang to life at a penny a pop. Some machines known as "shockers" were marketed as medical devices. In fact, one made by Mills, a huge manufacturer of coin-ops, was actually named Electricity is Life, and it would supposedly cure what ails you, according to Bill Petrochuk, an avid collector actively involved with the Coin Operated Collectors Association (http://coinopclub.org). Another lung tester, which operated by blowing into a mouthpiece attached to a hose causing water to rise in the device as a measurement tool, was eventually banned, ironically, due to the spread of tuberculosis.

Bat-A-Score Arcade Game, H.C. Evans, 1948, 5 cents to play, challenging baseball-themed game with pitcher throwing steel ball overhand to batter, considered Holy Grail game for advanced collectors with only five known examples, 79-1/2" h x 26-1/2" w x 46" d.............**$60,000**

Courtesy of Morphy Auctions, morphyauctions.com

There are also those aforementioned trade stimulators, some of which skirted gambling laws, according to Larry DeBaugh, a frequent consultant for Morphy Auctions (morphyauctions.com), who knows his stuff when it comes to devices powered by pocket change. These machines stimulated the trade of businesses like tobacco stores and bars by offering patrons a chance to win products, many times by spinning reels or playing a game. Later machines dispensed gum on the side for each coin spent. Customers received something for their money, and presto, law enforcement couldn't technically deem it gambling.

The earliest trade stimulators were cigar machines with no gambling involved, however. They were truly cigar dispensers, and for a nickel a customer would get one. What made it different from buying from the guy down the block is that you might get two or three for the same nickel using the machine. Petrochuk adds that these were used to free up some of the tobacco shop clerk's time as well. When taxes were imposed on cigars, requiring that they be sold from original boxes, these machines were no longer serviceable. They're now considered rare collectibles and sell for $10,000 and up in most instances, when you can find them.

There were also slot machines designed for use outside casinos that would vend a pack of mints, or do a bit of fortune telling, in the same way as later trade stimulators. Authorities fought these machines for decades, according to DeBaugh. Finally, in the 1950s and 1960s, vending-style gambling machines of this sort were outlawed, and their makers concentrated their marketing efforts on Las Vegas going forward.

Traditional slot machines are quite popular today as well, and collectors like DeBaugh, who've studied, bought, and sold these types of items for 35-40 years, have seen a bit of everything including those in pretty rough shape.

"An average machine, one that's seen a lot

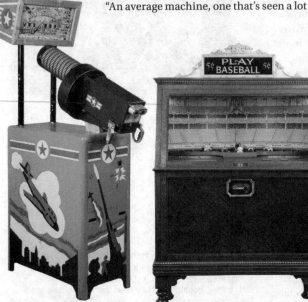

Genco's Sky Gunner Arcade Machine, 1953, 10 cents to play, patron shoots at 3-dimensional planes in a cinematic war scene, 81" h x 24" w x 48" d................ **$4,800**

Courtesy of Morphy Auctions, morphyauctions.com

Amusement Machine Co. All American Baseball Arcade Machine, rare, popular machine, restored, 5 cents to play, 68" h x 42" w x 27" d. **$54,000**

Courtesy of Morphy Auctions, morphyauctions.com

Love Tester Arcade Game, Exhibit Supply Co., 1929-1933, 1 cent to play, allows players to measure their sex appeal by squeezing machine grip, ranges from "No Sex Appeal" to "You Have It," 83" h x 23" w x 18" d..... **$3,300**

Courtesy of Morphy Auctions, morphyauctions.com

of play from the '40s or late '30s and is basically worn out, will run about $1,000. But they won't be worth anything unless they are restored. After they're running, you might have a $3,000 machine."

Petrochuk notes that collectors of coin-ops in general look for "nice, clean, original machines," but a small percentage falls into that category. He likes to use the term "preservation" when referring to giving old coin-ops new life, as in keeping things as original as possible. He sees restoration as more of a redo that might require totally new paint or extensive replating. "These old machines took a real beating. A few battle scars are acceptable," he adds.

Preserving coin-ops means using as many original parts as possible to replace those that are worn, and fabricating new ones out of appropriate materials when needed. DeBaugh actually supplies Rick Dale of the History Channel's hit television series, "American Restoration," with many parts salvaged from old slot machines that can't be repaired. He also notes that it's tough to find older slots from the early 1900s in anything but poor condition. The wood usually needs work, and sometimes the nickel or copper finishes will need to be replated as well.

Other unusual coin-ops beyond the familiar "one-armed bandits" include devices that sold matchbooks, collar buttons, and sprays of perfume. Going even further into the unimaginable zone are machines that actually dispensed live lobsters via a game of sorts. Others even provided live bait for fishing excursions. Or, maybe a machine that dispensed gold bars in airports might pique your curiosity?

Nut and gum dispensers are the most common vending models, but unusual brands in this category most definitely appeal to advertising collectors in addition to coin-op enthusiasts. In fact, many coin-ops are direct extensions of advertising collectibles since vending machines made in the 1920s and '30s, unlike those that dispense multiple types of snacks today, usually focused on a single brand. Hershey's machines dispensed chocolate bars. Wrigley's dispensers rotated to deliver packs of gum. There were even coin-operated dispensers for Dixie Cups. Add an unusual shape or size to the equation and advanced collectors will pay big bucks to own them.

Even those old-fashioned red, white, and blue stamp dispensers used in post offices 30-40 years ago appeal to collectors of newer machines, and those can be found for less than $100. If you want a slot machine for use in a "man cave" or game room, DeBaugh suggests looking at a Mills machine from the 1940s or '50s. Both high top and half top models can be found for around $1,000 in good working order. What's even better, they're dependable and reliable for home use for hours of coin-op fun.

— *Pamela Y. Wiggins*

Ten Strike Classic Arcade Game, H.C. Evans, produced from 1939-1953, 5 cents to play, patron plays five frames, 58" h x 19-1/2" w x 64" d.
.....................................**$25,200**

Courtesy of Morphy Auctions, morphyauctions.com

Undersea Raider Submarine Arcade Game, Bally, circa 1946, 5 cents to play, patron uses telescope to sight and fire torpedoes at enemy ships, professionally restored.....**$11,400**

Courtesy of Morphy Auctions, morphyauctions.com

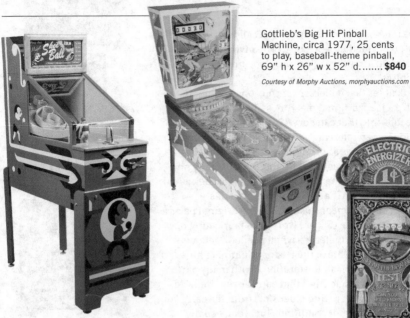

Gottlieb's Big Hit Pinball Machine, circa 1977, 25 cents to play, baseball-theme pinball, 69" h x 26" w x 52" d........ **$840**

Courtesy of Morphy Auctions, morphyauctions.com

Chicago Coin's Midget Skee Ball Arcade Machine, 1949, 5 cents to play, handle grip controls manikin throwing a ball in any of six scoring holes, museum quality condition, 70-1/2" h x 21-1/2" w x 44-1/2" d. **$30,000**

Courtesy of Morphy Auctions, morphyauctions.com

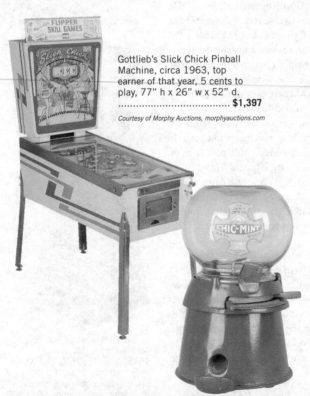

Gottlieb's Slick Chick Pinball Machine, circa 1963, top earner of that year, 5 cents to play, 77" h x 26" w x 52" d. **$1,397**

Courtesy of Morphy Auctions, morphyauctions.com

Spear The Dragon Arcade Machine, Exhibit Supply Co., 1926-1929, 1 cent to play, electric energizer housed in cabinet, patron grasps two metal knobs to feel electric current, which starts out gently and increases in strength as knight figure approaches dragon, 80" h x 20" w x 16-1/2" d. **$5,100**

Courtesy of Morphy Auctions, morphyauctions.com

Ball Gum Vending Machine, Chic-Mint Gum Co., Wilmington, DE, 1915, countertop vendor with red sheet metal base and flat-topped glass globe, restored, 11-1/2" h. **$420**

Courtesy of Morphy Auctions, morphyauctions.com

Mills Regular O.K. Mint Vendor Slot Machine,
1926, Iowa Novelty Co., Cedar Rapids, gooseneck
bell and three reel strip, good condition, 24" h x
19" w x 15" d... **$6,875**

Courtesy of Morphy Auctions, morphyauctions.com

Twin Double Upright Slot Machine, Centaur slot
on one side and an Eclipse on the other, circa
early 1900s, both sides accepting nickels, serial
number 848, 68" h x 47" w x 15" d...........**$96,000**

Courtesy of Morphy Auctions, morphyauctions.com

Watling Cherry Front Rol-A-Top Twin Jackpot
Slot Machine, 1938, 5 cents to play, upturned
cornucopia spilling out bright red cherries and a
twin jackpot reserve feature, 26" h x 15" d
x 16" w. **$3,900**

Courtesy of Morphy Auctions, morphyauctions.com

Wizard Fortune Teller Trade Stimulator, Mills
Novelty, 1919-1927, 1 cent to play, patron
selects from six questions, 18-1/2" h x 13-1/2" w
x 6" d... **$1,320**

Courtesy of Morphy Auctions, morphyauctions.com

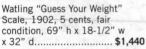

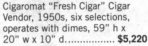

Cigaromat "Fresh Cigar" Cigar Vendor, 1950s, six selections, operates with dimes, 59" h x 20" w x 10" d................. **$5,220**

Courtesy of Morphy Auctions, morphyauctions.com

Mills Two Bits Chicago Upright Slot Machine, 1904, 5 cents to play, floor model machine housed in an oak cabinet, machine plays and pays with working cylinder music box, 67" h x 26-1/2" w x 14-1/2" d. **$30,000**

Courtesy of Morphy Auctions, morphyauctions.com

Watling "Guess Your Weight" Scale, 1902, 5 cents, fair condition, 69" h x 18-1/2" w x 32" d............................ **$1,440**

Courtesy of Morphy Auctions, morphyauctions.com

Smiling Sam The Voo Doo Man Fortune Teller, Exhibit Supply Co., 1939, 1 cent to play, Smiling Sam's face changes as he "thinks" and then dispenses a small fortune card, professionally restored, 78" h x 22" w x 19" d. **$8,400**

Courtesy of Morphy Auctions, morphyauctions.com

Zoltan Horoscope Fortune Teller, Prophetron, 1969, 10 cents to play, patron selected zodiac sign and received fortune from Zoltan, fiberglass, phone receiver, 70" h x 30" w x 22" d................. **$1,980**

Courtesy of Morphy Auctions, morphyauctions.com

COINS

INTEREST IN COIN COLLECTING in the United States surged in the late 1850s when the smaller, copper-nickel Flying Eagle cent replaced the old large copper one-cent coin. Just two years later, the Indian Head cent replaced the Flying Eagle cent. People started putting aside the obsolete coins, and demand and prices for them rose. Professional coin dealers emerged to meet the demand, and by the 1870s, most major Eastern cities had coin clubs.

The next major development in coin collecting occurred in 1888 when Dr. George Heath of Monroe, Michigan — a physician by profession who moonlighted as a mail-order coin dealer — published the first issue of *The American Numismatist*. Like many other publications of the time, the magazine was a marketing tool for Heath's coin business. By 1891, Heath had shortened the serial's title to *The Numismatist*, and its readership formed the basis for the founding of the American Numismatic Association.

Coin collecting continued to grow in the early 20th century as exciting new designs made old coins obsolete. Ironically, the Great Depression brought another major development in coin collecting. In 1934, the Whitman Publishing Co. of Racine, Wisconsin, introduced the "penny board." It was essentially a big piece of cardboard with holes in it for each date and mint mark of Lincoln cents, starting in 1909. The boards sold for 25 cents each and were widely available in hardware stores, dime stores, shoeshine parlors, and gasoline stations.

The boards provided cheap entertainment during the economic struggles of the 1930s as people of all ages checked the one-cent coins in their pocket change for dates and mint marks that would fill an empty hole in the board. The boards developed into the modern-day coin folder, which many collectors use to store their holdings today.

Coin collecting enjoyed a boom period in the 1950s. War veterans and others had disposable income to devote to a hobby and could find coins of the late 1800s and early 1900s in circulation. What they couldn't find they could buy from the growing number of dealers who operated shops, set up at coin shows, or advertised in coin publications such as the newly founded *Numismatic News*.

U.S. $5 Indian head gold 1913 half eagle, Philadelphia, mint, obverse features a Native American chief, reverse depicts the perched American eagle, 8.3 grams. **$330**

Courtesy of Florida Estate Sales, LLC, floridaestatesalesexperts.com

United States 1926 Philadelphia mint $10 Indian gold eagle coin, designed by Saint-Gaudens, the obverse features Lady Liberty adorned in a full Indian war bonnet with star-tipped feathers, reverse depicts perched eagle and stars around rim, 16.7 grams. **$600**

Courtesy of Florida Estate Sales, LLC, floridaestatesalesexperts.com

Coin collecting is enjoying another renaissance thanks in part to U.S. Mint programs such as the America the Beautiful Quarters, which again provide a forum for collecting coins from circulation. Meanwhile, on the high end of the market, traditionally popular coins — such as Standing Liberty quarters, Walking Liberty half dollars, Morgan silver dollars, and gold coins — make hobby headlines when they sell at auction for eye-popping prices in top grades.

What makes a coin valuable? Precious-metal content provides the base value for any gold or silver coin. Prices for precious metals have surged in recent years, so the base values of gold and silver coins have surged with them.

Gold and silver coins with collectible or numismatic value sell for a premium above their precious-metal value. The extent of the premium depends on the coin's grade, its rarity, and the demand for the coin in the collector market. Premiums over precious-metal content can vary from a few percentage points for bullion coins to several hundred percent for high-quality or rare collectible coins. If the premium is high, the coin is not affected as much by fluctuating market prices for silver and gold bullion. If the premium is low, the coin's value is more likely to be affected by the ups and downs of the bullion markets. Base-metal coins, such as one-cent and five-cent pieces, can also sell for well above their intrinsic value on the collector market because of their rarity, desirability, and condition.

Condition is stated in commonly used grading terms. Uncirculated coins, which show no signs of wear, are termed "mint state" or MS. A number usually follows to indicate varying degrees of condition within mint state (MS-67, MS-65, or MS-63, for example). Terms used to describe circulated coins, or coins showing wear, include "about uncirculated," "extremely fine," and "very fine," in descending order. Most coins valuable enough to justify the fee have

U.S. Liberty gold $2.50 coin, Philadelphia mint,1903, obverse features the crowned image of Lady Liberty, reverse depicts American eagle with shield, 4.1 grams. **$290**

Courtesy of Florida Estate Sales, LLC, floridaestatesalesexperts.com

20 Veinte Peso Mexican gold coin, 1917, obverse features the Mayan calendar, reverse features eagles triumph over the serpent, 16.6 grams.... **$625**

Courtesy of Florida Estate Sales, LLC, floridaestatesalesexperts.com

50 Peso Mexican gold coin, 1922, Mexico Independence of 1821 gold fifty peso coin, 41.6 grams. **$1,400**

Courtesy of Florida Estate Sales, LLC, floridaestatesalesexperts.com

U.S. $20 gold Saint Gaudens double eagle coin, 1924, Philadelphia mint, originally commissioned by Theodore Roosevelt, the obverse features Lady Liberty and the United States Capitol visible at lower left in background, reverse depicts American eagle with full motto, 33.4 grams. . **$1,400**

Courtesy of Florida Estate Sales, LLC, floridaestatesalesexperts.com

been graded by one of several professional coin grading services, a trend that started in the mid-1980s. Which service graded the coin is usually noted with the coin's grade when it is offered for sale.

ABBREVIATIONS

CAC – Certified Acceptance Corporation

ICCS – International Coin Certification Service

PCGS – Professional Coin Grading Service

PMG – Paper Money Guaranty

For more on grading, see *The Official American Numismatic Association Grading Standards for United States Coins.*

1880-S San Francisco mint $10 gold coin, eagle, 16.5 grams. **$600**

Courtesy of Florida Estate Sales, LLC, floridaestatesalesexperts.com

1882-O/S $1 VAM-4, Early Die State, AU53 NGC, Ex: Gene L. Henry Legacy Collection, a Top 100 Variety, extremely rare early die state of the VAM-4 overmintmark variety, has light gray surfaces with traces of luster beneath subtle champagne toning, census: 1 in 53, 10 finer (3/18), (NGC ID# CVKK, Variety PCGS# 133892, Base PCGS# 7138), 26.7 grams, metal: 90% silver, 10% copper. ... **$360**

Courtesy of Heritage Auctions, ha.com

1896 S-7 Bryan Dollar, MS63, Plentiful Gorham Variety, Uniface, Gorham Mfg. Co., MS63 NGC, Zerbe-6, HK-781, Schornstein-7, Ex: Zerbe-Ostheimer-Perkins, silver, 52 mm, plain edge, exhibits light gold and pale blue toning over reflective silver surfaces. **$720**

Courtesy of Heritage Auctions, ha.com

1951 50C MS67 PCGS, CAC, gold toning appears on the obverse, with pastel gold, blue, and lavender on the reverse, both sides highly lustrous, population: 5 in 67, 7 in 67 Full Bell Lines, 0 finer, CAC: 3 in 67, 0 finer (3/18). (Registry values: N2998) (NGC ID# 24SY, PCGS# 6658), 12.50 grams, metal: 90% silver, 10% copper.**$1,020**

Courtesy of Heritage Auctions, ha.com

1936 50C Norfolk MS68 PCGS, CAC, both sides are essentially unmarked with dappled orange-russet and antique-gold shadings at the borders, fully original and attractive Superb Gem, PCGS reports two finer examples, and there is one finer coin at CAC (3/18), 12.50 grams, metal: 90% silver, 10% copper. **$1,200**

Courtesy of Heritage Auctions, ha.com

1921-D $1 MS66 PCGS. CAC. PCGS Population: (435/10), NGC Census: (262/10), CDN: $650 Whsle, bid for problem-free NGC/PCGS MS66, Mintage 20,345,000, (Registry values: P3, N1793) (NGC ID# 256Y, PCGS# 7298), 26.7 grams, metal: 90% silver, 10% copper. **$1,020**

Courtesy of Heritage Auctions, ha.com

1924-S Dime, MS64 Full Bands, Uncentered Broadstrike, PCGS. Any 1924-S dime is highly desirable in Gem condition, but this piece is also noteworthy as a mint error. The design is complete on both sides with a broad arc of unstruck surface centered at 6:30. Dove-gray and caramel-gold toning on satiny and unabraded surfaces. Characteristic of a strike without the restraint of a collar die, the outer legends exhibit spreading toward the rims. **$840**

Courtesy of Heritage Auctions, ha.com

1870 25C standard silver quarter dollar, Judd-901, Pollock-1016, High R.6, PR62 PCGS, bust of Liberty faces right on the obverse, with UNITED STATES OF AMERICA around and the motto IN GOD WE TRUST on a scroll below, Liberty's hair is tied in a bun, headband ornamented with a star; on reverse, the denomination 25 CENTS and date 1870 are in a wreath of cotton and corn, with the inscription STANDARD above. Struck in silver with a plain edge. These patterns were sold to collectors for $15 a set. About 12 Judd-901 examples are known.................................... **$1,200**

Courtesy of Heritage Auctions, ha.com

1868 1C One Cent, Judd-605, Pollock-670, R.5, PR64 NGC, obverse design is similar to the regular issue three cent nickel, in a reduced scale for this smaller diameter pattern, reverse has a small scale version of the wreath that is familiar to collectors of Flying Eagle cents, Type Two and Type Three gold dollars, and three dollar gold pieces. The wreath encloses an unribbed Roman Numeral I as the sole indication of the denomination, struck in nickel with a plain edge. This is an early die state of a pattern that is usually found with severe obverse die breaks. These pieces were issued in two-coin sets along with five cent patterns, either Judd-623, 633, or 634. This sharply defined light gray example has flashy fields with strongly mirrored surfaces beneath hazy champagne toning. A strike-through appears on Liberty's cheek, and a few toning flecks on the obverse confirm the originality of this diminutive pattern. **$1,140**

Courtesy of Heritage Auctions, ha.com

1926 5C Buffalo MS66+ PCGS Secure, CAC, PCGS Population: (477/48 and 47/4+), NGC Census: (166/16 and 3/1+), CDN: $450 Whsle. Bid for problem-free NGC/PCGS MS66, Mintage 44,693,000. (Registry values: N491) (NGC ID# 22S5, PCGS# 3957), 5 grams, metal: 75% copper, 25% nickel.. **$557**

Courtesy of Heritage Auctions, ha.com

COMIC BOOKS

BACK IN 1993, Sotheby's auctioned a copy of *Fantastic Four #1* (1961) that was said to be the finest copy known to exist. It sold for $27,600, which at the time was considered an unheard-of price for a 1960s comic. A few years ago, Heritage Auctions sold that same copy for $203,000 ... and it's not even the finest known copy anymore.

It used to be that only comics from the 1930s or 1940s could be worth thousands of dollars. Now, truly high-grade copies of comics from the Silver Age (1956-1969 by most people's reckoning) can sell for four, five, or even six figures. Note I said truly high-grade. Long gone are the days when a near mint condition copy was only worth triple the price of a good condition copy. Now near mint is more like 10-20 times good, and sometimes it's as much as a factor of 1,000.

A trend of the last couple of years has been that the "key" issues have separated even further from the pack, value-wise. Note that not every key is a "#1" issue — if you have *Amazing Fantasy* #15, *Tales of Suspense* #39, and *Journey into Mystery* #83, you've got the first appearances of Spider-Man, Iron Man, and Thor. (Beware of reprints and replica editions, however.)

The most expensive comics of all remain the Golden Age (1938-1949) first appearances, like Superman's 1938 debut in *Action Comics #1*, several copies of which have sold for $1 million or more. However, not every single comic from the old days is going up in value. Take western-themed comics. Values are actually going down in this genre as the generation that grew up watching westerns is at the age where they're looking to sell, and there are more sellers than potential buyers.

Comics from the 1970s and later, while increasing in value, rarely reach anywhere near the same value as 1960s issues, primarily because in the 1970s, the general public began to look at comics as a potentially valuable collectible. People took better care of them, and in many cases hoarded multiple copies.

What about 1980s favorites like *The Dark Knight Returns* and *Watchmen*? Here the demand is high, but the supply is really high. These series were heavily hyped at the time and were done by well-known creators, so copies were socked away in great quantities. We've come across more than one dealer who has 20-30 mint copies of every single 1980s

Aquaman #1 (DC Comics, 1962), CGC NM- 9.2.
....**$6,570**

Courtesy of Heritage Auctions, ha.com

comic socked away in a warehouse, waiting for the day when they're worth selling.

I should mention one surprise hit of the last couple of years. When Image Comics published *The Walking Dead* #1 in 2003, it had a low print run and made no particular splash in the comics world. Once AMC made it into a television series, however, it was a whole different story. High-grade copies of #1 have been fetching $1,000 and up lately.

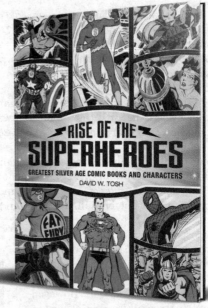

One aspect of collecting that has absolutely exploded in the last 20 years has been original comic art, and not just art for the vintage stuff. In fact, the most expensive piece Heritage Auctions has ever sold was from 1990: Todd McFarlane's cover art for *Amazing Spider-Man* #328, which sold for more than $650,000. It's not unusual for a page that was bought for $20 in the 1980s to be worth $5,000 now.

If you want to get into collecting original comic art, McFarlane would not be the place to start unless you've got a really fat wallet. I suggest picking a current comic artist you like who isn't yet a major "name." Chances are his originals will be a lot more affordable. Another idea is to collect the original art for comic strips. You can find originals for as little as $20, as long as you're not expecting a *Peanuts* or a *Prince Valiant*. Heritage Auctions (ha.com) maintains a free online archive of every piece of art they've sold and it is an excellent research tool.

For more information on the Silver Age of comic books, see *Rise of the Superheroes – Greatest Silver Age Comic Books and Characters* by David W. Tosh.

As expensive as both comic books and comic art can be at the high end of the spectrum, in many ways this is a buyer's market. In the old days you might search for years to find a given issue of a comic; now you can often search eBay and see 10 different copies for sale. Also, comic conventions seem to be thriving in almost every major city — and while the people in crazy costumes get all the publicity, you can also find plenty of vintage comic dealers at these shows. From that point of view, it's a great time to be a comic collector.

— Barry Sandoval

Barry Sandoval is Director of Operations for Comics and Comic Art, Heritage Auctions. In addition to managing Heritage's Comics division, Sandoval is a noted comic book evaluator and serves as an advisor to the *Overstreet Comic Book Price Guide.*

CGC GRADING

If you've bought comics at an auction house or on eBay, you might have seen some in CGC holders. Certified Guaranty Co., or CGC, is a third-party grading service that grades a comic book on a scale from 0.5 to 10. These numbers correspond with traditional descriptive grades of good, very fine, near mint, and mint, with the higher numbers indicating a better grade. Once graded, CGC encapsulates the comic book in plastic. The grade remains valid as long as the plastic holder is not broken open. CGC has been a boon to the hobby, allowing people to buy comics with more confidence and with the subjectivity of grading taken out of the equation. Unless extremely rare, it's usually only high-grade comics that are worth certifying.

Tales to Astonish #27 (Marvel, 1962), CGC-graded VF 8.0, first appearance of Ant-Man, illustrated by Jack Kirby and Steve Ditko. **$2,400**

Courtesy of Heritage Auctions, ha.com

Avengers #1 (Marvel, 1963), CGC-graded 9.6 (near mint+), cover by Jack Kirby, Pacific Coast pedigree copy from the Doug Schmeel Collection. **$274,850**

Courtesy of Heritage Auctions, ha.com

Captain America #100 (Marvel, 1968), CGC NM/ MT 9.8, Captain America's origin is retold, and there's a Black Panther appearance. Cover and art by Jack Kirby.. **$650**

Courtesy of Heritage Auctions, ha.com

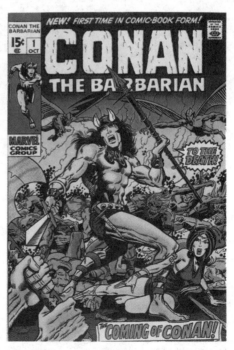

Conan the Barbarian #1 (Marvel, 1970), CGC-graded 9.8 (near mint/mint), from the Empire Comics Collection. **$3,884**

Courtesy of Heritage Auctions, ha.com

Daredevil #1 (Marvel, 1964), CGC NM+ 9.6, first appearance of Daredevil, cover by Jack Kirby/Bill Everett..**$37,350**

Courtesy of Heritage Auctions, ha.com

Doctor Strange #169 (Marvel, 1968), CGC NM+ 9.6, first Dr. Strange-titled comic book, Dan Adkins cover... **$430**

Courtesy of Heritage Auctions, ha.com

Fantastic Four #1 (Marvel, 1961), CGC-graded 9.2 (near mint-), White Mountain pedigree copy from the Doug Schmeel Collection.............**$203,150**

Courtesy of Heritage Auctions, ha.com

Flash Comics #1 (DC Comics, 1940), the introduction of Flash, CGC-rated 9.6 (near mint)...**$273,125**

Courtesy of Heritage Auctions, ha.com

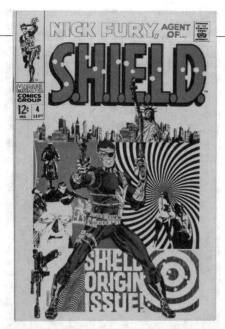

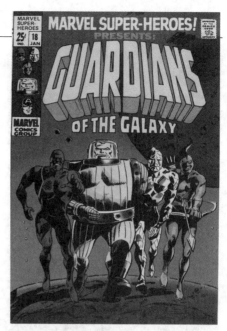

Nick Fury, Agent of S.H.I.E.L.D. #4 (Marvel, 1968), CGC-graded 9.8 (near mint/mint). **$1,135**

Courtesy of Heritage Auctions, ha.com

Marvel Super-Heroes #18 *Guardians of the Galaxy* (Marvel, 1969), CGC NM+ 9.6, origin and first appearance of The Guardians of the Galaxy with cover art by Gene "The Dean" Colan; from the Don and Maggie Thompson Collection. **$10,157**

Courtesy of Heritage Auctions, ha.com

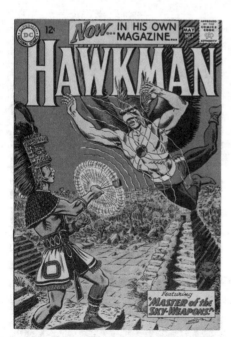

Hawkman #1 (DC Comics, 1964), CGC NM+ 9.6, the first Hawkman title, Murphy Anderson cover. **$4,480**

Courtesy of Heritage Auctions, ha.com

The Incredible Hulk #1 (Marvel, 1962), CGC-graded 9.2 (near mint). **$125,475**

Courtesy of Heritage Auctions, ha.com

Tales of Suspense #39 (Marvel, 1963), CGC-graded 9.6 (near mint+), first appearance of Iron Man, Pacific Coast pedigree copy from the Doug Schmeel Collection. **$262,900**

Courtesy of Heritage Auctions, ha.com

Fantastic Four #50 (Marvel, 1966), CGC NM/MT 9.8, part three of the "Galactus Trilogy," the Silver Surfer battles Galactus in the third appearance of both characters, Jack Kirby cover. **$35,850**

Courtesy of Heritage Auctions, ha.com

The Amazing Spider-Man #1 (Marvel, 1963), CGC NM+ 9.6, second appearance of Spider-Man and first appearance John Jameson, J. Jonah Jameson, and the Chameleon, Jack Kirby and Steve Ditko are credited with the cover, Curator Pedigree. ..**$262,900**

Courtesy of Heritage Auctions, ha.com

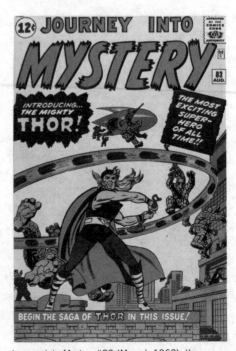

Journey into Mystery #83 (Marvel, 1962), the introduction of Thor, CGC-graded 9.2 (near mint-) **$83,650**

Courtesy of Heritage Auctions, ha.com

Wolverine (Limited Series) #1 (Marvel, 1982),
CGC-graded 10 (mint)...............................**$15,535**

Courtesy of Heritage Auctions, ha.com

Wonder Woman #122 (DC Comics, 1961), CGC
NM 9.4, first appearance of Wonder Tot. **$573**

Courtesy of Heritage Auctions, ha.com

X-Men #1 (Marvel, 1963), the introduction of the
X-Men, CGC-graded 9.8 (near mint/mint), from
the Doug Schmeel Collection. **$492,938**

Courtesy of Heritage Auctions, ha.com

COOKIE JARS

COOKIE JARS EVOLVED from the elegant British biscuit jars found on Victorian-era tables. These 19th century containers featured bail handles and were often made of sterling silver and cut crystal.

As the biscuit jar was adapted for use in America, it migrated from the dining table to the kitchen and, by the late 1920s, it was common to find a green-glass jar (or pink or clear), often with an applied label and a screw-top lid, on kitchen counters in the typical American home.

During the Great Depression — when stoneware was still popular but before the arrival of widespread electric refrigeration — cookie jars in round and barrel shapes arrived. These heavy-bodied jars could be hand-painted after firing, and the decorations were easily worn away by eager hands reaching for Mom's baked goodies. The lids of many stoneware jars typically had small tapering finials or knobs that also contributed to cracks and chips.

The Brush Pottery Co. of Zanesville, Ohio, produced one of the first ceramic cookie jars in about 1929, and Red Wing's spongeware line from the late 1920s also included a ridged, barrel-shaped jar. Many established potteries began adding a selection of cookie jars in the 1930s.

The golden age of cookie jars began in the 1940s with the arrival of two of the most famous creations: Shawnee's Smiley and Winnie, two portly, bashful little pigs who stand with eyes closed and heads cocked, he in overalls and bandana, she in flowered hat and long coat. A host of Disney characters also made their way into American kitchens. This golden age lasted for less than three decades, but the examples that survive represent an exuberance and style that have captivated collectors.

A rare full-fired (including interior) lidded blackware cookie jar by Margaret Tafoya, matriarch of Santa Clara Pueblo potters. The cookie jar, with her famous bear-paw imprint, is one of only a handful that she made, and was purchased in 1975 for $300. Very good condition, 8" x 8".............. **$2,500**

Courtesy of Allard Auctions, Inc., allardauctions.com

In the 1950s, the first television-influenced jars appeared, including images of Davy Crockett and Popeye. This decade also saw the end of several prominent American potteries, including Roseville, and the continued rise of imported ceramics.

A new collection of cartoon-inspired jars was popular in the 1960s, featuring characters drawn from the Flintstones, Yogi Bear, Woody Woodpecker, and Casper the Friendly Ghost. Jars reflecting the race for space included examples from McCoy and American Bisque. This decade also marked the peak production era for a host of West Coast manufacturers, led by twin brothers Don and Ross Winton.

Thanks to many collectors who started investing their money in cookie jars during the 1970s, cookie jars started evolving from merely storage vessels for baked goods into a contemporary art form.

For more information, see *Warman's Cookie Jars Identification and Price Guide* by Mark F. Moran.

GOLDEN AGE OF COOKIE JARS

Shawnee's famous Smiley and Winnie, each 11-1/2" h, excellent condition, the pair: **$225**

Courtesy of Dan Morphy Auctions, morphyauctions.com

Two little portly pigs ushered in the golden age of cookie jars beginning in the 1940s: Smiley and Winnie, shown at left, are the most famous creations by Shawnee Pottery. These bashful pigs stand with eyes closed and heads cocked, he in overalls and bandana, she in flowered hat and long coat. This golden age lasted for less than three decades, but the examples that survive represent an exuberance and style that have captivated collectors.

Vintage McCoy bear cookie jar, marked "McCoy" on the bottom, 10-3/4" h x 7" w x 7" d. **$20**

Courtesy of Martin Auction Co., martinauctionco.com

Betsy Ross cookie jar, 10" h x 7-1/2" w. **$30**

Courtesy of Martin Auction Co., martinauctionco.com

Buick convertible cookie jar, USA, 1979, glazed ceramic, signed and dated, 7" x 15" x 9". **$70**

Courtesy of Rago Arts and Auction Center, ragoarts.com

▶ Shawnee Lucky Elephant cookie jar, gold trim floral decals, 1940s, original tag on jar, 11-1/2" h. **$70**

Courtesy of Judd's Auction Gallery, Inc., juddsauction.com

Vintage McCoy clown cookie jar, marked "McCoy" on bottom, 7" x 11". **$40**

Courtesy of Desert West Auction, desertwestauction.com

Peter Max-designed ceramic "Zero" cookie jar, 1989, 8-1/2" x 8" x 4". **$400**

Courtesy of RoGallery.com

Vintage McCoy kitten in a pink basket, marked "McCoy" on the bottom, 10" h x 6" w x 5-1/2" d. **$40**

Courtesy of Desert West Auction, desertwestauction.com

Redwing Pottery monk cookie jar "Thou Shall Not Steal," 1940s, 11" h........................ **$70**

Courtesy of Auctions by Adkins, LLC, auctionsbyadkins.com

McCoy pear cookie jar, marked "McCoy USA" on bottom, 10" h x 7-1/2" w. **$60**

Courtesy of Martin Auction Co., martinauctionco.com

Shawnee ceramic pig cookie jar, slight chipping on rim, 8" x 12"....................................... **$40**

Courtesy of Desert West Auction, desertwestauction.com

Ceramic Pillsbury Doughboy cookie jar, off-white with navy blue painted details, marked as copyright of the Pillsbury Company 1973, 11" h x 6" w x 4" l...................................... **$40**

Courtesy of The Benefit Shop Foundation, Inc., thebenefitshop.org

Glenn Appleman ceramic cookie jar, Sid's Radio Taxi, 15" l x 9-1/2" w, 8" h. **$150**

Courtesy of Hughes Estate Sales, Inc., hughesestatesales.com

Hull Regal China Poinsettia Little Red Riding Hood, marked "Little Red Riding Hood Pat Des No. USA," 13" h......... **$160**

Courtesy of Matthew Bullock Auctioneers, bullockauctioneers.com

Winterthur rooster cookie jar, hand painted, marked China, colorful, lidded, 9" l, 14" h...**$15**

Courtesy of The Benefit Shop Foundation, Inc., thebenefitshop.org

Waterford cut crystal lidded biscuit or cookie jar, excellent condition, 8" h....................**$70**

Courtesy of Blackwell Auctions, blackwellauctions.com

Roseville Pottery Zephyr Lily cookie jar. Zephyr Lily is a late period pattern introduced by Roseville Pottery in 1946, jar is marked with the raised Roseville script mark, and 5-8"....................................**$95**

Courtesy of Corbett's Auction House, corbettsauctionhouse.com

Early Ransburg or Redwing Pottery fruit motif cookie jar, double handled, 9-1/2" x 6"..**$30**

Courtesy of Desert West Auction, desertwestauction.com

Sprout cookie jar, marked on bottom "©1988 The Pillsbury Company Made in Taiwan," 1-3/4" w x 7-3/4" h..............**$25**

Courtesy of Martin Auction Co., martinauctionco.com

Gibson House Wares ceramic John Deer tractor cookie jar, paper label on bottom "John Deere Licensed Product," 12" l x 8" h x 7" w. **$40**

Courtesy of Desert West Auction, desertwestauction.com

COUNTRY STORE

FEW CATEGORIES OF FINE COLLECTIBLES are as fun and colorful as country store memorabilia. The staple of quality antiques shows and shops nationwide, the phrase often refers to such an expansive field of items that it's often difficult to decide where "country store collectibles" begin and "advertising collectibles" end. However, that's one of the very reasons why the category remains so popular and one of the two reasons why this market is growing in value and appeal.

Country store collectibles are associated with items in use in general or frontier retail establishments dating from the mid-1800s and well into the 1940s. The country store was a natural evolution of the pioneer trading post as the more affordable source of day-to-day living items, baking and cooking supplies, or goods for general household and home garden use. Country store furniture is rare, but larger pieces usually include retail countertops and dry goods bins.

The appeal of country store memorabilia has never really waned during the last 40 years; however, the emergence of online trading in the late 1990s redefined items dealers once described as rare. Much like how mid-20th century rock and roll and entertainment memorabilia is used to decorate Applebee's Bar and Grill restaurants, so have country store collectibles been used to line the walls of Cracker Barrel Restaurant and Old Country Store establishments to evoke big appetites for comfort food.

Honest Scrap store tin display bin, great graphics showing a dog and a cat going after a pack of Honest Scrap tobacco, some light scrapes and rubs showing, excellent condition, 18" l. **$2,337**

Courtesy of Morphy Auctions, morphyauctions.com

Among items in high demand are original and complete store displays in top condition. These displays were originally intended to hold the product sold to customers and were not generally available for private ownership. Those that survive are highly sought after by collectors for their graphic appeal and their rarity. Until recently, restoration of these items would negatively impact auction prices. However, recent auction results show strong prices for these items if they are rare and retain most of the original graphics.

A great deal of time, talent, and production value was invested in these store displays. Think of them as the Super Bowl commercials of their day. With limited counter space and a captive audience, marketers used every technique and theme available to catch customers' eyes. And here is where the appeal of country store collectibles crosses over so many different categories of collectibles. A fine paper poster advertising DeLaval Cream Separators may appeal to those who collect farming items, cows, and country maidens in addition to country store items. The same principal applies to store displays. Are they collected as country store items or as well-preserved examples of vintage advertising, or both?

This category was extremely popular between the late 1970s and the mid-1990s. It appears the hobby is reaching a point at which longtime collectors are ready to begin a new phase of their lives — one that requires fewer items and less space — and are offering these collections for the first time in decades. So if the old adage, "The best time to buy an antique is when you see it" is true, the country store collectibles category stands grow as these large collections come to market and the crossover appeal catches the attention of a wide variety of collectors.

VISIT WWW.ANTIQUETRADER.COM

WWW.FACEBOOK.COM/ANTIQUETRADER

Painted French country store bin with drawers, 52-1/4" h, 88-3/4" l, 15" w........................ **$500**

Courtesy of Bright Star Antiques Co., brightstarantiques.com

Early country store glass display case, has a period Beeman's Pepsin Gum decal on the top right corner, most likely this was used to display food, two mesh sections on the back for ventilation, wood has moderate wear with soiling and scrapes, 35" x 27-1/2" x 23"................. **$122**

Courtesy of Morphy Auctions, morphyauctions.com

Country store curved glass display cabinet by J.Riswig of Chicago, mirrored back door and the glass is all intact, excellent condition, 18-1/2" x 9"... **$584**

Courtesy of Morphy Auctions, morphyauctions.com

▶ Country store paper cutter and bread holder, both with "Miss Sunbeam" advertising, wax paper dated 1944, excellent condition, 23" w.............**$150**

Courtesy of Rich Penn Auctions, richpennauctions.com

▼ Planter's Peanut counter top advertising jar, circa 1930, 9-3/4" x 9".................................. **$110**

Courtesy of Soulis Auctions, dirksoulisauctions.com

Lot of four old store stock unused fruit jar rings and Scott's Emulsion, fruit jar brands are Relio, American and Minneopa, soiling with some edge wear and scrapes; unused bottle of Scott's Emulsion is still in its original packing from 1921, excellent condition with minor wear to the bottom of the packaging. Largest box is 9-1/2" x 5-1/4" x 6-1/2"..... **$242**

Courtesy of Morphy Auctions, morphyauctions.com

Country store butcher block, has tag on the bottom: "John Boos & Co.," 34" h x 24" x 20". **$450**

Courtesy of Bright Star Antiques Co., brightstarantiques.com

▼ Vintage pine/oak country store cabinet, WC Heller & Co., Montpelier, Ohio, USA, 81-1/2" h, 94" w. **$550**

Courtesy of William J. Jenack Auctioneers, jenack.com

Country store Diamond Dyes cabinet, "Mansion" or "Children Skipping Rope," c. 1910-1914, Wells & Richardson Co., birch with tin litho front and back panels, 24-1/4" h x 15" w x 9" d.... **$500**

Courtesy of Rich Penn Auctions, richpennauctions.com

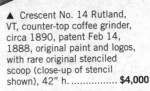

◄ "King Bee Coffee" coffee bin, "Canby, Ach & Canby, Dayton, O," softwood painted red with black stenciled lettering, hinged slant lid with molded edge, 26" h x 17-1/2" w x 13" d.............. **$550**

Courtesy of Conestoga Auction Company Division of Hess Auction Group, hessauctiongroup.com

▲ Crescent No. 14 Rutland, VT, counter-top coffee grinder, circa 1890, patent Feb 14, 1888, original paint and logos, with rare original stenciled scoop (close-up of stencil shown), 42" h. **$4,000**

Courtesy of Duane Merrill & Co, merrillsauction.com

Antique country store oak pie safe, marked on the bottom: "Wm Freihofer 99," very good with minor wear, 32" h x 22-1/2" square. **$200**

Courtesy of Conestoga Auction Company Division of Hess Auction Group, hessauctiongroup.com

Flower seed box, "Rice's Popular Flower Seeds Are the Best," quarter-sawn oak dovetailed box with pretty girl and flowers paper litho, VG+ condition, 4" h x 11" w x 8" d........................ **$125**

Courtesy of Rich Penn Auctions, richpennauctions.com

Three colorful country store counter top string holders, cast iron, all original paint, 7" h. **$300**

Courtesy of Bertoia Auctions, bertoiaauctions.com

Country store cast iron tape dispenser with scrollwork, attributed to Counterboy, Shelton, Connecticut, 24" x 11-1/2"......................... **$60**

Courtesy of Cordier Auctions & Appraisals, cordierauction.com

Tooley's Mercantile delivery wagon box, noted piece of Americana that has not come up for auction before, came out of the basement of the original general store in Danville, Pa. owned by John F. Tooley. This box was used to deliver groceries, dry goods and other smaller items to surrounding stores in the mid- to late 1800s, has wonderful hand-drawn advertisements for coffee, groceries and flour on all four sides, vibrant colors, 63" x 28" x 34 -1/2"....... **$6,000**

Courtesy of Morphy Auctions, morphyauctions.com

DISNEY COLLECTIBLES

COLLECTIBLES THAT FEATURE Mickey Mouse, Donald Duck, and other famous characters of cartoon icon Walt Disney are everywhere. They can be found with little effort at flea markets, garage sales, local antiques, and toys shows, and online as well as through auction houses and specialty catalogs.

Of Disney toys, comics, posters, and other items produced from the 1930s through the 1960s, prewar Disney material is by far the most desirable.

Mary Blair concept painting from *Alice in Wonderland*, Walt Disney Studios, 1951, rare, shows Alice beneath a hovering jellyfish during an underwater sequence, perhaps a precursor to the memorable "oyster" sequence in the final film. In addition to the central subjects, the artwork portrays a dazzling seascape in green and purple, fine condition, accomplished in tempera on 10" x 9-1/4 artist's board. **$6,624**

Courtesy of RR Auction, rrauction.com

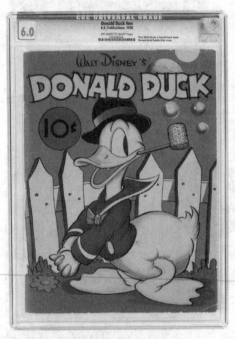

First Donald Duck/Walt Disney comic, *Donald Duck* #NN, 1938, CGC 6.0 Fine, K.K. Publications/Whitman. This is not only the first Donald Duck comic book, but the first Walt Disney comic book. Classic cover art, front features Donald with bubble pipe, back image is of him as an angel, off-white to white pages, cardboard cover, 80 pages in black and white featuring Sunday strip reprints from 1936-1937, including the first strips with Donald's nephews Huey, Dewey and Louie, scarce in this grade, same format as "Feature Books," 8-1/2" x 11-1/4". **$7,150**

Courtesy of Hake's Americana & Collectibles, hakes.com

▶ Disney RCA Victor 45 record player with Disney decals, turns on but doesn't spin, 10-1/2" x 8" x 9". **$60**

Courtesy of Echoes Antiques & Auction Gallery, Inc., echoesauctions.net

VISIT WWW.ANTIQUETRADER.COM

WWW.FACEBOOK.COM/ANTIQUETRADER

Pelham Disney store display puppets, oversized versions, include Mickey Mouse, Pluto, Donald Duck, and Goofy, Mickey has damage to one hand, overall very good to excellent condition, Goofy is 36" h. **$950**

Courtesy of Pook & Pook, Inc. with Noel Barrett, pookandpook.com

Davy Crockett Board Game, 1960s. **$16**

Courtesy of Pioneer Auction Gallery, pioneerantiqueauction.com

Painted wood adult Pinocchio chair, the ends with figural silhouette cutouts painted by a Disney artist in the 1960s, excellent condition, 48" h, 30" d. **$100**

Courtesy of Pook & Pook, Inc. with Noel Barrett, pookandpook.com

Walt Disney autograph in exhibit-quality framed presentation with vintage photographs at Disneyland, special piece acquired from a fan visiting Disneyland in the early 1960s. Walt Disney would occasionally eat inside the Red Wagon Inn, and accommodate kids and adults by signing autographs until a large crowd gathered. The three vintage black and white photographs are of Walt Disney at Disneyland, along with an information plaque about the piece, approx. 24-3/4" x 25-3/4". **$3,000**

Courtesy of GWS Auctions Inc., gwsauctions.com

Six Walt Disney serigraph animation cels featuring Dumbo with friend, Donald Duck golfing, Mickey with Pluto, Goofy golfing, Goofy fishing, and Goofy playing tennis, no COAs, all matted and framed, all approximately 21-1/2" x 19". **$175**

Courtesy of A-1 Auction, a1auctiongallery.com

Gumball machine with 1938 Disney decal, coin operated, made by Hamilton Products of Kansas City, Missouri, the iron base with graniteware enamel coating of green, the glass globe with Mickey Mouse and His Pals decal, copyrighted and dated 1938, text on the decal reads, "Manufactured by Hamilton Enterprises, Inc. Kansas City, Missouri" and "(c) 1938 Walt Disney Enterprises," very good condition, 15" x 7-1/2". **$700**

Courtesy of Soulis Auctions, dirksoulisauctions.com

Peter Pan TV advertising display sign, original prototype, folded pop-out, unmarked but for Admiral TV, which issued *Peter Pan* premiums including a series of cardboard countertop advertising standees. Sign prototype features all original art with exception of TV set (with cowboy image), rest is done in mixed media depicting Neverland at lower left and attached, three-dimensional image of the Lost Boys on cloud beside Tinker Bell, who is part of central pop-up display, which is dominated by large image of Michael flying in his trademark top hat. Bottom right has hand-lettered/painted "Look At The Picture" text, Fine/VF overall, from the archives of premium creators Sam & Gordon Gold, comes with letter of authenticity, 15" x 22-1/8", 18-3/4" h with pop-up display portion. **$990**

Courtesy of Hake's Americana & Collectibles, hakes.com

WALT DISNEY

December 12, 1963.

Dear Peter -

Your father brought me your letter this morning and I am happy to know that you watch our program every Sunday and that you also enjoy our pictures in the theatres.

MARY POPPINS is now being finished and should be ready for the theatres during the Fall of 1964. I hope you will see it because we think it is the best live action picture we have ever made.

I hope you enjoy THE SWORD IN THE STONE when you go to see it. This is all animation and is filled with interesting characters -- we're all very fond of this picture.

I hope you and your family have a very Merry Christmas and a Happy New Year.

Sincerely,

Master Peter Detmold,
5344 Golden Gate Avenue,
Oakland 18, California.

WD:DV

P.S. - I just thought you might like to have one of my autographed pictures with some of my many pets.
                                        W. D.

Walt Disney typed letter, signed TLS, one page, personal letterhead, December 12, 1963, letter to Peter Detmold, in full: "Your father brought me your letter this morning and I am happy to know that you watch our program every Sunday and that you also enjoy our pictures in the theatres. *Mary Poppins* is now being finished and should be ready for the theatres during the Fall of 1964. I hope you will see it because we think it is the best live action picture we have ever made. I hope you enjoy *The Sword in the Stone* when you go to see it. This is all animation and is filled with interesting characters--we're all very fond of this picture. I hope you and your family have a very Merry Christmas and Happy New Year." In fine condition, 7-1/4" x 10-1/2", accompanied by the original Walt Disney Productions mailing envelope. **$3,661**

Courtesy of RR Auction, rrauction.com

Original hand-drawn storyboard of circus elephant Mrs. Jumbo and her pride and joy, young Dumbo, Walt Disney, 1941, art is in nicely detailed graphite on paper, noted as SC 11 in the lower left, Very Good condition, images are 3-1/4" and 1-1/2", matted with an opening size of 7" x 5-1/4" and framed with Plexiglas for an overall size of 14" x 12-1/2"...$3,585

Courtesy of Heritage Auctions, ha.com

Classic "Mickey Mouse Walker" celluloid wind-up toy, built-in key on back and long wire metal tail, raised "Made In Japan" text on Mickey's back along with Disney copyright, 1930s, Mickey is designed with arms jointed at shoulders and attached by elastic string, toy works and his legs move back and forth rapidly as his body rambles about; when stationary, his tail serves as a prop to keep him upright for display, excellent overall condition, 7-1/4" h. **$399**

Courtesy of Hake's Americana & Collectibles, hakes.com

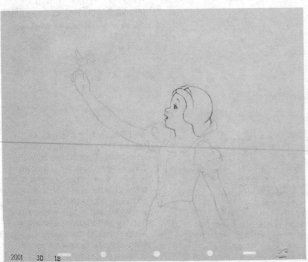

Original graphite and red pencil drawing of Snow White with a bird on her finger for the 1937 Walt Disney movie production, on artist paper, stamped production lower left, singed lower right and number 2, label bearing the signature of lead animator Shamus Calhane and COA on back of frame, 9-1/2" x 11-1/2", framed and matted 17-3/4" x 15-3/4"... **$300**

Courtesy of Burchard Galleries Inc., burchardgalleries.com

▶ Dopey La Mode Studios lamp and original matching shade, incised "Dopey" name on front of base with incised 1938 Walt Disney Enterprises copyright on back of base and original felt covering on underside, lamp has original power cord and plug, lamp works, by Doris Lamp Shade Co., shade depicts Dopey hiccupping bubbles, fine overall condition, scarce with correct matching shade, lamp is 7" h (9-1/4" to top of original socket), shade is 5-3/4". **$376**

Courtesy of Hake's Americana & Collectibles, hakes.com

DOORSTOPS

DOORSTOPS HAVE BEEN AROUND as long as there have been doors. They were originally improvised from garden stones, wedges of wood, pieces of furniture, or any other objects heavy enough to prop doors open to ensure air circulation. Early decorative ones, which date from the late 1700s, were generally round and made of sand-cast brass or metal with flat, hollow backs.

By the early 19th century, scores of French and English households boasted fashionable three-dimensional iron doorstops in the shape of animals, flowers, and figurines. Some, called door porters, incorporated convenient long handles that were used to lift and place them easily.

Homes with French double doors often featured matching pairs, like matching eagles or horse hooves, Punch and Judy, or lions opposing unicorns. Today these sets range from $400-$900 each, depending on condition and themes.

Doorstops migrated to American shores after the Civil War, where due to Yankee frugality, they became smaller and lighter than European models.

During the height of their popularity — the 1920s through the mid-1940s — American homemakers could purchase doorstops, or coordinated sets that included doorknockers and bookends, for pennies in gift stores and through mail-order catalogs. Fashionable Art Deco, circus, and nursery rhyme themes, along with figures like organ grinders, dapper gentlemen, Southern belles and flappers, reflected the times.

Cheery flower and flower-basket doorstops featuring bouquets of tulips, zinnias, pansies, black-eyed Susans or sunflowers, for example, celebrated the arrival of spring. Although some currently start at around $100 apiece, those that have survived with original paint in prime condition may fetch many times that amount.

Hubley's dog breed doorstops, which portray lifelike, highly detailed Doberman pinschers, German shepherds, cocker spaniels, French bulldogs, beagles, and various types of terriers, and more, were also extremely popular. So were arched, curled, springing, or sleeping cats.

Heron doorstop, B & H, beautiful casting and great depiction of wetland Heron sitting amongst foliage, 14 1/8" h...................................... **$9,500**

Courtesy of Bertoia Auctions, bertoiaauctions.com

John and Nancy Smith, avid collectors and leading doorstop and figural cast iron authorities, as well as authors of *The Doorstop Book: An Encyclopedia of Doorstop Collecting*, find that beginners generally concentrate on certain themes like flowers, animals, people, or wildlife. Some seek doorstops produced by a particular foundry, including Albany, National, Eastern

Grooming black and white cat on black base, nicely posed with double wedge back, rare and great design, marked, "Sculptured - Metal - Studios," 11" h.. **$8,000**

Courtesy of Bertoia Auctions, bertoiaauctions.com

Specialty, Judd, Wilton, Litto, Virginia Metalcrafters, Waverly, or Spencer.

As their collections grow, however, many explore other themes as well. Nautical enthusiasts may collect clipper ship, sailor, lighthouse, and anchor doorstops. Sports fans may seek skiers, golfers, caddies, or football players. Animal lovers may populate menageries with Hubley honey bears and horses or Bradley & Hubbard parrots. Some prefer pets portrayed in character, like rabbits in evening dress, Peter Rabbits chomping on carrots, and strutting ducks in tophats. These fancies currently sell from $300-$2,000.

Other collectors search for bright, sassy, desirable, and pricey Anne Fish Art Deco pieces like bathing beauties, Charleston dancers, and parrot, or Taylor Cook's brightly colored elephant on barrels, koalas, or fawns.

Doorstops that feature outstanding sculptural quality, form, and character are the most desirable of all. If they also bear identifying stamps, signatures, copyrights, studio names or production numbers (which often appear on their backs), their values rise even further.

In addition to desirability, rarity — possibly due to high production costs, short foundry existence, or even bad design — raises the value of vintage doorstops. Condition, however, determines their ultimate worth. Collectors should certainly buy doorstops that they like within a price range that they find comfortable. But they should be in the very best condition that they can afford. According to experts, only these will retain or increase in value over time. And some may increase considerably.

Today, for example, a rare, unusual, desirable doorstop that is also in mint condition – perhaps a vintage Uncle Sam, Halloween Girl, or Whistling Jim, may command as much as $10,000.

Because doorstops are cast objects, they lend themselves to reproduction, caution the Smiths. In addition to reuse of old molds, new designs are continually in production. "Older doorstops usually have smoother, more refined castings than reproductions, which are rougher or pebbly. Seams, if any, are usually tighter. Originals feature slotted screws or rivets, while reproductions, if cast in two or more pieces, are usually assembled with Philips-head screws. Moreover, artists generally painstakingly smoothed mold marks of vintage castings with hand files. Reproductions, however, are finished in minutes with power tools and tumblers. These leave coarser grinding marks," they said.

Collectors should also look carefully at the wear patterns on possible buys. Most old doorstops were used for their original purpose —holding doors open. So potential buyers are advised to look for wear in the logical places: on their tops, where they were handled, and around their bases, where they were scuffed along the floor. Reproductions rarely resemble the real thing.

Doorstops are readily found at antiques shows, shops, and auctions. It is recommended, however, to purchase them from reputable dealers who not only specialize in cast iron items, but also guarantee their authenticity.

— Melody Amsel-Arieli

Cast iron dog doorstop,
15-3/4" h x 10" w x 4" d......**$70**

*Courtesy of Westport Auction,
westportauction.com*

Cast iron painted doorstop by
Hubley of Peter Rabbit eating a
carrot, American, 9-1/4" h. . **$100**

*Courtesy of Cowan's Auctions, Inc.,
cowanauctions.com*

Advertising doorstop in shape
of milk bottle, Lake to Lake,
Sheboygan, WI. **$350**

Courtesy of Bertoia Auctions, bertoiaauctions.com

Rare koala bear cast iron doorstop, c. 1930, vibrant original
polychrome paint, half round hollow casting on integral log base,
backside marked "No 5. TAYLOR COOK 1930 C (opyright)," ref:
The Doorstop Book, Smith, P. 173, excellent untouched original
condition, 5-7/8" h x 7-3/4" w x 2" d.. **$340**

Courtesy of Jasper52, jasper52.com

Heavy brass eagle doorstop,
Tiffany and Co., cast by
Griffoul, of Newark, N.J.,
stamped "M. Peinlich Sc."
en verso, excellent condition,
7-1/2" h. **$514**

Courtesy of Heritage Auctions, ha.com

Cast iron whale with tail turned up, circa 1930s, very good condition, 7-1/4" h x 12-5/8" l x 3-1/2" w. **$360**

Courtesy of Jasper52, jasper52.com

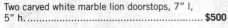

Two carved white marble lion doorstops, 7" l, 5" h. **$500**

Courtesy of William Bunch Auctions & Appraisals, bunchauctions.com

Large cast iron doorstop in full sails, circa 1920s, excellent condition, 9-7/8" h x 7-5/8" w. **$280**

Courtesy of Jasper52, jasper52.com

A.M. Greenblatt Studios cast iron ship, black paint, 12" x 8-1/2" **$100**

Courtesy of John McInnis Auctioneers, mcinnisauctions.com

Lighthouse, all original condition, 8" x 7". **$475**

Courtesy of Bertoia Auctions, bertoiaauctions.com

top lot!

An extremely rare and iconic doorstop sold at a March 2018 auction for a whopping $47,200 (including 18 percent buyer's premium). The important and exceptional multi-glazed redware doorstop, attributed to J. Eberly & Co., Strasburg, VA, circa 1890, is a molded figure of a sleeping lamb with well-detailed fleece coat, pierced nostrils, and incised mouth, the body dipped in cream-colored slip, heavily-decorated with streaks of copper and manganese, covered in a clear lead glaze, nice condition with strong luster to surface and some typical wear to glaze, 11-3/4" l. This particular lamb doorstop gained legendary status in 2002 when it set an auction record of $58,000 for an example of Shenandoah Valley multi-glazed redware at Green Valley Auctions in Mt. Crawford, Virginia. To date, this doorstop belongs to a small, coveted group of documented examples of this form and glaze, this example being among the best in terms of color and condition. Most Shenandoah Valley pottery pieces of this quality are held in museums or long-term private collections.

Noteworthy for their charming figural form and substantial size, the Eberly lamb has become an iconic image among collectors and scholars of Southern folk pottery. An 1888 J. Eberly & Co. price list, illustrated on P. 260 of H.E. Comstock's *The Pottery of the Shenandoah Valley*, lists "Lambs for Door Stops, per dozen, 3.00." This price most likely refers to the pottery's standardly produced, slip-coated lambs, as the word "fancy," used to denote Eberly's multi-glazed redware, is not mentioned.

Large cast iron floral doorstop, featuring a cluster of spring garden flowers in a handled wicker-style basket, 11-1/4" x 10". **$150**

Courtesy of Leland Little Auctions, lelandlittle.com

Man sitting on cotton bale, partial repaint on shirt, full figured, 9-1/8" x 7"........................ **$350**

Courtesy of Bertoia Auctions, bertoiaauctions.com

"The Patrol" doorstop, figure of a man, all original condition, solid casting, 8-3/4" x 3-3/8".
.... **$350**

Courtesy of Bertoia Auctions, bertoiaauctions.com

English figural Fox head doorstop riding crop above the fox head, 18" h. **$100**

Courtesy of Richard D. Hatch & Associates, richardhatchauctions.com

ENTERTAINMENT

ENTERTAINMENT AND MOVIE PROPS are big business in Hollywood, and studios are doing a better job at controlling their props from big-budget films. Props are now being sold by studios themselves or through small companies owned by the studio. It has turned the entertainment collecting world on its head as quality material gets more difficult to find for traditional brick and mortar dealers and auctioneers.

For the past four years, the Prop Store in London has had the Entertainment Memorabilia Live Auction. The latest event, in September 2017, was expected to raise more than $2 million, but collectors from around the world who gathered at this auction, pushed that amount to $5.13 million over 10 hours of intensive bidding. The sale featured 600 lots of original props, costumes, and production material from 200 films and television shows.

The top lot was the iconic Hero Helmet Chris Pratt wore as Peter "Star-Lord" Quill in *Guardians of the Galaxy* that sold for $181,170. Other top-selling items included a C-3PO special effects head from *Star Wars: The Empire Strikes Back* that went for $98,461, the jacket that Jack Nicholson wore as Jack Torrance in *The Shining*, which also went for $98,461, and the Alien creature costume from *Aliens* and Jules Winnfield's (Samuel L. Jackson) "Bad Mother F**ker" wallet from *Pulp Fiction* that each sold for $82,051. Other highlights were Indiana Jones' bullwhip from *Indiana Jones and the Last Crusade*, which sold for $106,666, the flight suit worn by Tom Cruise as Pete "Maverick" Mitchell in *Top Gun*, $61,538; the jumpsuit of Dr. Peter Venkman (Bill Murray) from *Ghostbusters*, $57,435; and another Jack Nicholson item: The Joker costume he wore in *Batman*, $53,333.

Prop Store sells original movie props and costumes and related memorabilia, regularly

One of the highlights of the Prop Store's Hollywood auction was this costume Jack Nicholson wore as The Joker in *Batman*, which sold for **$53,333**.

Courtesy of Prop Store, propstore.com

Another auction highlight was this pair of light-up Nikes worn by Michael J. Fox as Marty McFly in *Back to the Future II* that were snapped up for **$41,025**.

Courtesy of Prop Store, propstore.com

hosting live and online prop and costume auctions. Over 7,500 other items are also available for sale at propstore.com.

According to Julien's Auctions, one of the world's largest auctioneers of entertainment and film props, the market has been growing steadily for the last three decades. "In the past 35 years, the Entertainment Memorabilia auction market has gradually emerged to become an important and unequivocal collecting category," according to the company.

Collectors can pinpoint the exact year entertainment prop collecting became a mainstream collecting category. The seminal MGM Studios auction in 1970 was a watershed moment for film scholars and the auction business, which essentiality created a new market for an area of collecting that previously only existed among a few film enthusiasts. The studio's objective was to simply consolidate space on an already overcrowded lot by creating a three-day film memorabilia auction to clear seven soundstages. A vast assortment of costumes, film props, and related property from the studios beginnings dating from the 1920s were cataloged, tagged, and placed on the auction block.

Highlights recall the full size sailing ship from *Mutiny on the Bounty* (1935), Elizabeth Taylor's wedding gown worn in *Father of the Bride* (1950), Clark Gable's trench coat worn in several films, a group of swimsuits worn by Esther Williams and Johnny Weissmuller's loin cloth worn in *Tarzan* films of the 1940s. However, the most coveted pieces sold were from *The Wizard of Oz* (1939), which included a pair of ruby red slippers worn by Judy Garland that hammered on the auction block for $15,000 ($94,252 in today's dollars).

"With the auction's blockbuster success, film enthusiasts and collectors soon recognized film memorabilia as a fertile and profitable area of collecting. In the following years, small boutique shops, specialty companies, and private brokering businesses began to crop up and thrive selling recognized film props and screen-seen objects," according to Julien.

Since then, studios have recognized and embraced this booming market on their own, and this trend shows the market for film and TV gems is strong and will continue to grow.

Original screen-used movie prop ship from the classic black-and-white silent film, *Ben Hur: A Tale of the Christ* (Metro-Goldwyn-Mayer, 1925). This is one of the original ships used in the classic sea battle scene between the Romans and Macedonians. No expense was spared building these props for Fred Niblo. The battle scene was filmed in a small pool, and the boat was repurposed for the *Ben Hur* remake (Metro-Goldwyn-Mayer, 1959) starring Charleston Heston. The ship is made of copper and aluminum, highly detailed, front of the vessel has a figural ram's head, lattic rail runs along both sides of the hull, boat has been outfitted with sails, oars, anchors, and people. Most of these ships were destroyed during the battle scenes and left as partial hulls, but this is one of the few that survived intact with all the highlights and details still on it. This ship comes with a letter of authenticity, 6' l. **$7,000**

Courtesy of Milestone Auctions, milestoneauctions.com

Spades playing card prop from the production of the classic 1979 war movie, *Apocalypse Now* (United Artists, 1979), featuring the emblem of the First Air Cavalry Division with Colonel Kilgore's helicopter motto, "Death From Above," over a green-and-white lightning bolt design. In the film, Kilgore, played by Robert Duvall, marks the bodies of enemies by throwing these "death cards." The card is initialed "AT" by Alex Tavoularis, who worked in the film's art department. Housed in an acrylic display, fine condition, accompanied by a letter of provenance from Alex Tavoularis, 2-1/4" x 3-1/2. ..**$393**

Courtesy of RR Auction, rrauction.com

A Marilyn Monroe outdoor thermometer, circa 1970s, oblong, tin, depicting the star from *The Seven Year Itch*, (20th Century Fox, 1955) though text reads "Some / Like / It / Hot!," further text on the lower margin reads "Nostalgia Lane, Inc. New York, New York," 38" x 8". **$600**

Courtesy of Heritage Auctions, ha.com

Red lifeguard swimsuit of *Baywatch*'s Jordan Tate (Tracy Bingham), with a "Baywatch Lifeguard" patch. **$450**

Courtesy of Premiere Props, premiereprops.com

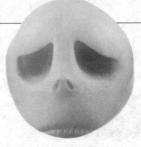

Extremely rare screen-used "Jack Skellington" animation heads used in the making of Tim Burtons' stop-motion animated musical film, *The Nightmare Before Christmas* (Touchstone, 1993). From the private collection of a cast member who worked on this film, there is a screw-in base on bottom of two and each one is just under 2"... **$5,019**

Courtesy of Heritage Auctions, ha.com

Mars Attacks! (Warner Bros., 1996) screen-used, life-size Martian Ambassador stand-in prop, from Warner Bros. archives, 48" x 12". **$1,500**

Prop courtesy of Premiere Props, premiereprops.com; movie still courtesy of Warner Bros.

Original title cards from the Tyrone Power western, *Pony Soldier* (20th Century Fox, 1953). Three total, all actual pieces of cowhide, organically cut around the margins, each hand-lettered with the film's opening credits, painted with Native American images, seen in the opening title sequence of the movie, each one approx. 20" x 30"............................**$312**

Courtesy of Heritage Auctions, ha.com

top lot!

Chris Pratt's Hero Helmet from *Guardians of the Galaxy* (Walt Disney Studios Motion Pictures/Marvel Studios, 2014) was the top lot at the Prop Store's annual Entertainment Memorabilia Live Auction, selling for $181,170. In the movie and its sequel, *Guardians of the Galaxy Vol. 2* (Walt Disney Studios Motion Pictures/Marvel Studios, 2017), Pratt plays Peter Quill/Star Lord, the half-human, half-alien leader of the Guardians, a band of misfits. The first movie was the highest-grossing film of 2014 in North America, earning $773 million at the Box Office; *Vol 2* has earned over $863 million, according to boxofficemojo.com.

Helmet photo courtesy of Prop Store, propstore.com; *Guardians of the Galaxy* movie still courtesy of Walt Disney Studios Motion Pictures/Marvel Studios.

Prop headstone from *Rocky Balboa* (aka *Rocky VI*; Metro-Goldwyn-Mayer, 2006). Lightweight (approximately 31 pounds), faux gray-colored stone reading "Adrian / Balboa / March 10, 1950 / January 11, 2002," mounted on a rectangular base; included with two black-and-white framed photographs showing Sylvester Stallone as Rocky Balboa in the graveyard scene where the headstone was used; actor who played Rocky's son in the film, Milo Ventimiglia, shot these photographs while on set, consigned directly by Stallone himself. Headstone: 28" x 30" x 6", photographs framed: 17" x 28". **$1,375**

Courtesy of Heritage Auctions, ha.com

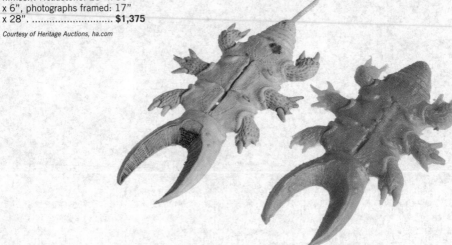

Star Trek: The Next Generation screen-used parasite props from the episode, "Conspiracy" (1988), season 1. Designed by senior illustrator Rick Sternbach, these could be seen streaming from a character's chest cavity after a larger creature bursts forth in the episode's climax. Crafted of latex, approx. 7". **$2,000**

Courtesy of Heritage Auctions, ha.com

Casino Royale (MGM, 2006) screen-used prop of a $500,000 casino plaque. These chip plaques were made uniquely for the poker scenes where James Bond 007 (Daniel Craig) beats Le Chiffre (Mads Mikkelsen) culminating in one final pot of $115 million, at a high-stakes tournament at the Hotel Splendide's Casino Royale's Salle Privé. BG-modified "nacre"-style plaques, this ultra-high-value plaque is pearlescent red with translucent black and gold, text "Casino Royale Montenegro" in black and gold, value of $500,000 printed on both sides of the chip, "Montenegro" and the BG logo and design plate appear printed in gold, also appears on both sides of this plaque. Very scarce to find, near mint+, 3" x 4-1/4" x 1/8"........ **$3,107**

Courtesy of Heritage Auctions, ha.com

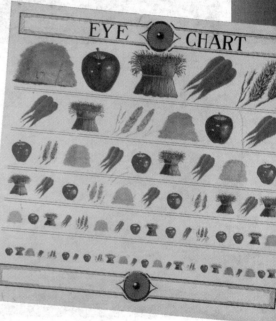

Deadpool (20th Century Fox, 2016) Wade (Ryan Reynolds) production-made test white Deadpool mask on Reynolds face cast (latex foam), 10" x 8"... **$600**

Courtesy of Premiere Props, premiereprops.com

Horse eye chart related to *Doctor Dolittle* (20th Century Fox, 1967), hand-painted in oil on illustration board, text on top margin reads "Eye Chart," funny images that repeat in six rows depict a haystack, apple, barley, and carrots, almost identical to the one used in the scene where Rex Harrison as the title character tests a horse for eye glasses; this one was likely used for publicity photographs or for a movie theater display, as it is slightly different from the one seen in the film, but it did originate from Fox via a former employee, 38" x 38". **$1,875**

Courtesy of Heritage Auctions, ha.com

A Bette Davis prop oil painting from *Mr. Skeffington* (Warner Bros., 1944). Rendered on canvas, depicting a beautiful and idealized portrait of the star as Fanny Trellis Skeffington, housed in an ornate gilt-painted wooden frame. Both Davis and Rains were nominated for Oscars in this sentimental tearjerker – her for Best Actress in a Leading Role and him for Best Actor in a Supporting Role. Framed: 44" x 34", painting only 36" x 24".. **$13,750**

Courtesy of Heritage Auctions, ha.com

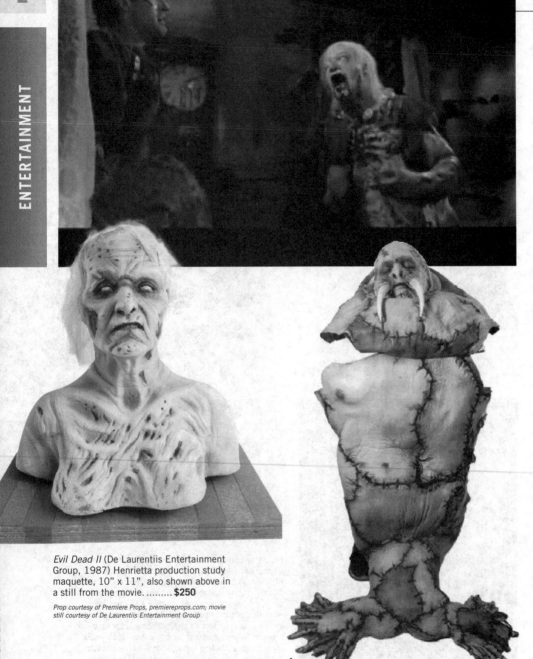

Evil Dead II (De Laurentiis Entertainment Group, 1987) Henrietta production study maquette, 10" x 11", also shown above in a still from the movie. **$250**

Prop courtesy of Premiere Props, premiereprops.com; movie still courtesy of De Laurentiis Entertainment Group

Tusk (A24, 2014) custom-made special effects rubber walrus body suit of Wallace Bryton (Justin Long), with head and face made to resemble a walrusized version of the character. Includes wearable shoulders and headpiece with whiskers and tusks, full lower body with raised stitching, and half human, half walrus webfeet, also includes extra "walrus skin" wrap..**$1,500**

Courtesy of Premiere Props, premiereprops.com

Cannon prop from *20,000 Leagues Under the Sea* (Walt Disney, 1954). This is a rare prop cannon from the movie, from long time Disney artist and producer Joe Hale. The cannons were mounted on the scale model of the ship that fought Captain Nemo's submarine, and in the movie, the cannons were actually fired by a powder charge that was set off electrically. The cannon has a cast iron barrel on a custom-made carriage, from the Joe Hale Archives, 7" x 3".
....**$1,016**

Courtesy of Heritage Auctions, ha.com

Star Trek: Deep Space Nine Sword of Kahless display prop designed by visual effects supervisor Dan Curry (1995), made of steel, with Klingon writing engraved into the two protruding side blades, Klingon insignia cut into the center, and handle wrapped in stripes of brown leather. Originally designed by Curry for the 81st episode of *Star Trek: Deep Space Nine*, this prop was crafted by master knife maker Gil Hibben (known for the Rambo knife), who was contracted by Paramount Pictures to fabricate a display piece for the MGM Grand "Star Trek Experience." Only two were made: one for the exhibit, and this one for the personal collection of Curry, who designed the original sword prop used in the television series. Includes an 8-1/2" x 11" photocopy of Curry's original concept sketch, measures a massive 59-3/4" x 16". **$50,000**

Courtesy of Heritage Auctions, ha.com

Star Trek: The Next Generation screen-used skeleton prop from the episode, "Loud as a Whisper" (1989), season 2. This Johns Hopkins functional model of the human skeleton with hanging display was used to show Riva's chorus being incinerated. Painted by visual effects supervisor Dan Curry with a bloody-ash color scheme to resemble residual burnt soft tissue, the skeleton is approximately 19", with the display measuring 22" x 8" x 6". **$1,062**

Courtesy of Heritage Auctions, ha.com

ENTERTAINMENT

A watch and pair of glasses from *Scream 3* (Dimension Films, 2000) worn by actress Neve Campbell, who played main character Sydney. Includes a framed photo of Campbell and certificate of authenticity from Premiere Props of California. **$175**

Courtesy of Saco River Auction, sacoriverauction.net

Geena Davis' *Thelma & Louise* (Metro-Goldwyn-Mayer, 1991) slippers, "Dearforms" dirty pink terry slip-ons, with lavender lace trim, bows and buttons, size 9-1/2 to 10-1/2, with wardrobe tag and certificate of authenticity.........................**$110**

Courtesy of GWS Auctions Inc., gwsauctions.com

Cameron Diaz *Gangs of New York* (Miramax, 2002) movie bag prop.
....**$275**

Courtesy of Saco River Auction, sacoriverauction.net

DOORS OF ICONIC HOTEL SELL FOR $400K

FOR OVER A CENTURY, New York City's Chelsea Hotel has been home to some of the most legendary, accomplished, and fascinating people of their time. Bob Dylan, Jackson Pollock, Mark Twain, Janis Joplin, Andy Warhol, Jimi Hendrix, Jack Kerouac — all of these people, and more, were residents and guests of the Chelsea. The hotel's bohemian environment led to wild parties, as well as inspiration for such iconic figures.

After being rescued from demolition by an enterprising former homeless man, 52 doors removed from Chelsea were offered at auction in April by Guernsey's auction house in New York. The door to the room Bob Dylan lived in for a few years was the top lot, selling for $125,000. The auction raised more than $400,000.

Since opening in 1884, the Chelsea Hotel was a refuge for writers, artists, and other entertainers, who would stay days, weeks, or indefinitely. The doors were rescued from the trash in 2012 by Jim Georgiou, who lived at the Chelsea from 2002 to 2011, when he was evicted for failing to pay rent. He moved across the street from the hotel and tried to make a living selling vinyl records. In 2012, Georgiou spotted workers preparing to throw out old doors and managed to recover the 52 with help from friends. After lengthy library research and interviews with neighbors, Georgiou identified 22 of the doors for association with famous residents.

"For me, they were history and beauty and connected to my heart. They're precious because there are so many people who've been through them," Georgiou told *The New York Times*.

Guernsey's said Georgiou pledged half of his proceeds to City Harvest, a nonprofit organization dedicated to feeding the needy.

Some other highlights include the doors of Janis Joplin/Leonard Cohen, $106,250;

Bob Dylan lived in Room 225 between 1968 and 1972 and is reportedly where he conceived his son, Jakob. Though the number plate on this door has been covered with whitewash, the number 225 is visible beneath. Dylan mentions the Chelsea in his song, "Sara," written to his first wife, Sara Lownds: "Staying up for days in the Chelsea hotel/writing 'Sad Eyed Lady of the Lowlands' for you." This door and all of the others are approx. 77' x 31-1/2"..........................**$125,000**

Andy Warhol/Edie Sedgwick, $65,625; Jack Kerouac, $37,500; Madonna/Isabella Rossellini, $16,250; Jimi Hendrix, $16,250; Joni Mitchell, $10,000; Bob Marley, $8,750; Jackson Pollock, $8,750; classical composer and critic Virgil Thomson, $2,000; and an unattributed red door with a striking painted eye, $12,500.

▶ Leonard Cohen lived in #424 the longest of all his stays at the hotel and apparently conducted an affair with singer-songwriter Janis Joplin in this room. Joni Mitchell also stayed in this room with Cohen. **$106,250**

▲ Madonna lived in Room #822 after moving to New York in the early 1980s, and shot photographs for her book, Sex, in the room as well. Shirley Clarke, Academy Award-nominated avant-garde filmmaker, also lived in this room. Clarke invited the Grateful Dead to perform on the roof of the Hotel, until apparently Andy Warhol's negative energies put the kibosh on the show. Isabella Rossellini also spent time in this room, and also appeared in Madonna's Sex book....**$16,250**

▲ American painter and abstract expressionist Jackson Pollock, under the auspices of Peggy Guggenheim, lived in Room 1017 and then moved out and reportedly relocated to this Room, 902, where he stayed briefly. **$8,750**

◀ Edie Sedgwick's room, #105, was used to shoot scenes for Andy Warhol's film, Chelsea Girls, and other of his Factory films. Directed by Warhol, with music by the Velvet Underground, and a budget of $3,000, Chelsea Girls is considered the first successful underground film in the United States. As the title suggests, the film focuses on residents and their lives within the Chelsea. **$65,625**

FARM COLLECTIBLES

THE HOBBY OF COLLECTING FARM TOOLS and other farming items continues to remain bright, with prices still solid.

Collecting farm memorabilia can take you on a long trip down Memory Lane. It is often the gathering of the memories and the search for the items that is more fun than the items themselves. Yes, value is important, but so is history. Farming's long history provides many collecting avenues and categories.

Some of the most popular farm collectibles are advertising items including barometers, thermometers, tape measures, yard sticks, tin signs in every size and shape imaginable, pens, pencils, glasses, kitchen containers, utensils, calendars, display stands, and toys. Values in this area are from a few dollars to thousands. It would be easy to spend a few hundred dollars on just one or two good signs, and a neon sign advertising a local tractor dealership could easily cost more than $1,000. Items of greatest value in general appear to be those that can be easily displayed in your home. This includes any of the tin or porcelain signs that are smaller than 24 inches by 24 inches. The really large signs are much harder to find display space for in the home.

Some kitchen items related to the preparation and preservation of food are not unique to farms, but are of special importance to farm kitchens, given their isolation from "store bought" food in many cases. Most farms had an extensive farm garden for family use, making the preservation of goods important.

Items most used by the farm family include canning items, pie safes, Hoosiers, early refrigerators, small utensils, etc.; and other items of interest around the household and farmstead. Things that immediately come to mind are the old apple corers and cherry pitters used in preservation of those fruits. Related items include the famous blue Ball jars and early tops and jars for preserving food.

Perhaps because of the recent farm-to-table food movement and a growing interest in early Americana, harvest items, like tools and canning jars, have also become popular with collectors.

Massey Harris neon advertising clock with yellow details around the border of the glass, clock face reads "Better-Built Farm Equipment," includes a wood wall-mount shelf measuring 8" h x 18" w x 11" d; clock is 18-1/4" h x 18-1/4" w x 7" d. **$850**

Courtesy of Dan Morphy Auctions, morphyauctions.com

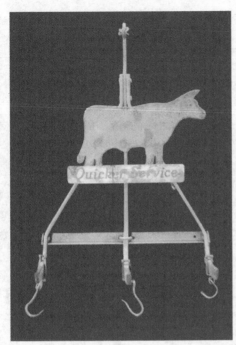

Dairy farm display rack, 34" x 19". **$350**

Courtesy of Bright Star Antiques Co., brightstarantiques.com

▶ Painted architectural farm house door, 81" x 33-1/4". **$225**

Courtesy of Bright Star Antiques Co., brightstarantiques.com

Painted two-piece farm house cupboard, 89" h, 88-1/4" l, 29" w. ...**$425**

Courtesy of Bright Star Antiques Co., brightstarantiques.com

Early Pennsylvania farm house painted dry sink, 33-1/2" h, 72" l, 30" w. **$500**

Courtesy of Bright Star Antiques Co., brightstarantiques.com

Primitive egg crate, made by OWOSSO MFG. CO., Owosso MICH & Benton, Arkansas E.B. Scott written on top, holds 9 dozen eggs, 11-5/8" w x 12-3/4" d x 11" h. **$50**

Courtesy of Long Auction Company, LLC, longauction.com

Original color American World War II Office of War Information poster (No. 59), published in 1943 (1943-0-520467), portraying two farmers with white text, "Work on a farm ... this Summer, Join the U.S. Crop Corps, See Your U.S. Employment Service or Your Local County Agent," 14-1/4" x 20". **$200**

Courtesy of RR Auction, rrauction.com

Mac-Cormick Farm Implement advertising poster, French poster is framed behind glass, original top and bottom metal strips, shows a farmer cutting grass on his Mac-Cormick machine, great illustration with strong colors, Very Good condition; framed dimensions: 37" x 29-1/4". . **$200**

Courtesy of Dan Morphy Auctions, morphyauctions.com

309

Painted wooden trade sign, "MOUNTAIN VIEW FARM/WALPOLE," 42-3/4" x 33". **$425**

Courtesy of Copake Auction, Inc., copakeauction.com

Osborne Farm Implements paper advertising poster, by Hayes Litho Co Buffalo N.Y., original top and bottom metal strips, colors and graphics fantastic, some edge wear, excellent condition, 29-3/4" x 19-3/4". **$1,500**

Courtesy of Dan Morphy Auctions, morphyauctions.com

Double-sided Registered Holstein farm sign, 48" x 39-1/2". **$450**

Courtesy of Bright Star Antiques Co., brightstarantiques.com

Birdsell Farm Wagon Works advertising cardboard sign, professionally framed behind glass, shows active factory scene, nice colors with some areas of soiling, Very Good+ condition; framed dimensions 37-1/4" x 28". **$850**

Courtesy of Dan Morphy Auctions, morphyauctions.com

Oliver Farm Implements porcelain sign with globe graphics, SSP sign, tough to find porcelain signs in the hobby, nice color and gloss, "Property Of Oliver Plows" ink stamped on the backside, 48" w x 14" h. .**$3,750**

Courtesy of Dan Morphy Auctions, morphyauctions.com

John Deere Farm Implements porcelain sign with neon border, SSP sign, great color and gloss, neon border has been added around it but the sign has not been drilled for neon, maker marked "Burdick," 72" w x 24" h x 10" d. **$4,500**

Courtesy of Dan Morphy Auctions, morphyauctions.com

▲ Scrub-top farm table, worn paint base, tapered legs, 51" x 36" x 29-1/2". **$170**

Courtesy of Hartzell's Auction Gallery, Inc., hartzellsauction.com

◄ A 1937 Zeller's Dairy Farm ad with working mercury thermometer, a calendar, and a photo of Kenneth Zeller aged 3-1/2 years, cardboard ad measures 23" x 13". **$30**

Courtesy of Keystone Auction, LLC, auctionsbykeystone.com

American farm table, 19th c., mixed wood, rectangular plank board top, over straight apron with single drawer, rising on tapered legs, joined by H stretcher, approx 28" h, 65-3/4" w, 36" d......**$375**

Courtesy of Austin Auction Gallery, austinauction.com

◄ Two farm tools, a pick and an apple picker, wood handles, apple picker is 62" l. **$20**

Courtesy of Greenwich Auction, greenwichauction.net

► Antique farm table tool to cut tobacco leaves or corn husks, made by Derby, late 19th/early 20th century, wood and cast iron, 36" h. **$30**

Courtesy of Greenwich Auction, greenwichauction.net

▲ Sheffield Farms toy horse-drawn wagon, 22" l. **$250**

Courtesy of Bertoia Auctions, bertoiaauctions.com

◄ Hand-crank cast iron corn sheller. **$50**

Courtesy of Auctions by Adkins, LLC, auctionsbyadkins.com

FINE ART

FINE ART, CREATED for aesthetic purposes and judged by its beauty rather than its utility, includes original painting and sculpture, drawing, watercolor, and graphics. It is appreciated primarily for its imaginative, aesthetic, or intellectual content.

Total global sales of art in 2016 were $45 billion, a 1.7 percent increase on the comparable figure for 2015, according to the 2017 TEFAF Art Market Report by Art Economics.

The report paints a picture of "a stable and resilient market, experiencing positive growth." However, sales are moving away from the auction houses to the private sector, both to private sales by auction houses and to dealers. In 2016, public auction sales of works of art, high-end jewelry, and decorative arts, reached $16.9 billion globally, a drop from $20.8 billion in 2015.

Despite a nearly 19-percent drop by dollar-value of art and antiques sold at auction, prices on an aggregate basis have not fallen as far, and are,

One of the established names collectors clamor for is Andy Warhol (American, 1928-1987). "The Star," original screenprint from artist's "Myths" portfolio, depicts screen legend Greta Garbo as Mata Hari, pencil signed and numbered 4 of 200, 37-7/8" x 37-7/8". **$52,000**

Courtesy of Bruneau & Co., bruneauandco.com

by contrast, down 8.6 percent. The report notes a drop in prices of modern art sold at auction in the U.S. and Europe, while contemporary art prices at auction in those region are about 4 percent higher.

The Asian auction market remained buoyant in 2016, despite that auction sales are down 1.6 percent and China is down 2.6 percent. Asia now accounts for a 40.5 percent share of world auction sales, up from a 31 percent share in 2015. China dominates auction sales with almost 90 percent share, the report said.

Perhaps not surprisingly, art fairs, both global and local, "are the most important point for acquiring new buyers, which is the largest concern of art dealers and galleries reporting to our annual survey," said the report.

Online sales are also a leading driver of fine art sales, which may surprise some, but

Ben Austrian (American, 1870-1921), "Shame on You," 1906, oil on canvas, 25-1/2" x 19-1/2". **$8,000**

Courtesy of Antiques & Modern Auction Gallery, antiquesmodern.com

Andre Brasilier (French, b. 1929), "Cavaliers sous les branches à Fère en Tardenois," 1970, oil on canvas, 38-1/2" x 51". **$78,000**

Courtesy of Shannon's Fine Art Auctioneers, shannons.com

collectors and dealers are comfortable making purchases with only a website between them. This segment is expected to grow a whopping 25 percent per year and is estimated to reach $10 billion in a few years.

Although multi-million dollar auction records tend to capture the most headlines, the market is seeing more art in general sold and at faster rates. Customers are much more selective about what they buy, so as condition sets the market for collectibles, the best examples of an artist's work influences prices. An artist's key works continue to bring the best prices, as collectors remain mindful of both aesthetics and resale.

Collectors are looking for established names including Andy Warhol, Roy Lichtenstein, Jasper Johns, Robert Rauschenberg, and Frank Stella. American artists like Jeff Koons, Jean Michel Basquiat, Christopher Wool, and Richard Prince top the charts. U.K. artists Peter Droig and Damien Hirst are also at the top of the list along with German artist Martin Kippenberg and Chinese artists Zeng Fanzhi, Luo Zhongli, Chen Yifei ,and Zhang Xioagang.

Romero Britto (Brazil, b. 1963), "Untitled," 2000, acrylic on board, signed, commissioned for the 2000 Rock and Roll Hall of Fame induction ceremony, painting was featured on the cover of the program catalog, 31-1/2" x 79-1/4". **$18,750**

Courtesy of Rago Arts and Auction Center, ragoarts.com

Cycladic (one of the three main branches of Aegean art), marble head, c. 2,500 B.C., from the estate of Annette Cravens. **$188,800**

Alexander Calder (American, 1898-1976), "Crayfish," c. 1946, painted red and black sheet metal, 3-3/8" x 2-1/4".............................**$153,400**

Robert Spear Duning (American, 1829-1905), "Fruit on a Tabletop," 1891, oil on canvas, 7" x 10"... **$3,438**

Abner Dubic (Haiti, b. 1944), "Haitian Village," features women and children tending animals, playing, and preparing food, 48" x 18"............ **$120**

Clementine Hunter (1887-1988), "Cotton Pickers," c. 1970, oil on board, signed lower right, 9-1/2" x 13-1/2". **$2,500**

Alice Mattern (American, 1909-1945), "Allegro," oil on canvas, 42-1/4" x 39". **$55,200**

Courtesy of Shannon's Fine Art Auctioneers, shannons.com

Ablade Glover (Ghanaian, b. 1934), "The Conversation," 1981, oil on canvas, signed and dated "GLO 1981" lower left, 30-1/4" x 24". **$3,000**

Courtesy of Crescent City Auction Gallery, crescentcityauctiongallery.com

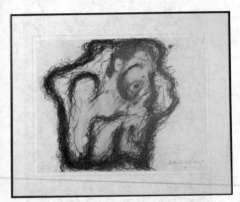

Arnulf Rainer (Austrian, b. 1929), "Stupid Prayers for Forgiveness," 1976, self portrait, mixed media charcoal on photograph, signed, 18-1/4" x 23-1/4"..**$13,640**

Courtesy of Ahlers & Ogletree Auction Gallery, aandoauctions.com

Miguel Martinez (Mexico, b. 1951), "Woman from Velarde," New Mexico, 1995, pastel and oil on paper, 30" x 40".. **$8,125**

Courtesy of Bruneau & Co., bruneauandco.com

Dale Nichols (American, 1904-1995), "Mid-Nation Winter," 1968, oil on canvas, 30" x 40". **$120,000**

Courtesy of Shannon's Fine Art Auctioneers, shannons.com

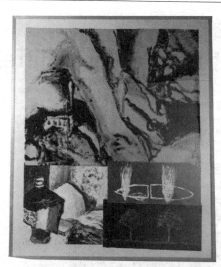

Nicola Simbari (Italian, 1927-2012), "Near Amalfi," 1965, oil on canvas, signed, 38-3/4" x 48-3/4"... **$5,700**

Courtesy of A.B. Levy's, ablevys.com

Juliao Sarmento (Portuguese, b. 1948), "Arena," 1985, collage of acrylic and charcoal on papers, unsigned, 69-1/4" x 59-1/2"......................**$19,360**

Courtesy of Ahlers & Ogletree Auction Gallery, aandoauctions.com

Kevin Red Star (American, b. 1943), "Mr. and Mrs. Choke Cherries," mixed media on canvas, signed, 33" x 44".. **$2,300**

Courtesy of Weiss Auctions, weissauctions.com

Charles J. F. Soulacroix (French-Italian, 1825-1879), "Enchantee," oil on canvas, 39-1/2" x 46-1/2"...**$60,000**

Courtesy of A.B. Levy's, ablevys.com

Francisco Viera Portuense (1765-1805), "Music's Allegory," 19th c., oil on canvas, unsigned, 38-3/4" x 28-3/4". **$1,000**

Courtesy of Crescent City Auction Gallery, crescentcityauctiongallery.com

FINE ART

10 Things You Didn't Know About Woodstock Art Colony (Byrdcliffe)

1 The Woodstock Byrdcliffe Guild (commonly referred to as the Woodstock Art Colony) came into existence in 1902. It's operated as a nonprofit organization since 1938.

2 Enamored with the natural beauty of Woodstock and the Catskill Mountains, husband-and-wife duo, Ralph Radcliffe Whitehead and Jane Byrd McCall, purchased an estimated 1,500 acres on Mount Guardian with the purpose of developing a utopian art colony. Fusing their middle names, the couple named it Byrdcliffe.

3 In May of 2017, collector Arthur Anderson donated 1,500 items of artwork by colony artists to the New York State Museum, in Albany. The selection of items includes early 20th century art by more than 170 members.

4 Various artistic disciplines are pursued at Byrdcliffe, including painting, metalwork, pottery, furniture making, design, weaving, and photography. As the landscape of artistic expression changed during the decades, it was represented in the instructors selected and the artistic offerings coming out of the colony. Examples of the Arts and Crafts movement, Impressionism, Cubism, Realism, abstract and folk art, and the Studio Movement are some influences represented in works attributed to the artists.

Eugene Speicher, "Martha," 1947, oil on canvas, 19" x 16".

Courtesy of The Historic Woodstock Arts Colony: Arthur A. Anderson Collection; photo by Eric R. Lapp

5 In 2014, an oil-on-canvas painting titled "January Thaw" by Woodstock Art Colony instructor Walter Koeniger realized $2,700 (w/BP) during an auction at George Costopulos Auctioneers.

6 The Woodstock Art Colony is reportedly one of the longest operating year-round arts colonies in America.

7 A bronze sculpture titled, "Young Greyhound," by Grace Mott Johnson, circa 1919, is one of the items by a member of the Woodstock Art Colony recently given to the New York Art Museum.

8 In the mid-1930s, Woodstock became the site of a WPA office, part of the Federal Art Project. In a couple years' time, 400 lithographs for all Woodstock artists had been printed, according to an article posted at the site of D. Wigmore Fine Art, Inc. In addition, colony artists were often selected to create murals commissioned by the Federal Art Project.

Grace Mott Johnson, "Young Greyhound" (Greyhound Pup), 1911, bronze, 9" x 6" x 6-1/2".

Courtesy of The Historic Woodstock Arts Colony: Arthur A. Anderson Collection; photo by Eric R. Lapp

9 The Colony has drawn and continues to attract artists and visitors from across the globe, including leading educator John Dewey, musicians Leon Barzin and Bob Dylan, painter George Bellows, actress Helen Hayes, and comedian and performer Chevy Chase.

10 It wasn't always sunshine and harmony at Byrdcliffe, though. There were moments of disenchantment among artists and instructors and at one point, a group branched off to create the Maverick art colony, which involved a music festival loosely deemed as a precursor to the 1969 Woodstock Music and Art Festival.

– Compiled by Antoinette Rahn

Sources: ArtFixDaily; woodstockguild.org; nysm.nysed.gov; nytimes.com; dwigmore.com/woodstock_essay.html.

FINE ART-REGIONALISM

AN AMERICAN TERM, Regionalism refers to the work of a number of rural artists, mostly from the Midwest, who came to prominence in the 1930s.

Regionalist artists often had an idiosyncratic style or point of view. What they shared, among themselves and among other American Scene painters, was a humble, anti-modernist style and a desire to depict everyday life. However, their rural conservatism tended to put them at odds with the urban and leftist Social Realists of the same era.

The three best-known regionalists are John Steuart Curry, Thomas Hart Benton, and Grant Wood, the painter of the best-known and one of the greatest works of American art, "American Gothic."

—Artcyclopedia.com

Like Jazz and Bluegrass, Regionalism is a truly unique American form of art. The American realist modern art movement included paintings, murals, lithographs, and illustrations depicting realistic scenes of rural and small-town America. The artworks keep tight to the country's early agrarian roots and the hardscrabble life many experienced during the Great Depression. Think *The Grapes of Wrath* immortalized in oil and pencils.

The movement arose surprisingly during the strongest years of the sleek and streamlined Art Deco movement. It ended in the 1940s due to the end of World War II. Critics look back and now point to the five-year span between 1930 and 1935 as the peak of the movement, although some artists created their greatest works well into the early 1950s, basing their influence and education by the movement's three most influential artists: Wood, Benton, and Curry. Despite major differences between the three (and their students), Regionalist art is often conservative and traditional, directly opposite of the rather flamboyant Continental art being produced, say, in France at the time.

Maurine Cantey (American, 1901-1982), "Girl in Yellow Raincoat," oil on board, signed lower left: "Maurine Cantey," 14" l x 10" w. **$4,518**

Courtesy of David Dike Fine Art, daviddikefineart.com

During the mid-1970s, Regionalist paintings were out of favor in the art world. Collectors often sold their paintings cheaply or quality examples could be found favorably at auction or even directly from the artists themselves. Critics derided the genre's stark, plain imagery in the age of Andy Warhol's modern take on Campbell's Soup cans.

Perhaps the most famous American Regional painting is Wood's "American Gothic," which is annually ranked as American's favorite painting. Artists of the era built entire careers on murals painted during the Depression and the early 1940s. These works went on to influence artists whose most important work kept Regionalism alive after World War II and the rise of

Henry Gasser (American, 1909-1981), "Mining Town," Pennsylvania, gouache on paper, signed "H. GASSER (II)," 21-5/8" l x 25-5/8" w................... **$4,375**

Courtesy of Doyle New York, doyle.com

Claude Flynn Howell (North Carolina, 1915-1997), "Flower Market," (Howell #1796), signed lower right "Howell" and signed and inscribed verso, oil on plywood, 18" x 22".
.... **$16,640**

Courtesy of Brunk Auctions, brunk.com

Modernism and Modernist artists.

The market for American Regional art is strong and growing stronger every year. Large-size, important works easily top seven figures and murals and mural studies command a half-million dollars. Price points for even lesser quality works span five figures and lithographs from the greats are attainable between $500 and $2,000 depending on the artist and the subject.

An ideal example is Merritt Mauzey's "Uncle Fud and Aunt Boo." Painted in the 1930s, the oil on Masonite depicts two figures exhausted from working their fields. Ironically, Uncle Fud, and Aunt Boo were well-known comedic radio characters created in the early 1930s by radio personality Bob Burns. They were happy-go-lucky, barefoot, tobacco chewing, dirt-poor sharecroppers. Merritt Mauzey places these normally happy and carefree characters in the firm and horrible grip of the Dust Bowl. Instead of the light-hearted comic characters Americans were used to, Mauzey presents them toiling against the awful forces of the drought. The sky is not blue, but gray, brown, and orange — filled with blowing topsoil. Mauzey replaces the romantic images of Thomas Hart Benton's regionalism with his own regionalism of stark truth and the plight of the sharecropping farmer.

Mauzey's accurate, however dispiriting and bleak, assessment of the farmer's plight held a place of pride in his heart. Mauzey kept "Uncle Fud and Aunt Boo" in his personal collection until his last days, always declining to sell them. To pay for medical care, he finally sold both of the prized paintings to a long-time cotton broker, knowing at that point in time (the mid-1970s) only someone in the cotton industry would appreciate them.

Molly Burroughs Luce (American, 1896-1986), "Landscape with Farm," 1957, oil on canvas, signed "Molly Luce 57," at the lower left, 36" l x 47-1/2" w. **$4,600**

Courtesy of Aspire Auctions, Inc., aspireauctions.com

Alexandre Hogue (American, 1898-1994), "Glen Rose," 1926, oil on canvas laid on Masonite, signed lower right: "Alexandre / Hogue," from the estate of Mildred Mcknight, 16-1/4" l x 20-1/4" w. **$78,125**

Courtesy of Heritage Auctions, ha.com

▲ Florence McClung (American, 1894-1992), "Carrolton Station," Texas, oil on board, signed lower left: "F McClung," 20" l x 24" w. **$42,175**

Courtesy of David Dike Fine Art, daviddikefineart.com

◄ John McCrady (American/ Louisiana, 1911-1968), "Pipe Fitters," watercolor on illustration board, signed lower right, "Downtown Gallery, Julia St., NO," label with artist and title, and typewritten artist's label with title en verso, 16" l x 22" w. **$7,360**

Courtesy of Neal Auction Company, nealauction.com

Jackson Lee Nesbitt (American, 1913-2008), "The Matthew W. Johnston Family," 1990, etching, pencil-signed, titled, dated and numbered "135/250" lower margin, 9-1/2" l x 12-1/4" w. $320

Courtesy of Neal Auction Company, nealauction.com

Aaron Pyle (1903-1972), "Waiting," lithograph, pencil signed, dedication lower center reads "To Jack Nesbitt" for fellow regional artist Jackson Nesbitt (1913-2008), signed lower right, 9" l x 15" w. $825

Courtesy of Soulis Auctions, dirksoulisauctions.com

Frederick Emanuel Shane (American, 1906-1992), "Artists Sketching," 1949, gouache on board, signed lower left margin: "F Shane / (C Shane)," dated and titled on the reverse: "Artists Sketching / California / 1949," 18-1/2" l x 28-1/4" w. $1,250

Courtesy of Heritage Auctions, ha.com

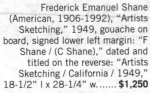

Sanford Ross (American, 1907-1954), Connecticut Valley, 1936, lithograph, pencil signed, titled and penciled edition 4/25 with dedication "For Margaret" lower left, signed by the artist lower right and dated 1936, 10" l x 14" w. $250

Courtesy of Soulis Auctions, dirksoulisauctions.com

Anthony Thieme (Massachusetts/ California, 1888-1954), "Easter Sunday," oil on canvas (lined), signed at lower right, "SS," 24-1/5" l x 29-1/4" w......**$24,600**

Courtesy of Leland Little Auctions, lelandlittle.com

Grant Wood (American, 1891-1942), "In the Spring," 1939, lithograph, Ed. 250, signed in pencil in lower margin, published by Associated American Artists, New York, 9" l x 11-7/8" w. **$2,750**

Courtesy of Heritage Auctions, ha.com

Hale Woodruff (American, 1900-1980), "The First Snow," 1927, oil on canvas, signed, dated and inscribed lower left: "To Jack Stephens / Hale Woodruff '27'," 16" l x 20" w................**$12,500**

Courtesy of Heritage Auctions, ha.com

Joseph Paul Vorst (German/American, 1897-1947), "Untitled," circa 1941, lithograph depiction of Vorst's friend and teacher Thomas Hart Benton (1889-1975), pencil signed, a rare and previously unrecorded litho by Vorst, 13-1/5" l x 12" w. **$5,310**

Courtesy of Soulis Auctions, dirksoulisauctions.com

Russell T. Limbach (American, 1904-1971), "Circus No.3," lithograph, signed twice in pencil "Limbach" lower right, numbered in rubber stamp "00051," 12-5/16" l x 8-5/8" w..................... **$190**

Courtesy of Grant Zahajko Auctions, LLC, gzauctions.com

Roger Medearis (American, 1920-2001), "The Homesteader," tempera on polymer canvas bonded to hardboard panel, signed "l.l.," titled, dated 1973, and description of medium on reverse panel, 15-3/4" l x 23-1/5" w. **$4,612**

Courtesy of LiveAuctioneers.com

Barse Miller (American, 1904-1973), "Harvest, Getting the Hay," watercolor on paper, signed lower left: "Barse Miller," 14" l x 21-1/4" w. **$6,875**

Courtesy of Heritage Auctions, ha.com

FOLK ART/AMERICANA

FOR A NATION that takes deep pride in calling itself a nation of immigrants, American folk art and Americana acts like the ribbon tying our collective heritage together. Rich with evidence of German woodworking, Scottish ship-carving, or perhaps African tribal motifs, each work is one-of-a-kind and stands on its own, backed by good ol' American individuality. The fact that most works were completed by self-taught artists who had little to no formal training enhances the appeal to the collectors of American folk art and Americana. In one sense, the vernacular charm symbolizes the country's reputation for ambition, ingenuity, and imagination. There's little wonder why American folk art and Americana is more popular than ever.

Another sign of this category's growing interest with collectors and the general public is the popularity of the only museum dedicated to the scholarly study and exhibition of the country's self-taught artisans, the American Folk Art Museum (folkartmuseum.org), New York City. The museum's more than 5,000 items were collected almost entirely through gifts. Collectors cheered in December 2013 when the museum digitized and gave away 118 free issues of *Folk Art* magazine (formerly *The Clarion*), originally published between winter 1971 and fall 2008. The trove may be accessed online at issuu.com/american_folk_art_museum.

For the last two weeks in January 2018, in observance of Americana Week, New York was the main destination for collectors, dealers, curators, and scholars, as the city hosted antiques shows, auctions, exhibitions, and lectures dedicated to antiques, modern art, and fine art. Two auction houses, Christie's and Sotheby's, racked up millions of dollars in sales for their Americana offerings.

Americana Week at Christie's New York included three distinct sales with pieces that explored collecting in the fields of Chinese export, American furniture, folk art and silver, and outsider and vernacular art. The auction house's "Important American Furniture, Folk Art and Silver" auction on Jan. 19 saw sales

Three carved and painted Canada goose field decoys, probably by Stacey Bryanton, Prince Edward Island, c. 1930, expected wear, 30-1/2"...**$3,660**

Courtesy of Pook & Pook, Inc., pookandpook.com

A rare and important silk-and-metal-on-linen needlework pictorial wrought by Mary Russell (B. 1779), Marblehead, Massachusetts or Bristol, Rhode Island, dated 1791, signed and dated, "Mary Russell workd in the 13th Year 1791" along lower edge, 18-1/4" x 21-3/4". **$324,500**

Courtesy of Christie's, christies.com

of $4.1 million. One of the highlights of the sale was a needlework pictorial that sold for $324,500 — almost four times its high estimate of $90,000.

Sotheby's annual Americana Week sales brought in $13.9 million, with nearly 1,000 lots sold across two auctions. The week kicked off with the sale of important printed and manuscript Americana, including cartography, which was led by *The Declaration of Independence*, printed by E. Russell, that sold for $1.2 million. The important Americana sale achieved $9.6 million and saw strong results across a diverse group of works, including American furniture, silver, and ceramics.

Painted Eggs trade sign, 19th c., original paint, wear consistent with age and use, good condition, writing only on one side, 5-1/2" h. **$7,320**

Courtesy of Pook & Pook, Inc., pookandpook.com

Carved and painted ship diorama, late 19th c., signed S. Arneger Chester, PA, wear, wired for two bulbs at top, 23-3/4" x 33". **$915**

Courtesy of Pook & Pook, Inc., pookandpook.com

Painted pine dower chest, Centre County, Pennsylvania, dated 1817, inscribed Daniel Houser, retaining original decoration with two large trees, love birds and flowers on a salmon ground, wear, hardware replaced, repaired breaks to foot facings, 24-1/2" h, 47-1/2" w. **$19,520**

Courtesy of Pook & Pook, Inc., pookandpook.com

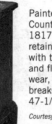

Painted pine bucket, 19th c., original blue surface with cat, bird, fruit, etc., wear, 1" strip patch to bottom, 5-3/4" h, 10-1/2" w. **$519**

Courtesy of Pook & Pook, Inc., pookandpook.com

Folk art carved and painted seated dog, early 20th c., with floppy ears, retaining putty color surface with black highlights, found in Zanesville, Ohio, 19-1/2" h... **$2,928**

Courtesy of Pook & Pook, Inc., pookandpook.com

Carved and painted folk art carnival Turk head, early 20th c., used at the entry to an amusement park in Pittsburgh, wear consistent with age and use, 22-1/2" h.............**$2,440**

Courtesy of Pook & Pook, Inc., pookandpook.com

Carved and painted Northern Pike fish trade sign, mid-20th c., good condition, 55" l......................... **$1,830**

Courtesy of Pook & Pook, Inc., pookandpook.com

Pair of carved and painted song birds, early 20th c., both with repairs to beak and chip to tail, 4" h, 8" w. **$458**

Courtesy of Pook & Pook, Inc., pookandpook.com

Pair of Portland, Maine polychrome painted swordfish bills, late 19th c., each with a carved handle and hilt, blades with small vignettes of Spring Point lighthouse and American shields, minor wear with few chips/worn spots to hilt, 40-1/2" l and 41-1/2" l. ... **$976**

Courtesy of Pook & Pook, Inc., pookandpook.com

Vermont ink on linen ditty bag, inscribed "Sarah P. Hammond Fair Haven 1820," the reverse with verse, minor staining, 8-3/4" x 8-1/2". **$650**

Courtesy of Pook & Pook, Inc., pookandpook.com

Sampler, likely Pennsylvania, 1849, wool on cotton, with brightly colored scene of a house with fruit baskets and instruments, signed at bottom "Rosanna I Spohn her work april 1849," in an old, grain painted frame, 16-1/2" x 16-1/2". ... **$554**

Courtesy of Cowan's Auctions, cowans.com

Charles II stumpwork panel, late 17th c., losses to edges, fraying and small holes, period frame with losses, 12-3/4" x 15-1/2". **$1,952**

Courtesy of Pook & Pook, Inc., pookandpook.com

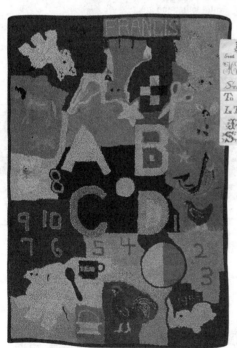

Two Hutterite samplers, American, 20th century, one with polychrome stitched alphabets, signed and dated at bottom, the other with stitched Bible verses, signed, larger 40-1/2" x 17-1/4"; smaller 15-3/4" x 16-1/4".. **$185**

Courtesy of Cowan's Auctions, cowans.com

American hooked rug, early/mid-20th c., with animals, ABCs, and numbers, mounted, good condition, 58" x 38". **$2,928**

Courtesy of Pook & Pook, Inc., pookandpook.com

American hooked rug with rabbits, early 20th c., some fraying to edges, 21" x 36"......................**$200**

Courtesy of Pook & Pook, Inc., pookandpook.com

Watercolor and gouache folk portrait, girl with cat, 19th c., good condition, 8" x 6". **$1,952**

Courtesy of Pook & Pook, Inc., pookandpook.com

David Y. Ellinger (American, 1913-2003), oil on velvet theorem of an eagle, good condition, glass a little foggy, 11" x 11". **$600**

Courtesy of Pook & Pook, Inc., pookandpook.com

Wilhelm Schimmel (Cumberland Valley Pennsylvania, 1817-1890), carved and painted rooster, retaining original polychrome decoration, good condition, 6-3/8" h...**$10,980**

Courtesy of Pook & Pook, Inc., pookandpook.com

Carved and painted whirligig, early 20th c., of a gentleman with top hat and green jacket atop an arrow and cast iron base, wear consistent with age and use, 31-1/2" h. **$1,098**

Courtesy of Pook & Pook, Inc., pookandpook.com

Carved and painted walking stick, late 19th c., with bone grip, retaining its original green surface, good condition, wear consistent with age and use, 36-1/4" l. **$188**

Courtesy of Pook & Pook, Inc., pookandpook.com

American watercolor theorem, 19th c., with a basket of flowers, toning, few small stains, 10" x 13-1/2". **$100**

Courtesy of Pook & Pook, Inc., pookandpook.com

Handmade folk art copper over wood whale weathervane, late 19th c., with iron seam along back, retaining an old tarred black surface, wear consistent with age and use, 34" l. **$14,640**

American oil on canvas folk portrait of a girl with basket of cherries, c. 1840, relined, all over touch-up to craquelure, 39" x 29". **$2,440**

Courtesy of Pook & Pook, Inc., pookandpook.com

Watercolor folk portrait, c. 1850, child with horse pull toy, inscribed Gilbert Proctor, staining, loss to gilt liner of frame, 6-1/2" x 5". **$488**

Courtesy of Pook & Pook, Inc., pookandpook.com

Pencil view of Niagara Falls, 19th c., paper wavy, lacking backboards, 15-1/2" x 20-1/2". **$138**

Courtesy of Pook & Pook, Inc., pookandpook.com

Carved and painted Mother and Child, 19th c., worm damage, 15-1/4" h. **$175**

Courtesy of Pook & Pook, Inc., pookandpook.com

Hooked whale welcome mat, dated 1950, probably Cape Cod, mounted, 18" x 39-1/2". .. **$183**

Courtesy of Pook & Pook, Inc., pookandpook.com

Friedrich Krebs (Southeastern Pennsylvania, 1749-1815), watercolor fraktur, woman on horseback, laid down, several repaired tears, 9-1/4" x 7-1/4". **$915**

Courtesy of Pook & Pook, Inc., pookandpook.com

FURNITURE STYLES

american

PILGRIM CENTURY 1620–1700

MAJOR WOOD(S): Oak

GENERAL CHARACTERISTICS:

- **Case pieces:** Rectilinear low-relief carved panels; blocky and bulbous turnings; splint-spindle trim

- **Seating pieces:** Shallow carved panels; spindle turnings

WILLIAM AND MARY 1685–1720

MAJOR WOOD(S): Maple and walnut

GENERAL CHARACTERISTICS:

- **Case pieces:** Paint-decorated chests on ball feet; chests on frames; chests with two-part construction; trumpet-turned legs; slant-front desks

- **Seating pieces:** Molded, carved crest rails; banister backs; cane, rush (leather) seats; baluster, ball and block turnings; ball and Spanish feet

QUEEN ANNE 1720-1750

MAJOR WOOD(S): Walnut

GENERAL CHARACTERISTICS:

- **Case pieces:** Mathematical proportions of elements; use of the cyma or S-curve broken-arch pediments; arched panels, shell carving, star inlay; blocked fronts; cabriole legs and pad feet

- **Seating pieces:** Molded yoke-shaped crest rails; solid vase-shaped splats; rush or upholstered seats; cabriole legs; baluster, ring, ball and block-turned stretchers; pad and slipper feet

CHIPPENDALE 1750-1785

MAJOR WOOD(S): Mahogany and walnut

GENERAL CHARACTERISTICS:

- **Case pieces:** Relief-carved broken-arch pediments; foliate, scroll, shell, fretwork carving; straight, bow or serpentine fronts; carved cabriole legs; claw and ball, bracket or ogee feet

- **Seating pieces:** Carved, shaped crest rails with out-turned ears; pierced, shaped splats; ladder (ribbon) backs; upholstered seats; scrolled arms; carved cabriole legs or straight (Marlboro) legs; claw and ball feet

FEDERAL (HEPPLEWHITE) 1785–1800

MAJOR WOOD(S): Mahogany and light inlays

GENERAL CHARACTERISTICS:

- **Case pieces:** More delicate rectilinear forms; inlay with eagle and classical motifs; bow, serpentine or tambour fronts; reeded quarter columns at sides; flared bracket feet

- **Seating pieces:** Shield backs; upholstered seats; tapered square legs

FEDERAL (SHERATON) 1800–1820

MAJOR WOOD(S): Mahogany, mahogany veneer, and maple

GENERAL CHARACTERISTICS:

- **Case pieces:** Architectural pediments; acanthus carving; outset (cookie or ovolu) corners and reeded columns; paneled sides; tapered, turned, reeded or spiral-turned legs; bow or tambour fronts; mirrors on dressing tables

- **Seating pieces:** Rectangular or square backs; slender carved banisters; tapered, turned or reeded legs

CLASSICAL (AMERICAN EMPIRE) 1815–1850

MAJOR WOOD(S): Mahogany, mahogany veneer, and rosewood

GENERAL CHARACTERISTICS:

- **Case pieces:** Increasingly heavy proportions; pillar and scroll construction; lyre, eagle, Greco-Roman and Egyptian motifs; marble tops; projecting top drawer; large ball feet, tapered fluted feet or hairy paw feet; brass, ormolu decoration

- **Seating pieces:** High-relief carving; curved backs; out-scrolled arms; ring turnings; sabre legs, curule (scrolled-S) legs; brass-capped feet, casters

VICTORIAN – EARLY VICTORIAN 1840–1850

MAJOR WOOD(S): Mahogany veneer, black walnut, and rosewood

GENERAL CHARACTERISTICS:

- **Case pieces:** Pieces tend to carry over the Classical style with the beginnings of the Rococo substyle, especially in seating pieces

VICTORIAN – GOTHIC REVIVAL 1840–1890

MAJOR WOOD(S): Black walnut, mahogany, and rosewood

GENERAL CHARACTERISTICS:

- **Case pieces:** Architectural motifs; triangular arched pediments; arched panels; marble tops; paneled or molded drawer fronts; cluster columns; bracket feet, block feet or plinth bases

- **Seating pieces:** Tall backs; pierced arabesque backs with trefoils or quatrefoils; spool turning; drop pendants

VICTORIAN – ROCOCO (LOUIS XV) 1845–1870

MAJOR WOOD(S): Black walnut, mahogany, and rosewood

GENERAL CHARACTERISTICS:

- **Case pieces:** Arched carved pediments; high-relief carving, S- and C-scrolls, floral, fruit motifs, busts and cartouches; mirror panels; carved slender cabriole legs; scroll feet; bedroom suites (bed, dresser, commode)

- **Seating pieces:** High-relief carved crest rails; balloon-shaped backs; urn-shaped splats; upholstery (tufting); demi-cabriole legs; laminated, pierced and carved construction (Belter and Meeks); parlor suites (sets of chairs, love seats, sofas)

VICTORIAN – RENAISSANCE REVIVAL 1860-1885

MAJOR WOOD(S): Black walnut, burl veneer, painted and grained pine

GENERAL CHARACTERISTICS:

- **Case pieces:** Rectilinear arched pediments; arched panels; burl veneer; applied moldings; bracket feet, block feet, plinth bases; medium and high-relief carving, floral and fruit, cartouches, masks and animal heads; cyma-curve brackets; Wooton patent desks

- **Seating pieces:** Oval or rectangular backs with floral or figural cresting; upholstery outlined with brass tacks; padded armrests; tapered turned front legs, flared square rear legs

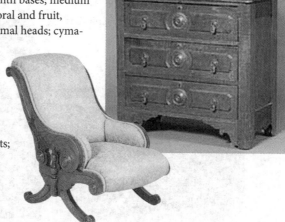

VICTORIAN – LOUIS XVI 1865-1875

MAJOR WOOD(S): Black walnut and ebonized maple

GENERAL CHARACTERISTICS:

- **Case pieces:** Gilt decoration, marquetry, inlay; egg and dart carving; tapered turned legs, fluted

- **Seating pieces:** Molded, slightly arched crest rails; keystone-shaped backs; circular seats; fluted tapered legs

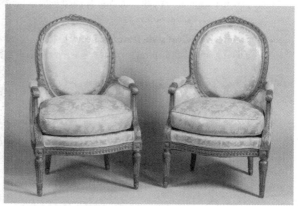

VICTORIAN – EASTLAKE 1870–1895

MAJOR WOOD(S): Black walnut, burl veneer, cherry, and oak

GENERAL CHARACTERISTICS:

- **Case pieces:** Flat cornices; stile and rail construction; burl veneer panels; low-relief geometric and floral machine carving; incised horizontal lines

- **Seating pieces:** Rectilinear; spindles; tapered, turned legs, trumpet-shaped legs

VICTORIAN JACOBEAN AND TURKISH REVIVAL 1870–1890

MAJOR WOOD(S): Black walnut and maple

GENERAL CHARACTERISTICS:

- **Case pieces:** A revival of some heavy 17th century forms, most commonly in dining room pieces

- **Seating pieces:** Turkish Revival style features: oversized, low forms; overstuffed upholstery; padded arms; short baluster, vase-turned legs; ottomans, circular sofas

- **Jacobean Revival style features:** heavy bold carving; spool and spiral turnings

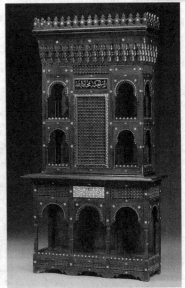

VICTORIAN – AESTHETIC MOVEMENT 1880–1900

MAJOR WOOD(S): Painted hardwoods, black walnut, ebonized finishes

GENERAL CHARACTERISTICS:

- **Case pieces:** Rectilinear forms; bamboo turnings, spaced ball turnings; incised stylized geometric and floral designs, sometimes highlighted with gilt

- **Seating pieces:** Bamboo turning; rectangular backs; patented folding chairs

ART NOUVEAU 1895–1918

MAJOR WOOD(S): Ebonized hardwoods, fruitwoods

GENERAL CHARACTERISTICS:

- **Case pieces:** Curvilinear shapes; floral marquetry; whiplash curves

- **Seating pieces:** Elongated forms; relief-carved floral decoration; spindle backs, pierced floral backs; cabriole legs

FURNITURE STYLES

TURN-OF-THE-CENTURY (EARLY 20TH CENTURY) 1895–1910

MAJOR WOOD(S): Golden (quarter-sawn) oak, mahogany, hardwood stained to resemble mahogany

GENERAL CHARACTERISTICS:

- **Case pieces:** Rectilinear and bulky forms; applied scroll carving or machine-pressed designs; some Colonial and Classical Revival detailing

- **Seating pieces:** Heavy framing or high spindle-trimmed backs; applied carved or machine-pressed back designs; heavy scrolled or slender turned legs; Colonial Revival or Classical Revival detailing such as claw and ball feet

MISSION (ARTS & CRAFTS MOVEMENT) 1900–1915

MAJOR WOOD(S): Oak

GENERAL CHARACTERISTICS:

- **Case pieces:** Rectilinear through-tenon construction; copper decoration, hand-hammered hardware; square legs

- **Seating pieces:** Rectangular splats; medial and side stretchers; exposed pegs; corbel supports

COLONIAL REVIVAL 1890–1930

MAJOR WOOD(S): Oak, walnut and walnut veneer, mahogany veneer

GENERAL CHARACTERISTICS:

- **Case pieces:** Forms generally following designs of the 17th, 18th, and early 19th centuries; details for the styles such as William and Mary, Federal, Queen Anne, Chippendale, or early Classical were used but often in a simplified or stylized form; mass-production in the early 20th century flooded the market with pieces that often mixed and matched design details and used a great deal of thin veneering to dress up designs; dining room and bedroom suites were especially popular

- **Seating pieces:** Designs again generally followed early period designs with some mixing of design elements

ART DECO 1925–1940

MAJOR WOOD(S): Bleached woods, exotic woods, steel, and chrome

GENERAL CHARACTERISTICS:

- **Case pieces:** Heavy geometric forms
- **Seating pieces:** Streamlined, attenuated geometric forms; overstuffed upholstery

MODERNIST OR MID-CENTURY 1945-1970

MAJOR WOOD(S): Plywood, hardwood, or metal frames

GENERAL CHARACTERISTICS: Modernistic designers such as the Eames, Vladimir Kagan, George Nelson, and Isamu Noguchi led the way in post-war design. Carrying on the tradition of Modernist designers of the 1920s and 1930s, they focused on designs for the machine age that could be mass-produced for the popular market. By the late 1950s, many of their pieces were used in commercial office spaces and schools as well as in private homes.

- **Case pieces:** Streamlined or curvilinear abstract designs with simple detailing; plain round or flattened legs and arms; mixed materials including wood, plywood, metal, glass, and molded plastics

- **Seating pieces:** Streamlined or abstract curvilinear designs generally using newer materials such as plywood or simple hardwood framing; fabric and synthetics such as vinyl used for upholstery with finer fabrics and real leather featured on more expensive pieces; seating made of molded plastic shells on metal frames and legs used on many mass-produced designs

DANISH MODERN 1950-1970

MAJOR WOOD(S): Teak

GENERAL CHARACTERISTICS:

- **Case and seating pieces:** This variation of Modernistic post-war design originated in Scandinavia, hence the name; designs were simple and restrained with case pieces often having simple boxy forms with short rounded tapering legs; seating pieces have a simple teak framework with lines coordinating with case pieces; vinyl or natural fabric were most often used for upholstery; in the United States dining room suites were the most popular use for this style although some bedroom suites and general seating pieces were available.

FURNITURE STYLES

english

JACOBEAN MID-17TH CENTURY

MAJOR WOOD(S): Oak, walnut

GENERAL CHARACTERISTICS:

- **Case pieces:** Low-relief carving; geometrics and florals; panel, rail and stile construction; applied split balusters
- **Seating pieces:** Rectangular backs; carved and pierced crests; spiral turnings ball feet

WILLIAM AND MARY 1689–1702

MAJOR WOOD(S): Walnut, burl walnut veneer

GENERAL CHARACTERISTICS:

- **Case pieces:** Marquetry, veneering; shaped aprons; 6-8 trumpet-form legs; curved flat stretchers
- **Seating pieces:** Carved, pierced crests; tall caned backs and seats; trumpet-form legs; Spanish feet

QUEEN ANNE 1702–1714

MAJOR WOOD(S): Walnut, mahogany, veneer

GENERAL CHARACTERISTICS:

- **Case pieces:** Cyma curves; broken arch pediments and finials; bracket feet
- **Seating pieces:** Carved crest rails; high, rounded backs; solid vase-shaped splats; cabriole legs; pad feet

GEORGE I 1714–1727

MAJOR WOOD(S): Walnut, mahogany, veneer, and yew wood

GENERAL CHARACTERISTICS:

- **Case pieces:** Broken arch pediments; gilt decoration, japanning; bracket feet
- **Seating pieces:** Curvilinear forms; yoke-shaped crests; shaped solid splats; shell carving; upholstered seats; carved cabriole legs; claw and ball feet, pad feet

GEORGE II 1727-1760

MAJOR WOOD(S): Mahogany

GENERAL CHARACTERISTICS:

- **Case pieces:** Broken arch pediments; relief-carved foliate, scroll and shell carving; carved cabriole legs; claw and ball feet, bracket feet, ogee bracket feet

- **Seating pieces:** Carved, shaped crest rails, out-turned ears; pierced shaped splats; ladder (ribbon) backs; upholstered seats; scrolled arms; carved cabriole legs or straight (Marlboro) legs; claw and ball feet

GEORGE III 1760-1820

MAJOR WOOD(S): Mahogany, veneer, satinwood

GENERAL CHARACTERISTICS:

- **Case pieces:** Rectilinear forms; parcel gilt decoration; inlaid ovals, circles, banding or marquetry; carved columns, urns; tambour fronts or bow fronts; plinth bases

- **Seating pieces:** Shield backs; upholstered seats; tapered square legs, square legs

REGENCY 1811–1820

MAJOR WOOD(S): Mahogany, mahogany veneer, satinwood and rosewood

GENERAL CHARACTERISTICS:

- **Case pieces:** Greco-Roman and Egyptian motifs; inlay, ormolu mounts; marble tops; round columns, pilasters; mirrored backs; scroll feet

- **Seating pieces:** Straight backs; latticework; caned seats; sabre legs, tapered turned legs, flared turned legs; parcel gilt, ebonizing

GEORGE IV 1820–1830

MAJOR WOOD(S): Mahogany, mahogany veneer and rosewood

GENERAL CHARACTERISTICS: Continuation of Regency designs

WILLIAM IV 1830–1837

MAJOR WOOD(S): Mahogany, mahogany veneer

GENERAL CHARACTERISTICS:

- **Case pieces:** Rectilinear; brass mounts, grillwork; carved moldings; plinth bases

- **Seating pieces:** Rectangular backs; carved straight crest rails; acanthus, animal carving; carved cabriole legs; paw feet

VICTORIAN 1837–1901

MAJOR WOOD(S): Black walnut, mahogany, veneers and rosewood

GENERAL CHARACTERISTICS:

- **Case pieces:** Applied floral carving; surmounting mirrors, drawers, candle shelves; marble tops

- **Seating pieces:** High-relief carved crest rails; floral and fruit carving; balloon backs, oval backs; upholstered seats, backs; spool, spiral turnings; cabriole legs, fluted tapered legs; scrolled feet

EDWARDIAN 1901–1910

MAJOR WOOD(S): Mahogany, mahogany veneer and satinwood

GENERAL CHARACTERISTICS: Neo-Classical motifs and revivals of earlier 18th century and early 19th century styles

FURNITURE

antique

FURNITURE HAS BEEN a major part of the collecting world for more than 100 years. It is interesting to note how this market has evolved.

In past decades, 18th century and early 19th century furniture was the mainstay of the American furniture market, but now the market is dominated by Modern and Mid-Century tastes, ranging from Art Deco through quality designer furniture of the 1950s and beyond (see "Modern Furniture" later in this section).

Today more furniture is showing up on internet sites, and sometimes good buys can be made. However, it is important to deal with honest, well-informed sellers and have a good knowledge of what you want to purchase.

As in the past, it makes sense to purchase the best pieces you can find, whatever the style or era of production. Condition is still important if you want your example to continue to appreciate in value in the coming years. For 18th century and early 19th century pieces, the original finish and hardware are especially important as it is with good furniture of the early 20th century Arts & Crafts era. These features are not quite as important for most manufactured furniture of the Victorian era and furniture from the 1920s and later. However, it is good to be aware that a good finish and original hardware will mean a stronger market when the pieces are resold. Of course, whatever style of furniture you buy, you are better off with examples that have not had major repair or replacements. On really early furniture, repairs and replacements will definitely have an impact on the sale value, but they will also be a factor on newer designs from the 20th century.

A George III satinwood and marquetry bookcase, top and bottom associated, with a pair of glazed doors enclosing five adjustable shelves, with two short drawers below, above a pair of cupboard doors, the left hand cupboard enclosing three short drawers the right cupboard with one shelf, 8'10-2/3" x 4'6-3/4" x 1'3".......... **$4,321**

Courtesy of Heritage Auctions, ha.com

VISIT WWW.ANTIQUETRADER.COM

WWW.FACEBOOK.COM/ANTIQUETRADER

As with all types of antiques and collectibles, there is often a regional preference for certain furniture types. This was proved in a big way when the most significant piece of Kentucky furniture ever offered at auction sold for a record price in October 2017 (see Top Lot). Although the American market is much more homogenous than it was in past decades, there still tends to be a preference for 18th century and early 19th century furniture along the Eastern Seaboard, whereas Victorian designs tend to have a larger market in the Midwest and South. In the West, country furniture and "western" designs definitely have the edge except in major cities along the West Coast.

Whatever your favorite furniture style, there are still fine examples to be found. Just study the history of your favorites and the important points of their construction before you invest heavily. A wise shopper will be a happy shopper and have a collection certain to continue to appreciate as time marches along.

A carved beech bench, Louis XV, on six cabriole legs, upholstered with yellow silk with flowers, 17-1/3" h, 51-1/2" w, 15" d. **$3,990**

Courtesy of Heritage Auctions, ha.com

A French Art Deco marquetry buffet in the style of Jules Leleu, circa 1930, 37" h x 90-1/2" w x 21-1/2" d. **$5,000**

Courtesy of Heritage Auctions, ha.com

L & JG Stickley Onondaga Shops glazed bookcase, 55-3/8" h x 30" w x 12" d...........................$2,750

Courtesy of Heritage Auctions, ha.com

A Renaissance Revival carved oak armchair, 19th century, 58-3/4" h x 26" w x 24" d.................$325

Courtesy of Heritage Auctions, ha.com

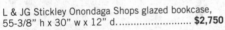

Pair of Georgian uphol-stered mahogany arm-chairs, England, 19th century, each carved overall, with acanthus-decorated serpentine crest, red silk-covered back and seat, open curvate arms, shaped apron with centralized shell motif, and legs with foliate knees extending to hairy paw feet, 45-1/8" h, 27-1/2" w, 31" d. $1,599

Courtesy of Skinner Auctioneers and Appraisers, skinnerinc.com

Set of four matched Hepplewhite revival shield back side chairs made by the Biggs Antique Furniture Company of Richmond, circa mid-20th century, form with carved tapered legs and "H" stretcher, satin covered seats with carved shield back, 21-1/2" x 17-1/4" x 38" h. **$1,100**

Courtesy of Cordier Auctions & Appraisals, cordierauction.com

An L & JG Stickley oak telephone table, 29-1/2" h x 20" w x 18" d................... **$550**

Courtesy of Heritage Auctions, ha.com

Fine Federal figured maple, mahogany and cherrywood serpentine top one-drawer stand, New England, circa 1800, 29-3/8" h x 20-3/8" w x 15" d...................................... **$3,750**

Courtesy of Heritage Auctions, ha.com

top lot

A two-piece desk and upper bookcase, American, 1796, constructed entirely of walnut (both primary and secondary), the desk with ogee bracket feet, molded base, the case with fluted quarter columns, four graduated drawers, each fitted with a dustboard, the battened fall board supported by lopers, the desk interior with a prospect door featuring a carved concave fan outlined by pricking, the base of the fan pricked MJ 1796. Two columned drawers flank the central shell, with four valanced pigeonholes, above four drawers. A total of nine "secret drawers" are hidden behind the removable central document drawer. The upper case has two doors, with two square, and two rectangular sunken panels of matching crotch walnut, and a broken arch pediment with carved sunflower rosettes, topped by three well-carved flame finials; desk: 102-2/4" h, 47-3/4" w, 43-1/4" d; bookcase: 23-1/4" h, 55-1/2" w, 43-1/2" d $498,750

A two-piece desk once belonging to one of the first settlers of Kentucky shattered the record for furniture made in the Bluegrass State when it sold for $498,750 at Cowan's Auctions in October 2017.

The most significant piece of Kentucky furniture to ever come to market was the top lot of an exciting two days at Cowan's Fall Fine & Decorative Art Featuring Americana Auction that saw prices soar across most categories, propelling the sale to a $1.8 million total (including buyer's premium).

The piece, conservatively estimated to sell between $50,000 to $75,000, not only set the new standard for Kentucky furniture, it was also the second most expensive piece of Southern furniture ever sold at auction. This was the first time the desk had been available to the public in over 220 years after remaining in the family of Kentucky pioneer Capt. John Cowan for six generations, according to Cowan's.

"We're thrilled," said Wes Cowan, Cowan's principal auctioneer and executive chairman (no relation to Capt. John Cowan). "But more importantly, the piece demonstrates conclusively that the market recognized this as an incomparable rarity. For scholars of Kentucky furniture, it is validation for what some have said for years: that great high-style furniture was being made in the 18th-century Bluegrass region."

Capt. John Cowan (1748-1823) was one of the first settlers of Kentucky in 1773, arriving with Thomas Bullit at the Falls of Ohio, where he helped survey the land that is now Louisville. A year later, he was one of the founders of Harrod's Town, the first permanent European settlement in Kentucky. By 1784, Cowan was a prominent enough citizen that his plantation was labeled on John Filson's map of Kentucky, one of the first maps of the territory. At the top of that first map, Cowan, alongside Daniel Boone and four others, was acknowledged for his assistance in constructing what was said to be the most accurate Kentucky map of its time.

Marble-top marquetry commode, France, late 19th/early 20th century, overall inlaid with chain-work motif, molded shaped top over conforming two-drawer case, on cabriole legs with sabot-mounted claw feet, 34-1/2" h, 42-1/2" w, 21" d. **$3,998**

Courtesy of Skinner Auctioneers and Appraisers, skinnerinc.com

Two Stickley Harvey Ellis nightstands, cherry, copper manlius, rectangular top over single drawer, single door with decorative inlay, copper hardware, metal tag, 29-1/8" h, 20" w, 16" d. **$1,353**

Courtesy of Skinner Auctioneers and Appraisers, skinnerinc.com

▼ Baroque-style fruitwood side table, probably Spain, late 19th century, molded rectangular top over stylized vasiform supports with downswept curvate stretchers, 21" h, 28-3/4" w, 16-5/8" d. **$738**

Courtesy of Skinner Auctioneers and Appraisers, skinnerinc.com

◀ Regency mahogany Étagère, England, early 19th century, urn-topped supports suspending four shelves with three drawers, base resting on turned feet, 63-1/8" h, 18" w, 16" d. **$738**

Courtesy of Skinner Auctioneers and Appraisers, skinnerinc.com

FURNITURE

▶ A German Empire mahogany and gilt bronze upholstered Schrank sofa, Schleswig-Holstein, North Germany, early 19th century, 43" h x 82" w x 29" d. **$750**

Courtesy of Heritage Auctions, ha.com

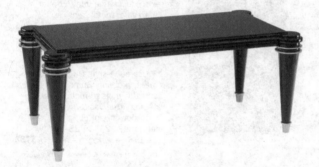

An Art Deco ebonized coffee table, 17" h x 41-1/4" w x 22" d. **$312**

Courtesy of Heritage Auctions, ha.com

Three-piece Louis XVI-style upholstered giltwood salon suite, circa 1870, 41" h x 66" w x 26" d. **$3,250**

Courtesy of Heritage Auctions, ha.com

FURNITURE

modern

MODERN DESIGN IS EVERYWHERE, evergreen, and increasingly popular. Modernism has never gone out of style. Its reach into the present day is as deep as its roots in the past. Just as it can be seen and felt ubiquitously in the mass media of today — on film, television, in magazines, and department stores — it can be traced to the mid-1800s post-Empire non-conformity of the Biedermeier Movement, the turn of the 20th century anti-Victorianism of the Vienna Secessionists, the radical reductionism of Frank Lloyd Wright and the revolutionary post-Depression thinking of Walter Gropius and the Bauhaus school in Germany.

"The Modernists really changed the way the world looked," said John Sollo, a partner in Sollo Rago Auction of Lambertville, New Jersey. Sollo's partner in business, and one of the most recognizable names in the field, David Rago, takes Sollo's idea a little further by saying that Modernism is actually more about the names behind the design than the design itself, at least as far as buying goes.

No discussion of Modern can be complete, however, without examining its genesis and enduring influence. Modernism is everywhere in today's pop culture. Austere Scandinavian furniture dominates the television commercials that hawk hotels and mutual funds. Post-war American design ranges across sitcom set dressings to movie sets patterned after Frank Lloyd Wright houses and Hollywood Modernist classics set high in the hills.

You have to look at the dorm rooms of college students and the apartments of young people whose living spaces are packed with the undeniably Modern mass-produced products of IKEA, Target, Design Within Reach, and the like.

There can be no denying that the post-World War II manufacturing techniques and subsequent boom led to the widespread acceptance of plastic and bent plywood chairs along with low-sitting coffee tables, couches and recliners.

George Nakashima pair of Conoid chairs, New Hope, Pennsylvania, 1969, walnut, hickory, manufactured by Nakashima Studios, signed with client's name, 35-1/2" x 20" x 21-1/2".......**$13,750**

Courtesy of Rago Arts and Auction Center, ragoarts.com

"The modern aesthetic grew out of a perfect storm of post-war optimism, innovative materials, and an incredible crop of designers," said Lisanne Dickson, director of 1950s/Modern Design at Treadway-Toomey.

"I think that the people who designed the furniture were maybe ahead of society's ability to accept and understand what they were doing," Sollo said. "It's taken people another 30 to 40 years to catch up to it."

There are hundreds of great Modern designers, many who worked across categories — furniture, architecture, fine art, etc. — and many contributed to the work of other big names without ever seeking that glory for themselves.

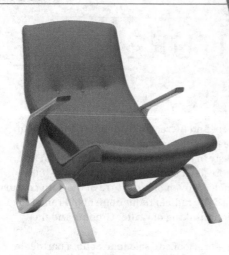

Grasshopper chair, Eero Saarinen design, 1945, manufactured by Knoll, Model No. 61U, 35-1/2" x 26-1/2" x 33".................. **$1,800-$2,500**

Courtesy of Rago Arts and Auction Center, ragoarts.com

Wing lounge chair (No. 503), United States, 1970s, sculpted walnut, wool, unmarked, designed by Vladimir Kagan, manufactured by Vladimir Kagan Designs, Inc., 42" x 31" x 33". **$10,000**

Courtesy of Rago Arts and Auction Center, ragoarts.com

Hans Wegner design Sawbuck chair, Denmark, mid-20th century, beech and oak, molded plywood seat and back, 30-1/2 h x 29" w x 27" d...................... **$1,350**

Courtesy of Skinner, skinnerinc.com

Hans Wegner Papa Bear Chair, Denmark, c. 1958, reupholstered in black wool, 39" h x 36-1/4" w x 35-1/2" d. **$7,995**

Courtesy of Skinner, skinnerinc.com

Paul Frankl two-drawer side tables (No. 464-393), United States, 1940s, lacquered cork, mahogany, brass, branded and stenciled, designed by Paul Frankl, manufactured by Johnson Furniture Co., 24-1/4" x 24" x 19". **$10,000**

Courtesy of Rago Arts and Auction Center, ragoarts.com

Hans Wegner contemporary Ox Chair, leather and metal, designed in 1960. ....**$8,000-$10,000**

Courtesy of Rago Arts and Auction Center, ragoarts.com

Georg Jensen Rocker, Model No. 97, manufactured by Kubus, Denmark, c. 1965, striped green and navy wool, 30" h x 25" w x 30" d.. **$523**

Courtesy of Skinner Auctioneers and Appraisers, skinnerinc.com

Sven Ivar Dysthe Planet Chair, Lunning Collection, Division of Georg Jensen Inc., Norway, blue wool upholstery, half-sphere swivels on base of chrome steel and rosewood, some surface rust, 29" h x 30" w x 27" d.. **$492**

Courtesy of Skinner Auctioneers and Appraisers, skinnerinc.com

Hans Wegner folding end table, Andreas Tuck Cabinetmakers, Denmark, mid-20th century, teak and steel, cube-form fitted with a drawer, exposed joinery, opens to a storage compartment, 19-1/2" h x 19 1/2" w x 20-1/2 d............... **$5,228**

Courtesy of Skinner Auctioneers and Appraisers, skinnerinc.com

Hans Wegner dining table and six chairs, teak, cane, Denmark, c. 1958, rectangular-top table with two leaves on cylindrical legs, table height 28-3/4" x 76" l x 41-1/4 w. **$28,290**

Courtesy of Skinner Auctioneers and Appraisers, skinnerinc.com

Hans Wegner sideboard, teak, fiber, Model RY-26, Denmark, 78-3/4" l x 31" w. **$1,968**

Courtesy of Skinner Auctioneers and Appraisers, skinnerinc.com

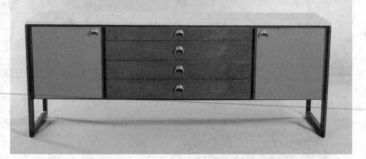

Jens Risom Credenza, mid-20th century, teak, travertine marble top over four center drawers flanked by two cabinets finished in safe green, raised on U-shaped legs, 34" h x 86-3/4" l x 19" d. **$2,460**

Courtesy of Skinner Auctioneers and Appraisers, skinnerinc.com

George Nakashima cabinet, New Hope, PA, 1957, walnut and natural fiber cloth, two sliding doors, originally designed as a radio cabinet, 32-1/2" h x 80" l x 21" d.............**$22,140**

Courtesy of Skinner Auctioneers and Appraisers, skinnerinc.com

George Nakashima walnut double dresser, New Hope, PA, 1959, manufactured by Nakashima Studios, signed with client name, 31-3/4" x 60" x 20". **$18,750**

Courtesy of Rago Arts and Auction Center, ragoarts.com

Hans Wegner sideboard with overcabinet, Denmark, c. 1958, teak and natural fiber, rectangular with overcabinet, two sliding doors, two banks of three drawers, 71" h x 70-1/2" w x 19-1/2" d... **$1,230**

Courtesy of Skinner Auctioneers and Appraisers, skinnerinc.com

Jens Risom chest of drawers, c. 1957, United States, teak, nine-drawer chest with crescent-shaped brass-tone pulls, raised on U-shaped base, Jens Risom Inc. label, 55-3/8" h x 34" w x 19-1/8"d... **$2,000**

Courtesy of Skinner Auctioneers and Appraisers, skinnerinc.com

George Nelson home office desk, 1946, manufactured by Herman Miller, Model Nos. 4658 & 601. This example contains the original Pendaflex file basket, which was a special order, 40-1/2" x 54-1/2" x 28"............................. **$6,875**

Courtesy of Rago Arts and Auction Center, ragoarts.com

George Nelson, Howard Miller, large walnut "Spike" clock, Howard Miller label, 30" diameter. **$732**

Courtesy of Rago Arts and Auction Center, ragoarts.com

GLASS

bride's baskets and bowls

THESE BERRY OR FRUIT BOWLS were popular late Victorian wedding gifts, hence the name bride's basket was adopted. They were produced in a variety of quality art glasswares and sometimes were fitted in ornate silver-plate holders.

Art glass bride's bowl, white opal with cream exterior, pink trim, melon ribbed with enamel floral design, 4-3/4" dia x 10-1/4". $600

Courtesy of Woody Auction LLC, woodyauction.com

Victorian bride's basket, c. 1890, blue ruffled bowl with gold leaves encircling interior, Rogers triple-plated frame, very good condition, 12" dia, 14" h. $150

Courtesy of A-1 Auction, liveauctioneers.com

Victorian colored glass and Vaseline bride's baskets, late 19th c, lot of two: one having a blue molded glass insert, mounted to a gilt metal stand with leaves throughout, 7-1/2" h, 10" l; and the other of vaseline glass with footed stand having foliate detailing to handle, 5" h, 4-1/2" dia. $80

Courtesy of DuMouchelles, dumouchelle.com

VISIT WWW.ANTIQUETRADER.COM

WWW.FACEBOOK.COM/ANTIQUETRADER

Victorian enameled milk glass bride's basket, pink to white ruffled collar, with berry leaf and vine hand-painted patterning and fired gold accents to interior, housed within a metal frame having scrolling details to handle, 11-1/2" h, 11-1/2" l. **$90**

Courtesy of DuMouchelles, dumouchelle.com

Cased art glass ruffled bride's bowl with polished pontil on silver-plated base, bowl is 4-1/2" dia, base is 3-15/16", 8-1/2" h overall.....................**$55**

Courtesy of Turkey Creek Auctions, turkeycreekauctions.com

Bride's basket, pink cased art glass ruffled bowl with white exterior, heavy enamel floral décor, set on Aurora #744 silver-plate stand, 13-1/2" x 13-3/4"............................**$175**

Courtesy of Woody Auction LLC, woodyauction.com

Mt. Washington art glass bride's basket, unmarked, white opaline with pink highlights and enamel floral décor, set on Meriden #185 silver-plate stand with child teaching dog to sit up, 14-1/2" x 7-1/2"..**$750**

Courtesy of Woody Auction LLC, woodyauction.com

Mt. Washington decorated Burmese bride's bowl, plush with polychrome-enamel decoration, spider-mum decoration, boldly ruffled and tooled rim, polished pontil mark, original quadruple-plate stand marked for "PAIRPOINT MFG CO." and numbered "2262," Mt. Washington Glass Co., fourth quarter 19th century, bowl is 5-1/4" h, 10" dia, 11" h overall.....................................**$550**

Courtesy of Jeffrey S. Evans & Associates, jeffreysevans.com

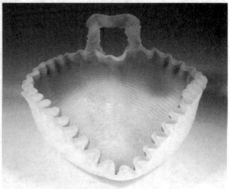

Victorian mother-of-pearl air-trap satin glass bride's bowl, opaque white exterior, shaded apricot interior, heart-form with an applied frosted colorless branch handle, frosted colorless rim, polished pontil mark, maker unverified, late 19th/ early 20th century, 9" x 10-1/4".......................**$50**

Courtesy of Jeffrey S. Evans & Associates, jeffreysevans.com

GLASS

carnival

CARNIVAL GLASS IS what is fondly called mass-produced iridescent glassware. The term "carnival glass" has evolved through the years as glass collectors have responded to the idea that much of this beautiful glassware was made as give-away glass at local carnivals and fairs. However, more of it was made and sold through the same channels as pattern glass and Depression glass. Some patterns were indeed giveaways, and others were used as advertising premiums, souvenirs, etc. Whatever the origin, the term "carnival glass" today encompasses glassware that is usually pattern molded and treated with metallic salts, creating that unique coloration that is so desirable to collectors.

Early names for iridescent glassware, which early 20th century consumers believed to have all come from foreign manufacturers, include Pompeian Iridescent, Venetian Art, and Mexican Aurora. Another popular early name was "Nancy Glass," as some patterns were believed to have come from the Daum, Nancy, glassmaking area in France. This was at a time when the artistic cameo glass was enjoying great success. While the iridescent glassware

Lot of three marigold carnival glass bolo ties, two with windmills, one with berries. $30
Courtesy of Tom Hall Auctions Inc., tomhallauctions.com

VISIT WWW.ANTIQUETRADER.COM

WWW.FACEBOOK.COM/ANTIQUETRADER

being made by such European glassmakers as Loetz influenced the American market place, it was Louis Tiffany's Favrile glass that really caught the eye of glass consumers of the early 1900s. It seems an easy leap to transform Tiffany's shimmering glassware to something that could be mass produced, allowing what we call carnival glass today to become "poor man's Tiffany."

Carnival glass is iridized glassware that is created by pressing hot molten glass into molds, just as pattern glass had evolved. Some forms are hand finished, while others are completely formed by molds. To achieve the marvelous iridescent colors that carnival glass collectors seek, a process was developed where a liquid solution of metallic salts was put onto the still hot glass form after it was unmolded. As the liquid evaporated, a fine metallic surface was left which refracts light into wonderful colors.

Classic carnival glass production began in the early 1900s and continued about twenty years, but no one really documented or researched production until the first collecting wave struck in 1960.

For more information on carnival glass, see *Warman's Carnival Glass Identification and Price Guide*, 2nd edition, by Ellen T. Schroy.

CARNIVAL GLASS COMPANIES

Much of vintage American carnival glassware was created in the Ohio valley, in the glasshouse-rich areas of Pennsylvania, Ohio, and West Virginia. The abundance of natural materials, good transportation, and skilled craftsmen that created the early American pattern glass manufacturing companies allowed many of them to add carnival glass to their production lines. Brief company histories of the major carnival glass manufacturers follow:

CAMBRIDGE GLASS CO.

Cambridge Glass was a rather minor player in the carnival glass marketplace. Founded in 1901 as a new factory in Cambridge, Ohio, it focused on producing fine crystal tablewares. What carnival glass it did produce was imitation cut-glass patterns.

Colors used by Cambridge include

Carnival glass Thistle bowl, 7-1/2" x 2-1/2"........$25
Courtesy of Martin Auction Co., martinauctionco.com

Carnival glass bowl, amethyst bowling, Fish (trout) and Fly pattern, 2" x 8-1/2"..........................$220
Courtesy of Tom Hall Auctions Inc., tomhallauctions.com

Carnival glass plate, Peacock on Fence pattern, excellent luster, 9"........................$150
Courtesy of Martin Auction Co., martinauctionco.com

Carnival glass two-handled centerpiece,
iridescent... **$140**

Courtesy of Fifth Avenue Estate Gallery, fifthavenueestategallery.com

Northwood carnival glass cracker jar and lid,
Grape & Cable pattern, dark purple, 6" dia,
5-1/4" h. **$90**

Courtesy of Long Auction Company, LLC, longauction.com

Carnival glass spooner, Cherry & Cable
Thumbprint, 6". **$20**

Courtesy of Martin Auction Co., martinauctionco.com

marigold, as well as few others. Forms found in carnival glass by Cambridge include tablewares and vases, some with its trademark "Near-Cut."

DIAMOND GLASS CO.

This company was started as the Dugan brothers (see Dugan Glass Co.) departed the carnival glass-making scene in 1913. However, Alfred Dugan returned and became general manager until his death in 1928. After a disastrous fire in June of 1931, the factory closed.

DUGAN GLASS CO.

The history of the Dugan Glass Co. is closely related to Harry Northwood (see Northwood Glass Co.), whose cousin, Thomas Dugan, became plant manager at the Northwood Glass Co. in Indiana, Pennsylvania, in 1895. By 1904, Dugan and his partner, W. G. Minnemayer, bought the former Northwood factory from the now defunct National Glass conglomerate and opened as the Dugan Glass Co. Dugan's brother, Alfred, joined the company and stayed until it became the Diamond Glass Co. in 1913. At this time, Thomas Dugan moved to the Cambridge Glass Co., later Duncan and Miller and finally Hocking, Lancaster. Alfred left Diamond Glass, too, but later returned.

Colors attributed to Dugan and Diamond include amethyst, marigold, peach opalescent, and white. The company developed deep amethyst shades, some almost black. Forms made by both Dugan and Diamond mirrored what other glass companies were producing. The significant contribution by Dugan and later Diamond were feet — either ball or spatula shapes. They are also known for deeply crimped edges.

FENTON ART GLASS CO.

Frank Leslie Fenton and his brothers, John W. Fenton and Charles H. Fenton, founded this truly American glassmaker in 1905 in Martins Ferry, Ohio. Early production was of blanks, which the brothers soon learned to decorate themselves. They moved to a larger factory in Williamstown, West Virginia.

By 1907, Fenton was experimenting

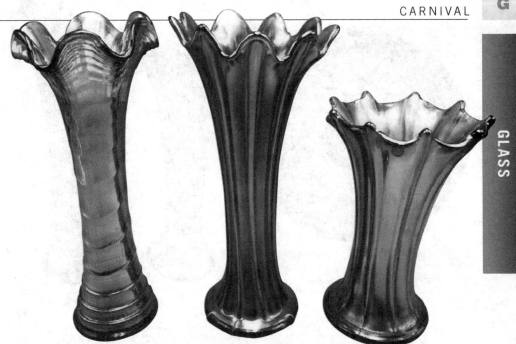

Lot of three carnival glass vases: green, Ribbed pattern, 10"; green, Northwood, 7-1/2"; and bright green swirl with fluted top, 12".. **$45**

Courtesy of Tom Hall Auctions Inc., tomhallauctions.com

with iridescent glass, developing patterns and the metallic salt formulas that it became so famous for. Production of carnival glass continued at Fenton until the early 1930s. In 1970, Fenton began to reissue carnival glass, creating new colors and forms as well as using traditional patterns.

Colors developed by Fenton are numerous. The company developed red and Celeste blue in the 1920s; a translucent pale blue, known as Persian blue, is also one of its more distinctive colors, as is a light yellow-green color known as vaseline. Fenton also produced delicate opalescent colors including amethyst opalescent and red opalescent. Because the Fenton brothers learned how to decorate their own blanks, they also promoted the addition of enamel decoration to some of their carnival glass patterns.

Forms made by Fenton are also numerous. What distinguishes Fenton from other glassmakers is its attention to detail and hand-finishing processes. Edges are found scalloped, fluted, tightly crimped, frilled, or pinched into a candy ribbon edge, also referred to as 3-in-1 edge.

IMPERIAL GLASS CO.

Edward Muhleman and a syndicate founded the Imperial Glass Co. at Bellaire, Ohio, in 1901, with production beginning in 1904. It started with pressed glass tableware patterns as well as lighting fixtures. The company's marketing strategy included selling to important retailers of its day, such as F. W. Woolworth and McCrory and Kresge, to get glassware into the hands of American housewives. Imperial also became a major exporter of glassware, including its brilliant carnival patterns. During the Depression, it filed for bankruptcy in 1931, but was able to continue on. By 1962, it was again producing carnival glass patterns. By April 1985, the factory was closed and the molds sold.

Colors made by Imperial include typical carnival colors such as marigold. It added

Carnival glass bowl, Dragon and Lotus pattern,
cobalt blue, 8". $45
Courtesy of Tom Hall Auctions Inc., tomhallauctions.com

Lot of two carnival glass vases, amethyst ribbed,
10" and 12". $90
Courtesy of Tom Hall Auctions Inc., tomhallauctions.com

interesting shades of green, known as helios, a pale ginger ale shade known as clambroth, and a brownish smoke shade.

Forms created by Imperial tend to be functional, such as berry sets and table sets. Patterns vary from wonderful imitation cut glass patterns to detailed florals and naturalistic designs.

MILLERSBURG GLASS CO.

John W. Fenton started the Millersburg Glass Co. in September 1908. Perhaps it was the factory's more obscure location or the lack of business experience by John Fenton, but the company failed by 1911. The factory was bought by Samuel Fair and John Fenton, and renamed the Radium Glass Co., but it lasted only a year.

Colors produced by Millersburg are amethyst, green, and marigold. Shades such as blue and vaseline were added on rare occasions. The company is well known for its bright radium finishes.

Forms produced at Millersburg are mostly bowls and vases. Pattern designers at Millersburg often took one theme and developed several patterns from it. Millersburg often used one pattern for the interior and a different pattern for the exterior.

NORTHWOOD GLASS CO.

Englishman Harry Northwood founded the Northwood Glass Co. He developed his glass formulas for carnival glass, naming it "Golden Iris" in 1908. Northwood was one of the pioneers of the glass manufacturers who marked his wares. Marks range from a full script signature to a simple underscored capital N in a circle. However, not all Northwood glassware is marked.

Northwood created many colors, except for red. Collectors prefer its pastels, such as ice blue, ice green, and white. It is also known for several stunning blue shades.

Forms of Northwood patterns range from typical table sets, bowls, and water sets to whimsical novelties, such as a Corn pattern, which realistically depicts an ear of corn.

Lot of three carnival glass rose bowls, all 4": three-footed, amethyst, Daffidil pattern; six-footed, amethyst, Grape and Cable pattern; and three-footed, amethyst, Bead and Cable pattern. **$40**

Courtesy of Tom Hall Auctions Inc., tomhallauctions.com

UNITED STATES GLASS CO.

In 1891, a consortium of 15 American glass manufacturers joined together as the United States Glass Co. This company was successful in continuing pattern glass production, as well as developing new glass lines. By 1911, it had begun limited production of carnival glass lines, often using existing pattern glass tableware molds. By the time a tornado destroyed the last of its glass factories in Glassport in 1963, it was no longer producing glassware.

Colors associated with US Glass are marigold, white, and a rich honey amber.

Forms tend to be table sets and functional forms.

WESTMORELAND GLASS CO.

Started as the Westmoreland Specialty Co., Grapeville, Pennsylvania, in 1889, this company originally made novelties and glass packing containers, such as candy containers. Researchers have identified its patterns being advertised by Butler Brothers as early as 1908. Carnival glass production continued into the 1920s. In the 1970s, Westmoreland, too, began to reissue carnival glass patterns and novelties. However, this ceased in February of 1996 when the factory burned.

Colors originally used by Westmoreland were typical carnival colors, such as blue and marigold.

Forms include tablewares and functional forms, containers, etc.

Northwood carnival glass bowl, Fruits & Flowers, 10". **$25**

Courtesy of Martin Auction Co., martinauctionco.com

GLASS

consolidated

THE CONSOLIDATED LAMP & GLASS CO. of Coraopolis, Pennsylvania, was founded in 1894. For a number of years it was noted for its lighting wares but also produced popular lines of pressed and blown tableware. Highly collectible glass patterns of this early era include the Cone, Cosmos, Florette, and Guttate lines.

Lamps and shades continued to be good sellers, but in 1926 a new "art" line of molded decorative wares was introduced. This "Martelè" line was developed as a direct imitation of the fine glassware being produced by Renè Lalique of France, and many Consolidated patterns resembled their French counterparts. Other popular lines produced during the 1920s and 1930s were Dancing Nymph, the delightfully Art Deco Ruba Rombic introduced in 1928, and the Catalonian line, which debuted in 1927 and imitated 17th century Spanish glass.

Although the factory closed in 1933, it was reopened under new management in 1936 and prospered through the 1940s. It finally closed in 1967. Collectors should note that many later Consolidated patterns closely resemble wares of other competing firms, especially the Phoenix Glass Co. Careful study is needed to determine the maker of pieces from the 1920-1940 era.

For more information, see *Phoenix & Consolidated Art Glass, 1926-1980*, by Jack D. Wilson (Antique Publications, 1989).

Reuben Haley, Consolidated Lamp and Glass Co., smoky topaz Ruba Rombic toilet water and perfume bottles, Coraopolis, PA, 1920s, partial original foil label to toilet water bottle, 7-3/4", 5" **$1,200**

Courtesy of Rago Arts and Auction Center, ragoarts.com

Consolidated Glass blue frosted charger, features a bacchanalian scene of dancing nymphs with sapphire blue coloring, unsigned, good condition, 17-3/4" dia...**$1,100**

Courtesy of Hill Auction Gallery, hillauctiongallery.com

Consolidated water lily console bowl, colorless with blue staining, design with three open blooms and three bulbs to the interior, factory-polished rim, second quarter 20th century, 3-3/8" h, 14-1/4" d rim. **$150**

Courtesy of Jeffrey S. Evans & Associates, jeffreysevans.com

Reuben Haley, Consolidated Lamp and Glass Co., jungle green Ruba Rombic vase and banana boat, Coraopolis, PA, 1920s, glass unmarked, 6-1/2" x 5", 4-1/4" x 12" x 6". **$1,900**

Courtesy of Rago Arts and Auction Center, ragoarts.com

Reuben Haley, Consolidated Lamp and Glass Co., jungle green Ruba Rombic whiskey decanter and six shot glasses, Coraopolis, PA, 1920s, glass unmarked; decanter: 9" x 7-1/4" x 3-1/2", glasses: 2-5/8" x 2". **$1,900**

Courtesy of Rago Arts and Auction Center, ragoarts.com

Consolidated "open heart arches" master berry bowl with hand-painted flowers, 8-1/4" dia. **$20**

Courtesy of Dennis Auction Service, Inc., dennisauction.com

Reuben Haley, Consolidated Lamp and Glass Co., smoky topaz Ruba Rombic whiskey decanter, tray, and six shot glasses, Coraopolis, PA, 1920s, glass unmarked; decanter: 9" x 7" x 3-3/4", tray: 1" x 11-1/4" x 10-1/2", glasses: 2-1/2" x 2"....................................**$3,250**

Courtesy of Rago Arts and Auction Center, ragoarts.com

Reuben Haley (American, 1872-1933), Consolidated Lamp & Glass Co. Ruba Rombic smoky topaz glass vase, from the estate of renowned historical and architectural author William Robert Mitchell, Jr. of Atlanta, Georgia, approx. 6-1/2" h. **$1,000**

Courtesy of Ahlers & Ogletree Auction Gallery, aandoauctions.com

Consolidated Glass lovebirds vase, features a bulbous body with raised decoration consisting of pairs of lovebirds on leafy branches, unsigned, good condition, 10-1/2" x 9"..........................**$200**

Courtesy of Hill Auction Gallery, hillauctiongallery.com

Consolidated Glass blackberry vase, features detailed raised blackberry and branch decoration with frosted amethyst coloration, unsigned, good overall condition with small chip to base, 18" x 8"... **$200**

Courtesy of Hill Auction Gallery, hillauctiongallery.com

GLASS

custard

"CUSTARD GLASS," AS COLLECTORS CALL it today, came on the American scene in the 1890s, more than a decade after similar colors were made in Europe and England. The Sowerby firm of Gateshead-on-Tyne, England, had marketed its patented "Queen's Ivory Ware" quite successfully in the late 1870s and early 1880s.

There were many glass tableware factories operating in Pennsylvania and Ohio in the 1890s and early 1900s, and the competition among them was keen. Each company sought to capture the public's favor with distinctive colors and, often, hand-painted decoration. That is when "custard glass" appeared on the American scene.

The opaque yellow color of this glass varies from a rich, vivid yellow to a lustrous light yellow. Regardless of intensity, the hue was originally called "ivory" by several glass manufacturers who also used superlative sounding terms such as "Ivorina Verde" and "Carnelian." Most custard glass contains uranium, so it will "glow" under a black light.

Five souvenir pieces of Lancaster, PA, including pitchers, bowl and toothpick holders, tallest is 5-1/4" h...................... **$190**

Courtesy of Conestoga Auction Company Division of Hess Auction Group, hessauctiongroup.com

The most important producer of custard glass was certainly Harry Northwood, who first made it at his plants in Indiana, Pennsylvania, in the late 1890s and, later, in his Wheeling, West Virginia, factory. Northwood marked some of his most famous patterns, but much early custard is unmarked. Other key manufacturers include the Heisey Glass Co., Newark, Ohio; the Jefferson Glass Co., Steubenville, Ohio; the Tarentum Glass Co., Tarentum, Pennsylvania; and the Fenton Art Glass Co., Williamstown, West Virginia.

Custard glass fanciers are particular about condition and generally insist on pristine quality decorations free from fading or wear. Souvenir custard pieces with events, places, and dates on them usually bring the best prices in the areas commemorated on them rather than from the specialist collector. Also, collectors who specialize in pieces such as cruets, syrups, or salt and pepper shakers will often pay higher prices for these pieces than would a custard collector.

Key reference sources include William Heacock's *Custard Glass from A to Z*, published in 1976 but not out of print, and the book *Harry Northwood: The Early Years*, available from Glass Press. Heisey's custard glass is discussed in Shirley Dunbar's *Heisey Glass: The Early Years* (Krause Publications, 2000), and Coudersport's production is well-documented in Tulla Majot's book, *Coudersport's Glass 1900-1904* (Glass Press, 1999). The Custard Glass Society holds a yearly convention and maintains a web site: www.homestead.com/custardsociety.

— James Measell

French Art Deco custard glass compote, gold border with floral, 5-1/2" h x 9" w.....................$40

Courtesy of Premier Auction Galleries, premierauctiongalleries.com

Fenton blue custard burmese glass ruffle vase, hand-painted roses, 1950s, satin, signed on the bottom, 7" h...$35

Courtesy of Vidi Vici Gallery, vidivicigallery.com

Scarce bee and beehive custard glass salt and pepper set...$15

Courtesy of Col. Christie Hatman Auctioneers, christiehatman.com

Heisey ring band syrup pitcher, custard with floral polychrome and gilt decoration, with period lid, A. H. Heisey & Co., late 19th/early 20th century, glass un-damaged, lid lacking thumbrest, 7" h......$90

Courtesy of Jeffrey S. Evans & Associates, jeffreysevans.com

Custard glass luster, 14".........................$30

Courtesy of Leonard's Auction Service, leonardauction.com

Lot of two custard glass syrup pitchers, comprising a sunset and a creased bale example, each with a period lid and applied handle, various makers, late 19th/first quarter 20th century, undamaged with the creased bale lid-top being loose, 6" h..$80

Courtesy of Jeffrey S. Evans & Associates, jeffreysevans.com

Assorted custard glass toothpick holders, lot of four, comprising a Heisey Winged Scroll with gilt decoration, a Bees on Basket with blue-staining, and a Ribbed Drape example with polychrome-enamel decoration, together with an opaque white Heisey Bead Swag toothpick holder with polychrome-enamel decoration, various makers, fourth quarter 19th/first quarter 20th century, 2-1/4" to 2-1/2" h. $80

Courtesy of Jeffrey S. Evans & Associates, jeffreysevans.com

GLASS

daum nancy

DAUM NANCY FINE GLASS, much of it cameo, was made by Auguste and Antonin Daum, who founded the factory in 1875 in Nancy, France. Most of their cameo and enameled glass was made from the 1890s into the early 20th century.

Cameo glass is made by carving into multiple layers of colored glass to create a design in relief. It is at least as old as the Romans.

Daum Nancy glass bowl, 3-1/2" h x 6-1/5" w... **$550**
Courtesy of Bruce Kodner Galleries, brucekodner.com

Daum Nancy cameo glass covered powder or dresser box, depicting orchids, signed "Daum Nancy" with the Croix de Lorraine, 3-1/4" dia x 2" h. **$450**

Courtesy of Clarke Auction Gallery, clarkeny.com

Exceptional Daum Nancy sugar and creamer with mushrooms, France, ca. 1900, acid-etched and enameled internally decorated glass, each signed Daum Nancy with Croix de Lorraine, 5-1/2", 4". **$6,500**
Courtesy of Rago Arts and Auction Center, ragoarts.com

VISIT WWW.ANTIQUETRADER.COM

WWW.FACEBOOK.COM/ANTIQUETRADER

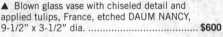

▲ Blown glass vase with chiseled detail and applied tulips, France, etched DAUM NANCY, 9-1/2" x 3-1/2" dia. **$600**

Courtesy of Rago Arts and Auction Center, ragoarts.com

◄ Daum Nancy wall sconce In green Pate De Verre shade in stylized foliage design, signed along lower edge in engraved "Daum France," includes original box for shade, 7" dia x 9" h with original bronzed metal wall mounted torchiere fixture, 33" h, total height 38-1/2". **$550**

Courtesy of Forsythes' Auctions, LLC, forsytheauctions.com

French cameo art glass vase, signed with Cross of Lorraine (Daum Nancy) mark, cased orange background with dark lavender overlay, pine branch and needles decoration, chip repair to base, 10-3/4". **$270**

Courtesy of Woody Auction LLC, woodyauction.com

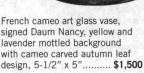

Daum Nancy French cameo art glass vase, signed Daum Nancy, fall scene, 4-3/4" h. **$3,000**

Courtesy of Woody Auction LLC, woodyauction.com

French cameo art glass vase, signed Daum Nancy, three blackbirds on winter scene background, 4-1/2" x 5". . **$3,500**

Courtesy of Woody Auction LLC, woodyauction.com

French cameo art glass vase, signed Daum Nancy, yellow and lavender mottled background with cameo carved autumn leaf design, 5-1/2" x 5". **$1,500**

Courtesy of Woody Auction LLC, woodyauction.com

▲ Art Nouveau wrought iron and glass lamp, signed, Daum Nancy, excellent condition, 12" h, 12" d. **$500**

Courtesy of Louvre Antique Auction, liveauctioneers.com

▶ Daum Nancy eagle sculpture, limited edition in multi-colored Pate De Verre glass, titled "Aigle" and numbered 249/1000, etched signature on base Daum France/249/1000, spread winged eagle clutching tree branch, original box with numbered certificate, booklet, and other paper work, 11" x 9" x 9-1/4" h. **$750**

Courtesy of Forsythes' Auctions, LLC, forsytheauctions.com

Daum Nancy orange flower drinking cup, 5" h. **$850**

Courtesy of World Auction Gallery LLC, worldauctiongallery.com

Daum Nancy silver mounted perfume bottle, 6" h. **$400**

Courtesy of World Auction Gallery LLC, worldauctiongallery.com

Daum Nancy mushroom table lamp, green and blue, signed Daum Nancy, heat crack in shade, 15" h. **$400**

Courtesy of Nadeau's Auction Gallery, nadeausauction.com

GLASS

depression glass

DEPRESSION GLASS IS the name of colorful glassware collectors generally associated with mass-produced glassware found in pink, yellow, crystal, or green in the years surrounding the Great Depression in America.

The homemakers of the Depression-era were able to enjoy the wonderful colors offered in this new inexpensive glass dinnerware because they received pieces of their favorite patterns packed in boxes of soap, or as premiums given at "dish night" at the local movie theater. Merchandisers, such as Sears & Roebuck and F. W. Woolworth, enticed young brides with the colorful wares that they could afford even when economic times were harsh.

Because of advancements in glassware technology, Depression-era patterns were mass-produced and could be purchased for a fraction of what cut glass or lead crystal cost. As one manufacturer found a pattern that was pleasing to the buying public, other companies soon followed with their adaptation of a similar design. Patterns included several design motifs, such as florals, geometrics, and even patterns that looked back to Early American patterns like Sandwich glass.

As America emerged from the Great Depression and life became more leisure-oriented again, new glassware patterns were created to reflect the new tastes of this generation. More elegant shapes and forms were designed, leading to what is sometimes called "Elegant Glass." Today's collectors often include these more elegant patterns when they talk about Depression-era glassware.

Depression-era glassware is one of the best-researched collecting areas available to the American marketplace. This is due in large part to the careful research of several people, including Hazel Marie Weatherman, Gene Florence, Barbara Mauzy, Carl F. Luckey, and Kent

Lot of blue Depression glass, most items in the Caprice pattern. **$60**
Courtesy of Donny Malone Auctions, donnymaloneauctions.com

Washburn. Their books are held in high regard by researchers and collectors today.

Regarding values for Depression glass, rarity does not always equate to a high dollar amount. Some more readily found items command lofty prices because of high demand or other factors, not because they are necessarily rare. As collectors' tastes range from the simple patterns to the more elaborate patterns, so does the ability of their budget to invest in inexpensive patterns to multi-hundreds of dollars per form patterns.

For more information on Depression glass, see *Warman's Depression Glass Identification and Price Guide*, 6th Edition, or *Warman's Depression Glass Handbook*, both by Ellen T. Schroy.

Lot of blue Depression pressed glass and Jeanette cake platter, 5"-5-3/4" h, 3-3/4" dia. **$20**
Courtesy of Donny Malone Auctions, donnymaloneauctions.com

Depression glass pink Candlewick Bubble cake plate, trimmed and in relief, with beaded detail, approx. 11" dia, 5" h. **$25**
Courtesy of The Benefit Shop Foundation Inc., thebenefitshop.org

Green flower console and candle sticks, etched glass, with matching candlesticks, 2-1/2" h, 12" w and 1-1/2" h, 5" w. **$10**
Courtesy of Donny Malone Auctions, donnymaloneauctions.com

Children's dishes, 23 pieces, Jeanette Cherry Blossom in pink, seven dinner plates, five cups, eight saucers, two sugars and one creamer, all excellent condition, largest 6" dia........**$70**
Courtesy of Rich Penn Auctions, richpennauctions.com

PATTERN SILHOUETTE **Identification Guide**

Depression-era glassware can be confusing. Many times a manufacturer came up with a neat new design, and as soon as it was successful, other companies started to make patterns that were similar. To help you figure out what pattern you might be trying to research, here's a quick identification guide. The patterns are broken down into several different classifications by design elements.

ART DECO

Ovide

BASKETS

Lorain

BEADED EDGES

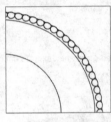

Beaded Edge

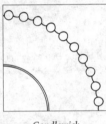

Candlewick

BIRDS

Delilah

Georgian

Parrot

Peacock & Wild Rose

BLOCKS

BOWS

COINS

Coin

CUBES

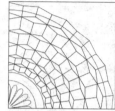

American

Cube

DIAMONDS

Cape Cod

Diamond Quilted

English Hobnail

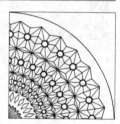

Holiday

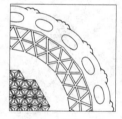

Laced Edge

Miss America

Peanut Butter

Waterford

Windsor

ELLIPSES (FANS)

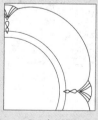

Crow's Foot

Newport

Romanesque

GLASS

FIGURES

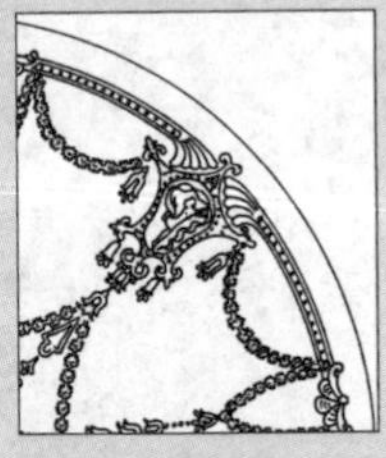

FLORALS

Cameo

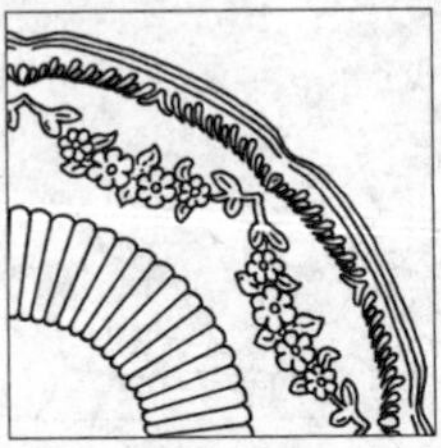

Alice

Cherry Blossom

Cloverleaf

Cupid

Daisy

Dogwood

Doric

Doric & Pansy

Floragold

Floral

Floral and Diamond Band

Flower Garden with Butterflies

Indiana Custard

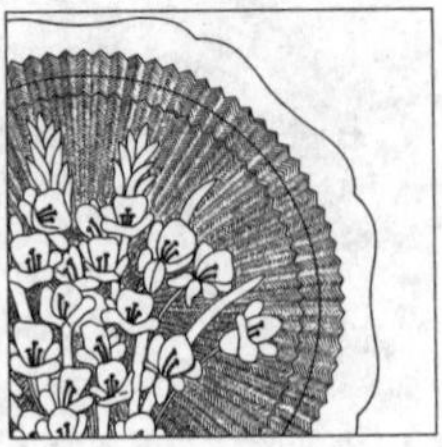

Iris

Jubilee

FLORALS

Mayfair (Federal)

Mayfair (Open Rose)

Normandie

Orange Blossom

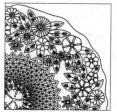

Pineapple & Floral

Primrose

Rosemary

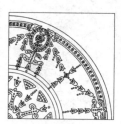

Rose Cameo

Royal Lace

Seville

Sharon

Sunflower

Thistle

Tulip

Vitrock

Wild Rose

FRUITS

Avocado

Cherryberry

Della Robbia

Fruits

Paneled Grape

Strawberry

GEOMETRIC & LINE DESIGNS

Cracked Ice

Cape Cod

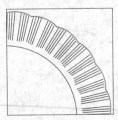

Cremax

Early American Prescut

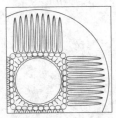

Park Avenue

Pioneer

Sierra

Star

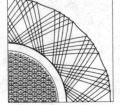

Starlight

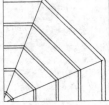

Tea Room

HONEYCOMB

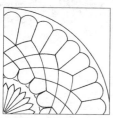

Aunt Polly

Hex Optic

HORSESHOE

Horseshoe

LEAVES

Laurel Leaf

Sunburst

LACY DESIGNS

Harp

Heritage

S-Pattern

*Sandwich
(Duncan Miller)*

Sandwich (Hocking)

Sandwich (Indiana)

LOOPS

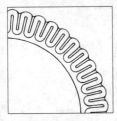
Christmas Candy

Crocheted Crystal

Pretzel

PETALS

Aurora

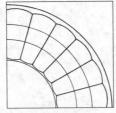
Block Optic

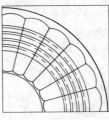
Circle

Colonial

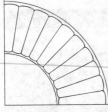
National

New Century

Old Café

Ribbon

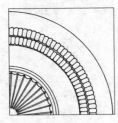
Roulette

Round Robin

Victory

PETALS/RIDGES WITH DIAMOND ACCENTS

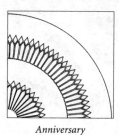

Anniversary

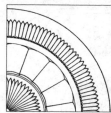

Coronation

Fortune

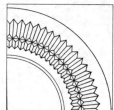

Lincoln Inn

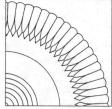

Petalware

Queen Mary

PLAIN

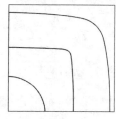

Charm

Mt. Pleasant

PYRAMIDS

Pyramid

RAISED BAND

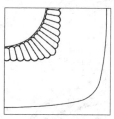

Charm

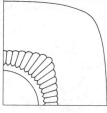

Forest Green

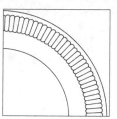

Jane Ray

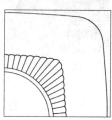

Royal Ruby

GLASS

RAISED CIRCLES

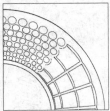

American Pioneer

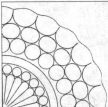

Bubble

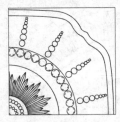

Columbia

Dewdrop

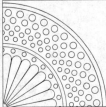

Hobnail

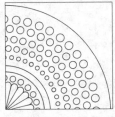

Moonstone

Oyster & Pearl

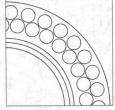

Raindrops

Radiance

Ships

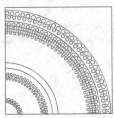

Teardrop

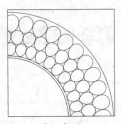

Thumbprint

RIBS

Homespun

RINGS (CIRCLES)

Manhattan

Moderntone

Moondrops

Moroccan Amethyst

Old English

Ring

SCENES

Chinex Classic

Lake Como

SCROLLING DESIGNS

Adam

American Sweetheart

Florentine No. 1

Florentine No. 2

Madrid

Patrick

Philbe

Primo

Princess

Rock Crystal

Roxana

Vernon

SWIRLS

Colony

Diana

Fairfax

Jamestown

Spiral

Swirl

Swirl (Fire King)

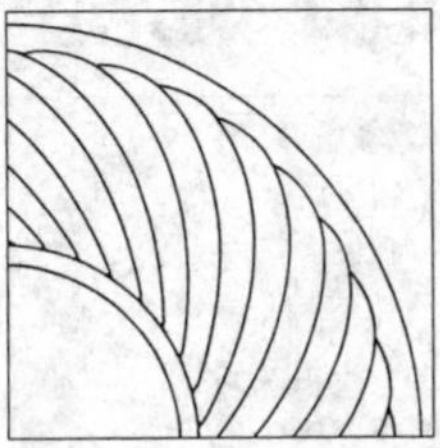

Twisted Optic

TEXTURED

Lot of 17 assorted pieces in the Diamond Cube pattern, diameter range: 5" to 13-1/5". **$40**

Courtesy of Donny Malone Auctions, donnymaloneauctions.com

▲ Depression glass set in the Iris and Herringbone pattern, features an amber iridescent hue garnished by embossed iris patterns enveloped by textured herringbone patterns, comprises a vase, pitcher, and a pair of two light candelabras, early 20th century, vase is 9" h, 5-1/2" dia; pitcher is 9" h; candelabras 5-3/8" h, 6" l. **$100**

Courtesy of Akiba Antiques, akibaantiques.com

Lot of pink Mayfair ice tea tumblers, footed, 6" to 6-3/4". **$50**

Courtesy of Strawser Auction Group, strawserauctions.com

GLASS

Four assorted Open Lace pink bowls, 2-1/2" h, 9-1/2" d, 3-1/4" h, 7" d..$15
Courtesy of Donny Malone Auctions, donnymaloneauctions.com

Set of 17 Miss America pink sherbets, 3-3/4" h, 3-1/2" d..$40
Courtesy of Donny Malone Auctions, donnymaloneauctions.com

Set of 14 Miss America pink luncheon plates, 8-1/2" d..$50
Courtesy of Donny Malone Auctions, donnymaloneauctions.com

GLASS

durand

FINE DECORATIVE GLASS similar to that made by Tiffany and other outstanding glasshouses of its day was made by Vineland Flint Glass Works Co. in Vineland, New Jersey, first headed by Victor Durand Sr. and subsequently by his son, Victor Durand Jr., in the 1920s.

Durand Ribbed-Optic art glass amethyst pieces comprising an unsigned champagne, a signed tazza, each with a polished pontil mark, with two Ribbed-Optic finger bowls, each with a polished pontil mark, Vineland Flint Glass Works, 1924-1931, 2-1/4" h to 6" h, 6-3/4" d tazza rim. **$170**

Courtesy of Jeffrey S. Evans & Associates, jeffreysevans.com

Moorish crackle art glass ginger jars, golden yellow luster with opal and ruby overlay, each with original cover with applied finials, each with a polished pontil mark, each signed, "DURAND," Vineland Flint Glass Works, 1924-1931, 9" h, 3-1/4" dia. vase rims, 3-3/4" dia. cover rims. **$900**

Courtesy of Jeffrey S. Evans & Associates, jeffreysevans.com

J.G. Durand French art glass single-light candlesticks, original label to each, 10" h.**$125**

Courtesy of DuMouchelles, dumouchelle.com

King Tut art glass vase, Lady Day Rose with gold decoration, polished pontil mark, signed, Vineland Flint Glass Works, 1924-1931, 5-7/8" h, 2-7/8" d rim. **$1,300**

Courtesy of Jeffrey S. Evans & Associates jeffreysevans.com

Cameo art glass vase, blue over opal over ambergris, spherical form, polished pontil mark, signed "DURAND/V/1995-8," Vineland Flint Glass Works, 1924-1931, 6-7/8" h, 4" dia. rim.................................. **$3,750**

Courtesy of Jeffrey S. Evans & Associates, jeffreysevans.com

Iridescent glass Zig-Zag vase, circa 1910, 5" h. **$550**

Courtesy of Heritage Auctions, ha.com

Optic-Ribbed large art glass trumpet vase, amethyst, applied circular foot, polished pontil mark, signed "DURAND/V/20120-16," Vineland Flint Glass Works, 1924-1931, 15-1/2" h, 5-3/8" dia. rim. **$475**

Courtesy of Jeffrey S. Evans & Associates, jeffreysevans.com

Pulled Feather art glass cut vase, yellow luster with blue decoration, urn form with floral decoration, polished pontil mark, signed "DURAND," Vineland Flint Glass Works, 1924-1931, 7-1/4" h, 4-1/2" dia. rim. **$250**

Courtesy of Jeffrey S. Evans & Associates, jeffreysevans.com

Iridescent glass King Tut covered compote, late 20th century, 6-3/8" h. **$800**

Courtesy of Heritage Auctions, ha.com

◀ Blue aurene art glass vase converted into a table lamp, raised on a wooden plithe just above the brass base, having a brass neck and fixture, complete with a bell-shaped milk glass shade, approx. 30-1/2" h. **$250**

Courtesy of Auction Gallery of Boca Raton, LLC, liveauctioneers.com

Hearts and Vines art glass vase, iridized gold with trailing heart and vine decoration, signed under the base, 6-1/4" x 4". **$725**

Courtesy of Soulis Auctions, dirksoulisauctions.com

Iridescent peacock blue ribbed glass bud vase/genie bottle, original purchase sticker on bottom with a price of $2,800, approx. 12-1/4" h, 8" w. **$500**

Courtesy of Burchard Galleries Inc., burchardgalleries.com

King Tut art glass ginger jar, green luster with gold decoration, shape 1964, original cover, polished pontil mark, faint signature, Vineland Flint Glass Works, 1924-1931, 7" h, 5-1/2" w. **$2,600**

Courtesy of Jeffrey S. Evans & Associates, jeffreysevans.com

Durand-attributed peacock feather whimsy/dish, ruby to colorless with ruby and opal loopings, applied central button, five-petal flower in the base, applied opal rim, Vineland Flint Glass Works, 1924-1931, 5-1/2" dia. **$120**

Courtesy of Jeffrey S. Evans & Associates, jeffreysevans.com

GLASS

fenton

THE FENTON ART GLASS CO. was founded in 1905 by Frank L. Fenton and his brother, John W., in Martins Ferry, Ohio. They initially sold hand-painted glass made by other manufacturers, but it wasn't long before they decided to produce their own glass. The new Fenton factory in Williamstown, West Virginia, opened on Jan. 2, 1907. From that point on, the company expanded by developing unusual colors and continued to decorate glassware in innovative ways.

Lot of three hand-painted Fenton art glass deer figures, 3-3/4" h. $80
Courtesy of Dennis Auction Service, Inc., dennisauction.com

Two more brothers, James and Robert, joined the firm. But despite the company's initial success, John W. left to establish the Millersburg Glass Co. of Millersburg, Ohio, in 1909. The first months of the new operation were devoted to the production of crystal glass only. Later iridized glass was called "Radium Glass." After only two years, Millersburg filed for bankruptcy.

Fenton's iridescent glass had a metallic luster over a colored, pressed pattern and was sold in dime stores. It was only after the sales of this glass decreased and it was sold in bulk as carnival prizes that it came to be known as carnival glass.

Fenton became the top producer of carnival glass, with more than 150 patterns. The quality of the glass and its popularity with the public enabled the new company to be profitable through the late 1920s. As interest in carnival glass subsided, Fenton moved on to stretch glass and opalescent patterns. A line of colorful blown glass (called "off-hand" by Fenton) was also produced in the mid-1920s.

During the Great Depression, Fenton survived by producing functional colored glass tableware and other household items, including water sets, table sets, bowls, mugs, plates, perfume bottles, and vases. Restrictions on European imports during World War II ushered in the arrival of Fenton's opaque colored glass, and the lines of "Crest" pieces soon followed. In the 1950s, production continued to diversify with a focus on milk glass, particularly in hobnail patterns. In the third quarter of Fenton's history, the company returned to themes that had proved popular to preceding generations and began adding special lines such as the Bicentennial series.

Innovations included the line of Colonial colors that debuted in 1963, including amber, blue, green, orange, and ruby. Based on a special order for an Ohio museum, Fenton in 1969 revisited its early success with "Original Formula Carnival Glass." Fenton also started marking its glass in molds for the first time.

The star of the 1970s was the yellow and blushing pink creation known as Burmese. This was followed closely by a menagerie of animals, birds, and children. In 1975, Robert Barber was hired by Fenton to begin an artist-in-residence program, producing a limited line of art glass vases in a return to the off-hand, blown-glass creations of the mid-1920s. Shopping at home via television was a phenomenon in the late 1980s when the "Birthstone Bears" became the first Fenton product to appear on QVC. In August 2007, Fenton discontinued all but a few of its more popular lines, and the company ceased production altogether in 2011.

For more information on Fenton Art Glass, see *Warman's Fenton Glass Identification and Price Guide*, 2nd edition, by Mark F. Moran.

Fenton art glass candy dish, iridescent blue-toned glass dish with curved, scalloped edges and handles, raised, dimensional butterfly design, approx. 2" h x 9" w x 6" l. **$10**

Courtesy of The Benefit Shop Foundation Inc., thebenefitshop.org

▲ Multicolored Fenton art glass centerpiece, pink, blue, and green glass, in a bowl shape with excess glass on the ends, 12" x 14-1/2" x 9-1/2" **$50**

Courtesy of Greenwich Auction, greenwichauction.net

◄ Fenton amber glass compote, 5-1/4" dia x 5" h. ...**$12**

Courtesy of Pioneer Auction Gallery, icollector.com; liveauctioneers.com

Drapery water pitcher, green with polychrome-enamel decoration, globular-form with flared star-crimped rim and applied handle, floral decoration, Fenton Art Glass Co., circa 1910, 9-1/2" h. **$40**

Courtesy of Jeffrey S. Evans & Associates, jeffreysevans.com

Fenton art glass peachblow frog, artist J Dowler for Janet Dowler. $29

Courtesy of Franckearth, franckearth.com

Fenton cranberry opalescent swirl water pitcher and four tumblers, circa 1938, pitcher with ruffled and pinched rim/spout, reeded clear glass applied handle, 9-1/2" h. $175

Courtesy of Stony Ridge Auction, stonyridgeauction.com

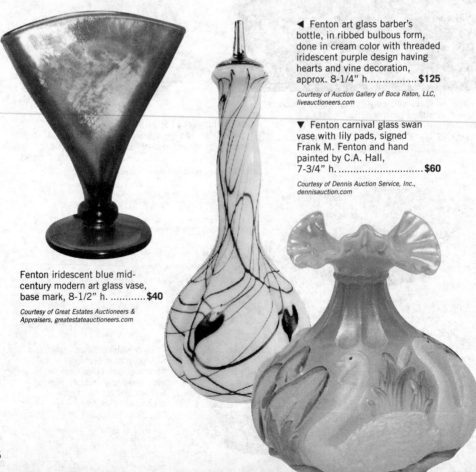

◀ Fenton art glass barber's bottle, in ribbed bulbous form, done in cream color with threaded iridescent purple design having hearts and vine decoration, approx. 8-1/4" h.................$125

Courtesy of Auction Gallery of Boca Raton, LLC, liveauctioneers.com

▼ Fenton carnival glass swan vase with lily pads, signed Frank M. Fenton and hand painted by C.A. Hall, 7-3/4" h. $60

Courtesy of Dennis Auction Service, Inc., dennisauction.com

Fenton iridescent blue mid-century modern art glass vase, base mark, 8-1/2" h. $40

Courtesy of Great Estates Auctioneers & Appraisers, greatestateauctioneers.com

GLASS

fostoria

THE FOSTORIA GLASS CO., founded in 1887, produced numerous types of fine glassware over the years. During its first ten years, Fostoria made pressed ware, but early in the 20th century, the company realized the importance of developing fine quality blown stemware.

In 1924, the company was one of the first to start a program of national advertising, and the first to produce complete dinner services in crystal. Besides their regular line of blown, etched, and pressed patterns, Fostoria did custom work such as providing glass with government seals for officials in Washington. All the presidents from Eisenhower through Reagan ordered glassware from them. At one time, Fostoria was the largest maker of handmade glassware in the United States, employing nearly 1,000 people. The American pattern, introduced in 1915, is still being produced by Lancaster Colony (who bought the Fostoria company in 1983), making it the most successful pattern in glass-making history. Fostoria's business peaked in 1950 when it made more than 8 million pieces of glass.

Fostoria's factory in Moundsville, West Virginia, closed in 1986.

There is an active group today, The Fostoria Glass Society of America, Inc., whose mission is to acquire and disseminate detailed knowledge concerning Fostoria Glass, and to establish and maintain a museum for housing and displaying Fostoria glass. For more information about this nonprofit, tax-exempt corporation, fostoriaglass.org.

Lot of 9 Fostoria "Colonial Dame" dark green and clear glass water goblets, unmarked, having swirl standard and base, approx. 6-3/4" h, 3-3/4" dia. **$50**

Courtesy of Austin Auction Gallery, austinauction.com

Fostoria June Pink cream and covered sugar, 3-3/4" h. **$40**

Courtesy of Specialists of the South, Inc., specialistsofthesouth.com

Four Fostoria June Pink parfait glasses, 5-1/4" h. **$100**

Courtesy of Specialists of the South, Inc., specialistsofthesouth.com

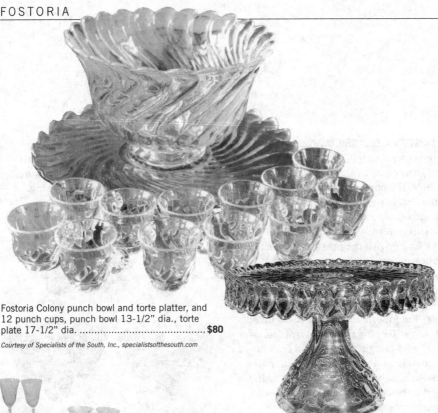

Fostoria Colony punch bowl and torte platter, and 12 punch cups, punch bowl 13-1/2" dia., torte plate 17-1/2" dia. **$80**

Courtesy of Specialists of the South, Inc., specialistsofthesouth.com

Fostoria American Crystal round glass pedestal cake plate, 1930s, scalloped edges above and below plate, molded to have old-fashioned "brandy well" in the center so you can fill it if you want to keep the cake moist or catch the liquor that was poured over some types of cakes during this era, classic round shape, excellent condition, 7" h x 10" w. **$70**

Courtesy of Jasper52, jasper52.com

A 54-piece Fostoria Trojan pattern table and stemware service in Topaz, comprising: 10 iced tea glasses, 5-3/4" h; eight water goblets, 8-1/4" h; eight champagne stems, 6" h; 10 plates, 8-3/4" dia; eight small side plates, 6" dia.; one console bowl, 12" dia.; three small dishes, one folded, one divided, and one handled; pair creamer and sugar; one service dish, 11" dia.; pair candlesticks; together with one unassociated colorless lidded dish, with cut to clear amber accent, 6-1/2" h. **$175**

Courtesy of Austin Auction Gallery, austinauction.com

Five-piece Fostoria amethyst   glass water set, includes four water glasses and water pitcher, pitcher 11" h, glasses measures 5-3/8" h. **$50**

Courtesy of Kodner Galleries Inc., kodner.com

Gone with the Wind table lamp, brown and pink tones with large poppy blossom decoration, original kerosene font, 25-1/2" h. **$550**

Courtesy of Woody Auction, LLC, woodyauction.com

Original Gone with the Wind table lamp, red satin Beaded Acanthus pattern, original fittings, excellent condition, 23" h. **$300**

Courtesy of Woody Auction, LLC, woodyauction.com

Gone with the Wind lamp, white satin Beaded Acanthus pattern, tank has been modified, glass in very good condition, 23-1/2" h. **$400**

Courtesy of Woody Auction, LLC, woodyauction.com

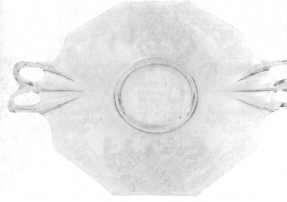

Fostoria "Elite Princess" peg lamps, cased soft pink with satin finish melon-form fonts, acid-etched rubina shades with molded bead and bulge pattern, floral etching and lightly crimped rims, No. 1 Taplin-Brown collars, pegs with metal sleeves and spring tabs, fitted with period Argand-style slip burners marked for Plume & Atwood Victor, non-period colorless slip chimneys, fitted in brass baluster-form candlesticks with push-up mechanisms and octagonal bases, Fostoria fonts/shades, fourth quarter 19th century; overall 14-3/4" h, fonts are 3-3/4" h to top and 4" dia, shade 4" h, 2-1/4" d fitter. **$250**

Courtesy of Jeffrey S. Evans & Associates, jeffreysevans.com

Fostoria June Pink cheese and cracker plate, 10" dia. **$45**

Courtesy of Specialists of the South, Inc., specialistsofthesouth.com

GLASS

gallé

GALLÉ GLASS WAS MADE in Nancy, France, by Emile Gallé, founder of the Nancy School and leader in the Art Nouveau movement in France. Much of his glass, both enameled and cameo, is decorated with naturalistic motifs. The finest pieces were made in the last two decades of the 19th century and the opening years of the 20th.

Pieces marked with a star preceding the name were made between 1904, the year of Gallé's death, and 1914.

Emile Gallé art glass cameo vase, circa 1900, vibrant purple with naturalistic and scrolling cameo motifs, signed Gallé paper label to underside, 9-1/2" h x 8-1/2" dia. **$700**

Courtesy of Peachtree & Bennett, peachtreebennett.com

Large marquetry glass crocus vase of tapering, flattened cylindrical form, the front decorated with three flowers, the back with two flowers, having internal decoration with engraved Gallé signature, 14" h....................................**$26,000**

Courtesy of Hidden Treasures Antiques & Fine Art, htantiques.com

Cameo glass bowl, circa 1900, the clear glass sides boldly streaked with crimson, overlaid in crimson and opalescent blue-green and finely wheel carved with a grasshopper amongst unfurling fern fronds, signed in cameo "Cristallerie/d'Emile Gallé/a Nancy" within a fern, 3-7/8" h. **$4,000**

Courtesy of Hidden Treasures Antiques & Fine Art, htantiques.com

VISIT WWW.ANTIQUETRADER.COM

WWW.FACEBOOK.COM/ANTIQUETRADER

Bulbous scenic cameo glass vase with palm trees, signed Gallé, 11"........................ **$400**

Courtesy of Berman's Auction Gallery, bermansauctiongallery.com

A small French enameled and gilt decorated ewer, circa 1900, signed intaglio for Gallé, full signature in intaglio reads "Emile Galle/Nancy/Modéle et décor depose," 3-1/2" h... **$3,250**

Courtesy of Hidden Treasures Antiques & Fine Art, htantiques.com

Cameo glass cup, circa 1910, signed Gallé, 8-1/8" h. **$5,000**

Courtesy of Hidden Treasures Antiques & Fine Art, htantiques.com

French cameo art glass vase, signed Gallé, frosted white background with orange cameo carved floral overlay, fire polished, 4" x 5"................ **$450**

Courtesy of Woody Auction LLC, woodyauction.com

Cameo glass lamp, circa 1900, shade is signed in cameo Gallé, base is signed in intaglio Gallé, mint condition, 28" h, 14" w. **$20,000**

Courtesy of Hidden Treasures Antiques & Fine Art, htantiques.com

Vase, amber-colored cameo sunflower decoration, sunflowers have stylized leaves and stems surrounding body of the vase with stylized sunburst on side, each flower has applied glass center, sunburst has amber glass applied center with foil inclusions, main sunflower has large silver foil inclusion behind the flower, two other floral centers are cameo carved, amber decoration is set on amber shading to cream background with fire polished finish, signed on the underside with elaborate signature "Gallé Depose," 8" dia, 6" h...............**$6,000**

Courtesy of Hidden Treasures Antiques & Fine Art, htantiques.com

GLASS

GLASS

heisey

NUMEROUS TYPES OF fine glass were made by A.H. Heisey & Co., Newark, Ohio, from 1895. The company's trademark, an H enclosed within a diamond, has become known to most glass collectors. The company's name and molds were acquired by Imperial Glass Co., Bellaire, Ohio, in 1958, and some pieces have been reissued.

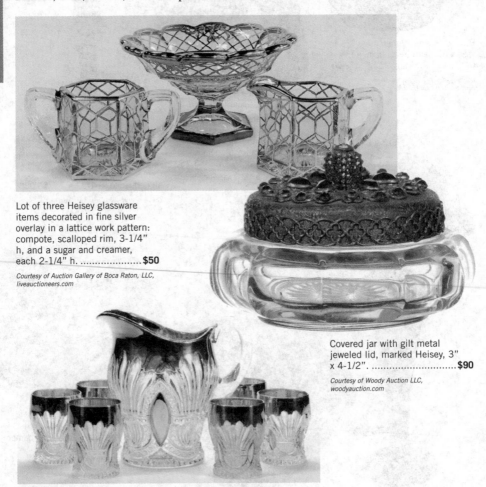

Lot of three Heisey glassware items decorated in fine silver overlay in a lattice work pattern: compote, scalloped rim, 3-1/4" h, and a sugar and creamer, each 2-1/4" h. **$50**

Courtesy of Auction Gallery of Boca Raton, LLC, liveauctioneers.com

Covered jar with gilt metal jeweled lid, marked Heisey, 3" x 4-1/2". **$90**

Courtesy of Woody Auction LLC, woodyauction.com

No. 335 Prince of Wales seven-piece water set, colorless with gilt decoration, comprising a water pitcher and six tumblers with factory-polished table rings, pitcher with H-in-diamond trademark to the base, circa 1902, pitcher 8-5/8" h, tumblers 4" h......................**$140**

Courtesy of Jeffrey S. Evans & Associates, jeffreysevans.com

VISIT WWW.ANTIQUETRADER.COM

WWW.FACEBOOK.COM/ANTIQUETRADER

A rare Eva Zeisel Town & Country salad serving set, contained in original packaging, comprising a mold-blown glass salad bowl and underplate in Limelight, silverplate serving fork and spoon by Three Crowns Silversmiths, Pottstown, Pennsylvania, held in an A.H. Heisey & Co. blue silver cloth slipcover, 1953-1954, contained in the original Heisey printed box with label indicating it was shipped from Heisey to Zinsmaster Bread Company of Duluth, Minnesota, in December 1955. Salad bowl, 11-1/4" dia.; underplate 14" dia.; spoon 11-5/8"; fork 11-7/8". **$550**

Courtesy of John Atzbach Antiques, atzbach.com

No. 1401 Empress salt and pepper shakers, Alexandrite, with original colorless lids, first half 20th century, 3-3/8" h....................................**$110**

Courtesy of Jeffrey S. Evans & Associates, jeffreysevans.com

Rectangular ice bucket, cut crystal, canted corners, mounted with a bail handle and encased in a footed ormolu frame with laurel rails and garland festoons, each end centering a standing female in classical gown, laurel wreaths and other symbols of empire, Heisey signature under the base, 10" x 8-1/2" x 5". **$375**

Courtesy of Soulis Auctions, dirksoulis.com

Heisey No. 335 Prince of Wales ruby-stained three-piece table set, colorless, comprising a covered butter dish, a covered sugar bowl, and creamer, each with H-in-diamond trademark to the base, circa 1902, 5-1/4" h to 7" h...**$275**

Courtesy of Jeffrey S. Evans & Associates, jeffreysevans.com

No. 160 Locket on Chain ruby-stained tumbler, colorless with gilt decoration, 1896-1904, 3-3/4" h. **$170**

Courtesy of Jeffrey S. Evans & Associates, jeffreysevans.com

GLASS

GLASS

imperial

FROM 1902 UNTIL 1984, Imperial Glass Co. of Bellaire, Ohio, produced hand-made glass. Early pressed glass production often imitated cut glass and may bear the raised "NUCUT" mark in the interior center. In the second decade of the 1900s, Imperial was one of the dominant manufacturers of iridescent or carnival glass. When glass collecting gained popularity in the 1970s, Imperial again produced carnival glass and a line of multicolored slag glass. Imperial purchased molds from closing glasshouses and continued many lines popularized by others including Central, Heisey, and Cambridge. These reissues may cause confusion but they were often marked.

Free-hand cut art glass vase, colorless and cobalt blue, Free Hand No. 514, decoration No. 16, two flowers to the vase with branching foliate decoration, applied double handles and circular base, retains manufacturing label, Imperial Glass Co., circa 1925, 10-1/8" h, 6-1/4" dia. **$2,300**

Courtesy of Jeffrey S. Evans & Associates, jeffreysevans.com

Lace Band ruby-stained covered condiment jar, colorless, Imperial Glass Co., circa 1902, 4-3/4" h. $80

Courtesy of Jeffrey S. Evans & Associates, jeffreysevans.com

Glass dish with cover in a lion form, good condition, 6-1/2" h x 7-1/2" x 6"...................... $40

Courtesy of Martin Auction Co., martinauction.com

DeVilbiss, art glass atomizer, 1926, gilt acid-cut design, orange interior, metal hardware, DeVilbiss mark, 5-1/4" h. **$600**

Courtesy of Perfume Bottles Auction, perfumebottlesauction.com

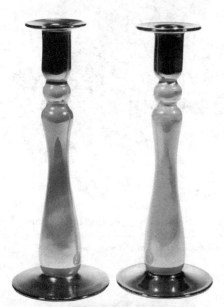

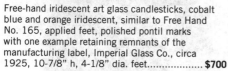

Free-hand iridescent art glass candlesticks, cobalt blue and orange iridescent, similar to Free Hand No. 165, applied feet, polished pontil marks with one example retaining remnants of the manufacturing label, Imperial Glass Co., circa 1925, 10-7/8" h, 4-1/8" dia. feet................... **$700**

Courtesy of Jeffrey S. Evans & Associates, jeffreysevans.com

Free-hand Heart and Vine art glass atomizer, orange iridescent with blue decoration, original metal mounts and bulb, Imperial Glass Co., circa 1925, 10" h. **$425**

Courtesy of Jeffrey S. Evans & Associates, jeffreysevans.com

Free-hand Heart and Vine art glass table lamp, orange iridescent with blue decoration, tall urn form, original metal mounts, central pole and sockets, amber glass faceted finial, Imperial Glass Co., circa 1925, 20-1/2" h, 5-1/2" dia. base... **$350**

Courtesy of Jeffrey S. Evans & Associates, jeffreysevans.com

Seven-piece water set, good condition, pitcher
8-1/2" h, cups 4" h.. **$50**

Courtesy of Martin Auction Co., martinauction.com

Free-hand Heart and Vine art glass vase, opal with
green decoration, urn form with a deep orange
iridescent interior, polished pontil mark, retains
manufacturing label, Imperial Glass Co., circa
1925, 6" h, 5" dia. **$850**

Courtesy of Jeffrey S. Evans & Associates, jeffreysevans.com

Free-hand Loop art glass jack-in-the-pulpit vase,
pale orange ground with blue loopings, Free
Hand No. 240, applied cobalt blue rim and foot,
polished pontil mark, Imperial Glass Co., circa
1925, 10-1/4" h, 7" dia. plume. **$750**

Courtesy of Jeffrey S. Evans & Associates, jeffreysevans.com

Free-hand Heart and Vine art glass vase, cobalt
blue iridescent with opal decoration, Free Hand
No. 265, applied opal handles and rim, applied
circular foot, polished pontil mark, Imperial Glass
Co., circa 1925, 9-1/4" h, 4-1/2" dia. **$1,600**

Courtesy of Jeffrey S. Evans & Associates, jeffreysevans.com

GLASS

lalique

RENÉ JULES LALIQUE was born on April 6, 1860, in the village of Ay, in the Champagne region of France. In 1862, his family moved to the suburbs of Paris.

In 1872, Lalique began attending College Turgot where he began studying drawing with Justin-Marie Lequien. After the death of his father in 1876, Lalique began working as an apprentice to Louis Aucoc, who was a prominent jeweler and goldsmith in Paris.

Lalique moved to London in 1878 to continue his studies. He spent two years attending Sydenham College, developing his graphic design skills. He returned to Paris in 1880 and worked as an illustrator of jewelry, creating designs for Cartier, among others. In 1884, Lalique's drawings were displayed at the National Exhibition of Industrial Arts, organized at the Louvre.

At the end of 1885, Lalique took over Jules Destapes' jewelry workshop. Lalique's design began to incorporate translucent enamels, semiprecious stones, ivory, and hard stones. In 1889, at the Universal Exhibition in Paris, the jewelry firms of Vever and Boucheron included collaborative works by Lalique in their displays.

In the early 1890s, Lalique began to incorporate glass into his jewelry, and in 1893 he took part in a competition organized by the Union Centrale des Arts Decoratifs to design a drinking vessel. He won second prize.

Lalique opened his first Paris retail shop in 1905, near the perfume business of François Coty. Coty commissioned Lalique to design his perfume labels in 1907, and he also created his first perfume bottles for Coty.

In the first decade of the 20th century, Lalique continued to experiment with glass manufacturing techniques, and mounted his first show devoted entirely to glass in 1911.

During World War I, Lalique's first factory was forced to close, but the construction of a new factory was soon begun in Wingen-sur-Moder, in the Alsace region. It was completed in 1921, and still produces Lalique crystal today.

In 1925, Lalique designed the first "car mascot" (hood ornament) for Citroën, the French automobile company. For the next six years, Lalique would design 29 models for companies such as Bentley, Bugatti, Delage, Hispano-Suiza, Rolls Royce, and Voisin.

Lalique's second boutique opened in 1931, and this location continues to serve as the main Lalique showroom today.

René Lalique died on May 5, 1945, at the age of 85. His son, Marc, took over the business at that time, and when Marc died in 1977, his daughter, Marie-Claude Lalique Dedouvre, assumed control of the company. She sold her interest in the firm and retired in 1994.

Penthievre pattern vase c.1926, clear and frosted amber glass, signed "R Lalique France" underneath, 10-1/4" h. **$14,000**

Courtesy of Leslie Hindman Auctioneers, lesliehindman.com

For more information on Lalique, see *Warman's Lalique Identification and Price Guide* by Mark F. Moran.

Pinsons bowl, with birds, 9-1/4" w. **$160**

Courtesy of Vero Beach Auction, verobeachauction.com

"Flora" yellow arched panel with satin finish in intaglio of a young woman's bust with bed of spring leaves, includes custom Lucite stand, marked "R. Lalique" at bottom, 14" x 9-1/2" and 17-1/2" x 20-1/2" with wood panel.............. **$2,500**

Courtesy of Vero Beach Auction, verobeachauction.com

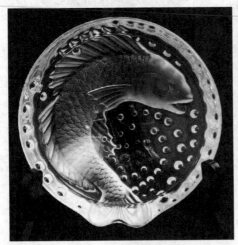

Rare Lalique glass bowl with a molded image of a mermaid with long flowing tail swimming freely in the bubbly waters, hint of green, raised signature "R. Lalique" on the underside of the rim, 9-1/4" dia... **$800**

Courtesy of Scheerer McCulloch Auctioneers, Inc., scheerermcculloch.com

Xi'an dragon koi fish bowl, French crystal, incised signature to underside, 1960s, 6" dia. **$100**

Courtesy of Main Auction Galleries, mainauctiongalleries.com

Green frosted glass frog, post-1945, marks: "Lalique, France," 3-1/8" h. **$575**

Courtesy of Heritage Auctions, ha.com

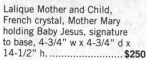

Lalique Mother and Child, French crystal, Mother Mary holding Baby Jesus, signature to base, 4-3/4" w x 4-3/4" d x 14-1/2" h. **$250**

Courtesy of Main Auction Galleries, mainauctiongalleries.com

Eight colored glass angelfish, post-1945, marks: "Lalique, France," 1-3/4" h. **$688**

Courtesy of Heritage Auctions, ha.com

Set of six purple small bowls and plates, bowl is 2" h x 3-3/4" dia, plate 5-3/4" dia. **$300**

Courtesy of World Auction Gallery LLC, worldauctiongallery.com

GLASS

"Danaides" gray glass vase, model introduced 1926, molded signature "R. LALIQUE," Marcilhac 972, 7-1/2" h.. **$2,000**

Courtesy of A.B. Levy's Palm Beach, ablevys.com

Set of five crystal wine glasses in the "Angel" pattern, each having a bowl engraved with wings and partially frosted above a knop containing the face of an angel, rising on a slender stem and ending in a circular foot, engraved "Lalique France," 8" h x 2-3/4" dia... **$800**

Courtesy of Great Gatsby's Auction Gallery, Inc., greatgatsby.com

Glass dresser box, circa 1935, Art Deco satin glass with four raised panels, bottom marked "Lalique," 3" h, 4-1/2" dia. **$850**

Courtesy of Oakridge Auction Gallery. oakridgeauctiongallery.com

Perruches pattern vase, c.1919, clear and frosted blue glass, signed "R Lalique France" to underneath, 10-1/4" h.............................**$11,000**

Courtesy of Leslie Hindman Auctioneers, lesliehindman.com

Ball-form green-stained ferns vase, inscribed "Lalique" on bottom, edge of foot has faint "R. Lalique," excellent condition, 4-1/2" h, 4-1/4" dia.
....**$450**

Courtesy of Oakridge Auction Gallery. oakridgeauctiongallery.com

Set of six "Algues Noir" glass plates, each signed, good condition, 7-3/4" dia.....................................**$175**
Courtesy of Kodner Galleries Inc., kodnergalleries.com

R. Lalique for Erasmic de Lui (From Him) clear glass perfume bottle and stopper, sepia patina, 1925, label, box, Lalique mark, 3-1/2".....**$11,000**

Courtesy of Perfume Bottles Auction, perfumebottlesauction.com

R. Lalique for Canarina Les Yeux Bleus (The Blue Eyes) blue glass perfume bottle and dauber stopper, 1928, molded label, Lalique mark, 2". ... **$2,600**

Courtesy of Perfume Bottles Auction, perfumebottlesauction.com

R. Lalique for Maison Lalique "Trois Paons" powder box, 1919, clear/frost glass, sepia patina, Lalique mark, 2-3/4" dia. **$1,400**

Courtesy of Perfume Bottles Auction, perfumebottlesauction.com

R. Lalique for Maison Lalique "Marguerites" powder box, 1920, clear/frost glass, blue patina, Lalique mark, 3" dia.**$600**

Courtesy of Perfume Bottles Auction, perfumebottlesauction.com

"Poissons" large opalescent glass plate, model introduced 1931, Marcilhac 3056, molded signature R.Lalique, 11-3/4" dia. **$500**

Courtesy of A.B. Levy's Palm Beach, ablevys.com

GLASS

libbey

IN 1878, WILLIAM L. LIBBEY obtained a lease on the New England Glass Co. of Cambridge, Massachusetts, changing the name to the New England Glass Works, W.L. Libbey and Son, Proprietors. After his death in 1883, his son, Edward D. Libbey, continued to operate the company at Cambridge until 1888, when the factory was closed. Edward Libbey moved to Toledo, Ohio, and set up the company subsequently known as Libbey Glass Co. During the 1880s, the firm's master technician, Joseph Locke, developed the now much desired colored art glass lines of Agata, Amberina, Peach Blow, and Pomona. Renowned for its cut glass of the Brilliant Period, the company continues in operation today as Libbey Glassware, a division of Owens-Illinois, Inc.

Two Libbey Nash clear and opalescent glass Silhouette giraffe compotes and elephant center bowl, Toledo, Ohio, second quarter 20th century, stenciled Libbey, lot was part of Libbey's Silhouette line designed in 1933 by former Tiffany & Co. executive Douglas Nash, 7-1/2" h x 11" dia (elephant bowl)...................**$800**

Courtesy of Heritage Auctions, ha.com

A collection of seven Libbey Glass Peachblow rose bowls, vases and cup from the World's Columbian Exposition, Chicago, 1893, white to rose, with gilt decoration, unsigned, largest dimensions: 5-3/4" h x 4" dia............................ **$850**

Courtesy of Gray's Auctioneers, graysauctioneers.com

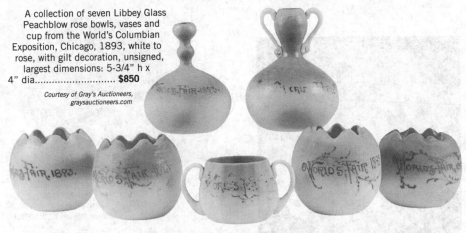

Libbey "Lovebirds/Wisteria" intaglio cut glass bowl, circa 1920, round bowl having a silver diamond cut band framing vines and leaves, engraved lovebirds among wisteria blooms, acid etch signature at the center, 8-7/8" dia x 4-1/4" h. **$130**

Courtesy of Cordier Auctions & Appraisals, cordierauction.com

Libbey Brilliant Period cut glass compote, Drape pattern, Libbey mark, 5-1/4" x 7-7/8". **$3,750**

Courtesy of Brunk Auctions, brunkauctions.com

Libbey Brilliant Period cut glass plate, Columbia pattern, 7". **$6,000**

Courtesy of Brunk Auctions, brunkauctions.com

A late 19th century American Brilliant Period cut glass flowers center in Libbey's "Ellsmere" pattern (variation), heavy deeply cut design with stars and cross hatching, slight wear some tiny point flakes, 1" hairline crack in one of the neck facets, 11-1/2" dia x 7-1/2" h. **$275**

Courtesy of Schmidt's Antiques Inc., schmidtsantiques.com

Libbey Brilliant cut glass punch bowl, American, ca. 1896-1906, footed, acid etched mark, having a scalloped rim and spiral design featuring hobstars, 7-1/2" dia., 14" h. **$900**

Courtesy of Cowan's Auctions, Inc., cowanauction.com

◄ Libbey Brilliant Period cut glass rum jug, cranberry cut to clear with stopper, Flute pattern, 6-1/2". **$400**

Courtesy of Brunk Auctions, brunkauctions.com

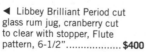

▶ Libbey amberina art glass vase, signed Libbey, 6-1/4" x 6". ...**$275**

Courtesy of Woody Auction LLC, woodyauction.com

413

GLASS

GLASS

milk glass

THOUGH INVENTED IN Venice in the 1500s, the opaque glass commonly known as milk glass was most popular at the end of the 19th century. American manufacturers including Westmoreland, Fenton, Imperial, Indiana, and Anchor Hocking produced it as an economical substitute for pricey European glass and china.

After World War I, the popularity of milk glass waned but production continued. Milk glass made during the 1930s and 1940s is often considered of lower quality than other periods because of the economic Depression and wartime manufacturing difficulties.

"Milk glass" is a general term for opaque colored glass. Though the name would lead you to believe it, white wasn't the only color produced.

"Colored milk glasses, such as opaque black, green, or pink, usually command higher prices," according to *Warman's Depression Glass* author and expert Ellen Schroy.

"Beware of reproductions in green and pink. Always question a milk glass pattern found in cobalt blue. Swirled colors are a whole other topic and very desirable."

Care should be taken when purchasing, transporting, and using this era of milk glass, as it is intolerant of temperature changes. "Don't buy a piece at a flea market unless you can protect it well for its trip to your home, and when you get it home, let it sit for several hours so its temperature evens out to what your normal home temperature is. It's almost a given if you take a piece of cold glass and submerge it into a nice warm bath, it's going to crack. And never, ever expose it to the high temps of a modern dishwasher," Schroy said.

Victorian condiment set, pink over milk glass, open salt, pepper and mustard jar with floral decoration, set on Meriden #69 silverplate frame featuring cherub, 6-1/2" x 5-1/2". **$500**

Courtesy of Woody Auction LLC, woodyauction.com

So how do you tell the old from the new? Schroy said getting your hands on it is often the only way to tell. "Milk glass should have a wonderful silky texture. Any piece that is grainy is probably new," she said. "The best test is to look for the 'ring of fire,' which will be easy to see in the sunlight: Hold the piece of milk glass up to a good light source (I prefer natural light) and see if there is a halo of iridescent colors right around the edge, look for reds, blues, and golds. This ring was caused by the addition of iridized salts into the milk glass formula. If this ring is present, it's probably an old piece." However, 1950s-era milk glass does not have this telltale ring, she said.

Old milk glass should also carry appropriate marks and signs, like the "ring of fire";

appropriate patterns for specific makers are also something to watch for, such as Fenton's Hobnail pattern. Collectors should always check for condition issues such as damage and discoloration. According to Schroy, there is no remedy for discolored glass, and cracked and chipped pieces should be avoided, as they are prone to further damage.

— Karen Knapstein

◄ Antique decorated milk glass barber's bottle, with hand-enameled "Sea Foam" label and transfer print rocaille pattern, upper portion painted sky blue, approx. 8-3/4" h. **$150**

Courtesy of Auction Gallery of Boca Raton, LLC, liveauctioneers.com

► Milk glass bowl, 8" l. **$30**

Courtesy of EDEN Fine Antiques Galleries, liveauctioneers.com

Milk glass hen on nest, 6" h. **$15**

Courtesy of Specialists of the South, Inc., specialistsofthesouth.com

► Early English rare Victorian milk glass child's hand-shaped ring holder, painted ruffled cuff, registry mark on bottom, 2-1/2" x 2-1/2" x 3-3/4". **$170**

Courtesy of Charleston Estate Auctions, charlestonestateauctions.com

Bryan & Kern jugate milk glass bank in the form of Uncle Sam's hat, painted red and blue, containing a paper label "liner" on the underside depicting the "Democratic Nominees," hard to find these labels present or without serious faults, "high grade" condition for the type, 2-1/2" h... **$420**

Courtesy of Heritage Auctions, ha.com

Large jagged-edged egg-shaped bowl/vase, footed orb form, rim intricately cut, gold-toned edges, with underplate, approx. 11" h, 7" w........**$90**

Courtesy of The Benefit Shop Foundation, Inc., thebenefitshop.org

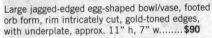

◀ Milk glass pedestal hobnail swung stretch vase, 21-1/4" h...........................**$35**

Courtesy of Specialists of the South, Inc., specialistsofthesouth.com

Unmarked pair of Victorian figural salt and pepper shakers, milk glass, painted chicks with silverplate heads, 3"......................................**$500**

Courtesy of Woody Auction LLC, woodyauction.com

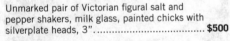

◀ German milk glass beer stein, having a lithophane in base of a monk holding a glass, molded figural thumb rest on metal lid, polychrome enamels, and a German saying, additional German engraving on top of lid with date "9.2.03," unmarked, late 19th/early 20th century, 7" h...**$180**

Courtesy of Jeffrey S. Evans & Associates, jeffreysevans.com

GLASS

moser

LUDWIG MOSER (1833-1916) founded his polishing and engraving workshop in 1857 in Karlsbad, Austria. Today this Czech Republic city is known as Karlovy Vary. He employed many famous glass designers, e.g., Johann Hoffman, Josef Urban, and Rudolf Miller. In 1900, Moser and his sons, Rudolf and Gustav, incorporated Ludwig Moser & Sons.

Moser art glass included clear pieces with inserted blobs of colored glass, cut colored glass with classical scenes, cameo glass and intaglio cut. Many inexpensive enameled pieces were also made. Moser was one of the few Czechoslovakian glassmakers to sign their pieces. The slogan "King of Glass, Glass of Kings" is associated with the company because of its famous clientele who, in addition to Edward VII and the Austrian Imperial Court, include Pope Pius XI, the Turkish sultan Abdul Hamid II, King Luís I of Portugal and his wife, Maria Pia of Savoy.

In 1922, Leo and Richard Moser brought Meyr's Neffe, their biggest Bohemian rival in art glass. Moser executed many pieces for the Wiener Workstatte in the 1920s.

Moser decorated art glass cut overlay cruet, cobalt cut to clear with painted gilt decoration, ground base marked in gilt, original stopper, 7" h.**$170**

Courtesy of Forsythes' Auctions, LLC, forsythesauctions.com

▲ Vintage Moser cobalt blue Bohemian Czech glass candlesticks, with dolphin-form stems and drip discs, 8-1/4" h. **$100**

Courtesy of Auctions at Showplace, nyshowplace.com

◀ Moser four-handled art glass vase, green shading to clear with extensive gold enamel highlights, 9". **$350**

Courtesy of Woody Auction LLC, liveauctioneers.com

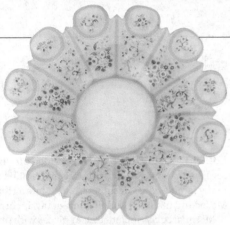

Moser pink to clear gilt glass teacup and saucer, square form, saucer 4-1/2"................................$60

Courtesy of Antiques & Modern Auction Gallery, antiquesmodern.com

Moser decorated cut overlay art glass plate, cobalt cut to clear with polychrome enameled roses with gilt trim, 8-1/8" dia. $475

Courtesy of Forsythes' Auctions, LLC, forsythesauctions.com

Purple Moser glass blown vase, enamel decoration depicting birds and flowers, 5" h x 7" l x 3-1/2" w...$260

Courtesy of Tom Hall Auctions Inc., tomhallauctions.com

Moser Victorian Aesthetic enameled amethyst glass bronze mounted bowl, decorated with a hummingbird confronting a snake coiled around a branch as it attempts to fetch the bird's nestling over a background of blue aestheticized foliage, reverse of the bowl is decorated with an applied butterfly gilt glass element between enameled white and purple blossoming florals with blue and green foliage, rim decorated with a thick applied amber glass drip edge with large terminating elements, underside bears a ground and polished pontil, mounted in a scrolled leg bronze base, exceptional example of sculptured Moser enameled glass, Czechoslovakia, 19th century, 7-1/8" h, 8-1/2" dia. $300

Courtesy of Bruneau & Co. Auctioneers, bruneauandco.com

▶ A Moser/Harrach glass sailfin lizard vase, topaz urn form with amethyst crimped rim continuing to applied sailfin lizard handles, with enamel and gilt accents, overall good condition, 10-1/4" h.....$1,000

Courtesy of Schmidt's Antiques Inc., schmidtsantiques.com

GLASS

mt. washington

A WIDE DIVERSITY of glass was made by the Mt. Washington Glass Co. of New Bedford, Massachusetts, between 1869 and 1900. It was succeeded in 1900 by the Pairpoint Manufacturing Co. Throughout its history, the Mt. Washington Glass Co. made different types of glass including pressed, blown, art, lava, Napoli, cameo, cut, Albertine, Peachblow, Burmese, Crown Milano, Royal Flemish, and Verona.

Mt. Washington art glass Burmese rose bowl, octagon rim on bulbous base, decorated with berries on leafy vines, 3-1/2" h. **$125**

Courtesy of Stony Ridge Auction, stonyridgeauction.com

A Mt. Washington "Royal Flemish" glass biscuit jar, square body with chrysanthemum motif on a gray and tan ground, fitted with a white metal cover, rim, and swing handle, glass is marked "RF/523" in red underneath, underside of cover is stamped "M. W. 4413," 7-3/4" h to cover. **$260**

Courtesy of Schmidt's Antiques Inc. Since 1911, schmidtsantiques.com

◄ Two Mt. Washington glass powder jars, pink satin ground with polychrome flowering branch decoration, each has a silverplate cover, overall, good condition, 4" dia......... **$120**

Courtesy of Schmidt's Antiques Inc. Since 1911, schmidtsantiques.com

GLASS

▲ Mt. Washington Melon Ribbed sugar shaker, blue and white tones with pink floral decoration, 2-1/2" x 4"........**$70**

Courtesy of Woody Auction LLC, woodyauction.com

▲ Mt. Washington art glass sweetmeat, cream tones with embossed star design, decorated with lily of the valley, flowers embossed, 3-3/4" x 6"...........................**$250**

Courtesy of Woody Auction LLC, woodyauction.com

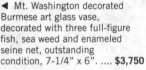

◀ Mt. Washington decorated Burmese art glass vase, decorated with three full-figure fish, sea weed and enameled seine net, outstanding condition, 7-1/4" x 6". **$3,750**

Courtesy of Woody Auction LLC, woodyauction.com

Mt. Washington cameo parlor lamp, circa 1890, yellow cut to opal, symmetrical design depicting the portrait of a woman within a reserve, flanked by floral decoration, metal base with brass finish, brass connector and spill ring, fitted with a "Meriden" brass drop-in font with a spider shade ring, topped with an opal-cased yellow ribbed umbrella shade, slip chimney, Mt. Washington Glass Co., 16-1/2" h, 7-3/4" h to spill ring, 7-1/4" square base......................**$110**

Courtesy of Jeffrey S Evans & Associates, jeffreysevans.com

Mt. Washington Crown Milano melon rib syrup pitcher, opal with pale yellow ground and polychrome and gilt stylized floral decoration, original quadruple-plate hinged lid with integral handle having the patent information on the interior, Mt. Washington Glass Co., fourth quarter 19th century, 6" h.. **$425**

Rare ribbed coupe, ovoid form with a scalloped rim decorated with red and purple mums with gold tracery, marked with the Royal Flemish R in diamond, good condition, 4-3/4" h. **$375**

Courtesy of Jaremos, jaremos.com

GLASS

murano

IN THE 1950S, the American home came alive with vibrant-colored decorative items, abstract art, and futuristic-designed furniture. The colorless geometry of the 1930s was out.

Over the last decade, mid-century design has once again gained favor with interior decorators, magazines, shows, and stores dedicated solely to this period. The bold colors and free-form shapes of mid-century modern Italian glass are emblematic of 1950s design. This distinctive glass has become a sought-after collectible.

Prices realized at auction for 1950s glass have seen a resurgence. However, there are still many items readily available and not always at a premium.

Italian glass can be found in many American homes. In fact, it is likely that some of the familiar glass items you grew up with were produced in Italy — the candy dish on the coffee table with the bright colors, the ashtray with the gold flecks inside. Modern glass objects from Italy were among the most widely distributed examples of 1950s design.

As with any decorative art form, there are varying levels of achievement in the design and execution of glass from this period. While you should always buy what you love, as there is never a guarantee return on investment, buying the best representation of an item is wise. In considering modern Italian glass, several points make one piece stand above another.

Italy has a centuries-old tradition of glassmaking, an industry whose center is the group of islands known as Murano in the lagoon of Venice. The most recognized and desirable Italian glass comes from three companies: Seguso, Venini and Barovier & Toso.

Italy offers a vast array of talented glass artists. Top end collectors seem to favor Carlo Scarpa from Venini, Napoleone Martinuzzi (who worked at Venini from 1925-1932), and Dino Martens of Aureliano Toso. You can expect to pay several thousand dollars for a fine piece by one of these artists.

For slimmer collecting budgets, good quality examples by other artists are available and more affordable. Alfredo Barbini and Fulvio Biaconi (for Venini) are two of them. While some of their work does command top dollar, many of their pieces are priced for the novice collector.

A few mid-century designs can still be found that could prove to be sleepers in the near future. Look for Inciso vases by Venini, Aborigeni pieces by Barovier & Toso, and Soffiati examples by Giacomo Cappellin. Each of these designs is totally different from the other, yet all are reasonably priced in today's market.

Collectors should be aware that the most popular glass form is the vase, with glass sculpture following next in line. Popular sculptural forms include male or female nude figurals and pasta glass animals by Fulvio Biaconi.

Vases are the most popular Murano glass form with collectors. Venini glass vase, mid-century modern Venetian, in alternating stripes of opaque turquoise and transparent yellow, marked underneath, 12" h. **$3,250**

Courtesy of Auctions at Showplace, nyshowplace.com

VISIT WWW.ANTIQUETRADER.COM

WWW.FACEBOOK.COM/ANTIQUETRADER

An Alfredo Barbini glass duck group, 7-1/4" h x 10" w x 3-1/2" d..**$750**

Courtesy of Heritage Auctions, ha.com

Murano art glass trapped three-color fish, artist signed "Shislow," 17" l.....................................**$86**

Courtesy of Skinner Auctioneers and Appraisers, skinnerinc.com

Murano glass rooster figure, approx. 8" l x 6" h.**$110**

Courtesy of Pasarel, pasarel.com

Venetian mid-century modern glass lamp, a bull sculpture by Gino Cenedese, mounted on an electrified chrome base, base lacking bottom plate, 9" h. **$150**

Courtesy of Auctions at Showplace, nyshowplace.com

Dino Rosin signed Murano glass sailboat with two sails. Murano glass has its decorative colored pattern on one side using the glass' natural refraction rate to create a kinetic art form that changes on the viewers perspective/location, signature is located on base, 30" h, 18" w. **$1,200**

Courtesy of Donny Malone Auctions, donnymaloneauctions

Vintage Murano pink pastel swan bowl, mint condition, 5-1/2" h. .. **$45**
Courtesy of Auction Kings Gallery, liveauctioneers.com

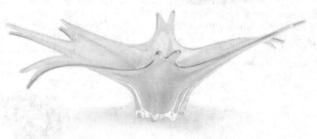

Pink glass splash centerpiece, 28" w... **$190**
Courtesy of Leslie Hindman Auctioneers, lesliehindman.com

Fratelli Toso Filigrana stoppered bottle, twisting ribbon pattern in red, pink and gold, foil label on bottom, "Murano Glass Made in Italy." **$175**
Courtesy of Concept Art Gallery, conceptartgallery.com

Murano Sommerso lidded glass box, Italy, 20th century, hand-wrought, composed of thick, faceted glass with blown-out well banded in gold plate where the cover meets the base, marked "G.S.E Ottone Galvanizatto ORO K.24," 5-1/8" h, 7-1/8" w, 4-7/8" d. **$492**
Courtesy of Skinner Auctioneers and Appraisers, skinnerinc.com

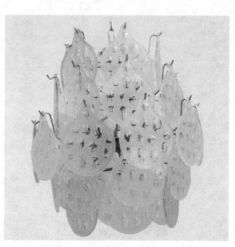

Vistosi chandelier, 1960s, with opal one and clear glass convenes disks suspended from a chromed metal frame, 24" h, 20" d. **$330**
Courtesy of Pierre Anthony Galleries, pierreanthonygalleries.com

Sculpture, Andrea Tagliapietra &
Mario Badioli, Italian, man in profile,
signed underfoot, 11"h, 6-1/2" w,
2-3/4" d. **$275**

Courtesy of Austin Auction Gallery, austinauction.com

Four covered glass bowls, 20th century, each cover modeled to show
a perched bird, 11" h. **$18**

Courtesy of Leslie Hindman Auctioneers, lesliehindman.com

Vintage Lino Tagliapietra (Italian b. 1934) Oggetti
Egg sculpture, Effetre International Vetri Murano
Egg, 1982, 8" h x 6-1/4" dia. **$500**

Courtesy of Antiques & Art International, antiquesandartsinternational.com

R. Antra signed large glass
Moderne sculpture, pink hand-
blown art glass swirl on a glass
pedestal, 27" h, 9" w. **$160**

*Courtesy of Donny Malone Auctions,
donnymaloneauctions*

Glass shell, Murano, Italy, 1984, signed and dated, 4-1/2" x 11" x 4". **$350**

Courtesy of Rago Arts and Auction Center, ragoarts.com

A Murrini glass vase with foil inclusions, attributed to Fratelli Toso, Murano, Italy, 11-1/2" h x 5-1/2" dia. **$500**

Courtesy of Heritage Auctions, ha.com

A pair of Fratelli Toso glass vases with white caning and turquoise Murrine, Murano, Italy, 9" h x 3" dia. **$437**

Courtesy of Heritage Auctions, ha.com

Glass vase with internal cane decoration, Murano, Italy, 1983, signed and dated, 28/100, 13-1/2" x 5-1/2" dia. **$700**

Courtesy of Rago Arts and Auction Center, ragoarts.com

A Dino Martin for Aureliano Toso Lattimo glass handkerchief vase, Murano, Italy, 8" h x 9" dia. **$375**

Courtesy of Heritage Auctions, ha.com

GLASS

GLASS

northwood

NORTHWOOD GLASS CO. was founded by Harry Northwood, son of prominent English glassmaker John Northwood, who was famous for his expertise in cameo glass.

Harry migrated to America in 1881 and, after working at various glass manufacturers, formed the Northwood Glass Co. in 1896 in Indiana, Pennsylvania. In 1902, he created H. Northwood and Co. in Wheeling, West Virginia. After Northwood died in 1919, H. Northwood and Co. began to falter and eventually closed in 1925.

Northwood produced a wide variety of opalescent, decorated, and special effect glasses, and colors like iridescent blue and green, which were not widely seen at the time.

Opaline Brocade/Spanish Lace bitters or barber's bottle, cranberry opalescent, pinched waist form, Northwood Glass Co. pattern introduced 1899, 7-1/2" h. **$700**

Courtesy of Jeffrey S. Evans & Associates, jeffreysevans.com

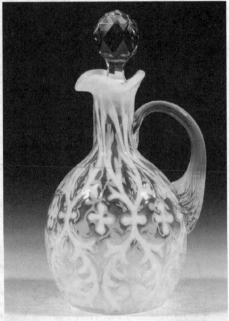

Opaline Brocade/Spanish Lace cruet, Vaseline (black lighted) opalescent, cut-facet stopper, applied reeded Vaseline (black lighted) handle, Northwood Glass Co. pattern introduced 1899, 7-1/4" h. **$160**

Courtesy of Jeffrey S. Evans & Associates, jeffreysevans.com

Opaline Brocade/Spanish Lace salt and pepper shakers, blue opalescent, period lids, Northwood Glass Co. Pattern introduced 1899, 3-5/8" h.....**$475**

Courtesy of Jeffrey S. Evans & Associates, jeffreysevans.com

Royal Ivy miniature lamp, rubina with satin finish, ball-form font, matching pattern ball-form shade, period collar with patent information, period nutmeg burner, colorless chimney, Northwood Glass Co., fourth quarter 19th/early 20th century, 6" h to top of shade, 2-7/8" h to top of collar, 3" d font. **$140**

Courtesy of Jeffrey S. Evans & Associates, jeffreyevans.com

Inverted Fan and Feather toothpick holder, pink slag, Northwood Glass Co./Dugan Glass Co., circa 1904, 2-3/8" h. **$250**

Courtesy of Jeffrey S. Evans & Associates, jeffreysevans.com

Chrysanthemum Sprig/Pagoda (OMN) toothpick holder, opaque blue with blue-staining and gilt decoration, signed with "Northwood" script, Northwood Glass Co., circa 1899, 2-5/8" h. **$70**

Courtesy of Jeffrey S. Evans & Associates, jeffreysevans.com

◀ National/S-Repeat syrup pitcher, green with gilt decoration, period lid with a figural bird finial and patent information on the interior, Northwood Glass Co./Dugan Glass Co., circa 1901, 7-1/4" h. **$275**

Courtesy of Jeffrey S. Evans & Associates, jeffreysevans.com

Ribbed Coinspot tumbler, cranberry opalescent, Northwood Glass Co., circa 1888, 3-1/2" h. **$250**

Courtesy of Jeffrey S. Evans & Associates, jeffreysevans.com

Frosted blue cased art glass water set, Leaf Umbrella pattern by Northwood, pitcher and four matching tumblers, pitcher is 8-3/4" h. **$175**

Courtesy of Woody Auction LLC, liveauctioneers.com

Northwood No. 333/ Leaf Mold syrup pitcher, canary/Vaseline (black lighted) with cranberry and opal spatter, satin finish, applied handle, period lid, Northwood Glass Co. pattern introduced in 1891, 6-1/4" h..........**$200**

Courtesy of Jeffrey S. Evans & Associates, jeffreysevans.com

Northwood No. 263/Leaf Umbrella syrup pitcher, ruby/cranberry, colorless applied handle, period lid with patent information, Northwood Glass Co. pattern introduced 1889, 6-1/2" h. **$250**

Courtesy of Jeffrey S. Evans & Associates, jeffreysevans.com

GLASS

opalescent

NORTHWOOD GLASS CO. was founded by Harry Northwood, son of prominent English glassmaker John Northwood, who was famous for his expertise in cameo glass.

Harry migrated to America in 1881 and, after working at various glass manufacturers, formed the Northwood Glass Co. in 1896 in Indiana, Pennsylvania. In 1902, he created H. Northwood and Co. in Wheeling, West Virginia. After Northwood died in 1919, H. Northwood and Co. began to falter and eventually closed in 1925.

Northwood produced a wide variety of opalescent, decorated, and special effect glasses, and colors like iridescent blue and green, which were not widely seen at the time.

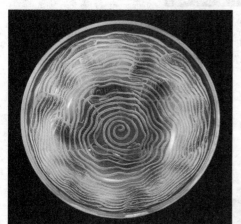

Pressed rosette curtain pins/tie backs, lot of 6, fiery opalescent, each with beaded petals, shaped rim, and period metal shank, Boston & Sandwich Glass Co., 1840-1870, 2"-3" d. **$70**

Courtesy of Jeffrey S. Evans & Associates, jeffreysevans.com

Rene Lalique art deco opalescent and sepia stained glass bowl, designed beautifully with molded swimming fish amidst a spiraling wave pattern, circa: 1930s, signed to base "R. Lalique France," 9-1/4" dia x 3-1/2" h. **$950**

Courtesy of Auction Gallery of Boca Raton, LLC, liveauctioneers.com

BT-8 "Lafayet" rare steamboat pressed open salt, opalescent medium blue with light mottling, marked "B. &. S. / GLASS. / Co" on stern and "SANDWICH" on interior and under base, Boston & Sandwich Glass Co., 1830-1845, 1-5/8" h, 1-7/8" x 3-5/8". **$425**

Courtesy of Jeffrey S. Evans & Associates, jeffreysevans.com

Continental glass dresser box, colorless opalescent, rectangular form with metal mounts, second half 19th century, 3" h x 4" w. **$130**

Courtesy of Jeffrey S. Evans & Associates, jeffreysevans.com

A Sabino opalescent molded glass perfume bottle in the "La Ronde Fleurie" pattern, Paris, France, circa 1930-1945, the ovoid form bottle with five partially draped dancing female figures holding floral chains with artichoke form stopper, engraved "Sabino, Paris" on the bottom, 6" h, 2-3/8" dia................... **$125**

Courtesy of Simpson Galleries, LLC., simpsongalleries.com

Opalescent swirl art glass shade, early 20th century, bullet form, spiral pattern, unmarked, 11" h, 4" fitter rim. **$50**

Courtesy of Leland Little Auctions, lelandlittle.com

Opaline Brocade/Spanish Lace wine decanter, colorless opalescent, bulge form with tri-corner rim, matching patterned ball-form stopper, National Glass Co., Northwood Glass Works, circa 1901, 9-1/2" h, 5-1/2" d. **$225**

Courtesy of Jeffrey S. Evans & Associates, jeffreysevans.com

Vase molded in relief with nude maidens at harvest, Paris, France, early to mid-20th c., opalescent glass, marked, 6-3/4" x 6-3/4" dia. **$325**

Courtesy of Rago Arts and Auction Center, ragoarts.com

Victorian Diamond Quilt water pitcher, colorless opalescent glass, bulbous form, circular rim, applied handle, polished pontil mark, maker unverified, late 19th/early 20th century, 7-1/2" h. **$160**

Courtesy of Jeffrey S. Evans & Associates, jeffreysevans.com

Beatty Swirl syrup pitcher, colorless opalescent, period lid with patent date, A. J. Beatty & Sons, circa 1889, 7" h. **$170**

Courtesy of Jeffrey S. Evans & Associates, jeffreysevans.com

GLASS

pattern

THOUGH IT HAS NEVER been ascertained whether glass was first pressed in the United States or abroad, the development of the glass-pressing machine revolutionized the glass industry in the United States, and this country receives the credit for improving the method to make this process feasible. The first wares pressed were probably small flat plates of the type now referred to as "lacy," the intricacy of the design concealing flaws.

In 1827, both the New England Glass Co., Cambridge, Massachusetts, and Bakewell & Co., Pittsburgh, took out patents for pressing glass furniture knobs; soon other pieces followed. This early pressed glass contained red lead, which made it clear and resonant when tapped (flint). Made primarily in clear, it is rarer in blue, amethyst, olive green, and yellow.

By the 1840s, early simple patterns such as Ashburton, Argus, and Excelsior appeared. Ribbed Bellflower seems to have been one of the earliest patterns to have had complete sets. By the 1860s, a wide range of patterns was available.

In 1864, William Leighton of Hobbs, Brockunier & Co., Wheeling, West Virginia, developed a formula for "soda lime" glass that did not require the expensive red lead for clarity. Although "soda lime" glass did not have the brilliance of the earlier flint glass, the formula came into widespread use because glass could be produced cheaply.

Green opalescent pattern glass table set in Pettipoint Pattern, attributed to Fenton, includes butter dish, creamer, sugar, spooner and cruet. **$150**

Courtesy of Woody Auction LLC, liveauctioneers.com

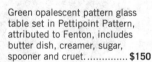

Pair of George Duncan & Sons glass rose globes in Snail pattern, c. 1891, unmarked, pattern No. 360, 4-1/4" h and 4-3/8" w. **$75**

Courtesy of Neal Auction Company, nealauction.com

Pair of Boston & Sandwich Glass Company Sweetheart colorless flint pattern glass EAPG whale oil lamps, 19th c., 10" x 4-1/2". **$100**

Courtesy of Duane Merrill & Company, merrillsauction.com

Daisy and Button pattern glass drink set, including six goblets and double-handled tray, blue glass, good condition. **$30**

Courtesy of Premier Auction Galleries, premierauctiongalleries.com

English pattern-molded opaque-twist wine glass, colorless lead glass, ogee bowl with 16 basal flutes, raised on a stem containing four spiral threads, conical foot with rough pontil mark, circa 1750, 5-3/4" h, 2-3/4" foot dia..... **$190**

Courtesy of Jeffrey S. Evans & Associates, jeffreysevans.com

▶ Pattern-molded and decorated two-handle vase, blue-green bottle glass, lightly molded with 20 vertical ribs, compressed globular body and tall, slightly flaring neck flanked with applied hollow handles, applied rigaree to body, lower neck, and handles, applied threading below rim, raised on an applied ten-petal foot with rough pontil mark and excellent wear, possibly South Jersey, 19th or 20th century, 8-1/2" h, 4-3/8" rim dia, 4-1/8" foot dia. **$50**

Courtesy of Jeffrey S. Evans & Associates, jeffreysevans.com

GLASS

peach blow

SEVERAL TYPES OF GLASS produced by half a dozen glasshouses are lumped together by collectors as Peach Blow. Hobbs, Brockunier & Co., Wheeling, West Virginia, made Peach Blow as a plated ware that shaded from red at the top to yellow at the bottom and is referred to as Wheeling Peach Blow. Mt. Washington Glass Works produced a homogeneous Peach Blow shading from rose at the top to pale blue in the lower portion. The New England Glass Works' Peach Blow, called Wild Rose, shaded from rose at the top to white. Gundersen-Pairpoint Co. also reproduced some of the Mt. Washington Peach Blow in the early 1950s, and some glass of a somewhat similar type was made by Steuben Glass Works, Thomas Webb & Sons, and Stevens & Williams of England. New England Peach Blow is one-layered glass and the English is two-layered.

Another single-layered shaded art glass was produced early in the 20th century by New Martinsville Glass Mfg. Co. Originally called "Muranese," collectors today refer to it as New Martinsville Peach Blow.

Hobbs Coral (Omn)/Peach Blow pitcher, glossy, unusual scalloped rim, applied amber handle, polished pontil mark, Hobbs, Brockunier & Co., circa 1885, 6-5/8" h. **$450**

Courtesy of Jeffrey S. Evans & Associates, jeffreysevans.com

Mt. Washington decorated Peach Blow No. 145 vase, plush with polychrome-enamel Queen's decoration, polished pontil mark, Mt. Washington Glass Co., 1886-1890, undamaged, 7-3/4" h, 4-1/2" dia... **$3,000**

Courtesy of Jeffrey S. Evans & Associates, jeffreysevans.com

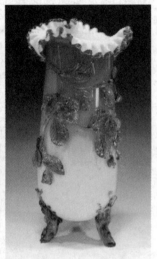

Stevens and Williams cased Peach Blow vase with applied amber glass feet, flowers and vines, ruffled and turned rim, no chips or cracks, 10-1/2" h. **$175**

Courtesy of Stony Ridge Auction, stonyridgeauction.com

Hobbs Coral (Omn)/Peach Blow No. 13 vase, glossy, globular base with an elongated neck, factory-polished rim, polished pontil mark, Hobbs, Brockunier & Co., circa 1885, undamaged, 10-5/8" h. **$225**

Courtesy of Jeffrey S. Evans & Associates, jeffreysevans.com

New England Glass Co./Mt. Washington Peach Blow lily/ trumpet form vase, glossy deep rose to cream color, excellent condition, 15" h. **$350**

Courtesy of Stony Ridge Auction, stonyridgeauction.com

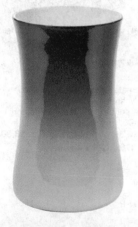

◀ Hobbs Coral (Omn)/Peach Blow celery vase, glossy, slightly waisted form, factory-polished rim, polished pontil mark, Hobbs, Brockunier & Co., circa 1885, 6-1/4" h. **$350**

Courtesy of Jeffrey S. Evans & Associates, jeffreysevans.com

Peach Blow vase with ruffled rim, applied amber glass feet, no cracks or chips, 12" h. ...**$125**

Courtesy of Stony Ridge Auction, stonyridgeauction.com

GLASS

phoenix

THE PHOENIX GLASS CO. of Beaver, Pennsylvania, was established in 1880. Known primarily for commercial glassware, the firm also produced a molded, sculptured, cameo-type line from the 1930s until the 1950s.

Phoenix Drape-Optic small pitcher, opal cased amberina, squat form with square neck, applied colorless reeded handle, and slight foot with polished pontil mark, Phoenix Glass Co., 1883-1888, 5-1/4" h, 2-1/2" square rim, 3-1/2" foot dia. **$170**

Courtesy of Jeffrey S. Evans & Associates, jeffreysevans.com

Phoenix Diamond-Optic craquelle water pitcher, cranberry opalescent, ball-form with circular plain rim, applied colorless handle, polished pontil mark, Phoenix Glass Co., 1883-1888, 7-1/4" h. **$350**

Courtesy of Jeffrey S. Evans & Associates, jeffreysevans.com

Vintage Phoenix Glass vase, approx. 9-1/2" h x 11-1/2" w....**$30**

Courtesy of Time & Again Auction Gallery, timeandagaingalleries.com

Phoenix Glass vase, original label, 11" x 8"..... **$50**

Courtesy of Martin Auction Co., martinauctionco.com

GLASS

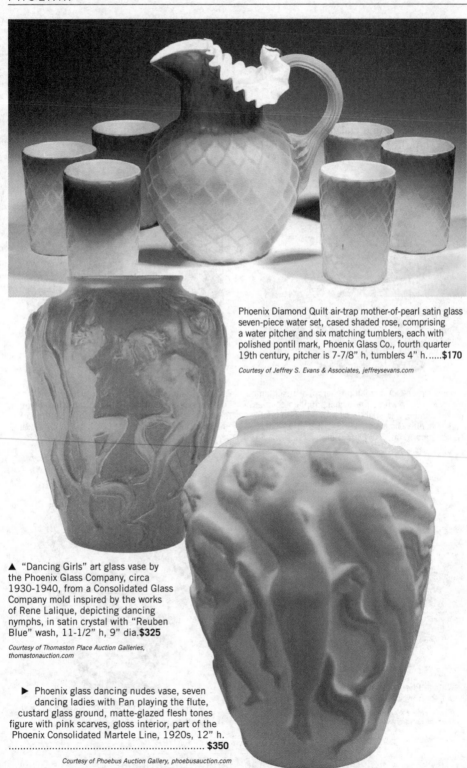

Phoenix Diamond Quilt air-trap mother-of-pearl satin glass seven-piece water set, cased shaded rose, comprising a water pitcher and six matching tumblers, each with polished pontil mark, Phoenix Glass Co., fourth quarter 19th century, pitcher is 7-7/8" h, tumblers 4" h.......**$170**

Courtesy of Jeffrey S. Evans & Associates, jeffreysevans.com

▲ "Dancing Girls" art glass vase by the Phoenix Glass Company, circa 1930-1940, from a Consolidated Glass Company mold inspired by the works of Rene Lalique, depicting dancing nymphs, in satin crystal with "Reuben Blue" wash, 11-1/2" h, 9" dia.**$325**

Courtesy of Thomaston Place Auction Galleries, thomastonauction.com

▶ Phoenix glass dancing nudes vase, seven dancing ladies with Pan playing the flute, custard glass ground, matte-glazed flesh tones figure with pink scarves, gloss interior, part of the Phoenix Consolidated Martele Line, 1920s, 12" h. **$350**

Courtesy of Phoebus Auction Gallery, phoebusauction.com

GLASS

pressed glass

PRESSED GLASS is one of the largest collecting categories in all of antiques, and the number of pieces sold at auction each year easily surpasses more than 3,500 examples in today's market.

Pressed glass was originally produced to imitate expensive cut glass owned mainly by the wealthy. It is made by pressing molten glass either mechanically or manually into textured molds. Unless removed by hand, each piece will retain mold lines, even on pieces with extensive detailing.

In recent years, three lots stunned the collecting community and refocused attention on a category many had not thought about in years. Each gives an inside look at how the hobby is changing as longtime collections are finally offered after years in private hands.

A bidding war broke out over a 2-1/4-inch high x 3-1/8-inch wide pressed glass rectangular salt made by the Providence Flint Glass Works of Providence, Rhode Island. The diminutive blue salt is signed "Providence" on the base and its auctioneers, the Hess Auction Group, dated the piece sometime between 1831 and 1833. It sold for $4,720, fully 10 times its low estimate of $400. The salt was from the private collection of renowned glass and china specialist Corinne Machmer, a familiar face at many Pennsylvania shows and shops. Machmer's lifelong collection also turned out a unique dark purple salt in the form of a boat, which sold to a phone bidder for $7,316. One of a group offered in the auction, the 1-1/2" high x 3-3/4" wide boat salt is signed on the stern "Pittsburgh" and was produced by the Sturbridge Flint Glass Works of Pittsburgh, Pennsylvania, between 1828 and 1835.

Rather than lament over the generally lower prices for mid-range examples in less-than-mint condition, we see the pressed glass hobby as an ideal time to begin collecting and learning about America's diverse history of glass making. On every front, the hobby is welcoming new students: Once expensive reference books are now affordable; online auction hosting sites make it easy to buy functional and historical American glassware made during the late 1700s and 1800s for less than $75; and newcomers to the hobby can still learn a great deal from a generation that researched glassmaking and founded glass museums more than any other.

Assorted pressed Lacy dishes, lot of 4, colorless, comprising two different Panelled Rose and Thistle, a Feather and Quatrefoil, and a Beehive and Thistle, Boston & Sandwich Glass Co. and possibly others, 1835-1850, 5-1/2" to 9-3/4" dia. **$170**

Courtesy of Jeffrey S. Evans & Associates, jeffreysevans.com

VISIT WWW.ANTIQUETRADER.COM

WWW.FACEBOOK.COM/ANTIQUETRADER

GLASS

Assorted Heisey pressed-panel glass syrup pitchers, lot of six, comprising a pink, green, and amber with matching underplate, and a colorless example with a matching underplate, each with a period sanitary lid, each signed with H-in-diamond trademark, maker unverified, first half 20th century, 5" h syrups, 4-1/4" and 5-1/2" dia underplates. **$110**

Courtesy of Jeffrey S. Evans & Associates, jeffreysevans.com

Pressed Lacy Gothic Arch sugar bowl, translucent blue, octagonal with two different arch designs and a plain rim, raised on a circular foot and scalloped foot, lacking cover, Boston & Sandwich Glass Co., 1840-1850, 3-1/2" h, 5-1/8" dia rim, 2-7/8" dia foot. **$130**

Courtesy of Jeffrey S. Evans & Associates, jeffreysevans.com

Pressed Star and Punty spoon holder/spill, brilliant canary yellow (black lighted), hexagonal bowl raised on a low circular foot, Boston & Sandwich Glass Co., 1850-1870, 4-5/8" h, 3-5/8" dia. **$350**

Courtesy of Jeffrey S. Evans & Associates, jeffreysevans.com

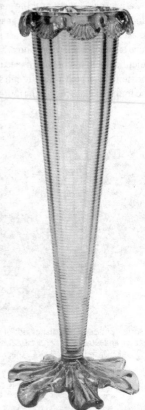

Pressed and threaded glass vase, green shaded to rose, tapered form with applied decoration to the rim, floral-form foot, probably English, late 19th/early 20th century, 12-1/2" h. **$40**

Courtesy of Jeffrey S. Evans & Associates, jeffreysevans.com

Pressed glass cologne bottles, lot of two, medium green and emerald green, comprising a hexagonal arches example with a blown stopper, and a diamond-motif with a cut-fluted stopper, various makers, second half 19th century, 6" h and 7-1/2" h.............................. **$110**

Courtesy of Jeffrey S. Evans & Associates, jeffreysevans.com

Pressed Lacy No. 1 socket on crossbar base candlestick, colorless, stem with interior prisms, beaded under base, wafer construction, Boston & Sandwich Glass Co., 1828-1835, 7" h, 4-1/4" sq base. **$130**

Courtesy of Jeffrey S. Evans & Associates, jeffreysevans.com

◀ Pressed Block/Grooved Bigler finger bowl, deep violet blue, deep bowl with nine panels and plain rim, base with a 12-point star, polished pontil mark, Boston & Sandwich Glass Co., 1850-1870, 3" h, 4-1/2" d rim. **$225**

Courtesy of Jeffrey S. Evans & Associates, jeffreysevans.com

▶ Pressed hexagonal candlestick, violet blue, thick-lipped hexagonal socket and compressed knop extension raised on a flared hexagonal base, wafer construction, Patrick F. Slane's American Glass Co., Boston, possibly Boston & Sandwich Glass Co., 1840-1860, 7-1/4" h, 4-1/4" d base. **$275**

Courtesy of Jeffrey S. Evans & Associates, jeffreysevans.com

Assorted early pressed glass items, lot of three, comprising a red amber Plume and Acorn nappie, a cobalt blue Daisy with Peacock Eye nappie, and a crude green bottle glass Scrolls, Flowers, and Quatrefoil plate, Boston & Sandwich Glass Co. and Midwestern, 1835-1860, 5-1/4" to 6-3/8" dia. **$160**

Courtesy of Jeffrey S. Evans & Associates, jeffreysevans.com

▶ Pressed lacy Peacock Eye shell-shaped dish with open handle, colorless, scalloped rim with beads underneath, Boston & Sandwich Glass Co., second quarter 19th century, 1-1/4" h, 7-5/8" x 9-1/2". **$650**

Courtesy of Jeffrey S. Evans & Associates, jeffreysevans.com

439

DN-1 dolphin pressed glass open salt, colorless lead glass, extremely rare, France, 1830-1850, 2-1/2" h, 2-3/8" x 3" d rim............................ **$350**

Courtesy of Jeffrey S. Evans & Associates, jeffreysevans.com

SL-1 shell pressed glass open salt, cobalt blue, shaped rim, rare, possibly Boston & Sandwich Glass Co., 1835-1850, 1-5/8" h, 2" x 3"......... **$160**

Courtesy of Jeffrey S. Evans & Associates, jeffreysevans.com

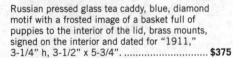

Russian pressed glass tea caddy, blue, diamond motif with a frosted image of a basket full of puppies to the interior of the lid, brass mounts, signed on the interior and dated for "1911," 3-1/4" h, 3-1/2" x 5-3/4". **$375**

Courtesy of Jeffrey S. Evans & Associates, jeffreysevans.com

Henry Schlevogt (Czech, 1904-1984) pressed malachite glass "Wheat Harvest" vase, for Desna/ Ornela, designed circa 1934, the flaring trumpet form vase in imitation of a block of carved malachite with male and female figures harvesting wheat on the sides, sandblasted "DESNA" mark on the bottom, 9-5/8" h, 5-3/4" dia. **$250**

Courtesy of Simpson Galleries, LLC, simpsongalleries.com

GLASS

pyrex

PYREX IS AN example of an invention born of necessity. As word has it, the concept of Pyrex cookware came to be during the first quarter of the 20th century.

Physicist Jesse Littleton, who was employed by Corning Industries, put his scientific mind and creative spirit to use to come up with a glass casserole dish to replace the one his wife said cracked during the cooking process. His solution was to use clear borosilicate, the material Corning Industries used to manufacture railroad sign lanterns, among other industrial goods, to create cookware that could withstand the heat of cooking. The test run was with the bottom of a battery jar, which his wife used to bake a cake and put in motion the creation of Pyrex cookware. By 1915, Pyrex was being sold nationwide.

In addition to pieces appearing on shelves and at quite affordable prices at antiques shops and malls and occasionally at auction, Pyrex remains a notable symbol of retro nostalgia. It's also receiving modern-day revival, as pieces are available for purchase new, boasting designs and themes made popular in the past. With adorable and memorable pattern names like Gooseberry, Butterprint, Atomic Eyes, and Daisy, it's no wonder this durable and delightful cookware stays the course after more than a century.

Five Autumn Harvest pattern nesting mixing bowls in hues of orange, circa late 1970s into mid-1980s, good used condition with some wear to the outer coloring, largest bowl is 10-1/2" d. **$52**

Courtesy of Scheerer McCulloch Auctioneers, scheerermcculloch

Five nesting bowls, two measuring 10" dia, largest is 12" dia.....**$23**

Courtesy of Specialists of the South, specialistsofthesouth.com

Pair of white-toned milk glass mixing bowls painted with green-toned floral design, date to mid-20th century, largest piece measures about 4" h x 9" w x 8" l, marked on bottom as Pyrex. $20

Courtesy of The Benefit Shop Foundation, Inc., thebenefitshop.org

Soft opal white, sweet pink shiny milk glass Pyrex dishes, Gooseberry pattern features sprigs of gooseberry leaves and striped berries, includes a 4-quart, 2-1/2-quart, 1-1/2-quart and 1-1/2-pint dish, good minor paint loss. $75

Courtesy of The Velvet Cricket, velvetcricket.com

Mid-century covered casserole dish, aqua blue with wheat design motif, settled on a metal stand. $55

Courtesy of Denise Ryan Auction Co., deniseryanauction.com

Carnival glass line insulator inscribed "Pyrex T.M. Reg. U.S. PAT. OFF. Made in U.S.A." and stamped with the date "APR 20, 1942," with the purpose to insulate the electrical wires that the piece would carry, so the electrical signal would not seep into the wooden electrical poles, in very good condition, virtually no damage, fantastic sheen in the carnival glass, 10" dia, 4" h. **$90**

Courtesy of North American Auction Company, northamericanauction.com

Vintage Pyrex primary colors mixing bowls, 401-404.................................**$80**

Courtesy of Specialists of the South, specialistsofthesouth.com

Two 1-1/2-cup vintage covered Amish butter dishes and one 1-1/2-pint covered dish..**$23**

Courtesy of Specialists of the South, specialistsofthesouth.com

GLASS

quezel

IN 1901, MARTIN BACH and Thomas Johnson, who had worked for Louis Tiffany, opened a competing glassworks in Brooklyn, New York, called the Quezal Art Glass and Decorating Co. Named for the quetzal, a bird with brilliantly colored features, Quezal produced wares closely resembling those of Tiffany until the plant closed in 1925. In general, Quezal pieces are more defined than Tiffany glass, and the decorations are brighter and more visible.

Quezel, two-light wall sconces, pair, Queens, NY, iridescent glass, brass, shades signed, 11" w x 6" d x 11" h overall. **$400**

Courtesy of Treadway Gallery, treadwaygallery.com

Quezel art glass shade with hearts, small chip on top rim, 5-3/8" h. **$70**

Courtesy of JMW Auction Service, jmwauction.com

Set of 3 shades by Quezel, gold iridescent, individually threaded, 5-1/2" l x 5" w. ..**$300**

Courtesy of Dutch Auction Sales, dutchauctionsales.com

Art glass Quezel lamp shade, excellent, 7". **$110**

Courtesy of Milestone Auctions, milestoneauctions.com

Quezel art glass bowl, calcite exterior with iridescent gold interior, 8" dia, 2-1/4" h...**$70**

Courtesy of Rachel Davis Fine Arts, racheldavisfinearts.com

GLASS

sandwich

NUMEROUS TYPES OF glass were produced at the Boston & Sandwich Glass Co. in Sandwich, Massachusetts, on Cape Cod, from 1826 to 1888. Founded by Deming Jarves, the company produced a wide variety of wares in differing levels of quality. The factory used free-blown, blown three-mold, and pressed glass manufacturing techniques. Both clear and colored glasses were used.

Jarves served as general manager from 1826-1858, and after he left, emphasis was placed on mass production. The development of a lime glass (non-flint) led to lower costs for pressed glass. Some free-blown and blown-and-molded pieces were made. By the 1880s the company was operating at a loss, and the factory closed on Jan. 1, 1888.

Pressed rosette curtain pins/ tie backs, lot of six, fiery opalescent, each with beaded petals, shaped rim, and period metal shank, Boston & Sandwich Glass Co., 1840-1870, 2" d and 3" d. **$70**

Courtesy of Jeffrey S. Evans & Associates, jeffreysevans.com

Assorted pressed Lacy nappies, lot of two, comprising a sapphire blue Crossed Swords and a strong fiery opalescent Stippled Bull's Eye, each with scallop-and-point rim, Boston & Sandwich Glass Co., 1835-1850, 4-1/2" dia. and 6-7/8" dia. **$120**

Courtesy of Jeffrey S. Evans & Associates, jeffreysevans.com

Antique Sandwich poinsettia lampwork paperweight, six green leaves, Lutz rose central cane, slightly concave polished base, Boston & Sandwich Glass Co., circa 1850, 2-1/2" d. **$450**

Courtesy of Jeffrey S. Evans & Associates, jeffreysevans.com

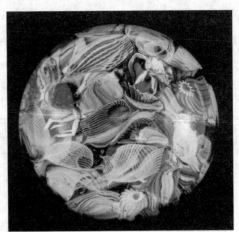

New England scrambled millefiori paperweight, scrambled ground of latticinio ribbons and millefiori canes, polished pontil mark, 1850-1887, 1-5/8" h, 2-1/2" dia. **$275**

Courtesy of Jeffrey S. Evans & Associates, jeffreysevans.com

Free-blown mottled witch ball, opaque white with rose and blue mottling, rough pontil mark with a 1/2" dia opening, chain and hook, 1840-1880, 4" dia. **$110**

Courtesy of Jeffrey S. Evans & Associates, jeffreysevans.com

EE-3B eagle and shield pressed open salt, opaque white with some fiery opalescence, on four feet, Boston & Sandwich Glass Co., 1830-1845, 2-1/8" h, 2" x 3-1/4". **$1,100**

Courtesy of Jeffrey S. Evans & Associates, jeffreysevans.com

Sandwich glass amethyst vase, 19th century, trumpet form with flared scalloped rim, six sided base, bullseye and oval decoration on panels, 8-3/4" h. **$350**

Courtesy of Brunk Auctions, brunkauctions.com

Blown-molded GIII-23 open salt, hat form, colorless, wide folded rim, Rayed Type III base with rough pontil ring, Boston & Sandwich Glass Co., 1825-1835, 2-1/4" h, 2-5/8" d rim. **$120**

Courtesy of Jeffrey S. Evans & Associates, jeffreysevans.com

Unlisted blown-molded GIII-8 mug/handled whiskey, colorless, cylinder form with applied handle, rayed Type VIA base, Boston & Sandwich Glass Co. and others, 1825-1840, 2-3/4" h..... **$120**

Courtesy of Jeffrey S. Evans & Associates, jeffreysevans.com

Blown-molded GIII-16 pint decanters, colorless, each with plain neck, rayed base with rough pontil mark, appropriate pressed wheel stopper, Boston & Sandwich Glass Co., 1825-1835, 9" h, 7-3/8" dia mouth. **$375**

Courtesy of Jeffrey S. Evans & Associates, jeffreysevans.com

◄ Free-blown fish globe on foot, colorless, globular with plain flared rim, raised on a funnel-form foot with folded rim, rough pontil mark, Boston & Sandwich Glass Co., Bakewell, Pears & Co., Pittsburgh, and others, 1840-1890, 8-1/2" h, 4-1/8" d rim, 5" d foot. **$130**

Courtesy of Jeffrey S. Evans & Associates, jeffreysevans.com

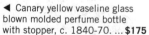

◄ Canary yellow vaseline glass blown molded perfume bottle with stopper, c. 1840-70. ... **$175**

Courtesy of Terri Peters & Associates Auction and Estate Marketing, terripetersandassociates.com

▶ Rare early American blue pressed sandwich glass three Printie block oil lamp, Boston & Sandwich Glass Co., 1840-1860, has octagonal standard on a square base, brilliant blue color, threaded brass camphene burner with "snuffers," 11-1/2" h. **$650**

Courtesy of Terri Peters & Associates Auction and Estate Marketing, terripetersandassociates.com

GLASS

steuben

FREDERICK CARDER, an Englishman, and Thomas G. Hawkes of Corning, New York, established Steuben Glass Works in 1903 in Steuben County, New York. In 1918, the Corning Glass Co. purchased the Steuben company. Carder remained with the firm and designed many of the pieces bearing the Steuben mark. Probably the most widely recognized wares are Aurene, Verre De Soie and Rosaline, but many other types were produced. The firm operated until 2011.

▲ Lot of two Steuben Aurene perfume bottles, blue iridized glass, both have the original stoppers, signed "Aurene," largest is 5-3/4" h. **$350**

Courtesy of Dan Morphy Auctions, morphyauctions.com

▶ Steuben art glass perfume bottle, original stopper, 6" h. **$750**

Courtesy of Dan Morphy Auctions, morphyauctions.com

Steuben Bristol yellow cologne bottle, rectangular bottle in yellow glass with overall black threading and black faceted stopper, 5" h......................**$150**

Courtesy of Jaremos, jaremos.com

▶ Steuben art glass bowl, signed "Aurene 565," iridescent gold, rolled rim, ribbed with star highlights, lightly etched, 3" x 5-1/2"...............................**$225**

Courtesy of Woody Auction LLC, liveauctioneers.com

Steuben Wisteria glass candlesticks, baluster form in wisteria, decorated with cut panels and fans, diachronic effect shading from blue to purple depending on light source, 8" h. **$1,000**

Courtesy of Jaremos, jaremos.com

Steuben Twist-Stem and Optic-Ribbed art glass candlestick, Pomona green and rosa, shape 6107, wide flared socket, wise flaring foot with a pinched dome, signed, "STEUBEN/F CARDER," Steuben Glass Works, first quarter 20th century, 10-1/4" h............. **$250**

Courtesy of Jeffrey S. Evans & Associates, jefferysevans.com

Steuben art glass sculpture depicting a trout leaping for an 18k yellow gold royal coachman fly, with oval wooden stand, designed by James Houston and introduced in 1966, signed "Steuben" on base, sculpture is 8" h x 6-1/4" x 3", base is 3/4" h x 6" x 3-3/4". **$1,100**

Courtesy of Thomaston Place Auction Galleries, thomastonauction.com

Steuben art glass tree stump bud vase, signed "Aurene #2744," blue iridescent, excellent color, 6-1/4". **$700**

Courtesy of Woody Auction LLC, liveauctioneers.com

Frederick Carder (1863-1963) for Steuben blue Aurene glass fan vase with applied threading, Corning, NY, unmarked, 8-1/2" x 7" x 4". **$375**

Courtesy of Rago Arts and Auction Center, ragoarts.com

A Steuben Aurene etched "Grape" pattern glass vase, urn form, gold Aurene ground with acid-etched continuous grapevine motif, signed "Steuben Aurene 2683" underneath, good condition, 10-1/2" h. **$1,300**

Courtesy of Schmidt's Antiques Inc. Since 1911, liveauctioneers.com

GLASS

tiffany glass

TIFFANY & CO. was founded by Charles Lewis Tiffany (1812-1902) and Teddy Young in New York City in 1837. Originally called Tiffany, Young and Ellis, the name was shortened to Tiffany & Co. in 1853 when Charles Tiffany took control and shifted the firm's focus to jewelry.

By the 1860s, Tiffany & Co. had established itself as America's most prestigious and reputable firm, first by importing the best of European goods and then by manufacturing its own wares of the highest quality. From 1867 until the end of the century, Tiffany exhibited and won medals at international expositions in Paris and the United States.

Charles' son, Louis Comfort Tiffany (1848-1933), was an American artist and designer who worked in the decorative arts and is best known for his work in stained glass. This outstanding American glass designer established Tiffany Glass Co. in 1885, and in 1902, it became known as Tiffany Studios, producing glass until the early 1930s.

Tiffany revived early techniques and devised many new ones. His work in large part defined both the Art Nouveau and Aesthetic movements. In the world of antiques and collectibles, his name is ubiquitous – even those who do not collect Tiffany Studios items know who he is and what his work looks like.

Because Tiffany Studios' glass is so widely loved and collected, there is a significant market in fakes, especially at the higher end of the spectrum, most specifically in lamps. This makes verification the most important thing to look for when it comes to Tiffany Studios.

Tiffany bronze and glass paperweight, iridescent glass turtlebacks, bears impressed signature, 1-1/4" h x 5-1/2" w x 4" d...**$325**

Courtesy of Hudson Valley Auctions, hudsonvalleyauctions.com

VISIT WWW.ANTIQUETRADER.COM

WWW.FACEBOOK.COM/ANTIQUETRADER

Tiffany art glass decanter, signed "L.C. Tiffany-Favrile 5501H," gold iridescent with green heart and vine decoration, nice fitted stopper, 8"........**$2,000**

Courtesy of Woody Auction LLC, liveauctioneers.com

Art glass vase, signed "L.C. Tiffany Favrile 8324J," rare Tiffany Cypriot, 5-1/5". **$6,000**

Courtesy of Woody Auction LLC, liveauctioneers.com

Tiffany art glass vase, paper Tiffany label, gold iridescent with pulled white design, ruffled rim, "04762" on base, 3-3/4"..............................**$350**

Courtesy of Woody Auction LLC, liveauctioneers.com

◄ Tiffany Studios inlaid bronze and glass tray, iridescent glass inlay, bears signature, 16-3/4" dia..........**$450**

Courtesy of Hudson Valley Auctions, hudsonvalleyauctions.com

▲ Tiffany art glass salt dip, signed "L.C.T. Favrile," blue iridescent, 2-1/2"......................**$300**

Courtesy of Woody Auction LLC, liveauctioneers.com

A Tiffany Studios patinated bronze and glass "Pine Needles" inkwell, early 20th century, marked "Tiffany Studios/New York/847," domed hinged top opening to a glass-lined well in a squat body, 3-3/4" h x 7" dia. **$600**

Courtesy of Hidden Treasures Antiques & Fine Art, htantiques.com

Tiffany Studios inkwell in the "American Indian" pattern, model #1183, New York, NY, early 20th c., bronze, glass insert, marked, 3-1/2" x 5-1/2" dia....**$475**

Courtesy of Rago Arts and Auction Center, ragoarts.com

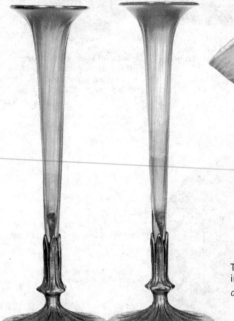

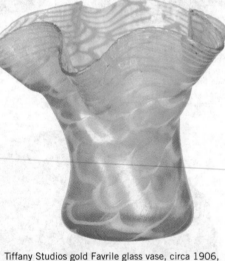

Tiffany Studios gold Favrile glass vase, circa 1906, inscribed "L.C. Tiffany Favrile," 10-3/4" h. **$800**

Courtesy of A.B. Levy's Palm Beach, ablevys.com

▲ Pair of Tiffany art glass trumpet vases, signed "L.C.T. Favrile," gold iridescent , set on signed Louis C. Tiffany Furnaces #159 bronze bases, 11-3/4". **$1,400**

Courtesy of Woody Auction LLC, liveauctioneers.com

▶ Tiffany art glass fingerbowl and underplate, signed "L.C.T.," gold iridescent with engraved beaded garland motif, 2-1/2" x 6". **$500**

Courtesy of Woody Auction LLC, liveauctioneers.com

GLASS
wave crest

NOW MUCH SOUGHT AFTER, Wave Crest was produced by the C.F. Monroe Co., Meriden, Connecticut, in the late 19th and early 20th centuries. It was made from opaque white glass blown into molds, then hand-decorated in enamels, and metal trim was often added. Boudoir accessories such as jewel boxes, hair receivers, etc., predominated.

Large Kelva Wave Crest dresser box, opal glass, hinged lid, relief decorated gilt metal collar and latch, has a leafy green paint decorated exterior with large pink and white flowers having enamel highlights, signed with "Kelva, Trade Mark" stamp on the bottom, 3-3/4" h x 8" dia................ **$175**

Courtesy of Fontaine's Auction Gallery, fontainesauction.com

Wave Crest lot of three glass items, opaque white with polychrome-enamel decoration, comprising a cylindrical vase, a signed cigar holder, and a signed oval dish, fourth quarter 19th century, 1-3/4" to 6" h. **$130**

Courtesy of Jeffrey S. Evans & Associates, jeffreysevans.com

Wave Crest lot of three toothpick holders, opaque white with polychrome-enamel decoration, two with brass rims, one set on a brass stand, each signed, fourth quarter 19th century, 1-3/4" to 2-1/4" h.............. **$110**

Courtesy of Jeffrey S. Evans & Associates, jeffreysevans.com

HARRY POTTER

AFTER MAKING HIS DEBUT in the June 1997 book, *Harry Potter and the Philosopher's Stone*, by J.K. Rowling, Harry Potter has become the favorite wizard of millions of Muggles all over the world.

Twenty years on, Harry Potter has also become one of the most successful franchises in the world and continues to expand with new films, books, plays, amusement parks, and more on the horizon. Whenever there's fan frenzy about a new book, movie, or any other development, it boosts the franchise across the board and one of the areas that continues to rapidly grow is the collectibles market of items associated with the books and movies.

Some of these items often have no trouble auctioning for hundreds of thousands of dollars, such as Rowling's writing chair that sold for almost $400,000 — or even millions, like a handwritten copy of *The Tales of Beedle the Bard* that Amazon paid $4 million for. Many movie props like wands and quidditch brooms, and books, particularly first editions, also sell for five figures or more.

Values for early *Harry Potter* first edition books continue to climb. As if written in the stars, the first edition, first printing is the rarest and most valuable of all editions. Securing an original copy is extremely difficult and even former library copies fly through auction houses like a seeker during a quiddich match.

Just seven years ago, a first edition, first printing copy (signed and inscribed by Rowling) with solid provenance to her early years as a writer sold for $23,900. Now standard copies from the late 1990s routinely sell between $10,000 and $16,000 on up. Condition makes all the difference: A copy "virtually as new" sold for an astounding $43,750 at auction. The former owner knew the book had value and wrapped it inside a first edition, later printing dust jacket.

Courtesy of Heritage Auctions, ha.com

ROWLING CHAIR

The April 2016 purchase of the chair used by J.K. Rowling while writing the first two *Harry Potter* books for $394,000 by Jeff Bezos, founder and CEO of Amazon, raised the ceiling on such collectibles and refocused collector attention on the wide world of unique items relating to the books and movies.

With the books a near-instant hit with children and later adults, it was only natural for them to be adapted into motion pictures. Assorted collectibles produced in 2001 in conjunction with the first eight *Harry Potter* movies are deep and diverse and among the most valuable and rare items, including limited edition original movie posters, baseball caps, movie props, LEGO sets, first edition book sets, and even period bronze sculptures that are increasing in value on the secondary market.

VISIT WWW.ANTIQUETRADER.COM

WWW.FACEBOOK.COM/ANTIQUETRADER

"The world of Harry Potter is one that reaches all ages," said John Lohmann, owner at *Harry Potter* prop seller Animation Ink Archives, which has been selling animation art and movie props for 25 years. "They were not just books for kids, but for everyone. With the movies, when they could actually see the world of Harry Potter, everyone wants a piece of it — not a toy or a theme park replica, but the real thing. Something when watching the movies, they can point to and say, 'Hey, that's mine!'

"To some collectors, having a robe worn by Daniel Radcliffe in the films is almost like having Darth Vader's black cape from the *Star Wars* films."

Despite this demand, there exists very little *Harry Potter* film props available to the public, making the material that is available all the more valuable. The challenge with collecting prop items is that Warner Brothers has only ever officially released a limited amount of them from the productions.

"Hero wands, robes, and broom sticks are highly collectible and sought-after," Lohmann said. He should know. His company once sold a single wand for $16,000.

HARRY POTTER GLASSES

A pair of $20,000 silver metal wire frame glasses with round clear lenses, shown below, worn by Daniel Radcliffe in his role as Harry Potter in *Harry Potter and the Sorcerer's Stone* is one of several pairs of glasses made for the film.

The most obvious prop from the films might be Harry's own eyeglasses, a pair of which, from the collection of Simon Murray, spectacle maker, were sold at auction. The iconic glasses were first described by author J.K. Rowling and became an integral part of Harry's signature look and persona.

"Props from the first film are generally most desired," said Lohmann. "It's such a joy to

Courtesy of Julien's Auctions, juliensauctions.com

see people's faces when we can offer them a piece of film and animation history. Even to see them get a piece of their childhood back."

Movie posters can be bought for much obtainable prices because of their size. Framing and displaying a poster of gigantic proportions is expensive and requires custom frames. Without framing, the posters risk being damaged every time the owner unrolls them to enjoy the artwork. You could say that big posters are like Godric Gryffindor's Sword — double edged. Many can be bought for under $50 and upward to $150+. One of the rarest and most valuable posters is a lenticular one-sheet prototype for *Harry Potter and the Prisoner of Azkaban* (Warner Brothers, 2004) that was never issued by Warner Brothers. It depicts Harry Potter's long-suffering Uncle Sirius Black (Gary Oldman) and in a brilliant marketing ploy, Warner's created this poster to mimic the "Wanted" posters used in the movie itself. What's exciting about these wanted posters is that you can see Sirius laughing with insanity on the poster and Warner's tried to duplicate a motion effect with the lenticular versions. As you move back and forth before this poster, the image of Black begins to disappear. After creating six of these full-size prototypes at a facility in Michigan, Warner Bros. decided that it was too expensive to put them into full production and so the project was dropped. They are valued between $3,800 and $4,000.

For more information on Harry Potter collectibles, see *Harry Potter: The Unofficial Guide to the Collectibles of Our Favorite Wizard* by Eric Bradley.

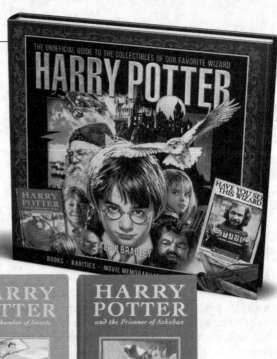

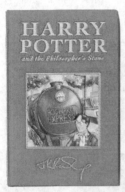

▲ ▶ A rare, complete set of all seven *Harry Potter* titles (U.K. editions), each copy is signed by J.K. Rowling. $13,750

Courtesy of Heritage Auctions, ha.com

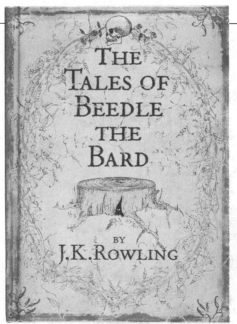

A signed copy of J.K. Rowling's *The Tales of Beedle the Bard*, translated from the *Original Runes* by Hermione Granger. **$896**

Courtesy of Heritage Auctions, ha.com

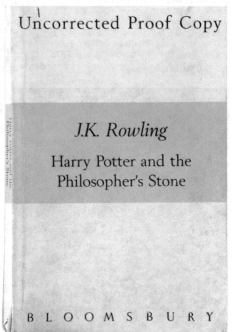

In the original Bloomsbury binding of white wrappers with a yellow band around the middle and lettered in black, is a prohibitively rare example of the uncorrected proof of *Harry Potter and the Philosopher's Stone*. The title page bears the error: "J. A Rowling," while the copyright page states: "Joanne Rowling" and has the complete number row descending from 10 to 1. ....**$4,780**

Courtesy of Heritage Auctions, ha.com

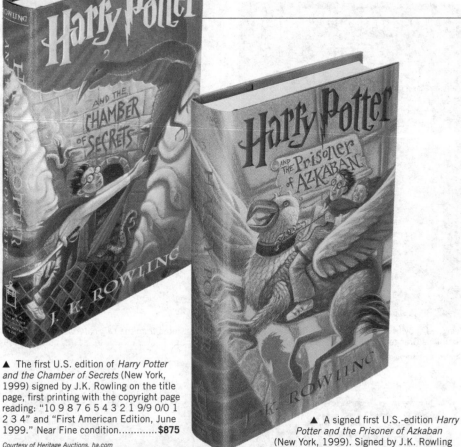

▲ The first U.S. edition of *Harry Potter and the Chamber of Secrets* (New York, 1999) signed by J.K. Rowling on the title page, first printing with the copyright page reading: "10 9 8 7 6 5 4 3 2 1 9/9 0/0 1 2 3 4" and "First American Edition, June 1999." Near Fine condition.............**$875**

Courtesy of Heritage Auctions, ha.com

▲ A signed first U.S.-edition *Harry Potter and the Prisoner of Azkaban* (New York, 1999). Signed by J.K. Rowling on the title page. First printing with the copyright page reading: "10 9 8 7 6 5 4 3 2 1 9/9 0/0 1 2 3 4" and "First American Edition, October 1999."......**$688**

Courtesy of Heritage Auctions, ha.com

DID YOU KNOW?

While rolled posters often are preferred by collectors, do not be afraid to purchase a folded poster. The folding does not distract from the value. Folded posters are usually the ones sent directly to movie theaters.

Harry Potter and the Sorcerer's Stone (Warner Brothers, 2001), DS advance style A one-sheet movie poster with owl image, rolled, Very Fine+, 27" x 40".................................**$84**

Courtesy of Heritage Auctions, ha.com

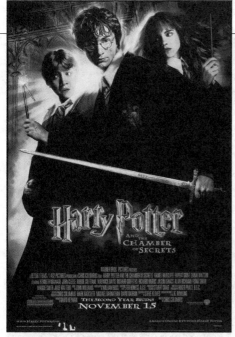

Harry Potter and the Chamber of Secrets (Warner Brothers, 2002), one-sheet DS poster, rolled, Fine/Very Fine, 27" x 40"..................................**$38**

Courtesy of Heritage Auctions, ha.com

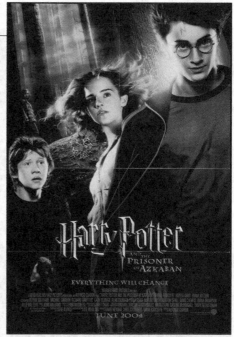

Harry Potter and the Prisoner of Azkaban (Warner Brothers, 2004), one-sheet DS advance movie poster, Very Fine+, 27" x 40". **$60**

Courtesy of Heritage Auctions, ha.com

Harry Potter and the Goblet of Fire (Warner Brothers, 2005), one-sheet SS advance movie poster, rolled, Very Fine/Near Mint, 27" x 40"....**$42**

Courtesy of Heritage Auctions, ha.com

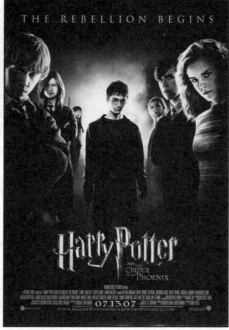

Harry Potter and the Order of the Phoenix (Warner Brothers, 2007), one-sheet DS advance movie poster, rolled, Very Fine-, 27" x 40". **$50**

Courtesy of Heritage Auctions, ha.com

▲ Two small British lenticular posters for *Harry Potter and the Deathly Hollows: Part 2* (Warner Brothers, 2011), full images of Harry and Voldemort, have never been used or displayed. Lenticular movie posters are unusually rare and costly for a studio to produce and give the viewer a 3D effect without special glasses. Examples from the *Harry Potter* film franchise are among the most popular with collectors. These posters were exclusively used at movie theaters at studio-approved outlets only. Mint condition, 11-1/2" x 16-1/2".......... **$40-$60**

Courtesy of Heritage Auctions, ha.com

Movie props that never made it to the screen are even valuable. This piece of sheet music with gold wording was from a scene that was cut from *Harry Potter and the Sorcerer's Stone*; 8" x 9-3/4".
.... **$600**

Courtesy of Animation Ink Archive, animationinkarchive.com

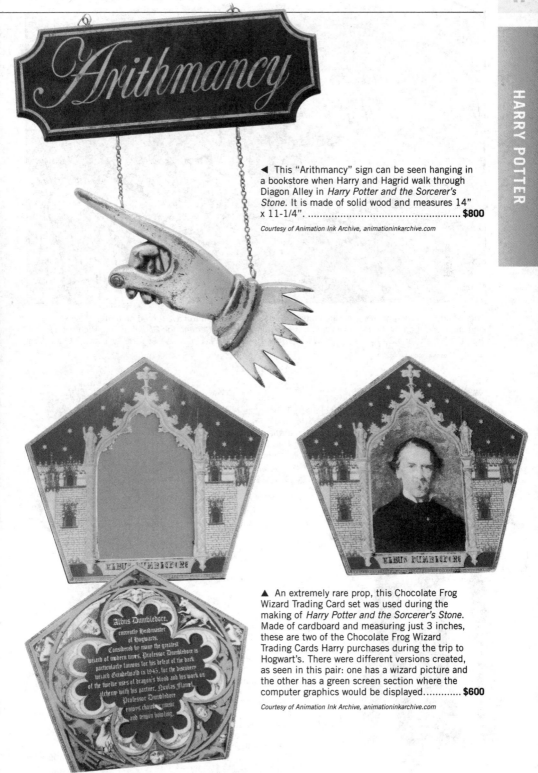

◀ This "Arithmancy" sign can be seen hanging in a bookstore when Harry and Hagrid walk through Diagon Alley in *Harry Potter and the Sorcerer's Stone*. It is made of solid wood and measures 14" x 11-1/4". **$800**

Courtesy of Animation Ink Archive, animationinkarchive.com

▲ An extremely rare prop, this Chocolate Frog Wizard Trading Card set was used during the making of *Harry Potter and the Sorcerer's Stone*. Made of cardboard and measuring just 3 inches, these are two of the Chocolate Frog Wizard Trading Cards Harry purchases during the trip to Hogwart's. There were different versions created, as seen in this pair: one has a wizard picture and the other has a green screen section where the computer graphics would be displayed............. **$600**

Courtesy of Animation Ink Archive, animationinkarchive.com

461

Original art, Tom Richmond's *MAD* illustration. Harry's friends seem to have turned on him in this amusing illustration by Richmond based on the hit film, *Harry Potter and the Goblet of Fire*. Richmond drew the fun art for a 2005 story in *MAD* Magazine; 16-1/5" x 11-1/5"...**$55**

Courtesy of Heritage Auctions, ha.com

◄ Original art by Tommy Lee Edwards, "Sorting Hat." For his interpretation of the famous Hogwarts' Sorting Hat, Edwards added long ribbons and braids to it; 10-3/4" x 15-1/2". **$529**

Courtesy of Heritage Auctions, ha.com

► Among the many pieces Warner Bros. Studios created to promote the *Harry Potter* movies was this life-sized Dobby, the House Elf statue. Only 200 were made for around 2003-04 for Walmart stores across the country and in many cases, it was only given to certain Walmart stores as a top sales bonus and then later raffled off to the employees. The statue is attached to a Plexiglass base; 28" h.
....**$350-$700**

Courtesy of HowCool.com

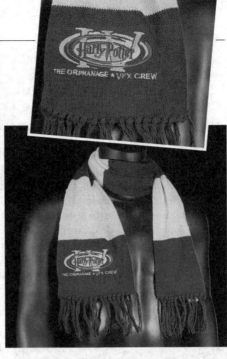

▲ Crew members working on the third and fourth installments of the *Harry Potter* film franchise were gifted Gryffindor House scarves when the films were complete. Both scarves are tassel-edged and made from knitted synthetic material in burgundy and gold, the Gryffindor House colors. One is burgundy with thin gold-colored stripes and features a faux-gold *Harry Potter and the Prisoner of Azkaban* logo, the other scarf displays thicker stripes and features an embroidered *Harry Potter and the Goblet of Fire* logo along with a logo for visual effects company called The Orphanage. The longest scarf is 76-1/2 inches long; the set: .... **$200-$300**

Courtesy of Prop Store, propstore.com

◀ Harry Potter Wizard Chess Set includes replica pieces as seen in the film, *Harry Potter and the Sorcerer's Stone*, sold by The Noble Collection and officially authorized by Warner Bros., pieces are 2"-4" h; playing board is 18-1/5" x 18-1/2".
.... **$50**

Courtesy of The Noble Collection, noblecollection.com

▶ The greatest wizard of all time, Dumbledore owned one of the most powerful wands ever created, the Elder Wand. Known as the Wand of Destiny, it was fated to become the tool that Harry would use to defeat Voldemort. Includes replica of the original Ollivander's wand box; 15" l. **$50**

Courtesy of The Noble Collection, noblecollection.com

HISTORICAL AMERICANA

HISTORICAL AMERICANA WALKS A FINE LINE between so many collecting genres: Folk art, manuscripts, political pinbacks and ceramics can all easily fall within their own collecting category. Historical Americana collectors seek to document America's political and cultural heritage, from its birth as a republic to the present, so although it may appear to be a 'catch-all' category on its surface, historical Americana is a thriving collecting category for that very reason.

Some items show America at its best — a U.S. flag arranged in the "Great Star" pattern of 33 stars, depicting America's struggle during Antebellum, or the very light bulbs developed by Thomas A. Edison in his New Jersey laboratory, a shining example of American ingenuity. Some show the country at its worst. Take Charles Guiteau, the radical who assassinated President James A. Garfield. An important private collection of artifacts and documents

Rembrandt Peale (1778-1860), after Charles Willson Peale (1741-1827), portrait of George Washington as a colonel of the Alexandria Militia, early 19th Century, oil on canvas, 50-1/8" x 40"
....**$852,500**

Courtesy of Christie's, christies.com

relating to the Presidential assassin, including a newly discovered manifesto in which he "justifies" shooting President Garfield, made its auction debut in mid-2017. Most of the items were saved by the warden of the jail in which Guiteau was being held and passed down through his family. The collection sold for just shy of $10,000, but to the country, the archive was an invaluable look at the inside of a man who changed U.S. history.

For the last two weeks in January 2018, in observance of Americana Week, New York was the main destination for collectors, dealers, curators, and scholars of historical Americana, as the city hosted antiques shows, auctions, exhibitions, and lectures dedicated to antiques, modern art, and fine art. Two auction houses, Christie's and Sotheby's, racked up millions of dollars in sales for their Americana offerings.

Sotheby's annual Americana Week sales brought in $13.9 million, with nearly 1,000 lots sold across two auctions. The week kicked off with the sale of important printed and manuscript Americana, including cartography, which was led by *The Declaration of Independence* printed by E. Russell that sold for $1.2 million. The important Americana sale achieved $9.6 million and saw strong results across a diverse group of works, including American furniture, silver, and ceramics.

Other sale highlights included a Federal inlaid cherrywood and mahogany tall-case clock by famed cabinetmaker Nathan Lumbard, circa 1800, that sold for $471,000 to the Museum of Fine Arts, Boston; one of the earliest and most important Wainscot armchairs, circa 1640-

1660, ever to appear at auction that sold for $375,000; and an American silver and copper "Indian" punch bowl and ladle created circa 1900-15 and attributed to metal molder and finisher Joseph Heinrich that fetched $312,500 - far surpassing its high estimate of $175,000.

Americana Week at Christie's New York included three distinct sales with pieces that explored collecting in the fields of Chinese export, American furniture, folk art and silver, and outsider and vernacular art. The auction house's "Important American Furniture, Folk Art and Silver" auction on Jan. 19 saw sales of $4.1 million. The leading lot was a portrait of George Washington as a military colonel that sold for $852,500 — considerably more than the high estimate of $600,000.

Another Washington item, an inaugural button, which is the earliest artifact referring to George Washington as the "Father of His Country," not only set a world record when it sold for $225,000 in Heritage Auction's Feb. 24, 2018 "American & Political Auction," but the sale itself set a world record as the highest-grossing auction of political memorabilia collection ever offered.

The David and Janice Frent Collection of Political & Presidential Americana, Part II, realized a record $1.2 million from 641 bidders. The sale eclipsed the previous world auction record when The Frent Collection debuted at Heritage in October 2017, generating $911,538.

"To say this auction was a pulse-pounder is an understatement," said Tom Slater, Director of Americana Auctions at Heritage. "It's been a career highlight bringing this collection to auction and the results have just been astounding."

The rare Washington artifact is now the world's most valuable Washington button, created to celebrate the first president's 1789 Inauguration. It features a crisp, stamped bust of Washington and the words "Pater Patriæ," a Latin phrase meaning "Father of his Country." Modern collectors avidly seek a wide variety of coat button designs honoring Washington that were sported by patriotic Americans. The Frent Collection featured some 50 assorted examples, believed to be the largest such holding ever assembled.

Surprises did not stop with Washington, Heritage said. Other highlights included an 1868 silk campaign flags for Ulysses S. Grant, one of just three believed known in this design, which raced to $62,500, more than triple its presale estimate; a stunning 1860 brooch featuring an ambrotype portrait of Abraham Lincoln by Mathew Brady, depicting the president in the iconic "Cooper Union" pose, which sold for $35,000 — a new high water mark for this item at auction; and an outstanding example of the "Ship of State" silk campaign flag from Henry Clay's 1844 campaign ended at $32,500.

The record-setting Holy Grail of George Washington inaugural buttons: Albert WI-19B, DeWitt GW-1789-41, 25 mm copper shell with lead-filled back, half-length military bust of Washington facing one-quarter left or dexter, inscribed "General Washington Pater Patriæ." This is the only portrait button in the accepted canon of Washington inaugural buttons and has always been at the top of the want list for anyone interested in the period. From the David and Janice Frent Collection. **$225,000**

Courtesy of Heritage Auctions, ha.com

▶ Whiskey bottle with jugate paper label, reddish-brown glass bottle with paper label on the front advertising "Harrison & Morton Old Bourbon Whiskey From Louis Taussig & Co. 26-28 Main St. San Francisco Cal.," 11-1/2" h. **$1,625**

Courtesy of Heritage Auctions, ha.com

▼ Annie Oakley signed iconic cabinet card by J. Wood of the Bowery, New York, titled "Annie Oakley, (Little Sure Shot)," popular markswoman wears a shooting award around her neck and a trademark star on brim of her hat, verso signed "Compliments of Annie Oakley," 4" x 6". **$4,375**

Courtesy of Heritage Auctions, ha.com

An important "Wild West" badge, inscribed to Johnny Baker's wife, Della Farrell, from "Cody & (Nate) Salsbery," engraved with a detailed description of a woman wearing a skirt on horseback intended to represent Della, who was also a star performer in Buffalo Bill's Wild West, where she and Baker met; reverse engraved "Kind wishes of Cody & Salsbery [sic] to Della Farrell," 1-1/4" x 1-1/2"... **$4,500**

Courtesy of Heritage Auctions, ha.com

White House Police Captain's badge, embossed brass and enamel badge depicting the White House and the Presidential Seal, inscribed "White House Police Captain," official full-sized badge worn by the Uniformed Division of the United States Secret Service from 1951-1962, 2-1/4" x 2-1/4".. **$812**

Courtesy of Heritage Auctions, ha.com

William Jennings Bryan's Ear of Corn Delegates Badge for the 1908 Democratic Convention, celluloid oval picturing Bryan, calling him the "Nation's Commoner," attached to a red, white, and blue ribbon suspended from a "Delegate" hanger, button reads, "Two of America's Great Essentials To Peace and Prosperity Known the World Over," referring to Bryan and corn. The voters thought differently, though, and Bryan went down to defeat for the third and last time. The badge is 1-1/2" x 2-1/4"..... **$687**

Courtesy of Heritage Auctions, ha.com

Superb 1840 campaign ribbon for William Henry Harrison, great design and slogans ("Poor Man's Friend"), crisp and fresh, 3" x 7". From the David and Janice Frent Collection........ **$600**

Courtesy of Heritage Auctions, ha.com

Important 1864 jugate silk campaign ribbon for Lincoln and Johnson. Rarity, red, white, and blue color, and condition work together to make this the premium 1864 Lincoln ribbon variety; other than a trivial light water stain at the top, it is in near mint condition, 2-14/16" x 7-14/16". From the David and Janice Frent Collection....**$21,250**

Courtesy of Heritage Auctions, ha.com

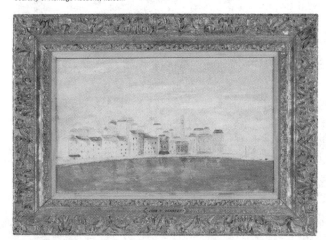

A rare signed original painting by the 35th U.S. President John F. Kennedy, oil with pencil on canvas board, depicts the skyline of a town, possibly in the South of France, as viewed from the water, in original frame with "Kennedy" nameplate, signed "Kennedy" in lower right corner, with a date which appears to be "1955," 21-1/2" x 15-1/2". **$162,500**

Courtesy of Heritage Auctions, ha.com

Ulysses S. Grant 1868 silk campaign flag, colors are deep and strong, a little light water staining, scattered small holes, generally great condition, 33" x 24". From the David and Janice Frent Collection. **$62,500**

Courtesy of Heritage Auctions, ha.com

James Montgomery Flagg's iconic "Uncle Sam I Want You" sketch, artist-signed, charcoal sketch of Uncle Sam pointing his finger at the viewer, inscribed by the artist "I Want You! James Montgomery Flagg," not dated, but probably 1942-1943, image most associated with illustrator Flagg, appearing on recruiting posters from WWI and WWII, 24-1/2" x 35"...**$13,750**

Courtesy of Heritage Auctions, ha.com

Abraham Lincoln cased sixth plate tintype, embossed copper mat and preserver, pressed paper case, no glass covering the tin, when open, portrait is accented by two small, original fabric flags that hold the top and bottom of the case together, 2-3/4" x 3-1/4". **$875**

Courtesy of Heritage Auctions, ha.com

Thomas E. Dewey rebus pin by Philadelphia Badge, advises Democrats and Truman partisans to "Get Your [Ass] off the Grass. It's Dewy," White House appears in the background, key button for any Dewey collection, 1-3/4". **$875**

Courtesy of Heritage Auctions, ha.com

Franklin D. Roosevelt cartoon contributor's pin, with caricature of FDR smoking a cigarette, inscribed "He Is Worth A Buck To Me! Local 9 CIO Shipyard Workers," made by Bastian Brothers, mint condition, 1". **$1,000**

Courtesy of Heritage Auctions, ha.com

A molded copper and zinc rooster weathervane, American, late 19th century, 18" h, 15" l..... **$5,000**

Courtesy of Christie's, christies.com

Impressive and colorful jugate poster of Roosevelt and Fairbanks, stone lithograph featuring large, natural color, overlapping portraits of the 1904 Republicans, titled "For President/ Theodore Roosevelt/ For Vice President/ Charles W. Fairbanks/ 1904," published by Louis Roesch Company of San Francisco, design elements include Lady Liberty, billowing flags, sprigs of laurel, a shield and the Washington Monument, framed, 25-1/2" x 40". **$5,125**

Courtesy of Heritage Auctions, ha.com

HUNTING AND FISHING COLLECTIBLES

FOR DIE-HARD HUNTERS, there's nothing better than spending time surrounded by vintage examples of the brands and tools they use in the field and on the water. The market for vintage hunting and fishing collectibles has seen prices creep ever northward out of the hundreds and into the thousands in recent years. The diverse category touches on thousands of different items and price points, with even nominally priced items finding new homes every day.

Decoys are one of the most popular collectibles. Collectors may be drawn to derelicts or those carved by the most well-respected artisans in North America.

Hunting and fishing ephemera is among the scarcest of all collectibles in this category. It doesn't always have to be paper, as the word is so often associated. Ephemera, including wooden boxes, labels, hunting tags and licenses, and even specialty magazines, all find a price among hunting and fishing collectors.

Hunting- and fishing-themed advertising items are among the most sought-after today. The market bull's-eye still revolves around the biggest names in advertising displays: Winchester, Peters, Remington, and Western Powder. Even pieces in compromised condition are bringing good prices on eBay.

Demand is so great for early Winchester paper that aluminum signs are being mass-produced by the thousands in the United States — not overseas.

These fakes and fantasy pieces are designed after 19th century cartridge boards. Rectangular signs measure 12-1/5 inches x 16 inches and 16 inches x 8-1/2 inches, and circular signs are often 11 inches or 12 inches in diameter.

The popularity of these signs is overwhelming, mostly because prices are less than $10 shipped and lots of collectors really want a piece of Winchester lore and history.

Perhaps unsurprisingly, a nice collection of vintage lures spanning a full century can be assembled for less than $500. Most lures sell at auction for between $1 and $100. Lures valued greater than $1,000 are generally early examples, uncataloged examples, in excellent condition, rare finds with original boxes, or prototypes.

William Aiken Walker (American/South Carolina, 1839-1921), "Hunting Dog," oil on canvas, signed lower right, presented in a giltwood frame, 17" x 14", framed 22-1/2" x 19-1/2". **$18,000**

Courtesy of New Orleans Auction Galleries, neworleansauction.com

Lot of two guns, top: Remington Model 700 BDL, .30-06 caliber, standard rifle with Weaver scope, excellent stock, barrel suffers from poor storage and there is salt and pepper corrosion on barrel and muzzle. Bottom gun: Ruger 1022 Deluxe, features the deluxe checkered pistol grip walnut stock and blued finish, Bushnell 3 x 9 scope, retains majority of original finish, couple of storage marks on wood. Fine pair of cabin guns. Serial number-6656769, 122-81493; manufacturer-Remington, Ruger; Model-700, 10/22; caliber-.30-06, .22 RF; barrel length 23", 19"; FFL Status-Curio & Relic. **$475**

Courtesy of Dan Morphy Auctions, morphyauctions.com

Custom-made Damascus steel hunting bowie knife, deer-antler handle with Case Factory mark, blade is hand-forged with 1095 and 15N20 high and low carbon steel with over 200 layers, 3/4 tang, brass steel guards, comes with leather sheath, overall length is 15", blade 9". **$180**

Courtesy of Connoisseur Auctions, liveauctioneers.com

Original, untouched early Maynard sporting rifle in fine condition, Model 1865, serial no. 2362, caliber: .350, barrel length 26", improved hunting and target rifle No. 3. Features case colored frame with traces of color, long range tang sight, walnut buttstock with patchbox that is stamped "Maynard Patentee May 27 1851 June 17 1856," lower tang lanyard ring, takedown, octagon to round barrel with an excellent clean bore, original walnut dealer case has a decal that reads, "A. McComas Maker & Importer of Guns Rifles & Pistols 51 Calvert, Baltimore." Comes with a wooden cleaning, pull-through, cleaning brush, bullet mold. Original stock excellent condition retaining the majority of original varnish; traces of blue on patchbox, generous amounts of blue on tang sight, case colors under sight, traces of colors on frame. Barrel has 90 percent original factory blue finish with areas of toning to patina, lever gray patina with color in hidden areas. Barrel sports a fixed rear sight and German nickel front sight. . **$2,500**

Courtesy of Dan Morphy Auctions, morphyauctions.com

H

HUNTING AND FISHING

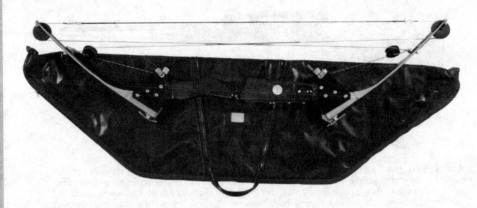

Allen prototype compound bow, hand-inscribed "#7303-50/60#-29 1/4-Ser. 7603ZS49L-Allen Pat. Second,"appears unused, with Allen Original Compound decal and calibration hang tag, padded black vinyl carrying case, excellent condition, 12" x 51"..$150

Courtesy of Rich Penn Auctions, richpennauctions.com

▼ American folk art powder horn, circa 1850, well carved, depicts a hunter packing down the powder in his musket with a ramrod, his faithful hunting dog and three trees populated with doves and a menacing serpent, unsigned, but carver likely of Pennsylvania origin, 12" h. $625

Courtesy of Heritage Auctions, ha.com

▲ Vintage leather hunting bag with original canvas strap, initials D.G.L. on front, 10-1/2" x 8-1/4" x 2".........$300

Courtesy of Auctions at Showplace, nyshowplace.com

German carved wood and cast brass powder flask, probably Augsburg or Nuremberg, 19th century, the branching wood form carved on either side with low-relief hunting scenes, the brass fittings with anthemion, foliage, and figurals on the original chain, 9-3/4" l x 6-1/4" w...............$125

Courtesy of Auctions at Showplace, nyshowplace.com

Laflin and Rand Hunting Season Show Cards, all four seasons depicting young boys with their season-appropriate catch, advertising on back, 8" x 12" each. **$850**

Courtesy of Auctions at Showplace, nyshowplace.com

Engraving of Lady Juliana Berners in her habit, 1825, noted for her writings on hunting and hawking, very good condition, 5" x 8". **$50**

Courtesy of Jasper52, jasper52.com

Cowbrand Soda advertising poster with hunting motif by artist G. Muss Arnolt, original bands top and bottom, excellent condition, 17" x 25". . **$1,500**

Courtesy of Auctions at Showplace, nyshowplace.com

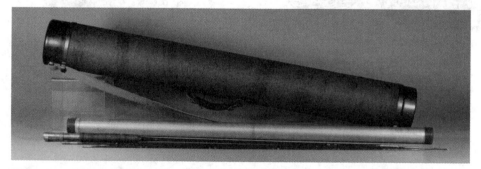

Vintage Weber Henshall 12 ft. bamboo fly fishing rod, labeled "J A Henshall, The Weber Lifelike Fly Co, Stevens Point WI,"together with Turner Brothers Delight rod case and an unbanded fly rod. **$300**

Courtesy of William Bunch Auctions & Appraisals, bunchauctions.com

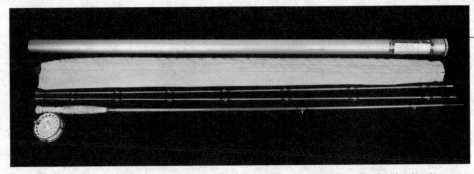

Orvis Superfine (2) fly fishing rod, comes with protective sheath and hard case, outfitted with a Hardy Bros Ltd. L.R.H. lightweight reel, both items very good condition, rod weighs 3-1/3 oz, 7-1/2' l. **$675**

Courtesy of Scheerer McCulloch Auctioneers, Inc., scheerermcculloch.com

S.E. Bogdan Nashua, NH, fly fishing reel, excellent condition, 3-1/2" dia. **$1,400**

Courtesy of Scheerer McCulloch Auctioneers, Inc., scheerermcculloch.com

Edward Vom Hofe fly fishing reel, believed to be an earlier model with patented date of Sept. 2, 1879, and Jan 23, 1883, reads "Fulton St. NY," inscribed with the name "George Raymond," void of any identifiable numbers, probably used for salmon fishing, very good condition, 4-1/4" dia. **$1,000**

Courtesy of Scheerer McCulloch Auctioneers, Inc., scheerermcculloch.com

STH Reels, DDR-C3 disk drag cassette reel 3, Argentina, comes in original box with a leather Arne Mason fishing reel pouch, excellent condition, 4" dia. **$120**

Courtesy of Scheerer McCulloch Auctioneers, Inc., scheerermcculloch.com

Arthur L. Walker 100 2/0 salmon fishing reel, #677, 1950s. A machinist by trade, Walker used German silver and hard rubber to handcraft his reels. This reel is in very good working condition. **$2,600**

Courtesy of Scheerer McCulloch Auctioneers, Inc., scheerermcculloch.com

Charlie Joiner Canvasback Drake decoy, 1950, wood and canvas over wire, full-sized Charlie "Speed" Joiner, Jr. (1921-2015) of Chestertown, MD, signed and dated 1950, famous Roman-nose style with tight crack on one side, rare early decoy......................... **$600**

Courtesy of Jasper52, jasper52.com

Lot of three duck decoys, early carved wood with glass eyes, one stamped "Stoney Point Decoys-Glen Burnie, MD" in block letters, all hand-painted with original paint, very good/excellent condition, all approx. 16-1/2" l...**$175**

Courtesy of Rich Penn Auctions, richpennauctions.com

▼ Lot of three duck decoys, early carved wood with glass eyes, hand-painted with original paint, makers unknown, all very good/excellent condition, 14" to 16" l.. **$80**

Courtesy of Rich Penn Auctions, richpennauctions.com

◄ Hollow-carved New Jersey black duck decoy in sleeping or preening position, cedar body is pegged, bird retains original painted surface, head has carved details (nostrils, mouth, nail and eye rings) and mottled paint decoration. The bird is a worker, with evidence of having been shot-over, retains original lead weight and an old leather rig loop, about 14" front-to-back, and about 6" h; at the widest, body about 5-1/2"... **$150**

Courtesy of Jasper52, jasper52.com

First edition of *How to Hunt and Trap*, J.H. Batty, 1878. The book served as a hunting and trapping guide for game animals such as moose, deer, geese, ducks, wolves, bears, etc., contains numerous illustrations, decorated gilt cover and spine, good condition, 5-1/4" x 7-3/4"......................................**$425**

Lot of two lures: Heddon Dowagath, glass eyes, three treble hooks, missing some paint on the top and the hooks are rusty but solid, 4-1/2" l; and a South Bend Bass-Oreno No. 973, good condition, with original box, which is missing an end on the bottom portion, 3-3/4" l. **$40**

Courtesy of Scheerer McCulloch Auctioneers, Inc., scheerermcculloch.com

Lot of nine vintage fishing lures, includes jitterbugs, spoon spinners, some signed, good condition, largest is 5" l.**$25**

Courtesy of Kodner Galleries Inc., kodner.com

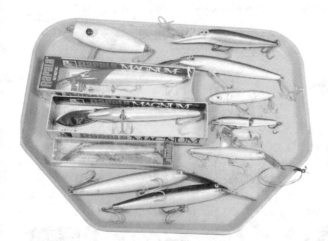

Lot of 12 vintage fishing lures, several Rapala sinking magnum lures, original Rapala wobbler-Finnish minnow, Big Mac, jointed two-part lure, three in original boxes, 3-1/2" h, 9" w, 1-1/2" d. **$70**

Courtesy of Uniques & Antiques, Inc., uniquesandantiques.com

Three-piece lot consists of a fly fishing wallet, small tackle box, and fly fishing reel. Wallet is made of textured brown leather, closes with a snap, has rivets on the bottom where the pages are connected, of vintage K&L "Common Sense" design with two pages with springs for holding flies tied to line, four felt pages, and two end pockets, gold-colored maker's mark shows nicely inside with "Common Sense" inside a jumping fish and "MADE IN U.S.A." printed beneath, 32 tied flies inside, 7" x 4-1/2"; metal tackle box is painted black with gold-colored accents, two separate compartments that close with a bar latch, tray in one side with several loops of leader tied to hooks of varying sizes, other side has organizational sections and found inside are several sinkers of varying sizes, 4" x 8" x 1-3/4" h; fly fishing reel is made of wood and metal and has a scalloped edge where the arm is secured to the wheel, knobs made of wood and metal, functional, overall measurements 8" x 7-3/4"................................. $90

Courtesy of Worth Auctions, worthauctions.com

Collection of vintage fishing accouterment, lot includes flies, lures, fish scales, worm box. **$150**

Courtesy of Kodner Galleries Inc., kodner.com

▼ Lot of 21 vintage fishing lures, most wood with glass eyes, includes Heddon Dowasiag models, many five-hook models with front and rear spinners. **$900**

Courtesy of Austin Auction Gallery, austinauction.com

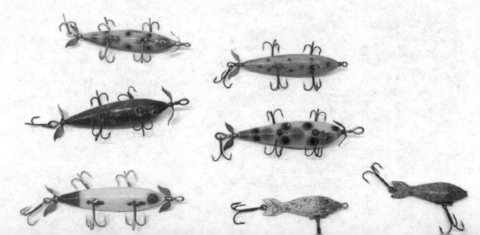

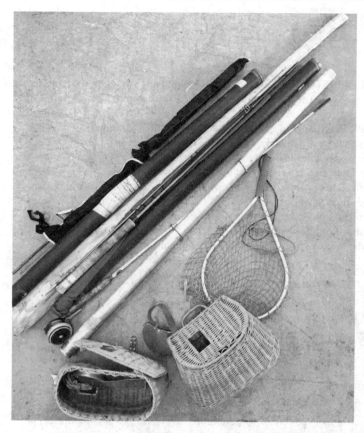

A group of vintage 1950s-era spin fishing items including six rods (Shakespeare Wonder with automatic reel), two creels, and net. **$70**

Courtesy of Duane Merrill & Company, merrillsauction.com

Vintage all metal Bomber Lure Bait and Tackle sign, depicts fishing lure at top middle of sign, excellent condition, 66" x 21" x 3"........................**$230**

Courtesy of Ole Hound Auction House, liveauctioneers.com

Vintage wooden fly fishing lure box with four-partitioned drawers having a latched front panel, 18" x 22" x 16".....**$90**

Courtesy of Greenwich Auction, greenwichauction.net

ILLUSTRATION ART

EXPOSURE PLAYS AN IMPORTANT ROLE in collector demand and values for illustration art, which has proven itself over the last decade as one of the most popular and dynamic art genres in the country.

Take for instance "Hello Everybody!," a calendar illustration originally produced for Brown & Bigelow in the late 1920s. Artist Rolf Armstrong created the carefree pastel on board of a young lady with a bright smile at the nexus of the Roaring '20s and the Great Depression. Popular reaction was enthusiastic. The artwork appeared as a calendar illustration, on playing cards, puzzles, a die-cut advertising sign for Orange Kist soda pop, and as the cover for the March 1929 edition of *College Humor* magazine. According to Janet Dobson's *Pin Up Dreams: The Glamour Art of Rolf Armstrong*, early works such as "Hello Everybody!" defined the vision of feminine beauty for the next 40 years and earned Armstrong the title of "Father of the Pin-Up Artists." The exposure and reputation of the artist generated strong demand when the original work finally came up for auction when its sale price was pushed to $30,000.

Ludwig Bemelmans (American, 1898-1962), "And here we're back - all twelve no less - Happy New Year and Togetherness!"; rear cover illustration from "Madeline's Christmas" first published in *McCall's*, 1956; ink and watercolor on paper laid down to board, signed "Bemelmans" in lower right, 17-3/4" x 14-1/2".
....**$75,000**

Courtesy of Swann Auction Galleries, www.swanngalleries.com

"Hello Everybody!" represents the type of subject matter that is attracting mainstream attention.

"It's really what we think of as classic images in all genres that speak directly and powerfully to a specific time period — whether it's a 1940s *Saturday Evening Post* cover, 1950s science-fiction paperback cover, or 1960s Gil Elvgren calendar pin-up," said Todd Hignite, vice president at Heritage Auctions, the world's largest auctioneer of illustration art and related works.

Interestingly, as the market for illustration art matures, auctioneers are reclassifying works as American fine art and offering works by artists with household names along with other artists such as Grandma Moses, Leroy Neiman, or by the Wyeths. Norman Rockwell's works now routinely bring in excess of $2 million at auction, but his early illustration art, steeped in sentimentality and strong national pride, may be found for less than $100,000.

"Well-known artists such as Rockwell did indeed work in advertising — many illustrators did — and it's certainly less expensive than a magazine cover by the same artist," Hignite said.

Although industry watchers are excited to see many illustration artists make the leap from illustration art to American fine

VISIT WWW.ANTIQUETRADER.COM

WWW.FACEBOOK.COM/ANTIQUETRADER

art, there are dozens, perhaps thousands, of artists whose identity is still lost but whose art lives on. Currently these works are anonymously attributed simply as "American artist," but that doesn't mean research has stopped looking into the identity of these artists. Scholars have been given a boost in recent years thanks to collectors who remain fascinated by various styles.

"The scholarship and research in the field is very active and between exhibitions, publications, and more dealers handling the work, is increasing all the time, but there's still a lot of work to be done in terms of identifying art," Hignite said. "Oftentimes artists didn't sign their paintings, and if their style isn't immediately identifiable, there's a good deal of digging to do. Much of the best research actually comes from devoted fans and collectors, who doggedly put together extensive checklists and track down publication histories, check stubs from publishers, biographies, etc., to try and enhance our understanding of the history."

This confluence of awareness, appreciation, and a growing nostalgia for mid-century works have more than doubled values for pieces offered just a few short years ago. Hignite credits the increase to a matter of supply and demand. "I think simply the opportunity to see a steady supply of great art by Elvgren has increased the demand," he said. "If you see one of his paintings in person, there's no question of his painting talent, and collector confidence increases as we see such a steady growth and consistent sales results."

Ludwig Bemelmans (American, 1898-1962), "Madeline's Rescue," original book illustration, circa 1953, watercolor and ink on paper laid on board, signed "Bemelmans" in lower right, 7/8" x 29-7/8".
......................................$37,500

Courtesy of Heritage Auctions, ha.com

Jerry Pinkney (American, b. 1939), "Brer Rabbit went in the house and him and Brer Bear sat down in the den," illustration appears on double spread of pages 62-63 in "Further Tales of Uncle Remus" as told by Julius Lester (New York: Dial Books, 1990), watercolor, pen and ink on paper, 10-1/4" x 14"..$27,500

Courtesy of Swann Auction Galleries, www.swanngalleries.com

Dr. Seuss (Theodor Geisel) (American, 1904-1991), "Tadd and Todd," published in *Redbook* magazine, August 1950, with dated publisher's label on verso, ink and watercolor on board, signed in lower left image, 8" x 7-1/4".
......................................$23,750

Courtesy of Swann Auction Galleries, www.swanngalleries.com

Norman Rockwell (1894-1978), study for "Triple Self Portrait," 1960. Rockwell's oil study of his self-described "masterpiece" was created for a 1960 cover of the *Saturday Evening Post,* signed and inscribed lower right, oil on photographic paper laid on panel, 11-1/2" x 9-1/4". $1,332,500

Courtesy of Heritage Auctions, ha.com

Joseph Christian Leyendecker (American 1874-1951), original cover illustration for *The Saturday Evening Post,* August 25, 1923, oil on canvas, 26" x 20", signed lower right with a monogram. $71,700

Courtesy of Heritage Auctions, ha.com

Erté (Romain de Tirtoff) (Russian born, French artist, 1892-1990), "La Cage Improvisée," cover art *Harper's Bazaar,* July 1922, signed "Erté" in right image, gouache on board, 13-3/4" x 10-1/4". $45,000

Courtesy of Swann Auction Galleries, www.swanngalleries.com

top lot

William Oden Waller, set design for 1927 Broadway production Manhattan Mary, featuring a jazz band amid a vibrant and highly detailed Art Deco background, with United Scenic Artists and "W. Oden Waller Studios" stamps on verso. Gouache over graphite on board, 11-1/4" x 19", $77,500. The two-act Broadway musical comedy was a "Roaring Twenties" New York extravaganza at the famed Apollo Theatre, replete with a jazz score by Ray Henderson, brightly colored sets by Waller and a story line that regaled with a classic rags-to-riches tale. Produced by the prolific George White, it ran from September 26, 1927 to May 12, 1928 and starred Ed Wynn, Ona Munson and White himself.

COURTESY OF SWANN AUCTION GALLERIES,
WWW.SWANNGALLERIES.COM

top lot

E.T. the Extra-Terrestrial by John Alvin (1948-2008), original promotional movie illustration, 1982, acrylic on board, 41" x 27", signed, $394,000. Alvin is among the greatest cinematic artists in history and created iconic images for more than 135 films, including *Blade Runner*, *The Goonies*, *Aladdin*, *The Princess Bride*, *Batman Returns*, *Jurassic Park*, and *The Lion King*. Alvin's first movie poster was *Blazing Saddles* in 1974 and Mel Brooks, loving the quirky representation of his film, commissioned the artist for the *Young Frankenstein* poster the same year. Alvin became the go-to cinematic artist for any budding blockbuster. Later in his career, he produced movie posters for series such as *Lord of the Rings*, *Harry Potter*, *Pirates of the Caribbean*, and the *30th Anniversary Star Wars Celebration*. According to the advertising executive at Walt Disney Pictures, John Sabel, "There was a reason why (movies) became a big success. It's because of the images that were produced, and a lot of those were John Alvin's paintings." Utilizing his daughter's hand as a model and taking inspiration from Michelangelo's "The Creation of Adam," Alvin created this world-renowned image for E.T. Seen as director Steven Spielberg's masterpiece and by some critics, as the greatest movie of all time, *E.T. the Extra-Terrestrial* was the highest grossing film of the 1980s and was nominated for nine Academy Awards, including Best Picture.

John Gannam (American, 1907-1955), "Impromptu Concert" U.S. Brewers Foundation advertisement, 1950, gouache on board, signed lower left, 23" x 19"..**$11,250**

Courtesy of Heritage Auctions, ha.com

Stevan Dohanos (American, 1907-1994), "Mutually Beneficial Friendship," *The Saturday Evening Post* cover, October 11, 1958, gouache on board, signed lower left: *Stevan Dohanos*, 28-3/4" x 26-1/4". **$31,250**

Courtesy of Heritage Auctions, ha.com

Hy (Henry) Hintermeister (American, 1897-1972), "Rocket Pad Keep Out," oil on canvas, signed lower left, 24" x 20". **$37,500**

Courtesy of Heritage Auctions, ha.com

Hy (Henry) Hintermeister (American, 1897-1972), "Shore Patrol Post No. 2," oil on canvas, signed lower left, 36" x 29". **$11,950**

Courtesy of Heritage Auctions, ha.com

Hugh Joseph Ward (American, 1909-1945), *Undercover Man, Private Detective* magazine cover, April 1942, oil on canvas, signed center right, 30-1/4" x 21". **$81,250**

Courtesy of Heritage Auctions, ha.com

Gil Elvgren (American, 1914-1980), "Cover, Girl!" oil on canvas, 1965, signed lower right, 30" x 24"...**$100,000**

Courtesy of Heritage Auctions, ha.com

Patrick Nagel (American, 1945-1984), *Joan Collins, #411*, 1982, acrylic on canvas signed and dated lower right, 47-1/2" x 40". Nagel gained fame for his distinct style of the female form that graced *Playboy* magazine and the cover of *Rio*, the 1982 best-selling album by Duran Duran. Nagel was at the forefront of a new wave of illustration in Los Angeles. His cool, minimalist style defined an era. Joan Collins became a star/celebrity playing the wicked and vengeful Alexis Colby in the 1980s prime-time TV soap opera *Dynasty*. **$100,000**

Courtesy of Heritage Auctions, ha.com

Roger Hane (American, 1939-1974), *The Lion, The Witch, and The Wardrobe* book cover, 1970, acrylic on canvas board, signed lower right. Illustration was used as the cover for *The Lion, The Witch, and The Wardrobe*, *The Chronicles of Narnia*, book 1 by C.S. Lewis, Collier, 1970, 15" x 9". **$26,250**

Courtesy of Heritage Auctions, ha.com

Robert McGinnis (American, b. 1926), "Casino Royale," original DVD illustration, 2002, gouache and pencil on board, signed, 23-1/2" x 30-1/2".........**$47,500**

Courtesy of Heritage Auctions, ha.com

Chris Van Allsburg (American, b. 1949), *The Stranger,* interior book illustration, 1986, colored pencil on paper, signed and dated "85" lower left, 10-1/2" x 13". Van Allsburg has written and illustrated more than 20 books and earned Caldecott Medals for *Jumanji* and *The Polar Express*, two books that were made into films. **$16,250**

Courtesy of Heritage Auctions, ha.com

Chesley Bonestell (American, 1888-1986), "Atomic Bombing of New York," *Collier's Magazine* interior illustration, 1948, mixed media on photograph, signed lower left, 15 1/2" x 18-1/4........................ **$27,500**

Courtesy of Heritage Auctions, ha.com

JEWELRY

JEWELRY HAS HELD a special place for humankind since prehistoric times, as an emblem of personal status and decorative adornment. This tradition continues today. We should keep in mind, however, that it was only with the growth of the Industrial Revolution that jewelry first became cheap enough so that even a person of modest means could wear a piece or two.

Only since around the mid-19th century did certain forms of jewelry, especially pins and brooches, begin to appear on the general market as a mass-produced commodity and the Victorians took to it immediately. Major production centers for the finest pieces of jewelry remained in Europe, especially Italy and England, but less expensive pieces were also exported to the booming American market and soon some American manufacturers also joined in the trade. Especially during the Civil War era, when silver and gold supplies grew tremendously in the U.S., did jewelry in silver or with silver, brass or gold-filled (i.e. gold-plated or goldplate) mounts begin to flood the market here. By the turn of the 20th century, all the major mail-order companies and small town jewelry shops could offer a huge variety of inexpensive jewelry pieces aimed at not only the feminine buyer but also her male counterpart.

Inexpensive jewelry of the late 19th and early 20th century is still widely available and often at modest prices. Even more in demand today is costume jewelry, well-designed jewelry produced of inexpensive materials and meant to carefully accent a woman's ensemble. Today costume jewelry of the 20th century has become one of the most active areas in the field of collecting and some of the finest pieces, signed by noted designers and manufacturers, can reach price levels nearly equal to much earlier and scarcer examples.

Jewelry prices, as in every other major collecting field, are influenced by a number of factors including local demand, quality, condition, and rarity. As market prices have risen in recent years it has become even more important for the collector to shop and buy with care. Learn as much as you can about your favorite area of jewelry and keep abreast of market trends and stay alert to warnings about alterations, repairs or reproductions that can be found on the market.

Seeing a lot of auction action in the past couple of years are colored diamonds, and many have been setting huge records. Christie's sold the 14.62-carat "Oppenheimer Blue" ring for $58 million in 2016, while Sotheby's sold the 59.6-carat "Pink Star" ring for $71 million in April 2017. Sotheby's also set a record in May 2017 for the auction price of a pair of earrings that are the world's most expensive to date.

Named after Greek gods, the "Apollo Blue" fancy vivid blue diamond, weighing 14.54 carats, and the "Artemis Pink" fancy intense pink diamond, at 16 carats, sold at Sotheby's "Magnificent Jewels and Noble Jewels" auction for an astounding $57.4 million.

"Individually, these captivating diamonds

The pear-shaped and brilliant-cut diamond earrings Apollo and Artemis.
Courtesy of Sotheby's, sotheby.com

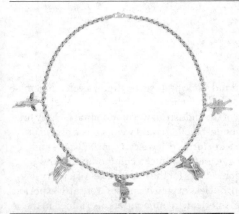

are truly exceptional stones and when considered as a pair, they enter a class of their own: the most important earrings ever to appear at auction," Sotheby's said.

An anonymous buyer purchased the pear-shaped Apollo and Artemis for $42.1 million and $15.3 million, respectively, and renamed them "The Memory of Autumn Leaves" and "The Dream of Autumn Leaves," the house said.

The previous record price for earrings was set by a pair of pear-shaped white diamond earrings, "Miroir de l'Amour," that Christie's sold for $17.7 million in November 2016.

Back on earth, where mortal jewelry collectors don't have such huge pocketbooks, there are luckily vast choices of affordable pieces to choose from.

As founder of GemGossip.com, Danielle Miele has seen trends in vintage jewelry come and go and circle back around.

"When I first got into collecting vintage and antique fine jewelry, which was about ten years ago, Art Deco was really popular — things like rock crystal pieces, jewelry with a lot of filigree, and even the late deco pieces that were predominately geometric," Miele said. "Now, I would say people are really getting back into charms, as in the past we saw charm bracelets being extremely popular, where today charm necklaces have been the hot item. This also gives a resurgence to long, sturdy gold chains and wire collars in solid gold, which have both been the preference to wear these charms on."

Another trend is big and bold pieces made from natural materials.

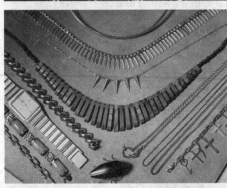

Vintage jewelry collectors have been gravitating toward bold and chunky rings, bracelets, and necklaces from the 1960s and '70s made of gold, lapis, malachite, and tiger's eye.

Photos courtesy of Danielle Miele, gemgossip.com

"I've also seen jewelry from the 1960s and 1970s become popular as of late — chunky gold rings, bracelets, and necklaces with malachite, lapis, and tiger's eye gemstones in bold shapes. What is old is new again, and you never know what will come be in style!" Miele said.

Celebrating its 10th anniversary in 2018,

GemGossip.com focuses on jewelry trends, antique and period jewelry, and celebrity jewelry, as well as exclusive designer interviews. It is also a hub for gemstone and jewelry education, considering Miele is a graduate gemologist from the Gemological Institute of America. She is currently traveling the world covering jewelry stories, visiting stores, and collecting rings. For more information about her blog, jewelry, and her jewelry adventures, visit gemgossip.com.

Two other great resources to learn more about jewelry are *Warman's Jewelry Identification and Price Guide*, 5th edition, by Christie Romero and *Warman's Costume Jewelry Identification and Price Guide* by Pamela Y. Wiggins.

JEWELRY STYLES

Jewelry has been a part of every culture throughout time, reflecting the times as well as social and aesthetic movements. Jewelry is usually divided into periods and styles. Each period may have several styles, with some of the same styles and types of jewelry being made in both precious and non-precious materials. Elements of one period may also overlap into others.

Georgian, 1760-1837. Fine jewelry from this period is quite desirable, but few good-quality pieces have found their way to auction in recent years. Sadly, much jewelry from this period has been lost.

Victorian, 1837-1901. Queen Victoria of England ascended the throne in 1837 and remained queen until her death in 1901. The Victorian period is a long and prolific one, abundant with many styles of jewelry. It warrants being divided into three sub-periods: Early or Romantic period dating from 1837-1860; Mid or Grand period dating from 1860-1880; and Late or Aesthetic period dating from 1880-1901.

Sentiment and romance were significant factors in Victorian jewelry. Often, jewelry and clothing represented love and affection, with symbolic motifs such as hearts, crosses, hands, flowers, anchors, doves, crowns, knots, stars, thistles, wheat, garlands, horseshoes and moons. The materials of the time were also abundant and varied. They included silver, gold, diamonds, onyx, glass, cameo, paste, carnelian, agate, coral, amber, garnet, emeralds, opals, pearls, peridot, rubies, sapphires, marcasites, cut steel, enameling, tortoiseshell, topaz, turquoise, bog oak, ivory, jet, hair, gutta percha and vulcanite.

Sentiments of love were often expressed in miniatures. Sometimes they were representative of deceased loved ones, but often the miniatures were of the living. Occasionally, the miniatures depicted landscapes, cherubs, or religious themes.

Hair jewelry was a popular expression of love and sentiment. The hair of a loved one was placed in a special compartment in a brooch or a locket, or used to form a picture under a glass compartment. Later in the mid-19th century, pieces of jewelry were made completely of woven hair. Individual strands of hair would be woven together to create necklaces, watch chains, brooches, earrings and rings.

Georgian black onyx, seed pearl, gold, and silver earrings, circa 1820, French, feature half-pearls set in silver, mounted on top of black onyx tablets, set in 18kt gold, French hallmarks, gross weight 7.90 grams, 2-3/4" x 3/4"h. **$1,500**

Courtesy of Heritage Auctions, ha.com

JEWELRY

Victorian diamond, platinum-topped gold, gold pendant-necklace, horseshoe shaped, features mine-cut diamonds weighing approx. 2.30 carats, set in platinum-topped gold, gross weight 8 grams, 1-3/8" x 5/8". **$1,250**

Courtesy of Heritage Auctions, ha.com

Edwardian enamel and diamond open-face pendant watch, with guilloche enamel case, the goldtone metal dial with Arabic numeral indicators, framed by rose-cut diamonds, platinum and gold mount, stem-wind, stem-set, 26 mm, suspended from a watch pin set with old European-cut diamonds............................. **$2,091**

Courtesy of Skinner Auctioneers and Appraisers, skinnerinc.com

In 1861, Queen Victoria's husband, Prince Albert, died. The queen went into mourning for the rest of her life, and Victoria required that the royal court wear black. This atmosphere spread to the populace and created a demand for mourning jewelry, which is typically black. When it first came into fashion, it was made from jet, fossilized wood. By 1850, there were dozens of English workshops making jet brooches, lockets, bracelets and necklaces. As the supply of jet dwindled, other materials were used such as vulcanite, gutta percha, bog oak, and French jet.

By the 1880s, somber mourning jewelry was losing popularity. Fashions had changed and the clothing was simpler and had an air of delicacy. The Industrial Revolution, which had begun in the early part of the century, was now in full swing and machine-manufactured jewelry was affordable to the working class.

Edwardian, 1890-1920. The Edwardian period takes its name from England's King Edward VII. Though he ascended the throne in 1901, he and his wife, Alexandria of Denmark, exerted influence over the period before and after his ascension. The 1890s were known as La Belle Epoque. This was a time known for ostentation and extravagance. As the years passed, jewelry became simpler and smaller. Instead of wearing one large brooch, women were often found wearing several small lapel pins.

In the early 1900s, platinum, diamonds, and pearls were prevalent in the jewelry of the wealthy, while paste was being used by the masses to imitate the real thing. The styles were reminiscent of the neo-classical and rococo motifs. The jewelry was lacy and ornate, feminine and delicate.

Arts & Crafts, 1890-1920. The Arts & Crafts movement focused on artisans and craftsmanship. There was a simplification of form where the material was secondary to the design. Guilds of artisans banded together. Some jewelry was mass-produced, but the most highly prized examples of this period are handmade and signed by their makers. The pieces were simple and at times abstract. They could be hammered, patinated, and acid etched. Common

Arts & Crafts amethyst, pearl, and gold pendant, Edward Oakes, reversible cross features square and round-cut amethyst, accented by half pearls measuring 4.50 mm and 7.30 mm, set in 18kt gold, gross weight 21.68 grams, 2-3/4" x 1-15/16". **$5,250**

Courtesy of Heritage Auctions, ha.com

Two pairs of Art Nouveau 14kt gold cufflinks, one decorated with lion heads, total 9.2 dwt., 3/4". **$400**

Courtesy of Skinner Auctioneers and Appraisers, skinnerinc.com

materials were brass, bronze, copper, silver, blister pearls, freshwater pearls, turquoise, agate, opals, moonstones, coral, horn, ivory, base metals, amber, cabochon-cut garnets, and amethysts.

Art Nouveau, 1895-1910. In 1895, Samuel Bing opened a shop called "Maison de l'Art Nouveau" at 22 Rue de Provence in Paris. Art Nouveau designs in the jewelry were characterized by a sensuality that took on the forms of the female figure, butterflies, dragonflies, peacocks, snakes, wasps, swans, bats, orchids, irises, and other exotic flowers. The lines used whiplash curves to create a feeling of lushness and opulence.

1920s-1930s. Costume jewelry began its steady ascent to popularity in the 1920s. Since it was relatively inexpensive to produce, it was mass-produced. The sizes and designs of the jewelry varied. Often, it was worn a few times, disposed of and then replaced with a new piece. It was thought of as expendable, a cheap throwaway to dress up an outfit. Costume jewelry became so popular that it was sold in both upscale and "five and dime" stores.

During the 1920s, fashions were often accompanied by jewelry that drew on the Art Deco movement, which got its beginning in Paris at the "Exposition Internationale des Arts Décoratifs et Industriels Modernes" held in 1925. The idea behind this movement was that form follows function. The style was characterized by simple, straight, clean lines, stylized motifs, and geometric shapes. Favored materials included chrome, rhodium, pot metal, glass, rhinestones, Bakelite, and celluloid.

One designer who played an important role was Coco Chanel. Though previously reserved

JEWELRY

Coco Chanel was reportedly a huge fan of constellations and astrology, and Chanel's Comet Collection wonderfully exhibits the designer's affinity. Done in white 18kt gold with 39 full-cut 0.65 carat diamonds, this comet ring features a shooting star design, good to very good condition, size 6. .... **$3,000**

Courtesy of Heritage Auctions, ha.com

Ladies retro 14kt yellow gold freeform diamond ring, in unique retro modern freeform design, set with four centralized round brilliant cut diamonds in a diagonal position, diamond weight is approx. .20 cts, weighs approx. 5.1 grams, hallmarked and stamped "14K," size 7-1/2. .... **$125**

Courtesy of Auction Gallery of Boca Raton, LLC, liveauctioneers.com

for evening wear, the jewelry was worn by Chanel during the day, making it fashionable for millions of other women to do so, too.

With the 1930s came the Depression and the advent of World War II. Perhaps in response to the gloom, designers began using enameling and brightly colored rhinestones to create whimsical birds, flowers, circus animals, bows, dogs and just about every other figural form imaginable.

Retro Modern, 1939-1950. Other jewelry designs of the 1940s were big and bold. Retro Modern had a more substantial feel to it and designers began using larger stones to enhance the dramatic pieces. The jewelry was stylized and exaggerated. Common motifs included flowing scrolls, bows, ribbons, birds, animals, snakes, flowers, and knots.

Sterling silver now became the metal of choice, often dipped in a gold wash known as vermeil.

Designers often incorporated patriotic themes of American flags, the V-sign, Uncle Sam's hat, airplanes, anchors, and eagles.

Postwar Modern, 1945-1965. A movement that emphasized the artistic approach to jewelry making, it is also referred to as Mid-Century Modern. This approach was occurring at a time when the Beat Generation was prevalent. These avant-garde designers created jewelry that was handcrafted to illustrate the artist's own concepts and ideas. The materials often used were sterling, gold, copper, brass, enamel, cabochons, wood, quartz, and amber.

1950s-1960s. The 1950s saw the rise of jewelry that was made purely of rhinestones: necklaces, bracelets, earrings, and pins. The focus of the early 1960s was on clean lines: pillbox hats and A-line dresses with short jackets were a mainstay for the conservative woman. The large, bold rhinestone pieces were no longer the must-have accessory.

Postwar Modern Antonio Pineda Mexican silver and amethyst bracelet, Taxco, circa 1953, marks: ANTONIO (crown), SILVER, HECHO EN MEXICO, 970, (eagle-12), 4.10 troy oz, 7-3/4" circumference. **$1,250**

Courtesy of Heritage Auctions, ha.com

They were now replaced with smaller, more delicate gold-tone metal and faux pearls with only a hint of rhinestones.

At the other end of the spectrum were psychedelic-colored clothing, Nehru jackets, thigh-high miniskirts, and go-go boots. Beads, large metal pendants, and occasionally big, bold rhinestones accessorized the look. By the late 1960s, the hippie look was born and the rhinestone had, for the most part, been left behind.

Vintage signed "Coro" purple rhinestone brooch, a classic arrangement of icy purple and sparkle, 2-1/4" x 2-1/4"... **$30**

Courtesy of Matthew Bullock Auctioneers, bullockauctioneers.com

Antique gold, turquoise, and diamond bangle bracelet, 14kt, signed SA, c. 1869, with personal engraving, approx. 27.4 dwts, inner circumference 6-1/2".. **$2,000**

Courtesy of Doyle New York, doyle.com

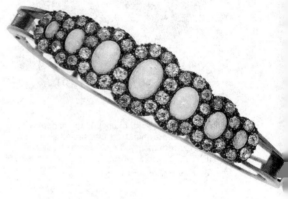

Art Deco mixed metal and enamel bracelet, c. 1930, the tapering hinged cuff with black and green enamel, articulated fringe, maker's mark GC, interior circumference 7"....................... **$3,813**

Courtesy of Skinner Auctioneers and Appraisers, skinnerinc.com

Victorian opal and diamond, silver-topped gold bracelet, features oval-shaped opal cabochons ranging in size from 3.45 x 2.40 mm to 7.60 x 5.55 mm, accented by European-cut diamonds weighing a total of approximately 2.25 carats, set in silver-topped 10kt gold, gross weight 19 grams, 6-1/2" x 1/2"... **$1,312**

Courtesy of Heritage Auctions, ha.com

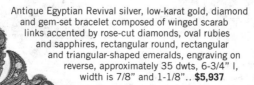

Antique Egyptian Revival silver, low-karat gold, diamond and gem-set bracelet composed of winged scarab links accented by rose-cut diamonds, oval rubies and sapphires, rectangular round, rectangular and triangular-shaped emeralds, engraving on reverse, approximately 35 dwts, 6-3/4" l, width is 7/8" and 1-1/8".. **$5,937**

Courtesy of Doyle New York, doyle.com

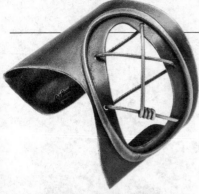

Sterling silver cuff bracelet, Art Smith, with wirework, signed, 2-3/4" w, interior circumference 6-1/2", opening at back approx. 1-1/4"........ **$1,722**

Courtesy of Skinner Auctioneers and Appraisers, skinnerinc.com

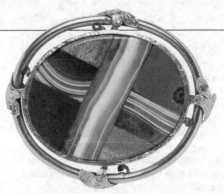

Antique Scottish agate brooch, gold mount, 1-7/8" l... **$431**

Courtesy of Skinner Auctioneers and Appraisers, skinnerinc.com

Pair of retro 14kt gold, diamond, and sapphire clip brooches, Raymond Yard, designed as ribbed gold leaves with diamond melee accents, signed, 1-7/8" l. **$6,765**

Courtesy of Skinner Auctioneers and Appraisers, skinnerinc.com

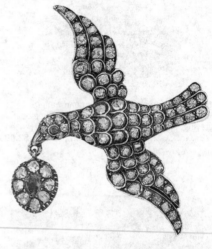

Georgian silver, gold, diamond, and ruby bird pin, flying swallow set throughout with small rose- and old-mine-cut diamonds, with one round ruby eye, ruby bright medium pinkish-red, drop-shaped pendant centering one pear-shaped ruby, edged by rose-cut diamonds, reverse of pendant with glazed compartment with woven hair, circa 1780, approximately 4.2 dwts, 1-1/2" x 1-5/8". **$1,625**

Courtesy of Doyle New York, doyle.com

Antique 14kt gold, diamond, and seed pearl brooch, designed as a sunburst, prong-set with old European-cut diamonds, 4.8 dwt, 1" l. **$246**

Courtesy of Skinner Auctioneers and Appraisers, skinnerinc.com

Two gold, cultured pearl, lapis, ruby insect pins, 14kt, approx. 11.8 dwts gross, 1-1/2" x 1"...... **$562**

Courtesy of Doyle New York, doyle.com

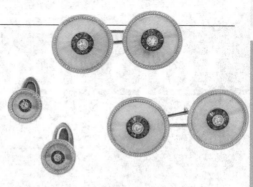

Art Deco rock crystal, sapphire, and diamond dress set, comprising a pair of cufflinks and two shirt studs, with carved rock crystal and channel-set sapphires, single-cut diamond accents, platinum-topped gold mounts, Continental hallmarks, in a box for Julius Hugler, Vienna. **$1,353**

Courtesy of Skinner Auctioneers and Appraisers, skinnerinc.com

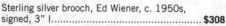

Sterling silver brooch, Ed Wiener, c. 1950s, signed, 3" l... **$308**

Courtesy of Skinner Auctioneers and Appraisers, skinnerinc.com

Gold cufflinks, 18kt, France, designed as griffins, 5.3 dwt, guarantee stamps. **$349**

Courtesy of Skinner Auctioneers and Appraisers, skinnerinc.com

Gold, gold coin, and lapis cufflinks, 18kt, each with 1920 cinco pesos coin, 15.4 dwt............. **$861**

Courtesy of Skinner Auctioneers and Appraisers, skinnerinc.com

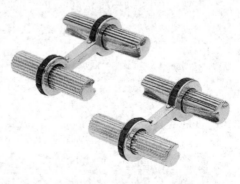

Enamel and gold cheetah cufflinks, orange, red, and black enamel applied onto 18kt gold, gross weight 20.40, 7/8" x 15/16" x 7/8"................ **$750**

Courtesy of Heritage Auctions, ha.com

Sapphire and gold cufflinks, Cartier, French, feature square-cut sapphires weighing a total of approximately 0.50 carat, set in 18kt gold, marked Cartier Paris, C2028, O14579 with French hallmarks, gross weight 11.80 grams, 1-1/16" x 7/8"... **$2,750**

Courtesy of Heritage Auctions, ha.com

top lot

She is famous for singing "Diamonds are a girl's best friend," but in this case, simulated diamonds are, too. A pair of gold-plated earrings featuring filigree spheres accented with simulated diamonds, once worn by Marilyn Monroe in a series of Fox publicity photos used to promote the film, *Gentlemen Prefer Blondes* (20th Century Fox, 1953), recently sold for $90,000 at auction.

The November 2017 Julien's Auctions, "Joseff of Hollywood: Treasures from the Vault," featured an exquisite collection of more than 600 unique pieces of costume jewelry and accessories worn in films and on the red carpet by Hollywood's most glamorous stars of the 1920s-1940s. Eugene Joseff, master jeweler to the stars, designed the pieces. The earrings worn by Monroe are clip-on, stamped "sterling patented," and 2-3/4 inches long. Fox staff photographer Frank Powolny shot the publicity photos, and his photo shoot produced legendary images of Monroe wearing the racy gold pleated gown designed by Travilla for *Gentlemen Prefer Blondes*. Although the gown was deemed too revealing because of its plunging neckline and was cut from the film, Monroe liked it and insisted on wearing it to the 1953 Photoplay Awards ceremony, as well as this photo shoot, together with these earrings, producing some of the most iconic images of her.

Joseff was the custom designer on over 1,000 films before his untimely death in 1948. Upon his passing, his wife, J.C., continued the company's relationship with Hollywood by serving as costume jeweler on more than 450 films until 2006. This collection encompassed exquisitely crafted pieces worn by Hollywood's most legendary stars in some of the most iconic films of Hollywood's Golden era.

A small sampling of highlights from the auction include a silver-plated, simulated diamond and sapphire winged brooch worn by Marlene Dietrich ($22,500) as both a

necklace and a hair ornament in studio publicity portraits used to promote *Destry Rides Again* (1939); a pair of silver-plated star earrings accented with simulated diamonds ($1,000) and silver-plated celestial costume ornaments ($1,750) worn by Greta Garbo in *Camille* (1936); a multi-strand, tiered necklace with bezel-set simulated diamonds and amethysts worn by Vivien Leigh ($45,000) and a cigar case used by Clark Gable ($25,000) in *Gone with the Wind* (1939); a pair of simulated pearl earrings also worn by Monroe ($65,000) in *Gentlemen Prefer Blondes* (1953); and a double-strand order chain comprising gold-plated filigree panels worn by Katharine Hepburn ($1,500) in *Mary of Scotland* (1936

Gold and tiger's-eye quartz earrings, 18kt, 3/4" l......................**$185**

Courtesy of Skinner Auctioneers and Appraisers, skinnerinc.com

Pair of gold and coral pendant earrings, Cartier, 18kt, topped by clusters of dimpled gold balls, fringed by three strands of similar motif, accented by small round cabochon corals, signed Cartier, nos. 55236, 55326, with French import marks, approximately 14.2 dwts, clip-backs, 1-13/16" x 9/16"...........**$4,062**

Courtesy of Doyle New York, doyle.com

Gold, peridot, tourmaline, and diamond earrings, 14kt, oval-cut peridot framed by blue-green tourmalines and full-cut diamonds, 8.1 dwt, 7/8" l..**$492**

Courtesy of Skinner Auctioneers and Appraisers, skinnerinc.com

Shell, multi-stone, gold earrings, Seaman Schepps, feature turbo shell, accented by turquoise and coral cabochons, set in 14kt gold, with partial marks for Seaman Schepps, who created one of America's most avant-garde jewelry companies of the 20th century. Gross weight 28.20 grams, designed for non-pierced ears, 1-1/4" x 1-1/16"...**$1,313**

Courtesy of Heritage Auctions, ha.com

Turquoise, colored diamond, and gold earrings, Eli Frei, feature pear-, round-, and square-shaped turquoise cabochons, accented by full-cut black diamonds weighing a total of approximately 1.95 carats, set in 18kt white gold with a black rhodium finish, marked Frei, gross weight 17.70 grams, for pierced ears, 2-5/8" x 1/2".....................**$906**

Courtesy of Heritage Auctions, ha.com

Antique silver, enamel, and garnet serpent fringe necklace, articulated links applied with periwinkle blue enamel with black enamel detail, spaced by red and white enamel discs, suspending thirty-two stylized serpents tipped by flexibly-set heart-shaped garnets, circa 1840, enamel loss, approximately 41.7 dwts., overall good condition, width with fringe 1-1/4", 16-1/2" l...**$5,000**

Courtesy of Doyle New York, doyle.com

Victorian seed pearl, black onyx, gold locket-pendant-brooch-necklace, features seed pearls set in gold atop a rectangular black onyx tablet measuring 35 x 27 x 6.50 mm, framed in 14kt gold, suspending from a 14kt gold chain, back reveals an oval photo pane, gross weight 31.08 grams, pendant is 1-1/2" x 1-1/8" (not including bail), chain is 22-1/4" l.............. **$750**

Courtesy of Heritage Auctions, ha.com

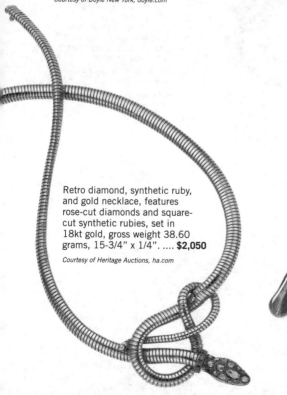

Retro diamond, synthetic ruby, and gold necklace, features rose-cut diamonds and square-cut synthetic rubies, set in 18kt gold, gross weight 38.60 grams, 15-3/4" x 1/4". **$2,050**

Courtesy of Heritage Auctions, ha.com

Jugendstil .935 silver and amethyst necklace, Theodor Fahrner, the shaped plaque set with an oval cabochon amethyst, suspending a drop, and suspended from paperclip chain, Continental hallmarks, signed, 20" l...................... **$861**

Courtesy of Skinner Auctioneers and Appraisers, skinnerinc.com

A 14kt gold, kunzite, enamel, and diamond ring, set with a large cushion-shape kunzite measuring approx. 23 x 18.50 x 14 mm, and weighing approx. 45.80 cts., the shoulders designed as enamel and diamond butterflies, size 7 (with sizing beads)........... **$1,169**

Courtesy of Skinner Auctioneers and Appraisers, skinnerinc.com

An 18kt gold, ruby, and diamond ring, Van Cleef & Arpels, France, set with four heart-shape rubies, total wt. 1.47 cts., and full-cut diamonds, total wt. 0.77 cts., No. B5663679, maker's mark and guarantee stamp, signed, size 7. .... **$7,380**

Courtesy of Skinner Auctioneers and Appraisers, skinnerinc.com

An 18kt gold, coral, and diamond dome ring, set with oval and pear-shape coral cabochons, full-cut diamond melee accents, 9.8 dwt, size 7-3/4. .... **$1,230**

Courtesy of Skinner Auctioneers and Appraisers, skinnerinc.com

Chalcedony and gold ring, features a chalcedony sphere measuring 24 mm, set in 18kt gold, marked C. Vollrath for Claus Vollrath, gross weight 40.70 grams, size 8 (sizeable). **$1,750**

Courtesy of Heritage Auctions, ha.com

Art Deco jadeite jade, ruby, and gold necklace, features navette and cushion-shaped jadeite jade cabochons, accented by round-cut rubies weighing a total of approximately 0.20 carat, set in 18kt gold, gross weight 13.40 grams, drop length 2-1/4", 16-1/8" l. **$2,750**

Courtesy of Heritage Auctions, ha.com

A 14kt white gold and diamond solitaire, c. 1940s, the full-cut diamond weighing approx. 0.25 cts., further set with single-cut diamond melee, with band, size 6-1/4 to 6-1/2.............. **$277**

Courtesy of Skinner Auctioneers and Appraisers, skinnerinc.com

Antique silver and pietra dura brooch and earrings, depicting roses, bellflowers, and forget-me-nots, brooch 1", earrings 1-5/8" l. **$308**

Courtesy of Skinner Auctioneers and Appraisers, skinnerinc.com

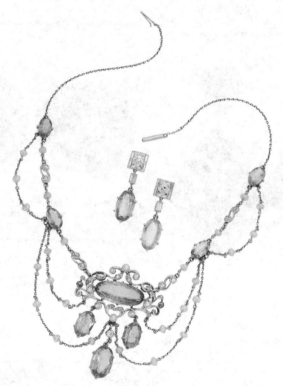

Edwardian topaz, diamond, pearl, platinum, and gold suite, includes a necklace featuring oval-shaped topaz ranging in size from 9.60 x 6.20 x 3.60 mm to 22 x 9.40 x 6.30 mm and weighing a total of approximately 27.50 carats, set in 14kt gold, enhanced by rose-cut diamonds and pearls, set in platinum; together with a pair of earrings suspending oval-shaped topaz measuring 13.10 x 7.75 x 3.90 mm and weighing a total of approximately 5.70 carats, surmounted by European and baguette-cut diamonds weighing a total of approximately 1.40 carats, set in platinum and 14kt gold. Gross weight 33.10 grams. Necklace is 15" l x 2" w, earrings, for pierced ears, are 2-1/4" l x 5/16" w. **$3,250**

Courtesy of Heritage Auctions, ha.com

COSTUME JEWELRY

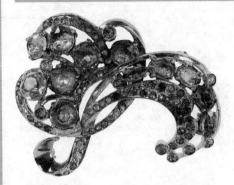

Eisenberg Original large sterling brooch, rare early example, marked sterling and signed Eisenberg, excellent condition, approx. 3" l. **$140**

Courtesy of Auction Gallery of Boca Raton, LLC, liveauctioneers.com

Trifari Jelly Belly spider brooch, c. 1940s, signed, 2" l. **$225**

Courtesy of Greenwich Auction, greenwichauction.net

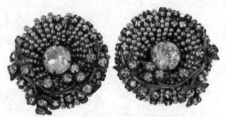

Pair of Miriam Haskell rhinestone earrings with faux seed pearls, marked on backs, approx. 1-1/4" dia. **$125**

Courtesy of Greenwich Auction, greenwichauction.net

Pair of Kenneth Jay Lane jeweled costume earrings, encrusted with rhinestones and colored glass cabochons, approx. 3-1/2" l. **$250**

Courtesy of Auction Gallery of Boca Raton, LLC, liveauctioneers.com

Large Hattie Carnegie butterfly-form statement necklace, fit with simulated gemstones and held on a double-strand chain approx. 24-1/2" l. **$175**

Courtesy of Auction Gallery of Boca Raton, LLC, liveauctioneers.com

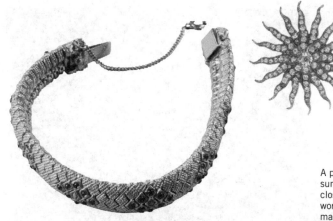

A pair of simulated diamond sun brooches with bar pin closures, one signed "Ciner," worn by Vivien Leigh on her masquerade ball gown in *That Hamilton Woman* (United Artists, 1941), 3-1/4" l.... **$2,000**

Courtesy of Julien's Auctions, juliensauctions.com

Ciner gold-plated bracelet, set with turquoise, ruby and sapphire cabochons, approx. 7".. **$25**

Courtesy of Hilliard & Co., hilliardandco.com

Miriam Haskell costume pearl bracelet, set with faux baroque pearls, signed, 2-1/2" wide across opening... **$70**

Courtesy of Greenwich Auction, greenwichauction.net

Coro Victorian-style brooch, faux amethyst, 1-1/2" l. **$20**

Courtesy of Auction Gallery of Boca Raton, LLC, liveauctioneers.com

Vintage signed Coro enameled floral pin, very good condition, 3-1/2" l. **$40**

Courtesy of Auction Gallery of Boca Raton, LLC, liveauctioneers.com

Ciner rhinestone costume jewelry pin, blue and clear stones, marked, missing one small stone, 2-1/2" h, 2-1/2" w, 1-1/2" d. **$100**

Courtesy of Uniques & Antiques, Inc., uniquesandantiques.com

Miriam Haskell rhinestone necklace, marked on back, multi-strand of faux seed pearl, with large faux pearl and rhinestone clasp/pendant, 16-1/2" l. **$250**

Courtesy of Greenwich Auction, greenwichauction.net

Two pairs of Eisenberg clip earrings in original box, unsigned, 1-3/4" and 1-1/2". **$30**

Courtesy of Martin Auction Co., martinauctionco.com

Gold and lapis bead necklace and pair of costume earclips, 34 lapis beads approx. 10 mm. **$750**

Courtesy of Doyle New York, doyle.com

KITCHENWARE

EVERYONE KNOWS THAT the kitchen is the hub of the home, so it's no surprise that the market for vintage kitchenware collectibles remains strong. From antique rolling pins and cookie cutters to vintage toasters and wooden bowls, and everything in between, these items hold much nostalgia.

Stephen White of White & White Antiques & Interiors of Skaneateles, New York, said interest in vintage antique kitchenware remains steady. He was quick to feature his rare whale ivory-crested Nantucket rolling pin valued at $425. "I have unusual kitchen antiques, from hand food choppers to copper pots," he said.

"What I see is a more gradual demand for these items," said Jimmy Roark of Nashville, Tennessee, who operates a small antiques collectibles shop in his garage. "I sell a lot of my cookie cutters, antique wooden bowls, and vintage mixer beaters during the holidays."

"When you think of Pittsburgh, you can't escape the long history that the H.J. Heinz Co. has here," said Toni Bahnak of Candlewood Antiques in Ardara, Pennsylvania. "We have rare old vinegar bottles and ketchup bottles that denote an era when the Heinz Co. made its own glass," Bahnak said.

Industry experts say ketchup and pickle collectibles rose in value because of the business deal that saw the H.J. Heinz Co. purchased by Warren Buffett's Berkshire Hathaway and 3G Capital, which was co-founded by Jorge Lemann, one of Brazil's richest men. Even before the blockbuster deal was announced, some Heinz memorabilia collectors reported that their antique bottles and jars were fetching higher prices than normal.

Early country primitive apple peeler, painted, original stencil decoration, 36" l, 32" h.......... **$950**
Courtesy of Robert Slawinski Auctioneers, Inc., slawinski.com

"I had one of my antique vinegar bottles sell for about $225 and I think I could have gotten more for it," said Ruth Oslet, an antiques collector from Waynesburg, Pennsylvania. She sold it to a marketing executive who collects business memorabilia.

Tom Purdue, a long-time collector of food company antiques, said history and nostalgia play an important role in what people remember and want to save for their modern kitchens. "I can remember the distinct smell of my grandmother's old pickle jars and Heinz horseradish in her musty old kitchen where she used a hand pump to wash dishes," said Purdue, an 89-year-old former blacksmith from Wheeling, West Virginia.

The ever-expanding business reaches back to 1869 when Henry John Heinz and neighbor L. Clarence Noble began selling grated horseradish, bottled in clear glass to showcase its purity. It wasn't until 1876 that the company introduced its flagship product, marketing the country's first commercial ketchup.

Not all history, though, is tied to corporate America. Family memories still stoke the

Lot of seven butter molds: swan, cat, acorns, letter "B," sheath of wheat and floral designs, all excellent condition, 2-1/2" h to 7-1/4" h......... **$125**

Courtesy of Rich Penn Auctions, richpennauctions.com

Vintage kitchen cabinet brochure, Youngstown Kitchens, by Mullins Manufacturing Company of Warren, Ohio, circa 1950, includes kitchen illustrations and information about kitchen planning, when folded approx. 3-1/8" x 6-1/4", completely opened: 18-3/4" x 12-1/2".
.... **$20**

Courtesy of Jasper52, jasper52.com

Antique Fries Co. metal cream beater, rare with lid, 9-1/2" h. **$79**

Courtesy of Matthew Bullock Auctioneers, bullockauctioneers.com

embers of home cooking although many young people today find fast food the fuel of the future.

"I still have my family's old cornbread recipe and I use it all the time," said Elizabeth Schwan, gallery director for Aspire Auctions in Pittsburgh.

Schwan, who scans the country for antiques, admits she has a soft spot for old kitchen utensils. "Flour-sifters, antique copper mixing bowls, and rolling pins were all part of my heritage because my family grew up on a Kentucky farm," Schwan said. "I can still smell the homemade bread and jams."

And like most farm families, the kitchen served as a meeting place and refuge from a long day's work. "Between verbal debates about what to plant on the south flats, we would help our parents churn butter and chop wood for the old country stove," said Myrtle Bench, 91, of Washington, Pennsylvania.

Lot of two copper kitchenware pieces, Continental, 19th c., scattered dents, verde patina: handled pitcher, approx. 18-1/2" h, 10-1/4"dia, and coated copper milk pail, with iron handle, approx. 14-1/2" h, 12-1/2" dia,16-1/2 lbs total **$175**

Courtesy of Austin Auction Gallery, austinauction.com

Salter kitchen scale, circa 1880, 12.5" h. **$140**

Courtesy of Tiroche Auction House, tiroche.co.il

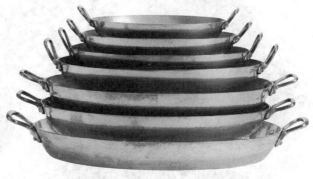

Seven copper handled low cookers/paella skillets, 20th century, stamped: Bridge Kitchenware, made in France, largest without handles, 19-1/2" w x 14" d, smallest 10-1/2" w x 7" d. **$750**

Courtesy of John Moran Auctioneers, johnmoran.com

Hanging spice cabinet, primitive, 11 drawers with pressed lettering and porcelain pulls, late 1800s, very good condition, 25" h x 10" w..... **$430**

Courtesy of Rich Penn Auctions, richpennauctions.com

Two vintage Bromwells flour sifters. **$36**

Courtesy of Estate Auction Company, estateauctionco.com

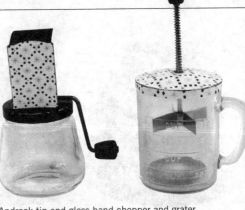

Shallow flat-bottomed pot, swing handle, tripod feet, cover, 7" x 14-1/2"...............................**$215**

Courtesy of John McInnis Auctioneers, mcinnisauctions.com

Androck tin and glass hand chopper and grater, chopper has Hazel Atlas hallmark and A-14, grater marked Androck 49 2 Made in the U.S.A., largest measures 8" h...**$30**

Courtesy of Desert West Auction, desertwestauction.com

Child's iron kitchenware, includes Griswold cast iron griddle No. 0, unmarked fry pan, Griswold No. 262 crispy corn or wheat stick pan, Wagner Ware tea size Kristy Korn Kobs 1317 Pat'd July 6, 1920, and an unmarked iron trivet with paw feet, trivet 6" dia. **$160**

Courtesy of Stephenson's Auction, stephensonsauction.com

Three vintage buttermold rolling pins, one has remnants of original box, Heureka made in Germany, good condition, all are 15" l...**$50**

Courtesy of Ascendant Auction Galleries, ascendantauctions.com

LAMPS AND LIGHTING

LIGHTING DEVICES HAVE BEEN AROUND for thousands of years, and antique examples range from old lanterns used on the farm to high-end Tiffany lamps. The earliest known type of lamp was the oil lamp, which was patented by Aimé Argand in 1784 and mass-produced starting in the 19th century. Around 1850, kerosene became a popular lamp-burning fluid, replacing whale oil and other fluids.

In 1879, Thomas A. Edison invented the electric light, causing fluid lamps to lose favor and creating a new field for lamp manufacturers. Decorative table and floor lamps with ornate glass lampshades reached their height of popularity from 1900-1920, due to the success of Tiffany and other Arts & Crafts lamp makers such as Handel.

French gilt-painted spelter electrified figural lamp sculpture of "La Veillee du Forgeron" (The Watch of the Blacksmith), 1920s, with identifying plaque on front of base, 17-1/4" h x 8-1/2" w.. **$200**

Courtesy of Auctions at Showplace, nyshowplace.com

Philip Johnson and Richard Kelly mid-century modern floor lamp for Edison Price Inc., circa 1953, brass frame with aluminum shade, 42" h x 25" dia... **$4,500**

Courtesy of Auctions at Showplace, nyshowplace.com

VISIT WWW.ANTIQUETRADER.COM

WWW.FACEBOOK.COM/ANTIQUETRADER

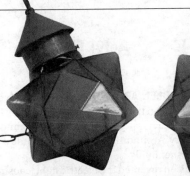

Pair of vintage Czech art glass geodesic hanging light fixtures, aquamarine blue glass lamp shades with copper mounts, 14", 11" dia. **$450**

Courtesy of MG Neely Auction, neelyauction.com

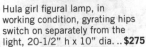

Hula girl figural lamp, in working condition, gyrating hips switch on separately from the light, 20-1/2" h x 10" dia. .. **$275**

Courtesy of Westport Auction, westportauction.com

Pair of hardwood Chinese lantern-style lamps, carved rosewood with pierced designs and brass inlays, international power plugs, 17" h, 7" w, 10" d. **$325**

Courtesy of Sterling Associates, antiquenj.com

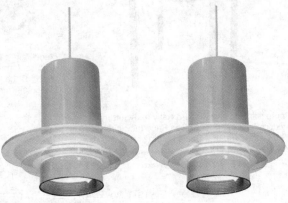

Vintage Neptune ship's lantern, brass frame enclosing glazed panes and holding an oil lamp with colorless hurricane shade, 6 lbs, 15" h. **$80**

Courtesy of Austin Auction Gallery, austinauction.com

Mid-century modern pendant lamps or chandeliers, in sea foam green, 11" h x 12" dia. **$325**

Courtesy of Auctions at Showplace, nyshowplace.com

Two Steuben lamps, art glass, ceramic, Corning, New York, 20th century, conical colorless form with trapped bubbles rest on box shaped under lights, one with chips to tip, lamps are 7-1/2" h, box diameter is 4-3/4". **$861**

Courtesy of Skinner Auctioneers & Appraisers, skinnerinc.com

Anton Chotka, Austria, 1881-1955, vintage cold painted bronze lamp, signed Chotka, Oriental figural building with a tower and brightly decorated oriental rugs and figures, working condition, glass panels in tower.................... **$4,600**

Courtesy of Tremont Auctions, tremontauctions.com

Large and impressive Tiffany Studios-style leaded glass and bronze floor lamp, 20th century, shade with foliate and rose motif, pigtail heat cap, raised on bronze tree trunk base, 73-1/4" h x 26" dia. **$1,750**

Courtesy of Heritage Auctions, ha.com

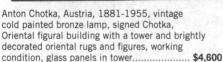
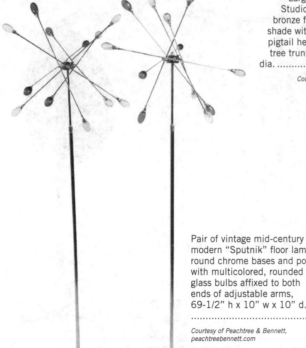

Pair of vintage mid-century modern "Sputnik" floor lamps, round chrome bases and posts with multicolored, rounded glass bulbs affixed to both ends of adjustable arms, 69-1/2" h x 10" w x 10" d.
.... **$450**

Courtesy of Peachtree & Bennett, peachtreebennett.com

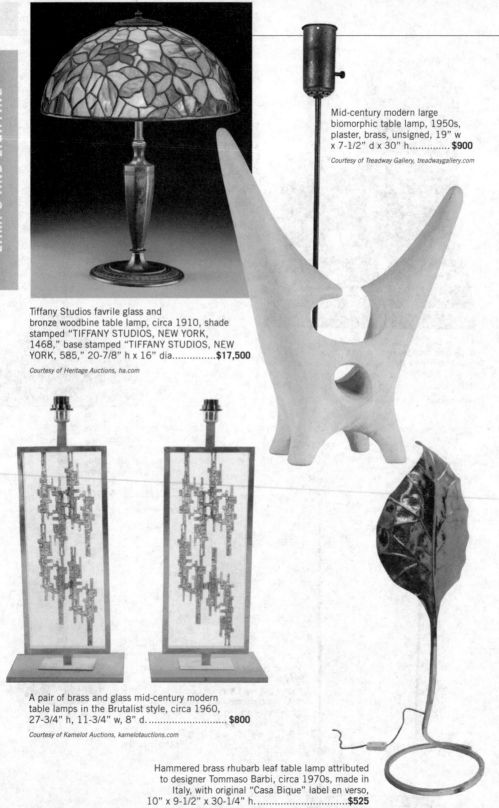

Mid-century modern large biomorphic table lamp, 1950s, plaster, brass, unsigned, 19" w x 7-1/2" d x 30" h............. **$900**

Courtesy of Treadway Gallery, treadwaygallery.com

Tiffany Studios favrile glass and bronze woodbine table lamp, circa 1910, shade stamped "TIFFANY STUDIOS, NEW YORK, 1468," base stamped "TIFFANY STUDIOS, NEW YORK, 585," 20-7/8" h x 16" dia...............**$17,500**

Courtesy of Heritage Auctions, ha.com

A pair of brass and glass mid-century modern table lamps in the Brutalist style, circa 1960, 27-3/4" h, 11-3/4" w, 8" d...........................$800

Courtesy of Kamelot Auctions, kamelotauctions.com

Hammered brass rhubarb leaf table lamp attributed to designer Tommaso Barbi, circa 1970s, made in Italy, with original "Casa Bique" label en verso, 10" x 9-1/2" x 30-1/4" h...............................$525

Courtesy of MG Neely Auction, neelyauction.com

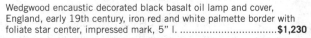

Wedgwood encaustic decorated black basalt oil lamp and cover, England, early 19th century, iron red and white palmette border with foliate star center, impressed mark, 5" l. **$1,230**

Courtesy of Skinner Auctioneers & Appraisers, skinnerinc.com

Vintage cobalt turtleback and cobalt glass globe, form lamp on stand, 17" w x 13" h. . **$1,400**

Courtesy of Clarke Auction Gallery, clarkeny.com

Hanging lamp, mixed metal, Mexico, 20th century, pierced metal oval form decorated with lion, bird, jack rabbit, butterfly, foliate, and floral designs, with coiled metal near base, opening to fit a fixture, suspended from a chain, 21-5/8" drop height, aperture 1-1/8" dia.............**$431**

Courtesy of Skinner Auctioneers & Appraisers, skinnerinc.com

Mid-century modern articulating table lamp, functional, 10-1/2" h x 10" dia............**$170**

Courtesy of Westport Auction, westportauction.com

Tiffany Studios gilt bronze table lamp with feather-pull glass shade, circa 1910, stamped "TIFFANY STUDIOS, NEW YORK, 419," engraved "L.C.T.," 13" h, shade is 4-1/8" x 7-1/8"... **$3,125**

Courtesy of Heritage Auctions, ha.com

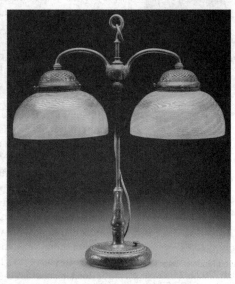

Tiffany Studios damascene favrile glass and bronze double-student lamp, circa 1900, stamped "TIFFANY STUDIOS, NEW YORK, 9908," engraved "L.C.T.," both shades marked "L.C.T." at aperture opening, shade diameter is approx. 10", opening to shade diameter at upper aperture is approx. 4"; lamp is 26-1/8" h x 22"......... **$8,750**

Courtesy of Heritage Auctions, ha.com

LEGO SETS AND MINIFIGURES

THERE HAVE BEEN approximately 10,000 LEGO sets created over the past 50 years, and it's estimated that by 2019, minifigures will outnumber the human race, with close to eight billion peanut-sized plastic people inhabiting human homes and stores throughout the world.

It's safe to say that LEGO is one of the biggest franchises in the universe; it's also popular with collectors.

ICONIC TOYS

There are many reasons why LEGO sets are valuable: They are iconic toys, creative, and exceptionally produced, but they mostly create a bond with fans and future buyers. Each set also has a limited production run — some for a couple of months, some for several years. The more unique and rare a set, usually the higher the value it has. The one factor that works differently from other collectibles is age. Older is not always more valuable, and although some collectors are fond of pre-2000 sets, the most popular sets are those released from 2000 and after. Besides being more relative to many fans and collectors, sets that were created after 2000 are on a different level of creativity and complexity. In addition to a change in set design, bold business decisions by LEGO to add licensed movie/TV properties such as *Star Wars*, *Harry Potter*, and *The Lord of the Rings*, have paid off considerably. The first and foremost of these more elaborate, licensed themes is the *Star Wars* Ultimate Collector Series, which launched in 2000. The UCS sets are more complex builds and accurate in appearance to their movie counterparts. They are large sets, designed with adult fans in mind, but even the smaller, more cost-effective licensed sets help drive new fans to LEGO. With every new *Star Wars* or *Harry Potter* movie, children flock to the stores to buy new sets based on it. Non-licensed themes also benefit from the more intricate designs and larger set sizes. The largest retail LEGO set ever produced (piece count), the 10189 Taj Mahal, is a beautiful rendition of one of the "Wonders of the World." LEGO is no longer a toy for just children, and adults are now buying sets for themselves and this practice drives up prices on many new and retired sets.

Some sets will plateau and may even drop in value over time. LEGO sets are valuable because of their connections to potential buyers. Many current fans are unfamiliar with older sets and place little value on them, yet some newer sets can fetch thousands of dollars. A potential buyer might have wanted a set as a child and could not afford it, so when they get older and have some extra discretionary income, they pay top dollar for it. Other sets are bought by collectors who are completists and enjoy collecting entire themes.

Advanced Models, 3450 Statue of Liberty, 2000, 2,882 pieces, 0 minifigures, $198.99 retail. **. $1,510 (new); $1013 (used)**

The fact that all LEGO sets do retire at some point creates a limited time to buy them from primary retailers. Short-term resellers and long-term investors capitalize on this and will stock up on new sets, waiting for a LEGO set to retire or go EOL (end of line), then will proceed to list these retired sets on eBay at a price higher than the manufacturer's suggested retail price. Some resellers even "flip" sets short term, basically reselling a hot or popular LEGO set before they retire. This usually occurs around Christmas or when a popular set is in short supply.

Values of LEGO sets can range greatly. It is not an exact science. Determining the exact value depends on the set itself. How rare is it? How popular is it? How badly does a buyer want one? Many sets have an emotional tie to a particular buyer, and they are willing to pay over and above the going rate for a set because they want it. It's that simple. Also, the size of sets with regards to piece count and weight can also play an important factor in the value. LEGO bases their MSRPs on the weight of a set, for the most part. The more ABS (acrylonitrile butadiene styrene) plastic used to produce a set, the more it will cost at retail and on the secondary market.

LITTLE PLASTIC POWERHOUSES

LEGO minifigures also play a major role in the value of a set, and these peanut-sized plastic people produce huge profit potential. Many of the most valuable and profitable LEGO sets are because of a rare minifigure or because it contains multiple minifigures.

HELPFUL COLLECTING TIPS

HERE ARE SOME THINGS A NOVICE SHOULD LOOK FOR WHEN CHOOSING LEGO SETS TO COLLECT:

- LEGO sets with rare pieces and minifigures: Minifigures are often called the "currency" of the LEGO world and are highly collectible and popular. Some individual minifigures can sell for tens, if not hundreds, of dollars.

- Licensed sets can appreciate very well after retirement and many contain valuable and highly collectible minifigures.

- Large sets, with 1,000 pieces or more, seem to exhibit strong returns on investment. The largest set of any LEGO theme can be the safest choice.

- LEGO sets with a low Price Per Piece ratio, usually around $0.07 a brick (based on MSRP), can be profitable. Sometimes new LEGO sets are "parted" out and resold to fans as individual pieces. This is a huge market and helps many fans and builders acquire pieces they could not buy otherwise.

- Sets with short production runs usually equate to rarity, thus are more valuable. Many have a two-year production run, so anything less is optimal.

- Collector or limited edition sets can appreciate to higher levels than unmarked sets.

- Small sets and polybags can also show strong returns, and those with rare minifigures or small seasonal or holiday sets are solid choices.

- Unique sets can also be profitable in the long term.

Things change quickly in the LEGO world. Sets get retired. Sets get remade. What was once rare becomes commonplace when newer versions are produced. The bottom line is that these little plastic ABS bricks are valuable. Even sets that are incomplete can be sold for more money than was originally paid for at retail. Keep your sets in good condition. Save the boxes and instructions. Store them carefully. If possible, keep your valuable sets and pieces separate from the rest of your LEGO collection in case you ever want to resell your collection. Most importantly, enjoy your LEGO sets and bricks. They are a wonderful toy that stimulates the imagination and, quite possibly, your bank account.

LEGO minifigures have become a highly collectible and profitable hobby over the past ten to fifteen years, basically matching the LEGO set investment phenomena step by step. In fact, The LEGO Group itself has even promoted the minifigure as a collectible item, releasing the Collectible Minifigures theme in 2010. This theme is one of the most popular and has accounted for hundreds of highly creative and valuable minifigures. LEGO minifigures have become so valuable in some instances that they can be sold for more money than the original price of the LEGO set they were in.

The values of minifigures exploded in growth in direct correlation to the popularity of eBay and other secondary marketplaces. From the 1970s to the early 1990s, there really were no major outlets where a person could resell a LEGO set or minifigure, so when eBay grew in scope and popularity, savvy collectors and investors realized that sets could be broken down into smaller components and sold for a profit. People learned quickly that LEGO minifigures could be removed from new sets and resold on eBay or sites like Bricklink.com for more than the original set cost at retail. This is called "parting out" a LEGO set, and it has become a multimillion-dollar business for thousands of collectors, investors, and resellers across the world. These pint-sized plastic people have been and will continue to be a driving force in the LEGO Universe.

With the LEGO Group's continued production of creative and innovative sets that are of the highest quality, the future is bright for this hobby. More and more fans worldwide will be introduced to products, and those who loved LEGO as a child will once again be drawn back into the hobby, either because of their own kids or because some new set connected with them on an emotional level. All in all, it's a great time to be involved in the world of LEGO collecting, whether focusing on sets, minifigures, or both.

For more information on collectible LEGO sets and minifigures, see *The Ultimate Guide to Collectible LEGO Sets: Identification and Price Guide* and *The Collectible LEGO Minifigure*, both by Ed Maciorowski and Jeff Maciorowski.

Note: All images are courtesy of Ed Maciorowski and Jeff Maciorowski.

Price note and sources: Secondary-market prices for LEGO sets and minifigures are always fluctuating, so for the latest values, visit Brickpicker.com, Bricklink.com, and other online sources. Minifigure prices here are for new ones and based on average values for January-July, 2018 at Bricklink.com.

SETS

Advanced Models, 10196 Grand Carousel, 2009, 3,263 pieces, 9 minifigures, $249.99 retail.
.... **$1,749 (new); $848 (used)**

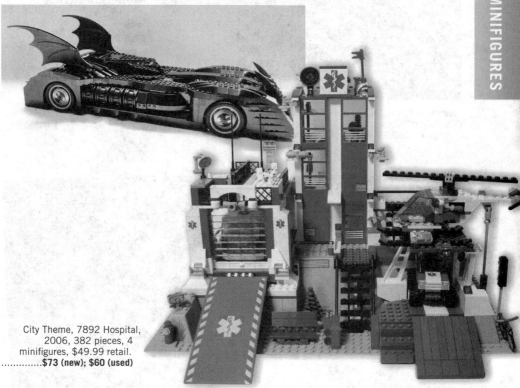

Batman, 7784 The Batmobile: Ultimate Collector Edition, 2006, 1,045 pieces, 0 minifigures, $69.99 retail.
..............$326 (new); $180 (used)

City Theme, 7892 Hospital, 2006, 382 pieces, 4 minifigures, $49.99 retail.
..............$73 (new); $60 (used)

Dino Theme, 5882 Ambush Attack, 2012, 80 pieces, 1 minifigure, $11.99 retail.
.... $32 (new); $16 (used)

Friends Theme, 3185 Summer Riding Camp, 2012, 1,112 pieces, 4 minifigures, $99.99 retail. .... $203 (new); $93 (used)

Legends of Chima Theme, 70014-1 The
Croc Swamp Hideout, 2013, 647 pieces, 5
minifigures, $69.99 retail. ....**$120 (new); $63 (used)**

Hero Factory Theme, 2283 Witch Doctor, 2011,
331 pieces, 0 minifigures, $29.99 retail.
....**$71 (new); $49 (used)**

Ideas/Cuusoo Theme, 21104 Mars Science
Laboratory Curiosity Rover, 2014, 295 pieces, 0
minifigures, $29.99 retail. ..**$212 (new); $140 (used)**

Marvel Superheroes Theme, 6866 Wolverine's Chopper Showdown, 2012, 199 pieces, 3 minifigures, $19.99 retail. ....**$109 (new); $59 (used)**

L

LEGO SETS AND MINIFIGURES

Pirates of the Caribbean Theme, 4195 Queen Anne's Revenge, 2011, 1,097 pieces, 9 minifigures, $119.99 retail.
.... **$437 (new); $189 (used)**

Monster Fighters Theme, 9468 Vampyre Castle, 2012, 949 pieces, 7 minifigures (including two Bat Monsters which are exclusive to it), $99.99 retail.
.... **$133 (new); $111 (used)**

Ninjago Theme, 2521 Lightning Dragon Battle, 2011, 645 pieces, 4 minifigures, $79.99 retail.
.... **$171 (new); $84 (used)**

Space Theme, Galaxy Squad 70709 Galactic Titan, 2013, 1,012 pieces, 5 minifigures, $99.99 retail. .... **$99 (new); $56 (used)**

Seasonal Theme, 10199 Winter Village Toy Shop, 2009, 815 pieces, 7 minifigures, $59.99 retail.
....$100 (new); $64 (used)

Star Wars UCS Theme, "First Edition" 10179 Millennium Falcon (one of 20,000 made), 2007, 5,192 pieces, 5 minifigures, $499.99 retail.
.... $1,958 (new); $1,092 (used)

Star Wars UCS Theme, 10143 Death Star II, 2005, 3,441 pieces, 0 minifigures, $269.99 retail. ....**$1,511 (new); $752 (used)**

Vintage (pre-2000) Theme, 6286 Skull's Eye Schooner, 1993, 912 pieces, 9 minifigures, $126.99 retail. .... **$143 (new); $313 (used)**

Trains Theme, 10219 Maersk Train, 2011, 1,237 pieces, 3 minifigures, $99.99 retail. .... **$339 (new); $244 (used)**

Vintage (pre-2000) Theme, 5571 Giant Truck, 1996, 1,757 pieces, 0 minifigures, $138.99 retail. .... **$395 (new); $262 (used)**

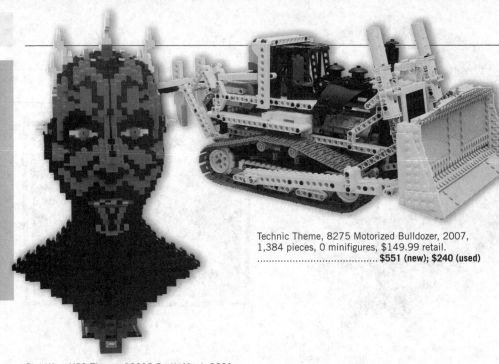

Technic Theme, 8275 Motorized Bulldozer, 2007, 1,384 pieces, 0 minifigures, $149.99 retail.
.... **$551 (new); $240 (used)**

Star Wars UCS Theme, 10018 Darth Maul, 2001, 1,868 pieces, 0 minifigures, $149.99 retail.
.... **$799 (new); $533 (used)**

MINIFIGURES

Bumblebee Girl, Collectible Minifigures (Series 10) Theme, 2013, obtained at general retail (polybag). **$31**

Alfred the Butler, Batman Theme, 2006, obtained in set 7783 The Batcave: The Penguin And Mr. Freeze's Invasion................................ **$38**

Dragon Knights - Dragon Master (Yellow/Red/Blue White Plumes, Dragon Cape), Castle Theme, 1993, obtained in set 6082 Fire Breathing Fortress. .... **$35 (Yellow)**

Zombie Bride, Monster Fighters Theme, 2012, obtained in set 9465 The Zombies. **$68**

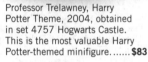

Professor Trelawney, Harry Potter Theme, 2004, obtained in set 4757 Hogwarts Castle. This is the most valuable Harry Potter-themed minifigure. **$83**

Mr. Gold, Collectible Minifigures (Series 10) Theme, 2013, obtained in Random Series 10 Polybag (only 5,000 made. **$760**

Kobe Bryant (NBA, Los Angeles Lakers, Home #8), Sports Theme, 2003, obtained in 3500 Kobe Bryant, 3563 NBA Collectors #4. ....**$13**

Davy Jones, Pirates of the Caribbean Theme, 2011, obtained in set 4184 The Black Pearl. In the world of LEGO minifigures, the undead equals more value. **$79**

Samukai, Ninjago Theme, 2011, obtained in set 2505 Garmadon's Dark Fortress, 2507 Fire Temple. **$25**

Darth Vader (Chrome Black), Star Wars Theme, 2009, obtained in 4547551 Chrome Darth Vader polybag. The black chrome finish of this particular version of Darth Vader is a subtle difference in appearance, yet makes a major difference in its value, effectively making it one of the most valuable non-comic con/toy fair minifigures of all time. **$146**

4521221 Gold chrome plated C-3PO, Star Wars Theme, 2007, obtained in random 2007 Star Wars sets. The 4521221 Gold chrome-plated C-3PO was a promotional item that LEGO released in 2007 in 10,000 random sets that sold for retail. The promotion was in honor of the 30th Anniversary of Star Wars. This C-3PO has a unique gold chrome coating on it like the movie C-3PO. **$557**

Boba Fett (Cloud City, printed arms and legs), Star Wars Theme, 2003, obtained in set 10123 Cloud City. The printing on the arms and legs of the 10123 Cloud City Boba Fett was the first of its kind and makes him valuable on the LEGO secondary markets. **$321**

Superman (in Black Costume), Super Heroes Theme, 2013, 2013 San Diego Comic-Con exclusive, only 200 were handed out. **$1,200**

Zurg, Toy Story Theme, 2010, obtained in set 7593 Buzz's Star Command Spaceship...... **$37**

LITHOGRAPH PRINTS

A PRINT IS any work of art made in multiple iterations, created through a transfer process. There are many different types of prints and the process is constantly evolving, but the four best-known techniques are etching, lithography, screen print, and woodcut.

An advantage of owning a print is often economics. Prints can present the opportunity to own an authentic and iconic subject far more inexpensively than an original piece of art with a seven-figure price tag attached to it. Prints can also be a great way to get acquainted with styles and artists in the same mode as other mediums, but at a different price point.

In lithography, the artist draws onto stone using a grease-based medium — normally special lithographic crayons, or greasy ink known as tusche. The stone is treated with a chemical solution, ensuring the image attracts printing ink and that blank areas repel ink and attract water. A solvent "fixes" the image, and the surface is dampened with water. Oil-based ink is then applied to the stone with a roller, adhering only to the image. Finally, the stone is placed on a lithographic press and covered with damp paper and board — a pressure bar ensuring force is evenly applied across the image. The image is printed in reverse, with separate stones used for complex images of multiple colors.

Lithography opened up printmaking to artists otherwise reluctant to learn the technical skills needed to create woodcuts or etchings, since many of the same tools, such as brushes and pencils, can be used. Lithography was first made famous by Henri de Toulouse-Lautrec in the 19th century, but has been embraced by many of the major artists of the Post-War period, including Pablo Picasso, Joan Miró, David Hockney, and Jasper Johns.

Poster, "Liz," 1964, Andy Warhol (1928-1987), offset lithograph in colors, from an edition of approximately 300, signed and dated "65" in ballpoint pen in lower margin, published by Leo Castelli Gallery, New York, 21-7/8" x 21-7/8" (image), 23" x 23" (sheet). **$60,000**

Courtesy of Heritage Auctions, ha.com

Artists make prints for a variety of reasons. They might be drawn to the collaborative nature of the print studio, or the potential for innovation the medium offers, or for a print's potential to document each stage of a creative process. Prints can offer a completely different creative outlet to the artist's primary working method.

An "original" print is technically a unique work. It is generally produced as a limited number of impressions (collectively known as an edition), and each print is given an edition number, typically written as a fraction — for example, 13/50. The number to the right of the slash indicates the edition size (in this case, 50), while the figure to the left is the individual print's number.

An artist may also produce a limited number of artist's proofs, often marked A/P, that are identical in nature to the standard edition. Here again, fractions may be used to indicate the total number of proofs, and the print number (e.g. A/P 1/4). Other proofs may be made at an earlier stage, as the artist and printer develop an image or test different compositions. These are known as state proofs, trial proofs, or color proofs. These can be unique, with differences in color combinations, paper types, or size. Andy Warhol started to sell his trial proofs as unique color-combinations separate from the edition, and they're now some of the most coveted works in his print market.

When the image is perfected, a proof is made and signed B.A.T. (an abbreviation of the French bon à tirer, or "ready to print"). The rest of the edition is matched to this image, which is unique and traditionally kept by the printer.

Paper is also an important component of the process. A sign of a true print specialist is not only their interest in technique but also their obsession with paper. Paper can directly influence the nature of what the printed image looks like. Jasper Johns is famous for pushing for higher quality, heavier paper for his prints, while Andy Warhol loved cheaper, thinner paper for his Soup Can prints from the 1960s to emphasize they were meant to be enjoyed by the masses.

Along with type of paper used, condition reports should also note whether an item is the full sheet or with full margins, which means that the paper has not been trimmed in some fashion, itself an issue that affects the value.

Not all prints are singed. Andy Warhol and Pablo Picasso both stamp-signed some of their prints, and some larger portfolio editions were only signed on the title page. Don't be alarmed if a print is only initialed. It doesn't mean that it is worth less — indeed, some artists only initial their prints, such as Richard Diebenkorn and Lucian Freud.

Poster, "Savarin," 1977, Jasper Johns (American, b. 1930), lithograph in colors, Ed. 42/50, signed, dated, and numbered in pencil on bottom edge, published by ULAE, West Islip, New York, 38-1/4" x 28-1/4".....................................**$100,000**

Courtesy of Heritage Auctions, ha.com

Poster, "L"Anglais au Moulin Rouge," 1892, Henri de Toulouse-Lautrec (French, 1864-1901), color lithograph, 29/100, signed and numbered in pencil lower left: HTLautrec / No. 29. Printed by Ancourt on wove paper, 18-5/8" x 14-5/8". .**$50,000**

Courtesy of Heritage Auctions, ha.com

Poster, "Crying Girl," 1963, Roy Lichtenstein (American, 1923-1997), offset lithograph in colors on woven paper, signed in pencil in bottom margin, published by Leo Castelli Gallery, New York, 17-1/8" x 23-1/4"..............................**$56,250**

Courtesy of Heritage Auctions, ha.com

Souvenir United Confederate Veterans (UCV) chromolithograph poster titled "Heroes and Leaders of the Civil War / Let Us Have Peace," published by Peter Tracy, Memphis, Tennessee, 1901, issued for the occasion of the United Confederate Veterans 11th Annual Reunion in Memphis, TN, May 28-29, 1901, 20-3/8" h x 26-1/2" w...**$960**

Courtesy of Case Antiques Auctions & Appraisals, caseantiques.com

Poster, "Gstaad" by Alex Walter Diggelmann (1902-1987), lithograph, 1934, backed on Japan paper. Diggleman was a Swiss graphic artist and book designer best known for his sports posters; 50" h x 35-1/2" w.....................................**$35,965**

Courtesy of Christie's, christies.com

! top lot

Harry Houdini enthralled audiences worldwide with daring acts of extrication from shackles, ropes, handcuffs, and various locked containers. Arguably the greatest and most sensational of all of Harry Houdini's escapes was his "Chinese Water Torture Cell." In the trick, Houdini (1874-1926) mesmerized audiences by escaping from a contraption resembling a water-filled fish tank. Placed head down into the glass and metal tank, and with feet manacled to the top of the tank, Houdini would use a full two minutes of suspense before emerging from his watery grave. Houdini first performed the outrageous trick in 1912 at the Circus Busch in Berlin. He continued to perform the escape until his death in 1926.

A rare poster depicting Houdini performing the trick sold for $114,000 in 2017 at Potter & Potter Auctions in Chicago, setting a record as the most expensive magic poster ever sold at public auction. Printed in London in 1912, the poster is 88" h x 40" w.

Poster, World War I, "War Exposition," marked
Otis Lithograph Company World War #4148,
38-3/4" h x 26" w. $80

*Courtesy of Leonard of Auction - Auctioneers & Appraisers,
leonardauction.com*

WWI Crayon Lithograph Poster, by James
Montgomery Flagg, printed by American
Lithographic Co, NY. $175

Courtesy of The Cobbs Auctioneers, thecobbs.com

Poster, 1900, stone lithograph featuring a bold
portrait of the Democratic candidate William
Jennings Bryan beneath an eagle, surrounded
by draped flags, industrial, farming, and mining
scenes, as well as campaign slogans, 22-1/5" h x
15-1/5" w. $6,875

Courtesy of Heritage Auctions, ha.com

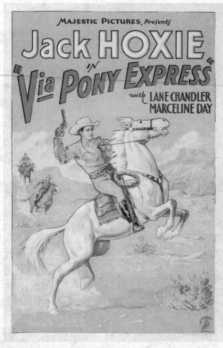

Movie poster, *Via Pony Express* (Majestic, 1933)
one sheet, 41" h x 27" w. $239

Courtesy of Heritage Auctions, ha.com

Poster, "Winter-Luft-verkehr" by Herbert Matter, printed signature to lower right corner, 40" h x 25" w. **$1,500**

Courtesy of Wright20 Auctions, wright20.com

Eberhardt & Ober Brewing Company of Allegany, Pennsylvania, lithograph poster, depicts the buildings of the brewery with Pennsylvania countryside in background, framed, 31-1/2" h x 45-7/8" w. **$810**

Courtesy of Case Antiques Auctions & Appraisals, caseantiques.com

Color lithograph advertising poster for "The Great Chang and Fak-Hong's United Magicians Presents The Noe Ark" depicting a group of various animals, birds, and reptiles with an ark in the background, "Made in Spain" lower right margin. This was an illusionist magic trick using live animals departing from what had appeared to be an empty ark, 28" h x 40-1/2" w. **$530**

Courtesy of Case Antiques Auctions & Appraisals, caseantiques.com

Window card, "Josephine Baker," National Theatre, (Sherman S. Krellberg Presents, 1964), printed on card stock for a series of shows in Washington, D.C., dated March 16-21, printed by Artcraft Litho. & Ptg. Co. Inc., N.Y.C., 22" h x 14" w. **$750**

Courtesy of Heritage Auctions, ha.com

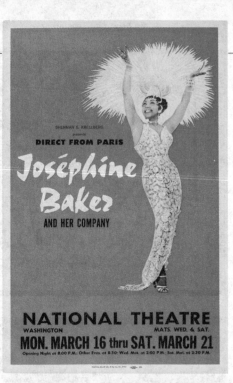

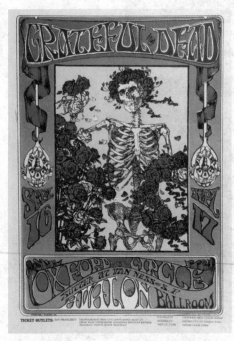

Poster, Stanley Mouse and Alton Kelley, "Grateful Dead: Skeleton and Roses," 1966, Family Dog Presents at Avalon Ballroom vintage lithographic rock poster in colors, original first printing, plate signed lower left and dated, printed by The Bindweed Press (San Francisco, CA), 20" h x 14-1/4" w, world record. **$19,000**

Courtesy of Clars Auction Gallery

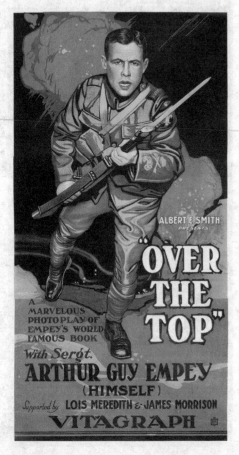

Movie poster, "Over the Top" (Vitagraph, 1918), three sheet, Fredric C. Madan artwork, 80" h x 41-1/4" w. **$1,673**

Courtesy of Heritage Auctions, ha.com

Movie poster, *Casablanca*, first Post-War release of the Warner Brothers film starring Humphrey Bogart, Ingrid Berman, Paul Henreid, Claude Rains, Peter Lorre, Sydney Greenstreet and Conrad Veidt. As of 2017, the Italian poster, featuring Luigi Martinati artwork, matched the world record for the most valuable movie poster ever sold at public auction, 55-1/2" x 78-1/4". **$478,000**

Courtesy of Heritage Auctions, ha.com

Insert, "A Night in the Show" (Terra Films, R-1927), Swedish, 35" h x 23" w................ **$1,015**

Courtesy of Heritage Auctions, ha.com

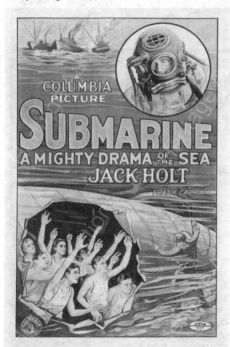

Movie poster, *Submarine* (Columbia, 1928), one sheet, 40" h x 26" w. **$10,755**

Courtesy of Heritage Auctions, ha.com

Movie poster, *Riptide* (MGM, 1934), one sheet, style c, 41" h x 27" w.................................. **$9,560**

Courtesy of Heritage Auctions, ha.com

Movie poster, *Spitfire* (RKO, 1934), one sheet, 41" h x 27" w. **$23,900**

Courtesy of Heritage Auctions, ha.com

Movie poster, *Brennan of the Moor* (Exclusive Supply Corp., 1913), six sheet, 88" h x 80" w. **$717**

Courtesy of Heritage Auctions, ha.com

MAPS AND GLOBES

MAP COLLECTING IS growing in visibility thanks to discoveries and sales of historically important maps. It remains a surprisingly affordable hobby when you consider that most maps made in the early 19th century are hand-colored and represent the cutting edge of scientific knowledge at the time. Most examples from the last 400 years are available for less than $500, and engravings depicting America or its states may be owned for less than $150. Larger maps are usually worth more to collectors.

Globes, or terrestrial globes, have been around for centuries, taking back to the 1400s, when owning a globe was a rarity and reserved for only those with titles or riches. As time passed, globes became more widely available. Today antique globes offer collectors a unique view of the world as it existed in history.

GLOBES COMMANDING MORE AT AUCTION

The globe market is strong, said Kyle Lambalzer, who writes on his blog Collecting Antique and Vintage Globes [antiqueglobes.blogspot.com]. "Those in the best condition are very strong. Globes, like many antiques, I think, are very strong at the high end of the market. Quality and condition will always bring a high price," he said. "The past two years have been generally stable to up for globes. Auction prices recently have been very good for the best examples."

Lambalzer said the most popularly collected globes today are those with a mid-century look — black ocean globes in particular. Smaller globes, eight inches or less in diameter, are also hot. "Vintage Tellurion models are on fire right now," he said.

In late 2017, a few celestial globes sold at auction for more than $200,000: A glass celestial globe by John Cowley, the oldest surviving glass celestial globe known and estimated to have been made between 1730 and 1740, sold for $217,165 at Christie's; a rare pair of Vincenzo Coronelli Italian terrestrial and celestial 18-1/2-inch globes was the top lot at Bonhams' October 2017 auction, Important Instruments of Science & Technology, and sold for $207,681.

Colonial America map, hand colored, published by Emanuel Bowen of London, 1754, boundaries of the provinces bear little resemblance to the states as we now know them, Native American tribes are noted, as are forts, settlements and stockades. **$1,687**

Courtesy of Heritage Auctions, ha.com

New Orleans' Neal Auction Company offered a strong selection of antique and vintage globes in early 2017 to much collector interest. A circa 1866, fine American table globe, the cartouche reading, "Loring's Nine and half Inch Terrestrial Globe, Boston, Josia Loring, Drawn and Engraved by W.H. Annin" sold within estimate for $2,562. Collectors also zeroed in on the odd and unusual, such as a circa 1927 American 6-inch puzzle globe made by the Geographical Educator Company, New York, which sold for $1,708. The quizzical globe sphere is divided into seven sections, and then sub-divided with jigsaw maps of the continents. Another oddity also brought significant bidding as a 19th century German miniature novelty globe, attributed to Carl Bauer of Nuremburg, sold for $1,098. The unusual 1-3/4-inch diameter globe is tipped into a box and is actually an accordion strip showing 28 nationalities, labeled in French, English, and German.

The best advice for new collectors? From Lambalzer's perspective, newbie collectors should buy what they like: "But buy the best examples they can afford," he said. "Modern globes (those after WWII) are collectible to a point. But after 1960, there are few globes that are desirable, generally speaking.

"Globes pre-1930 and especially from before 1900 are harder to find but good examples still come up for sale on a regular basis. New collectors usually start collecting maps and globes because they like history, or they are interested in a certain region of the world. For example a person very interested in WWII might want a globe from before, during, and after the conflict."

Lambalzer said globe collectors are connected online much more than you might think. "I use social media in the form of my blog, Pinterest, and I link posts on Facebook occasionally," he said. "The collector market for globes is surprisingly larger than I thought when I started blogging. I've met collectors on four continents via the web."

MAPS HOLDING STEADY

Values for antique maps hinge on a variety of factors. Unlike globes, the market for maps is highly fragmented based on interest for particular areas, periods, colors, size, and budget. Once these factors are addressed, the collector has a good idea of exactly what to focus on at auction or from other collectors, according to the longtime map seller Geographicus.

The ideal place for the beginning collector to purchase maps is commonly used auction sites such as eBay and Etsy.com. The challenge facing new collectors is the rampant reproductions of vintage and antique maps. Even maps from the 1940s are being reproduced at a rapid rate, let alone maps from the mid- to late-19th century. It's a "buyer beware" world out there in the map category. Experienced collectors can turn to online websites such as fleaglass.com, which brings together the world's top sellers of antique scientific instruments, including maps and globes. Prices are higher at specialty sites but the sellers are vetted and what is represented is authentic.

One of the top resources to learn about antique and vintage maps is the David Rumsey Collection, a historical map collection of more than 76,000 maps and images online. The collection includes rare 16th through 21st century maps of America, North America, South America, Europe, Asia, Africa, Pacific, and the World. Rumsey has donated his entire physical map collection to Stanford University where it is housed at the David Rumsey Map Center in the Stanford Library.

Map of North America, printed 1852,
Philadelphia, cartographer S. Mitchell, color,
10-1/2" x 8"... **$60**

Courtesy of Jasper52, jasper52.com

Map of Florida showing Seminole Indian Districts,
printed 1846, cartography by Tanner and
engraved by J & C Walker, 16-1/2" x 13"......... **$300**

Courtesy of Jasper52, jasper52.com

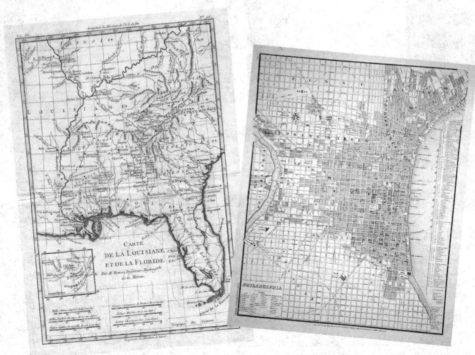

Map of Louisiana and Florida, printed 1780,
Paris, cartographer Bonne, detailed map of
Mississippi basin and southeastern North America
from Florida to Virginia, 8-1/2" x 12-1/2".......... **$80**

Courtesy of Jasper52, jasper52.com

Map of Philadelphia, printed 1849, from Meyer's
Auswanderungs-Atlas of America, with letter
key to city wards and number keys to buildings,
monuments, hotels, churches and banks,
11-3/4" x 14-1/2".. **$50**

Courtesy of Jasper52, jasper52.com

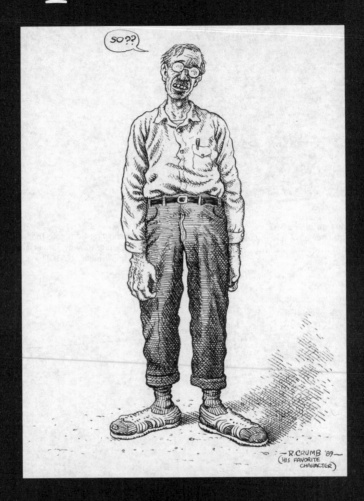

Not all maps are created equal, nor are they all particularly historical. But that doesn't mean odd maps can't be valuable, especially if the oddball who created it is famous. Robert Crumb is perhaps the most famous of the artists to work in the underground comix movement in the 1960s. He gained fame as the founder of Zap Comix and for creating such counterculture icons as "Fritz the Cat" and "Mr. Natural," as well as his "Keep on Truckin'" strip. Crumb's hand-drawn "Potter Valley Map" from the early 1970s is proof that original art maps can lead collectors to gold.

In 1970, using a $5,000 advance from Ballantine for his *Head Comix* book, Robert and his wife, Dana, bought a former commune in Potter Valley, Calif., practically sight-unseen, to escape the madness of the city's hippie scene. There, they lived with young son, Jesse, while Robert tended goats and chickens as he continued to pump out Underground comic books. This incredibly rare hand-drawn map done for a friend shows the route from San Francisco to their home, some 150 miles north. In the upper left, Crumb added a "Come to

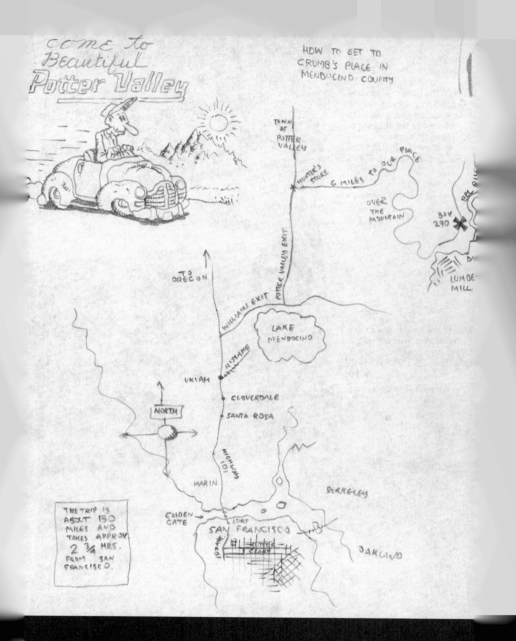

"Beautiful Potter Valley" illustration of Flakey Foont driving an old car (Dana in fact drove a 1947 Pontiac at that time). The art is in black marker, atypical of Crumb but logical for something like this, which was never meant to be published or seen outside of Crumb's close circle of friends. At auction, the matted and framed map sold for $5,019.

War of 1812 map, Walker/ Baines, printed 1816 after end of the War of 1812 between the United States and Great Britain, covers eastern U.S. including the palins to the west of the Mississippi River, features forts, early settlements, Indian tribal areas and villages, 10-3/4" x 15-1/2".
......................................$260

Courtesy of Jasper52, jasper52.com

Map of the Americas with new discoveries inset, printed in 1818, Paris, cartographer J.B. Nolin, rare, 28-1/2" x 20-1/4".
......................................$550.

Courtesy of Jasper52, jasper52.com

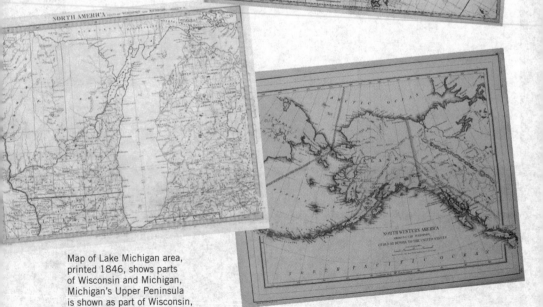

Map of Lake Michigan area, printed 1846, shows parts of Wisconsin and Michigan, Michigan's Upper Peninsula is shown as part of Wisconsin, cartography by Tanner, Smith, engraved by J&C Walker, 13" x 15-1/2"............................$200

Map of Alaska, printed in 1887, cartographer W. Bradley, printed in Philadelphia, 11-1/2" x 15"..$60

Courtesy of Jasper52, jasper52.com   *Courtesy of Jasper52, jasper52.com*

Map of Southern U.S. Provinces, printed 1817, drawn and engraved by Nathanial Robert Hewitt for John Thomson's "New General Atlas," 20-3/4" x 25"................................ **$700**

Courtesy of Jasper52, jasper52.com

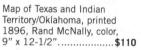

Map of Texas and Indian Territory/Oklahoma, printed 1896, Rand McNally, color, 9" x 12-1/2"....................**$110**

Courtesy of Jasper52, jasper52.com

Map of the West Indies, printed 1731, artist/cartographer/engraver: Johann Christoph Homann/Homann Heirs/Jean Baptiste Bourguignon d'Anville, 24-1/2" x 20-1/2"... **$1,000**

Courtesy of Jasper52, jasper52.com

Plan of New Orleans map, printed 1870, detailed and colored street plan of New Orleans from 1870 edition of Mitchell's popular New General Atlas, 10-7/8" x 9-1/2"..$75

Courtesy of Jasper52, jasper52.com

Bird's-eye view map of Helena, Montana, printed in 1890, cartographer Kessler Brewery/ American Pub. Co., printed in Milwaukee, Wis., offers excellent bird's-eye view of Helena with 16 insets of key buildings, 27-1/2" x 41"......................................$480

Courtesy of Jasper52, jasper52.com

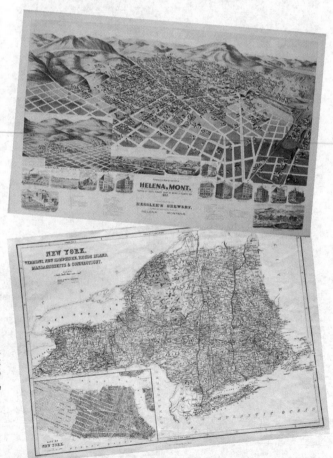

Map of New York, Vermont, New Hampshire, Rhode Island, Massachusetts and Connecticut, printed 1874, cartographer A. & C. Black., full color, 21-3/4" x 16".......................................$95

Courtesy of Jasper52, jasper52.com

MARITIME ANTIQUES

MARITIME FINE ART and collectibles are enjoying a resurgence in popularity as long-held collections come to market. This venerated collecting category spans ship models, navigational instruments, yachting memorabilia, journals and books, ship accoutrements, sailor-made handicrafts, and maritime-themed fine art paintings and sculptures.

Rare examples of scrimshaw are rapidly coming back into fashion despite recently passed laws that have limited the ability to sell later carvings, which may only be purchased in the state it was sold. Antique scrimshaw (defined as older than 100 years) can be sold intrastate.

The most alluring aspect of collecting maritime art is the connection to the artists (many of whom are well documented) and the recognition of America's strong whaling history.

In late 2017, a rare and extraordinary scrimshaw whale's tooth set a world record as part of a 500-lot auction offered by Eldred's Auctioneers & Appraisers. Carved by scrimshander expert Edward Burdett, the art depicts a whaling scene of the "William Tell" and the "George and Susan" and a coastal view of the whaleship "William Thomson" on the reverse. The scrimshaw tooth carved by Burdett hammered for $456,000 against a $160,000 estimate.

Burdett was a pioneer of American scrimshaw, and in his short but prolific career he produced what are widely considered masterpieces of the genre. "This is certainly one of the best pieces of scrimshaw to come on the market in years," said Bill Bourne, vice president and head of the Maritime Art Department at Eldred's.

Diver's helmet, 19th c., brass with ebonized finish, labeled "Siebe Gorman & Co. Ltd. London," 18-1/2" h......... **$2,645**

Courtesy of Eldred's Auctioneers & Appraisers, eldreds.com

Bell, 19th c., bronze, from "The Royal Charlotte" ship's name engraved on front, 14" h x 16-1/2" dia...**$2,300**

Courtesy of Eldred's Auctioneers & Appraisers, eldreds.com

VISIT WWW.ANTIQUETRADER.COM

WWW.FACEBOOK.COM/ANTIQUETRADER

Binoculars, 1940s, German, likely for submarine use, marked "Dienstaglas Beh 15 Fach," mounted on an adapted brass and iron adjustable pedestal base, 17" l, pedestal is 53-1/4" h.............**$1,840**

Courtesy of Eldred's Auctioneers & Appraisers, eldreds.com

Model, 19th c., depicting an 18th c. warship, made by a prisoner of war, well-detailed with four cannon decks, displayed in a marquetry inlaid wooden shadow box, 8-1/4" h x 10-1/2" w x 4" d.........**$18,400**

Courtesy of Eldred's Auctioneers & Appraisers, eldreds.com

Collection, early 20th c., display examples of various marine and sailing knots, in rope work frame, 21-3/4" h, x 32" w. **$345**

Courtesy of Eldred's Auctioneers & Appraisers, eldreds.com

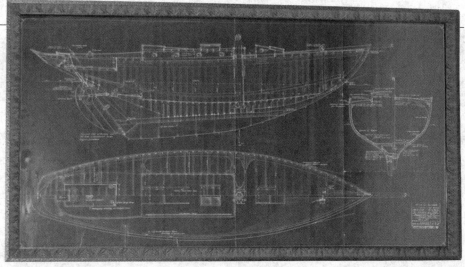

Blueprint, 1930, from the auxiliary cruising cutter construction plant by A. Nielsen, naval architect from the offices of John. G. Alden, issued Sept. 25, 1930, 23" h x 43-1/2" w... **$575**

Courtesy of Eldred's Auctioneers & Appraisers, eldreds.com

Foghorn, 19th c., rotary model, with painted decoration on a black background depicting the 1899 America's Cup yacht "Columbia, Captain Charles Barr" and "Designer N.G. Herreshoff," brass handle and cupper trumpet, 15" h x 22" l x 8" w.................... **$690**

Courtesy of Eldred's Auctioneers & Appraisers, eldreds.com

Flag, first half of 20th c., New York Yacht Club Burgee, high-grade bunting, 26" l x 40-1/2" w. **$420**

Courtesy of Eldred's Auctioneers & Appraisers, eldreds.com

top lot

A piece of pictorial scrimshaw by noted artist Edward Burdett set a world record when it sold at auction at Eldred's Auctioneers & Appraisers for $456,000. Believed to have been created circa 1830-1833, Burdett's eight-inch masterpiece depicts the American whaleship William Tell flying a large American flag off her stern, a whaleboat off her bow about to capture a surfaced sperm whale, and another American whaleship, near the tip. The reverse depicts the American whaleship William Thomson flying a large American flag, a coastal lighthouse and house is off the bow. The piece shows exceptional detail throughout.

"The quality of the workmanship, the size of the tooth, its varied colors, its inscription and the fact that it has not been on the market contributed to its desirability," said Bill Bourne, vice president of Eldred's auction house in Massachusetts.

Burdett was the earliest American maker of pictorial scrimshaw, producing all of his work during an active whaling career in the 1820s and early 1830s. He was born on Nantucket in October 1805, the son of a merchant sea captain. He was one of the first practitioners of a relatively new art form — the decorative engraving of sperm whale teeth and whale jawbone panels.

Although he lacked formal training, Burdett was a superb artisan whose work displays a distinctive power and beauty rare in scrimshaw. It is believed he created more than 20 pieces in his short life. Burdett met a grisly fate as a first officer of a Nantucket whaleship when in November 1933 he became entangled in the whale line and was yanked overboard and drowned.

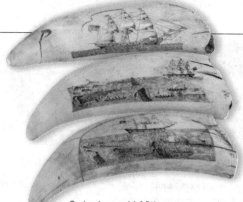

Scrimshaw, mid-19th c., whale's teeth, attributed to the Arch Engraver, teeth from same jawbone, scenes correlate with each other, first tooth depicts an American flagged whaleship, three whaleboats in the water and eight whales, second tooth depicts a three-masted ship flying a long pennant from the center mast and a polychrome American flag off the stern, third tooth depicts a spread-wing eagle clutching a banner inscribed "Prosper - The Whaler."...**$240,000**

Courtesy of Eldred's Auctioneers & Appraisers, eldreds.com

Scrimshaw, pair, whale's teeth, circa 1840, one tooth with highly detailed polychrome work in green, black and brown sepia depicting a woman in Victorian dress. Reverse with sizable whaler portrait depicting the ship sighting whales with watch figure on foremast and two figures on the mid-mast, including one holding a telescope, 6-1/2" l; second tooth with a seated portrait of John Hancock, and on reverse a sizable whale portrait with the same whale ship as the first tooth, dropping her jib, 6-3/4" l. **$8,050**

Courtesy of Eldred's Auctioneers & Appraisers, eldreds.com

Ship's iron-bound wooden water keg, 19th c., 22" l. **$138**

Courtesy of Eldred's Auctioneers & Appraisers, eldreds.com

Valentine, late 19th-early 20th c., in an octagonal walnut frame, multi-shell design of a central heart and anchor surrounded by concentric bands, 13-3/4" l x 13-3/4" w. **$2,280**

Courtesy of Eldred's Auctioneers & Appraisers, eldreds.com

Sextant, 19th c., ebony and brass, no maker's mark, 13" l. **$240**

Courtesy of Eldred's Auctioneers & Appraisers, eldreds.com

Weather vane, 20th c., wooden, carved in the manner of Clark G. Voorhees, Jr., on a contemporary wooden stand, 24" l x 13-1/5" w. **$360**

Courtesy of Eldred's Auctioneers & Appraisers, eldreds.com

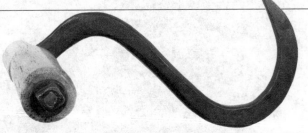

Hook, mid-19th c., whaleman's hand-held blubber hook, wrought iron with turned whalebone handle, 8-1/4" l. **$540**

Courtesy of Eldred's Auctioneers & Appraisers, eldreds.com

Tugboat light, 20th c., two red lenses, 29" h. **$161**

Courtesy of Eldred's Auctioneers & Appraisers, eldreds.com

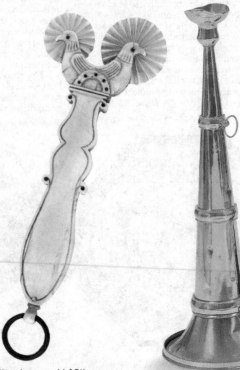

Ship's wheel, 19th c., brass and oak, hub marked "Isle of Innisfree," 66-1/2" dia. ... **$1,265**

Courtesy of Eldred's Auctioneers & Appraisers, eldreds.com

Pie crimper, mid-19th c., walrus ivory, two wheels supported by a mount in the form of conjoined birds, scrolled handle with incised conforming border and brass pique inlay, baleen hanging ring at end of handle opposite wheels, 7-3/4" l. **$16,800**

Courtesy of Eldred's Auctioneers & Appraisers, eldreds.com

Yachtsman's trumpet, 20th c., with carrying rings, knurled trim, oval mouthpiece, 17-3/4" l, 6" dia. **$460**

Courtesy of Eldred's Auctioneers & Appraisers, eldreds.com

Quarterboard, early 20th c., John W. Wells, pine board with relief carved gilt lettering and trim on black background, 96" l. **$1,800**

Courtesy of Eldred's Auctioneers & Appraisers, eldreds.com

MOVIE POSTERS

A GREAT MOVIE POSTER not only encapsulates the film it represents, it captures the era in which it was produced and reflects the state of the world at its time of production.

Few people are as well situated to discuss the movie poster market as Grey Smith, Heritage Auctions' Director of Rare & Vintage Movie Posters. Over the last 20 years, and throughout his life as a collector, he has handled the greatest movie posters of all time, including the 2017 sale of a First Post-War Release Italian 4-Fogli movie poster for *Casablanca* (Warner Brothers, 1946), a never-before-sold poster from what is widely considered one of the best films ever made. The poster sold for $478,000.

A short time later, that amount was surpassed when the stunning poster for *Dracula*, the 1931 horror classic, sold at auction for $525,800. (See Top Lot feature in this section.)

After a few years in which the poster market looked a little bit thin, it has come roaring back in the last few, as collectors look to pay top dollar for the best possible posters of their respective collecting genres.

A few truisms hold in the market, currently, such as the old Universal Horror movie posters are always the top of the heap, but we are also seeing that great examples of hit movies, from all decades, are selling well and bringing top dollar. If it is rare, and it is quality, then it will be highly collectible.

Below, Grey shares a few of his insights:

WHAT IS THE CURRENT STATE OF THE MOVIE POSTER MARKET?

Grey Smith (GS): The market seems very healthy as prices seem to grow yearly for the majority of the more scarce higher end pieces. Good and rare titles are also bringing record prices. Some of the more common material of the last 40 years has not held up as well due to the quantity found in today's Internet market.

Grey Smith
Heritage Auctions

WHAT MAKES SOMETHING A GREAT MOVIE POSTER?

GS: First and foremost, the film title. The scarcity of that title is what really drives this hobby. Second is the star power of the title and, finally, the graphic appeal.

IS THERE STILL GREAT FILM ART BEING PRODUCED?

GS: I'm fairly jaded and believe the older material is great, especially pre-1960s posters. These outshine newer posters in all respects. There are some very well done posters produced today, such as *Walk the Line* (2005) or *The Dark Knight* (2008), not to mention the "alternate" posters of such companies as Mondo, which is brilliantly rethinking movie posters today. That said, I think the majority of current posters are all a photo shop jobs done on a formulaic premise. It keeps going back to the desirability of the title or star, but in my opinion, there is little great poster art being produced anymore by the studios.

WHAT ARE SOME OF THE TOP GENRES SELLING RIGHT NOW – BESIDES HORROR, WHICH SEEMS TO ALWAYS BE THE TOP?

GS: The top selling posters now are the great and scarce titles, not necessarily genres. If the title or poster is scarce in the market, it sells. For example, a *Lady Eve* one sheet sold for more than $80,000 in Heritage's July 2017 auction – a very scarce one sheet and from a classic film that exceeded our previous sale of the poster by five-fold.

ANY ADVICE FOR THE STARTING COLLECTOR?

GS: Collect what you love from the films you appreciate, and what you can afford. By educating yourself you will find your way in this fascinating hobby. Very good posters can be found at reasonable prices, if one is willing to put in the time and effort.

It Happened One Night (Columbia, 1934), one sheet, starring Clark Gable and Claudette Colbert, directed by Frank Capra, 27" x 41".............**$11,950**

Courtesy of Heritage Auctions, ha.com

Assassin of Youth (Roadshow, 1937), silk-screen one sheet, exploitation film from director Elmer Clifton, 28" x 42". **$4,000**

Courtesy of Heritage Auctions, ha.com

Stagecoach (United Artists, 1939), six sheet, starring John Wayne and directed by John Ford, 78-3/4" x 80-1/4"....................................**$59,750**

Courtesy of Heritage Auctions, ha.com

The Day the Earth Stood Still (20th Century Fox, 1951), six sheet, directed by Robert Wise, 79-1/2" x 80-1/4".....................................**$38,240**

Courtesy of Heritage Auctions, ha.com

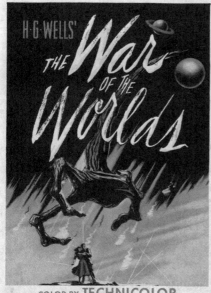

The War of the Worlds (Paramount, 1953), one sheet, directed by Byron Haskin, 27" x 41".. **$3,700**

Courtesy of Heritage Auctions, ha.com

Some Like It Hot (United Artists, 1959), insert, comedy, starring Marilyn Monroe, Tony Curtis and Jack Lemmon, directed by Billy Wilder, 14" x 36".. **$500**

Courtesy of Heritage Auctions, ha.com

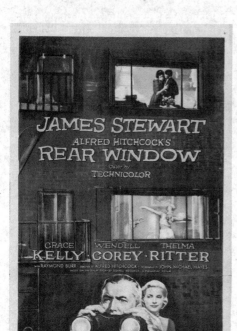

Rear Window (Paramount, 1954), one sheet, starring James Steward and Grace Kelly, directed by Alfred Hitchcock, 27" x 41".................... **$4,000**

Courtesy of Heritage Auctions, ha.com.

top lot

Scary Good
Dracula Poster Sets World Record

One of only two surviving movie posters for the 1931 horror classic, *Dracula*, became the most valuable movie poster in history in 2017. Showcasing the menacing visage of actor Bela Lugosi, whose career would be defined by the role, the 27" x 41" poster sold for $525,800 during a Heritage Auctions' event.

"The *Dracula* poster is a rare, important poster that sparked intense bidding among some of our elite collectors," Heritage Auctions Vintage Posters Director Grey Smith explained. "Considering the sheer beauty of the poster and the timeless popularity of the film, it's not a surprise that the demand was so high."

Contemporary films have a variety of marketing materials at their disposal but in the 1930s, studios mostly had to rely on a movie poster image to captivate an audience.

"It is a matter of opinion, but this poster probably is the most beautiful of all of the styles," Smith said. "And one of only two styles that pictures Bela Lugosi in realistic terms or a faithful rendering — the other is a photographic image."

The poster surpassed the previous auction record of $478,000, set twice by Heritage. In July 2017, Heritage sold the only known surviving Italian issue movie poster from 1946 for *Casablanca*. That sale matched the previous world record from November 2014 for an only-known 1927 copy of the poster for *London After Midnight*.

Lt. Col. George J. Mitchell, Jr., an associate member of the American Society of Cinematographers, owned the *Dracula* poster since the 1950s. Mitchell was a longtime cinematographer and photographer, who after World War II and a 20-year career in the U.S. Army, started a small film production company in San Diego.

"The reason my dad purchased the poster is because he loved horror films. He was drawn to the Bela Lugosi poster because it brought back childhood memories of seeing the film when it was first released," Mitchell's son, Arthur Mitchell, said. "He remembered going to the theater … and remembered that there was an ambulance stationed in the lobby, in case anyone was so scared they needed medical attention."

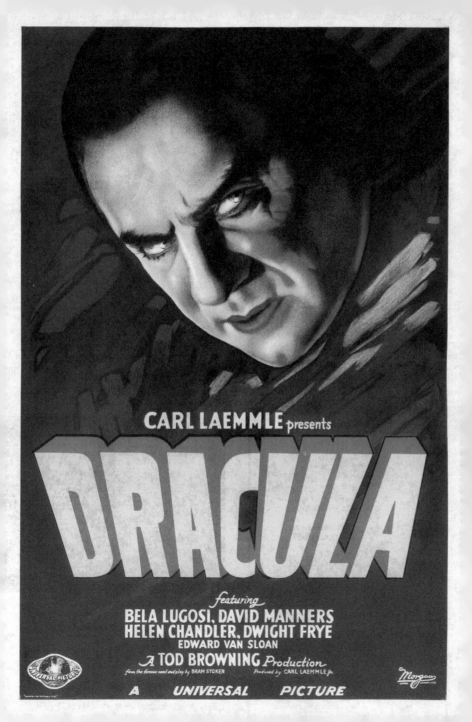

Breakfast at Tiffany's (Paramount, 1961), one sheet, starring Audrey Hepburn and George Peppard, directed by Blake Edwards; Robert McGinnis artwork, 27" x 41"......................**$13,145**

Courtesy of Heritage Auctions, ha.com

Lawrence of Arabia (Columbia, 1962), one sheet, Roadshow Style B, starring Peter O'Toole, Alec Guinness, Anthony Quinn, and Omar Sharif, directed by David Lean, 27" x 41"............... **$3,585**

Courtesy of Heritage Auctions, ha.com

Jaws (Universal, 1975), subway credits style, starring Roy Scheider, Richard Dreyfuss, and Robert Shaw, directed by Steven Spielberg, Roger Kastel artwork, 47" x 59". **$3,100**

Courtesy of Heritage Auctions, ha.com

American Graffiti (Universal, 1973), one sheet, comedy, starring Ron Howard, Richard Dreyfuss, Cindy Williams, Charles Martin Smith, Paul LeMat, Mackenzie Phillips, Harrison Ford, and Wolfman Jack, directed by George Lucas and produced by Francis Ford Coppola, 27" x 41"..**$388**

Courtesy of Heritage Auctions, ha.com

Rocky (United Artists, 1977), starring Sylvester Stallone and Talia Shire, 30" x 40". **$500**

Courtesy of Heritage Auctions, ha.com

Star Wars (20th Century Fox, 1977), first-printing one sheet, starring Mark Hamill, Harrison Ford, and Carrie Fisher, directed by George Lucas, 27" x 41"... **$1,500**

Courtesy of Heritage Auctions, ha.com

E.T. The Extra-Terrestrial (Universal, 1982), one sheet bicycle style, poster never released to theaters; directed by Steven Spielberg, 26-3/4" x 40-1/2"... **$1,900**

Courtesy of Heritage Auctions, ha.com

Footloose (Paramount, 1984), starring Kevin Bacon, Lori Singer, John Lithgow, Dianne Wiest, Chris Penn, and Sarah Jessica Parker, directed by Herbert Ross, 40" x 60". **$50**

Courtesy of Heritage Auctions, ha.com

10 Things You Didn't Know About Lon Chaney

1 Long before the advanced movie-making magic of today, Lon Chaney (April 1, 1883-Aug. 26, 1930) approached acting with an incomparable ability to truly transform himself into characters that became legends of early cinema. Fusing his skills of movie makeup application, physical dexterity, and unparalleled commitment to the craft of storytelling, Chaney revolutionized character development. This was accomplished during a short 17-year career, which included his appearance in more than 150 motion pictures (all silent films, with the exception of one 'talkie' — the remake of *The Unholy Three*).

2 Among his most memorable performances were that of Quasimodo in 1923's *The Hunchback of Notre Dame*, and Erik (the Phantom) in 1925's *Phantom of the Opera*. However, Quasimodo was not Mr. Chaney's first time as a hunchback. In his first recorded film role (1913) he played the part of Barnacle Bill, a fisherman who was a hunchback, in *The Sea Urchin*.

3 An original stone lithograph one sheet (in Very Fine-plus condition) promoting the 1927 film, *London After Midnight*, starring Mr. Chaney in the lead actor role of Scotland Yard Inspector Burke, realized $478,000 during a 2014 auction presented by Heritage Auctions.

4 The son of deaf parents, the Colorado-native's earliest forms of communication included sign language, pantomime, and intentional and exaggerated facial expressions. As his film credits reveal, these well-honed skills were instrumental in his acting career. Prior to Mr. Chaney's birth, his grandfather (Jonathan Ralston Kennedy) was involved in a foundation of a school for the deaf in 1874. The school became what is today the Colorado School for the Deaf and Blind.

Gelatin silver glossy print of Lon Chaney Sr. from *The Phantom of the Opera* (Universal, 1925), uncommon portrait of Chaney in full monster makeup, as his monstrous visages were generally withheld from advance publicity for anticipation effect, very good condition, 7-1/2" x 9-3/4"..................... **$676**

Photo courtesy of Profiles in History, profilesinhistory.com

5 Not one to seek the limelight outside of theater or film productions, items of memorabilia bearing a message from Mr. Chaney are scarce for that reason and the age of most items. However, during a 2010 auction presented by Profiles in History, a black and white portrait of him, dressed as his character Chuck Collins from the 1928 film, *The Big City*, with the inscription, "To Martha from Macon Always a friend Sincerely Lon Chaney," commanded $2,242.

6 Another segment of collectible with appeal to fans of Mr. Chaney, as well book collectors and early film enthusiasts, are photoplay edition books. Most were published in tandem with films of the 1920s and 1930s. With so many films starring Mr. Chaney and other icons of this period considered "lost," the photoplay books provide an opportunity to enjoy the storyline of these classic films, as well as intriguing dust jackets depicting scenes from the films and sometimes including original film stills within the book's interior. *Collecting Tip from seasoned collector, film buff, and numismatics expert and author Tom Michael: Photoplay editions can be found on online auction sites including eBay with great regularity, and knowing what to look for makes a big difference. In some cases, books without dust jackets can be acquired for under $20, while original photoplay books accompanied by clearly marked quality color reproduction scans of the dust jacket image sell in the $200 to $300 range; also original photoplay books with original dust jackets are known to command upward of $500.

▲ *London After Midnight* lithograph one sheet.
....**$478,000**

Courtesy of Heritage Auctions, ha.com

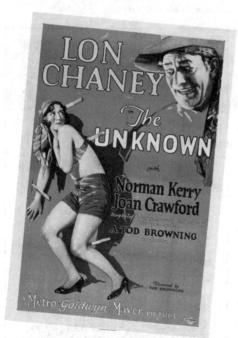

7 In his personal life, Mr. Chaney, like most people, experienced near tragedy and triumph. His first wife was noted cabaret performer "Cleva" Creighton. The birth of their son in 1906 nearly ended in tragedy when the baby was born premature and unresponsive. Following unsuccessful attempts to revive the baby, reports state Mr. Chaney gathered up the child, hustled outside and immediately immersed him into an ice-cold lake nearby. The baby survived, and followed in his performer parents shoes. In 1939, now using the name Lon Chaney, Jr., he earned a New York Critics Choice Award for his performance of Lennie in the stage performance "Of Mice and Men." He is best known for his iconic portrayal of Lawrence Talbot in the 1941 film, *The Wolf Man.*

8 A gelatin silver matte portrait of Mr. Chaney as Echo from his only non-silent and ultimately his last film, *The Unholy Three*, sold for $4,425 during an auction offered by Profiles in History.

9 His talents and skills on the stage and screen also led to a few unique writing credits. The 14th edition of the *Encyclopedia Britannica*, published in 1929, includes Mr. Chaney's input regarding the subject of motion picture make-up. In addition, his frequent performances of 'outsider' characters resulted in a significant fan base among incarcerated individuals. This led Mr. Chaney to research and pen articles on the topic of treatment of inmates and prison operations (penology).

10 *The Phantom of the Opera* brought a flurry of positive reviews from the public and the press when it debuted in 1929. *The New York World*'s review of the film is a great example of this: *"It is something of a pleasure to be able to sit back and hurl the word horrible at a motion picture star and still realize that the fellow is getting a dandy notice ... If this boy (Chaney) doesn't thrill you with his underground-kidnapping of the beautiful Parisian opera singer he will positively, and I guarantee it, send you home determined to leave the lights burning all night long."*

– Compiled by Antoinette Rahn

◄ Genius director Tod Browning and Lon Chaney created a masterful, disturbing, horror classic with *The Unknown* (MGM, 1927). One sheet, Very Fine-, 27" x 41". **$38,837**

Courtesy of Heritage Auctions, ha.com

Sources: lonchaney.com, *The Films of Lon Chaney* by Michael F. Blake, Heritage Auctions (ha.com), Profiles in History (profilesinhistory.com), PBS' *American Masters Film: Lon Chaney: A Thousand Faces*, blog.historygeo.com, "Colorado Biographical Dictionary."

Ghostbusters (Columbia, 1984), starring Bill Murray, Dan Aykroyd, Sigourney Weaver, Harold Ramis, Rick Moranis, Annie Potts, William Atherton, and Ernie Hudson, directed by Ivan Reitman, 40" x 60"...................................... **$200**

Courtesy of Heritage Auctions, ha.com

Pulp Fiction (Miramax, 1994), one sheet, starring John Travolta, Samuel L. Jackson, Bruce Willis, and Uma Thurman, directed by Quentin Tarantino, 27" x 40".. **$2,000**

Courtesy of Heritage Auctions, ha.com

Toy Story (Buena Vista, 1995), one sheet, animation, starring voices of Tom Hanks, Tim Allen, Don Rickles, John Ratzenberger, and Annie Potts, directed by John Lasseter, 27" x 40". **$90**

Walk the Line (20th Century Fox, 2005), one sheet, starring Joaquin Phoenix and Reese Witherspoon, directed by James Mangold, 27" x 40"... **$203**

Courtesy of Heritage Auctions, ha.com

Courtesy of Heritage Auctions, ha.com

MUSIC MEMORABILIA

THE STATE OF the hobby for those who collect music and related memorabilia is healthy. Before the economy went south in 2008, multiple buyers might be in the market for a pricey item, such as a fully signed photo of The Beatles. The resulting bidding battle could drive the price up to $10,000. Today, pristine and rare examples of coveted items can bring hundreds of thousands of dollars. Quality items from recognizable and popular performers are always in demand. The Beatles and Elvis remain the most popular but other artists are emerging as well.

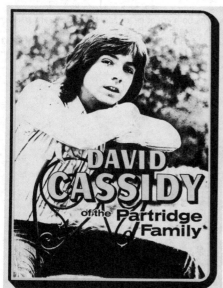

Artists from the late 1970s and 1980s, especially hard rock, heavy metal and pop acts, are poised to be the next generation of headlining acts for collectors. Bruce Springsteen, Nirvana and Punk memorabilia is growing in value. Memorabilia from recently deceased stars such as Prince and David Bowie is commanding top dollar.

And just as the desired artists are changing, so, too, are some of the items that are being collected. Concert posters are practically nonexistent today because there isn't much of a need for them anymore. Also on the endangered species list: ticket stubs, printed magazines, handbills, and promotional materials. These items from the 1950s through early 1990s are collected with great enthusiasm today.

Vinyl records, once thought dead, have rebounded dramatically for listening pleasure and collecting. As with any collectible, demand, rarity and condition are key with vinyl.

David Cassidy concert poster and Partridge Family toy bus, 1970s. Poster promotes a show from "David Cassidy of the Partridge Family" on Saturday, March 27, at the Portland Auditorium, printed on card stock, 15" x 22-1/2"; Partridge Family toy bus from Remco, 1973, with plastic figurines and original box, box measures 16" x 8" x 7-1/4". From the David Gest Memorabilia Archive................**$475**

Courtesy of Heritage Auctions, ha.com

VISIT WWW.ANTIQUETRADER.COM

WWW.FACEBOOK.COM/ANTIQUETRADER

561

MUSIC MEMORABILIA

Other than major players, music memorabilia can be fluid. Always collect what you like. Investing in music memorabilia can be a risky proposition for newbies. Build a collection around your passion, be it punk, disco, concert posters, or all things Neil Diamond.

Strive to acquire items that are in the best condition possible and keep them that way. Always put a priority on provenance while weighing quantity and rarity. And most of all: have fun!

A Frankie Avalon and Bob Denver pair of director's chair backs, circa 1987, both made of blue canvas with a white canvas strip bearing each star's name in black. As both are of nearly identical appearance, they are likely from the 1987 beach film, *Back to the Beach*, starring both Denver and Avalon; each measures approximately 22" x 6-3/4". From the David Gest Memorabilia Archive. **$163**

Courtesy of Heritage Auctions, ha.com

A vintage 1958 Dick Clark "Autograph" doll, 25", and a 1959 American Bandstand "Platter Puss" mascot plush toy, 22". From the David Gest Memorabilia Archive. **$200**

Courtesy of Heritage Auctions, ha.com

Help! The Beatles hardcover book, Random House, 1965. A rare hardcover book from the movie *Help!* starring The Fab Four, book is the first time the movie was transferred in color with actual color photos from the film, complete movie song lyrics, exclusive behind-the-scenes snapshots, and more Beatles memorabilia, 28 pages, 8-1/4" x 11-1/4". **$145**

Courtesy of Heritage Auctions, ha.com

▶ A George M. Cohan cut signature, penned in black fountain ink on a small piece of paper "Yankee Doodle fella / Geo. M. Cohan," matted with a black and white photograph, matted: 14" x 11", signature only: 3" x 2". **$163**

Courtesy of Heritage Auctions, ha.com

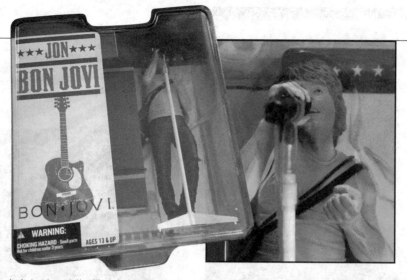

Jon Bon Jovi stand-up doll still sealed in plastic carton, made in China by McFarlane Toys Brothers, holding a guitar and upright microphone, excellent condition. **$49**

Courtesy of a private seller on eBay

A wonderful group of memorabilia relating to the 1960s psychedelic pop act, Cowsills, including a 12-1/4" drum head autographed by Bill, Paul, Dick, Susan, John, Barry, Barbara, William, and Bob Cowsill in black felt pen; a 12" x 12" 1960s Cowsills concert program; and a sealed stereo copy of the band's 1967 landmark album, *The Cowsills* (MGM SE-4498). From the David Gest Memorabilia Archive. **$750**

Courtesy of Heritage Auctions, ha.com

▼ A Connie Francis collection of wigs, circa 1980s-1990s, seven total, all variously styled, all worn by the singer to various functions, included with a "Certificate of Authenticity" hand-signed by Francis. **$67**

Courtesy of Heritage Auctions, ha.com

Spinners' "I'll Be Around" RIAA White Matte Gold Sales Award (Atlantic 45-9204, 1972), framed in wood to an overall 13" x 17". From the David Gest Memorabilia Archive. **$475**

Courtesy of Heritage Auctions, ha.com

Bob Marley's custom T-shirt gifted to a road crew member, circa 1980, verbal provenance indicates that this T-shirt was gifted to the soundman by Bob Marley at a Santana/Bob Marley concert, Marley told him that there were only two such T-shirts made. **$200**

Courtesy of Heritage Auctions, ha.com

An Annette Funicello handwritten interview, circa 1970s, 10 questions submitted by fans, typed on three sheets of Mickey Mouse/Walt Disney Notebook paper, all answers handwritten (except question #7, which is unanswered), in blue ballpoint ink, includes an 8-1/2" x 11" color photo of Funicello. From the David Gest Memorabilia Archive. **$163**

Courtesy of Heritage Auctions, ha.com

Three records and photographs of Marilyn Monroe, framed, 22" x 28". **$400**

Courtesy of USA Live Auctions, usaliveauctions.com

A 1969 Woodstock Music and Art Fair unused three-day ticket, each section of the piece is good for one admission to each day of the now-historic music festival, 2" x 6". **$84**

Courtesy of Heritage Auctions, ha.com

ODDITIES

LONG SINCE THE tradition centuries ago of the "cabinets of curiosity," featuring an array of fantastical objects from the dawn of life to the present day, people have been fascinated with the odd and unusual.

Increasingly more collectors are expressing this interest through items they collect, from human skeletons, insect and fish fossils, tree root sculptures, shaman ritual suits, works of art, anatomical wax heads, and everything in between.

If you want to start collecting weird and wonderful things, a good place to start may be the Oddities Flea Market in New York, now in its second year. Organized by artist Ryan Matthew Cohn, a star of the former realities show, "Oddities," on the Discovery Channel and the Science Channel, and his wife, Regina, the flea market features an assemblage of vendors from across the country bringing you an extensive variety of peculiar items curated by Cohn including medical history ephemera, anatomical curiosities, natural history items, osteological specimens, taxidermy, obscure home decor, jewelry, one-of-a-kind dark art, and more.

The Oddities Flea Market Facebook page says that as time goes on, the event grows significantly while inviting new talent along the way, and the team plans on eventually bringing their creation on the road to cities all over the country, and possibly even the globe.

More information about the event and vendors can be found at facebook.com/Odditiesfleamarket/ and at instagram.com/odditiesfleamarket/?hl=en.

Collecting oddities is a way to express your creativity and build a collection that really stands out from the norm. It's exciting to discover something that perhaps no one else has — whether it's a two-headed taxidermy snake or steel corset. These kinds of antiques and collectibles tell strange and wondrous stories. Plus they are just freakin' cool.

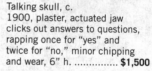

Talking skull, c. 1900, plaster, actuated jaw clicks out answers to questions, rapping once for "yes" and twice for "no," minor chipping and wear, 6" h. **$1,500**

Courtesy of Potter & Potter Auctions, potterauctions.com

Vintage grass-growing heads, 13 assorted caricatures of soldiers, monkeys, burghurs, everyman figures such as soda jerks, criers, smilers, celebrities such as W.C. Fields, in various shades of clay, some in paint, made in Germany, USA, Mexico, Japan, etc.; some trademarked or named on base, early-mid 20th c., accompanied by booklet, "Vintage Grass Growing Clay Heads: The Collection of Alan Olswing." Generally good condition, some with chips, tallest is 8". **$625**

Courtesy of Rago Arts and Auction Center, ragoarts.com

top lot

This exceptional example of a life-size articulated artist mannequin with a finely carved face, France, 1860, (chair not included), 60" h, recently sold at Rago Arts and Auction Center for $45,000. This is the example from Ann Morris' Manhattan shop window, which has never before been offered for sale. The mannequin is in very good condition, commensurate with age, and has beautiful patina and an exceptionally carved face. It was purchased by the grandfather of the consignor.

Artists' models, the articulated figures found among the stocks of art supply merchants, date back several centuries. Ranging in size from under 7 inches to larger-than-life size, the earliest and finest examples are of South German origin from the early 16th century. Italian examples are also known. Minute and meticulous attention was paid to every articulation of these exquisite, earliest boxwood examples of male and female figures. Engineered with an ingenious system of gut bands, they were not suitable for rigorous use in artist studios and were likely made for display in Kunstkammer collections (cabinet of curiosity), reflecting the interest in the human body during the Renaissance.

Artist mannequins, or lay figures, became more androgynous from the 18th into the 19th century, by which time they were constructed in pine, linden or walnut with wooden pegs and ball joints. Reaching their peak of manufacture and popularity in France c. 1850, ownership was coveted. "Mannequin Articulé" would be listed in the inventory of important artists' possessions at that time. Keenly sought after by collectors, desirability and rarity is defined by size, quality, condition, antiquity and, particularly, the deftness of the carving.

Lighted skull and bones wooden fraternity sign, etched onto verso "1934/Beta," shield form, painted in black and gilt, depicting a skull and bones and Greek lettering, socketed wiring to skull's eyes and around border, 44" x 28"..$1,500

Courtesy of Potter & Potter Auctions, potterauctions.com

Charles Eames (1907-1978) and Ray Eames (1912-1988) Evans Products leg splint, USA, 1943, birch plywood, manufacturer marks, overall very good condition, mounted on stand, 43-3/4" x 8" x 5". **$594**

Courtesy of Rago Arts and Auction Center, ragoarts.com

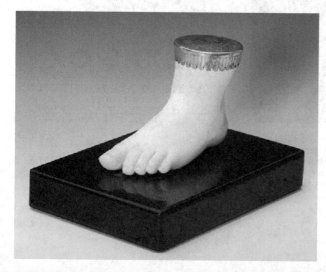

Cast of Tom Thumb's foot, 1847, Parian porcelain, engraved brass plaque at the top of the foot states: "Charles S. Stratton. Known as General Tom Thumb. Born Jan 11th 1832 at Bridgeport Connecticut US. Age 15 Years. Measuring 25 inches high and weighing 15 pounds. 1847." Mounted to black marble base, fine condition. **$7,500**

Courtesy of Potter & Potter Auctions, potterauctions.com

Tilt-A-Whirl car, metal and wood with detachable shell, repainted, with new decals, upholstered seat in very good condition, 35" x 68" x 68". **$1,700**

Courtesy of Potter & Potter Auctions, potterauctions.com

Five boxes of Beech-Nut Fancy Fruit 100-count tab gum for vending...**$225**

Courtesy of Potter & Potter Auctions, potterauctions.com

Antique tattoo folk art flash panel on board, (San Francisco), c. 1920s, thirty-two designs, inked and glazed on board, containing portraits of ethnic and folkloric characters, creatures, and other designs, weathered at edges and right side, 24" x 18"...**$2,600**

Courtesy of Potter & Potter Auctions, potterauctions.com

Advertisement: "Grand & Moral Exhibition. The Celebrated 3 Horned and 3 Eyed Ox." Dayton, c. 1880, woodcut illustration of the anatomically incorrect ox by Tuttle of New Orleans, advertising an exhibition of the beast at No. 31 Market Street, Dayton, Ohio, unmounted, framed: 11-1/2" x 14-1/2"...**$300**

Courtesy of Potter & Potter Auctions, potterauctions.com

Book about Millie and Christine McKoy: *History and Medical Description of the Two-Headed Girl*. Buffalo: Warren, Johnson & Co., 1870. Blue pictorial wraps, 16mo, wraps chipped and soiled, good condition.. **$475**

Courtesy of Potter & Potter Auctions, potterauctions.com

Barnello, *E. Barnello's Voodoo Incantations, or How to Eat Fire*. New York: Benedict, c. 1890. Color pictorial wrappers depicting a fire-eating imp, rear advts. of publisher's dime handbooks. With photographic portrait of the author, previously tipped-in, annotated by Grossman: "From W.W. Durbin Collection, presented to me by Dave Price/ 3/56." Spine reinforced, wrappers chipped, yellowing inside from photo adhesive, Grossman bookplate front inside cover, ownership stamps of Jacob Eilperin. **$350**

Courtesy of Potter & Potter Auctions, potterauctions.com

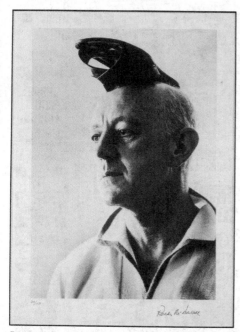

Roddy McDowall (photographer, British, 1928-1998), Alec Guinness portrait, New York City, 1966, gelatin silver print, 1990; signed and editioned "20/125" in ink in margin recto, 14" x 9-1/2"... **$188**

Courtesy of Heritage Auctions, ha.com

Philippe Halsman (American, 1906-1979), Marilyn-Mao, 1952; gelatin silver, printed later, numbered "192/250" in pencil in the photographer's stamp on verso, 12-3/4" x 10". **$438**

Courtesy of Heritage Auctions, ha.com

Sergio Bustamante (Mexico, b. 1943), alligator, painted papier-mâché, signed and numbered 3/100 under mouth left side, structurally sound, breaks to tops of four toes (two partially detached), few other small surface losses scattered throughout, 13" h x 27" w x 73" l. $375

Courtesy of Heritage Auctions, ha.com

Lyman Metal Products Turnpike Toll Gun, Norwalk, Conn., ca. 1960, load this little gun up with coins and fire them into the toll basket... $150

Courtesy of Potter & Potter Auctions, potterauctions.com

Post Cereals vintage sample cereal boxes collection, over 100 boxes, 1970s, prototype boxes with premium advertisements, most flattened complete boxes, plus some trimmed panels, gathered in parcels and comprising the varieties: Honey Comb, Alpha Bits, Post Toasties, Raisin Bran, Grape Nuts Flakes, Sugar Coated Corn Flakes, Bran Flakes, and Corn Flakes. Provenance: Collection of Larido Corporation, premiums supplier to Post/General Foods. $3,200

Courtesy of Potter & Potter Auctions, potterauctions.com

Quack medical device, American, late 19th century, W.H. Burnap, New York, in wooden case with original label to lid interior, opens to reveal geared mechanism, with ivory-handled crank, 4-1/2" x 10" x 4-1/2"...................... **$150**

Courtesy of Cowan's Auctions, cowans.com

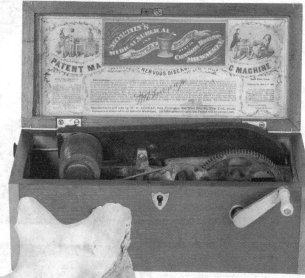

▼ Giant clam shell, *Tridacna gigas*, South Pacific; 11" x 26" x 21". **$2,250**

Courtesy of Rago Arts and Auction Center, ragoarts.com

Didactic collection of rubber mushrooms, 31 mushroom specimens, designated as edible, poisonous or fatal, cast from nature in rubber, each labeled with its botanical name, France, c. 1930, excellent original condition commensurate with age, all with original labels and parts, tallest: 7-1/2". **$7,500**

Courtesy of Rago Arts and Auction Center, ragoarts.com

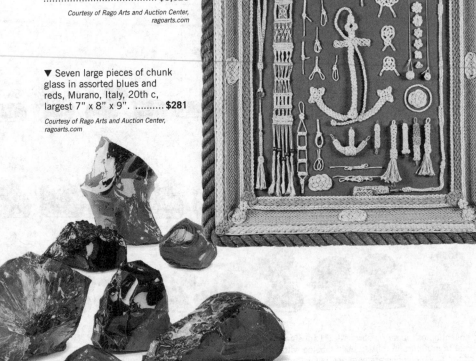

Burl specimen and druid seats, 19th c., burl specimen on stand, England, along with five "druid seats" of ancient petrified fungus with hooks for hanging, burl shelf missing a foot, burl: 11" x 21" x 6"; largest seat: 8" x 9" x 5".
.... **$563**

Courtesy of Rago Arts and Auction Center, ragoarts.com

Monumental framed sailor's knot sample board, 40 samples arrayed on a green field surrounded by three borders of ornamental knotwork and an outermost frame of burnished gold rope, USA, older giltwood frame, overall good condition, 41-1/2" x 48" x 4".
.... **$3,625**

Courtesy of Rago Arts and Auction Center, ragoarts.com

▼ Seven large pieces of chunk glass in assorted blues and reds, Murano, Italy, 20th c, largest 7" x 8" x 9". **$281**

Courtesy of Rago Arts and Auction Center, ragoarts.com

PAPERWEIGHTS

ANTIQUE PAPERWEIGHTS MADE in the 19th century captured floral designs, reptiles, and millefiori canes in traditional Victorian styles encased in a solid sphere of clear crystal.

Artists of the 19th century generally produced paperweights in factory settings along with other decorative glass objects. Rarely signed by individual artists, most antique paperweights are attributed to a factory by motif, color palette, canes, and shape. Little is known about individual artists who created the work.

In a 19th century society with fancy desks and paper, paperweights were functional objects of art. Flowers were a large part of Victorian society and both ladies and gentleman of the time were attracted to fauna and flora. Paperweights were considered fascinating objects of art and conversation pieces in Victorian homes.

Factories producing paperweights were primarily located in France, Italy, Czechoslovakia, America, and China. Factory-made paperweights often had similar motifs. Factories would also produce special pieces. These rare designs showcased fantastic capabilities and secret techniques only known to each factory. Today these special pieces bring staggering auction results.

In the mid-20th century there was a revival in modern paperweights. At first artists began creating updated versions using glass-working techniques of antique traditions. This revival began alongside the studio art glass movement in America. Individual glass artists opened homegrown studios in garages and basements. The pioneer and dean of the American paperweight revival was Charles Kaziun of Brockton, Massachusetts. Kaziun set new artistic standards and methods for creating paperweights at that time. He worked alone in his own small home studio creating the path that all subsequent contemporary paperweight artists followed.

In the early years of collecting paperweights, few collectors knew much about them and even less about how they were made. In 1955, Paul Jokelson, an avid antique paperweight collector and importer, founded the Paperweight Collectors Association. He promoted paperweights and created a forum for educating collectors and helping artists like Kaziun show and sell their new work. Jokelson published many early books on paperweights; other authors followed, creating a library of books on paperweights. The PCA has biannual paperweight conventions.

Today many artists all over the world are creating fine paperweights. The finest modern paperweights have made their way into private and museum art collections. The Bergstrom-Mahler Museum of Glass in Neenah, Wisconsin, houses one of the world's largest collections of paperweights

Stanislaw Borowski special order paperweight, whimsical blue-eyed Kilroy-style head wearing a green and yellow curled cap, engraved GSB beneath. The Borowski Glass Studio was founded in Poland in 1990 by Stanislaw Borowski, who became an internationally acclaimed glass artist, producing intriguing and amusing sculptures; 5-1/2" x 4-3/4" w. **$70**

Courtesy of Mark Mussio, Humler & Nolan, humlernolan.com

Jon Kuhn (b. 1949) heart paperweight, Winston-Salem, N.C., 2017, ground, polished, and laminated glass, signed and dated, 1-1/2" x 5" sq. .. **$938**

Courtesy of Rago Arts and Auction Center, ragoarts.com

Jon Kuhn (b. 1949) paperweight, Winston-Salem, N.C., 2017, ground, polished, and laminated glass, signed and dated, 3-1/4" x 3-3/4" x 4"............................... **$1,750**

Courtesy of Rago Arts and Auction Center, ragoarts.com

Richard Marquis, "Noble Effort" spherical murrini glass paperweight, Washington State, 1989, signed in murine, 1/4 of detachable base is ground along edge, good condition, 2-1/2" dia.......................... **$813**

Courtesy of Rago Arts and Auction Center, ragoarts.com

Amalric Walter (1870-1959), moth paperweight, Nancy, France, early 20th c, pâte-de-verre, molded A. WALTER NANCY, couple shallow, minor flecks around outer edge under base, 2" x 4-1/2" x 4"..... **$1,188**

Courtesy of Rago Arts and Auction Center, ragoarts.com

Debbie Tarsitano Studio art glass lampwork magnum paperweight, colorless, depicting two crossing pink dahlia with a bloom at the center, polished pontil mark, signature cane to the underside, fourth quarter 20th c, 4" dia. **$1,521**

Courtesy of Jeffrey S. Evans & Associates, jeffreysevans.com

St. Louis pear-form paperweight, cased deep rose to orange, applied to a colorless square base with a polished pontil mark, France, moderate shelf wear, second half 19th c, 2-1/4" h, 3" sq. base.......... **$351**

Courtesy of Jeffrey S. Evans & Associates, jeffreysevans.com

▲ New England Glass Co. blown apple-form paperweight, 1860-1880, cased deep rose shaded to yellow, the stem visible, green button-like rough pontil, on a colorless circular base, 2-3/4" h, base 3-5/8" dia. **$468**

Courtesy of Jeffrey S. Evans & Associates, jeffreysevans.com

▲ White frit To My Wife paperweight, over a central crown, striations in glass, 3-3/8" dia............................ **$38**

Courtesy of Pook & Pook, Inc., pookandpook.com

Paul Joseph Stankard Botanical Sculpture, fall colors, brandywine bouquet, dried flowers, seeds and pods over a snowing ground, a natural fire polished finish at sides with a cut front, signed at the base of one side panel "Paul J. Stankard F34 1989," VG to excellent condition, 5" h x 2-3/4" w..**$6,050**

Courtesy of James D. Julia Auctioneers, jamesdjulia.com

in the United States. It's second only to the holdings of the Corning Museum of Glass in New York. Other institutions such as The Chicago Art Institute, Museum of Fine Arts in Boston, and The Currier Museum of Art in Manchester, New Hampshire, among others, also have modern paperweights on view.

Collectors love paperweights because, unlike other forms of art, they can hold them in their hands and be drawn into a fascinating miniature world.

Lifeless bird bronze paperweight, unmarked, plaster filling, 1" h x 6" l..................$130

Courtesy of Mark Mussio, Humler & Nolan, humlernolan.com

Steven Lundberg paperweight, bluebell flowers and green leaves accented by a bright red field, engraved Steven Lundberg, Lundberg Studios, 1984, 010301, excellent condition, 2-1/2" h. $150

Courtesy of Mark Mussio, Humler & Nolan, humlernolan.com

Jon Kuhn (b. 1949) heart paperweight, Winston-Salem, N.C., 2012, internally decorated laminated glass, signed and dated, excellent condition, 4" x 4-1/4" x 4". $1,000

Courtesy of Rago Arts and Auction Center, ragoarts.com

Three Orient & Flume paperweights, factory signed, clockwise from top right: tri-flowers and pulled feathers on cobalt, engraved 137 Jn, dated 1978, factory sticker, 2-1/2"; butterfly and flower with pulled feathers, engraved I71 Jn, 1978, company sticker, 2-3/8"; and golden peacock feather, engraved 212, May 1979, company sticker, 2-1/2". Each engraved Orient & Flume with registration and dates and having original boxes and felt bags. $350

Courtesy of Mark Mussio, Humler & Nolan, humlernolan.com

David Schwarz (b. 1952) spherical paperweight, Vancouver, Wash., 1993, blown and polished glass, signed and dated, short scratch to top, 9" dia. $625

Courtesy of Rago Arts and Auction Center, ragoarts.com

PAPERWEIGHTS

Paul Joseph Stankard floral botanical, pink blossoms with bud, white wild flower, painted green leaves, ant, honeybee hovering over the design, dimensional design also having several "spirits under the earth," hollow cut at the base, and a line cutting surrounding the exterior side near the base, VG to excellent condition, 5" h x 2-3/4" w. **$3,025**

Courtesy of James D. Julia Auctioneers, jamesdjulia.com

Melissa Ayotte Apache basket sculpture, exterior overlaid in brown with blue design, engraved by hand with staves, and patterns resembling a basket, interior holds a bouquet of flowers in pink, yellow and cobalt with white buds and green leaves, VG to excellent condition, approx. 5" dia x 4" h overall..................... **$1,089**

Courtesy of James D. Julia Auctioneers, jamesdjulia.com

Rick Ayotte Illusion sculpture, central bouquet of flowers and green leaves, faceted in panels surrounding the topsides and back, signed on one side facet "Ayotte 2 of 3," VG to excellent condition, 4" h x 4-1/2" w.**$3,025**

Courtesy of James D. Julia Auctioneers, jamesdjulia.com

Modern St. Louis France pedestal paperweight, 16 colorful patterned millefiori canes, ground of white stardust canes, latticino pedestal in pink and white, marked on the underside "103/150," comes in original fitted Saint Louis France box (tear to one edge), approx. 3" h x 3" w............. **$968**

Courtesy of James D. Julia Auctioneers, jamesdjulia.com

St. Louis faceted upright bouquet sculpture, central upright bouquet, white, yellow, pink, cobalt flowers, deep green leaves, overall faceting, signed on the underside "Saint Louis 1995 2/10," comes in fitted Saint Louis box, VG to excellent condition, 5" h x 3" w......... **$787**

Courtesy of James D. Julia Auctioneers, jamesdjulia.com

▲ Modern St. Louis France four-color pedestal newel post, alternating green and white ribbon cane, pink and blue ribbon cane, white latticino chaplet bead, marked on the top "SL 1991" within a signature cane. With original fitted Saint Louis France box, VG to Excellent condition, approx. 5" h x 3-1/2" w. **$484**

Courtesy of James D. Julia Auctioneers, jamesdjulia.com

◀ Colin Richardson paperweight, contemporary, orchid on clear ground, brown, white and orange orchids with green leaves growing on a moss-covered log, signed on the side in etched letters "Colin Richardson 2012 – (illegible) Ill. 19 1/1," one broken green leaf at bottom of design and a floating green leaf at left of log in the making, 3-1/2" dia....**$484**

Courtesy of James D. Julia Auctioneers, jamesdjulia.com

PETROLIANA

GASOLINE- AND OIL-RELATED COLLECTIBLES are called petroliana. Signs dominate the category, but it also includes posters, cans, premiums, lights, and service station items. Pieces are collected for display and a premium is placed on eye appeal and condition.

As with all advertising items, factors such as brand name, intricacy of design, color, age, condition, and rarity drastically affect value. Signs enjoying the hottest demand are those measuring 30 to 42 inches, in near mint condition, and with interesting graphics and bright colors.

Reproductions, fantasy pieces, and fakes have plagued petroliana collectors for decades. The relatively recent boon in the category has ushered in a new and diverse tidal wave of merchandise designed for fast profit, particularly porcelain signs. Brands such as Sinclair, Indian, Oilzum, and Mobilgas are actively sold on websites and at flea markets across the nation. These mass-produced signs are getting increasingly more difficult to distinguish from authentic, vintage survivors of the early 20th century.

The only way to avoid reproductions is experience: making mistakes and learning from them; talking with other collectors and dealers; finding reputable resources (including books and websites), and learning to invest wisely, buying the best examples one can afford.

Marks can be deceiving, paper labels and tags are often missing, and those that remain may be spurious. Adding to the confusion are "fantasy" pieces, globes that have no vintage counterpart, and that are often made more for visual impact than deception. There is another important factor to consider. A contemporary maker may create a "reproduction" sign or gas globe in tribute of the original, and sell it for what it is: a legitimate copy. Many of these are dated and signed by the artist or manufacturer, and these legitimate copies are highly collectible today. Such items are not intended to be frauds.

But a contemporary piece may pass through many hands between the time it leaves the maker and wind up in a collection. When profit is the only motive of a reseller, details about origin, ownership, and age can become a slippery slope of guesses, attribution, and – unfortunately – fabrication.

Although signs dominate this hobby, service station items are also highly valuable and collected. This restored air scale model jr. with air hose was the top lot at Morphy Auctions' Automobilia & Petroliana auction in February 2018. It sold for more than $20,000 against the high bid estimate of $8,000. There is little to no wear on the restoration and all of the stripping and "Air" letters are painted and not decals. It's a great display piece of early automotive service station memorabilia; 46" h x 22" w.
......................................**$21,600**

Courtesy of Morphy Auctions, morphyauctions.com

A few tips to keep in mind when purchasing petroliana signs:

1. No two porcelain signs are ever truly identical. The original process used to make them was imperfect to begin with – each color layer of enamel was added and baked on in a special kiln at temperatures specific to each color. It's entirely natural that imperfections would occur, and authenticators now rely on these variations in much the same way as the FBI uses fingerprints.
2. Original signs are made of steel, not aluminum. A magnet will be attracted to an authentic sign.
3. Most circular signs are 28, 30, 42, or 48 inches in diameter. Look for telltale signs of use: scratches and deep chips around hang holes, even scratches around the perimeter from frames, rust on exposed steel in place of missing enamel.

For more information about petroliana, consult *Warman's Gas Station Collectibles* by Mark Moran. For more advice on how to intelligently buy petroliana signs, check out *Picker's Pocket Guide – Signs: How to Pick Antiques Like a Pro.*

◀ Eco Tireflator Air Meter Model 46, restored, 70" h x 15" w. .. **$9,600**

Courtesy of Morphy Auctions, morphyauctions.com

▼ Dependable Dodge Service porcelain sign with arrow crest, 42" dia.
.... **$3,750**

Courtesy of Morphy Auctions, morphyauctions.com

FINDING A FAKE

AUTHENTICATING A SIGN IS BEST LEFT TO PROFESSIONALS, BUT HERE ARE A FEW TIPS THAT CAN HELP:

- Be leery of rust spots that have not darkened with age.
- Enamel chips that expose gleaming steel is a bad sign.
- Watch out for uneven application of the porcelain.
- Missing mounting holes or grommets that appear unused are red flags
- Missing or smudged maker's marks are concerns.
- Authentic signs often, but not always, feature some type of stamp or markings on the back, either a maker's initials or a number denoting the enamel colors used on the front.
- Different enamel colors were layered on top of one another in the making of the sign, beginning with a white base coat. If you can feel the transition between one color and another then chances are the sign is original.

Coca-Cola Gas Today embossed tin sign, includes chalkboard and bottle graphic, a great example of soda pop and gas advertising, 23-1/2" w x 15" h. **$8,400**

Courtesy of Morphy Auctions, morphyauctions.com

Oldsmobile Service porcelain sign with crest graphic, 60" dia. **$5,100**

Courtesy of Morphy Auctions, morphyauctions.com

Red Crown & Polarine Summer or Winter double-sided tin sign, 1913, Passaic Metal Ware Co., Passaic, N.J., 27-1/2" h x 19-1/2" w. **$10,800**

Courtesy of Morphy Auctions, morphyauctions.com

Racine Tires tin flange sign, maker marked Shonk Litho Company, Chicago, 14" dia. **$3,300**

Courtesy of Morphy Auctions, morphyauctions.com

Husky Gasoline porcelain service shield sign, nice example of a hard-to-find sign, 48" x 42". .... **$7,995.**

Courtesy of Morphy Auctions, morphyauctions.com

Calso's Supreme Gasoline globe with Ethyl logo, 15" single lens in a high-profile metal body. **$1,600+**

Courtesy of Morphy Auctions, morphyauctions.com

Blue Crown gas globe, one-piece, possibly original paint, rare, metal collar, 17" h...................... **$800+**

Courtesy of Morphy Auctions, morphyauctions.com

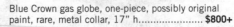

Co-op Gasoline globe single lens in a narrow glass body. ....**$2,000+**

Courtesy of Morphy Auctions, morphyauctions.com

Conoco globe with Ethyl logo, green plastic body, 13-1/2" lenses. .... **$900+**

Courtesy of Morphy Auctions, morphyauctions.com

United Motors Service diecut porcelain arrow sign,
42" w x 16" h.. **$4,800**

Courtesy of Morphy Auctions, morphyauctions.com

Gurney Seed globe, showing radio station,
Yankton, S.D., in a wide white glass body, 13-1/2"
lenses...**$1,500+**

Courtesy of Morphy Auctions, morphyauctions.com

Koolmotor jewel-body globe, circa 1930s, 15"
lenses, 19-1/2" h overall...........................**$5,000+**

Courtesy of Morphy Auctions, morphyauctions.com

The Petroleum Products Co. Kansas Made Dog-On
Good Gasoline Globe, rare, only-known example,
17-1/4" x 15-1/2"....................................**$10,455**

Courtesy of Morphy Auctions, morphyauctions.com

12 Things You Didn't Know
About Vintage Road Signs

1 From humble, but helpful, beginnings, the road signs we see today reportedly evolved from carved marble milestones erected in Ancient Rome. The first example of the Roman milestones was the Milliarium Aureum, a column that served as the central point from which all primary roads in Rome radiated. Roman milestones were invented as a means of measuring distance, since the space between two milestones was typically a mile.

2 A must-visit destination for anyone with a love of road signs, and signs in general, is the American Sign Museum, in Cincinnati, Ohio. Within the 20,000-square-foot museum are examples of more than 100 years of American signage. In addition to road signs, the museum boasts thousands of examples of road art and vintage advertising signage, among other items.

3 Lack of consistency among road signs caused more challenges than conformity when it came to road travel in 20th century America. In 1935, the *Manual on Uniform Traffic Control Devices for Streets and Highways* was put in place to standardize travel signs and control traffic mobility. Elements of this manual remain active within American roadway travel today. As a side note, the year the manual was unveiled, a gallon of gas cost 10 cents, according to the U.S. Department of Transportation website.

4 Although the invention of the automobile certainly prompted an increase in road sign development in the U.S., the earliest process for creating road signs came out of Germany. The process of creating porcelain enamel signs included flattening a piece of iron, coating it with colored powdered glass and firing it in a kiln. Porcelain enamel signs were first used in Germany before the turn of the 20th century.

5 Long before the 21st century popular practice of "bedazzling" items with shiny glass, beads, and jewels, the early generation of road signs boasted a form of bedazzling to add reflectiveness. It's reported that the revolutionary invention of an adhesive in 1937 by the 3M company, led to production of reflective road signs featuring glass beads attached with the adhesive. Two years later, 3M came out with retro-reflective sheeting, changing the presentation and effectiveness of traffic road signs for generations.

6 An active preservation and education effort of the American Sign Museum is the Save Old Signs (SOS) initiative. It involves tracking preservation projects, reporting on legislative issues involving signs, listing endangered sign movements, and encouraging sharing of sign stories. You can also view the Museum's archive online at americansignmuseum.org.

Metal vintage California Route 66 sign featuring glass beads on the numbers for reflective purpose, 24" x 24"...................... **$650**

Courtesy of Meissner's Auction Service, meissnersauction.com

Idaho Highway 36 sign, 24" x 24"............... **$2,500**

Courtesy of Mecum Auctions, mecum.com

Shield-style Route 66 road sign with an example of the cat's-eye design in the number six. The appearance of a cat's eye in Route 66 signs often increases interests among collectors. This sign is one of 21 different Route 66 signs to sell as a single lot.. **$26,000**

Courtesy of RM Auctions, live.rm-auctions.com

A vintage New Mexico U.S. Route 66 highway sign with a great rustic look. **$325**

Courtesy of North American Auction Company. Northamericanauctioncompany.com

7 Pre-war American road signs are among the most sought after and elusive, according to David Purvis, director of road signs for Mecum Auctions, mecum.com. Purvis' own appreciation of signs, road art, and classic vehicles was forged early in life, while spending time with his father who owned a car museum. The limited availability of early 20th century road signs is due to most retired signs being scrapped for use in the war effort, Purvis adds. This also contributes to increased secondary-market values for road signs manufactured between the 1920s and 1930s.

8 Early in American road sign history, the majority of sign production (and automotive license plates) took place in state penitentiaries. The practice of federal contracted signs produced by inmates ceased during the Great Depression, in an effort to strengthen the private business sector, according to some reports. Eventually the practice was renewed and is in use in some U.S. states today.

9 Automobile clubs in states across the nation spearheaded the placement of road signs on the nation's highways and byways. According to the AllState Insurance blog, in 1905 the Buffalo Automobile Club erected a series of signs across New York, which was followed by the Automobile Club of California placing signs in 13 counties, beginning in 1906.

10 The shape and color of road signs are not a matter of happenstance or highway department's getting in on a great deal at the paint store; it's tied to psychological reactions within the mind, according to Dr. David Cowell, a psychologist specializing in the impact of color on the brain, as reported in an article by BBC News. For example, Dr. Cowell said orange and yellow "suggest a positive future," which in turn is meant to encourage drivers to look forward to traveling beyond a construction zone. In terms of shapes, rectangular signs have the appearance of an open book - serving as a source of information, while triangular signs, with their sharp points, indicate danger - and for that reason, are often used to present warning signs.

11 Vintage road signs indicating U.S. Route 66 are among the most popular within the collectible road sign market. The highway was established in November of 1926, but the road signs didn't appear along the original 2,400-mile route until 1927, according to Route66World.com. Often the familiar black-and-white shield-shaped road signs would include the state name above the 66. Although the iconic Route 66 was formally decommissioned in 1985, various segments of the historic roadway continue to welcome travelers daily.

12 Acquiring vintage road signs is a treasure-hunt adventure to be enjoyed at flea markets, collector shows (petroliana and advertising shows are great places to start), online bidding and selling sites including eBay, Etsy, etc., and auctions.

– Compiled by Antoinette Rahn

Sources: http://penelope.uchicago.edu/~grout/encyclopaedia_romana/romanforum/milliariumaureum.html; https://mutcd.fhwa. dot.gov/mutcd_80_bday.htm; https://www.americansignmuseum.org; https://www.justcollecting.com/miscellania/antique-road-signs; http://www.vintagetrafficsigns.com; https://blog.allstate.com/from-rome-to-detroit-a-history-of-street-signs; http:// www.caltrafficsigns.com/history.php; http://news.bbc.co.uk/2/hi/uk_news/magazine/7628908.stm; http://www.madehow.com/ Volume-2/Road-Sign.html; http://www.smithsonianmag.com/travel/endangered-site-historic-route-66-usa-52145829/; http:// www.route66world.com/66_history/

Ride with Rose Regular Gasoline globe, 13-1/2" single lens in Capco body. ....**$2,750+**

Courtesy of Morphy Auctions, morphyauctions.com

Sinclair Oils one-piece globe, etched, 15" h.**$2,000+**

Courtesy of Morphy Auctions, morphyauctions.com

Standard's Supreme (with Ethyl) Gasoline globe, 15" lenses in a high-profile metal body. ....**$2,300+**

Courtesy of Morphy Auctions, morphyauctions.com

Mobiloil Gargoyle large oval globe, one-piece body, probably new old stock. ....**$2,900+**

Courtesy of Morphy Auctions, morphyauctions.com

▶ Texaco leaded stained-glass metal body globe, slight fading, smaller size. ....**$4,500+**

Courtesy of Morphy Auctions, morphyauctions.com

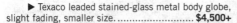

PINBACKS

CONSIDERED THE DEAN OF THE PINBACK BUTTON, Ted Hake, namesake of Hake's Americana & Collectibles, says at least 2 million buttons have crossed his palms since 1960. It was in his junior year of high school when he discovered the little metal disks with interesting sayings or promotional images. Since then, he has gone to manage the sale of some of the largest and most important collections of pinback buttons to ever come to market — and he says that market remains strong and vibrant. You can take his word to the bank, as his auction house sold a world-record political pinback in November 2017 for more than $47,000 (see Top Lot).

"After some 57 years and 2 million buttons, almost every day I still come upon buttons I'm seeing for the first time," he said. "Now is an ideal time to get into the hobby of collecting pinback buttons in the two broad categories of both political and non-political buttons."

The pinback button has been used in the United States since the first presidential inauguration in 1789, as George Washington supporters produced a slogan button which was designed to be sewn to the lapel of a coat or worn as a pendant. It wasn't until modern times that the pinback as we know it came to be. Benjamin S. Whitehead patented the first innovation to the design in 1893 by inserting a sheet of transparent film made of celluloid over a photograph mounted on a badge to protect the image from scratches and abrasion. The innovation opened the door to his company (eventually renamed Whitehead & Hoag) to produce any manner of political or promotional button imagination would allow.

Advertising pinback, 1914, Daisy Air Rifle, text reads: "The Happy Daisy Boy," additional text denoting 'Honorable Mention' Daisy Letter Contest 1914 (given only to a small select group of contest entrants), Bastian Bros. back paper, rare, 1-1/5" dia...................... **$2,596**

Courtesy of Hake's Americana & Collectibles, hakes.com

"My first large collection, about 50,000 buttons, came in the mid-1970s from the estate of Joe Stone in Toledo, Ohio, who started his collection as a boy in 1921 when he picked up a button from the street while on an errand for his mother," Hake recalls. "His collection became the basis for my book, *Collectible Pin-Back Buttons 1896-1986.*" By far my largest collection, around a million pieces in all categories, came from the estate of Greenwich Village collector Marshall Levin. From the 1960s through 1999, Marshall was the consummate button collector of the modern era. He established relationships with most of the New York City area button manufacturers and attended every protest rally and industry trade show he possibly could."

Advertising pinback, 1912, premium from Wyman's Department Store of South Bend, Indiana, desirable Santa Claus wearing aviator goggles, Whitehead & Hoag Co. back paper, rare in this condition, 1-1/2" dia. **$746**

Courtesy of Hake's Americana & Collectibles, hakes.com

Advertising pinback, 1901, popular devil design, text reads: "Begone! Dull Care/May 6-11/1901/ Sacramento Street Fair," possibly promoting live play or performance, 1-3/4" dia. **$118**

Courtesy of Hake's Americana & Collectibles, hakes.com

POLITICAL PINBACKS

Following World War II, a handful of presidential campaign button collectors somehow found each other, joined forces, and established the American Political Items Collectors (www.apic.us). The club had its first real growth spurt in the mid-1960s. There was little documentation of the material at that point and what existed focused on the pre-button era items (mostly campaign tokens) prior to 1896.

Hake was the first to begin to document presidential campaign items with his 1974 book on the subject, *The Encyclopedia of Political Buttons 1896-1972*. He followed up in 1977 with *Political Buttons Book II 1920-1976* and *Political Buttons Book III 1789-1916*. All three books catalog some 15,000 buttons and other types of presidential campaign artifacts. Between these books and later books on particular types of items (ribbons, textiles, china, inaugural medals, etc.) collectors today have many resources for learning which items are common and which are scarce to rare. This is enhanced even more by internet sites such as eBay, Worthpoint, and prices realized records for the past auctions of many different auction houses.

"The easy availability of historical pricing information, I feel, is the key factor contributing to the significant prices being paid for select and seldom offered presidential campaign items," Hake said.

For politicals, there are two reasons this is a great time to collect. For the collector on a budget, between eBay and auction houses, there is much historic but "common" material steadily available at very collector friendly prices. From 1896, the first year buttons were used, "common" McKinley or Bryan presidential campaign buttons can be bought in the $10-$25 range for beautiful, undamaged, pieces over 120 years old.

Pinback, circa 1820-1840, depicting the U.S. Capitol Building, hand-engraved, gilt metal, banner below image reads "WASHINGTON'S TOWN," back stamped with numbers: 6018 and 35, 1-3/4" dia. **$2,000**

Courtesy of Early American History Auctions and History Store, earlyamerican.com

Campaign pinback, 1900, for William McKinley and Theodore Roosevelt, Whitehead & Hoag Co. imprint, silk ribbon attached with thread reading "N.Y. Press," from the Ron Koot Collection, 4" dia. **$9,086**

Courtesy of Hake's Americana & Collectibles, hakes.com

Campaign pinback, 1960, jugate button for John F. Kennedy and Lyndon Johnson, text reads: "VOTE STRAIGHT/ DEMOCRATIC TICKET," scarce, from the Ron Koot Collection, 3" dia................................ **$431**

Courtesy of Hake's Americana & Collectibles, hakes.com

Campaign pinback, circa 1960s, John F. Kennedy presidential campaign, from the Ron Koot Collection, 2-1/4" dia. **$118**

Courtesy of Hake's Americana & Collectibles, hakes.com

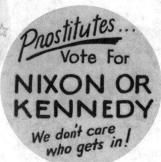

Pinback, 1960, text reads: "Prostitutes/Vote For NIXON OR KENNEDY/We don't care who gets in!," from the Fred Noye Collection, 2-1/5" dia. **$259**

Courtesy of Hake's Americana & Collectibles, hakes.com

Jugate button, 1901, commemorating U.S. President Theodore Roosevelt's disregard for segregation laws by hosting educator Booker T. Washington to a meal at the White House (the first President to invite an African American to dine at the White House), rare in this largest size, from the David and Janice Frent Collection, 1-3/4" dia. **$8,125**

Courtesy of Heritage Auctions, ha.com

Advertising pinback, May
1942, DC Comics, premium
for Sensation Comics, a comic
book series published by DC
Comics, bold profile of Wonder
Woman, the series' lead
character, from the Robert M.
Overstreet Collection,
1-1/8" dia..........................$778

*Courtesy of Hake's Americana & Collectibles,
hakes.com*

Advertising pinback, circa
1907-1920, candy, text reads:
"Knut Butter Kisses/Have A
Kiss/J.H. Phelps of Cleveland
(candy maker)," Bastain Bros.
Co., back paper, 1-1/4" dia. $162

*Courtesy of Hake's Americana & Collectibles,
hakes.com*

Advertising pinback, circa
1900, gunpowder, text reads
"DU PONT/SMOKELESS
POWDER," Whitehead & Hoag
Co. back paper, 1-1/4" dia. . $118

*Courtesy of Hake's Americana & Collectibles,
hakes.com*

Advertising pinback, 1915,
features Ty Cobb, from
10-button premium set issued
by Schmelzer's Sporting Goods
of Kansas City, Mo., set is
noted as the first baseball
celluloid pinback issue to
feature lithographic artwork
juxtaposed with an actual
player photo, finest-known
example, rare, 1-1/4" dia. $6,490

*Courtesy of Love of the Game Auctions,
loveofthegameauctions.com*

Advertising pinback, circa
1900-1903, earliest-
known pinback button to
promote a teddy bear, text
reads: "JORDAN MARSH
CO." (United States' first
"departmentalized" store),
Ehrman, Boston back paper,
1-1/4" dia............................$233

*Courtesy of Hake's Americana & Collectibles,
hakes.com*

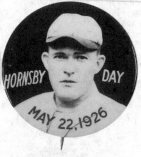

Advertising pinback, 1926,
issued May 22 for "Rogers
Hornsby Day" in what was then
called Sportsmen's Park, St.
Louis, Mo., 1-3/4" dia. $861

*Courtesy of Love of the Game Auctions,
loveofthegameauctions.com*

top lot

The "holy grail" of jugate buttons set a world-record price at a November 2017 auction at Hake's Americana & Collectibles. Considered the most iconic button among collectors of political campaign material, the James M. Cox/ Franklin D. Roosevelt pinback jugate sold for $47,278. The 1920 button with the slogan, "AMERICANIZE AMERICA VOTE FOR COX AND ROOSEVELT," is from the Democratic presidential campaign. Cox was the governor of Ohio at the time and Roosevelt was the assistant secretary of the Navy. The button has Whitehead & Hoag Co. back paper, is in high-grade condition, one of eight examples known to exist, and 13/16 inches in diameter.

According to Hake's, the jugate is akin to the Honus Wagner T206 tobacco card or *Action Comics* #1, the first appearance of Superman. Of the six varieties in sizes, from 5/8 inches to 1-1/4 inches, four are unique or are one of three known examples. These varieties have long been locked in major collections and the nine examples owned by the Cox family media empire are unlikely to ever change hands.

"We are aware of eight examples of the presently offered design, all of which are cornerstone pieces of advanced collections not expected to be offered soon, including one in the Cox family holdings. Three are known to have condition issues, making this offering one of only four potentially high-grade examples known and likely the only one to be available to the many collectors seeking to complete their jugate collections. This example is arguably the most desirable of all potentially available specimens," said Hake's.

One of the biggest questions many collectors have about these buttons is what makes them so rare. According to Hake's, the best theory is that, given the Democrats 1920 low probability of victory, combined with limited resources at the local level, no quantities of any variety were ever ordered, thus making all surviving examples likely samples issued by their manufacturers; this is supported by the fact that no more than three Cox/FDR jugates have been found together at one time — and this with collectors scouring the country for them since the button first set a record after selling for more than $200 in 1964, an event that forever changed the hobby. Since then, the Cox/FDR button has maintained its iconic status. Many advanced collectors spend a lifetime in pursuit of any example in any condition, viewing it as the last mile marker to having a "great collection," said Hake's.

Pinback, 1966, The Beatles, caricature drawing by artist David Levine, text reads: "A-14 'The Beatles' By David Levine 1963-64-65-66 New York Review," acetate covering, 6" dia....... **$118**

Courtesy of Hake's Americana & Collectibles, hakes.com

Protest pinback, March 1971, created to protest U.S. Army officer William Calley, Jr., court-martialed for murdering 22 South Vietnamese civilians in the March 16, 1968 My Lai Massacre, text reads: "Lt. William Calley, Jr. Rather Than Words," rare, 2-1/8" dia....... **$906**

Courtesy of Hake's Americana & Collectibles, hakes.com

Pinback, 1896, commemorates the 20th anniversary of Gen. George A. Custer's death at the Battle of Little Bighorn, Whitehead & Hoag Co. back paper................................... **$275**

Courtesy of Early American History Auctions and History Store, earlyamerican.com

Souvenir pinback, 1902, text reads: "THE MOUNTAIN AND PLAIN FESTIVAL ASSOCIATION/OCTOBER 7-8, DENVER/1902/WORLD'S CHAMPIONSHIP/STICK TO YOUR SADDLE," Whitehead & Hoag Co. back paper, rare (one of three known to exist), 1-1/4" dia.......................... **$118**

Courtesy of Hake's Americana & Collectibles, hakes.com

Pinback, circa 1929-1934, real photograph of football player Red Grange (considered the first football superstar), likely issued while Grange played for the Chicago Bears, possibly unique, 1-1/4" dia. **$651**

Courtesy of Hake's Americana & Collectibles, hakes.com

Set of two rare fan club-issued buttons, c. 1964-1967, first button reads: "THE SHANGRI-LAS FAN CLUB," 3" dia., second button reads: "Mitch Ryder of The DETROIT WHEELS," 3-1/5" dia. **$118**

Courtesy of Hake's Americana & Collectibles, hakes.com

POKÉMON CARDS

SINCE 1995, POKÉMON has been a worldwide phenomenon loved by people of all ages, and Pokémon trading cards have been a huge part of that success.

Since the late 1990s, starting with Base Set, the Pokémon Trading Card Game (TCG) has continued printing new sets every year, with 78 expansion sets and counting and over 8,000 different cards. Children worldwide who ruthlessly collected Pokémon TCG cards may have been making an investment with these collectible critters.

TCG cards are in high demand and some can sell online for thousands, with one copy of the ultra rare Pikachu illustrator card valued at $100,000. Another one of these Pikachu cards, in mint condition, recently sold at Heritage Auctions for $54,970. Other valuable cards include a Japanese holographic Charizard worth $30,000, shadowless holographic cards like Blastoise worth $1,000 or more, and even common and uncommon shadowless cards like Charmander that sell for more than $50. Even many of the current TCG cards being produced can earn a quick $15.

When collecting, it is usually more exciting to obtain cards by opening sealed products. In the Pokémon TCG, there are usually four new sets released each year. The official Pokémon website (pokemon.com/us/), Bulbapedia (bulbapedia.bulbagarden.net), and PokéBeach (pokebeach.com) are three great sites for TCG news. With each new set released, there are theme decks, booster packs, booster boxes, and other items available for purchase.

The best way to collect Pokémon cards is to buy the cards individually. It is much more expensive, although a lot more fun, to open sealed products when collecting. If collecting sealed products is the preferred way, booster boxes are the best value, and it is much cheaper to collect new sets as soon as they are released. Usually within two to three years after official release date, prices for sealed products start to increase dramatically. However, beware that there are no guarantees with certain cards in packs. It could take several booster boxes to pull one specific card from a set.

If the goal is to complete sets and collect cards from individual card purchases, the opposite applies.

Charizard 4/102, Holo Rare, Base Set, 1999. .... **$75**

Basic Pokémon
Pikachu
40 HP
Mouse Pokémon. Length: 1' 4", Weight: 13 lbs.
Gnaw
10
Thunder Jolt Flip a coin. If tails, Pikachu does 10 damage to itself.
30
weakness
resistance
retreat cost
When several of these Pokémon gather, their electricity can cause lightning storms. LV. 12 #25
Illus. Mitsuhiro Arita ©1995, 96, 98 Nintendo, Creatures, GAMEFREAK. ©1999 Wizards. 58/102

Pikachu 58/102, Common, Base Set, 1999............ **$2**

When sets get older, they no longer can be used in the Pokémon TCG, so the demand for the cards diminish, making the cards decrease in value. Shortly after a set is rotated out of the TCG is when single cards should be purchased. Those who only play the TCG will be looking to sell those in-demand cards for new cards, therefore increasing the supply of cards for sale and dropping prices. After several years, cards start to increase in value again, usually very slowly, unless the card was extremely hard to pull or the Pokémon is popular.

When searching sites such as eBay, better deals are usually found when buying Pokémon lots, since bulk buying results in a better price per card. Most retail stores like Walmart and Target sell Pokémon cards, which are usually located near one of the checkout aisles in the front. Booster boxes are only sold online or in hobby shops, like comic book stores or card shops.

There are tons of sites online for buying Pokémon cards, both sealed products and singles. eBay is the best place to buy individual Pokémon cards, since most times the cards for sale are the cards in the pictures of the listing; for value, it is important that both the card's front and back are in good shape.

Other reliable sites that sell individual Pokémon cards are Troll and Toad, PokeOrder, Professor-Oak, Collector's Cache, and TCG Player. When buying Pokémon cards online, it is important that the condition is identified before purchasing. Most sites indicate the rarity, with the best-condition cards in near mint and the worst cards in used or played condition.

Some of the best online sites for buying sealed products are Troll and Toad, Collector's Cache, PokeOrder, Blowout Cards, Dave and Adam's Card World, and The Card Kid. Most sites have similar prices, so it is just a matter of finding a site that has the product in stock. It is important to note that packs can be weighed, so be weary of buying single booster packs online. Pack weighing means that booster packs are put on a scale, and packs that weigh less only have rare non-holo cards in them, never ultra rares, holo, or secret rare cards, so these packs are sold at a discount; the packs with good cards in them are opened and sold individually.

As far as any collecting hobby goes, resale is key to being able to continue purchasing new cards. There are many avenues to sell Pokémon cards, whether it is through eBay, which results in the highest prices for the seller, or selling to sites online that sell cards. There are profits to be made in Pokémon card collecting. As far as newly released sets go, it is best to buy booster boxes, or cases, which include six booster boxes of the same set, as this makes the booster packs much cheaper than if they were bought individually. Any good cards pulled, such as ultra rares or secret rares, can immediately be sold for a significant amount.

Prices of new cards are usually higher because of the demand for the cards in the TCG. Prices follow this pattern when a new set is released: First, right before the set is released, if any seller is able to obtain the cards early, the prices are high for all cards; right after the set is released, demand is still high, although the prices drop a little from pre-release prices, mainly due to a high supply of cards. About two weeks after the official set release date, almost all prices drop; then for the next year or two, whatever cards work best in the TCG greatly increase in price, and for the most part, stay high the whole time the set is used in the TCG.

So, if you are looking to sell, the best time to sell new cards is immediately when the set is released, or waiting a few weeks after the set is released and seeing what cards are best in the TCG. For older sets and cards, usually those no longer playable in the TCG, the cards on the whole aren't worth much, unless they are extremely rare. Usually it takes five years after a card is released to see an increase in value after it is no longer usable in the TCG.

For sellers, it is best to sell the cards at a fixed price, setting the price a little higher than the card is worth, and waiting for a buyer to come along. As a seller, it is worth buying large lots of cards, hoping that some valuable cards are in the lot and make up for the purchase price of it.

Another great way to make a profit on Pokémon cards is to keep sealed products. No matter the item, but especially booster boxes, it is a guarantee that the product will greatly increase in value in the coming years. Base Set booster boxes, even in unlimited print, cost well over $1,000 per box. While it makes zero sense as a collector to buy one to open, since all of the cards in the set can be purchased for less than $200, it makes for a great profit for sellers. So if card collecting isn't your goal, but making a profit is, only open brand new sets; do not open older sets — keep those products sealed and sell the products like this. Getting cards graded is also a good way to increase the value of cards and make a profit on them.

Pokémon card rarity is the easiest way to quickly determine if a card is worth something. There are three different card rarities: common, uncommon, and rare.

Common: For the most part, common cards are worth very little, no matter how old, and are almost always worth less than $.35.

Uncommon: Uncommon cards are $.45 or less.

Rare: Rare cards that are non-holo are worth $.75 or less. The only cards that have some value to them are rare cards that are holo, ultra rare, or secret rare. These types of rare cards are harder to pull in packs, with holo cards one in every three booster packs at best. The harder a card is to pull, the more likely it is a valuable card.

For more information on Pokémon cards, consult *Pokémon Cards: The Unofficial Ultimate Collector's Guide* by Ryan Majeske.

Jolteon 20/64, Non Holo, Jungle Set, 1999.... **$2.50**

Gyarados 7/130, Holo Rare, Base Set 2, 2000.....**$7**

Tyranitar 31/75, Non Holo, Neo Discovery, 2001..**$4**

Venusaur 18/110, Holo Rare, Legendary
Collection, 2002. ....**$20**

Flareon, 5/100, Holo Rare, EX Sandstorm, 2003..**$8**

Charmander 113/112, Secret Rare, EX FireRed & LeafGreen Set, 2004. ....**$8**

Ghetsis 101/116, Uncommon, Plasma Freeze Set, 2013. ....**$5**

Lysandre 104/106, Full Art Trainer, Flashfire Set, 2014..**$12**

Shaymin EX 77/108, Roaring Skies Set, 2015, one of seven EX cards in this set. $7

Glaceon EX 20/124, Ultra Rare, Fates Collide Set, 2016..$4

Ultra Ball 161/149, Sun & Moon Set, 2017, one of six Secret Rare Trainer cards in the set. $55

Regirock 91/92, Gold Star, EX Legend Maker, 2006..$90

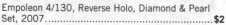

Empoleon 4/130, Reverse Holo, Diamond & Pearl
Set, 2007...$2

Vulpix SH6, Shiny Holo, Platinum Set, 2009. ....$12

Undaunted Set, 2010, Kyogre &
Groudon LEGEND 87/90 (top). $14
Kyogre & Groudon LEGEND 88/90
(bottom). $15

Raikou SL9, Shiny Legendary, Call of Legends Set, 2011..$20

Reshiram EX 22/99, Ultra Rare, Next Destinies Set, 2012...$4

POSTCARDS

IN 1913, DURING THE HEIGHT of postcard mania, the United States Post Office estimates that more than 900 million postcards were sent by mail. This is a staggering statistic when you consider that the population of the United States during the same year was less than 97.5 million people. That averages out to just more than nine postcards a year mailed for every person in the country. With hundreds of millions of postcards mailed each year during the Golden Age of Postcards (1907-1915), it is not surprising that antique postcards are so popular and still readily available to collectors.

In identifying and dating postcards, there are specific eras, defined by both style and dates; however, these dates do not account for the transition from one era to the next. It is important to remember that these "eras" refer to the printing on the back of the postcard, whereas postcards identified as Real Photo, Art Nouveau, and Art Deco are classified by the image on the front of the postcard. Real Photo, Art Nouveau, and Art Deco period postcards were produced in more than one of the classic postcard eras. For example, Art Nouveau-period postcards were produced during the Pioneer Era, Private Mailing Card Era, Undivided Back Era, and the Divided Back Era. Changes in style and production format overlap.

Postcard eras begin with the Pioneer Era (1889-1898), which has its roots in the Columbian Exposition in Chicago in May 1893 when vendors exhibited and sold picture postcards to the public. Although pre-stamped postcards had been introduced decades earlier, the Columbian Exposition was the first venue that introduced postcards to the masses.

Cards from the Pioneer Era are scarce and easily identifiable by certain indicators. Those most prized by collectors are known as the "Gruss aus" cards. These were German postcards from the Pioneer Era that usually had several views on the front of the card with the words "Gruss aus," which is German for "Greetings from."

It wasn't long before the American and British markets produced their own domestic multi-view cards with the words "Greetings from" on them. The back of American pioneer

Pioneer Era postcards have undivided backs. They may bear the words, "Souvenir Card" or "Mailing Card," and do not have the "Act of Congress" acknowledgment.

cards are not divided, often bear the words, "Souvenir Card" or "Mailing Card," and there is no "Act of Congress" acknowledgment. Government-printed postcards during this time required one-cent postage and have pre-printed stamps of Grant or Jefferson. Privately printed postcards required two cents of postage and used U.S. postage stamps. Many Pioneer Era postcards have multiple views on the front of the card along with the words, "Greetings From" or "Souvenir of." The back of the card was meant for the address only; any message had to be written on the front of the card.

The next era is the Private Mailing Card Era (1898-1901). As of May 19, 1898, private vendors were allowed to print and sell postcards. These cards bear the words, "Private Mailing Card," and the government notice "Authorized by Act of Congress May 19, 1898." Postcards still have undivided backs reserved for the address of the recipient; any sentiment or message was limited to the front of the card. Some postcards from this period have a blank white area on the front of the card below the image for a written message. Some cards bear an image on only a portion of the card with most of the front left for a message, and others have no place for a message, which is why many cards from this era have a message written on the image itself. Private Mailing Cards with messages written across the image are no longer considered inferior; they are scarce enough that those with messages written on the image are prized.

The Undivided Back Era (1901-1907) is the next milestone in the production of postcards. Although all postcards prior to this time have undivided backs, this is the first time the use of the words "Post Card" was permitted. On December 24, 1901, the government also allowed private printers to use a logo; the back of the card was still reserved for the address of the recipient.

Perhaps the most famous and easily recognizable logo to the postcard collector is the Tuck lion and unicorn logo, which was first used during this postcard era. The majority of postcards produced during this time were from Europe, especially Germany, which was well known for rich chromolithography. By this time, postcards were so popular it is estimated that production doubled every six months. It was during this era that postcards in series of two or more were first printed. Popular topics for series included: romance, fantasy, fashion, comedy, art, theatrical themes, and anthropomorphism, especially with cats, dogs, bears, fowl, and rabbits.

These "Gruss aus" postcards are German Pioneer Era cards that preceded the emergence of the American Pioneer Card; both have messages written on the front of the postcard. Gruss aus postcards are prized by collectors.

The Divided Back Era (1907-1915), also known as the Golden Age of Postcards, began on March 1, 1907, and for the first time in the short history of postcards, messages were permitted on the back of the card alongside the address.

It was during this Golden Age that the most vibrant, memorable, imaginative, and nostalgic images were produced. Companies in Germany printed many of these brightly colored images. Suddenly there were postcards for every holiday. There were postcards for New Years, Valentine's Day, St. Patrick's Day, Washington and Lincoln's birthdays, April Fool's Day, Fourth of July, Halloween, Thanksgiving, Christmas, birthdays, souvenir images, comic cards, and postcards to simply send well wishes. There were even postcards in Hebrew celebrating Jewish holidays and New Year's Day. Most of these cards, although printed in Germany, were in English; however, there were many greetings in German sent within the United States and to the United States.

One type of postcard that is rarely addressed is the puzzle postcard. These are a series of four to six postcards with each card being a portion of the image. Once all components in a series were received, they could be placed together like a picture puzzle to complete the entire image. These are difficult to encounter as they have usually been separated through the years.

The outbreak of World War I dealt a devastating blow to the postcard industry from which it never recovered. Most of the large postcard companies were based in Europe, and mostly in Germany. The Divided Back Era ended and the Golden Age of postcards yielded to the next era known as the White Border Era (1915-1930).

During the White Border Era, many Italian artists such as Umberto Brunelleschi, M. Montedoro, and Sofia Chiostri produced some of the most dazzling images in the Art Deco style — especially of women, but these are rarities. Many American companies attempted to satisfy the demand for postcards but the quality was not up to the standards of the chromolithographs from Germany. The stock was often insubstantial, even flimsy, the colors dull, and the subject matter mediocre; white borders economized on ink. The term White Border Era is loosely descriptive in the sense that a majority of postcards produced during this time were printed with a white border around the image. It is not an absolute, however, in that not every postcard with a white border is from this time period nor does every postcard from this time period have a white border. It is not unusual to find postcards from the Golden Era reprinted with a white border during the White Border Era; however, when comparing the quality, the difference is obvious at once.

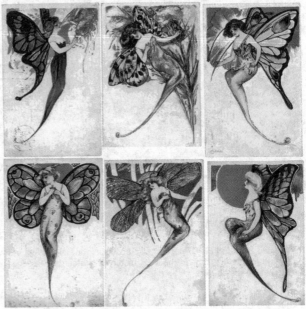

During the Golden Age of postcards (1907-1915), incredibly talented artists created some of the most enduring images of the 20th century, from realistic and adorable depictions of children to fantasy images such as fairies and gnomes. This rare set of six Butterfly Girls from the Detroit Publishing Company in 1907 was created by American artist Samuel L. Schmucker, who was famous for his exquisite depictions in the Art-Nouveau style. This complete set in good condition can sell from **$1,500 to $1,800.**

There are many books and price guides about antique and vintage postcards that include three more "eras" identified as Real Photo, Art Nouveau, and Art Deco (an abbreviation of the French "Arts Décoratifs"). I hesitate to include the last two as eras since they are actually styles of art and in terms of postcards the Art Nouveau and Art Deco styles overlap the postcard eras. Art Nouveau-style postcards existed during the Pioneer Era, Private Mailing Card Era, Undivided Back Era, and the Divided Back Era. Art Deco postcards existed during the Divided Back Era, White Border Era, Linen Era, and the early part of the Photochrome Era. Some postcard collectors, even experts, may disagree, but I'm holding fast.

Because the average "antiques dealer," flea market vendor, and garage sale merchant know little about postcards, it is a field of collectibles that is forever ripe and rife with little treasures at bargain prices. Even if you are a novice in the field of postcards, you will be able to start hunting tomorrow prepared with what you have just read and probably make some great finds. Most of my pioneer era and Gruss aus cards came from bargain boxes where they were relegated because they had writing on the front (I know, I know, you're shaking your head in profound disbelief).

If you do decide to collect postcards, I recommend you obtain an informative postcard book and study it — the reading will pay off — such as *Postcard Collector, Greetings From The Way We Were* by Barbara Andrews. Learn about condition, care, and rarities and have fun collecting.

— Dr. Anthony J. Cavo

Dr. Anthony J. Cavo *is an honors graduate of the Asheford Institute of Antiques and a graduate of Reisch College of Auctioneering. He has extensive experience in the field of buying and selling antiques and collectibles; at age 18, he became one of the youngest purchasers and consigners of antiques and art for a New York auction house. Dr. Cavo is an active dealer in the antiques and collectibles marketplace in the U.S. and abroad.*

Three in a series of embossed and textured postcards, alternately referred to as Cowgirl Cards, Annie Oakley Cards, and Cheyenne Series (the sender has written the name "Shyenne" [sic] at the top of one of the cards), 1906, S. Langsdorf & Co., New York, made in Germany, rider's clothing is silk velour and the rest of card is heavily embossed. These cards are in very good, age-appropriate, used condition, bright, crisp colors, some blunting at corners. Individually, these cards are valued at $14-$16; a set of three: **$60**

Courtesy of the Dr. Anthony Cavo Collection

Raphael Tuck and Sons Happy Childhood series No. 728, 1905, undivided back for address only, back of postcard reserved for the address only during this time period therefore the Raphael Tuck and Sons name along with the series title and hand-written sentiment are on the front of the card alongside the image. At one time, postcards with the message written in the image were shunned by dealers and collectors, but today they are prized; the handwritten message in the image denotes their early production date. Very good, used condition, slight blunting of corners, some edge wear, good coloration, 5-1/2" x 3-1/2"..........**$5**

Courtesy of the Dr. Anthony Cavo Collection

Silk embroidered postcard: From Your Soldier Boy silk embroidered butterfly with colors representing the flags of the Allied Powers: Serbia, Russia, France, the United Kingdom, Italy, Belgium, and the United States, silk in excellent condition, fine, bright colors. The card, made in Paris, is in very good used condition, slight discoloration of embossed white matting, 5-1/4" x 3-1/2"... **$15-$20**

Courtesy of the Dr. Anthony Cavo Collection

The R. M. S. Lusitania woven in silk Stevengraph postcard matted in embossed white card, 1908, printed in England by Thomas Stevens, in very good, used condition, slight soiling of embossed white matte, 5-1/2" x 3-1/2"..................**$250-$450**

Courtesy of the Dr. Anthony Cavo Collection

▶ Embossed postcard with silk velour textured dress, A Highball, 1907, Illustrated Postcard Company, New York and Leipzig, very good, used condition, slight blunting of corners, slight bend to lower left corner, cancellation ink top left, 5-1/2" x 3-1/2". **$10**

Courtesy of the Dr. Anthony Cavo Collection

▲ Ethnic-themed cards were quite popular during the early days of the postcard, such as these two Dutch-themed ones: "I vill cry mine eyes out ...," 1913, by S. Bergman, New York, very good, used condition, slight discoloring along the borders, 5-1/2" x 3-1/2"; and "If I had viskers ...," 1913, by S. Bergman, NY, in very good, used condition with slight blunting of corners, 5-1/2" x 3-1/2". "Used" describes a card that bears a hand-written message and or has been mailed and bears a canceled stamp. Each: **$4**

Courtesy of the Dr. Anthony Cavo Collection

Illustrated Postcard Company postcard of a bathing beauty, "Siesta," postmarked 1905, fair to good condition, light surface soiling, postmark in image, message on bottom, some corner blunting from album corner mounts, 3-1/2" x 5-1/2"... **$4**

Courtesy of the Dr. Anthony Cavo Collection

Raphael Tuck and Sons ASTI series 6295 Rosalind, 1906, by Italian artist Angelo Asti, in very good, used condition, 5-1/2" x 3-1/2" **$5**

Courtesy of the Dr. Anthony Cavo Collection

迎歓

Issued by the Department of Communications in commemoration of the Visit of the American Fleet, Oct. 1908.

Commemoratives have always been a desirable category of postcard collecting. This postcard commemorates the Great White Fleet of 16 American battleships that sailed around the world from December 1907 to February 1908. It was dubbed the Great White Fleet because the hulls of the ships were painted stark white. This postcard commemorates the visit of the fleet to Yokohama, Japan, in October 1908 and bears a photograph of Rear Admiral Charles Stillman Sperry. Unused, circa 1908, Tokyo Printing Company, very good to excellent condition, 3-1/2" x 5-5/8"...$50

Courtesy of the Dr. Anthony Cavo Collection

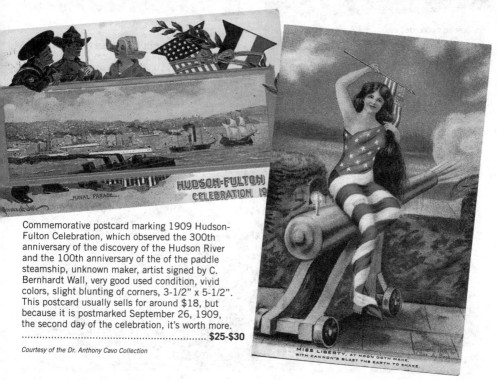

Commemorative postcard marking 1909 Hudson-Fulton Celebration, which observed the 300th anniversary of the discovery of the Hudson River and the 100th anniversary of the of the paddle steamship, unknown maker, artist signed by C. Bernhardt Wall, very good used condition, vivid colors, slight blunting of corners, 3-1/2" x 5-1/2". This postcard usually sells for around $18, but because it is postmarked September 26, 1909, the second day of the celebration, it's worth more.
.... $25-$30

Courtesy of the Dr. Anthony Cavo Collection

Patriotic postcard, one of a set of four, depicting "Miss Liberty," circa 1908, Photo-Color-Graph Company, New York, used, very good condition, bright colors, slight chipping at the corners, 3-1/2" x 5-1/2"...$8-$10

Courtesy of the Dr. Anthony Cavo Collection

Embossed postcard, circa 1912, depicting Santa Claus at the North Pole atop the world, artist signed by Ellen H. Clapsaddle, rare, printed in Germany by the International Art Publishing Company, very good used condition, sharp colors, minimal blunting of corners, 3-1/2" x 5-1/2". .... **$68-$80**

Courtesy of the Dr. Anthony Cavo Collection

Postcard of Santa Claus in a biplane, unusual depiction of St. Nick and utilizes the new wonder of flight, printed by the Fairman Company of Cincinnati, circa 1910, very good condition, minor surface soiling, slight blunting of corners, 3-1/2" x 5-1/2". **$30**

Courtesy of the Dr. Anthony Cavo Collection

Three Hamilton King artist-signed bathing beauty postcards: Asbury Park Girl, Newport Girl, and Long Branch Girl, copyright 1907, J. T. Wilcox, bright colors, light soiling, blunting at corners, all are 3-1/2" x 5-1/2", each:... **$27-$30**

Courtesy of the Dr. Anthony Cavo Collection

Vintage Halloween postcard, 1908, Illustrated Postcard Company, depicts a pumpkin scarecrow against a night sky, very good, used, condition, slight blunting of corners, 3-1/2" x 5-1/2"......... **$48**

"IF in the mirror your lover is seen You'll surely be happy on Hallowe'en!"

▲ Embossed Art Nouveau Halloween postcard, circa 1911, L. S. C. Company, depicts a young woman holding a pumpkin while staring at the face of her lover in a mirror on which an owl is perched, used, fair condition, album mounted creasing at all corners, slight soiling, discoloration, minimal fading, 3-1/2" x 5-1/2" ... **$36**

Courtesy of the Dr. Anthony Cavo Collection

◄ Easter postcard, German American Novelty Art Series No. 655, printed in Germany, circa 1906, depicts a hen selling colored eggs to rabbits, very good, used condition, colors bright, edges sharp, slight chipping, some blunting at corners, hand-written greeting on bottom, 3-1/2" x 5-1/2".
.... **$12-$14**

Courtesy of the Dr. Anthony Cavo Collection

Embossed postcard, postmarked 1907, Illustrated Post Card Company, depicts a railroad train "Limited Express," colors vivid, corners sharp, very good, used condition with an undivided back and message written on the image side at the bottom. The railroad theme is desirable to collectors, 3-1/2" x 5-1/2". $18

Courtesy of the Dr. Anthony Cavo Collection

Raphael Tuck and Sons Playful Bunnies Easter postcard series "Oilette," No. 1004, postmarked 1918, excellent used condition, 3-1/2" x 5-1/2". **$8**

Courtesy of the Dr. Anthony Cavo Collection

Raphael Tuck and Sons Zodiac Series of Valentine postcards, No. 128, depicting the signs of Aries and Virgo, artist-signed, used, very good, condition, bright colors, sharp corners, embossed margins, signed "DWIG," which is the early signature for Clare Victor Dwiggins, 3-1/2" x 5-1/2". The entire set is worth $380-$400, but individually, each is worth: .... **$30-$40**

Courtesy of the Dr. Anthony Cavo Collection

POSTWAR DESIGN

POSTWAR DESIGN, OR mid-century modern, describes mid-20th century developments in modern design, architecture, and urban development. It is a style that is now recognized by scholars and museums worldwide as a significant design movement. It is also the lone segment of the furniture market that is still seeing significant price increases and volume movement among dealers and auction houses in today's market. However, demand is not limited to furniture.

The period collectors now seek spans from 1945 through 1979. This includes posters, objets d'art, lamps, and even electronics. Naturally, a 34-year period will see a tremendous amount of change in taste and style, but it is just this very reason why the period appeals to so many people — particularly Millenials and other young buyers.

The period distinguishes itself from Modernism, which lasted from 1920 to 1945. After this period, mass-produced wares brought high-design into the home at an affordable cost. Made from cast aluminum to chrome to brightly colored plastics, the period embraced new technologies to create an array of consumer goods that are now in high demand on the secondary market.

According to Noel Riley in her book, *The Elements of Design*, the 1940s and 1950s were a period of transition between the austerity of the Second World War and its aftermath of rationing and shortages, and the youthful, exuberant design revolution of the 1960s. Impelled by the Modernist principles of functionalism, the contemporary aesthetic was defined by new materials and the development of technologies, as well as a spirit of optimism and confidence. It was a vigorous period in design, with bold shapes, bright colors, and practical solutions to the needs of daily life.

PLASTICS

A perfect example of these bold colors, new technologies, and practical design are popularly collected bowls made of melamine plastic, popular among American home makers through the 1940s, 50s, 60s, and 70s.

Aaronel DeRoy Gruber
(American, 1918-2011),
Small Equilibrial Wonder,
1969, plastic, signed Aaronel,
dated 1969 and numbered 2/5,
3-1/2" h. **$1,750**

Courtesy of Doyle New York, doyle.com

During the 1940s, new technologies made the production of plastic dinnerware possible and it subsequently became extremely popular in homes across America. According to JustCollecting.com, melamine, a thermo set plastic material, was used in many factories and in much dinnerware production by the late 1940s. American Cyanamid was one of the leading manufacturers and distributors of melamine powder to various plastics molders. They name-branded their version "Melmac." Melamine, and more specifically "Melmac," was marketed by American Cyanamid as a wonder plastic. These bowls, now collected under the term Texas ware, sell for as much as $50 each on auction sites such as eBay and commerce sites such as Etsy.com.

Paul Evans (American, 1931-1987) armchairs, circa 1970s, Paul Evans Studio, New Hope, Pa., pair in bronze, composite and upholstery, unmarked, 27" l x 25-1/2" w x 20" d..........**$33,750**

Courtesy of Rago Arts and Auction Center, ragoarts.com

CERAMICS

Post-war ceramics enjoyed the same explosion of color and style as artists tossed conventions out and ushered in a new era of elegant shapes and progressive patterns. The hourglass form was favored in the 1950s and this form is an excellent method to date ceramics from this period.

Although genre busting, the ceramics of the Postwar era strictly adhered to functionality, combining organic shapes with ease of use. This period saw the emergence of Danish studio potters who took influence from Japan and organic forms from nature to create distinctive and innovative soft shapes.

Artist Berndt Friberg's hand-thrown hare's fur vases (now valued at $600 and up) exemplify this approach, as do bell-form tall mid-century vintage lamps, dating from the 60s. These familiar lamps feature a smooth and textured ceramic body with drip glazed decoration in vivid hues. The stem and base are often wood.

TEXTILES

A bolt of circa 1949-50 Salvador Dali surreal art fabric recently sold for $3,750 at auction. Schiffer Prints commissioned an assortment of Modernist artists, architects, and industrial designers to create a Modern textile range. Designers included: Salvador Dali, Ray Eames, George Nelson, Bernard Rudofsky, Abel Sorenson, George Nelson, Irving Harper, Paul McCobb, and Edward J. Wormley.

Schiffer didn't alter or modify the patterns and did not impose a theme or color palette. The results were dramatic. "Unquestionably it is the most brilliant single collection of all modern prints introduced since the war," declared *The New York Times* on June 22, 1949, when Schiffer Prints introduced their Stimulus line at the Architectural League of New York.

Dali designed three Surrealist prints chosen by Schiffer for production in 1949: Seste Elenique, Afternoon Stones, and Sonata d'Ete. Later that year, Schiffer issued a second collection incorporating Dali's final two prints for them, Leaf Hands and Spring Rain.

The results set the tone for post-war draperies, dresses, shirts, pants, and nearly every other form of textile worn or seen through the period.

Charles Ormond Eames, Jr. (American, 1907–1978) and Bernice Alexandra "Ray" Kaiser Eames (American, 1912–1988), set of six low plywood chairs with metal frames, designed 1940, mfg. by Herman Miller, original labels, 26-1/4" h x 22" w x 25-1/4" d. **$1,534**

Courtesy of Eldred's Auctioneers & Appraisers, eldreds.com

Modernist armchair, circa 1970s, possible Italian, tufted leather, lace-up back, chrome frame, two quadrilateral legs joined by stretchers, unmarked, 30-1/4" h x 42-1/5" w x 28" d................. **$216**

Courtesy of Eldred's Auctioneers & Appraisers, eldreds.com

Mogens Lassen (Danish, 1901-1987), Mogens Lassen Stool, circa 1942, teak, carved saddle seat on tripod base, paper label on underside for "Manufacturer K. Thomsen Snedkermester Bredgade 36- Kbh. K. Telf. Pala: 2554," 20" h. **$330**

Courtesy of Eldred's Auctioneers & Appraisers, eldreds.com

George Nakashima (American, 1905-1990), stool and Wepman table, 1966/81, Nakashima Studio, New Hope, Pa., walnut, larger signed Berenson, smaller signed S.R., table: 17" l x 24" w x 13" d, stool: 13" l x 21-1/2" w x 15" d. **$5,625**

Courtesy of Rago Arts and Auction Center, ragoarts.com

William Hinn (Swedish, 20th Century) chest on chest, circa 1955, The Swedish Furniture Guild for Urban Furniture, walnut, 34" l x 44-1/2" w x 24" d. **$1,000**

Courtesy of Heritage Auctions, ha.com

▼ Charlotte Perriand (French, 1903-1999), Le Corbusier (French, 1887-1965), and Pierre Jeanneret (French, 1896-1967), LC1 Chair, designed 1928, mfg. by Cassina, red leather, steel, brass, 25-3/4" l x 23" w x 25" d. **$425**

Courtesy of Heritage Auctions, ha.com

▶ T.H. Robsjohn-Gibbings (British, 1905-1976) Widdicomb Mesa (coffee table), circa 1950s, Grand Rapids, MI, walnut, retaining manufacturer label and stenciled markings, 17" l x 73-1/2" w x 49" d. **$93,750**

Courtesy of Rago Arts and Auction Center, ragoarts.com

George Nakashima (American, 1905-1990), settee, 1965, Nakashima Studio, New Hope, Pa., walnut, upholstery, unmarked; provenance: Collection of Dr. Milton and Bryna Bronstein, Edison, NJ; 30-1/2" l x 59-3/4" w x 36" d. **$8,750**

Courtesy of Rago Arts and Auction Center, ragoarts.com

Frederick H. Rhead (English/American, 1880-1942), Arequipa, 1912, vase, squeezebag-decorated with stylized flowers, Fairfax, Ca., blue pot under tree mark/AREQUIPA CALIFORNIA/1912/506A; important (one of the best examples known to exist), 6-1/4" l x 5-1/2" w........**$93,750**

Courtesy of Rago Arts and Auction Center, ragoarts.com

Harry Bertoia (Italian/American, 1915 - 1978), Untitled sculpture (Bush), circa 1950s, Pennsylvania, patinated bronze, copper, unmarked, 16" l x 15" w..........................**$43,750**

Courtesy of Rago Arts and Auction Center, ragoarts.com

Rene Buthaud (French, 1886-1986), Untitled vase, glazed earthenware, depicting nude male figures, signed RB, 14" l x 10" w. **$11,250**

Courtesy of Rago Arts and Auction Center, ragoarts.com

Henning Koppel (Danish, 1917-1982), coffee and tea service, model 1017, circa 1952, mfg. the Georg Jensen Co., sterling silver, four-piece service, hand-raised sterling silver with guaiacum wood handles, no monogram (Koppel won his second Gold Medal at the Milan Triennale for this set design, subsequently granting him the prestigious Lunning Prize in 1953), 55.05 oz total weight.......**$12,800**

Courtesy of Alex Cooper Auctioneers, Inc., alexcooper.com

George Nelson (American, 1908-1986), tray, circa 1950, mfg. by Herman Miller, laminated walnut, 15-1/4" l x 15-1/4" w............. **$162**

Courtesy of Heritage Auctions, ha.com

Floor lamps, metal and ribbon, circa 1950s, pair, unknown designer and manufacturer, patinated, 56" h, 10" dia. **$1,125**

Courtesy of Doyle New York, doyle.com

Loet Vanderveen (Danish/American, 1921-2015), Stalking Cheetah, .999 silver, signed on underside with incised "Loet Vanderveen," silver purity ".999," edition designation "20/250," and "142 T," noted example of artist's application of patina and polished finishes, 14-1/4" l. **$3,690**

Courtesy of Bruneau & Co. Auctioneers, bruneauandco.com

Hans Hedberg (Swedish, 1917-2007), egg box with stand, circa 1960, crackle glazed earthenware, iron, 11-1/2" l. **$1,375**

Courtesy of Heritage Auctions, ha.com

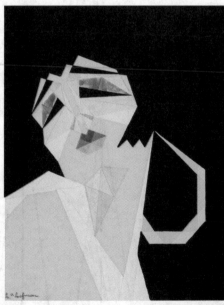

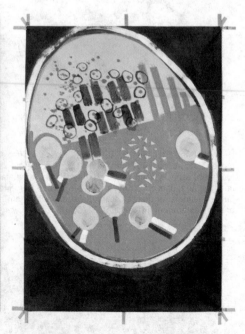

Hans O. Hofman (American, 1893-1973), "Woman at Night," gouache and graphite on paper laid to card, signed H.O. Hofman (II), 11-1/2" l x 9" w.. **$1,250**

Courtesy of Doyle New York, doyle.com

Noriko Yamamoto (Japanese, b. 1929), kite, circa 1960, tempera on rice paper over bamboo stretchers, signed Noriko, dated 62 and inscribed "Tokyo" on the reverse, estate of Murray and Carol Tinkelman, 36" l x 53" w................. **$750**

Courtesy of Doyle New York, doyle.com

QUILTS

EACH GENERATION MADE quilts, comforters, and coverlets, all intended to be used. Many were used into oblivion and rest in quilt heaven, but for myriad reasons, some have survived. Many of them remain because they were not used but stored, often forgotten, in trunks and linen cabinets.

A quilt is made up of three layers: the top, which can be a solid piece of fabric, appliquéd, pieced, or a combination; the back, which can be another solid piece of fabric or pieced; and the batting, the center layer, which can be cotton, wool, polyester, a blend of poly and cotton, or even silk. Many vintage quilts are batted with an old blanket or even another old, worn quilt.

The fabrics are usually cotton or wool or fine fancy fabrics like silk, velvet, satin, and

Baltimore Album colorful hand-sewn appliqué quilt. The famed Baltimore Album Quilt first appeared around 1840 as a style used by only quilt makers in the Baltimore, Maryland, area. This quilt features 20 individual blocks of uniquely designed and hand-sewn appliquéd patterns each by a different artisan. A significant block features a circle of stars design with four flags flying and embroidered dates 1776 and 1861, placing the making of this quilt at the later date. Above the date of 1861 is stenciled the name Rachel A. Weeks, the block's maker. Several others helped with this quilt and each block is attributed with the maker's name or initials: B.C.W., M.Z., A.M.H., C.J. T. Embroidered full names are Jane Demarest, and Maria Tice. A common practice by 1845 was to stencil your name on a quilt in ink. The names found stenciled are Caroline and Ellen Ackerman and J. M. Ruskirk, as well as Rachel A. Weeks. Each block is approximately 16-1/2" square with a swag motif border adding another 5-1/4". **$5,000**

Courtesy of Heritage Auctions, ha.com

taffeta. The layers of a true quilt are held together by the stitching — or quilting — that goes through all three layers and is usually worked in a design or pattern that enhances the piece overall.

Quilts made from a seemingly single solid piece of fabric are known as wholecloth quilts, or if they are white, as whitework quilts. Usually such quilts are constructed from two or more pieces of the same fabric joined to make up the necessary width. They are often quilted quite elaborately, and the seams virtually disappear within the decorative stitching. Most wholecloth quilts are solid-colored, but prints were also used. Whitework quilts were often made as bridal quilts and many were kept for "best," which means that they have survived in reasonable numbers.

Wholecloth quilts were among the earliest type of quilted bedcovers made in Britain, and the colonists brought examples with them according to inventory lists that exist from colonial times. American quiltmakers used the patterns early in the nation's history, and some were carried with settlers moving west across the Appalachians.

Appliqué quilts are made from shapes cut from fabric and applied, or appliquéd, to a background, usually solid-colored on vintage quilts, to make a design. Early appliqué quilts dating back to the 18th century were often worked in a technique called broderie perse, or Persian embroidery, in which printed motifs were cut from a piece of fabric, such as costly chintz, and applied to a plain, less-expensive background cloth.

Appliqué was popular in the 1800s, and there are thousands of examples, from exquisite, brightly colored Baltimore Album quilts made in and around Baltimore between circa 1840 and 1860, to elegant four-block quilts made later in the century. Many appliqué quilts are pictorial with floral designs the predominant motif. In the 20th century, appliqué again enjoyed an upswing, especially during the Colonial Revival period, and thousands were made from patterns or appliqué kits that were marketed and sold from 1900 through the 1950s.

Pieced or patchwork quilts are made by cutting fabric into shapes and sewing them together to make a larger piece of cloth. Patchwork became popular in the United States in the early 1800s. The patterns are usually geometric, and their effectiveness depends heavily on the contrast of not just the colors themselves, but of color value as well.

Colonial clothing was almost always made using cloth cut into squares or rectangles, but after the Revolutionary War, when fabric became more widely available, shaped garments were made, and these garments left scraps. Frugal housewives, especially among the westward-bound pioneers, began to use these cutoffs to put together blocks that could then be made into quilts. Patchwork quilts are by far the most numerous of all vintage-quilt categories, and the diversity of style, construction, and effect that can be found is a study all its own.

Dating a quilt is a tricky business unless the maker included the date on the finished item, and unfortunately for historians and collectors, few did. The value of a particular example is affected by its age, of course, and educating yourself about dating methods is invaluable. There are several aspects that can offer guidelines for establishing a date. These include fabrics, patterns, technique, borders, binding, batting, backing, quilting method, and colors and dyes.

In recent years, many significant quilt collections have appeared in the halls of museums around the world, enticing both quilters and practitioners of art appreciation. One of the most noted collections to become a national exhibition in 2014 was the Pilgrim/Roy Collection. The selection of quilts included in the "Quilts and Color" exhibition, presented by the Museum of Fine Arts in Boston, was a mix of materials and designs, represented in nearly 60 distinct 19th and 20th century quilts.

For more information on quilts, see *Warman's Vintage Quilts Identification and Price Guide* by Maggi McCormick Gordon.

Vintage appliqué quilt with flowers and swag
border, Lancaster, PA, 79" x 96". **$100**

Courtesy of William J. Jenack Auctioneers, jenack.com

Red hearts hand appliquéd over blue circles and
diamonds on white fabric, blocks are machine
stitched together, corner diamonds have machine
top stitching around the perimeters, hand quilted,
red fabric binding, 83-1/2" x 72". **$140**

Courtesy of Soulis Auctions, dirksoulisauctions.com

Solid red and green tulips on a white background,
hand appliquéd and quilted, embroidered details
on the tulips, appliquéd sashing, red inner border
and binding, white backing, 80" x 70". **$350**

Courtesy of Soulis Auctions, dirksoulisauctions.com

Vintage quilt, 20th century, repeating squares
with circular patched pattern, unmarked, 58" x
78". **$210**

Courtesy of Leland Little Auctions, lelandlittle.com

Mennonite Log Cabin quilt, Waterloo County Ontario, Canada, c. 1930, bold pattern using light and dark shades of blue, violet, and black cloth arranged in log cabin blocks forming alternating dark and light bands, 84" l, 69" w. **$800**

Courtesy of Skinner Auctioneers and Appraisers, skinnerinc.com

Mennonite quilt in shades of green, blue, and red wool, and with a bar border, the whole backed with polished black cotton, 84"x 68". **$225**

Courtesy of Auctions at Showplace, nyshowplace.com

Vintage hand-stitched petal quilt, quilt top with hand-stitched gold and dark blue petals, 95" x 85". **$70**

Courtesy of Ascendant auction Galleries, ascendantauctions.com

Vintage pieced quilt, ivory ground with pieced blue squares and all over quilting stitch, 74" x 96". **$460**

Courtesy of Leland Little Auctions, lelandlittle.com

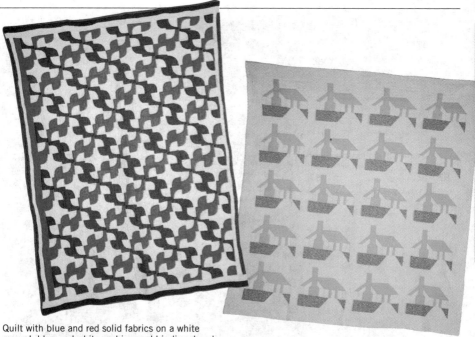

Quilt with blue and red solid fabrics on a white ground, blue and white sashing, red binding, hand quilted, 83" x 60-1/2"...................................**$180**

Courtesy of Soulis Auctions, dirksoulisauctions.com

Quilt of twenty house blocks in solid yellow and printed green fabric on a white background fabric, hand embroidered details, hand pieced and creatively hand quilted, white sashing and binding, 77-1/2" x 72-1/2". **$90**

Courtesy of Leland Little Auctions, lelandlittle.com

Vintage Lonestar patchwork quilt, 74" x 76"....**$130**

Conestoga Auction Company Division of Hess Auction Group, hessauctiongroup.com

Mennonite "Log Cabin" or "Barn Raising" quilt, made by Angela Martin, Hawksville, Waterloo County, Ontario, c. 1910, strips of cloth in various hues of black, blue, red, and purple forming a layered effect of alternating light and dark tones of log cabin blocks with a maroon chevron border, 81-1/2" l, 66" w. **$615**

Courtesy of Skinner auctioneers and Appraisers, skinnerinc.com

Mid-20th century patchwork
quilt with squares motif,
87" h x 74" w. **$75**

Courtesy of Roland New York, rolandantiques.com

Pieced wool and cotton Amish quilt, circa 1920, the
triangular patches on indigo ground within a light
red inner border heightened with leaf quilting and a
black outer border and inner panel heightened with
cube quilting, 45" x 76". **$4,000**

Courtesy of Sotheby's, sothebys.com

10 Things You Didn't Know About Manly Wartime Quilts

1 Little did the military agencies of the 18th and 19th centuries know that the durability and pliability of the felted wool military uniforms would also serve an important role in hand-stitched quilts. These historic and scarce quilts represent a fascinating story of quilt making during wartime.

2 A selection of 29 never-before-displayed antique wartime quilts hand-stitched by soldiers from Australia, Austria, England, and the United States, told the tale of 'stitching soldiers' through the exhibit "War and Pieced: The Annette Gero Collection of Quilts from Military Fabrics." The exhibition was displayed at the American Folk Art Museum in New York City and Quilt Study Center & Museum at the University of Lincoln-Nebraska.

3 Quilts featuring geometric patterns are unexpectedly common among the antique examples made by servicemen and prisoners of war that were created from 'found' materials, including military uniforms and blankets. However, the effort and elements involved in creating these quilts was not common, given the availability of materials in the locations 'stitching soldiers' were occupying, and the soldiers' inexperience.

4 Wartime quilt patterns were not limited to geometric shapes, as some of the earliest examples demonstrate. It's reported that the technique intarsia, referenced in quilting as well as woodworking, was utilized in quilts made during the Austro-Turkish, Prussian and Napoleonic wars. This also speaks to the real possibility that trained tailors serving as soldiers in wartime were behind the creation of advanced quilts, as the quilts appear to be assembled without a seam allowance.

5 One of the more rare quilts discovered depicts soldiers and musicians from a Prussian regiment, villagers, flowers, celestial symbols, a central star image, and even a character who appears to be sporting fashion of a court jester. The wool quilt bears signs of hand-applique and embroidery work and measures 55 x 43 inches. It dates to 1760-1780.

Soldier's mosaic quilt, artist unidentified, Crimea, India, or United Kingdom, c. 1850, wool with applied cording; inlaid and hand-corded, 93-1/2" x 75-1/2".

Courtesy of International Quilt Study Center & Museum, University of Nebraska-Lincoln

6 At one time, these wartime quilts made by soldiers were referred to as 'convalescent quilts.' This came from the idea that many of the quilts were the result of therapy techniques taught to soldiers who were recovering from war wounds.

7 Since 2003 and 2010, respectively, the national non-profit organizations Quilts of Valor and Quilts of Honor have been presenting veterans with quilts as tokens of appreciation for their sacrifices, strength, and steadfast commitment to serving, protecting and defending. If you would like to learn more about these groups and their mission, ways you can help, or to inquire about requesting a quilt for a serviceperson, visit quiltsofhonor.org. As of July 31, 2017, more than 164,631 and 4,000 have been awarded to veterans.

8 Dr. Annette Gero, owner of the quilts featured in the "War and Pieced" exhibit, has been a seasoned quilt historian for more than 30 years. The native Australian is recognized globally for her work researching and documenting Australian quilt history. She's also written books on the subject, including *The Fabric of Society — Australia's Quilt Heritage from Convict Times to 1960*.

9 Soldier quilts are also viewed by some as a form of trench art, which is defined as artistic objects created using remnants of wartime materials. Soldiers and prisoners of war are most often viewed as the artists of these items, but it also extends to civilians making objects with links to a conflict.

10 The opportunity to view antique quilts stitched by soldiers — during wartime — using castoff military uniforms and blankets is extraordinary for a few reasons. Largely it has to do with the fact that estimates put the number of soldier quilts in existence today at less than one hundred.

– Compiled by Antoinette Rahn

Sources: www.annettegero.com; www.mgnsw.org.au; www.iwm.org.uk

A vividly colored Pineapple pattern quilt in a variety of fabric types including wovens, brocade, velvet and velveteen, blocks feature red centers and corners, all on a black background fabric, hand pieced and tied, gray binding, light blue backing, 85" x 66-1/2"................................. **$110**

Courtesy of Soulis Auctions, dirksoulisauctions.com

Quilt with yellow field with star pattern, 20th century, not signed, 63" x 73"........................ **$170**

Courtesy of Leland Little Auctions, lelandlittle.com

Polychrome fabrics on a sprigged blue ground, blue sashing, striped ticking binding and backing, high loft, hand quilted, 74" x 69".................... **$130**

Courtesy of Soulis Auctions, dirksoulisauctions.com

RECORDS

BEFORE YOU CAN determine a record's worth, you need to grade it. When visually grading records, use a direct light, such as a 100-watt desk lamp, to clearly show all defects. If you're dealing with a record that looks worse than it sounds, play grade it. You also need to assess the condition of each sleeve, cover, label, and insert. Think like the buyer as you set your grades. Records and covers always seem to look better when you're grading them to sell to someone else than when you're on the other side of the table, inspecting a record for purchase. If in doubt, go with the lower grade. And, if you have a still sealed record, subject it to as many of these same grading standards as you can without breaking the seal.

GOLDMINE GRADING

MINT (M): Absolutely perfect. Mint never should be used as a grade unless more than one person agrees the item meets the criteria; few dealers or collectors use this term. There is no rule for calculating mint value; that is best negotiated between buyer and seller.
- Overall Appearance: Looks as if it just came off the manufacturing line.
- Record: Glossy, unmarred surface.
- Labels: Perfectly placed and free of writing, stickers, and spindle marks.
- Cover/Sleeve: Perfectly crisp and clean. Free of stains, discoloration, stickers, ring wear, dinged corners, sleeve splits, or writing.

NEAR MINT (NM) OR MINT MINUS (M-): Most dealers and collectors use NM/M- as their highest grade, implying that no record or sleeve is ever truly perfect. It's estimated that no more than 2% to 4% of all records remaining from the 1950s and 1960s truly meet near-mint standards.
- Overall Appearance: Looks as if it were opened for the first time. Includes all original pieces, including inner sleeve, lyric sheets, inserts, cover, and record.
- Record: Shiny surface is free of visible defects and surface noise at playback. Records can retain NM condition after many plays provided the record has been stored, used, and handled carefully.
- Labels: Properly pressed and centered on the record. Free of markings.
- Cover/Sleeve: Free of creases, ring wear, cutout markings, and seam splits. Picture sleeves look as if no record was ever housed inside. Hint: If you remove a 45 from its picture sleeve and store it separately, you will reduce the potential for damage to the sleeve.

VERY GOOD PLUS (VG+) OR EXCELLENT (EX+): Minor condition issues keep these records from a NM grade. Most collectors who want to play their records will be happy with VG+ records.
- Overall Appearance: Shows slight signs of wear.
- Record: May have slight warping, scuffs or scratches, but none that affects the sound. Expect minor signs of handling, such as marks around the center hole, light ring wear, or discoloration.
- Labels: Free of writing, stickers, or major blemishes.
- Cover/Sleeve: Outer cover may have a cutout mark. Both covers and picture sleeves may have slight creasing, minor seam wear or a split less than 1" long along the bottom.

VERY GOOD (VG): VG records have more obvious flaws than records in better condition, but still offer a fine listening experience for the price.

- Overall Appearance: Shows signs of wear and handling, including visible groove wear, audible scratches and surface noise, ring wear, and seam splits.
- Record: Record lacks its original glossy finish and may show groove wear and scratches deep enough to feel with a fingernail. Expect some surface noise and audible scratches (especially during a song's introduction and ending), but not enough to overpower the music.
- Labels: May have minor writing, tape, or a sticker.
- Cover/Sleeve: Shows obvious signs of handling and wear, including dull or discolored images; ring wear; seam splits on one or more sides; writing or a price tag; bent corners; stains; or other problems. If the record has more than two of these problems, reduce its grade.

VERY GOOD MINUS (VG–), GOOD PLUS (G+) OR GOOD (G): A true G to VG- record still plays through without skipping, so it can serve as filler until something better comes along; you can always upgrade later. At most, these records sell for 10% to 15% of the near mint value.

- Overall Appearance: Shows considerable signs of handling, including visible groove wear, ring wear, seam splits, and damaged labels or covers.
- Record: The record plays through without skipping, but the surface sheen is almost gone, and the groove wear and surface noise is significant.
- Labels: Worn. Expect stains, heavy writing, and/ or obvious damage from attempts to remove tape or stickers.
- Cover/Sleeve: Ring wear to the point of distraction; dinged and dog-eared edges; obvious seam splits; and heavy writing (such as radio station call letters or an owner's name).

Baseball The First 100 Years vinyl record, 1969, narrated by Curt Gowdy and James Stewart, lot also includes a Terry Cashman record titled Willie, Mickey, and The Duke. **$46**

Courtesy of Heritage Auctions, ha.com

FAIR (F) OR POOR (P): Only outrageously rare items ever sell for more than a few cents in this condition, if they sell at all. More likely, F or P records and covers will end up in the trash or be used to create clocks, journals, purses, jewelry, bowls, coasters, or other art.

- Overall Appearance: Beat, trashed, and dull. Records may lack sleeves or covers.
- Record: Vinyl may be cracked, scratched, and/or warped to the point it skips.
- Labels: Expect stains, tears, soiling, marks, and damage, if the label is even there.
- Cover/Sleeve: Heavily damaged or absent.

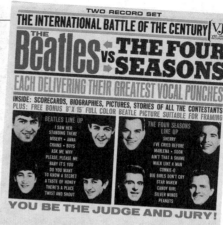

Bon Jovi, "You Give Love A Bad Name" 12-inch
33rpm single, Mercury 434, VG+. **$50**

Courtesy of a private seller, eBay.com

The Beatles Vs. The Four Seasons sealed mono
double LP (Vee-Jay VJ DX 30, 1964), two-record
set comprised of Introducing The Beatles and
Golden Hits of The Four Seasons. That it wasn't a
big seller in 1964 (peaked at #142 on Billboard's
Top Pop Albums chart) makes it all the more
collectible now, plus being still factory-sealed
makes it an incredible rarity, condition: EX 7/
MT 10, from the Stan Panenka Beatles Vinyl
Collection. **$1,750**

Courtesy of Heritage Auctions, ha.com

David Bowie "Starman" 7" Record Store Day
2012 picture disc, mint condition. **$291**

Courtesy of a private seller, eBay.com

James Bond original movie soundtrack, On Her
Majesty's Secret Service, (United Artists, 1970),
vinyl unrestored record with bright color and clean
overall appearance, Very Fine-, 12-1/2" x 12-
1/2". **$20**

Courtesy of Heritage Auctions, ha.com

Prince, "Little Red Corvette," 45rpm picture disc,
special limited edition, New condition. **$300**

Courtesy of a private seller, eBay.com

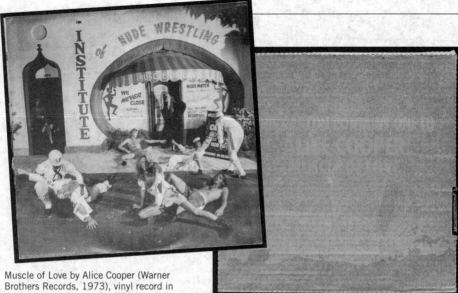

Muscle of Love by Alice Cooper (Warner Brothers Records, 1973), vinyl record in original packaging, packaging unique in that it forgoes the usual record jacket, the original LP was packaged with a shallow cardboard carton, with an intentionally printed "stain," inner sleeve shows the band as sailors out for a good time, and as an extra bonus the LP included a paper "book cover" that could be folded and used as a book jacket, Very Fine-, 12-1/2" x 12-1/2". **$23**

Courtesy of Heritage Auctions, ha.com

The Magical Music of Disney vinyl record box set (Ovation, 1978), four-album set featuring 50 years of music from Disney films, including instrumentals from early cartoon shorts, albums are housed in a slipcase cover, long out of print, Fine condition. **$31**

Courtesy of Heritage Auctions, ha.com

Robert Crumb "Ducks Yas Yas"/"Beautiful Missouri Waltz" and record with sleeve (Good Tone Records, 1972), first record by cartoonist Robert Crumb (as "Good Tone Banjo Boys" on side A, "Armstrong's Pasadenians" on side B, with Robert Armstrong), produced as a 78 RPM with "hippie"-style graphics for the front of the sleeve. These were originally sold through the mail and in head shops, next to the underground comix racks, sleeve is in Fine condition, vinyl record is a bit dusty, but appears Near Mint. **$74**

Courtesy of Heritage Auctions, ha.com

Grandmaster Flash & The Furious Five signed album *The Message*, 1982, inscribed to Rick James, signed by all seven original members of the group, each signature includes a note to mentor Rick James, an amazing album signed by the legendary hip-hop crew with one of the rarest signatures in Keef Cowboy, who passed in 1989, full LOA from PSA/DNA. **$960**

Courtesy of Heritage Auctions, ha.com

Dire Straits, *Communique*, Warner HS 3330 LP vinyl record, original shrink wrap, NM condition. **$14.95**

Courtesy of a private seller, eBay.com

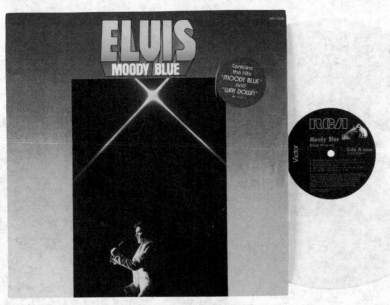

Elvis Presley, *Moody Blue*, white vinyl stereo LP (RCA AFL1-2428, 1977), final studio album released before Elvis passed away, any colored vinyl version aside from the black or blue was produced in incredibly limited numbers, and were intended for RCA Records in-house use only. Condition: NM 8 (sleeve)/ EX 7 (disc)..**$937**

Courtesy of Heritage Auctions, ha.com

Pink Floyd, *Animals*, rare pink vinyl/sleeve stereo LP (France - Harvest 2C 068-98434, 1977), there are two versions of this incredibly collectible pink vinyl version of Pink Floyd's 1977 masterpiece: pink vinyl with the standard jacket, and then the version offered here, which is ultra rare. It consists of the pink vinyl record with labels showing photos of animals, a plain pink inner sleeve, plain pink outer sleeve, and an 8-1/2" x 11" sheet of paper printed with the album's title, tracklist, songwriting credits, etc. The matrix/runout numbers are as follows: side 1 – "Pelle" (etched), "M6 315868 1 4 98434 A 21 B" (stamped, minus the "4," which is etched)/ side 2 – "Pelle" (etched), "M6 315805 1 98434 B 21 B" (stamped). Inner sleeve Excellent, credits list Fine. Condition: NM 8 (sleeve - handling wear, minor dent at the bottom-right corner, light red staining at the left side of the front, and fading to the edges)/MT 9 (disc)..**$275**

Courtesy of Heritage Auctions, ha.com

SCIENCE AND TECHNOLOGY

CASUAL SHOPPERS AND a growing number of established collections returning to market are just a couple of the reasons why vintage science and technology is a growing segment of the hobby. Much like the objects themselves, collectors' passion for vintage technology can be diverse and intricate. And unlike some categories, vintage tech is still in the early stages of developing strong demand, leaving lots of fresh-to-market discoveries for the historic-minded tinkerer.

Retired software engineer Bob Patton started collecting handheld calculators roughly 25 years ago and has 350 unique models in his collection, "but 569 have passed through my hands." He offered highlights from his collection priced from $10 to as much as $100. He sees the interest as rooted in a simpler time: "Any obsolete technology is just nostalgia and a curiosity in old technology," he said. "You can still find things that are valuable, you just need persistence and to look at garage sales, junk stalls, and antiques shops."

Science and technology is one of the broadest of all collecting categories and is generally thought to include fossils, fine minerals, medical and navigational devices, globes, and

This rare pair of Vincenzo Coronelli Italian terrestrial and celestial 18-1/2-inch globes on stands was the top lot at Bonhams' October 2017 auction, "Important Instruments of Science & Technology," and sold for $207,681. The terrestrial globe has two sets of twelve copper engraved half gores and two polar calottes, the sphere mounted in brass meridian with graduated scales, octagonal horizon ring and raised on five turned columns, the horizon applied with colored calendar, zodiac and degree scales; the celestial sphere mounted within brass meridian and stand to match the terrestrial globe, the sphere applied with two sets of copper-engraved half gores and two polar calottes. Coronelli was a Franciscan friar, cartographer, publisher, and encyclopedist known for globes and atlases, and wrote more than 100 works of terrestrial and celestial cosmography in Latin, French, and Italian.

Courtesy of Bonhams, bonhams.com

VISIT WWW.ANTIQUETRADER.COM

WWW.FACEBOOK.COM/ANTIQUETRADER

The Columbus Letter, or in its full title, De Insulis nuper in mari Indico repertis, is a book by Christopher Columbus, being details of his westward voyage across the Atlantic and the discovery of America, and sold for $751,500 at Bonhams in September 2017. It was published in the very infancy of book publishing, just 50 years after German Johannes Gutenberg introduced the printing press into Europe and became one of the first "best sellers" in history, though few original copies remain. Three illustrations from it, published in Basel in 1494, are, from left: Columbus's galleon, Oceanica Classis, in full sail, Columbus landing in a small boat, from a galleon in the foreground, on the island of "Insula Hyspana," and the first map depicting a part of America with Columbus's ships among the West Indian islands of Fernanda, Hyspana, Ysabella, Saluatorie, and Conceptionis Maria.

Courtesy of Bonhams, bonhams.com

more. As it finds a new generation of collectors — one well-versed in technology from the beginning — the field is inclusive of artworks, computers, portable computing, documents and manuscripts, and oddities. Collections are limited only by budget and imagination. Early specialization based on passion helps the collector avoid fakes, new creations, and inflated prices.

The public's fervent fascination and curiosity with the scientific and technological mind seems especially boundless for pioneers such as Galileo Galilei, Albert Einstein, and Leonardo da Vinci. Visitors flock to exhibits featuring da Vinci's *Codex Leicester*, the most famous of the inventor's 30 surviving journals. Bill Gates, the founder of Microsoft and one of the world's richest individuals, purchased the *Codex* from Christie's for $30 million in 1994 and has placed the book on continual display around the world, most recently in the United States.

Items of science's rock star, Einstein, especially personally written letters and documents, have a devoted collecting base. In 2017, Christie's auctioned five correspondences sent by him to his lifelong friend, Michele Besso, that sold for whopping prices. These correspondences not only cover their shared passion for physics — Besso was his only acknowledged collaborator on the groundbreaking theory of Special Relativity — but all aspects of life. An autographed letter dated December 1916 in which Einstein discusses the cosmological constant, a concept equal to the energy density of the vacuum of space, sold for $377,635; an autographed four-page letter about special and general relativity dated January 3, 1916 sold for $125,000; a letter dated October 31, 1916 acknowledging the first flush of acceptance of the general theory of relativity sold for $136,941; an autographed letter dated October 30, 1949 that contains one of his famous quotes, "I have defended the good Lord against the insinuation that he plays a continual game of dice," sold for $137,500; and an autograph postcard dated December 21, 1915 that was written shortly after Einstein's landmark presentation of four papers on the General Theory of Relativity to the Prussian Academy of Sciences in November 1915 sold for $150,000.

In 2017, Christies also sold a 1976 Apple I computer, one of only six known, for $355,000.

Bonhams also auctioned important items in 2017 including *De Insulis nuper in mari Indico repertis* by Christopher Columbus, detailing his westward voyage across the Atlantic and the discovery of America, for $751,500; a rare pair of Vincenzo Coronelli terrestrial and celestial globes on stands for $207,681; three important works by German theorist Albrecht Dürer for $175,000; and an archive of designs by Marc Brunel for the Thames Tunnel, one of the great achievements of the heroic age of engineering, for $263,251.

Sotheby's inaugural History of Science & Technology auction in December 2017 racked up $1,462,375 in sales and included books, manuscripts, scientific and technological instruments and other artifacts, spanning from the 16th to 20th centuries in categories ranging from physics, mathematics, cryptography and computing, to medicine, astronomy and space exploration. The top lot, which sold for $435,000, was an Enigma M4 fully operational four-rotor Kriegsmarine Enigma cipher machine, Berlin-Wilmersdorf, Germany, Heim Und Rinke, from 1944. The rarest and most desirable of all enigmas, the M4 was one of the hardest to decrypt and very few survived the war.

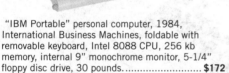

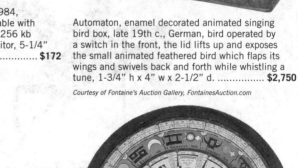

"IBM Portable" personal computer, 1984, International Business Machines, foldable with removable keyboard, Intel 8088 CPU, 256 kb memory, internal 9" monochrome monitor, 5-1/4" floppy disc drive, 30 pounds. **$172**

Courtesy of Auction Team Breker, breker.com

Automaton, enamel decorated animated singing bird box, late 19th c., German, bird operated by a switch in the front, the lid lifts up and exposes the small animated feathered bird which flaps its wings and swivels back and forth while whistling a tune, 1-3/4" h x 4" w x 2-1/2" d. **$2,750**

Courtesy of Fontaine's Auction Gallery, FontainesAuction.com

Terrestrial globe on mahogany stand, first half 19th c., mfg. by Smith & Son (London), 7-1/2" h. **$850**

Courtesy of Nye & Company Auctioneers, nyeandcompany.com

Perpetual calendar, c. 1900, "Le Chronoscope de Max Walter France," astrological for years 1876-2043, four rotating lithographed discs: zodiacal signs, years of birth, years of life, zodiacal houses, 21-1/4"dia. **$492**

Courtesy of Auction Team Breker, breker.com

Didactic model, c. 1930, French, set of 31 examples of mushroom specimens, designated as edible, poisonous or fatal, cast from nature in rubber, each labeled with its botanical name, each on bases, tallest: 7-1/2" h. **$7,500**

Courtesy of Rago Arts & Auction Center, ragoarts.com

▶ Horse and rider artist model, c. 19th c., France, walnut, supported by iron rod on wood base, 23" h....................**$11,250**

Courtesy of Rago Arts & Auction Center, ragoarts.com

Set of four staircase architectural models, 20th c., various woods, measurements vary: 29" h x 12" w, 13" h x 30" w, 11-1/4" h x 7-1/2" w, 29" h x 25" w...**$8,125**

Courtesy of Rago Arts & Auction Center, ragoarts.com

Nicolas Bion Butterfield Navigational Pocket Dial, circa 1685-1715, Paris, France, silvered, marks: N Bion A Paris, pocket dial having compass, latitudinal delineations, and pop-up gnomon with avian motif, scales for 55°, 50°, 45° and 40°, compass offset 17° West of North to allow for magnetic variation, cardinal and quadrantal point delineations, compass housed behind glass in well, reverse side of the dial-plate engraved with a table of latitudes of prominent cities, rare, 1-1/8" h x 2-1/4" w x 2-1/2" d... **$1,875**

Courtesy Heritage Auctions, ha.com

Cigarette lighter, c. 1920, electric, maker unknown, 220 V, wood handle with cable and push button. **$123**

Courtesy of Auction Team Breker, breker.com

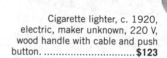

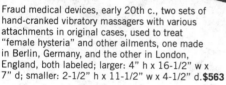

Fraud medical devices, early 20th c., two sets of hand-cranked vibratory massagers with various attachments in original cases, used to treat "female hysteria" and other ailments, one made in Berlin, Germany, and the other in London, England, both labeled; larger: 4" h x 16-1/2" w x 7" d; smaller: 2-1/2" h x 11-1/2" w x 4-1/2" d. **$563**

Courtesy of Rago Arts & Auction Center, ragoarts.com

▲ Lunar globe, 1961, Moscow, scale 1:13.600.000, dated Aug. 19, 1961, 12 green and cream-printed gores, labeled in Cyrillic script, named regions, craters and mountains, the then unexplored dark side of the moon without markings, Bakelite base, 14-3/4" h. **$923**

Courtesy of Auction Team Breker, breker.com

◀ Nikola Tesla's coil demonstration model, c. 1915, "Elektro Vulkan, Kromeriz" label, circular wood base, inner coil on porcelain isolator, outer coil on three glass columns, 15-3/4" h x 10-1/2" w. **$1,230**

Courtesy of Auction Team Breker, breker.com

Scale production model of Prudhoe Natural Gas drill site, late 20th c., the largest oil field in North America, 25-1/2" h x 60-1/4" w x 28-3/8" d. .. **$375**

Courtesy of Heritage Auctions, ha.com

▶ Octant, Hadley's Reflection Quadrant, circa 18th c., used in astronomy and navigation, mahogany frame, boxwood graduated arc (90-degrees), 26" index arm. **$675**

Courtesy of Auction Team Breker, breker.com

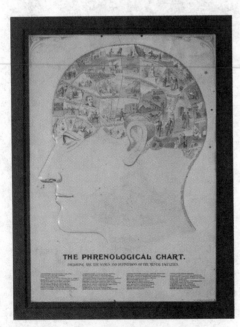

Phrenological chart, 1908, American, chart mfg. by Fowler and Wells Co., New York, painted tin, depicting the tenets of phrenology - the study of personality traits by examining the shape of, and bumps on, the head, 19" h x 14" w. **$3,125**

Courtesy of Rago Arts & Auction Center, ragoarts.com

Demonstration model, c. 1915, electro-magnetic motor with rotating Geissler Tube, 9-7/8" h, tube: 10-1/5" l. **$1,100**

Courtesy of Auction Team Breker, breker.com

Table organ, c. 1898, German, "Kalliston-Pankalon," mfg. by Ernst Erich Liebmann, crank-driven table organ, 42 notes, 36 double reeds including three contrabass reeds, two bell-strikers and four drum-beaters, with 10 metal music sheets, rare. **$17,200**

Courtesy of Auction Team Breker, breker.com

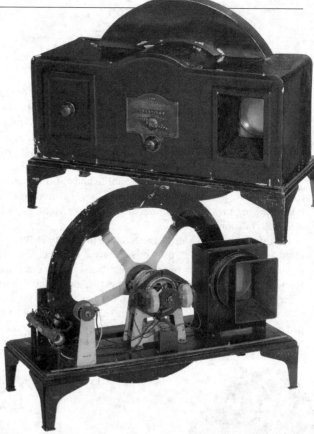

First commercially produced television set, 1928, mfg. by Plessey Co. for Baird Television Ltd., John Logie Baird (1888-1946), screen with approx. 4" h x 3" w, Mervyn mica tube, mechanism marked "Televisor" and stamped "J.L. Baird," brown-painted aluminum case with period Bakelite controls, scarce-less than 1,000 sets produced, 21" h x 27" w x 12" d. **$18,462**

Courtesy of Auction Team Breker, breker.com

◀ Shock machine, 19th c., France, "Le Cochon," mfg. by Maurice & Molle, Paris, embossed and painted zinc, figural pig, coin slot, two brass handles, turning the right handle while holding the left delivers mild electric shock to player, longer he can hold on, the greater his shock will be, until pig's eyes light up and a bell rings to signal his resistance, rare, 29" h. ...**$19,693**

Courtesy of Auction Team Breker, breker.com

▲ "Darling" typewheel pocket and desk typewriter (index) machine, 1910, American, mfg. Sullivan & Co., Berlin, with inking roll, 54 capital letters, desk clamp, original pouch, serial no. 3231, also marketed as "Trebla" and "Ha-Jo-Ma" for foreign markets.**$8,615**

Courtesy of Auction Team Breker, breker.com

SPORTS

THERE ARE COLLECTIBLE items representing nearly every sport, but baseball memorabilia is probably the most well-known segment. The "national pastime" has millions of fans, with enthusiastic collectors seeking out items associated with players such as Babe Ruth, Lou Gehrig, and others who became legends in their own lifetimes. Although baseball cards, issued as advertising premiums for bubble gum and other products, seem to dominate the field, there are numerous other items available, including game-worn jerseys and uniforms.

High-end sports cards and memorabilia had another banner year in 2017, as the market remains strong for the best of the best and several items sold for more than $2 million; 2018 is heading in that same direction, after a Mickey Mantle baseball card sold for a record of almost $3 million.

The mint-condition Mantle card, one of just six 1952 Topps Mantle cards that have been rated a "Mint 9" on a scale of 10 by Professional Sports Authenticator, sold at Heritage Auctions for $2.8 million in April 2018. That is the record price ever paid at auction for a post-World War II card and the second highest for any baseball card. The top record for that still belongs to a 1909 T206 Honus Wagner card, which sold for $3.1 million for in 2016.

Several other pieces of memorabilia sold for more than $2 million in 2017, including two prized Babe Ruth items owned by actor Charlie Sheen. At the first Lelands.com Invitational Auction in June 2017, the 1919 contract of Ruth's sale from the Red Sox to the Yankees went

Babe Ruth's 1927 World Series ring and the 1919 contract of Ruth's sale from the Boston Red Sox to the New York Yankees sold at auction for a combined bid of more than $4 million.

Courtesy of Lelands Auctions, lelands.com

for $2,303,320, while Ruth's 1927 World Series ring had a winning bid of $2,093,927. Both started with bids of $100,000.

"These record-breaking prices show once again that Babe Ruth dominates the baseball auction world the same way he did the game," said Josh Evans, Lelands.com founder and chairman.

The five-page contract is the Yankees' copy that Barry Halper once purchased from former owner Jacob Ruppert's estate. That Ruppert copy was sold to Sheen in 2005 and hadn't changed hands until 2017. There were three copies of the Ruth contract. The Red Sox copy was sold for $996,000 to a Yankees fan during an auction at Sotheby's in 2005. The American League copy has never surfaced, according to Lelands.

Other valuable pieces of sports memorabilia that sold at auction in 2017 include a Jackie Robinson 1947 game-worn jersey that sold for $2.05 million via Heritage Auctions, a 1937 Lou Gehrig game-worn pinstripe jersey for $870,000 via Heritage, a 1955 Sandy Koufax Brooklyn Dodgers rookie jersey for $667,189 via Lelands , a T206 Honus Wagner PSA 1 (J. Ross Greene Collection) for $609,294 via SCP, a 1916 Babe Ruth M101-4 Rookie Card PSA 7 for $600,000 via Robert Edward Auctions, another T206 Honus Wagner card, PSA 2, for $600,000 via Memory Lane, a 1947 Jackie Robinson rookie year cap, used to fend off racially motivated beanballs, for $590,994 via Lelands, a 1916 Babe Ruth M101-5 rookie card for $552,000 via Heritage Auctions, a 1948 Bowman Baseball Partial Wax Box for $514,746 via Mile High Card Co., and a 1968 Mickey Mantle autographed game-worn road jersey for $486,000 via Heritage.

Sports collectibles are more accessible than ever before because of online auctions and several auction houses that dedicate themselves to that segment of the hobby. Provenance is extremely important when investing in high-ticket sports collectibles. Being able to know the history of the object may greatly enhance the value, with a premium paid for items secured from the player or directly from their estate.

Circa 1938 Lou Gehrig original news photograph, PSA/DNA Type 2, a 1938 New York World's Fair patch is affixed on Gehrig's sleeve, two "World Wide Photos" rubber stamps are shown on back along with a detached caption, 7" x 9"............ **$576**

Courtesy of Heritage Auctions, ha.com

A 1948 Leaf Satchel Paige #8 PSA NM 7 rookie card. The '48 Leaf Paige is a short-print that is famous for being among the most difficult entries, accounting for this abridged census is the stunted availability and the popularity that Paige holds in the collecting community............................**$84,000**

Courtesy of Heritage Auctions, ha.com

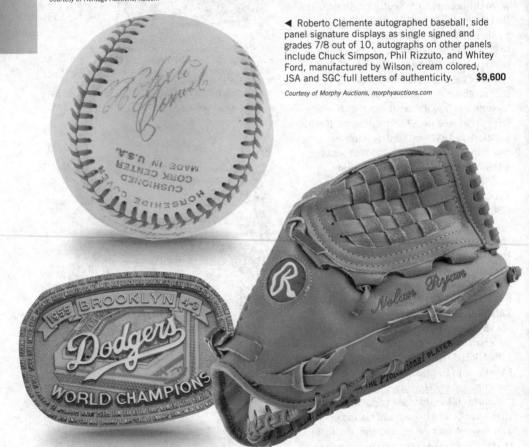

Detroit Tigers American League Champions scroll pennant, 1940, yellow graphics remain uncracked and tassels are still in-place, EX/MT, about 29" l. **$360**

Courtesy of Heritage Auctions, ha.com

◀ Roberto Clemente autographed baseball, side panel signature displays as single signed and grades 7/8 out of 10, autographs on other panels include Chuck Simpson, Phil Rizzuto, and Whitey Ford, manufactured by Wilson, cream colored, JSA and SGC full letters of authenticity. **$9,600**

Courtesy of Morphy Auctions, morphyauctions.com

Brooklyn Dodgers belt buckle by Josten's, 1955, features bird's eye view of Ebbets at center and the names of every World Championship roster member ringing perimeter, numbered 174/1955 of a limited edition, original Josten's case and packaging, mint, 2-1/2" x 3-1/2" **$780**

Courtesy of Heritage Auctions, ha.com

Circa 1993 Nolan Ryan game-issued glove, "Rawlings model Pro-6" constructed out of leather, never saw the field of action, has "Nolan Ryan" in cursive blue threads on the thumb. Because of the avalanche of requests for Ryan memorabilia his last season, extra gloves were created and most were sold through his charity. **$1,200**

Courtesy of Heritage Auctions, ha.com

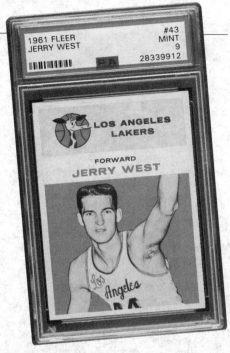

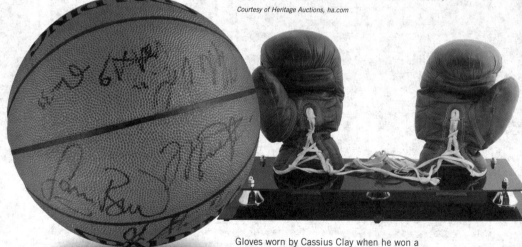

Near complete set of 1961 Fleer basketball cards, all of which have varying degrees of glue on the reverse, only missing Wilt Chamberlain and Jerry West for completion, fronts are exceptional bright, colorful, and sharp examples as they were straight from packs, cards are out of the Fleer Double Bubble archive books. **$5,100**

Courtesy of Morphy Auctions, morphyauctions.com

Fleer Jerry West #43 PSA Mint 9 1961 basketball card. PSA has graded well over 900 examples of this West card and only three have ranked higher, card displays flawless surfaces, corners and edges, and is immaculate. **$19,200**

Courtesy of Heritage Auctions, ha.com

Summer Olympics "Dream Team" signed basketball, 1992, included are Bird, Jordan, Stockton (last name light), Malone, Barkley, Pippen, Johnson, Robinson, Ewing, Drexler and Laettner, full letter of authenticity from SGC Authentic... **$5,040**

Courtesy of Heritage Auctions, ha.com

Gloves worn by Cassius Clay when he won a three-round decision vs Charlie Dobbins to win the Louisville Golden Gloves Championship on February 18, 1959. Gloves are red leather with Wilson labels at the wrist, there is a AAU 10 oz label on the inside of each glove, both gloves are marked "C.C." on the inside for Cassius Clay and both have an "OK" in a circle as well, stamped "Louisville G.G." on the inside, have a vintage tag that reads "Used by Cassius Clay 1959 Golden Gloves 2-18-59 Champ LT Heavy Weight," reverse says "Defeated Charlie Dobbins." The gloves originate from Cassius Clay trainer Joe Martin.**$9,225**

Courtesy of Morphy Auctions, morphyauctions.com

One of just six 1952 Topps Mickey Mantle baseball cards that have been rated a "Mint 9" on a scale of 10 by Professional Sports Authenticator sold for a hefty price of $2.88 million at an April 2018 auction at Heritage Auctions. The card was owned by former NFL offensive lineman Evan Mathis. An anonymous buyer won the prize after several rounds of vigorous bidding," Heritage said.

"This card is a towering symbol of American exceptionalism, from its celebration of our national pastime to the fearless ambition of creator Sy Berger's vision to the exaltation of a culture that could elevate a poor kid from the Oklahoma coal mines to the pinnacle of fame and acclaim. It is ten square inches of the American dream, preserved virtually flawlessly for eternity. It is a commodity recognized and coveted by millions, yet available to only a tiny handful of the most sophisticated collectors," according to Heritage.

"The supremacy of the 1952 Topps Mickey Mantle #311 card in the entirety of post-war trading card collecting is a matter of record. Likewise is the known population of that card assessed

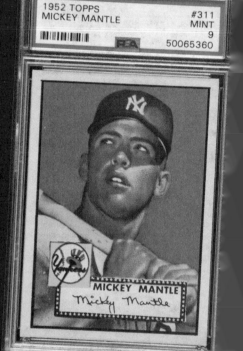

The record-breaking 1952 Topps Mickey Mantle baseball card.
.... **$2,880,000**

COURTESY OF HERITAGE AUCTIONS, HA.COM

by the leading trading card grading service, and the quantity at each grade level. archive of sales data, from hundreds or thousands of transactions across innume selling venues, charts a steady ascent at every grade level (though, admittedly, th data tails off as we climb to the upper reaches-it's been a decade since the last M example tempted a bidding audience)," Heritage said.

Of more than 1,500 submissions for PSA assessment, only six 1952 Topps Ma cards have earned a Mint 9 rating, with just three rising higher, to a perfect Gem assessment. Heritage has recorded two world records for high-grade specimen the past twelve months: $660,000 for a NM-MT 8 example, and $1,135,250 for a MT+ 8.5.

"The sale of this Mint 9 representation, widely considered by the small cast o experts who have examined the half-dozen as one of the finest at the grade, wil new benchmark for the issue, and for post-war trading cards at large," Heritage

Boxing champion Rocky Marciano signed photograph with actor Jerry Lewis, lightly signed in the upper left corner "Best Wishes Rocky Marciano" (3/4 out of 10), photo is laid on heavy period cardboard, foil stamped "Grossinger's 1953" in the lower left corner, 7" x 9-3/4".. **$215**

Courtesy of Morphy Auctions, morphyauctions.com

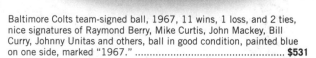

Punching bag that originates from Columbia Gym that was used by Cassius Clay during the time he trained there, tan bag measures 15" long and has a face drawn on it, speculated to be drawn by Ali himself, stamped "Columbia Gym Louisville KY," originates from early Cassius Clay trainer Joe Martin and includes a copy of a letter from him dated 1983. **$840**

Courtesy of Morphy Auctions, morphyauctions.com

Sugar Ray Robinson boxing poster for rare exhibition bout on Sept 10, 1957 in Philadelphia. Robinson defeated Otis Woodward 13 days before he faced Carmen Basilio. The main event was Harold Johnson vs. Wayne Bethea, a great bout in its own right. Both Johnson and Sugar Ray are pictured for this Tuesday night card at Philadelphia's Convention Hall, 22" x 28"......................... **$720**

Courtesy of Morphy Auctions, morphyauctions.com

Baltimore Colts team-signed ball, 1967, 11 wins, 1 loss, and 2 ties, nice signatures of Raymond Berry, Mike Curtis, John Mackey, Bill Curry, Johnny Unitas and others, ball in good condition, painted blue on one side, marked "1967." **$531**

Courtesy of Morphy Auctions, morphyauctions.com

Wright & Ditson dog ear leather youth-sized football helmet, model H400, padding and straps all original and intact, hand-written initials "D.F.F.H." and "Gibson City ILL," Excellent condition overall... **$875**

Courtesy of Morphy Auctions, morphyauctions.com

Topps Football Archive Collection with Joe Namath rookie card, 1965, collection includes the 1965 display box that has been re-assembled, 110 cards with stars including Joe Namath (front is NRMT) and Jack Kemp, 11 insert rub-offs, cards are out of the Fleer Double Bubble archive books, appears EX-MT.........................**$4,200**

Courtesy of Morphy Auctions, morphyauctions.com

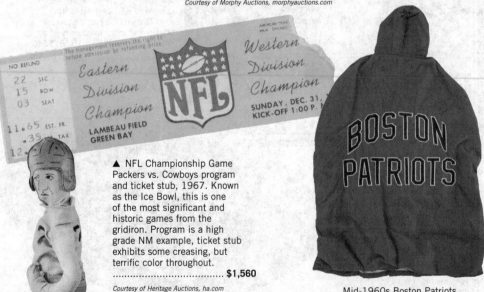

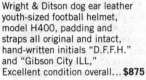

▲ NFL Championship Game Packers vs. Cowboys program and ticket stub, 1967. Known as the Ice Bowl, this is one of the most significant and historic games from the gridiron. Program is a high grade NM example, ticket stub exhibits some creasing, but terrific color throughout. **$1,560**

Courtesy of Heritage Auctions, ha.com

◄ Late 1920s Red Grange doll, rare, includes its original leather helmet and jersey, 19" h.. **$504**

Courtesy of Heritage Auctions, ha.com

Mid-1960s Boston Patriots game-worn sideline cape, red, white and blue, exhibiting solid wear throughout, displays sewn-on lettering on the back, and displays the proper "Holovak & Coughlin" size XXL tagging in the collar. **$1,020**

Courtesy of Heritage Auctions, ha.com

Arnold Palmer match-worn golf shoes, 1960s.**$1,020**

Courtesy of Heritage Auctions, ha.com

A 2005 multi-signed Masters Flag, includes array of signatures from stars of the PGA including the following notables: Fuzzy Zoeller, Trevor Immelman, Jack Nicklaus, Arnold Palmer, Gary Player, Craig Stadler, Mark O'Meara and Zach Johnson. Autographs average 9/10 to 10/10..... **$384**

Courtesy of Heritage Auctions, ha.com

Bobby Jones signed original oversized photograph by Bert Longworth, 1920s. Jones was golf's signature star at the time and signed a light spot on this original photograph and personalized the bold signature, graded Beckett 9, "To Will Smith With Best Wishes," "Bert Longworth Hollywood" studio stamp on the lower right corner, 10" x 13" **$7,200**

Courtesy of Heritage Auctions, ha.coms

A signed 1982 Donruss Jack Nicklaus card, graded PSA Gem MT 10, features a beautiful black signature of the "Golden Bear," PSA/DNA Certified.. **$408**

Courtesy of Heritage Auctions, ha.com

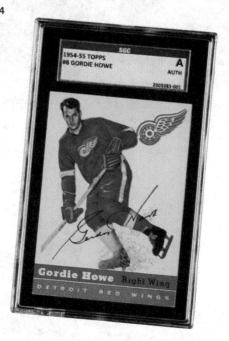

A 1954 Topps Gordie Howe #8 SGC Authentic rookie card, considered one of the most important hockey cards of the modern era, small amounts of white have been added to the top corners, encapsulated SGC Authentic.......................**$14,400**

Courtesy of Heritage Auctions, ha.com

Mario Lemieux of the Pittsburgh Penguins game-used hockey skate. Mario Lemieux was one of the most talented players to lace up a pair of skates in the NHL and this custom Nike Quest V12 skate was originally obtained from a team source, hand written tag in the back of boot reads "12-3/8" and a manufacturer ID number. **$256**

Courtesy of Morphy Auctions, morphyauctions.com

Wayne Gretzky game-worn Los Angeles Kings jersey, 1989-90. .... **$5,040**

Courtesy of Heritage Auctions, ha.com

Glenn Hall game-used St. Louis Blues hockey stick, 1967-68. Inducted into the Hockey Hall of Fame in 1975, Hall was a member of two Stanley Cup championships as a player, and another as a goaltender's coach. **$722**

Courtesy of Heritage Auctions, ha.com

Chicago Blackhawks pennant, 1966-67, moderate wear throughout, 30". **$102**

Courtesy of Heritage Auctions, ha.com

► Gallery-wrapped print on canvas of legendary Brazilian footballer, Pele, titled "Scissor Kick" and also autographed by him. Piece is authenticated by PSA/DNA, approx. 20" x 25". **$600**

Courtesy of Seized Assets Auctioneers, seizedassetsauctioneers.com

STAR WARS

THE FOUNDATION OF global popular culture was shaken to its core in 1977 when George Lucas released one of the most important films in modern American history: the science fiction space opera, *Star Wars: A New Hope.*

Over the past 40 years, eager fans have popularized *Star Wars* terms that have been indelibly stamped onto our collective consciousness and even introduced into the American lexicon words like "lightsaber," "Jedi Knight," and "droids"; expressions such as "May the Force Be With You," and the moral/psychic concept of "the dark side of the Force." Nearly 100 unique figures were produced in Kenner's vintage *Star Wars* line (discounting the company's *Droids* and *Ewoks* sub-lines released in 1985) between 1978 and 1985. Records show that the company sold almost 300 million action figures in total.

Yet little did 20th Century Fox realize the influence the film would have on children and adult collectors everywhere, and in a brilliant stroke of prescience, Lucas may have subconsciously realized the potential of the *Star Wars* franchise. Lucas alone contracted to retain all sequel and merchandising rights for the film, and what was to follow.

Kenner toys obtained the rights to produce 3-3/4-inch action figures, playsets, creatures, and vehicles based on important scenes from *Star Wars*. The smaller 3-3/4-inch scale was utilized in direct response to the oil shortages of the 1970s, scarcities that increased the cost of plastic production affecting many major toy companies such as Hasbro, Fisher Price, and Mego. Little would Kenner realize the overwhelming response that their more portable *Star Wars* figures would attract on retail shelves. Soon after their release, the 3-3/4-inch action figure format became the standard in the field. At this smaller size (as opposed to Hasbro's enormous 11-1/2-inch G.I. Joe figures or Mego's interchangeable 8-inch figure body), characters were easier to produce, simpler to manufacture, and could ultimately sell higher numbers in order to allow consumers to purchase many more units ("collect them all") — refreshing sold-out retail pegs much more quickly.

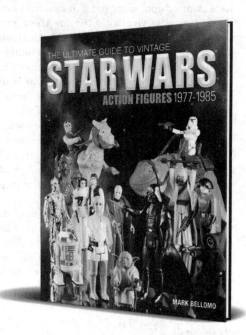

One of the top toy experts in the country, Mark Bellomo has written a number of bestselling books on toys and popular culture, including *The Ultimate Guide to Vintage Star Wars Action Figures, 1977-1985*; *The Ultimate Guide to Vintage Transformers Action Figures*; and *The Ultimate Guide to G.I. Joe, 1982-1994*.

Star Wars figures became a sensation — a phenomenon — in the late 1970s/early 1980s, and the items sold briskly throughout the release of the original trilogy, producing a bevy of toys for each of the three films: *A New Hope (Episode IV)*, *The Empire Strikes Back (Episode V)*, and *The Return of the Jedi (Episode VI)*. A total of 96 figures were available in the original "vintage" line (1977-1985), not including myriad figure variations (telescoping light sabers, vinyl-caped Jawas, etc.), or the Sy Snootles and the Rebo Band three-pack set. The most popular and valuable of these carded figures are the earliest *Star Wars* releases, those figures found on original "12-back cards" — those card backs that showed only the first 12 *Star Wars* action figures in 1977. Other pricey figures can be found within the final run of the line, 1984/85's "Power of the Force" collection, where figures (both new sculpts and previously released characters) were carded along with a collector's coin. A few of these carded samples are worth thousands of dollars in Mint on Card (MOC) condition.

Along with the standard 3-3/4-inch figures was a collection of deluxe 12-inch Large Size figures based on more popular characters from the films — these were the first deluxe 12-inch action figures made in the likenesses of the most popular characters from the original *Star Wars* trilogy, and are held in high regard by *Star Wars* aficionados.

Apart from releasing nearly one hundred *Star Wars* action figures, Kenner crafted 5 creatures, 31 vehicles (including store exclusives), 13 playsets (again, including exclusives), a few assorted accessories, and 7 action figure storage cases. Also adding to the collecting fun were assorted ephemera: proof of-purchase mail-away items, a Collector's Action Stand, an Action Figure Survival Kit, a Display Arena, myriad Power of the Force coins, pack-in posters, and special bagged figures solicited before their official retail carded release. These special offers added an air of anticipation to the hobby of collecting, and most kids couldn't wait for these packages to arrive in the mail: Kenner always treated kids as truly special customers.

Regardless of all of this, the vintage *Star Wars* line was cancelled in 1985 due to poor sales and a shrinking sci-fi marketplace. Sadly, it would be ten long years before *Star Wars* collectors would be treated to any new toys.

To much fanfare, Kenner released a new series of *Star Wars* action figures in 1995, and the "Power of the Force" line (or, as fans dubbed it, the "POTF II" line) was born. Although initially criticized for their bulky statures and poor facial sculpts, the POTF II action figure line lasted five years and yielded many excellent new figures, a slew of unproduced characters, and even improved paint applications, intricate figure sculpts, and added articulation.

Today, *Star Wars* toys are some of the most desirable action figures on the secondary market, and the people who collect them are often the most devoted in the hobby. Vintage figures and vehicles still sealed in their packages command outrageous prices on online auction sites such as eBay and in collectible stores.

The Star Wars toy universe is immense. For a complete look, please see *The Ultimate Guide to Vintage Star Wars Action Figures, 1977-1985*.

— Mark Bellomo

Star Wars Land Speeder (a.k.a. Landspeeder), #38020, 1978, Kenner, Mint In Sealed Box (characters not included).
..............................**$260-$300+**

One of the standouts of Hake's Russell Branton Star Wars Collection auction: Ben Kenobi double-telescoping MOC. **$76,700**

Courtesy of Hake's Americana and Collectibles, hakes.com

STAR WARS COLLECTION CENTERPIECE
OF RECORD-BREAKING AUCTIONS

HAKE'S AMERICANA WRAPPED ITS 50TH-ANNIVERSARY YEAR in 2017 with a November 14-16 auction that set multiple company and auction-industry records as it crossed the finish line at $1,754,464. Things only got better for the auction company in 2018 when another auction from March 13-15 totaled $2,357,183, which was the first auction to surpass $2 million for Hake's.

The centerpiece of both of these sales was the 100 percent AFA-graded Russell Branton Star Wars Collection, which produced some out-of-the-galaxy results. The superstar of both auctions was a Boba Fett rocket-firing prototype, which sold for a whopping $86,383 against a high estimate of $50,000. This L-slot action figure from the 1979 Kenner line was graded AFA 85 NM+. Another big seller was a 1978 Kenner Ben (Obi-Wan) Kenobi double-telescoping action figure presented on its original blister card that sold for $76,700. This represents the highest auction price ever paid for a *Stars Wars* production figure, and was one of three MOC double-telescoping figures auctioned. Needless to say, having a MOC DT of Ben is an incredible sight, rarely seen, very sought after, and ultimately extremely valuable in the world of *Star Wars* toys, said Hake's.

A Darth Vader double-telescoping 12-back-A AFA 70 EX+ ended at $64,900, nearly doubling the low-end estimate of $35,000. Other highlights include a Princess Leia 12-back-A, hammering for $29,500; a "Power of the Force" Admiral Ackbar 92-back proof card AFA 90 NM+/MT from 1984 that sold for $9,204, nearly doubling the high-end estimate of $5,000; and the highest-graded example of a 1978 "Yellow Hair" Luke Skywalker figure, which was hotly pursued to $50,622 against a pre-sale estimate of $10,000-$20,000. Its astonishing price set a new record for any Luke

647

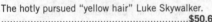

The hotly pursued "yellow hair" Luke Skywalker.
....$50,622

Courtesy of Hake's Americana and Collectibles, hakes.com

Skywalker figure. Another highlight was the Anakin Skywalker prototype figure from the 1985 toy line for the film *Star Wars: The Power of the Force*. It garnered 17 bids before settling at $34,981 against an estimate of $10,000-$20,000.

"This auction is uncharted territory for the hobby. While graded action figures have been around for several years, many of the extremely rare examples in Branton's collection have never before appeared at auction with the distinction of AFA grading," said Alex Winter, president of Hake's Americana.

From the day he began collecting in 2003, Branton has always focused on condition. "I wouldn't buy anything that had a low grade. That's why it took me 10 years to complete my collection," he said.

This leads to the reason why Branton chose to sell: He reached his goal of acquiring every original-trilogy character from Kenner's 1977-1986 production line, and all possess AFA grading.

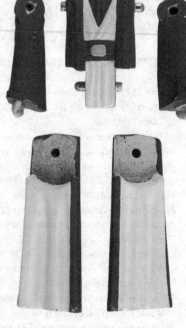

Another auction highlight was this Anakin Skywalker prototype figure from 1985. ....$34,981

Courtesy of Hake's Americana and Collectibles, hakes.com

X-Wing Fighter, made famous
by pilot Luke Skywalker,
#38030, 1978, Kenner, Mint
In Sealed Box..........**$520-$550+**

A-Wing Fighter, #93700,
1985, Kenner, Mint In Sealed
Box (character not included).
..................................**$475-$510**

Imperial TIE Fighter, #38040,
1978, Kenner, Mint Loose
Condition. .... **$80-$95+**

▲ Tatooine Skiff, featured in
Return of the Jedi, #715401,
1985, Kenner, characters
not included, Mint Loose
Condition. ....**$225-$250+**

Jabba the Hutt Action Playset, one of the most popular of all Kenner Star Wars playsets, #704901, 1983, Kenner, Mint In Sealed Box. ....**$165-$190+**

Bobba Fett (with Imperial Blaster), fearsome intergalactic bounty hunter, #39250, 1979, Kenner, Mint Loose Condition. ....**$25-$32**

Rancor Monster figure, #71060, 1984, Kenner, Mint in Sealed Box...........**$245-$275+**

Speed Bike Vehicle, #70500, 1983, Kenner, rider not included, Mint In Sealed Box. ...**$55-$70**

Millennium Falcon, the galaxy's most famous modified light freighter owned by Han Solo, #391101, 1979, Kenner, Mint In Sealed Box. ....**$2,800-$3,200**

AT-AT (Imperial All Terrain Armored Transport),
Empire Strikes Back, 1981, Mint In Sealed Box
(characters not included).......................**$825-975+**

◀ Scout Walker vehicle, #69800, 1982, Kenner,
Mint In Sealed Box (character not included).
....**$140-$175**

Rebel Armored Snowspeeder, #39610, 1980, Kenner, Mint In Box.. **$650-$725+**

TOOLS

Powerful
Compact, Convenient

This "Yankee" Push Brace No. 75 can be used in tight corners and places where the bit-brace is a clumsy tool.

No. 75 has famous "Yankee" Spiral Ratchet drive, all you do is "push." Quick on boring—holds all usual wood drills and bits with square shanks up to ⅜ inch. Speedier than any other tool for light drilling in metal, for driving or drawing heavy screws, or running-up nuts on bolts. On automobile or light machinery repair work, and about the garage it is a tool of big usefulness.

"YANKEE"
Push Brace
No. 75. Price $2.80

Heavily nickeled. Hardwood polished handle. Drop forged, hardened steel jaws. Length 16¾ inches closed—23⅝ inches extended. Every detail finished and surfaced with "Yankee" skill that reduces friction to a minimum, and built for strength and long life.

Your Dealer Can Supply You

Write for "Yankee Tool Book" FREE—for mechanics and amateurs. "Yankee" Tools in the Garage" for Motorists.

North Bros. Mfg. Co.
PHILADELPHIA

"YANKEE" TOOLS
make Better Mechanics

The Yankee No. 75 push brace was North Bros.' top seller.

IN THE 100 years spanning 1850 to 1950, new and innovative tools hit the retail market as often as new apps now appear for your smartphone or tablet computer. More than 2.68 million patents for new inventions and designs were granted during this period, according to the U.S. Patent and Trademark Office.

During this period, lots of tool-making companies prospered or closed based on how quickly they could bring new tool designs and technologies to market. The North Brothers Manufacturing Company of Philadelphia, Pennsylvania, is an excellent example of a company that produced both mundane tools and collector's items.

The company's iron foundry produced simple, utilitarian tools beginning in 1880. The company saw steady sales, but marketed nothing truly exceptional until the mid-1890s when it took on tool designer Zachary Furbish, after it acquired his company called the Forest City Screwdriver and Drill Company. It was perhaps the best decision the company ever made. Furbish had patented his own for a special type of ratchet screwdriver. In 1899, North Bros. launched its line of "Yankee" ratchet screwdrivers, which antique tool dealer Sanford Moss (sydnassloot.com) considers as "the most technically sound and mechanically innovative of any hand drill ever produced."

The company's top seller was the "Yankee" No. 75 push brace. Furbish's unique spiral ratchet design and the firm's bit and brace. The "Yankee" brand was quickly attached to hundreds of products, even a 19-inch, 10-pound bench-mounted, hand-crank drill press produced in 1914.

Eventually, the term "yankee screwdriver" was adopted to describe all types of push/pull type screwdrivers (just like how the brand name Kleenex is popularly used to describe all facial tissues). The company was purchased by The Stanley Works (yes, that Stanley) in 1946 and the Yankee brand is now owned by Germany's Schröder tool company. You can still buy a chromium-plated Yankee Spiral Ratchet screwdriver on Amazon.com — 120 years after the brand first hit the market.

Successes and failures by tool companies of yore leave collectors a rich source of articles to collect — some of which see prices swings based on several factors.

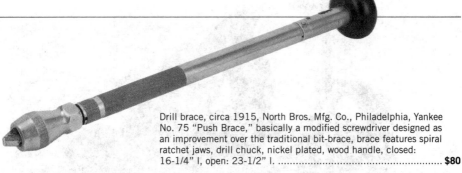

Drill brace, circa 1915, North Bros. Mfg. Co., Philadelphia, Yankee No. 75 "Push Brace," basically a modified screwdriver designed as an improvement over the traditional bit-brace, brace features spiral ratchet jaws, drill chuck, nickel plated, wood handle, closed: 16-1/4" l, open: 23-1/2" l. **$80**

Courtesy of stellers_j, eBay.com

Tool collectors can be a deep-pocketed bunch when the right piece comes to market. Brown Tool Auction holds many world records, including the most paid at auction for a tool when a Sandusky Three-arm plow plane sold for $114,400 in 2005. Other auction records include a Chelsea pencil sharpener for $17,000 and rosewood, Sandusky center-wheel plow for $22,000, along with many other great tools that are current records in their tool type.

Today's tool collecting community is small enough that the activities of a handful of collectors can have a significant impact on prices for some types of tools, said Jim Gehring.

No one knows the hobby better than Gehring. He owns both *The Fine Tool Journal*, the hobby's No. 1 collecting magazine, and Brown Tool Auctions, the record-holding auction house. Between the two entities, Gehring oversees seven tool auctions and just added another dedicated to farming antiques. He said that although tool prices have still not fully recovered from a 10-year decline, they are slowly recovering.

"Chisels, gouges and other edged tools are popular and command strong prices, as are anvils," Gehring said. "And as with all collectibles, the market is strongest for the highest quality and rarest items."

The hobby's biggest challenges are the availability of rare tools and an aging collector community, Gehring said. Unlike other collecting categories, reproductions and enhancements are limited yet still exist.

"Out and out reproductions are rare but do exist." Gehring said. "A lot of cast iron tools, particular planes, were 'japanned' (a type of hard enamel-type finish, usually black), which tends to wear and chip over the years, and it is common to find planes that have been repainted with common black paint," Gehrig said. "If well done, it doesn't affect the value that much, particularly if it's described in the auction listing."

Replaced blades, screws and other parts are also fairly common in many old tools but that fact is an accepted convention among collectors. Often the replacement was done by the original user of the tool without any fraudulent intent.

Except for the rarest tools, the cost of manufacturing a really good reproduction isn't that much less than the value of the original tool, which keeps reproductions down, Gehring said.

Gehring estimates there's a 50-50 split between those who buy to collect or buy to use. The highest-end tools tend to be purchased by collectors, he said; however, there is a large and growing community of people who are interested in wood and metal working, either as a hobby or profession, and who appreciate the value of older tools.

"A large percentage of collectors are people who use (or used) tools in their professional lives," Gehring said. "Relying solely on anecdotal evidence, it seems to me very high percentages are professional contractors and builders, as well as carpenters. There are also a large number who are enthusiastic, and sometimes very skilled, amateur woodworkers.

When we go to a woodworker›s convention, it's a completely different crowd than the typical tool collector convention," Gehring said.

For more information on tools, visit *The Fine Tool Journal* and Brown Tool Auctions at finetoolj.com.

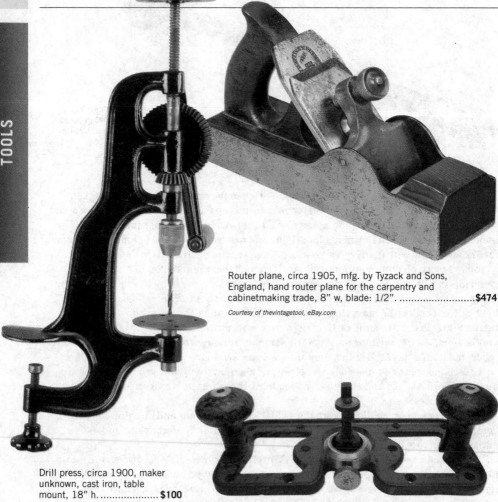

Router plane, circa 1905, mfg. by Tyzack and Sons, England, hand router plane for the carpentry and cabinetmaking trade, 8" w, blade: 1/2". **$474**

Courtesy of thevintagetool, eBay.com

Drill press, circa 1900, maker unknown, cast iron, table mount, 18" h. **$100**

Courtesy of Morphy Auctions, morphys.com

Plane, c. 1892, mfg by S. Tyzack and Sons, England, "Infill Smoothing Plane," marked "I. Sorby Sheffield," brass lever cap, dovetailed steel sole, 9" l. **$215**

Courtesy of Skinner Auctioneers & Appraisers, skinnerinc.com

Plane, 1905-1943, mfg. by Stanley Tools, Stanley No. 97, cast iron, edge plane used in cabinet making, original Japanned black varnish, 10" l. **$130**

Courtesy of Soulis Auctions, dirksoulisauctions.com

Plane, 1867, "Phillips Plow Plane," patented by Russell Phillips of Gardiner, Maine, with one original reversible blade stamped: "P.P.P./pat. Aug. 13, 1867." **$650**

Courtesy of John McInnis Auctioneers, mcinnisauctions.com

Stanley tool outfit, circa 1880s, Stanley Tools, original set including a Stanley Plane No. 45, with boxed cutters and fences, original boxes, smaller bearing the original paper label, plane: 11-1/2" l **$150**

Courtesy of Soulis Auctions, dirksoulisauctions.com

Scroll saw, 1886, mfg. Seneca Falls Mfg. Co., New York, "Victor," double-treadle with upper and lower spindles, marked: "The Seneca Falls Mfg. Co., VICTOR, throat arm marked Pat, June. 12, 1877 & Pat. Pend. and The Seneca Falls Mfg. Co. Seneca Falls, N.Y.," 59" h
....**$2,280**

Courtesy of Skinner Auctioneers & Appraisers, skinnerinc.com

Cobblestone hammer, circa 1810-30, mfg. by Jackson Bros., hand-wrought, cobblestone hammer, square poll and long adze-shaped bill for trimming and lifting paving stones, marked 'Jackson Bros.,' poll: 4" l, tail: 10" l..**$190**

Courtesy of Horst Auctioneers, horstauction.com

Wrench, circa late 19th c., American, hand-wrought, displayed in custom wood box, 8-1/4" l x 2-3/4" w x 3" d..**$40**

Courtesy of Material Culture, materialculture.com

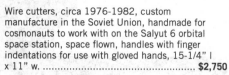

Wire cutters, circa 1976-1982, custom manufacture in the Soviet Union, handmade for cosmonauts to work with on the Salyut 6 orbital space station, space flown, handles with finger indentations for use with gloved hands, 15-1/4" l x 11" w. **$2,750**

Courtesy of Heritage Auctions, ha.com

Tool chest, c. 1900, unmarked, joiner's tool set, birch and oak dovetailed chest, iron strapping around hinged lid edge, wrought iron carrying handles, four compartments, assorted tools, handsaw compartment, collection of wood molding planes, on casters, 25" h x 37-3/4" w x 25-1/2" d. **$720**

Courtesy of Skinner Auctioneers & Appraisers, skinnerinc.com

Tusk cutters, mid-1900s, unknown maker, nickel plated, used to trim and cut boar tusks, marked: "47," rare. **$15**

Courtesy of Soulis Auctions, dirksoulisauctions.com

Tape loom, circa 18th century, simple country tool, (loom was gripped between the knees and used to weave "tapes," or narrow strips of fabric used to tie clothes for lack of buttons), 10" l. .. **$275**

Courtesy of Hap Moore Antiques-Auctions, hapmoore.com

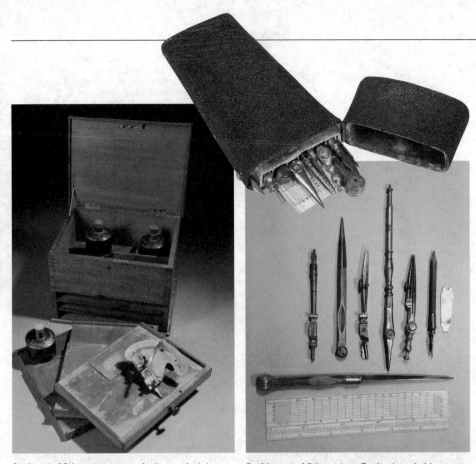

Goniostat, 19th century, unmarked, a goniostat is a device used in cutting gem facets, brass and steel goniostat with half-moon sector divided in 0-50 increments, with sharpening tool set, housed in dovetailed mahogany box, three pullout trays, 9" h x 7" w x 7" d. **$360**

Courtesy of Skinner Auctioneers & Appraisers, skinnerinc.com

Drafting set, 19th century, England, probably London, brass and steel instruments and bone rule, housed in a wood and shagreen fitted traveling carrying case with hinged lid, 7" l. **$984**

Courtesy of Skinner Auctioneers & Appraisers, skinnerinc.com

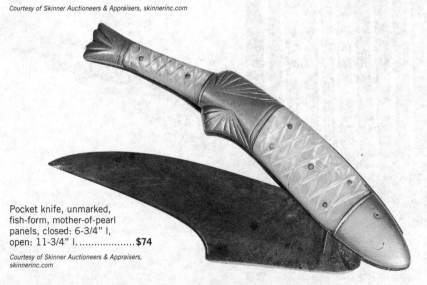

Pocket knife, unmarked, fish-form, mother-of-pearl panels, closed: 6-3/4" l, open: 11-3/4" l. **$74**

Courtesy of Skinner Auctioneers & Appraisers, skinnerinc.com

Mitre square, circa 1880s, unmarked, fixed bevel, brass, ebony, unusual form..**$70**

Courtesy of Soulis Auctions, dirksoulisauctions.com

Plumb bob, unmarked, brass, hardwood, exceptionally large, 10 pounds, 14-1/4" l, 2-1/2" w. **$170**

Courtesy of Soulis Auctions, dirksoulisauctions.com

Wheel cutting engine, circa 19th c., England, used for cutting watch clock wheels, ...**$1,495**

Courtesy of R.O. Schmitt Fine Arts, roschmitt.com

Woodworking bench, circa late 19th c., from Alfred, Maine, on keyed stretcher and shoe foot base, having dovetailed center storage drawer, 95" l..**$1,800**

Courtesy of Hap Moore Antiques-Auctions, hapmoore.com

TOYS - HOT WHEELS

AMERICA'S LOVE AFFAIR with the automobile was hot and heavy in 1968, and Detroit fed the affair with all the adrenaline it could. The bigger the car the better, and the more horsepower under the hood, the happier car owners were. The muscle car movement was firmly entrenched as the decade's end neared.

Fifty years after their introduction, it's easy to see that Mattel's Hot Wheels cars swung in at the perfect time. America's love affair with everything with four wheels was in full bloom, and with flashy Hot Wheels cars, there was finally a toy car that matched the excitement of the hot vehicles lining dealerships and the pages of popular car magazines. Slight rakes, opening hoods exposing V-8 engines, side-exiting exhaust pipes, hood scoops, and the metallic paint colors of Hot Wheels cars brought new-found electricity to toy shelves. These features further adorned the most energetic cars on the market: Chevrolet Camaros, Ford Mustangs, Plymouth Barracudas, and Ford Thunderbirds. The sparkling paint also dressed some of the most famous custom cars of the day, such as Ed "Big Daddy" Roth's Beatnik Bandit and Bill Cushenbery's Silhouette.

Mattel introduced 16 cars in 1968. Often referred to as The Sweet Sixteen, the cars were set off by red-striped tires, emulating performance cars of the day. These wheels were developed to roll faster and more smoothly than any other non-motorized toy vehicle of the day, particularly the well-established Matchbox cars. Known as "Redlines," these first releases quickly caught on. Although the look of Hot Wheels cars were the direct result of Mattel designer Harry Bentley Bradley's

Michael Zarnock is one of the leading Hot Wheels cars authorities in the world. He has written numerous books and has twice been selected a Guinness world record holder for his Hot Wheels collection. Mattel created a Hot Wheels car in 2009 based on a hot rod Zarnock built and raced throughout the Northeast.

Detroit-built 1964 El Camino, the combination of bright colors and hot subject vehicles gave Hot Wheels cars a "California cool" image. This West Coast image helped the cars ride a wave of popularity that has not wavered for 50 years. Some of the more desirable colors of these cars are Pink, Purple, and Magenta, with Pink being the most valuable of colors.

Once introduced, Hot Wheels were instantly popular, so much so that a second manufacturing facility was opened in Hong Kong. There are early Redline Hot Wheels cars with both USA and Hong Kong countries of production on their base, so pay attention to those bases. By 1972, all Hot Wheels cars were made in Hong Kong. Before Hot Wheels entered the scene, Matchbox cars ruled the toy-car world. But the English toy cars instantly became second choices among children as soon as Hot Wheels cars rolled into town. While there remains today a healthy collector base for Matchbox cars, there is no comparison to Hot Wheels cars in terms of popularity or demand.

From 1968 through 1972, Mattel used vibrant paint on Hot Wheels cars. Called Spectraflame, the paint process consisted of polishing the zinc-plated, die-cast metal bodies and then painting them with a thin layer of transparent, candy-colored paint. Some of the most desirable Redline cars feature the Spectraflame treatment. Mattel discontinued the process in 1973, and until the end of the Redline era in 1977, cars were painted in enamel colors, with the exceptions being the chrome 1976 "Super Chromes" and gold chrome 1977 "Super Chromes."

— By Michael Zarnock

Beatnik Bandit: The famous Ed "Big Daddy" Roth custom was immortalized in this casting. Beatnik Bandit is pictured here as a U.S. casting in olive with a clear bubble; Hong Kong versions have a blue-tinted bubble. **$90**

THE 1968 HOT WHEELS LINE-UP

consisted of sixteen custom vehicles now called "The Sweet Sixteen" by collectors. The cars hold a significant place in Hot Wheels history and remain coveted by collectors:

Custom Barracuda: A blue U.S.-built Custom Barracuda is popular with collectors in part because the pre-1970 Barracuda has been replicated so rarely in scale – and it looks great! The hood opens to reveal a metal engine.......... **$550**

Custom Camaro: As one of the first castings to be released, the Custom Camaro is an icon of the Redlines offerings. There are a dizzying amount of variations but the demand for the Custom Camaro remains strong.................... **$600**

WHAT TO LOOK FOR AND WHERE

There are many places you can find Hot Wheels cars: online, flea markets, yard sales, antiques shops, thrift stores, and auction houses. Truth is, you can find them just about anywhere if you look hard enough. When looking for Hot Wheels, there are a few key things that you always need to consider:

- **Condition**
- **Age**
- **Price**
- **What are you going to do with it?**

Condition is everything when it comes to buying and selling. The words "new in package" (NIP) and "mint" (M) are thrown around a lot by those who buy and sell. Even if a car is in the original package, that doesn't automatically mean that it's "mint" in the package. Mint means no chips, no roof or side rubs from the plastic blister that it comes in, no base tarnish, nothing! "Mint" means perfect. Cars do get damaged and even have the paint flake off in the package, so be aware.

Packages are also graded. The abbreviation (MIMP) Mint In Mint Package means the car is perfect and so is the package. No dents in the plastic blister, no bends or creases in the card, no soft corners on the card, no stains, no nothing.

It's OK to have a price sticker on the package though. That's something that does not affect the value.

Flea markets and antiques shops are places that you really need to be careful of. I have seen cars that are all busted up, no paint, broken windows and a missing wheel with a $20 price tag on it. The car is junk! It's not worth anything. These places think because it's old, it has value. It doesn't. Condition is everything when it comes to value and collectibility. If you think you're going to repair a car or repaint it, don't bother! Repaired or repainted cars with non-original parts have no value. Collectors do not want them. If it's something you want to do and keep for yourself, then that's a different story. You can do whatever makes you happy when it comes to your collection. But remember, if you're planning on selling it later, collectors know original from replacement.

When you're at a yard sale, look the place over. If you don't see anything in plain sight, ask if they have any old toys like Hot Wheels. Look in those big boxes on the floor that are full of small items. There are usually a lot of toy cars in the bottom of those boxes and more often than not, they are Hot Wheels. The cars in these boxes are always marked at very cheap prices.

Custom Corvette: The Custom Corvette, here in rose, features an opening hood........................ **$350**

Custom Cougar: The Custom Cougar features an opening hood and comes in an array of colors. The casting was built in both in U.S. and Hong Kong.
.... **$475**

Custom Eldorado: Not every Hot Wheels casting from 1968 was based on a muscle car or a street rod, as illustrated by the Custom Eldorado. The brainchild of Harry Bradley, who worked as a designer for Cadillac before going to Mattel, is shown here in green and blue, products of the Hong Kong plant...................**$250**

Custom Firebird: In the process of adding a California touch to the 1967 Pontiac Firebird convertible, Mattel exaggerated the length, making the Custom Firebird one long-looking Hot Wheels car. **$325**

Custom Fleetside: Designer Harry Bradley's personal tricked-out 1964 Chevrolet El Camino is credited as inspiration for the Hot Wheels look. The Custom Fleetwood incorporates nearly all of the features of Bradley's daily ride. Made in U.S. with opening back cover. **$300**

Custom T-Bird: The Custom T-Bird was available with or without a black-painted roof and with an opening hood exposing a metal engine...**$250**

Custom Mustang: The Custom Mustang comes in assorted colors. The green car shown, with closed hood scoops and no louvers: **$450**
Red or gold cars with open hood scoops:........ **$2,000**
Red, yellow, orange or blue cars with louvered
  rear window:... **$1,000**

top lot

Bruce Pascal has a Hot Wheels car collection of several thousand cars valued at more than $1 million, the highlight of which is this pre-production, ultra-rare 1969 Pink Rear-Loading Volkswagen Beach Bomb. The car was featured on an episode of the hit TV show "Pawn Stars," where Pascal was offered $70,000 for the car. He declined. Pascal calls the car the Holy Grail of Hot Wheels cars and says the car is worth about $150,000. What makes this Hot Wheels car so valuable? Pascal's Beach Bomb is a prototype that never made into stores. This model was never mass-produced because it was determined the car was top-heavy and too narrow to function and fit properly in the Hot Wheels Super Charger. Until the introduction of the Super-Charger, gravity race sets dominated the Hot Wheels market. The Super-Charger was a game-changer, propelling cars onto the track at racing speed lap after lap. Because Pascal's pink prototype wouldn't work with the Super-Charger the body style was scrapped. Pascal's Beach Bomb features clear windows and surfboards loaded into the back via a rear window. On the version that was eventually released, the surfboards slid into a side pocket.

COURTESY OF BRUCE PASCAL

Custom Volkswagen: Custom Volkswagens were offered from 1968 to 1971 and nearly all feature an opening sunroof...**$350**

Deora: With surfboards prominently displayed, the Deora was the ultimate California fantasy car. The Deora was based on a Dodge concept truck built by the Alexander Brothers.............................. **$400**

Ford J-Car: The Ford J-Car, with a hinged rear engine area, was the only original Hot Wheels casting to include a sticker sheet. **$90**

Hot Heap: The Hot Heap features all the goodies of a fine 1960s Model T street rod. Unlike others in the line, there are no moving parts, aside from the wheels. **$130**

Python/Cheetah: All U.S. castings and the bulk of Hong Kong castings of this car carry the best-known name Python. However, when the casting was originally built in Hong Kong it was stamped with the name "Cheetah on the base. Samples of such are extremely rare and valuable. **$120**

Silhouette: The Silhouette is one of the most popular but least valuable Hot Wheels castings from 1968. Because the car's popularity made it a common car when it was new, many examples still survive. **$85**

TOYS

NO OTHER HOBBY touches collectors, and people in general, quite like toys. The people who collect vintage toys are simply revisiting their first collection. In some cases, they never left it. That's the thing about toy collecting: You can find amazing examples in abundant supply from any time period — especially your own.

Sales data shows you'll have lots of company in your toy collecting hobby, but also lots of competition for finer examples. The collectible toy business is one of the largest in both the retail market and the secondary market, and is also perhaps one of the first types of established collecting genres ever defined. It's interesting to note that FAO Schwarz, founded in 1862 as America's first toy store, launched its "Toy Bazaar" antique toy department in the early 1960s to meet collector demand. Toy collecting is an old and venerated hobby.

No figures are kept for the number of vintage collectible toys sold every year, but the number sold at auction is growing. At any given time, more than five million toys are for sale or taking bids on eBay. LiveAuctioneers, one of the world's largest auction-hosting websites, shows an estimated half-million toys were sold by brick and mortar auction houses at auction during the last 20 years. In many cases, these sales have set new records as collections finally come to market after decades in private hands.

A comical-looking tin toy Mickey and Minnie, with big teeth and five fingers on each hand, ride atop a green motorcycle, Germany, c. 1932. This is one of the most desirable of the German automotive toys from this period because of its crossover appeal to motorcycle collectors, its robust size and edgy design. Excellent condition, 9-1/2" w. **$42,500**

Courtesy of Bertoia Auctions, bertoiaauctions.com

VISIT WWW.ANTIQUETRADER.COM

WWW.FACEBOOK.COM/ANTIQUETRADER

> **Condition is of the utmost importance in today's collector market. The most valuable items are in original condition with minimal restoration or alterations. This 'best or nothing' approach to condition has probably been the most influential change in the hobby during the last decade. Values of toys in mid-range to low condition have fallen, while values of rare toys in top condition often skyrocket beyond all expectations.**

Among these private collections, few reached the size, scope, and value of that owned by Donald Kaufman, whose family founded Kay Bee Toys in 1922, and who decided in 2009 to sell his collection. Kaufman felt collectors would care for the toys better than any museum ever could. It took four auctions to sell the great Kaufman collection of automotive toys for a record $12.1 million. The collection stands as the most valuable of its kind in history.

You don't need to spend $12 million on toys to have an amazing collection. But it certainly helps to bring a fraction of the passion Kaufman brought to his hobby. You probably have a few toys hanging around the house, and it's never been easier to find unusual examples. Adding to them can become addictive, especially when you find ones you had as a kid ... or the ones you always wanted.

Toy collecting allows for an infinite number of specialized collecting variations. Want cast iron cars made between 1930 and 1940? You could start with the Hubley Manufacturing Co. and collect by size. Only want dolls that were first introduced as paper dolls in the early 1950s? Betsy McCall is your gal. Have an affinity for pre-war metal squirt guns made in Michigan? Versions made by All Metal Products Co., better known as Wyandotte Toys, can be found for $20 on up, depending on condition. With toys, your collection can be as specialized or as general as you want it to be.

Toy values are chiefly influenced by demand, rarity and condition, but there are other factors as well: authenticity, exposure, provenance, quality and, most importantly, condition.

Authenticity is black or white. There are no gray areas with authenticity: Either the toy is right or it is wrong. It is either authentic or it is a fake.

Exposure influences demand for a work and brings prestige to its owner. When Steve Geppi, the president and CEO of Diamond Comic Distributors, paid $200,000 for the world's most valuable action figure — the first handcrafted prototype of the 1963 G.I. Joe action figure — the sale made international news and earned a Guinness World Record. Exposure is crucial for building collector demand around a single piece or an entire category.

Provenance explains an established history of ownership. Once a vintage toy has entered the secondary market, it develops a provenance. A famous owner can add at most 15 percent or more on the value of a toy, but there are exceptions and this changes dramatically depending on who owned the toy in the past. When Leonardo DiCaprio sold part of his action figure collection at Morphy Auctions in 2006, values were stronger than expected, thanks to his famous name.

Quality may be a subjective criterion; however, a well-constructed toy is hard to find and fewer still survive for decades or even centuries. The more time you spend looking at quality toys, the easier it is to recognize good craftsmanship when you see it.

Large wood and iron English model stagecoach, ca. 20th century, wooden cab with crown painted on doors, interior with seats and dome top trunk in back, spoke wheels, iron suspension, painted pink, turquoise and black, good condition, 38" l x 4" h. **$100**

Courtesy of White's Auctions, whitesauctions.com

Papier-mâché bulldog growler pull toy nodder, c1880, rare, has a pull chain that makes the dog's mouth move and growl, inlay glass eyes with straw collar, roller feet, 11" h, 19" l............. **$1,000**

Courtesy of Hill Auction Gallery, hillauctiongallery.com

Dachshund felt pull toy, on metal spoke wheel, early 1900s, painted face, button eyes and stitched nose, 20" l **$200**

Courtesy of White's Auctions, whitesauctions.com

Vintage remote control poodle, 1950s, Cragston Japan, in working condition, 11" l.....................**$14**

Courtesy of Pioneer Auction Gallery, pioneerantiqueauction.com

Life-size ride-on plush pony, Hansa Toys, 2002, original label Thomas Boland & Co, San Diego, California, tan plush fur, tail and mane, with vintage child's tooled leather saddle, leather bridle and breast plate, good condition, 55" l x 46" h. **$600**

Courtesy of White's Auctions, whitesauctions.com

Vintage teak hippo, Danish Modern, Kay Bojesen, 4-1/2" x 10" x 2-1/2".....................................**$275**

Courtesy of Ashcroft and Moore, ashcraftandmoore.com

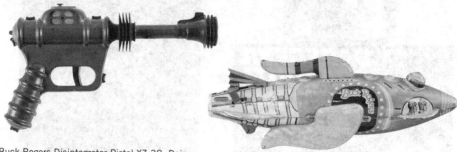

Buck Rogers Disintegrator Pistol XZ-38, Daisy, 1935, copper-finish, sold in stores and used as a premium by Cream of Wheat, and in 1939 by Popsicle, no holster or box, still flashes, fine condition, approx. 9-3/4" l. **$430**

Courtesy of Heritage Auctions, ha.com

Buck Rogers lithographed tin wind-up spaceship, Louis Marx, complete and in working order, makes an intermittent noise as it moves along, as intended, 12" l. **$275**

Courtesy of Heritage Auctions, ha.com

"Say Hey" Willie Mays Baseball Game and Mickey Mantle Baseball Action Game. Dating to the season of the New York Giants' four-game World Series sweep, the Willie Mays game by Oliver Game Toy Development Co. capitalizes on the persona of the sport's most exciting player. This is the larger of two versions, adding "1954's Most Valuable Player" text to the box, which opens to reveal a folded playing surface with three functioning spinners, original instructions, two unused scorecards and game pieces; 9-1/2" x 14 x 1-1/2". Also included is a 4" x 7" Official Mickey Mantle Baseball Action Game made by the Kohner Bros. in VG working condition. **$492**

Courtesy of Heritage Auctions, ha.com

Antique Japanese Kobe wooden articulated Eater, hand carved and stained wood lever-operated toy with amusing action: figure cuts and eats melon, good condition, 4-1/2" x 3-1/2" x 2-1/2" **$150**

Courtesy of Hill Auction Gallery, hillauctiongallery.com

Lot of 16 various Steadfast toy London and Scottish soldiers, very good condition. **$110**

Courtesy of Centurion Auctions, centurionauctions.com

Scream'n Demons Daredevil Dragout! and Lunatic Fringe lot of two, Hasbro, 1971. These 7" long custom Harley-Davidson choppers were made by Hasbro in 1971 and seemed to be a mixed tribute to both daredevil Evel Knievel and biker films like Born to be Wild and The Wild Ones. This group includes the large Daredevil Dragout! set that includes Dirty Devil and Doom Buggy. Also included is the individually packaged Lunatic Fringe motorcycle and rider. The kit is in its original box and is complete and fine condition. The Lunatic Fringe is still in its original box, which is in good condition, and toy is excellent. . **$57**

Courtesy of Heritage Auctions, ha.com

McFarlane Movie Maniacs Collectibles Edition Feature Film Figure of *The Crow*/Eric Draven, McFarlane Toys, 2000, with custom accessories including a black crow, black guitar, and stand for each, in original box, 12"................................**$25**

Courtesy of Heritage Auctions, ha.com

Superman Magical Television Party Favor, Gem Party Favor Co., c. 1960s. The directions read, "Moisten a screen of television lightly, then a funy [sic] picture come out in it." Made in Japan, still sealed in original cellophane packaging, which is in Very Good condition, with the card inside being in Excellent condition. **$25**

Courtesy of Heritage Auctions, ha.com

Mickey Mantle Backyard Baseball and Zoom Ball Toy, in original packaging, c. 1960s. The Mick's name and face were everywhere throughout the 1950s-'60s, including these vintage toys. Included are a Zoom Ball and a Backyard Baseball, both with original packaging in VG condition. **$192**

Courtesy of Heritage Auctions, ha.com

VINTAGE ELECTRONICS

THERE'S PLENTY OF HISTORY to collect in the ever-growing and expanding category of vintage electronics. From the dawn of the Electrical Age (which spans 1600-1800) to the household innovations of today, the depth and variety of vintage electronics makes it one of the fastest-growing collectible segments in the hobby. This is because of an influx of younger collectors (generally mid-20s to mid-40s) who happen to be the first generation to live with mobile, digital technology crucial to modern life.

Despite the innovation and constantly changing adaptations, the principals of electronics have remained unchanged for more than 100 years. Non-collectors might be surprised to learn that the same basic technology that made the original ViewMaster a commercial hit in 1938 is the basis of today's latest virtual reality technology. Presenting two photographs of the same object from slightly different angles is the basis of the Oculus Rift virtual reality device (which may itself be a hot collectible in the next 25 years).

Some of the most sought-after examples of vintage electronics in today's hobby include rare or mint condition video game consoles and games; calculators from the early 1970s; and personal computers from the very early years of the technology, such as the Hewlett Packard 9100A released in 1968 or the KENBAK – 1, which sold for $35,000 at auction in early 2015. By the time you read this chapter, the average cost of a laptop computer is about $600, while the resale value of its 40+ year-old-grandfather starts at about $1,200 and ends at more than $600,000 for one of the scant 63 surviving examples of the Apple 1 computer assembled by Steve Jobs and his friends in 1976. In 2017, Christies sold a 1976 Apple I computer for $355,000.

Vintage electronics fall into the category of "usable collectible"; vintage electronics collectors put a premium on usability over decorative value. A good example is the growing popularity of collecting vintage electronics that surround music. Collectors fuel a robust hobby by hunting down obscure and obsolete EL34 tubes made in the early 1960s in West Germany by Telefunken (generally found at $75-$100). The tubes were used in amplifiers made by companies such as Marshall and Hi-Watt and are now prized by collectors and audiophiles who restore amps for the sole purpose of recreating the unique "British-tone" that made the music of The Beatles and Led Zeppelin. Was the music produced by the young Eric Clapton rooted in his

Vintage Bally *Baby Pacman* video arcade game, 68" h x 22-1/2" w x 37" d............. **$650**

Courtesy of Clars Auction Gallery, clars.com

imagination and creativity? Absolutely. Were the unique British amps and EL34 tubes crucial in enhancing his harmonic consistency? Without a doubt. So while it might be easy to find parts of a vintage Marshall amp from the days of The British Invasion for about $50 to $200, a near-mint/mint amp in perfect working order will likely cost between $1,500 and $5,500. American examples from the 1950s can command five figures.

One popular niche to appear in the last five years is the emergence of the collection and restoration of vintage boombox stereos, which were a commercial hit in the 1970s and

1980s. Collectors have formed clubs across the country, founded an active Facebook page (Boomboxery), and even an annual event, the Boomboxery International Blaster Summit.

Resources: *Retro-Electro: Collecting Technology: From Atari to Walkman*, Pepe Tozzo, Universe Publishing.

Atari 2600 video game console system, 1980, with controllers, etc., unknown if complete, 24" x 13".............. **$50**

Courtesy of Stephenson's Auction, stephensonauction.com

Star Wars Electronic Laser Battle Game, encapsulated boxed set contains electronic (with AC adaptor or battery) game from Kenner's popular 1977 *Star Wars* toy line, ©1977 Twentieth Century-Fox Film Corporation, AFA-graded 80 NM, from the Russell Branton Star Wars Collection. Branton's peerless collection was sold at auction by Hake's Americana. For more on that, see P. 647. ....**$2,905**

Courtesy of Hake's Americana & Collectibles, hakes.com

Namco *Final Lap 2* arcade race car game, both sides power on and play, includes three keys to open the money depositor, minor damage to the driver side of the floor area, light water damage. **$900**

Courtesy of Great Expectations Auction Company, LLC, liveauctioneers.com

Colecovision video game system, expansion pack, gaming system, games, super action controller set, expansion module, controllers, power supply, owner's manuals, and 10 games including *Turmoil, Zaxxon, Frogger, Donkey Kong*, untested.......**$50**

Courtesy of Lemar Auctions and Estate Services, lemarauctions.com

Tetris cocktail table video game, manufactured by Atari Games, 1988, working condition............. **$250**

Courtesy of Centex Auction Group, centexauctiongroup.com

Working Pachislo *Jet Set Radio* Japanese Skill Stop Token Redemption Slot Machine with LCD display video screen, based on the Sega Dreamcast game of the same name, Model #7777, with keys, bag of tokens, operation manual. **$75**

Courtesy of Gulfcoast Coin & Jewelry, gulfcoastcoin.com

◄ Ted Nugent pinball machine, Stern Electronics, full size, plug-and-play ready, nice condition, 30" w x 52" l x 71" h................................. **$1,900**

Courtesy of Kraft Auction Service, kraftauction.com

▶ Miller Beer electronic message board, 35" w, 17" h, 4" d......**$60**

Courtesy of Dotta Auction Co., Inc., dottaauction.com

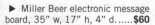

The "Bubbler" Jukebox, 25¢, Rock-Ola. One of the more recent versions of the most classic jukebox of all time, this "Bubbler" features a more contemporary electronic song selector with hundreds of songs to choose from and instead of playing the traditional vinyl record, this machine carries CDs, but the rest of its known characteristics remain the same such as the kaleidoscopic bubble lighting, the die cast front grill and the mirrored horizontal tiles on each side of the jukebox. With four keys, excellent condition, 60" h x 34" w x 26" d................. **$2,750**

Courtesy of Dan Morphy Auctions, morphyauctions.com

Freed Eisman battery radio and Victor Model VV-5 410 No. 605, 1920s, victrola also has an electronic reproducer, 38" w x 34-1/2" h. **$350**

Courtesy of Dennis Auction Service, Inc., dennisauction.com

▶ Leica "R3" electronic camera with lens and display case, two pieces, serial No. 1486161, with a Leitz Summicron-R 50mm f1.2 lens, accompanied by a Leica camera display case featuring Amatl wood veneer, camera also has a leather case, strap, and both pieces come with original box and paperwork, camera is 3-3/4" h, 5-3/4" w; case is 4" h, 11" w, 6-1/8" d. **$550**

Courtesy of DuMouchelle, dumouchelle.com

10 **Things** You Didn't Know About **Nikon**

1 The company has been in business for 100 years: Two of Japan's leading optical manufacturers merged, with capital investment from Koyata Iwasaki, the president of Mitsubishi, on July 25, 1917, forming Nippon Kogaku K.K. ("Japan Optical Industries Co., Ltd."). Immediately after the formation, it merged with Fuji Lens Manufacturing. Headquartered in Tokyo, the newly formed optics firm began researching optical glass in 1918, but suspended operations because of technical difficulties. (The company's name is changed to Nikon Corporation in 1988.)

2 First marketed in 1921, Nikon's MIKRON ultra-small-prism binoculars were one of the first binocular models developed, designed, and manufactured by the firm. MIKRON binoculars were re-released in 1997, proving popular with collectors.

3 The name "Nikon" was adopted for small-sized cameras in 1946. However, it wasn't until 1948 that a camera actually bore that name. It was first sold as simply "Nikon," but "Model I" was soon added to distinguish it from subsequent camera models.

4 Japan took the lead in professional photography equipment in 1959 thanks to the introduction of the Nikon F single-lens reflex (SLR) camera. With a motorized advance making the camera capable of exposing four frames per second, and lenses from 21mm to 1000mm, it offered photographers speed and diversity in addition to reliable image capturing. In November 1965, six years after the release, the 200,000th Nikon F was presented to photographer David Douglas Duncan, who made the Nikon and NIKKOR brand names known all over the world. Nikon F-series cameras were produced until May 1974; more than 850,000 were made.

5 A Nikon I SLR camera, in original condition and good working order with original shutter blinds, sold for 40,000 euro (about $45,929 U.S., excluding buyer's premium) on June 10, 2017, during the WestLicht Photographica Auction in Vienna, Austria. The early "5 digit" Nikon I features two film guide rails, fixed spool, uncovered base, matching serial number in back door and number "3" engraved inside (a chassis number which was used to complete the camera from its single parts), base plate engraved "MADE IN OCCUPIED JAPAN," with matching Tokyo Nikkor-H.C 2/5cm No. 708363 lens, UV filter, cap, black painted hood, original Nikon film spool, original yellow/white Nikon I instruction manual, and rare blue velvet maker's box.

6 A rare Nikon S3 rangefinder camera sold for 85,000 euro (about $97,600 U.S., excluding buyer's premium) during a June 2017 WestLicht Photographica Auction in Vienna. The outfit is reported to have been owned by a U.S. Navy intelligence officer stationed in Japan. The Nikon S3-M black camera with S72 motor drive in black, 1960, No. 18x24mm was in fully original, perfect working and near mint condition. The motor drive is number 94885 and registers up to 72 exposures, and the large, green Nikkor-S 1.4/5cm battery pack is number 413204.

7 The Nikon F's use by explorers is a testament to its toughness, durability and reliability. Influenced by Japanese climbing parties using Nikon cameras on their Mount Everest

WestLicht Photographica Auction in Vienna, Austria, sold this Nikkor Fisheye 5.6/6.2mm SAP, circa 1964, in November 2015. One of the rarest Nikon lenses in existence, the optical gadget sold for about $150,300.

Courtesy of WestLicht Photographica Auction, westlicht-auction.com

This Nikon I SLR camera, in original condition and good working order with original shutter blinds, sold about $45,929 on June 10, 2017, during the WestLicht Photographica Auction in Vienna, Austria.

Courtesy of WestLicht Photographica Auction, westlicht-auction.com

This rare Nikon S3 rangefinder camera sold for about $97,600 during the June 10 WestLicht Photographica Auction in Vienna.

Courtesy of WestLicht Photographica Auction, westlicht-auction.com

US astronaut Barry "Butch" Wilmore inspects one of the cameras aboard the International Space Station Jan. 25, 2015, in preparation for another photo session of station experiments. Barry is the Commander of Expedition 42. Photo by Barry Wilmore

Courtesy of International Space Station/NASA, nasa.gov

This aerial view of Cincinnati was acquired on April 10, 2015, with a Nikon D4 digital camera using an 800 millimeter lens, and is provided by the ISS Crew Earth Observations Facility and the Earth Science and Remote Sensing Unit, Johnson Space Center. This image was taken by a member of the Expedition 43 crew. The International Space Station Program supports the laboratory as part of the ISS National Lab to help astronauts take pictures of Earth that will be of the greatest value to scientists and the public, and to make those images available at images.nasa.gov.

Courtesy of International Space Station/NASA, nasa.gov

expeditions, in 1963, the American Mount Everest expedition purchased 20 Nikon F systems to document the adventure. The group, including James W. Whittaker, who is the first American to reach Everest's summit, reached the peak on May 1, 1963, and the Nikon Fs reportedly "delivered a fully satisfactory performance in the recording of valuable measurements and investigations."

8 Nikon cameras can be spotted in many iconic films from the last several decades. In Francis Ford Coppola's film, Apocalypse Now (1979), the photojournalist played by Dennis Hopper is outfitted with several Nikon cameras. In Stanley Kubrick's *Full Metal Jacket* (1987), J.T. "Joker" Davis, played by Matthew Modine, also carries a Nikon camera.

9 In November 2015, WestLicht Photographica Auction in Vienna, Austria, sold one of the rarest Nikon lenses in existence: the Nikkor Fisheye 5.6/6.2mm SAP, circa 1964. Covering a picture angle of 230 degrees, the lens captures views behind the camera. As number 1014, this is the first of only three lenses produced; it is in almost new condition with caps and leather case. Excluding the buyer's premium, the Nikkor Fisheye lens sold for 130,000 euro (about $150,300 U.S.).

10 Nikon made it to outer space in 1972: According to NASA, the equipment for the Apollo 16 mission included a 35mm Nikon F "fitted with a 55mm f/l.2 lens for astronomical and dim-light photographic experiments." The Nikons performed well. The ISS is equipped with several Nikons. As of July 2010, more than 700,000 photos had been snapped by Nikon cameras from outside the earth's atmosphere. Many of the images taken from space can be viewed at images.nasa.gov.

– Compiled by Karen Knapstein

Sources: liveauctioneers.com/westlicht-photographica-auction; pixelpluck.com; cameras.reviewed.com; eol.jsc.nasa.gov/FAQ/#camera; www.nikon.com; imaging.nikon.com

A pair of Shep International Ltd. Neve 31105 rackmount modules, made in England, from the collection of Neil Young. **$5,500**

Courtesy of Julien's Auctions, juliensauctions.com

Electronic Token slot machine, with a box of tokens, excellent working condition, 19" x 15" x 32" h. **$1,200**

Courtesy of Rockabilly Auction Company, rockabillyauction.com

A rare and unused 1983 Technics SL-D33 turntable, direct-drive automatic turntable system in silver and black, featuring die-cast construction, includes a high-line Audio Technica 140 LC cartridge, mounted in a special headshell: the MG6 which is magnesium with a special vibration-damping insert, system has a silver base with '80s modern square silver knobs and a black and silver stylus arm, has speeds of 33 and 45 rpm, power and audio cables included, along with the unique connector cable for the Technics remote control system, also included is the original Technics dust cover in mint condition. . **$400**

Courtesy of Jasper52, jasper52.com

Custom Gibson guitar and case, 1960s, black and yellow, Model ES335, serial number 891118, new replacement tuners marked West Germany, holes from past tuners, Bigsby front plate, comes with case, some wear........................ **$2,750**

Courtesy of Lemar Auctions and Estate Services, lemarauctions.com

Vintage Wurlitzer Model 140B electronic portable piano, featuring extra smaller legs, foot pedal, and key cover, manufactured and marketed by Wurlitzer, sound is generated by striking a metal reed with a hammer, which induces an electric current in a pickup. Wurlitzer manufactured several different models of electric pianos, including console models with built-in frames, and standalone stage models with chrome legs, good condition, 39" x 22" x 33". **$550**

Courtesy of Matthew Bullock Auctioneers, bullockauctioneers.com

WATCHES

A WRISTWATCH ONCE BELONGING to legendary superstar Paul Newman caused rousing excitement in the vintage watch hobby late last year when set a world record after selling at auction for $17.8 million (see Top Lot).

The auction by Phillips in Association with Bacs & Russo in October 2017 opened with a "startling and deliberate" phone bid of $10 million, which created a 12-minute bidding war for the "Paul Newman" Daytona Rolex, until it went to a final bidder on the phone. Watch enthusiasts from around the world followed this historic moment online, over the phone, and in a packed salesroom of more than 700 people, according to Phillips.

"Kicking off our fall season, 'Winning Icons' was a groundbreaking event for the international collecting community, realizing $28.8 million and establishing the highest total ever achieved for a watch auction in the United States. This historic sale was led by the one and only original 'Paul Newman' Daytona, the true 'Adam and Eve' of the watch-collecting world," said Aurel Bacs, Phillips senior consultant. "This record result is a testament to the historic importance and continued legacy of this Rolex."

Rolex and Patek Philippe watches remain at the top of the vintage and antique market. This Patek Philippe wristwatch, Ref. 3974J, is yellow gold, has an automatic perpetual calendar, minute repeating, (watch was produced with the Star Calibre in 1989 to celebrate Patek Philippe's 150th anniversary), each required four years of development and assembly with 467 individual parts, and is very rare and important.
....................................**$322,500**

Courtesy Heritage Auctions, ha.com

This timepiece is the only 'exotic'-dialed Daytona that Newman owned, inspiring the storied nickname for the most prestigious versions of Rolex's Daytona, and it was only fitting that this ultimate of sought-after lots would lead Phillips Watches' New York City debut following numerous successful seasons in Geneva and Hong Kong.

The atmosphere was electric throughout the entire sale of iconic watches from the 20th century, which featured rare and important models from Omega, Heuer, Audemars Piguet, Cartier, and other leading watchmakers, according to Phillips.

The total sale realized $28,875,750 — the all-time record for a U.S. watch auction — and saw participation from bidders across 43 countries.

For the hobby in general, the new audience for vintage watches is, in fact, global.

"The vintage watch market is in a very healthy state at the moment," Phillip's Auctions' Paul Maudsley recently told the Business of Fashion (BOF). "Each year new collectors come on board and gain an understanding of the various specialist collected brands, and prices rise steadily."

Rolex and Patek Philippe remain at the top of the vintage and antique watch market, which experts say is worth in the region of $2 billion annually. The market for watches priced below $10,000 is white hot at the moment even as early versions of emerging brands gain a young and affluent following.

It appears classic style never goes away — it just gets more expensive.

Interest, too, is increasing for watches that were once deemed too stuffy for a younger generation to wear. Brands such as Vacheron Constantin, Audemars Piguet, and Breguet are being seen through fresh eyes — all this despite the fact manufacturers pump dozens of new brands into the marketplace every year.

"Most people think that watch sales start with price, but that's not the case," says Lloyd Amsdon, one of the founders of WatchFinder & Co, which sells pre-owned and vintage watches online and through a small network of UK retail outlets, in an interview with BOF. "The biggest single factor is choice. Retailers don't sell Rolexes made over the last 50 years; they sell the new ones. Vintage and pre-owned open up the market and give consumers more choice."

MARKET GROWTH

Vintage watch collecting has been a robust hobby since the 1960s. But sellers of vintage watches are now turning to social media outlets such as Instagram, subject-exclusive blogs, and online storefronts to snag new watch fans and satisfy demand. The internet's most dependable vintage watch website, Hodinkee, opened an online store recently to help consumers locate dependable vintage watches at affordable prices.

Customers from the Middle East, London, China, and Hong Kong are making up much of the vintage watch consumption market in the United States. It's easier to own a vintage watch and it's now seen as chic to sport a brand that is different than the newest label. Collecting vintage watches can be an addictive hobby thanks to the thousands of brands and styles available produced across the last 125 years.

NOT AN INVESTMENT

Like any collectible, experts will warn collectors not to rely too heavily on the value of vintage watches increasing in the future. Just as the vintage watch market is seeing an uptick, the modern watch market is seeing a downswing. The same could happen to vintage watches at a moment's notice, according to Maudsley. "Whether its modern or vintage watches, they should be looked upon for their aesthetics, technical function and so on, not purely as investments — we have the stock market for that," he told BOF. "But that said, if a watch purchase is driven by a passion for the pieces, an understanding of the quality and rarity, and the buyer has done their research, then they have proven to have risen in price."

It is important to note the market for general pocket watches (as dependable as they may seem) is not nearly as strong as the market for vintage wristwatches. Tastes and clothing change and no one seem to have the pocket space for a pocket watch next to their iPhone. A vintage wristwatch makes a completely different statement.

FUTURE POTENTIAL

Here is one example of the boon in value vintage watches have experienced during the last 40 years. The Horological Society of New York recently unearthed four wrist and pocket watches that had spent the last 40 years in a long forgotten vault. They were donated to the society at a time when the vintage watch market was in its infancy, said Heritage Auctions watch expert Michael Fossner.

The vault held two wristwatches: an Audemars Piguet 18K Gold Square Wristwatch Ref. 5128BA Signed Tiffany & Co. Circa 1960, which sold for $5,0000, and a Patek Philippe Ref. 3514 18k Gold Automatic Wristwatch, which hammered for $15,000. And two pocket watches: an Audemars Piguet 18K Gold Ultra-Thin Pocket Watch Signed Tiffany & Co. Circa 1959, which sold for $4,600, and a Piaget $20 Saint Gaudens Gold Coin Watch Signed Cartier, which ended at $4,000. The proceeds benefited the HSNY Endowment Fund.

"These great watches by Patek, Audemars Piguet, Piaget and others were of modest value when donated to the Society, where they were consigned to a vault and forgotten, oblivious to the skyrocketing market outside," he said.

As the HSNY auction shows, the vintage watch market is still very much a new and unexploited marketplace. As thousands of people worldwide begin to gain interest in vintage watches, can the vintage market keep pace before demand outstrips supply? Only time will tell.

Pocket watch, 1936, Hamilton 23 Jewel 950 Elinvar, gold-filled case, bar over crown, screw back and bezel, double sunk dial, bold "box car" Arabic numerals, blued spade hands, sub seconds, No. 2639079, 16 size. **$750**

Courtesy of Heritage Auctions, ha.com

Pocket watch, circa 1934, mfg. Ball, Hamilton 23 Jewel Grade 999 Official RR Standard Rare Dial, 18 mm, gold filled display case, enamel dial,, Montgomery with inner 24 hour numerals, blued steel spade hands, movement: No. 644370,.. **$5,000**

Courtesy Heritage Auctions, ha.com

Movado, 1925, Movado, skeleton case front of a 1866 20 pesos gold coin, gold back with profile of Emperador Maximiliano, upper 18k gold frame work with griffins and swords, pin back, crown form winding crown, central eagle dial on a black enamel ground, unusual and rare, 35 mm. **$4,062**

Courtesy of Heritage Auctions, ha.com

Pocket watch, 1899, Illinois Watch Company, containing seven sets of small gold/quartz samples and one large gold quartz sample, engraved to a one John J. Kelly (Kelling), June 7, 1899, California. **$4,062**

Courtesy of Holabird Western Americana, fhwac.com

Wristwatch, Van Cleef & Arpels, gold, Concord, 14k and 18k mechanical, sweep seconds hands, date aperture, dia. ap. 22 mm., dial signed Van Cleef & Arpels, Concord, case nos. 2085241 & 387635, ap. 36.7 dwts. Gross, 6-1/2" dia... **$1,062**

Courtesy of Doyle New York, doyle.com

Wristwatch, Patek Philippe, 2005, Ref. 5970R-001, rose gold chronograph, perpetual calendar, moon phases, tachometer, 24-hour indication. **$125,000**

Courtesy Heritage Auctions, ha.com

Wristwatch, Hamilton, H385150 steel automatic, polished and brushed, transparent case back secured with screws, sapphire crystals, satin silver dial with raise steel dart indexes, numeral at 12, date aperture at six, 21 jewel movement, 40 mm. **$212**

Courtesy Heritage Auctions, ha.com

Wristwatch, 1997, Jaeger-Lecoultre, Ref. 270.8.68, case: 26mm wide, dial and movement signed, stainless steel and enamel wristwatch, No. 28 of 97 pieces, rare, 42 mm l. **$6,059**

Courtesy of Phillips, phillips.com

Wristwatch, 2015, Louis Vuitton, Ref. 05EK00, white gold, world-time, hand-painted dial, Case, dial and movement signed, 41 mm dia. **$30,295**

Courtesy of Phillips, phillips.com

Wristwatch, 2006, Franck Muller, lady's unused specimen, Ref. 1750 S6, steel tonneau, two-body case, stainless steel, sapphire crystal, 35 mm x 25 mm. **$2,250**

Courtesy of Heritage Auctions, ha.com

Wristwatch, 1940, Breitling, early chronograph, three body, stainless snap back, base metal center and bezel, silvered dial, luminous Arabic numerals, 45 minute register at twelve, sub seconds at six, blue telemeter scale, Venus 170 movement, nickel finished, 17 jewels, signed Pontiac, 35 mm. **$750**

Courtesy of Heritage Auctions, ha.com

Wristwatch, circa 1970s, Piaget lady's diamond, coral, black onyx with gold, oval-shaped 18k gold case, coral tablet dial with gold Dauphine hands, sapphire crystal, manual wind movement, 17 jewels, Piaget, 18k gold integral bracelet featuring pear and marquise-shaped black onyx and coral tablets, full-cut diamonds, 4 carat approx total weigh, 7-1/4" l. **$75,000**

Courtesy of Heritage Auctions, ha.com

top lot

Provenance matters, especially when it comes to items owned by legendary celebrities. A wristwatch that Oscar-winning actor, philanthropist, racing enthusiast, and style icon Paul Newman once wore around his wrist every day for 15 years became the world's most expensive wristwatch ever auctioned when it sold for a record-breaking $17.8 million.

Newman's own "Paul Newman" Rolex Cosmograph Daytona — a gift from his wife, actress Joanne Woodward — has long been considered the Holy Grail among watch collectors. It had been expected to sell for around $1.3 million, but after fierce bidding, the iconic watch was won by an anonymous bidder for almost 14 times the asking price.

According to Phillips, which auctioned the legendary watch, "It's a timepiece whose importance to 20th and 21st-century watch collecting cannot be understated. After all, once the watch community attributed the nickname to Daytona models fitted with Rolex's artistic 'exotic' dial, demand skyrocketed for all models of Daytona, making it perhaps the most widely sought after collectors' watch up to the present day."

Paul Newman (1925-2008) with his wife, actress Joanne Woodward, circa 1963. Joanne gave her husband the record-breaking Daytona as a gift.

Photo by Fotos International/Archive Photos/Getty Images

Woodward bought her husband the "exotic dial" Daytona likely from Tiffany & Co. in New York in 1968-1969, and had the back inscribed, "Drive Carefully Me." This is in reference to

Rolex Reference No: 6239, model Cosmograph "Paul Newman" Daytona, 1968, stainless steel chronograph wristwatch with off-white dial and tachymeter bezel, case No: 2'005'325, engraved "Drive Carefully Me," hand-engraved inventory number D61798 under side of top left lug, 17 jewelsc, crocodile "Bund-style" strap, 37mm dia.................................$17,752,500

Courtesy of Phillips, phillips.com

Newman's new interest in car racing after filming the 1969 movie, *Winning*, in which they co-starred. He wore the watch for years until giving it away in the 1980s to James Cox, the then-boyfriend of his daughter, Nell, according to Phillips.

The watch came accompanied with a signed letter written by Nell, documenting its provenance and her support of its sale. In the letter, she recounts the moment the watch got handed down to Cox: "… Pop asked James if he knew the time. Apparently Pop forgot to wind his wristwatch that morning. James responded that he didn't know the time and didn't own a watch. Pop handed James his Rolex and said, 'If you can remember to wind this each day, it tells pretty good time.'"

A portion of the proceeds went to The Nell Newman Foundation and Newman's Own Foundation, in support of Paul Newman's philanthropy, Phillips said.

Wristwatch, circa 1970s, Pierre Cardin, Jaeger France, unusual case: No: 591752, curved to fit on side of wrist, screw back, acrylic crystal, 45 mm x 36 mm. **$375**

Courtesy of Heritage Auctions, ha.com

Wristwatch, 1961, Hamilton Wear Test Pacer, yellow and white gold filled case, two body, asymmetric, charcoal gray dial, model 500 movement, electric, (Hamilton's design department considered different colors for dials in 1961, but this charcoal gray version was never marketed), 45 mm x 32 mm. **$2,000**

Courtesy of Heritage Auctions, ha.com

Wristwatch, circa 1946, Rolex Ref. 3372 Steel & Gold Bubble Back Chronometre, stainless steel case, gold bezel, case No. 488417, 'C' mark on back of upper left lug, three body, screw back, acrylic crystal, black dial, gold markers with outer luminous dot, luminous lozenge hands, center seconds, 31 mm. **$2,000**

Courtesy of Heritage Auctions, ha.com

Wristwatch, 1925, Hausmann & Co. gold single button split seconds chronograph, 18k yellow gold case, four body, hinged gold cuvette signed "Hausmann & Co. Roma, Napoli, Genova," moveable wire lugs, white enamel dial, open Arabic numerals, signed "Hausmann & Co.," rare, 46 mm. **$8,125**

Courtesy of Heritage Auctions, ha.com

Wristwatch, circa 1964, Hamilton Nautilus, dial commissioned by President Lyndon Baines Johnson, 10k rolled gold plate case, silver dial with applied gold numerals and engraved golden indexes, LBJ initials and the motto "Do Unto Others As You Would Have Them Do Unto You," 34 mm.**$875**

Courtesy of Heritage Auctions, ha.com

WILDLIFE ART

WILDLIFE ART IS BECOMING an increasingly popular genre for collectors and museum curators.

At the 2017 Coer d'Alene Art Auction in July, which realized more than $16 million in sales, the top lot for wildlife art was an oil painting by Carl Rungius that sold for nearly $500,000 (see Top Lot).

The decoy market is showing signs of a tremendous recovery after several years of lower-than-expected auction prices for even the most celebrated carvers. Investment-grade decoys are again brining close to six-figure sums and collectors are not afraid to bid aggressively to own key decoys that have had much exposure in either books on the topic or museum exhibitions.

"The most popular genre collected today seems to be animals from the farm, said Rod Zullo, a wildlife sculptor artist and fellow of the National Sculpture Society. "Horses and dogs continue to touch the personal needs of today's collectors."

Zullo says he personally continues to see an improvement of the market as the economy improves: "The better the economy, the more disposable income, hence better prices and more sales."

PAINTINGS

It appears 19th century oils are performing much better than they have in the recent past. The oil on canvas titled *Pointer and Quail*, 1892, by Edmund Henry Osthaus (born in Hildesheim, Germany, in 1858) seared its $30,000 pre-auction estimate to sell for $63,000 at Copley Fine Arts Auctions winter sale in 2017. And a second Osthaus' oil on canvas hunting scene titled *On Point*, depicting two hunting dogs who have spotted their quarry, sold for $44,400 against a $25,000 pre-auction estimate.

Katmai Bears, Ken Carlson (b. 1937), oil on board, signed lower right, 30" x 45". **$59,500**

Courtesy of The Coeur d'Alene Art Auction, cdaartauction.com

Frederick Stone Batcheller's *Woodcock and Quail*, circa 1855 — a stunning still life of a day's bounty — blew its $5,000 estimate out of the water when it sold for $11,400. Of course these high-flying auction prices generally do not attract first-time wildlife art collectors. Many start at smaller price points.

Zullo suggests finding a resource you can trust. "The best advice I can give to a new collector is to find a dealer you can trust and that has a proven track record of advising collectors," he said. "The collector should heed the advice from the dealer as to what subject matter and genre is a solid investment, but they should also remember that art is about what you like, not what someone else likes."

CONTEMPORARY SCULPTURE

When the well-known Judson C. and Nancy Sue Ball collection hit the market a few years ago, it released a number of contemporary wildlife sculptures to collecting acclaim. Jonathan Kenworthy's *Leaping Wildebeest*, 1991, a bronze with brown patina, hammered for $55,000 following interest from four bidders and Antoine-Louis Barye's *Bear Fleeing from Dogs*, a bronze with brown patina, sold for $10,625.

Two more lots exceeded estimates as Kenneth Rodney Bunn's *Vantage Point*, 1997, a wonderful depiction of a bear perched on a log, sold for $27,500, and Michael Coleman's *Moose*, 1998, a bronze with brown patina, ended at $23,125, beating out a renowned Albert Bierstadt *Pink Butterfly*, circa late 1800s, which sold for $18,875.

It appears collectors are seeking bold representations of wildlife scenes and portraits that capture the majesty of the wilderness and its big-game animals.

TODAY'S TALENT INCREASING SALES

Contemporary artists are increasingly taking advantage of social media as a way to promote their art and observations on the art world.

"Social media is today what websites where 15 years ago," Zullo said. "It's important to have a presence, but it can be overdone. You don't want the public to see so much of your work that they become overwhelmed.

"Sharing work and ideas is good, but be careful not to be so common," Zullo advises. "People become bored with your work. Try to keep it as special as it truly is. Social media is a balance of enough but not too much. It does connect the artist with other like minds and that is a good thing."

Follow the Leader (2017), Steve Burgess (b. 1960), oil on board, signed lower right, 24" x 44". **$16,660**

Disturbed Daydreams (1986), Carl Brenders (b. 1937), gouache on paper, signed and dated lower left, 28" x 22". **$8,925**

Courtesy of The Coeur d'Alene Art Auction, cdaartauction.com

Courtesy of The Coeur d'Alene Art Auction, cdaartauction.com

top lot

he top lot for wildlife art at the 2017 Coer d'Alene Art Auction was this painting, *Out* *e Canyon*, by visionary artist Carl Rungius (1869-1959), oil on canvas, signed lower t, 28" x 36", that sold for $476,000.

ccording to Peter Hassrick, now the director of The American Institute of Western erican Art at the Denver Art Museum, "For many, the symbol of the North American tinent lies not in the people or politics which guide it through history, but in the itself and the native animals which have long thrived there. It has not only been ts who have recognized in their observations of the natural world a pervasive force lematic of America's greatness — there seems to be a place in the hearts of all . Yet, there was one man, Carl Clemens Maritz Rungius, whose vision of that symbol eeded most others and whose acuteness of observation brought the natural beauty o world to those who could never see for themselves."

assrick said Rungius, born in Berlin in 1869, first came to America in 1894 to visit an e in Brooklyn and go moose hunting in Maine. "They found no moose that summer, t was for the best, as the disappointment caused Rungius to stay for another season following summar, at the invitation of the colorful Wyoming outfitter, Ira Dodge, gius spent five months on the East Fork of the Green River in the shadow of the natic Wind River Mountains. It was an area known to provide initial inspiration for many great western artists, Alfred Jacob Miller and Albert Bierstadt being two of the iest," Hassrick said. "From this time on, the Far West and Rockies became Rungius' dio, the abundant wildlife his models. He traveled to Yellowstone and Jackson Hole tching, hunting, and collecting specimens from which to work when he returned east, aid.

The Rifleman Bird, Raymond Harris Ching (b. 1939), gouache on paper, signed lower right, 21" x 19". **$3,570**

Courtesy of The Coeur d'Alene Art Auction, cdaartauction.com

Homestead Covey (1981), David Hagerbaumer (b. 1921), watercolor on paper, signed and dated lower left, 13" x 18". . **$595**

Courtesy of The Coeur d'Alene Art Auction, cdaartauction.com

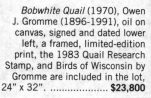

Bobwhite Quail (1970), Owen J. Gromme (1896-1991), oil on canvas, signed and dated lower left, a framed, limited-edition print, the 1983 Quail Research Stamp, and Birds of Wisconsin by Gromme are included in the lot, 24" x 32". **$23,800**

Courtesy of The Coeur d'Alene Art Auction, cdaartauction.com

Indian Summer (1999), Carl Brenders (b. 1937), mixed media on paper, signed and dated lower right, 28" x 39-1/2"... **$8,925**

Courtesy of The Coeur d'Alene Art Auction, cdaartauction.com

Grouse, George Browne (1918-1958), oil on canvas, signed lower right, 20" x 24". **$7,735**

Courtesy of The Coeur d'Alene Art Auction, cdaartauction.com

Three of a Kind (2017), Ken Carlson (b. 1937), oil on board, signed lower right, 18" x 22". **$17,850**

Courtesy of The Coeur d'Alene Art Auction, cdaartauction.com

Elk Topping Out, Bob Kuhn (1920-2007), acrylic on board, signed lower right, 10" x 12". **$19,040**

Courtesy of The Coeur d'Alene Art Auction, cdaartauction.com

Montana Traveler, Bob Kuhn (1920-2007), acrylic on board, signed lower left, 12" x 15". **$101,150**

Courtesy of The Coeur d'Alene Art Auction, cdaartauction.com

Shady Spot, Bob Kuhn (1920-2007), acrylic on board, signed lower right, 20" x 28-1/2". **$53,550**

Courtesy of The Coeur d'Alene Art Auction, cdaartauction.com

Caught in the Open (2017), Luke Frazier (b. 1970), oil on board, signed lower left, 30" x 48". **$17,850**

Courtesy of The Coeur d'Alene Art Auction, cdaartauction.com

Competition, Lynn Bogue Hunt (1878-1960), oil on canvas, signed lower right, 20" x 27". **$19,040**

Courtesy of The Coeur d'Alene Art Auction, cdaartauction.com

Fall Outing, Frank B. Hoffman (1888-1958), oil on board, signed lower left, 18" x 24". **$22,610**

Courtesy of The Coeur d'Alene Art Auction, cdaartauction.com

Tiger in the Snow (1997), Terry Isaac (b. 1958), oil on board, signed and dated lower left, 28" x 40". **$7,140**

Courtesy of The Coeur d'Alene Art Auction, cdaartauction.com

High Country Monarch (1907), Carl Rungius (1869-1959), oil on canvas, signed lower right, dated lower left, 25" x 34". **$386,750**

Courtesy of The Coeur d'Alene Art Auction, cdaartauction.com

The Predator (1997), Bob Kuhn (1920-2007), acrylic on board, signed and dated lower right, 24" x 40". **$119,000**

Courtesy of The Coeur d'Alene Art Auction, cdaartauction.com

Abrupt Departure – Black Ducks and Mallards, David Maass (b. 1929), oil on board, signed lower right, 24" x 32". **$6,545**

Courtesy of The Coeur d'Alene Art Auction, cdaartauction.com

To Noses that Read, A Smell that Spells Man, Charles M. Russell (1864-1926), bronze, stamped in base: top - To Noses that Read | a Smell that | Spells Man | side - CM Russell [skull] | R.B.W., 4-1/2" h.
....**$166,600**

Courtesy of The Coeur d'Alene Art Auction, cdaartauction.com

WORLD WAR II COLLECTIBLES

DURING THE MORE than seven decades since the end of World War II, veterans, collectors, and nostalgia-seekers have eagerly bought, sold, and traded the "spoils of war." Actually, souvenir collecting began as soon as troops set foot on foreign soil. Whether Tommies from Great Britain, Doughboys from the United States, or Fritzies from Germany, soldiers eagerly looked for trinkets and remembrances that would guarantee their place in the historic events that unfolded before them. Helmets, medals, Lugers, field gear, daggers, and other pieces of war material filled parcels and duffel bags on the way back home.

As soon as hostilities ended in 1945, the populations of defeated Germany and Japan quickly realized they could make money-selling souvenirs to the occupation forces. The flow of war material increased. Values became well established; a Luger was worth several packs of cigarettes, a helmet, just one. A Japanese sword was worth two boxes of K-rations, an Arisaka bayonet was worth a Hershey's chocolate bar.

Over the years, these values have remained proportionally consistent. Today, that "two-pack" Luger might be worth $5,000 and that one-pack helmet, $1,500. The Japanese sword might fetch $1,200 and the Arisaka bayonet $95. Though values have increased dramatically, demand has not dropped off. In fact, World War II collecting is the largest segment of the militaria hobby.

For more information on World War II collectibles, see *Warman's World War II Collectibles Identification and Price Guide*, 3rd edition, by John Adams-Graf.

USAAF flying helmet group: leather A-11 flying helmet in excellent condition with avionics, Type A-14 soft rubber oxygen mask with straps, and pair of AN-6530 flying goggles with clear lenses and soft rubber.

.... **$435**

Courtesy of Heritage Auctions, ha.com

U.S. 82nd Airborne soldier's jump jacket and trousers, including paratrooper M2 knife.
.... **$3,200-$3,865**

Courtesy of AdvanceGuardMilitaria.com

U.S. AAF 13th Air Force 5th Bomb Group aerial gunner's painted A2 flight jacket.................. **$2,650**

Courtesy of AdvanceGuardMilitaria.com

U.S. Red Cross Woman's Military Welfare Service uniform. ....**$385-$425**

Courtesy of AdvanceGuardMilitaria.com

German SS Judicial Service Sturmführer black tunic. ....**$10,000-$12,000**

Courtesy of HistoryHunter.com

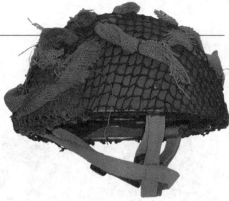

British MK II paratrooper helmet. ...... **$1,250-$1,700**

Courtesy of Peter Suciu

German reversible lace-up camouflage smock.
....**$11,000-$13,000**

Courtesy of HistoryHunter.com

German M35 SS double-decal helmet.
....**$8,000-$11,000**

Courtesy of HistoryHunter.com

U.S. Army officer's summer cap owned and used
by General Joseph W. "Vinegar Joe" Stilwell. . **$3,585**

Courtesy of Heritage Auctions, ha.com

◀ Luftwaffe Fallschirmjäger helmet, 2nd Model.
.... **$5,500-$7,000**

Courtesy of Hermann-Historica.de

Kriegsmarine rear admiral's service cap.
.... **$8,000-$9,000**

Courtesy of Hermann-Historica.de

British "Rupert" D-Day dummy paratrooper. **$3,346**

Courtesy of Heritage Auctions, ha.com

USAAF QAC A-5 parachute harness with A-4 parachute. .... **$800-$1,000**

Courtesy of AdvanceGuardMilitaria.com

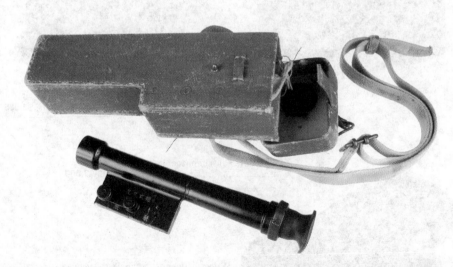

Japanese Type 99 4x sniper scope with case. .... **$2,500-$3,000**

Courtesy of Chris William

◄ "UNITED we are strong" propaganda poster, No. 64, U.S. Government Printing Office, 1943, issued by Office of War Information, near fine condition, folding creases, 28-1/2" x 40"..**$188**

Courtesy of Heritage Auctions, ha.com

◄ German factory-cased, gold-plated and relief-engraved Walther Model PP pistol as presented to SA officer, Viktor Lutze.. **$241,500**

Courtesy of Rock Island Auction Co., rockislandauction.com

▼ A 1933-1945 Nazi officer's sword with lion head handle, manufactured in Eichorn, Germany, excellent condition, 38" l. **$900**

Courtesy of Morphy Auctions, morphyauctions.com

▼ Winchester T3 carbine with original pattern M-2 infrared sniper scope and accessories. ....**$15,000-$30,000**

Courtesy of Rock Island Auction Co., rockislandauction.com

SPECIAL CONTRIBUTORS AND ADVISORS

The following collectors, dealers, sellers, and researchers have supported the *Antique Trader Antiques & Collectibles Price Guide* with their pricing and contacts over the years. Many continue to serve as a valuable resource to the entire collecting hobby, while others have passed away. We honor all contributors past and present as their hard work and passion lives on through this book.

John Adams-Graf

Andre Ammelounx

Mannie Banner

Tom Bartsch

Ellen Bercovici

Sandra Bondhus

James R. and Carol S.
  Boshears

Bobbie Zucker Bryson

Emmett Butler

Dana Cain

Linda D. Carannante

Dr. Anthony J. Cavo

David Chartier

Les and Irene Cohen

Amphora Collectors
  International

Les and Irene Cohen

Marion Cohen

Neva Colbert

Marie Compton

Susan N. Cox

Caroline Torem-Craig

Leonard Davis

Bev Dieringer

Janice Dodson

Del E. Domke

Debby DuBay

Susan Eberman

Steve Evans

Joan M. George

Roselyn Gerson

William A. and Donna J. Gray

Pam Green

Linda Guffey

Carl Heck

Alma Hillman

K. Robert and Bonne L. Hohl

Ellen R. Hill

Joan Hull

Hull Pottery Association

Louise Irvine

Helen and Bob Jones

Mary Ann Johnston

Donald-Brian Johnson

Dorothy Kamm

Edwin E. Kellogg

Madeleine Kirsh

Vivian Kromer

Curt Leiser

Gene Loveland

Mary McCaslin

Pat Moore

Mark F. Moran

Reg G. Morris

Craig Nissen

Joan C. Oates

Ed Pascoe

Margaret Payne

Gail Peck

John Petzold

Dr. Leslie Piña

Michael Polak

Joseph Porcelli

Arlene Rabin

John Rader, Sr.

Betty June Wymer

LuAnn Riggs

Tim and Jamie Saloff

Barry Sandoval

Federico Santi

Ellen Schroy

Arlyn Sieber

Mary Sieber

Peggy Sebek

Steve Stone

Michael Strawser

Phillip Sullivan

Chriss Swaney

Mark and Ellen Supnick

Tim Trapani

Jim Trautman

Bruce and Vicki Waasdorp

Elaine Westover

Kathryn Wiese

Pamela Y. Wiggins

Laurie Williams

Nancy Wolfe

Mark Wollemann

PRICING, IDENTIFICATIONS, AND IMAGES PROVIDED BY:

Dirk Soulis Auctions
529 W. Lone Jack Lees
Summit Road
Lone Jack, MO 64070
(816) 697-3830
www.dirksoulisauctions.com

Doyle New York
175 E. 87th St.
New York, NY 10128
(212) 427-2730
www.doylenewyork.com

Dreweatts &
Bloomsbury Auctions
24 Maddox St.
London, England W1S 1PP
+44 (207) 495-9494
www.dreweatts.com/

Dumouchelle Art Galleries
409 E. Jefferson Ave.
Detroit, MI 48226
(313) 963-6255
www.dumouchelle.com

Elite Decorative Arts
1034 Gateway Blvd., #108
Boynton Beach, FL 33426
(561) 200-0893
www.eliteauction.com

Fine Arts Auctions, LLC
324 S. Beverly Dr., #175
Beverly Hills, CA 90212
(310) 990-2150
www.fineartauctionllc.com

Fontaine's Auction Gallery
1485 W. Housatonic St.
Pittsfield, MA 01210
www.fontainesauction.net

Forsythes' Auctions, LLC
P.O. Box 188
Russellville, OH 45168
(937) 377-3700
www.forsythesauctions.com

Fox Auctions
P.O. Box 4069
Vallejo, CA 94590
(631) 553-3841
Fax: (707) 643-3000
www.foxauctionsonline.com

Frasher's Doll Auction
2323 S. Mecklin Sch. Rd.
Oak Grove, MO 64075
(816) 625-3786

J. Garrett Auctioneers, Ltd.
1411 Slocum St.
Dallas, TX 75207
(214) 683-6855
www.jgarrettauctioneers.com

Garth's Arts & Antiques
P.O. Box 369
Delaware, OH 43015
(740) 362-4771
www.garths.com

Glass Works Auctions
Box 180
East Greenville, PA 18041
(215) 679-5849
www.glswrk-auction.com

The Golf Auction
209 State St.
Oldsmar, FL 34677
(813) 340-6179
thegolfauction.com

Gray's Auctioneers
& Appraisers
10717 Detroit Ave.
Cleveland, OH 44102
(216) 226-3300
graysauctioneers.com

Great Gatsby's Antiques
and Auctions
5180 Peachtree Industrial Blvd.
Atlanta, GA 30341
(770) 457-1903
www.greatgatsbys.com

Grogan & Co.
22 Harris St.
Dedham, MA 02026
(781) 461-9500
www.groganco.com

Guyette & Deeter
24718 Beverly Rd.
St. Michaels, MD 21663
(410) 745-0485
Fax: (410) 745-0487
www.guyetteandschmidt.com

GWS Auctions, LLC
41841 Beacon Hill # E
Palm Desert, CA 92211
(760) 610-4175
www.gwsauctions.com

Ken Farmer Auctions
and Appraisals
105 Harrison St.
Radford, VA 24141
(540) 639-0939
www.kfauctions.com

Hake's Americana
& Collectibles
P.O. Box 12001
York, PA 17402
(717) 434-1600
www.hakes.com

Hamilton's Antique &
Estate Auctions, Inc.
505 Puyallup Ave.
Tacoma, WA 98421
(253) 534-4445
www.joe-frank.com

Norman Heckler & Co.
79 Bradford Corner Rd.
Woodstock Valley, CT 06282
www.hecklerauction.com

Heritage Auctions
3500 Maple Ave.
Dallas, TX 75219-3941
(800) 872-6467
www.ha.com

Hess Fine Auctions
1131 4th St. N.
St. Petersburg, FL 33701
(727) 896-0622
www.hessfineauctions.com

Hewlett's Antique Auctions
PO Box 87
13286 Jefferson St.
Le Grand, CA 95333
(209) 389-4542
Fax: (209) 389-0730
http://www.hewlettsauctions.com/

Holabird-Kagin Americana
3555 Airway Dr., #308
Reno, NV 89511
(775) 852-8822
www.holabirdamericana.com

Homestead Auctions
3200 Greenwich Rd.
Norton, OH 44203
(330) 807-1445
www.homesteadauction.net

Bill Hood & Sons Art &
Antique Auctions
2925 S. Federal Hwy.
Delray Beach, FL 33483
(561) 278-8996
www.hoodauction.com

Humler & Nolan
The Auctions at Rookwood
225 E. Sixth St., 4th Floor
Cincinnati, OH 45202
(513) 381-2041
Fax: (513) 381-2038
www.humlernolan.com

iGavel Auctions
229 E. 120th St.
New York, NY 10035
(212) 289-5588
www.igavelauctions.com

Ivy Auctions
22391 Hwy. 76 E.
Laurens, SC 29360
(864) 682-2750
www.ivyauctions.com

Jackson's International
Auctioneers & Appraisers
2229 Lincoln St.
Cedar Falls, IA 50613
jacksonsauction.com

Jasper52
101 Avenue of the Americas
Suite 900
New York, NY 10013
(212) 634 0978
jasper52.com

Jeffrey S. Evans
& Associates
2177 Green Valley Ln.
Mount Crawford, VA 22841
(540) 434-3939
www.jeffreysevans.com

John Moran Auctioneers
735 West Woodbury Rd.
Altadena, CA 91001
(626) 793-1833
www.johnmoran.com

Julien's Auctions
9665 Wilshire Blvd., Suite 150
Beverly Hills, CA 90210
(310) 836-1818
www.juliensauctions.com

Just Art Pottery
Greg and Lana Myroth
1184 Rentsch Drive
East Peoria, IL 61611
(309) 690-7966
www.justartpottery.com

Kaminski Auctions
564 Cabot St.
Beverly, MA 01915
(978) 927-2223
Fax: (978) 927-2228
www.kaminskiauctions.com/

Kennedy Auctions Service
160 West Court Ave.
Selmer, TN 38375
(731) 645-5001
www.kennedysauction.com

Lang's Sporting Collectibles
663 Pleasant Valley Rd.
Waterville, NY 13480
(315) 841-4623
www.langsauction.com

Legend Numismatics
P.O. Box 9
Lincroft, NJ 07738
(800) 743-2646
www.legendcoin.com

Legendary Auctions
17542 Chicago Ave.
Lansing, IL 60438
(708) 889-9380
www.legendaryauctions.com

Los Angeles
Modern Auctions
16145 Hart St.
Van Nuys, CA 91406
(323) 904-1950
www.lamodern.com

Leslie Hindman Auctioneers
1338 West Lake St.
Chicago, IL 60607
(312) 280-1212
www.lesliehindman.com

**Louis J. Dianni, LLC
Antiques Auctions**
May 1-Oct. 15:
982 Main St., Suite 175
Fishkill, NY 12524
Oct. 20-April 15:
1304 SW 160th Ave., Suite 228A
Sunrise, FL 33326
https://louisjdianni.com

Love of the Game Auctions
P.O. Box 157
Great Meadows, NJ 07838
loveofthegameauctions.com

Main Street Mining Co.
2311 East Loop 820 N.
Fort Worth, TX 76118
(817) 616-5001
https://mainstreetmining.com

Manifest Auctions
361 Woodruff Rd.
Greenville, SC 29607
(864) 520-2208
Fax: (864) 520-2210
manifestauctions.com

Manitou Auctions
205 Styer Dairy Rd.
Reidsville, NC 27320
(336) 349-6577
www.manitou-auctions.com

Manor Auctions
2415 N. Monroe St.
Tallahassee, FL 32303
(850) 523-3787
Fax: (850) 523-3786
www.manorauctions.com

**Mark Mattox Auctioneer & Real
Estate Broker, Inc.**
3740 Maysville Rd.
Carlisle, KY 40311
(859) 289-5720
http://mattoxauctions.com/
auctions/

Martin Auction Co.
100 Lick Creek Rd.
Anna, IL 62906
(618) 833-3589
www.martinauctionco.com
martinauctioncompany@gmail.com

**Martin J. Donnelly
Antique Tools**
5523 County Rd. 8
Avoca, NY 14809
(607) 566-2617
www.mjdtools.com

Matt Maring Auction Co.
P.O. Box 37
Kenyon, MN 55946
(507) 789-5227
www.maringauction.com

Material Culture
4700 Wissahickon Ave.
Philadelphia, PA 19144
(215) 849-8030
www.materialculture.com

Matthews Auctions
111 South Oak St.
Nokomis, IL 62075-1337
(215) 563-8880
www.matthewsauctions.com

**John McInnis Auctioneers
& Appraisers**
76 Main St.
Amesbury, MA 01913
(978) 388-0400
Fax: (978) 388-8863
www.mcinnisauctions.com

McLaren Auction Service
21507 Highway 99E
Aurora, OR 97002
(503) 678-2441
www.mclarenauction.com

**McMasters-Harris
Auction Co.**
P.O. Box 755
Cambridge, OH 43725
www.mcmastersharris.com

Michaan's Auctions
2751 Todd St.
Alameda, CA 94501
(510) 740-0220
www.michaans.com

Midwest Auction Galleries
925 North Lapeer Rd.
Oxford, MI 48371
(877) 236-8181
or (248) 236-8100
Fax: (248) 236-8396
www.midwestauctioninc.com

Mile High Card Co.
7200 S. Alton Way, Suite A230
Centennial, CO 80112
(303) 840-2784
www.milehighcardco.com

Milestone Auctions
3860 Ben Hur Ave., Unit 8
Willoughby, OH 44094
(440) 527-8060
www.milestoneauctions.com

Dan Morphy Auctions
2000 N. Reading Rd.
Denver, PA 17517
(717) 335-3435
morphyauctions.com

Mohawk Arms, Inc.
P.O. Box 157
Bouckville, NY 13310
(315) 893-7888
www.militaryrelics.com

Mosby & Co. Auctions
5714-A Industry Ln.
Frederick, MD 21704
(240) 629-8139
www.mosbyauctions.com

Neal Auction Co.
4038 Magazine St.
New Orleans, LA 70115
(504) 899-5329
www.nealauction.com

Nest Egg Auctions
30 Research Pkwy.
Meriden, CT 06450
(203) 630-1400
www.nesteggauctions.com

**New Orleans
Auction Gallery**
1330 St. Charles Ave.
New Orleans, LA 70130
www.neworleansauction.com

Nico Auctions
4023 Kennett Pike, Suite 248
Greenville, DE 19807
(888) 390-0201
www.nicoauctions.com

**Noel Barrett Vintage
Toys @ Auction**
P.O. Box 300
Carversville, PA 18913
(215) 297 5109
www.noelbarrett.com

**North American
Auction Co.**
78 Wildcat Way
Bozeman, MT 59718
(800) 686-4216
www.northamericanauction
company.com

Northeast Auctions
93 Pleasant St.
Portsmouth, NH 03801
(603) 433-8400
Fax: (603) 433-0415
www.northeastauctions.com

**O'Gallerie: Fine Arts, Antiques
and Estate Auctions**
228 Northeast 7th Ave.
Portland, OR 97232-2909
(503) 238-0202
www.ogallerie.com

Omaha Auction Center
7531 Dodge St.
Omaha, NE 68114
(402) 397-9575
www.omahaauctioncenter.com

Omega Auction Corp.
1669 W. 39th Pl.
Hialeah, FL 33012
(786) 444-4997
www.omegaauctioncorp.com

**Pacific Galleries Auction House
and Antique Mall**
241 South Lander St.
Seattle, WA 98134
(206) 441-9990
Fax: (206) 448-9677
www.pacgal.com

Past Tyme Pleasures
39 California Ave., Suite 105
Pleasanton, CA 94566
www.pasttyme1.com

PBA Galleries
133 Kearny St., 4th Floor
San Francisco, CA 94108
(415) 989-2665
www.pbagalleries.com

Phoebus Auction Gallery
18 East Mellen St.
Hampton, VA 23663
(757) 722-9210
www.phoebusauction.com

Pioneer Auction Gallery
14650 SE Arista Dr.
Portland, OR 97267
(503) 496-0303
www.pioneerantiqueauction.com

Pook & Pook, Inc.
463 East Lancaster Ave.
Downingtown, PA 19335
(610) 269-4040
www.pookandpook.com

Potter & Potter Auctions
3759 N. Ravenswood Ave., #121
Chicago, IL 60613
(773) 472-1442
www.potterauctions.com

Premier Auction Galleries
12587 Chillicothe Rd.
Chesterland, OH 44026
(440) 688-4203
Fax: (440) 688-4202
www.pag4u.com

Don Presley Auction
1319 West Katella Ave.
Orange County, CA 92867
(714) 633-2437
www.donpresley.com

Preston Hall Gallery
2201 Main St., Suite #820
Dallas, TX 75201
(214) 718-8624
www.prestonhallgallery.com

Profiles in History
26901 Agoura Rd., Suite 150
Calabasas Hills, CA 91301
(310) 859-7701
www.profilesinhistory.com

Purcell Auction Gallery
2156 Husband Rd.
Paducah, KY 42003
(270) 444-7599
www.purcellauction.com/

Quinn's Auction Galleries
360 S. Washington St.
Falls Church, VA 22046
(703) 532-5632
www.quinnsauction.com

Rago Arts & Auctions
333 N. Main St.
Lambertville, NJ 08530
(609) 397-9374
www.ragoarts.com

Red Baron's Antiques
8655 Roswell Rd.
Atlanta, GA 30350
(770) 640-4604
www.rbantiques.com

Richard Opfer
Auctioneering, Inc.
1919 Greenspring Dr.
Lutherville-Timonium, MD 21093
(410) 252-5035
www.opferauction.com

Rich Penn Auctions
P.O. Box 1355
Waterloo, IA 50704
(319) 291-6688
www.richpennauctions.com

RM Auctions
One Classic Car Dr.
Blenheium, Ontario
NOP 1A0 Canada
+1 (519) 352-4575
www.rmauctions.com

Robert Edward Auctions
P.O. Box 7256
Watchung, NJ 07069
(908) 226-9900
www.robertedwardauctions.com

Rock Island Auction Co.
7819 42 St. West
Rock Island, IL 61201
(800) 238-8022
www.rockislandauction.com

Roland Auction NY
80 E 11th St.
New York, NY 10003
(212) 260-2000
www.rolandauctions.com

RR Auction
5 Route 101A, Suite 5
Amherst, NH 03031
(603) 732-4280
www.rrauction.com

Saco River Auction Co.
2 Main St.
Biddeford, ME 04005
(207) 602-1504
www.sacoriverauction.com

Scheerer McCulloch
Auctioneers
515 E Paulding Rd.
Fort Wayne, IN 46816
(260) 441-8636
www.smauctioneers.com

SCP Auctions, Inc.
32451 Golden Lantern, Suite 308
Laguna Niguel, CA 92677
(949) 831-3700
www.SCPauctions.com

Seeck Auction Co.
Jim and Jan Seeck
P.O. Box 377
Mason City, IA 50402
www.seeckauction.com

SeriousToyz
1 Baltic Pl.
Croton on Hudson, NY 10520
(866) 653-8699
www.serioustoyz.com

Showtime Auction Services
22619 Monterey Dr.
Woodhaven, MI 48183-2269
(734) 676-9703
www.showtimeauctions.com

Skinner, Inc.
357 Main St.
Boston, MA 01740
(617) 350-5400
www.skinnerinc.com

Sloans & Kenyon Auctioneers
and Appraisers
7034 Wisconsin Ave.
Chevy Chase, MD 20815
(301) 634-2330
www.sloansandkenyon.com

Sotheby's New York
1334 York Ave.
New York, NY 10021
(212) 606-7000
www.sothebys.com

Specialists of the
South, Inc.
544 E. Sixth St.
Panama City, FL 32401
(850) 785-2577
www.specialistsofthesouth.com

Stanley Gibbons
399 Strand
London
WC2R 0LX
England
+44 (0)207 836 8444
www.stanleygibbons.com

Stanton Auctions
PO Box 326
106 E. Longmeadow Rd.
Hampden, MA 01036
(413) 566-3161
www.stantonauctions.com

Carl W. Stinson, Inc.
293 Haverhill St.
Reading, MA 01867
(617) 834-3819
www.stinsonauctions.com

Stefek's Auctioneers
& Appraisers
18450 Mack Ave.
Grosse Pointe Farms, MI 48236
(313) 881-1800
www.stefeksltd.com

Stephenson's Auctioneers
& Appraisers
1005 Industrial Blvd.
Southampton, PA 18966
(215) 322-6182
www.stephensonsauction.com

Stevens Auction Co.
301 North Meridian St.
Aberdeen, MS 39730-2613
(662) 369-2200
www.stevensauction.com

Strawser Auctions
P.O. Box 332
Wolcottville, IN 46795
www.strawserauctions.com
Sullivan & Son Auction, LLC
1995 E. County Rd. 650
Carthage, IL 62321
(217) 743-5200
www.sullivanandsonauction.com

Swann Auction Galleries
104 E 25th St., # 6
New York, NY 10010-2999
(212) 254-4710
www.swanngalleries.com

Teel Auction Services
619 FM 2330
Montabla, TX 75853
(903) 724-4079
www.teelauctionservices.com

Theriault's – The Doll Masters
P.O. Box 151
Annapolis, MD 21404
(800) 638-0422
www.theriaults.com

Thomaston Place
Auction Galleries
51 Atlantic Hwy.
Thomaston, ME 04861
(207) 354-8141
www.thomastonauction.com

John Toomey Gallery
818 North Blvd.
Oak Park, IL 60301
(708) 383-5234
http://johntoomeygallery.com

Tory Hill Auction Co.
5301 Hillsborough St.
Raleigh, NC 27606
(919) 858-0327
www.toryhillauctions.com

Tradewinds Antiques
& Auctions
24 Magnolia Ave.
Manchester-by-the-Sea,
MA 01944
(978) 526-4085
www.tradewindsantiques.com

Treadway Gallery, Inc.
2029 Madison Rd.
Cincinnati, OH 45208
www.treadwaygallery.com

Turkey Creek
Auctions, Inc.
13939 N. Hwy. 441
Citra, FL 32113
(352) 622-4611
(800) 648-7523
www.antiqueauctionsfl.com

Turner Auctions + Appraisals
461 Littlefield Ave.
South San Francisco, CA 94080
(415) 964-5250
(310) 997-0400
(888) 498-4450
www.turnerauctionsonline.com

Vero Beach Auction
492 Old Dixie Hwy.
Vero Beach, FL 32962
(772) 978-5955
Fax: (772) 978-5954
www.verobeachauction.com

Victorian Casino
Antiques Auction
4520 Arville St., #1
Las Vegas, NV 89103
(702) 382-2466
www.vcaauction.com

Wiederseim
Associates, Inc.
PO Box 470
Chester Springs, PA 19425
(610) 827-1910
www.wiederseim.com

Philip Weiss Auctions
74 Merrick Rd.
Lynbrook, NY 11563
(516) 594-0731
www.weissauctions.com

William J. Jenack Estate
Appraisers & Auctioneers
62 Kings Highway Bypass
Chester, NY 10918
(877) 282-8503
www.jenack.com

Witherell's Art & Antiques
300 20th St.
Sacramento, CA 95811
(916) 446-6490
witherells.com

Woodbury Auction, LLC
50 Main St. N.
Woodbury, CT 06798
(203) 266-0323
www.woodburyauction.com

Woody Auction
317 S. Forrest St.
Douglass, KS 67039
(316) 747-2694
www.woodyauction.com

Wright
1440 W. Hubbard St.
Chicago, IL 60642
(312) 563-0020
www.wright20.com

Zurko Promotions
115 E. Division St.
Shawano, WI 54166
www.zurkopromotions.com

INDEX